Microsoft® Official Academic Course

Windows 7 Enterprise Desktop Support Technician
Exam 70-685

Revised and Expanded Version

WILEY

Credits

EXECUTIVE EDITOR	John Kane
DIRECTOR OF SALES	Mitchell Beaton
EXECUTIVE MARKETING MANAGER	Chris Ruel
MICROSOFT SENIOR PRODUCT MANAGER	Merrick Van Dongen of Microsoft Learning
EDITORIAL PROGRAM ASSISTANT	Jennifer Lartz
CONTENT MANAGER	Micheline Frederick
SENIOR PRODUCTION EDITOR	Kerry Weinstein/John Curley
CREATIVE DIRECTOR	Harry Nolan
COVER DESIGNER	Jim O'Shea
TECHNOLOGY AND MEDIA	Tom Kulesa/Wendy Ashenberg

This book was set in Garamond by Aptara, Inc. and printed and bound by Bind Rite Graphics. The cover was printed by Bind Rite Graphics.

ISBN 978-1-118-13450-4

Printed in the United States of America

10 9 8 7 6 5 4 3 2

Foreword from the Publisher

Wiley's publishing vision for the Microsoft Official Academic Course series is to provide students and instructors with the skills and knowledge they need to use Microsoft technology effectively in all aspects of their personal and professional lives. Quality instruction is required to help both educators and students get the most from Microsoft's software tools and to become more productive. Thus our mission is to make our instructional programs trusted educational companions for life.

To accomplish this mission, Wiley and Microsoft have partnered to develop the highest quality educational programs for Information Workers, IT Professionals, and Developers. Materials created by this partnership carry the brand name "Microsoft Official Academic Course," assuring instructors and students alike that the content of these textbooks is fully endorsed by Microsoft, and that they provide the highest quality information and instruction on Microsoft products. The Microsoft Official Academic Course textbooks are "Official" in still one more way—they are the officially sanctioned courseware for Microsoft IT Academy members.

The Microsoft Official Academic Course series focuses on *workforce development*. These programs are aimed at those students seeking to enter the workforce, change jobs, or embark on new careers as information workers, IT professionals, and developers. Microsoft Official Academic Course programs address their needs by emphasizing authentic workplace scenarios with an abundance of projects, exercises, cases, and assessments.

The Microsoft Official Academic Courses are mapped to Microsoft's extensive research and job-task analysis, the same research and analysis used to create the Microsoft Certified Information Technology Professional (MCITP) exam. The textbooks focus on real skills for real jobs. As students work through the projects and exercises in the textbooks they enhance their level of knowledge and their ability to apply the latest Microsoft technology to everyday tasks. These students also gain resume-building credentials that can assist them in finding a job, keeping their current job, or in furthering their education.

The concept of lifelong learning is today an utmost necessity. Job roles, and even whole job categories, are changing so quickly that none of us can stay competitive and productive without continuously updating our skills and capabilities. The Microsoft Official Academic Course offerings, and their focus on Microsoft certification exam preparation, provide a means for people to acquire and effectively update their skills and knowledge. Wiley supports students in this endeavor through the development and distribution of these courses as Microsoft's official academic publisher.

Today educational publishing requires attention to providing quality print and robust electronic content. By integrating Microsoft Official Academic Course products and Microsoft certifications, we are better able to deliver efficient learning solutions for students and teachers alike.

Joseph Heider

General Manager and Senior Vice President

Preface

Welcome to the Microsoft Official Academic Course (MOAC) program for Windows 7 Enterprise Desktop Support Technician. MOAC represents the collaboration between Microsoft Learning and John Wiley & Sons, Inc. publishing company. Microsoft and Wiley have teamed up to produce a series of textbooks that deliver compelling and innovative teaching solutions to instructors and superior learning experiences for students. Infused and informed by in-depth knowledge from the creators of Windows 7 and crafted by a publisher known worldwide for the pedagogical quality of its products, these textbooks maximize skills transfer in minimum time. Students are challenged to reach their potential by using their new technical skills as highly productive members of the workforce.

Because this knowledgebase comes directly from Microsoft, architect of Windows 7 and creator of the Microsoft Certified Information Technology Professional exams (www.microsoft.com/learning/mcp/mcitp), you are sure to receive the topical coverage that is most relevant to students' personal and professional success. Microsoft's direct participation not only assures you that MOAC textbook content is accurate and current; it also means that students will receive the best instruction possible to enable their success on certification exams and in the workplace.

■ The Microsoft Official Academic Course Program

The *Microsoft Official Academic Course* series is a complete program for instructors and institutions to prepare and deliver great courses on Microsoft software technologies. With MOAC, we recognize that, because of the rapid pace of change in the technology and curriculum developed by Microsoft, there is an ongoing set of needs beyond classroom instruction tools for an instructor to be ready to teach the course. The MOAC program endeavors to provide solutions for all these needs in a systematic manner in order to ensure a successful and rewarding course experience for both instructor and student—technical and curriculum training for instructor readiness with new software releases; the software itself for student use at home for building hands-on skills, assessment, and validation of skill development; and a great set of tools for delivering instruction in the classroom and lab. All are important to the smooth delivery of an interesting course on Microsoft software, and all are provided with the MOAC program. We think about the model below as a gauge for ensuring that we completely support you in your goal of teaching a great course. As you evaluate your instructional materials options, you may wish to use the model for comparison purposes with available products.

■ Pedagogical Features

The MOAC textbook for Windows 7 Enterprise Desktop Support Technician is designed to cover all the learning objectives for that MCITP exam, which is referred to as its "objective domain." The Microsoft Certified Information Technology Professional (MCITP) exam objectives are highlighted throughout the textbook. Many pedagogical features have been developed specifically for *Microsoft Official Academic Course* programs.

Presenting the extensive procedural information and technical concepts woven throughout the textbook raises challenges for the student and instructor alike. The Illustrated Book Tour that follows provides a guide to the rich features contributing to *Microsoft Official Academic Course* program's pedagogical plan. Following is a list of key features in each lesson designed to prepare students for success on the certification exams and in the workplace:

- Each lesson begins with an **Objective Domain Matrix.** More than a standard list of learning objectives, the Objective Domain Matrix correlates each software skill covered in the lesson to the specific MCITP exam objective domain.

- Concise and frequent **Step-by-Step** instructions teach students new features and provide an opportunity for hands-on practice. Numbered steps give detailed step-by-step instructions to help students learn software skills. The steps also show results and screen images to match what students should see on their computer screens.

- **Illustration** such as screen images provide visual feedback as students work through the exercises. The images reinforce key concepts, provide visual clues about the steps, and allow students to check their progress.

- **Key Terms** are listed at the beginning of the lesson. When these important technical terms are first used later in the lesson, they appear in bold italic type and are defined.

- Engaging point-of-use **Reader aids,** located throughout the lessons, tell students why this topic is relevant (*The Bottom Line*), provide students with helpful hints (*Take Note*), or show alternate ways to accomplish tasks (*Another Way*). Reader aids also provide additional relevant or background information that adds value to the lesson.

- **Certification Ready** features throughout the text signal students where a specific certification objective is covered. They provide students with a chance to check their understanding of that particular MCITP exam objective and, if necessary, review the section of the lesson where it is covered.

- **Knowledge Assessments** provide progressively more challenging lesson-ending activities, including practice exercises and case scenarios.

- A **Lab Manual** accompanies this textbook package. The Lab Manual contains hands-on lab work corresponding to each of the lessons within the textbook. Numbered steps give detailed, step-by-step instructions to help students learn workplace skills associated with Windows 7. The labs are constructed using real-world scenarios to mimic the tasks students will see in the workplace.

■ Lesson Features

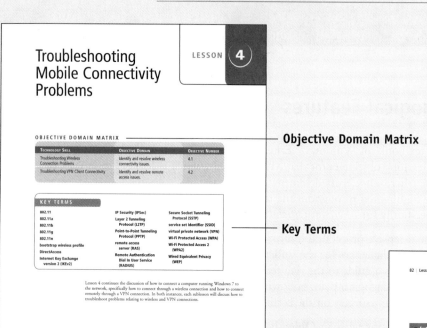

Objective Domain Matrix

Key Terms

Bottom Line Reader Aid

Certification Ready Alert

Easy-to-Read Tables

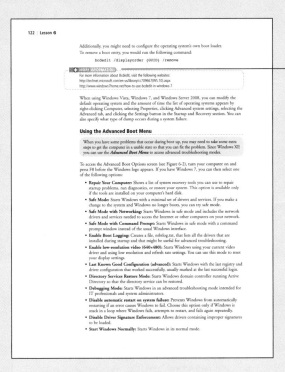

More Information Reader Aid

Take Note Reader Aid

Warning Reader Aid

Screen Images

Step-by-Step
Exercises

Informative
Diagrams

X-Ref Reader
Aid

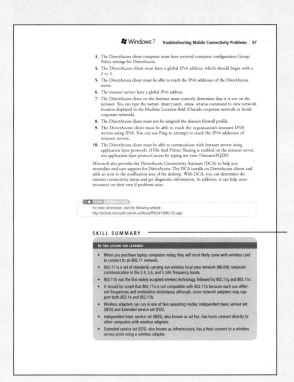

Skill Summary

Case Scenarios

Knowledge Assessment

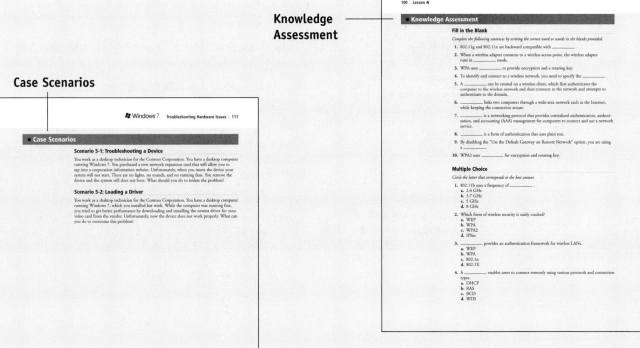

Conventions and Features Used in This Book

This book uses particular fonts, symbols, and heading conventions to highlight important information or to call your attention to special steps. For more information about the features in each lesson, refer to the Illustrated Book Tour section.

CONVENTION	MEANING
↓ THE BOTTOM LINE	This feature provides a brief summary of the material to be covered in the section that follows.
CERTIFICATION READY	This feature signals the point in the text where a specific certification objective is covered. It provides you with a chance to check your understanding of that particular MCITP objective and, if necessary, review the section of the lesson where it is covered.
TAKE NOTE*	Reader aids appear in shaded boxes found in your text. *Take Note* provides helpful hints related to particular tasks or topics.
⬥ ANOTHER WAY	*Another Way* provides an alternative procedure for accomplishing a particular task.
X REF	These notes provide pointers to information discussed elsewhere in the textbook or describe interesting features of Windows 7 that are not directly addressed in the current topic or exercise.
A *shared printer* can be used by many individuals on a network.	Key terms appear in bold italic on first appearance.

Instructor Support Program

The *Microsoft Official Academic Course* programs are accompanied by a rich array of resources that incorporate the extensive textbook visuals to form a pedagogically cohesive package. These resources provide all the materials instructors need to deploy and deliver their courses:

- Perhaps the most valuable resource for teaching this course is the software used in the course lab work. The **MSDN Academic Alliance (MSDN AA)** is designed to provide the easiest and most inexpensive developer tools, products, and technologies available to faculty and students in labs, classrooms, and on student PCs. A free 3-year membership to the MSDN AA is available to qualified MOAC adopters. *Note:* Windows 7 Enterprise Edition for lab deployment can be downloaded from MSDN AA for use by students in this course.

Resources available online for download include:

- The **Instructor's Guide** contains solutions to all the textbook exercises as well as chapter summaries and lecture notes. The Instructor's Guide and Syllabi for various term lengths are available from the Book Companion site (www.wiley.com/college/microsoft).

- The **Test Bank** contains hundreds of questions organized by lesson in multiple-choice, true-false, short answer, and essay formats and is available to download from the Instructor's Book Companion site (www.wiley.com/college/microsoft). A complete answer key is provided.

- Complete **PowerPoint Presentations and Images** are available on the Instructor's Book Companion site (www.wiley.com/college/microsoft) to enhance classroom presentations. Tailored to the text's topical coverage and Skills Matrix, these presentations are designed to convey key Windows 7 concepts addressed in the text.

  All figures from the text are on the Instructor's Book Companion site (www.wiley.com/college/microsoft). You can incorporate them into your PowerPoint presentations or create your own overhead transparencies and handouts.

  By using these visuals in class discussions, you can help focus students' attention on key elements of the products being used and help them understand how to use them effectively in the workplace.

- When it comes to improving the classroom experience, there is no better source of ideas and inspiration than your fellow colleagues. The **Wiley Faculty Network** connects teachers with technology, facilitates the exchange of best practices, and helps to enhance instructional efficiency and effectiveness. Faculty Network activities include technology training and tutorials, virtual seminars, peer-to-peer exchanges of experiences and ideas, personal consulting, and sharing of resources. For details visit www.WhereFacultyConnect.com.

MSDN ACADEMIC ALLIANCE—FREE 3-YEAR MEMBERSHIP AVAILABLE TO QUALIFIED ADOPTERS!

The Microsoft Developer Network Academic Alliance (MSDN AA) is designed to provide the easiest and most inexpensive way for universities to make the latest Microsoft developer tools, products, and technologies available in labs, classrooms, and on student PCs. MSDN AA is an annual membership program for departments teaching Science, Technology, Engineering, and Mathematics (STEM) courses. The membership provides a complete solution to keep academic labs, faculty, and students on the leading edge of technology.

Software available in the MSDN AA program is provided at no charge to adopting departments through the Wiley and Microsoft publishing partnership.

As a bonus to this free offer, faculty will be introduced to Microsoft's Faculty Connection and Academic Resource Center. It takes time and preparation to keep students engaged while giving them a fundamental understanding of theory, and the Microsoft Faculty Connection is designed to help STEM professors with this preparation by providing articles, curriculum, and tools that professors can use to engage and inspire today's technology students.

Contact your Wiley rep for details.

For more information about the MSDN Academic Alliance program, go to:

msdn.microsoft.com/academic/

Note: Windows 7 Enterprise Edition for lab deployment can be downloaded from MSDN AA for use by students in this course.

Important Web Addresses and Phone Numbers

To locate the Wiley Higher Education Rep in your area, go to www.wiley.com/college and click on the "Contact Us" link at the top of the page, or call the MOAC toll-free number: 1 + (888) 764-7001 (U.S. & Canada only).

To learn more about becoming a Microsoft Certified Professional and exam availability, visit www.microsoft.com/learning/mcp.

Book Companion Web Site

The students' book companion site for the MOAC series includes any resources, exercise files, and Web links that will be used in conjunction with this course. Use your book's ISBN or title to search www.wiley.com for the student companion site for this course.

Wiley Desktop Editions

Wiley MOAC Desktop Editions are innovative, electronic versions of printed textbooks. Students buy the desktop version for 50% off the U.S. price of the printed text and get the added value of permanence and portability. Wiley Desktop Editions provide students with numerous additional benefits that are not available with other e-text solutions.

Wiley Desktop Editions are NOT subscriptions; students download the Wiley Desktop Edition to their computer desktops. Students own the content they buy to keep for as long as they want. Once a Wiley Desktop Edition is downloaded to the computer desktop, students have instant access to all of the content without being online. Students can also print the sections they prefer to read in hard copy. Students also have access to fully integrated resources within their Wiley Desktop Edition. From highlighting their e-text to taking and sharing notes, students can easily personalize their Wiley Desktop Edition as they are reading or following along in class.

Microsoft Software

As an adopter of a MOAC textbook, your school's department is eligible for a free three-year membership to the MSDN Academic Alliance (MSDN AA). Through MSDN AA, Windows 7 Enterprise edition for lab deployment is available for your use with this course.

Preparing to Take the Microsoft Certified Information Technology Professional (MCITP) Exam

Microsoft Certified Information Technology Professional

The Microsoft Certified Technology Specialist (MCTS) and Microsoft Certified IT Professional (MCITP) credentials provide IT professionals with a simple and targeted framework to showcase their technical skills in addition to the skills that are required for specific developer job roles.

For organizations, the certification program provides better skills verification tools that help with assessing not only in-demand skills on Windows 7 and other Microsoft technologies but also the ability to quickly complete on-the-job tasks. Individuals will find it easier to identify and work toward the certification credential that meets their personal and professional goals.

To learn more about becoming a Microsoft Certified Information Technology Professional and exam availability, visit www.microsoft.com/learning/mcp/mcitp.

Preparing to Take an Exam

Unless you are a very experienced user, you will need to use a test preparation course to prepare to complete the test correctly and within the time allowed. The *Microsoft Official Academic Course* series is designed to prepare you with a strong knowledge of all exam topics, and with some additional review and practice on your own, you should feel confident in your ability to pass the appropriate exam.

After you decide which exam to take, review the list of objectives for the exam. You can easily identify tasks that are included in the objective list by locating the Lesson Skill Matrix at the start of each lesson and the Certification Ready sidebars in the margin of the lessons in this book.

To take an exam, visit www.microsoft.com/learning/mcp to locate your nearest testing center. Then call the testing center directly to schedule your test. The amount of advance notice you should provide will vary for different testing centers, and it typically depends on the number of computers available at the testing center, the number of other testers who have already been scheduled for the day on which you want to take the test, and the number of times per week that the testing center offers testing. In general, you should call to schedule your test at least two weeks prior to the date on which you want to take the test.

When you arrive at the testing center, you might be asked for proof of identity. A driver's license or passport is an acceptable form of identification. If you do not have either of these items of documentation, call your testing center and ask what alternative forms of identification will be accepted. If you are retaking a test, bring your identification number, which will have been given to you when you previously took the test. If you have not prepaid or if your organization has not already arranged to make payment for you, you will need to pay the test-taking fee when you arrive.

Acknowledgments

MOAC Instructor Advisory Board

We thank our Instructor Advisory Board, an elite group of educators who has assisted us every step of the way in building these products. Advisory Board members have acted as our sounding board on key pedagogical and design decisions leading to the development of these compelling and innovative textbooks for future Information Workers. Their dedication to technology education is truly appreciated.

Charles DeSassure, Tarrant County College

Charles DeSassure is Department Chair and Instructor of Computer Science & Information Technology at Tarrant County College Southeast Campus, Arlington, Texas. He has had experience as a MIS manager, system analyst, field technology analyst, LAN administrator, microcomputer specialist, and public school teacher in South Carolina. DeSassure has worked in higher education for more than ten years and received the Excellence Award in Teaching from the National Institute for Staff and Organizational Development (NISOD). He currently serves on the Educational Testing Service (ETS) iSkills National Advisory Committee and chaired the Tarrant County College District Student Assessment Committee. He has written proposals and makes presentations at major educational conferences nationwide. DeSassure has served as a textbook reviewer for John Wiley & Sons and Prentice Hall. He teaches courses in information security, networking, distance learning, and computer literacy. DeSassure holds a master's degree in Computer Resources & Information Management from Webster University.

Kim Ehlert, Waukesha County Technical College

Kim Ehlert is the Microsoft Program Coordinator and a Network Specialist instructor at Waukesha County Technical College, teaching the full range of MCSE and networking courses for the past nine years. Prior to joining WCTC, Kim was a professor at the Milwaukee School of Engineering for five years where she oversaw the Novell Academic Education and the Microsoft IT Academy programs. She has a wide variety of industry experience including network design and management for Johnson Controls, local city fire departments, police departments, large church congregations, health departments, and accounting firms. Kim holds many industry certifications including MCDST, MCSE, Security+, Network+, Server+, MCT, and CNE.

Kim has a bachelor's degree in Information Systems and a master's degree in Business Administration from the University of Wisconsin Milwaukee. When she is not busy teaching, she enjoys spending time with her husband Gregg and their two children—Alex and Courtney.

Penny Gudgeon, Corinthian Colleges, Inc.

Penny Gudgeon is the Program Manager for IT curriculum at Corinthian Colleges, Inc. Previously, she was responsible for computer programming and web curriculum for twenty-seven campuses in Corinthian's Canadian division, CDI College of Business, Technology and Health Care. Penny joined CDI College in 1997 as a computer programming instructor at one of the campuses outside of Toronto. Prior to joining CDI College, Penny taught productivity software at another Canadian college, the Academy of Learning, for four years. Penny has experience in helping students achieve their goals through various learning models from instructor-led to self-directed to online.

Before embarking on a career in education, Penny worked in the fields of advertising, marketing/ sales, mechanical and electronic engineering technology, and computer programming. When not working from her home office or indulging her passion for lifelong learning, Penny likes to read mysteries, garden, and relax at home in Hamilton, Ontario, with her Shih-Tzu, Gracie.

Margaret Leary, Northern Virginia Community College

Margaret Leary is Professor of IST at Northern Virginia Community College, teaching Networking and Network Security Courses for the past ten years. She is the Co-Principal Investigator on the CyberWATCH initiative, an NSF-funded regional consortium of higher education institutions and businesses working together to increase the number of network security personnel in the workforce. She also serves as a Senior Security Policy Manager and Research Analyst at Nortel Government Solutions and holds a CISSP certification.

Margaret holds a B.S.B.A. and MBA/Technology Management from the University of Phoenix and is pursuing her Ph.D. in Organization and Management with an IT Specialization at Capella University. Her dissertation is titled "Quantifying the Discoverability of Identity Attributes in Internet-Based Public Records: Impact on Identity Theft and Knowledge-Based Authentication." She has several other published articles in various government and industry magazines, notably on identity management and network security.

Wen Liu, ITT Educational Services, Inc.

Wen Liu is Director of Corporate Curriculum Development at ITT Educational Services, Inc. He joined the ITT corporate headquarters in 1998 as a Senior Network Analyst to plan and deploy the corporate WAN infrastructure. A year later he assumed the position of Corporate Curriculum Manager supervising the curriculum development of all IT programs. After he was promoted to his current position three years ago, he continued to manage the curriculum research and development for all the programs offered in the School of Information Technology in addition to supervising the curriculum development in other areas (such as Schools of Drafting and Design and Schools of Electronics Technology). Prior to his employment with ITT Educational Services, Liu was a Telecommunications Analyst at the state government of Indiana working on the state backbone project that provided Internet and telecommunications services to the public users such as K-12 and higher education institutions, government agencies, libraries, and health-care facilities.

Wen Liu has an M.A. in Student Personnel Administration in Higher Education and an M.S. in Information and Communications Sciences from Ball State University, Indiana. He was formerly the director of special projects on the board of directors of the Indiana Telecommunications User Association and used to serve on Course Technology's IT Advisory Board. He is currently a member of the IEEE and its Computer Society.

Jared Spencer, Westwood College Online

Jared Spencer has been the Lead Faculty for Networking at Westwood College Online since 2006. He began teaching in 2001 and has taught both on-ground and online for a variety of institutions, including Robert Morris University and Point Park University. In addition to his academic background, he has more than fifteen years of industry experience working for companies including the Thomson Corporation and IBM.

Jared has a master's degree in Internet Information Systems and is currently ABD and pursuing his doctorate in Information Systems at Nova Southeastern University. He has authored several papers that have been presented at conferences and appeared in publications such as the Journal of Internet Commerce and the Journal of Information Privacy and Security (JIPC). He holds a number of industry certifications, including AIX (UNIX), A+, Network+, Security+, MCSA on Windows 2000, and MCSA on Windows 2003 Server.

We thank Ray Esparza at Glendale Community College, Rachelle Hall at Glendale Community College in Arizona, Katherine James at Seneca College, Patrick Smith at Marshall Community and Technical College, Jared Spencer at Westwood College Online, Bonnie Willy at Ivy Tech Community College, and Jeff Riley for their diligent review and for providing invaluable feedback in the service of quality instructional materials.

Focus Group and Survey Participants

Finally, we thank the hundreds of instructors who participated in our focus groups and surveys to ensure that the Microsoft Official Academic Courses best met the needs of our customers.

Jean Aguilar, Mt. Hood Community College

Konrad Akens, Zane State College

Michael Albers, University of Memphis

Diana Anderson, Big Sandy Community & Technical College

Phyllis Anderson, Delaware County Community College

Judith Andrews, Feather River College

Damon Antos, American River College

Bridget Archer, Oakton Community College

Linda Arnold, Harrisburg Area Community College–Lebanon Campus

Neha Arya, Fullerton College

Mohammad Bajwa, Katharine Gibbs School–New York

Virginia Baker, University of Alaska Fairbanks

Carla Bannick, Pima Community College

Rita Barkley, Northeast Alabama Community College

Elsa Barr, Central Community College–Hastings

Ronald W. Barry, Ventura County Community College District

Elizabeth Bastedo, Central Carolina Technical College

Karen Baston, Waubonsee Community College

Karen Bean, Blinn College

Scott Beckstrand, Community College of Southern Nevada

Paulette Bell, Santa Rosa Junior College

Liz Bennett, Southeast Technical Institute

Nancy Bermea, Olympic College

Lucy Betz, Milwaukee Area Technical College

Meral Binbasioglu, Hofstra University

Catherine Binder, Strayer University & Katharine Gibbs School–Philadelphia

Terrel Blair, El Centro College

Ruth Blalock, Alamance Community College

Beverly Bohner, Reading Area Community College

Henry Bojack, Farmingdale State University

Matthew Bowie, Luna Community College

Julie Boyles, Portland Community College

Karen Brandt, College of the Albemarle

Stephen Brown, College of San Mateo

Jared Bruckner, Southern Adventist University

Pam Brune, Chattanooga State Technical Community College

Sue Buchholz, Georgia Perimeter College

Roberta Buczyna, Edison College

Angela Butler, Mississippi Gulf Coast Community College

Rebecca Byrd, Augusta Technical College

Kristen Callahan, Mercer County Community College

Judy Cameron, Spokane Community College

Dianne Campbell, Athens Technical College

Gena Casas, Florida Community College at Jacksonville

Jesus Castrejon, Latin Technologies

Gail Chambers, Southwest Tennessee Community College

Jacques Chansavang, Indiana University–Purdue University Fort Wayne

Nancy Chapko, Milwaukee Area Technical College

Rebecca Chavez, Yavapai College

Sanjiv Chopra, Thomas Nelson Community College

Greg Clements, Midland Lutheran College

Dayna Coker, Southwestern Oklahoma State University–Sayre Campus

Tamra Collins, Otero Junior College

Janet Conrey, Gavilan Community College

Carol Cornforth, West Virginia Northern Community College

Gary Cotton, American River College

Edie Cox, Chattahoochee Technical College

Rollie Cox, Madison Area Technical College

David Crawford, Northwestern Michigan College

J.K. Crowley, Victor Valley College

Rosalyn Culver, Washtenaw Community College

Sharon Custer, Huntington University

Sandra Daniels, New River Community College

Anila Das, Cedar Valley College

Brad Davis, Santa Rosa Junior College

Susan Davis, Green River Community College

Mark Dawdy, Lincoln Land Community College

Jennifer Day, Sinclair Community College

Carol Deane, Eastern Idaho Technical College

Julie DeBuhr, Lewis-Clark State College

Janis DeHaven, Central Community College

Drew Dekreon, University of Alaska–Anchorage

Joy DePover, Central Lakes College

Salli DiBartolo, Brevard Community College

Melissa Diegnau, Riverland Community College

Al Dillard, Lansdale School of Business

Marjorie Duffy, Cosumnes River College

Sarah Dunn, Southwest Tennessee Community College

Shahla Durany, Tarrant County College–South Campus

Kay Durden, University of Tennessee at Martin

Dineen Ebert, St. Louis Community College–Meramec

Donna Ehrhart, State University of New York–Brockport

Larry Elias, Montgomery County Community College

Glenda Elser, New Mexico State University at Alamogordo

Angela Evangelinos, Monroe County Community College

Angie Evans, Ivy Tech Community College of Indiana

Linda Farrington, Indian Hills Community College

Dana Fladhammer, Phoenix College

Richard Flores, Citrus College

Connie Fox, Community and Technical College at Institute of Technology West Virginia University

Wanda Freeman, Okefenokee Technical College

Brenda Freeman, Augusta Technical College

Susan Fry, Boise State University

Roger Fulk, Wright State University–Lake Campus

Sue Furnas, Collin County Community College District

Sandy Gabel, Vernon College

Laura Galvan, Fayetteville Technical Community College

Candace Garrod, Red Rocks Community College

Sherrie Geitgey, Northwest State Community College

Chris Gerig, Chattahoochee Technical College

Barb Gillespie, Cuyamaca College

Jessica Gilmore, Highline Community College

Pamela Gilmore, Reedley College

Debbie Glinert, Queensborough Community College

Steven Goldman, Polk Community College

Bettie Goodman, C.S. Mott Community College

Mike Grabill, Katharine Gibbs School–Philadelphia

Francis Green, Penn State University

Walter Griffin, Blinn College

Fillmore Guinn, Odessa College

Helen Haasch, Milwaukee Area Technical College

John Habal, Ventura College

Joy Haerens, Chaffey College

Norman Hahn, Thomas Nelson Community College

Kathy Hall, Alamance Community College

Teri Harbacheck, Boise State University

Linda Harper, Richland Community College

Maureen Harper, Indian Hills Community College

Steve Harris, Katharine Gibbs School–New York

Robyn Hart, Fresno City College

Darien Hartman, Boise State University

Gina Hatcher, Tacoma Community College

Winona T. Hatcher, Aiken Technical College

BJ Hathaway, Northeast Wisconsin Tech College

Cynthia Hauki, West Hills College–Coalinga

Mary L. Haynes, Wayne County Community College

Marcie Hawkins, Zane State College

Steve Hebrock, Ohio State University Agricultural Technical Institute

Sue Heistand, Iowa Central Community College

Heith Hennel, Valencia Community College

Donna Hendricks, South Arkansas Community College

Judy Hendrix, Dyersburg State Community College

Gloria Hensel, Matanuska-Susitna College University of Alaska Anchorage

Gwendolyn Hester, Richland College

Tammarra Holmes, Laramie County Community College

Dee Hobson, Richland College

Keith Hoell, Katharine Gibbs School–New York

Pashia Hogan, Northeast State Technical Community College

Susan Hoggard, Tulsa Community College

Kathleen Holliman, Wallace Community College Selma

Chastity Honchul, Brown Mackie College/Wright State University

Christie Hovey, Lincoln Land Community College

Peggy Hughes, Allegany College of Maryland

Sandra Hume, Chippewa Valley Technical College

John Hutson, Aims Community College

Celia Ing, Sacramento City College

Joan Ivey, Lanier Technical College

Barbara Jaffari, College of the Redwoods

Penny Jakes, University of Montana College of Technology

Eduardo Jaramillo, Peninsula College

Barbara Jauken, Southeast Community College

Susan Jennings, Stephen F. Austin State University

Leslie Jernberg, Eastern Idaho Technical College

Linda Johns, Georgia Perimeter College

Brent Johnson, Okefenokee Technical College

Mary Johnson, Mt. San Antonio College

Shirley Johnson, Trinidad State Junior College–Valley Campus

Sandra M. Jolley, Tarrant County College

Teresa Jolly, South Georgia Technical College

Dr. Deborah Jones, South Georgia Technical College

Margie Jones, Central Virginia Community College

Randall Jones, Marshall Community and Technical College

Diane Karlsbraaten, Lake Region State College

Teresa Keller, Ivy Tech Community College of Indiana

Charles Kemnitz, Pennsylvania College of Technology

Sandra Kinghorn, Ventura College

Bill Klein, Katharine Gibbs School–Philadelphia

Bea Knaapen, Fresno City College

Kit Kofoed, Western Wyoming Community College

Maria Kolatis, County College of Morris

Barry Kolb, Ocean County College

Karen Kuralt, University of Arkansas at Little Rock

Belva-Carole Lamb, Rogue Community College

Betty Lambert, Des Moines Area Community College

Anita Lande, Cabrillo College

Junnae Landry, Pratt Community College

Karen Lankisch, UC Clermont

David Lanzilla, Central Florida Community College

Nora Laredo, Cerritos Community College

Jennifer Larrabee, Chippewa Valley Technical College

Debra Larson, Idaho State University

Barb Lave, Portland Community College

Audrey Lawrence, Tidewater Community College

Deborah Layton, Eastern Oklahoma State College

Larry LeBlanc, Owen Graduate School–Vanderbilt University

Philip Lee, Nashville State Community College

Michael Lehrfeld, Brevard Community College

Vasant Limaye, Southwest Collegiate Institute for the Deaf – Howard College

Anne C. Lewis, Edgecombe Community College

Stephen Linkin, Houston Community College

Peggy Linston, Athens Technical College

Hugh Lofton, Moultrie Technical College

Donna Lohn, Lakeland Community College

Jackie Lou, Lake Tahoe Community College

Donna Love, Gaston College

Curt Lynch, Ozarks Technical Community College

Sheilah Lynn, Florida Community College–Jacksonville

Pat R. Lyon, Tomball College

Bill Madden, Bergen Community College

Heather Madden, Delaware Technical & Community College

Donna Madsen, Kirkwood Community College

Jane Maringer-Cantu, Gavilan College

Suzanne Marks, Bellevue Community College

Carol Martin, Louisiana State University–Alexandria

Cheryl Martucci, Diablo Valley College

Roberta Marvel, Eastern Wyoming College

Tom Mason, Brookdale Community College

Mindy Mass, Santa Barbara City College

Dixie Massaro, Irvine Valley College

Rebekah May, Ashland Community & Technical College

Emma Mays-Reynolds, Dyersburg State Community College

Timothy Mayes, Metropolitan State College of Denver

Reggie McCarthy, Central Lakes College

Matt McCaskill, Brevard Community College

Kevin McFarlane, Front Range Community College

Donna McGill, Yuba Community College

Terri McKeever, Ozarks Technical Community College

Patricia McMahon, South Suburban College

Sally McMillin, Katharine Gibbs School–Philadelphia

Charles McNerney, Bergen Community College

Lisa Mears, Palm Beach Community College

Imran Mehmood, ITT Technical Institute–King of Prussia Campus

Virginia Melvin, Southwest Tennessee Community College

Jeanne Mercer, Texas State Technical College

Denise Merrell, Jefferson Community & Technical College

Catherine Merrikin, Pearl River Community College

Diane D. Mickey, Northern Virginia Community College

Darrelyn Miller, Grays Harbor College

Sue Mitchell, Calhoun Community College

Jacquie Moldenhauer, Front Range Community College

Linda Motonaga, Los Angeles City College

Sam Mryyan, Allen County Community College

Cindy Murphy, Southeastern Community College

Ryan Murphy, Sinclair Community College

Sharon E. Nastav, Johnson County Community College

Christine Naylor, Kent State University Ashtabula

Haji Nazarian, Seattle Central Community College

Nancy Noe, Linn-Benton Community College

Jennie Noriega, San Joaquin Delta College

Linda Nutter, Peninsula College

Thomas Omerza, Middle Bucks Institute of Technology

Edith Orozco, St. Philip's College

Dona Orr, Boise State University

Joanne Osgood, Chaffey College

Janice Owens, Kishwaukee College

Tatyana Pashnyak, Bainbridge College

John Partacz, College of DuPage

Tim Paul, Montana State University–Great Falls

Joseph Perez, South Texas College

Mike Peterson, Chemeketa Community College

Dr. Karen R. Petitto, West Virginia Wesleyan College

Terry Pierce, Onandaga Community College

Ashlee Pieris, Raritan Valley Community College

Jamie Pinchot, Thiel College

Michelle Poertner, Northwestern Michigan College

Betty Posta, University of Toledo

Deborah Powell, West Central Technical College

Mark Pranger, Rogers State University

Carolyn Rainey, Southeast Missouri State University

Linda Raskovich, Hibbing Community College

Leslie Ratliff, Griffin Technical College

Mar-Sue Ratzke, Rio Hondo Community College

Roxy Reissen, Southeastern Community College

Silvio Reyes, Technical Career Institutes

Patricia Rishavy, Anoka Technical College

Jean Robbins, Southeast Technical Institute

Carol Roberts, Eastern Maine Community College and University of Maine

Teresa Roberts, Wilson Technical Community College

Vicki Robertson, Southwest Tennessee Community College

Betty Rogge, Ohio State Agricultural Technical Institute

Lynne Rusley, Missouri Southern State University

Claude Russo, Brevard Community College

Ginger Sabine, Northwestern Technical College

Steven Sachs, Los Angeles Valley College

Joanne Salas, Olympic College

Lloyd Sandmann, Pima Community College–Desert Vista Campus

Beverly Santillo, Georgia Perimeter College

Theresa Savarese, San Diego City College

Sharolyn Sayers, Milwaukee Area Technical College

Judith Scheeren, Westmoreland County Community College

Adolph Scheiwe, Joliet Junior College

Marilyn Schmid, Asheville-Buncombe Technical Community College

Janet Sebesy, Cuyahoga Community College

Phyllis T. Shafer, Brookdale Community College

Ralph Shafer, Truckee Meadows Community College

Anne Marie Shanley, County College of Morris

Shelia Shelton, Surry Community College

Merilyn Shepherd, Danville Area Community College

Susan Sinele, Aims Community College

Beth Sindt, Hawkeye Community College

Andrew Smith, Marian College

Brenda Smith, Southwest Tennessee Community College

Lynne Smith, State University of New York–Delhi

Rob Smith, Katharine Gibbs School–Philadelphia

Tonya Smith, Arkansas State University–Mountain Home

Del Spencer–Trinity Valley Community College

Jeri Spinner, Idaho State University

Eric Stadnik, Santa Rosa Junior College

Karen Stanton, Los Medanos College

Meg Stoner, Santa Rosa Junior College

Beverly Stowers, Ivy Tech Community College of Indiana

Marcia Stranix, Yuba College

Kim Styles, Tri-County Technical College

Sylvia Summers, Tacoma Community College

Beverly Swann, Delaware Technical & Community College

Ann Taff, Tulsa Community College

Mike Theiss, University of Wisconsin–Marathon Campus

Romy Thiele, Cañada College

Sharron Thompson, Portland Community College

Ingrid Thompson-Sellers, Georgia Perimeter College

Barbara Tietsort, University of Cincinnati–Raymond Walters College

Janine Tiffany, Reading Area Community College

Denise Tillery, University of Nevada Las Vegas

Susan Trebelhorn, Normandale Community College

Noel Trout, Santiago Canyon College

Cheryl Turgeon, Asnuntuck Community College

Steve Turner, Ventura College

Sylvia Unwin, Bellevue Community College

Lilly Vigil, Colorado Mountain College

Sabrina Vincent, College of the Mainland

Mary Vitrano, Palm Beach Community College

Brad Vogt, Northeast Community College

Cozell Wagner, Southeastern Community College

Carolyn Walker, Tri-County Technical College

Sherry Walker, Tulsa Community College

Qi Wang, Tacoma Community College

Betty Wanielista, Valencia Community College

Marge Warber, Lanier Technical College–Forsyth Campus

Marjorie Webster, Bergen Community College

Linda Wenn, Central Community College

Mark Westlund, Olympic College

Carolyn Whited, Roane State Community College

Winona Whited, Richland College

Jerry Wilkerson, Scott Community College

Joel Willenbring, Fullerton College

Barbara Williams, WITC Superior

Charlotte Williams, Jones County Junior College

Bonnie Willy, Ivy Tech Community College of Indiana

Diane Wilson, J. Sargeant Reynolds Community College

James Wolfe, Metropolitan Community College

Marjory Wooten, Lanier Technical College

Mark Yanko, Hocking College

Alexis Yusov, Pace University

Naeem Zaman, San Joaquin Delta College

Kathleen Zimmerman, Des Moines Area Community College

We also thank Lutz Ziob, Merrick Van Dongen, Bruce Curling, Joe Wilson, Rob Linsky, Jim Clark, Scott Serna, Ben Watson, and David Bramble at Microsoft for their encouragement and support in making the Microsoft Official Academic Course programs the finest instructional materials for mastering the newest Microsoft technologies for both students and instructors.

Brief Contents

www.wiley.com/college/microsoft or
call the MOAC Toll-Free Number: 1+(888) 764-7001 (U.S. & Canada only)

Contents

Main Text Brief Contents

Introduction to Windows 7

OBJECTIVE DOMAIN MATRIX

TECHNOLOGY SKILL	OBJECTIVE NUMBER
Installing Windows 7	
List system requirements for Windows 7.	Supplemental
Using the Control Panel	
Describe the Control Panel and its use.	Supplemental
Using Microsoft Management Console and Administrative Tools	
Describe the Administrative Tools and its use.	Supplemental
Using a Troubleshooting Methodology	
List and describe the basic steps in troubleshooting.	Supplemental

KEY TERMS

Action Center

Administrative Tools

Computer Management console

Control Panel

Event Viewer

Microsoft Management Console (MMC)

ports

registry

service

After completing this lesson, you will have a better understanding of the role that Windows 7 plays in today's computer world. You will know how to use the basic configuration tools used in Windows 7, which can be key in troubleshooting a wide range of problems. Lesson 1 will finish by looking at a basic troubleshooting methodology model, which can be used in troubleshooting problems with computers running Windows 7 as well as many other Information Technology platforms.

You were just hired as an administrator for the Acme Corporation. You have problems on several machines that you need to troubleshoot. Since you are new to the company and how the computers are set up, you decide to stick with the basics and first determine what the problems are and what each machine contains so that you can better troubleshoot the problem. Therefore, you use the tools that are available in the Control Panel and Administrative Tools to help troubleshoot these problems.

Introducing Windows 7

THE BOTTOM LINE

Windows 7 is the newest version of Microsoft Windows operating system for desktop computers for use on personal computers, including home and business desktops, laptops, netbooks, tablet PCs, and media center PCs. Windows 7 was released to manufacturing on July 22, 2009, and reached general retail availability on October 22, 2009, less than three years after the release of its predecessor, Windows Vista.

Windows 7 will become the dominant operating system to replace Windows XP and Windows Vista. Windows 7 is based on Windows Vista and was designed to address those points for which Windows Vista was criticized. Unlike its predecessor, which introduced a large number of new features, Windows 7 was intended to be a more focused, incremental upgrade to the Windows line, with its main goal being to continue compatibility with applications and hardware with which Windows Vista is already compatible. Similar to Windows Vista, one of the main goals of Windows 7 is to address security weaknesses found on the aging Windows XP.

Selecting Computer Hardware

When choosing what components to include in a computer that will run Windows 7, you should always favor components that offer the performance that you need along with reliability.

The primary subsystems that make up a computer are:

- Processor
- Memory
- Storage
- Network

If any of these fails, the entire system can fail. In addition, if any one of these is asked to do more than what it was designed for, it can cause a bottleneck that may affect the performance of the entire system.

The subsystems just listed are not the only components that make up the computer, but they are the primary ones that are often looked at when determining what a computer can handle. Two subsystems that are essential for gaming, presentation, and video applications are the video system (including the monitor and video cards/adapters) and the sound card/adapter.

LOOKING AT THE PROCESSOR

The computer is built around one or more integrated chips called the processor. It is considered the brain of the computer because all of the instructions it performs are mathematical calculations and logical comparisons. Today's processors are mostly produced by Intel and AMD.

Today, the clock speed of the processor is usually expressed in gigahertz (GHz). A gigahertz is 1 billion (1,000,000,000) cycles per second. During each cycle, a circuit will react in a predictable way (bring in a value, perform a calculation, or perform a comparison). It is these reactions that make the computer do what it does. Of course, if a processor runs at a faster speed, it would be safe to assume it could do more in less time.

Over the last several years though, speed is not the only factor that determines processor performance. Most processors sold today are multicore processors that are like having two or more processing cores packaged as one. In addition, they use other technologies to keep the processor working at peak efficiency, like using an assembly line approach or trying to anticipate what it needs to do first so that it can keep all pipelines working.

Another factor is how much data a processor can process. For years, processors were 32-bit processors that could process up to 4 GB or 64 GB of memory. The newer processors made today are 64-bit processors as compared to the older 32-bit processors. A 64-bit processor is a processor with a default word size of 64 bits and a 64-bit external data bus. Most people don't realize that today's processors can already handle 64-bit calculations (remember, every value, small and large numbers, and numbers with decimal points are broken down into 0s and 1s [bits]). Most processors internally can process 128, 256, and maybe larger numbers. But one of the main benefits of 64-bit processors is that they can process significantly more memory than 32-bit processors (4 GB with a 32-bit address bus and 64 GB with a 36-bit address bus). Technically a 64-bit processor can access up to 16.3 billion gigabytes (16 exabytes). The AMD64 architecture currently has a 52-bit limit on physical memory (which supports up to 4 petabytes or 4048 terabytes) and only supports a 48-bit virtual address space (256 terabytes). Usually, you will reach the limit of the motherboard or memory chips before you reach the limit of the processor.

With more data in memory, a 64-bit processor can work faster because it can access larger amounts of RAM instead of swapping data back and forth with the much slower disks. In addition, with the larger internal registers, it can process larger numbers without breaking them into several smaller numbers, and it can even take several smaller numbers and do some mathematical calculation or comparison to these numbers at the same time. Today, just about every computer processor sold is a 64-bit processor.

If an operating system and programs are written to use the larger 64-bit calculations and use the additional accessible memory, the processing power of a computer can be significantly increased. Most programs designed for a computer running a 32-bit version of Windows will work on a computer running 64-bit versions of Windows. Notable exceptions are some anti-virus programs and some hardware drivers. The biggest problem that you may encounter is finding 64-bit drivers for some of your older hardware devices.

LOOKING AT RAM

RAM (random access memory) is the computer's short-term or temporary memory. It stores instructions and data that the processor accesses directly. If you have more RAM, you can load more instructions and data from the disks. In addition, having sufficient RAM can be the largest factor in your overall computer performance. Unfortunately, if power is discontinued from the RAM such as what occurs when you shut off your PC, the contents of the RAM disappear. This is the reason you use disks for long-term storage.

LOOKING AT DRIVES

Traditionally, hard drives are half electronic/half mechanical devices that store magnetic fields on rotating platters. Today, some hard drives, known as solid-state drives, are electronic devices with no mechanical components.

Most systems today have some form of optical drive. Older systems will have compact disk drives, which use disks similar to a music CD player. Newer systems have either a DVD or

Blu-ray drive. The Windows 7 installation disk is a DVD. In either case, the optical drives store information using laser light. Traditionally, optical disks were considered read-only devices but many systems have burning capabilities that allow the user to write data to special optical disks.

LOOKING AT NETWORK CONNECTIONS

The last primary component that makes up a computer is the network connection. Without a network connection, the computer will not be able to communicate with other computers. Most personal computers have network interface cards or NICs that allow them to communicate over corporate networks or to connect to the Internet via a cable or DSL modem.

LOOKING AT THE MOTHERBOARD

Another component that brings these four subsystems together is the motherboard. For the processor to communicate with the rest of the system, it plugs in or connects to a large circuit board called the motherboard or system board. The motherboard allows the processor to branch out and communicate with all of the other computer components. The motherboard is considered the nervous system of the PC. While the capabilities of the motherboard have been greatly expanded (most include sound and network connectivity), you can further expand the capabilities of the system by installing expansion cards.

On the motherboard, you will find the processors and RAM. In addition, you will find the chipset and the BIOS on the motherboard. The chipset represents the nerve clusters that connect your various components including the keyboard, disk drives, and RAM. Depending on the design of the motherboard, one chipset will run faster than another chipset or have more redundant features. Of course, these types of systems usually cost more.

On the motherboard and expansion cards, you will find firmware. Firmware is software contained in read-only memory (ROM) chips. Different from RAM, ROM instructions are permanent and can't be changed or erased by normal means. When you shut off your computer, those instructions remain so that when you turn your computer on again, it knows how to boot the system, test the system, and find a boot device such as your hard drive.

Instructions that control much of the computer's input/output functions, such as communicating with disks, RAM, and the monitor kept in the system ROM chips are known as the BIOS (basic input/output system). You can think of the BIOS as the computer's instincts. By having instructions (software) written on the BIOS, the system already knows how to communicate with some basic components such as a keyboard and how to read some basic disks such as IDE drives. It also looks for additional ROM chips, which may be on the motherboard or on expansion cards that you add to the system. These ROM chips have additional instructions to operate additional devices such as adding SCSI or RAID drives.

If you have not realized it by now, the instructions written on the BIOS is software. Different from the normal software you purchase at a store or order off the Internet, it is not written on a disk. Unfortunately like any software, the BIOS may need to have a bug fixed or may need to be expanded to support a new type of hardware that did not exist when the BIOS was written. Sometimes a newer BIOS version can lead to better system performance. To overcome some problems, you would have to check with your system or motherboard manufacturer to see if they have a new version of the BIOS that you can download and apply to your system. The process of updating your system ROM BIOS is called flashing the BIOS.

Unfortunately, flashing the BIOS is a delicate process. If the process gets interrupted while you are flashing the BIOS or you install the wrong version, your system may no longer be accessible and you may need to replace your motherboard to overcome the problem.

Therefore, if it is your first time in flashing a system, you should do it a couple of times with someone who has done it before. In addition, you should enter your BIOS or CMOS Setup program and write down all of your current settings. This is usually done by pressing a key or combination of keys early during the boot process before the operating system loads. Common keys are usually the Delete or F10 key. To find out which key or keys to use, look at the screen during boot up or access the computer or motherboard manual. Finally, be sure to thoroughly review the system or motherboard manufacturer's website to determine what version of the BIOS your system has and which is the correct new version to download and install. You will then download the BIOS image and an executable program to flash the BIOS.

LOOKING AT POWER SUPPLIES AND CASES

Before moving on, we should discuss power supplies and cases. A case provides an enclosure that helps protect the components that are inside of the case. The case with the power supplies and additional fans are usually designed to provide a fair amount of airflow through the system to keep the system cool. Typically if you have items that are designed for performance, they will produce heat, and too much heat is always bad for electronic and mechanical devices.

The power supply can be thought of as the blood of the computer. The computer runs on electricity. Without it, the computer is just a box. Since power supplies are half electronic and half mechanical devices, they are considered high-failure items when you compare them to pure electronic devices such as memory chips or processors. Mechanical devices tend to wear out over a period of time.

LOOKING AT PORTS

With computers, you need to be able to add external devices. *Ports* are plug sockets that enable an external device such as a printer, keyboard, mouse, or external drive. These ports are usually identified by the shape of the plug socket, the number of pins, the number of rows of pins, and the orientation of the pins (male or female). The most popular ports (see Figure 1-1) are:

- **Parallel port:** 2-row, 25-pin female D port—Considered a legacy port that used to connect printers.
- **Serial port:** 2-row, 9-pin male D port—While considered a legacy port, it is often used to connect to switches and routers to configure them. It can also be used to connect legacy keyboards, mice, and printers.
- **Universal serial bus (USB):** A popular device that can be used to connect keyboards, mice, printers, modems, and external disk drives.
- **PS/2 mouse or keyboard port:** 6-pin Mouse mini-DIN—Port used to connect a legacy mouse.
- **RJ-45 connector:** Used to connect a 10Base-T/100Base-T/1000Base-T network cable.

Figure 1-1

PC Ports (PS/2 mouse port, PS/2 keyboard port, Serial port, Parallel port, 1394 port, USB ports, RJ-45 port, DVI port, and VGA port)

LOOKING AT VIDEO SYSTEMS

The video system consists of video cards/adapters and the monitor. The video card or adapter is an expansion card that generates output images to a display or monitor. Video hardware can be integrated on the motherboard, often occurring with early machines. In this configuration it is sometimes referred to as a video controller or graphics controller.

Many video cards offer additional functionality such as accelerated rendering of 3D scenes and 2D graphics, video capture, TV-tuner adapter, MPEG-2/MPEG-4 decoding, FireWire, TV output, or the ability to connect multiple monitors (multimonitor). Some systems require high-performance video cards for graphical demanding purposes such as PC games and video editing.

For the video card to process graphics for display, the video card needs video memory. Some of these adapters have their own dedicated memory while some that are built into the motherboard use part of the RAM.

The most common connection systems between the video card and the computer display are:

- **Video Graphics Array (VGA):** 3-row, 15-pin female D connector—Analog-based standard used for CRT displays.
- **Digital Visual Interface (DVI):** Digital-based standard designed for displays such as flat-panel displays (LCDs, plasma screens, wide high-definition television displays), and video projectors.
- **Video In Video Out (VIVO) for S-Video, Composite video, and Component video:** Used for televisions, DVD players, video recorders, and video game consoles. They often come in two 9-pin Mini-DIN connector variations, and the VIVO splitter cable generally comes with either 4 connectors (S-Video in and out + composite video in and out), or 6 connectors (S-Video in and out + component PB out + component PR out + component Y out [also composite out] + composite in).
- **High-Definition Multimedia Interface (HDMI):** An advanced digital audio/video interconnect commonly used to connect game consoles and DVD players to a display. HDMI supports copy protection through HDCP.

Basic characteristics include:

- **Size of the monitor:** Diagonal measurement of the screen.
- **Display resolution:** Specified as the width and height in pixels.
- **Color depth:** Measured in bits, which indicate how many colors can be displayed on the screen at one time.
- **Refresh rate:** Expressed in hertz, which specify how often the image is redrawn on the screen.
- **Aspect ratio:** The ratio of the width of the image to its height, expressed as two numbers separated by a colon. Until about 2003, most computer monitors had a 4:3 aspect ratio. Since then, many monitors have a 16:9 aspect ratio, which is similar to a wide-screen TV.

LOOKING AT SOUND SYSTEMS

A sound card or audio card is a computer expansion card that facilitates the input and output of audio signals to and from a computer used with multimedia applications such as music composition, editing video or audio, presentation, education, and entertainment (games). Many computers have sound capabilities built in, while others require additional expansion cards to provide for audio capability.

Connectors on the sound cards are color coded as per the PC System Design Guide. They also have symbols with arrows, holes, and sound waves. Common connectors include:

- **Pink (microphone symbol):** Analog microphone audio input. 3.5 mm TRS A microphone.
- **Light blue (an arrow going into a circle):** Analog line level audio input.

- **Lime green (arrow going out one side of a circle into a wave):** Analog line level audio output for the main stereo signal (front speakers or headphones).
- **Gold/gray game port (arrow going out both sides into waves):** 15-pin 2-row D pin connector—Used as a game port (joysticks) or Musical Instrument Digital Interface (MIDI).

UTILIZING DESKTOP VERSUS MOBILE COMPONENTS

Windows 7 is usually found in desktop computers and mobile computers such as laptops, note-books, and subnotebooks. While these components are very similar, there are some differences. First, mobile components are usually smaller than their desktop version. Second, mobile components are designed to use less power so that you can get longer battery life. Of course, depending on its design and configuration, this usually means a reduction in performance.

■ Installing Windows 7

THE BOTTOM LINE | Before you can start using, managing, or configuring an operating system, you will need to first install the operating system.

CERTIFICATION READY
If you are giving a computer, can you determine if you can install Windows 7 on the computer?
Supplemental

While installing Windows 7 is discussed in other Microsoft courses, you still need to keep in mind the system requirements to properly run Windows 7 and its applications. The system requirements are listed in Table 1-1.

For the 32-bit version of Windows 7, Windows can recognize up to 4 GB of memory except for the Windows 7 Starter edition, which only recognizes 2 GB of memory. For the 64-bit version of Windows 7, Windows 7 Ultimate, Enterprise, and Professional can recognize up to 192 GB. Windows 7 Home Premium 64-bit recognizes up to 16 GB, and Windows 7 Home Basic 64-bit recognizes up to 8 GB of memory. For more information, visit: http://msdn. microsoft.com/en-us/library/aa366778(VS.85).aspx.

Table 1-1

Windows 7 system requirements

	32-BIT	64-BIT
Processor	1 GHz 32-bit processor	1 GHz 64-bit processor
Memory (RAM)	1 GB	2 GB
Graphics card	To support Aero, DirectX 9 graphics processor with WDDM driver model 1.0	To support Aero, DirectX 9 graphics processor with WDDM driver model 1.0
HDD free space	16 GB	20 GB
Optical drive	DVD for installation	DVD for installation

To minimize problems, you should only choose hardware that is on the Hardware Compatibility List (HCL) for Windows 7 because new hardware models and devices are being created every day. The HCL is found at http://www.microsoft.com/whdc/hcl/default.mspx.

If you have a computer running Windows XP or Windows Vista, you can test your machine for any hardware or software compatibility issues. The Windows 7 Upgrade Advisor scans your PC for potential compatibility issues and lets you know about your upgrade options. Within minutes, you'll get a report that tells you whether your PC meets the system requirements, a list of any known compatibility issues with your hardware, devices, and installed programs, and guidance on what to do before installing Windows 7 on your PC.

A clean installation is installing the software from scratch on a new drive or on a newly reformatted drive. Many people find that doing a clean install of an operating system is the best way to go because it offers a fresh start. The disadvantage is that the system and all of its software needs to be reinstalled, patched and configured, and data copied over, something that may take hours or even days.

Often when you buy proprietary computers such as HP, IBM, or Dell, they include a disk (typically a CD or DVD) with drivers. Because the Windows installation program may not know how to access some SCSI or RAID drives, you may need to click the Load Driver disk during the installation to specify the driver. In other instances, you will boot the disk that comes with the computer, run the associated program on the disk, configure the RAID controller and associated drives, partition the drives, and specify which operating system you want to install. The computer will then copy the drivers to a folder on the drive and either install the operating system from the disk or prompt you to insert the operating system installation disk. If you don't use this disk, the operating system installation disk will not recognize the drivers and will not load the necessary drivers during the installation process.

In some instances, you may want to take a current system and upgrade from Windows Vista to Windows 7 using the upgrade installation. Unfortunately, you cannot perform an in-place upgrade from 32-bit to 64-bit architecture and from one language to another. You can perform an in-place upgrade from a lower edition of Windows 7 to a higher one using the Windows Anytime Upgrade tool. You cannot upgrade directly from Windows XP to Windows 7. Instead, you will first have to upgrade to Windows Vista, then upgrade Windows Vista to Windows 7.

When you want to upgrade to Windows 7, you should follow these guidelines:

- Verify that the current computer will support Windows 7.
- Update your anti-virus program, run it, and then disable it. After you install Windows, remember to re-enable the anti-virus program, or install new anti-virus software that works with Windows 7.
- Back up your files. You can back up files to an external hard disk, a DVD or CD, or a network folder.
- Connect to the Internet. Make sure your Internet connection is working so that you can get the latest installation updates. These updates include security updates and hardware driver updates that can help with installation. If you don't have an Internet connection, you can still upgrade or install Windows.

If your system is a production system, verify and/or test all applications to make sure they are compatible with Windows 7.

■ Using the Control Panel

↓
THE BOTTOM LINE As with previous versions of Windows, the main graphical utility used to configure the Windows environment and hardware devices is the *Control Panel*.

CERTIFICATION READY
Do you know how to configure the Windows environment?

To access the Control Panel, you can click the Start button on the taskbar and select Control Panel. You can also display the Control Panel in any Windows Explorer view by clicking the leftmost option button in the Address bar and selecting Control Panel. See Figure 1-2.

Figure 1-2

Windows 7 Control Panel
in category view

Of the eight categories listed, each includes a top-level link, and under this link are several of the most frequently performed tasks for the category. Clicking a category link provides a list of utilities in that category. Each utility listed within a category includes a link to open the utility, and under this link are several of the most frequently performed tasks for the utility.

As with current and previous versions of Windows, you can change from the default category view to classic view (large icon view or small icon view). Icon view is an alternative view that provides the look and functionality of Control Panel in Windows 2000 and earlier versions of Windows where all options are displayed as applets or icons (see Figure 1-3).

Figure 1-3

Windows 7 Control Panel
in large icon view

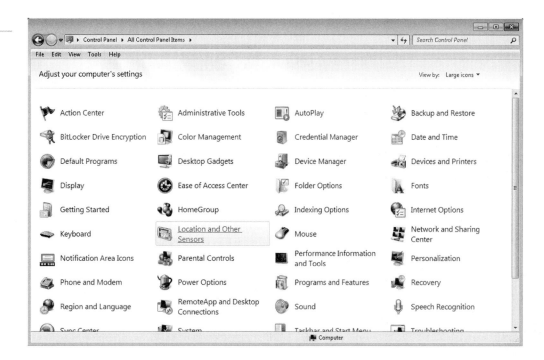

Looking at User Account Control

User Account Control (UAC) is a feature that started with Windows Vista and is included with Windows 7 that helps prevent unauthorized changes to your computer. If you are logged in as an administrator, UAC asks you for permission, and if you are logged in as a standard user, UAC will ask you for an administrator password before performing actions that could potentially affect your computer's operation or that change settings that affect other users. Since the UAC is designed to make sure that unauthorized changes are not made, especially by malicious software that you may not know you are running, you need to read the warnings carefully, and then make sure the name of the action or program that's about to start is one that you intended to start.

As a standard user, in Windows 7, you can do the following without administrative permissions or rights:

- Install updates from Windows Update.
- Install drivers from Windows Update or those that are included with the operating system.
- View Windows settings.
- Pair Bluetooth devices with the computer.
- Reset the network adapter and perform other network diagnostic and repair tasks.

When an application requests elevation or is run as administrator, UAC will prompt for confirmation and, if consent is given, allow access as an administrator.

UAC cannot be enabled or disabled for any individual user account. Instead, you enable or disable UAC for the computer, which affects all accounts running on the computer. If you disable UAC, you lose the additional security protections UAC offers, which may put the computer at risk. However, if you perform a lot of administrative tasks on a computer, the UAC prompts can be annoying and can stop you from doing certain activities including saving files to the root directory of a drive or the C:\Windows\System32 folder.

 ENABLE OR DISABLE UAC

GET READY. To enable or disable UAC, follow these steps:

1. If you are in the Control Panel's category view, click User Accounts. If you are in icon view, double-click User Accounts.
2. On the User Accounts page, click the Change User Account Control settings.
3. Then slide the slider to the appropriate options as shown in Table 1-2.
4. When prompted to restart the computer, click Restart Now or Restart Later as appropriate for the changes to take effect.

Besides manually configuring the UAC, some organizations may use group policies (including a computer's local policies) to ensure that the UAC is enabled so that the computer is protected from malware. The UAC settings group policy are located at Computer Configuration > Windows Settings > Security Settings > Local Policies > Security Options.

Table 1-2

UAC settings

SETTING	DESCRIPTION	SECURITY IMPACT
Always notify	You will be notified before programs make changes to your computer or to Windows settings that require the permissions of an administrator. When you're notified, your desktop will be dimmed, and you must either approve or deny the request in the UAC dialog box before you can do anything else on your computer. The dimming of your desktop is referred to as the secure desktop because other programs can't run while it's dimmed.	This is the most secure setting. When you are notified, you should carefully read the contents of each dialog box before allowing changes to be made to your computer.
Notify me only when programs try to make changes to my computer	You will be notified before programs make changes to your computer that require the permissions of an administrator. You will not be notified if you try to make changes to Windows settings that require the permissions of an administrator. You will be notified if a program outside of Windows tries to make changes to a Windows setting.	It's usually safe to allow changes to be made to Windows settings without notification. However, certain programs that come with Windows can have commands or data passed to them, and malicious software can take advantage of this by using these programs to install files or change settings on your computer. You should always be careful about which programs you allow to run on your computer.
Notify me only when programs try to make changes to my computer (do not dim my desktop)	You will be notified before programs make changes to your computer that require the permissions of an administrator. You will not be notified if you try to make changes to Windows settings that require the permissions of an administrator. You will be notified if a program outside of Windows tries to make changes to a Windows setting.	This setting is the same as "Notify only when programs try to make changes to my computer," but you are not notified on the secure desktop. Because the UAC dialog box isn't on the secure desktop with this setting, other programs might be able to interfere with the dialog's visual appearance. This is a small security risk if you already have a malicious program running on your computer.
Never notify	You will not be notified before any changes are made to your computer. If you are logged on as an administrator, programs can make changes to your computer without you knowing about it. If you are logged on as a standard user, any changes that require the permissions of an administrator will automatically be denied. If you select this setting, you will need to restart the computer to complete the process of turning off UAC. Once UAC is off, people who log on as administrator will always have the permissions of an administrator.	This is the least secure setting. When you set UAC to never notify, you open up your computer to potential security risks. If you set UAC to never notify, you should be careful about which programs you run, because they will have the same access to the computer as you do. This includes reading and making changes to protected system areas, your personal data, saved files, and anything else stored on the computer. Programs will also be able to communicate and transfer information to and from anything your computer connects with, including the Internet.

Configuring System Settings

One of the most important configuration settings for a Windows administrator is the system settings within the Control Panel. This includes gathering generation information about your system, changing the computer name, adding the computer to a domain, accessing the device manager, configuring remote settings, configuring startup and recovery options, and configuring overall performance settings.

To access system settings, you can do one of the following:

- If you are in Category view, click System and Security and click System, or click View amount of RAM and processor speed.
- If in classic view, double-click the System applet.
- Right-click Computer and select Properties.

In Windows, there are often several ways to do the same thing.

At the top of the screen you see the Windows edition you have and the system type (32-bit versus 64-bit). Toward the bottom of the screen you will see the computer name and domain (if any), if Windows is activated and the Product ID. See Figure 1-4.

Figure 1-4

Control Panel system settings

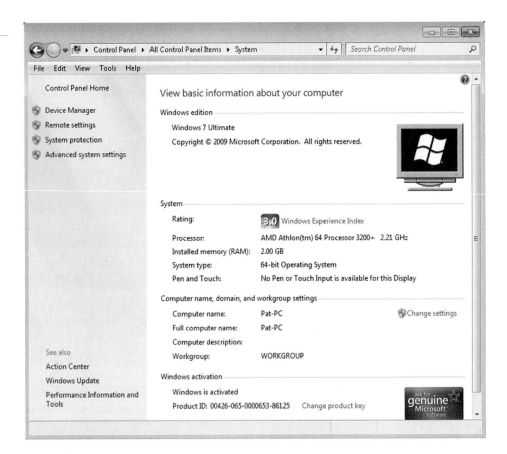

Changing Computer Name and Domain Settings

To help identify computers, you should name a computer with a meaningful name, which is done within the system settings in Control Panel. You can also add a computer to a domain or workgroup.

Every computer should have a unique computer name assigned to a network. If two computers have the same name, one or both of the computers will have trouble communicating on the network. To change the computer name, open System from the Control Panel. Then click the Change Settings option in the Computer name, domain, and workgroup settings. When the System Properties box appears with the Computer Name tab selected, you then click the Change button. See Figure 1-5.

Figure 1-5

Control Panel system properties

By default, a computer is part of a workgroup, which is usually associated with a peer-to-peer network where user accounts are decentralized and stored on each individual computer. If you have several users that need to access the computer (with unique usernames and passwords), you need to create a user account for each user on the computer. If you want those users to access another stand-alone computer, you will have to create the same computer accounts and passwords on that computer as well. As you can imagine, with several computers, this can become a lot of work as you keep creating and managing accounts on each individual machine.

A domain is a logical unit of computers that defines a security boundary and is usually associated with Microsoft's Active Directory. The security of the domain is generally centralized and controlled by Windows servers acting as domain controllers. As a result, you can manage the security much easier for multiple computers while providing better security.

When a computer is added to a domain, an account is created that represents the computer and information is stored on the computer to uniquely identify it, all of which contribute to a more secure work environment.

To add the computer to the domain, open the System Properties, and click the Change button. Then select the Domain option and type in the name of the domain. Click OK. The computer then prompts you to log in as a domain account with the ability to add computers to the domain. This is typically a domain administrator or account administrator. After you enter the credentials (username and password), a Welcome dialog box appears. After you click OK to close the Welcome dialog box and you have closed the System Properties dialog box, you will be prompted to reboot the computer.

To remove a computer from a domain, join an existing workgroup, or create a new workgroup, select the workgroup option and type in the name of the workgroup. Then click OK. If you are removing yourself from the domain, you will be asked for administrative credentials so that the account can be deleted from Active Directory.

Changing Date and Time

One of your easiest tasks is making sure that the computer has the correct date and time, which is essential for logging purposes and for security. If a secure packet is sent with the wrong date or time, the packet may be automatically denied because the date and time is used to determine if the packet is legit.

To access the date and time settings, do one of the following:

- Click Clock, Language, and Region in the Control Panel while in Category view and click Set the time and date.
- Double-click Date and Time while in Icon view.
- If the date and time show in the Notification area, double-click the date and time.

To set the clock:

1. Click the Date and Time tab and then click Change date and Time.
2. Double-click the hour, minutes, or seconds, and then click the arrows to increase or decrease the value.
3. When you are finished changing the time settings, click OK.

To change the time zone, click Change time zone and click your current time zone in the drop-down list. Then click OK.

If you are part of a domain, the computer should be synchronized with the domain controllers. If you have a computer that is not part of a domain, you can synchronize with an Internet time server by clicking the Internet Time tab and selecting the check box next to Synchronize with an Internet time server. Then select a time server and click OK.

Using the Action Center

Action Center is a central place to view alerts and take actions that can help keep Windows running smoothly.

Action Center lists important messages about security and maintenance settings that need your attention. Red items in Action Center are labeled Important and indicate significant issues that should be addressed soon, such as an outdated anti-virus program that needs updating. See Figure 1-6. Yellow items are tasks that you should consider addressing, like recommended maintenance tasks.

To view details about either the Security or Maintenance section, click the heading or the arrow next to the heading to expand or collapse the section. If you don't want to see certain types of messages, you can choose to hide them from view.

Figure 1-6

Action Center

You can quickly see whether there are any new messages in Action Center by placing your mouse over the Action Center icon in the notification area on the taskbar. Click the icon to view more detail, and click a message to address the issue. Or, open Action Center to view the message in its entirety.

If you're having a problem with your computer, check Action Center to see if the issue has been identified. If it hasn't, you can also find helpful links to troubleshooters and other tools that can help fix problems.

One tool hidden within the Action Center is the Reliability Monitor. This is an advanced tool that measures hardware and software problems and other changes to your computer. It provides a stability index that ranges from 1 (the least stable) to 10 (the most stable). You can use the index to help evaluate the reliability of your computer. Any change you make to your computer or problem that occurs on your computer affects the stability index.

To get to the Reliability Monitor, you just need to open the Action Center. Then under the Maintenance section, click View reliability history. You can then:

- Click any event on the graph to view its details.
- Click Days or Weeks to view the stability index over a specific period of time.
- Click items in the Action column to view more information about each event.
- Click View all problem reports to view only the problems that have occurred on your computer. This view doesn't include the other computer events that show up in Reliability Monitor, such as events about software installation.

Troubleshooting Using the Control Panel

The Control Panel contains several troubleshooting programs that can automatically fix some common problems with your computer, such as problems with networking, hardware, or devices using the web and program compatibility.

Troubleshooters are designed fix a variety of common problems. They are not designed to fix every problem but can fix common problems quickly. When you run a troubleshooter, it might ask you some questions or reset common settings as it works to fix the problem. Windows includes several troubleshooters, and more are available online when you select the Get the most up-to-date troubleshooters from the Windows Online Troubleshooting service check box at the bottom of Troubleshooting.

Troubleshooter tools and tasks allow you to:

- Run programs made for previous versions of Windows.
- Configure a device.
- Use a printer.
- Troubleshoot audio recording.
- Troubleshoot audio playback.
- Connect to the Internet.
- Access shared files and folders on other computers.
- Display Aero desktop effects.
- Fix problems with Windows Update.
- Run maintenance tasks.
- Improve power usage.
- Check for performance issues.

If the troubleshooter fixed the problem, you can close the troubleshooter. If it couldn't fix the problem, you can view several options that will take you online to find an answer. In either case, you can always view a complete list of changes made. If you click the Advanced link on a troubleshooter and then clear the Apply repairs automatically check box, the troubleshooter displays a list of fixes to choose from, if any problems are found.

■ Using Microsoft Management Console and Administrative Tools

THE BOTTOM LINE

The *Microsoft Management Console (MMC)* is one of the primary administrative tools used to manage Windows and many of the network services provided by Windows. It provides a standard method to create, save, and open the various administrative tools provided by Windows. When you open Administrative Tools, most of these programs are MMC.

To start an empty MMC, go to the command prompt, Start Search box or Run box, type mmc or mmc.exe. Every MMC has a console tree that displays the hierarchical organization of snap-ins (or pluggable modules) and extensions (a snap-in that requires a parent snap-in). By adding and deleting snap-ins and extensions, users can customize the console or access tools that are not located in Administrative Tools. You can add snap-ins to a MMC by opening the File menu and selecting Add/Remove Snap-ins. See Figure 1-7.

Figure 1-7

Adding snap-ins to a blank MMC

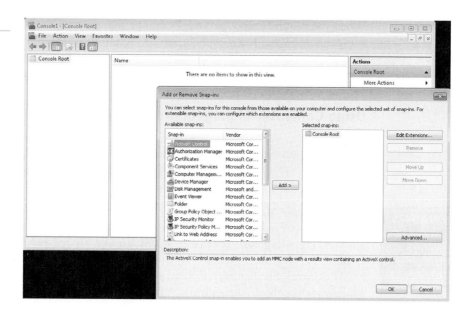

Administrative Tools is a folder in the Control Panel that contains tools for system administrators and advanced users. To access the Administrative Tools, open the Control Panel, open Administrative Tools by clicking Start, Control Panel, System and Security while in category view or double-click the Administrative Tools applet while in icon view. There is also a quick link on Windows that can be accessed by clicking the Start button.

Some common administrative tools in this folder include:

- **Component Services:** Configure and administer Component Object Model (COM) components. Component Services is designed for use by developers and administrators.

- **Computer Management:** Manage local or remote computers by using a single, consolidated desktop tool. Using Computer Management, you can perform many tasks, such as monitoring system events, configuring hard disks, and managing system performance.

- **Data Sources (ODBC):** Use Open Database Connectivity (ODBC) to move data from one type of database (a data source) to another.

- **Event Viewer:** View information about significant events, such as programs starting or stopping or security errors that are recorded in event logs.

- **iSCSI Initiator:** Configure advanced connections between storage devices on a network.

- **Local Security Policy:** View and edit Group Policy security settings.

- **Performance Monitor:** View Advanced system information about the processor, memory, hard disk, and network performance.

- **Print Management:** Manage printers and print servers on a network and perform other administrative tasks.

- **Services:** Manage the different services that run in the background on your computer.

- **System Configuration:** Identify problems that might be preventing Windows from running correctly.

- **Task Scheduler:** Schedule programs or other tasks to run automatically.

- **Windows Memory Diagnostics:** Check your computer's memory to see whether it is functioning properly.

- **Windows PowerShell Modules:** A task-based command-line shell and scripting language designed especially for system administration.

When you use these tools, you might assume that they are used only to manage the local computer. However, many of them can be used to manage remote computers as well. For example, you can use the Computer Management console to connect to and manage other computers, assuming you have administrative rights to the computer.

Using Computer Management Console

The Computer Management console is one of the primary tools to manage a computer running Windows 7 and includes the most commonly used MMC snap-ins.

CERTIFICATION READY
How can you access the Computer Management console?
Supplemental

The *Computer Management console* is available in Windows Server 2003, Windows Server 2008, Windows XP, Windows Vista, and Windows 7. It includes multiple snap-ins including Task Scheduler, Event Viewer, Shared Folders, Local Users and Groups, Performance, Device Management, Routing and Remote Access, Services, and WMI Control. See Figure 1-8. If you are using Windows 7, you can access the Computer Management console through the Administrative Tools or by right-clicking Computer and clicking Manage.

Figure 1-8

Computer Management console

■ Looking at Services

THE BOTTOM LINE

A *service* is a program, routine, or process that performs a specific system function to support other programs or to provide a network service. It runs in the system background without a user interface. Some examples include web serving, event logging, and file serving.

To manage the services, use the Services console located under Administrative Tools (see Figure 1-9). The Services snap-in is also included in the Computer Management console. You can also execute services.mmc from a command prompt, Start Search box or Run box.

To start, stop, pause, resume, or restart services, right-click on the service and click on the desired option. To the left of the service name is a description. To configure a service,

Figure 1-9

Services console

right-click the service and click on the Properties option or double-click the service. On the General tab, under the start-up type pull-down option, set the following:

- **Automatic:** Specifies that the service should start automatically when the system starts.
- **Automatic (Delayed Start):** Specifies that the service should start automatically after the services marked as automatic have started (which is approximately 2 minutes).
- **Manual:** Specifies that a user or a dependent service can start the service. Services with manual start-up do not start automatically when the system starts.
- **Disable:** Prevents the service from being started by the system, a user, or any dependent service.

If you like doing things at the command prompt or you have a need use a script to start or stop a service, you would use the sc command to communicate with the Service Control Manager and Services. The sc config command is used to modify a service entry in the registry and Service Database. You can also use the net start and net stop commands to start and stop services.

When you configure a service, you need to configure what account the service runs under. You can use the built-in accounts included with Windows or you can use a service account that you create locally or on the domain. The built-in accounts include:

- **Local System:** Highly privileged account that can access most resources on the local computer.
- **NT Authority/LocalService:** Has the same privileges of the local Users group on the computer. When it accesses Network resources, it uses no credentials and a null session.
- **NT Authority/NetworkService:** Has the same level of access as the Users group on the local computer. When it accesses network resources, it does so under the context of the local computer account.

You should always take care when changing the Startup parameters for a service including the Startup Type and Log On As settings since these changes might prevent key services from running correctly. In addition, Microsoft recommends that you do not change the Allow service to interact with desktop settings since this will allow the service to access any information displayed on the interactive user's desktop. A malicious user could then take control of the service or attack it from the interactive desktop. If you specify an account that does not have permission to log on as a service, the Services snap-in automatically grants the appropriate permissions to that account on the computer you are managing. If you use a local or domain account, make sure that the account uses a password that does not expire and that you use a strong password.

If you enable or disable a service and a problem occurs, you can try to start the service manually and see what happens. You can also look in the Event Viewer for more information on some of the errors. If the system does not boot because of the enabled or disabled service, you should try to start the computer in Safe mode, which will only start the core services needed to operate. By using Safe mode, you should have an opportunity to fix the problem.

If you are new to Windows, particularly in administering and configuring Windows, you should take some time, click on each service and read the description of each service. You will learn that many service names are very descriptive. For now, let's cover two specific services:

- **Server:** Supports file, print, and named-pipe sharing over the network. If Services is not started, you will not be able to access shared folders including administrative shares such as C$ and IPC$.

- **Workstation:** Creates and maintains client network connections to remote servers using the SMB protocol. Without this service, you will not be able to access shared folders on other computers.

■ Looking at the Registry

The *registry* is a central, secure database in which Windows stores all hardware configuration information, software configuration information, and system security policies. Components that use the registry include the Windows kernel, device drivers, setup programs, hardware profiles, and user profiles.

Most of the time, you will not need to access the registry because programs and applications typically make all the necessary changes automatically. For example, when you change your desktop background or change the default color for Windows, you access the Display settings within the Control Panel, and it saves the changes to the registry.

If you do need to access the registry to make changes, you should closely follow the instructions from a reputable source because an incorrect change to your computer's registry could render your computer inoperable. However, there may be a time when you need to make a change in the registry because there is no interface or program to make the change. To view and manually change the registry, you use the Registry Editor (Regedit.exe), which can be executed from the command prompt, Start Search box or Run box. See Figure 1-10.

The Registry is split into a several logical sections, often referred to as hives, which are generally named by their Windows API definitions. The hives beginning with HKEY are often abbreviated to a three- or four-letter short name starting with HK. For example, HKCU is HKEY_CURRENT_USER and HKLM is HKEY_LOCAL_MACHINE. Windows 7 has 5 Root Keys/HKEYs:

- **HKEY_CLASSES_ROOT:** Stores information about registered applications, such as file association that tells which default program opens a file with a certain extension.

Figure 1-10

Registry Editor

- **HKEY_CURRENT_USER:** Stores settings specific to the currently logged in user. When a user logs off, the HKEY_CURRENT_USER is saved to HKEY_USERS.
- **HKEY_LOCAL_MACHINE:** Stores settings specific to the local computer.
- **HKEY_USERS:** Contains subkeys corresponding to the HKEY_CURRENT_USER keys for each user profile actively loaded on the machine.
- **HKEY_CURRENT_CONFIG:** Contains information gathered at runtime. Information stored in this key is not permanently stored on disk, but rather regenerated at boot time.

Registry keys are similar to folders, which can contain values or subkeys. The keys within the registry follow a syntax that is similar to a Windows folder or file path using backslashes to separate each level. For example:

HKEY_LOCAL_MACHINE/Software/Microsoft/Windows refers to the subkey "Windows" of the subkey "Microsoft" of the subkey "Software" of the HKEY_LOCAL_MACHINE key.

Registry values include a name and a value. There are multiple types of values. Some of the common key types are shown in Table 1-3.

Reg files (also known as Registration entries) are text files for storing portions of the registry. They have a .reg filename extension. If you double-click a reg file, it will add the registry entries into the registry. You can export any registry subkey by right-clicking the subkey and choosing Export. You can back up the entire registry to a reg file by right-clicking Computer at the top of Regedit and selecting export or you can back up the system state with Windows Backup.

Table 1-3

Registry key types

NAME	DATA TYPE	DESCRIPTION
Binary value	REG_BINARY	Raw binary data; most hardware component information is stored as binary data is displayed in Registry Editor in hexadecimal format.
DWORD value	REG_DWORD	Data represented by a number that is 4 bytes long (a 32-bit integer); many parameters for device drivers and services are this type and are displayed in Registry Editor in binary, hexadecimal, or decimal format.
Expandable String value	REG_EXPAND_SZ	A variable-length data string; this data type includes variables that are resolved when a program or service uses the data.
Multi-String value	REG_MULTI_SZ	A multiple string; values that contain lists or multiple values in a form that people can read are generally this type. Entries are separated by spaces, commas, or other marks.
String value	REG_SZ	A fixed-length text string.
QWORD value	REG_QWORD	Data represented by a number that is a 64-bit integer; this data is displayed in Registry Editor as a Binary value and was introduced in Windows 2000.

Using a Troubleshooting Methodology

 THE BOTTOM LINE As a computer technician, you will eventually have to deal with problems. Some problems will have obvious solutions and be easy to fix. Many problems will need to be figured out by following a troubleshooting methodology.

The whole purpose of effective troubleshooting methodologies is to reduce the amount of guesswork and random solutions so that you can troubleshoot and fix the problem in a timely manner. Microsoft Product Support Service engineers use the "detect method," which consists of the following six steps:

1. **Discover the problem:** Identify and document problem symptoms, and search technical information resources including searching Microsoft Knowledge Base (KB) articles to determine whether the problem is a known condition.

2. **Evaluate system configuration:** Ask the client or customer and check the system's documentation to determine if any hardware, software, or network changes have been made including any new additions. Also check any available logs including looking in the Event Viewer.

3. **List or track possible solutions, and try to isolate the problem by removing or disabling hardware or software components:** You may also consider turning on additional logging or running diagnostic programs to gather more information and test certain components.

4. **Execute a plan:** Test potential solutions and have a contingency plan if these solutions do not work or have a negative impact on the computer. Of course, you don't want to make the problem worse, so if possible, back up any critical system or application files.

5. **Check results:** If the problem is not fixed, go back to track possible solutions.

6. **Take a proactive approach:** Document changes that you made along the way while troubleshooting the problem. Also notify the customer or client and document internal systems of the problem in case it happens in the future or if those changes that fixed the problem affect other areas.

So when troubleshooting problems, you do have several tools that can help isolate and fix the problems including:

- System Information
- Device Manager
- Event Viewer
- Task Manager
- Resource Monitor
- Performance Monitor
- System Configuration
- Memory Diagnostics tool
- Troubleshooting Wizard
- Boot Menu including Safe mode
- Windows Repair

When troubleshooting issues within Windows and related programs, you will eventually deal with problems where you do not know what to do. Therefore, you will have to ask co-workers and research on the Internet. Using good search engines, such as Google and Bing, is invaluable. You will also need to check the vendor websites including Microsoft's website (www.microsoft.com).

Most of the information available from Microsoft to design, plan, implement, manage, and monitor Microsoft products will be found on the Microsoft website, particularly at Microsoft TechNet (http://technet.microsoft.com), which includes Microsoft Knowledge Base, service packs, security updates, resource kits, technical training, operations and deployment guides, white papers, and case studies.

Information used mostly for troubleshooting can be found in Microsoft's Knowledge Base and at several online forums (such as http://social.microsoft.com/forums and http://social.technet.microsoft.com/Forums). These are helpful for a wide range of problems and allow you to leave messages for others to answer. The Microsoft Knowledge Base is a repository of thousand of articles made available to the public by Microsoft Corporation that contains information on many problems encountered by users of Microsoft products. Each article bears an ID number and is often referred to by its Knowledge Base (KB) ID. Access the Knowledge Base by entering keywords or the ID at http://support.microsoft.com/search/.

Viewing System Information

When you first start troubleshooting a computer, you need to know what is in the computer and what is running on the computer. Look at System properties for the processor and amount of RAM. Look at Device Manager to see what hardware is recognized and what drivers are loaded. The System Information program is a useful troubleshooting tool that you can use to see inside a system.

System Information (also known as msinfo32.exe) shows details about your computer's hardware configuration, computer components, and software, including drivers. It was originally included with Windows to assist Microsoft support people in determining machine specifics especially when talking to end users, but it can be used by anyone at any time.

System Information lists categories in the left pane and details about each category in the right pane. See Figure 1-11. The categories include:

- **System Summary:** Displays general information about your computer and the operating system, such as the computer name and manufacturer, the type of basic input/output system (BIOS) your computer uses, and the amount of memory that's installed.
- **Hardware Resources:** Displays advanced details about your computer's hardware, and is intended for IT professionals.
- **Components:** Displays information about disk drives, sound devices, modems, and other components installed on your computer.
- **Software Environment:** Displays information about drivers, network connections, and other program-related details.

Figure 1-11

System Information

To find a specific detail in System Information, type what you're looking for in the Find what box at the bottom of the window. For example, to find your computer's Internet protocol (IP) address, type ip address in the Find what box, and then click Find.

Using the Event Viewer

One of the most useful troubleshooting tools is the Event Viewer MMC snap-in, which essentially is a log viewer. Any time you have problems, you should look in the Event Viewer to check for any errors or warnings that may reveal what the problem is.

The *Event Viewer* is a Microsoft Management Console (MMC) snap-in that enables you to browse and manage event logs. It is included in the Computer Management console and is included in Administrative Tools as a stand-alone console. You can also execute the eventvwr.msc command.

You can perform the following tasks using Event Viewer:

- View events from multiple event logs; see Figure 1-12.
- Save useful event filters as custom views that can be reused.

Figure 1-12

Windows Event Viewer

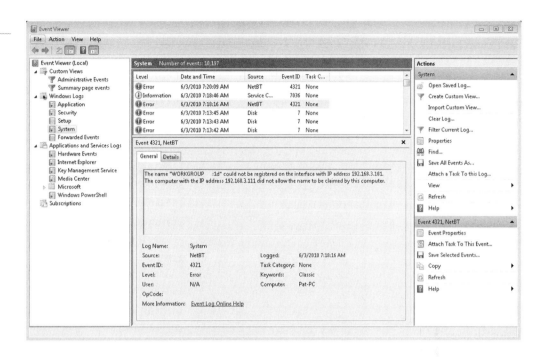

- Schedule a task to run in response to an event.
- Create and manage event subscriptions.

The Windows Logs category includes the logs that were available on previous versions of Windows. They include:

- **Application log:** Contains events logged by applications or programs.
- **Security log:** Contains events such as valid and invalid log on attempts and access to designated objects such as files and folders, printers, and Active Directory objects. By default, the Security log is empty until you enable auditing.
- **Setup log:** Contains events related to application setup.
- **System log:** Contains events logged by Windows system components including errors displayed by Windows during boot and errors with services.
- **ForwardedEvents log:** Used to store events collected from remote computers. To collect events from remote computers, you must create an event subscription.

Based on the roles and programs installed on a computer, Windows may have additional logs such as DHCP, DNS, or Active Directory.

Applications and Services logs were first introduced with Windows Vista. These logs store events from a single application or component rather than events that might have system-wide impact:

- **Admin events:** Primarily targeted at end users, administrators, and support personnel. The events that are found in the Admin channels indicate a problem and a well-defined solution that an administrator can use to solve the problem.
- **Operational events:** Used for analyzing and diagnosing a problem or occurrence. They can be used to trigger tools or tasks based on the problem or occurrence.
- **Analytic events:** Published in high volume. They describe program operation and indicate problems that cannot be handled by user intervention.
- **Debug events:** Used by developers troubleshooting issues with their programs.

Table 1-4 shows the common fields displayed in the Event Viewer logs.

Table 1-4

Event Viewer log fields

PROPERTY NAME	DESCRIPTION
Source	The software that logged the event, which can be either a program name, such as "SQL Server," or a component of the system or of a large program, such as a driver name.
Event ID	A number identifying the particular event type.
Level	A classification of the event severity:
	Information: Indicates that a change in an application or component has occurred, such as an operation has successfully completed, a resource has been created, or a service started.
	Warning: Indicates that an issue has occurred that can impact service or result in a more serious problem if action is not taken.
	Error: Indicates that a problem has occurred, which might impact functionality that is external to the application or component that triggered the event.
	Critical: Indicates that a failure has occurred from which the application or component that triggered the event cannot automatically recover.
	Success Audit: Shown in security logs to indicate that the exercise of a user right has succeeded.
	Failure Audit: Shown in security logs to indicate that the exercise of a user right has failed.

When you open any of these logs, particularly the Application, Security, and System logs, they will have thousands of entries. Unfortunately, it may take some time to find what you are looking for if you search entry by entry. To cut down on the time to find what you want, you can use a filter. To filter a log, open the Action menu and click Filter Current Log.

SKILL SUMMARY

IN THIS LESSON YOU LEARNED:

- While installing Windows 7, keep in mind the system requirements to properly run Windows 7 and its applications.

- To minimize problems, you should only choose hardware that is on the Hardware Compatibility List (HCL) for Windows 7.

- As with previous versions of Windows, the main graphical utility to configure the Windows environment and hardware devices is the Control Panel.

- One of the most important configuration settings for a Windows administrator is the System settings within the Control Panel. This includes gathering generation information about your system, changing the computer name, adding the computer to a domain, accessing the device manager, configuring remote settings, configuring startup and recovery options, and configuring overall performance settings.

- Action Center is a central place to view alerts and take actions that can help keep Windows running smoothly.

- Troubleshooting in the Control Panel contains several programs that can automatically fix some common problems with your computer, such as issues with networking, hardware, and devices, using the web, and program compatibility.

- The Microsoft Management Console (MMC) is one of the primary administrative tools used to manage Windows and many of the network services provided by Windows.

- Administrative Tools is a folder in the Control Panel that contains tools for system administrators and advanced users.

- The Computer Management console is one of the primary tools to manage a computer running Windows 7 and includes the most commonly used MMC snap-ins.

- A service is a program, routine, or process that performs a specific system function to support other programs or to provide a network service.

- The registry is a central, secure database in which Windows stores all hardware configuration information, software configuration information, and system security policies.

- Following a troubleshooting methodology to efficiently troubleshoot a problem will help you solve many problems.

- One of the most useful troubleshooting tools is the Event Viewer MMC snap-in, which essentially is a log viewer.

■ Knowledge Assessment

Fill in the Blank

Complete the following sentences by writing the correct word or words in the blanks provided.

1. The application that provides a central place to view alerts and take actions that can help keep Windows running smoothly is _____ .

2. The folder in the control panel that contains tools for system administrators and advanced users is the _____ .

3. A program, route, or process that performs a specific system function to support other programs or to provide a network service is known as _____ .

4. The central, secure database in which Windows stores all hardware configuration information, software configuration information, and system security policies is known as the _____ .

5. To view the Windows logs, you would use the _____ .

6. The step used in a troubleshooting methodology that allows you to identify and document problem systems would be _____ .

7. Typically, the 32-bit processor cannot see more than _____ or 64 GB of memory.

8. The chips that represent the instincts of the computer and control the boot process are known as _____ .

9. To change the name of a computer, you would use the _____ in the Control Panel.

10. The _____ is a feature that is used to prevent unauthorized changes to the computer.

Multiple Choice

Circle the letter that corresponds to the best answer.

1. To install Windows 7 on a 64-bit machine, you should have at least _____ MB of RAM.
   a. 512
   b. 1024
   c. 2048
   d. 4096

2. Which of these provides a single consolidated desktop from which to manage most administrative tools on a computer running Windows 7?
   a. Server Manager
   b. Component Services
   c. Computer Management console
   d. Data Sources (ODBC)

3. Which root key in the registry is used to store settings that are specific to the local computer?
   a. HKEY_CURRENT_USER
   b. HKEY_USERS
   c. HKEY_CURRENT_CONFIG
   d. HKEY_LOCAL_MACHINE

4. Which step in the troubleshooting methodology would you use to document the problem and its solution?
   a. Take a proactive approach
   b. Check results
   c. Execute a plan
   d. Discover the problem

5. Which program allows you to quickly see what hardware and software a system has?
   a. System Information
   b. System Configuration
   c. System Properties
   d. Computer Management console

6. Which log found in the Event Viewer will allow you to view errors generated during boot?
   a. Application log
   b. Security log
   c. Setup log
   d. System log

7. Administrative tools include Computer Management console and Event Viewer are based on the _____ .
   a. AppExe
   b. MMC
   c. CP applet
   d. HKEY_LOCAL_MACHINE

8. You are an administrator on a computer running Windows 7. You try to save a file to the root directory of the C drive but you are denied. What is causing this problem?
   a. UAC is turned on.
   b. Administrators have been removed from the computer.
   c. Drive C is not turned on.
   d. The drive C is not shared.

9. When you encounter a problem that you have never seen before, you should _____ .
   a. Boot into safe mode
   b. Research on the Internet
   c. Reboot the computer
   d. View the Device Manager for unknown devices

10. The most common port used for mice and other pointing devices is _____ .
    a. Parallel
    b. Serial
    c. PS/2
    d. USB

True / False

Circle T if the statement is true or F if the statement is false.

T F 1. 32-bit processors can only see 4 GB of memory.

T F 2. When using the Event Viewer, it is best to review each entry one by one when looking for what is causing problems during boot.

T F 3. Since video cards are not part of the main subsystems, they are not a factor in performance.

T F 4. To use Windows Aero, you need to have DirectX 9 graphics with WDDM driver model 1.0.

T F 5. UAC is turned off by default.

■ Case Scenarios

Scenario 1-1: Researching a Problem

You get a call from a client who says that her computer will not boot. When you visit the client, you see a blue screen and on the screen, you see the message, 0x0000007B INACCESSIBLE BOOT DEVICE. Use the Internet to research what causes this error and how to fix it.

Scenario 1-2: Using a Troubleshooting Methodology

You have a computer to that will not boot. Nothing displays on the monitor, you hear no beep codes, and you see no lights on the computer. Using the troubleshooting methodology, what steps would you use to troubleshoot and fix this problem?

2 LESSON

Resolving IP Connectivity Issues

OBJECTIVE DOMAIN MATRIX

TECHNOLOGY SKILL	OBJECTIVE DOMAIN	OBJECTIVE NUMBER
Connecting to a Network	Identify and resolve network connectivity issues.	2.2
Troubleshooting IP Network Problems	Identify and resolve network connectivity issues.	2.2
Understanding TCP/IP	Identify and resolve names resolution issues.	2.3

KEY TERMS

default gateway

Domain Name System (DNS)

host

Internet Protocol (IP)
  address

ipconfig command

Network address
  translation (NAT)

Network and Sharing Center

ping command

ports

private address

subnet mask

Windows Internet Name
  Service (WINS)

After completing this lesson, you will understand how hosts communicate over a TCP/IP network and how to configure Windows 7 to communicate on a TCP/IP network. Topics include IP addressing, name resolution, and network address translation. The lesson finishes by looking at the various tools in troubleshooting network connectivity problems.

You are an administrator for the Acme Corporation. You receive a phone call from a user on your network who cannot connect to the corporate intranet website. You go over to her machine and you use several tools to determine why she cannot connect to the intranet site. After reviewing her IP configuration and doing some isolation testing, you determine that there is nothing wrong with her computer, but there is a problem with network connections between her computer and the server that is running the intranet website.

Connecting to a Network

Before you can start networking, you have to physically connect the host to the network using a physical cable or wireless technology. While some networks are simple and others are complex, they all can be brought down by a faulty or misconfigured switch, access point, or network card. Networks can also be brought down by a faulty cable.

CERTIFICATION READY
Can you describe how to physically connect your computer and configure it so that the computer can connect on the network?
2.2

The most common cabling system used for wired computers is Ethernet. Most computers that use Ethernet connect with unshielded twisted-pair (UTP) cabling. Each end of the UTP cable has RJ-45 connectors. Today's workstations usually come with 100 Mb/s or 1 Gb/s connections for Ethernet, while some older machines only support 10 Mb/s. To connect a workstation to an Ethernet network, your host will connect to one end of the cable and the other end will be connected to a switch (or for legacy networks a hub).

If a client cannot communicate over the network, you should first check to make sure that the cable is firmly connected to the network. You should also look at the indicator lights on the network card or interface and the lights on the switch or hub to determine what the LEDs are telling you. If you have no lights on the switch or hub, make sure that the switch or hub has power and is turned on.

If the problem only affects one computer on a subnet, the problem is most likely with the computer itself, the network interface, or the cable that connects the host to the switch or hub. To help isolate a faulty cable, you can purchase a cable tester or you can swap with a known good cable. If there is a problem with the network interface card, you should verify that you have the proper drivers loaded and that the network interface is enabled.

If the problem is affecting more than one computer, you need to look for a centralized component to those computers. For example, if the switch or hub is down, the computers connected to that switch or hub will not be able to communicate.

Although wireless connections are discussed further in Lesson 4, the troubleshooting process is similar to wired networks. You must first determine if the problem is only affecting the single computer or multiple computers that are trying to access the same wireless access point. You will then need to check if the wireless network has been configured properly and if the access point is turned on. Besides checking Windows to see if the network interface is enabled, you should also look for buttons or switches on laptops that can enable or disable the wireless connections. Finally, if you can connect to other hosts within the same subnet as other wireless clients but you cannot connect to wired clients or servers, you should check on the network cable that connects the access point to the rest of the network.

Understanding TCP/IP

Since the Internet has become so popular, so has the TCP/IP protocol suite that the Internet runs on. One of the two main protocols mentioned in the name, is the IP protocol that is responsible for addressing and routing packets between hosts. Like when you send a letter through your post office to a specific street address located within a city or zip code, each host must have its own unique IP address so that it can send and receive packets.

A *host* is any device that connects directly to a network. While most hosts are computers, they can also include network printers, routers, layer 3 switches, managed switches, and any other device that has a network card or interface.

An *Internet Protocol (IP) address* is a logical address and numerical label that is assigned to a device that is connected to a computer network. While you have to follow certain guidelines based on the TCP/IP protocol suite, they are logical addresses that you assign as needed.

Today, most IP addresses are based on the traditional IPv4 addresses, which are based on 32-bit numbers. Unfortunately, since the Internet has grown in popularity, the 4 billion addresses used on an IPv4 network are almost depleted. Therefore, there are designs to migrate the Internet to IPv6 addresses, which are based on 128-bit addresses. Since each bit doubles the number of available addresses, the 128-bit addresses allow up to 3.403×10^{38} addresses.

Looking at IPv4 Networks

Today, most networks will be IPv4 networks. While the IPv4 allows 2^{32} or 4,294,867,296 addresses, IPv4 has matured through the years and various techniques were invented to utilize the addresses more efficiently.

As mentioned before, IPv4 addresses are based on 32 bits. When shown, an IPv4 address is expressed in dot-decimal notation consisting of four numbers (w.x.y.z), each ranging from 0 to 255. Each number is called an octet because it is based on 8 bits. Examples of IPv4 addresses are:

> 192.168.1.1
>
> 16.23.212.214
>
> 127.0.0.1

The earliest IPv4 addresses were based on a classful network design where the first three bits of the first octet would define the class—class A, B, and C. Using the information in Table 2-1, you can create 128 class A networks, 16,384 class B networks, and 2,097,151 class C networks. While a single class A network could have over 16 million hosts, a class C could only have 254 hosts. Of course, for you to create all of these networks, you will have to have your own large network that is not shared with the Internet. Most of these addresses are already in use.

Table 2-1

IPv4 classful network

Class	Range of First Octet	Default Subnet Mask	Network ID	Host ID	Number of Networks	Number of Addresses per Network
A	0–127	255.0.0.0	w	x.y.z	128	16,777,214
B	128–191	255.255.0.0	w.x	y.z	16,384	65,534
C	192–223	255.255.255.0	w.x.y	z	2,097,151	254

The *subnet masks* specify which bits are network bits and which bits are host bits. When you have a subnet mask of 255.0.0.0, it means that the first 8 bits are used to describe the network bits while the last 24 bits are used for the host bits. Therefore, if you have a 12.212.34.5 address with a subnet mask of 255.0.0.0, you have a 12.0.00 network address and a 0.212.34.5 host address.

Class A, B, and C addresses are known as unicast addresses that specify a single network device. Packets sent to a unicast address are delivered to the single node containing the interface identified by the address.

Class D addresses are defined from 224.0.0.0 to 239.255.255.255 used for multicast addresses. A multicast address is a single address that refers to multiple network devices. You can think of a multicast address as a group address that can be used to cut down traffic by sending one set of data packets meant for multiple hosts.

When using a classful network address, you automatically know which bits are assigned to define the network and which bits define the host on the network. For example, if you have 130.34.34.2, the default subnet mask is 255.255.0.0. Therefore, for a classful network, 130.34.0.0 would be the network address and the host address would be 0.0.34.2.

Unfortunately, with a classful network, many addresses were wasted. For example, while you might assign a class A address to a single network, most of the 16 million addresses were not used. Therefore, classless inter-domain routing (CIDR) was developed to utilize the networks more efficiently. Instead of using the pre-defined subnet masks, CIDR is based on variable-length subnet masking (VLSM) where you can take a network and subdivide the network into smaller subnets.

For example, you could use a class B network (130.5.0.0), which could be assigned to a large corporation. Every host within the corporation must begin with 130.5.0.0. You then assign a network address 130.5.1.0 to the first subnet or site and 130.5.2.0 to the second subnet or site. Each address located at the first subnet must start with 130.5.1.

CIDR notation uses a syntax that specifies the IP address, followed by a slash, followed by the number of masked bits. For example, if you have an IPv4 address of 12.23.52.120 with a subnet mask of 255.255.0.0, you would write the address as 12.23.52.120/16.

Using Private Networks and NAT

> While CIDR helped use IPv4 addresses more efficiently, additional steps were necessary to prevent the exhaustion of IPv4 addresses. *Network address translation (NAT)* is used with masquerading to hide an entire address space behind a single IP address. In other words, it allows multiple computers on a network to connect to the Internet through a single IP address.

NAT enables a local area network (LAN) to use one set of IP addresses for internal traffic and a second set of addresses for external traffic. The NAT box is usually a router (including routers made for home and small office Internet connections) or a proxy server. As a result, NAT serves two main purposes:

- Provides a type of firewall by hiding internal IP addresses
- Enables a company to use more internal IP addresses

The *private addresses* are reserved addresses not allocated to any specific organization. Since these private addresses cannot be assigned to global addresses used on the Internet and are not routable on the Internet, you must use a NAT gateway or proxy server to convert between private and public addresses. These are private network addresses as expressed in RFC 1918:

- 10.0.0.0–10.255.255.255
- 172.16.0.0–172.31.255.255
- 192.168.0.0–192.168.255.255

NAT obscures an internal network's structure by making all traffic appear originated from the NAT device or proxy server. To accomplish this, the NAT device or proxy server uses stateful translation tables to map the "hidden" addresses into a single address and then rewrites the outgoing Internet Protocol (IP) packets on exit so that they appear to originate from the router. As data packets are returned from the Internet, the responding data packets are mapped back to the originating IP address using the entries stored in the translation tables. See Figure 2-1.

Figure 2-1

Network address translation device that converts between public and private addresses

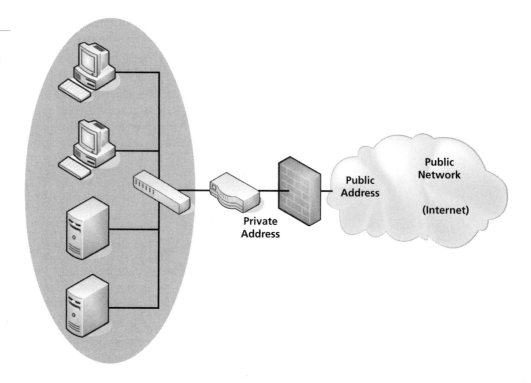

Looking at IPv6 Networks

As mentioned earlier, available public IPv4 addresses are running low. To overcome this problem as well as a few others, IPv6 was developed as the next-generation Internet Protocol version.

IPv6 provides a number of benefits for TCP/IP-based networking connectivity, including:

- 128-bit address space to provide addressing for every device on the Internet with a globally unique address.
- More efficient routing than IPv4.
- Support for automatic configuration.
- Enhanced security to protect against address and port scanning attacks and utilize IPSec to protect IPv6 traffic.

Since the IPv6 uses 128 bits, the addresses are usually divided into groups of 16 bits, written as 4 hex digits. Hex digits include 0, 1, 2, 3, 4, 5, 6, 7, 8, 9, A, B, C, D, E, and F. The groups are separated by colons. Here is an example of an address:

FE80:0000:0000:0000:02C3:B2DF:FEA5:E4F1

Similar to the IPv4 addresses, IPv6 are divided into network bits and host address. However, the first 64 bits define the network address and the second 64 bits define the host address. Therefore, for our example address, FE80:0000:0000:0000 defines the network bits and 02C3:B2DF:FEA5:E4F1 defines the host bits. The network bits are also further divided where a block of 48 bits is used as the network prefix and the next 16 bits are used for subnetting.

To facilitate simplified automatic addressing, the IPv6 subnet size has been standardized and fixed to 64 bits, and the MAC address is used to generate the host bits within the unicast network address or link-local address when stateless autoconfiguration is used.

With IPv6, you still have unicast and multicast addressing. However, unicast addressing can be divided into:

- **Global unicast address:** Public addresses that are globally routable and reachable on the IPv6 portion of the Internet.
- **Link-local addresses:** Private non-routable addresses confined to a single subnet. They are used by hosts when communicating with neighboring hosts on the same link but can also be used to create temporary networks for conferences or meetings, or to set up a permanent small LAN. Routers process packets destined for a link-local address, but they will not forward them to other links.
- **Unique local addresses:** Meant for private addressing, with the addition of being unique, so that joining two subnets does not cause address collisions.

You may also have an anycast address, which is an address that is assigned to multiple computers. When IPv6 addresses communication to an anycast address, only the closest host responds. You typically use this for locating services or the nearest router.

Using the Default Gateway

A **default gateway** is a device, usually a router, which connects the local network to other networks. When you need to communicate with a host on another subnet, you forward all packets to the default gateway.

The default gateway allows a host to communicate with remote hosts. Every time a host needs to send packets, it will first determine if the host is local (same subnet) or if it is remote (where it has to go through a router to get to the remote host). The router will then determine the best way to get to the remote subnet, and it forwards the packets to the remote subnet.

To determine if the destination address is local or remote, the router looks at the network bits of both the sending and destination hosts. If the network bits are the same, it will assume the destination host is local and send the packets directly to the local host. If the network bits are different, it will assume the destination host is remote and send the packets to the default gateway.

For example, you have the following:

> **Sending host address:** 10.10.57.3
>
> **Sending host subnet mask:** 255.255.255.0
>
> **Destination host address:** 10.10.89.37

By isolating the network address for the host, you have 10.10.57.0. By isolating the network address for the destination host address, you have 10.10.89.0. Since they are different, the packet will be sent to the default gateway, and the router will determine the best way to get to its final destination.

Of course, if the subnet mask is wrong, the host might misidentify a host as being local or remote. If the default gateway is wrong, packets may not be able to leave the local subnet.

Understanding Name Resolution

In today's networks, you assign logical addresses such as IP addressing. Unfortunately, these addresses tend to be hard to remember, especially with the newer more complicated IPv6 addresses. Therefore, you need to use some form of naming service that will allow you to translate logical names, which are easier to remember, to those logical addresses.

CERTIFICATION READY
Identify and resolve names resolution issues.
2.3

There are two types of names to translate. First is the host name, which resides in the Domain Name System and is the same system used on the Internet. When you type the name of a website or server that is on the Internet such as www.microsoft.com or cnn.com, you are specifying a domain/host name. The second name is your computer name, also known as the

NetBIOS name. If you are on a corporate network or your home network, the host name is usually the computer name.

USING HOSTS AND LMHOSTS FILES

Early TCP/IP networks used hosts (used with domain/host names associated with DNS) and lmhosts (used with NetBIOS/Computer names associated with WINS) files, which were text files that would list a name and its associated IP address. However, every time you needed to add or modify a name and address, you would have to go to every computer and modify the text file on every computer that needed to know the address. For larger organizations, this was very inefficient because it might include hundreds if not thousands of computers and the text files could become quite large.

In Windows, both of these files are located in the C:\Windows\system32\drivers\etc folder. The hosts file (see Figure 2-2) can be edited and is ready to use. The lmhosts.sam is a sample file and it will have to be copied as lmhosts without the .sam filename extension.

Figure 2-2

A sample hosts file

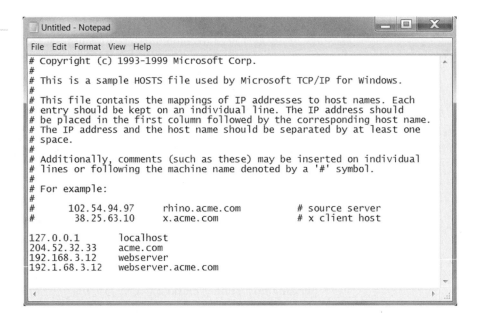

While the hosts and lmhosts files are considered legacy methods for naming resolution, they can still come in handy when troubleshooting or testing because name resolution will check these two files before contacting naming servers. For example, you just installed a new server but you do not want to make it available to everyone else. So you can add an entry in your local hosts file so that when your computer resolves a certain name it will resolve to the IP address of the new server. This keeps you from changing or adding a DNS entry, which would affect all users on your organization's network until you are ready.

USING THE DOMAIN NAME SYSTEM

Besides becoming the standard for the Internet, DNS, short for *Domain Name System,* is a hierarchical client/server-based distributed database management system that translates domain/host names to an IP address. In other words, while you may have a DNS server (or several servers), sometimes referred to as name servers, for your organization to provide naming resolution for your organization, all of the DNS servers on the Internet are linked together to provide worldwide naming resolution that allows you to manage the DNS for your organization.

The top of the tree is known as the root domain. Below the root domain, you will find top-level domains such as .com, .edu, .org, and .net and two-letter country codes such as .uk, .ca, and .us. Below the top-level domains, you will find the registered variable name that corresponds to the organization or other registered name. The second-level domain name must be registered by an authorized party such as networksolutions.com or godaddy.com.

For example, Microsoft.com is registered to the Microsoft Corporation. When you search for Microsoft.com, the host will first contact the .com DNS servers to determine the name server for microsoft.com. It will then contact the microsoft.com DNS servers to determine the address that is assigned to microsoft.com. For larger organizations, they may subdivide their DNS name space into subdomains such as technet.microsoft.com, msdn.microsoft.com, or social.microsoft.com.

A host name is a name assigned to a specific computer within a domain or subdomain to identify the TCP/IP host. Multiple host names can be assigned to the same IP address although only one name can be assigned to a physical computer or virtual computer.

A fully qualified domain name (FQDN) describes the exact position of a host with the DNS hierarchy. Some examples of full names include:

> www.microsoft.com
>
> technet.microsoft.com
>
> server1.sales.microsoft.com

USING WINDOWS INTERNET NAME SERVICE

Another name resolution technology is *Windows Internet Name Service* or WINS, which translates from NetBIOS (computer name) to specify a network resource. Since the growth of the Internet and the scalability of DNS, WINS is considered a legacy system.

A WINS sever contains a database of IP addresses and NetBIOS names that update dynamically. Unfortunately, WINS is not a hierarchical system like DNS so it is only good for your organization and was made only for Windows operating systems. Typically, other network devices and services cannot register with a WINS server. Therefore, you would have to add static entries for these devices if you want name resolution using WINS.

When you share a directory, drive, or printer on a PC running Microsoft Windows or Linux machines running Samba, you would access the resource by using the Universal Naming Convention (UNC), also known as Uniform Naming Convention to specify the location of the resources. Traditionally, UNC uses the following format:

> \\computername\sharednamed\optionalpathname

For example to access the shared directory on a computer called server1, you would type the following name:

> \\server1\data

However as DNS has become more popular, you can also use host names with the UNC. For example, you could use:

> \\Server1.microsoft.com\data

■ Configuring IP Address Settings

For a computer running Windows 7 to communicate with other hosts, it will need to connect to and communicate over the network. Therefore, you need to know how to connect the computer and configure the TCP/IP properties.

Network and Sharing Center provides real-time status information about your network. It can be used to configure and manage your network connections including managing your wireless networks, the type of connections you have, and the level of access you have to other

Figure 2-3

Network and Sharing Center

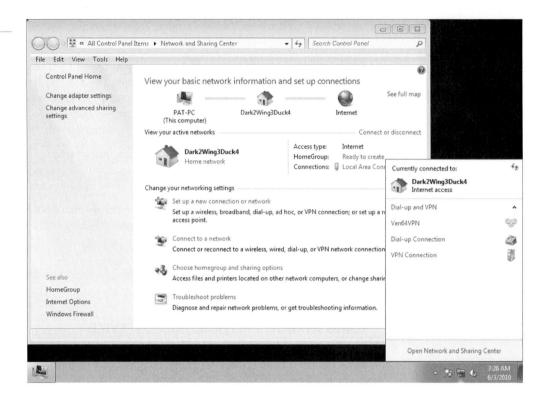

computers and devices on the network. See Figure 2-3. It can also be used to help trouble-shoot network connectivity problems by providing detailed information about your network in the network map. The Network and Sharing Center can be accessed from the Control Panel or from the Notification Area.

Within the Network and Sharing Center, you will set up IP configuration for Windows 7 including:

- IP address and its corresponding subnet mask (uniquely identifies the computer using a logical address)
- Default gateway (nearest router that connects to the other networks or the Internet)
- One or more DNS servers (provides name resolution [domain/host name to IP address])

The IP address, subnet mask, default gateway, and DNS servers can be configured manually or automatically via a DHCP server.

 SET UP IP CONFIGURATION

GET READY. To set up IP configuration in Windows 7:

1. Open the Control Panel.
2. To access the network connection properties, do one of the following:
   - While in Category view, click Network and Internet, click Network and Sharing Center, and click Change adapter settings.
   - If you are in Icon view, double-click Network and Sharing Center, and click Change adapter settings.
   - Right-click the network icon in the notification area, select Open Network and Sharing Center and click Change adapter settings.
3. Right-click the connection that you want to change, and then click Properties.
4. Under the Networking tab, click either Internet Protocol Version 4 (TCP/IPv4) or Internet Protocol Version 6 (TCP/IPv6), and then click Properties.

To specify IPv4 IP address settings, do one of the following:

- To obtain IP settings automatically from a DHCP server, click Obtain an IP address automatically, and then click OK.
- To specify an IP address, click Use the following IP address, and then, in the IP address, Subnet mask, Default gateway, Preferred DNS server, and Alternate DNS server boxes, type the appropriate IP address settings. See Figure 2-4.

Figure 2-4

Configuring IPv4

To specify IPv6 IP address settings, do one of the following:

- To obtain IP settings automatically, click Obtain an IPv6 address automatically, and then click OK.
- To specify an IP address, click Use the following IPv6 address, and then, in the IPv6 address, Subnet prefix length, and Default gateway boxes, type the IP address settings. See Figure 2-5.

Figure 2-5

Configuring IPv6

SET UP ALTERNATE IP CONFIGURATION

GET READY. Windows 7 provides the ability to configure alternate IP address settings (a second IP address) to support connecting to different networks. You configure dynamic and alternative addressing by completing the following steps:

1. Open the Control Panel.

2. While in Category view, click Network and Internet, click Network and Sharing Center, and click Change Adapter Settings instead of Manage Network Connections.

3. In the Local Area Connection Status dialog box, click Properties. This displays the Local Area Connection Properties dialog box.

4. Double-click Internet Protocol Version 6 (TCP/IPv6) or Internet Protocol Version 4 (TCP/IPv4) as appropriate for the type of IP address you are configuring.

5. Select Obtain An IPv6 Address Automatically or Obtain An IP Address Automatically as appropriate for the type of IP address you are configuring. If desired, select *Obtain DNS Server Address Automatically.* Or select *Use The Following DNS Server Addresses* and then type a preferred and alternate DNS server address in the text boxes provided.

6. When you use dynamic IPv4 addressing with desktop computers, you should configure an automatic alternative address. To use this configuration, on the Alternate Configuration tab, select *Automatic Private IP Address*. Click OK twice, click Close, and then skip the remaining steps.

7. When you use dynamic IPv4 addressing with mobile computers, you'll usually want to configure the alternative address manually. To use this configuration, on the Alternate Configuration tab, select User Configured. Then in the IP Address text box, type the IP address you want to use. The IP address that you assign to the computer should be a private IP address, and it must not be in use anywhere else when the settings are applied.

8. With dynamic IPv4 addressing, complete the alternate configuration by entering a subnet mask, default gateway, DNS, and WINS settings. When you're finished, click OK twice and then click Close.

9. To specify DNS server address settings for IPv4 and IPv6, do one of the following:

   • To obtain a DNS server address automatically, click Obtain DNS server address automatically, and then click OK.

   • To specify a DNS server address, click Use the following DNS server addresses, and then, in the Preferred DNS server and Alternate DNS server boxes, type the addresses of the primary and secondary DNS servers.

Managing Network Discovery and Sharing Services

To make your computer more secure, Windows 7 is designed to run only the services that you need to run and disable those services that you do not need. This would include allowing your computer to be seen on the network and utilizing file and printer sharing.

The Network and Sharing Center also allows you to configure certain network services such as network discovery and sharing. These settings include:

• **Network discovery:** Allows this computer to see other network computers and devices and makes it visible to other network computers.

• **File and printer sharing:** Allows people on the network to access files and printers that you have shared on this computer.

• **Public folder sharing:** Allows people on the network to access files in the public folder.

- **Media streaming:** People and devices on the network can access pictures, music, and videos on the computer. In addition, the computer can find media on the network.
- **Password protected sharing:** Only people who have a user account and password on the computer can access shared files, printers attached to the computer, and the public folders. To give other people access, you must turn off password protected sharing.

 ENABLE NETWORK DISCOVERY

GET READY. To enable network discovery:

1. Open the Network and Sharing Center.
2. Click Change advanced sharing settings.
3. Select Turn on network discovery. See Figure 2-6.
4. Click the Save changes button.

Figure 2-6

Network discovery

Understanding Ports

THE BOTTOM LINE

You access a remote computer by address (or by name, which is translated to an address). What most people don't realize is that usually when a host communicates over a network, it has multiple connections working in the background. Each of these connections are handled by a process or program. A host uses *ports* to identify which packets belong to a network service or program.

You can have a total of 65,535 TCP ports and another 65,535 UDP ports. When a program on your computer sends or receives data over the network, it sends that data to an IP address and a specific port on the remote computer and usually receives the data on a random port on its own computer, which means that the computer can handle several connections using the same network protocol at the same time. For example, you can connect to several different websites on different servers/IP addresses. Since most websites use port 80, you can connect to each server over port 80 and the web server will communicate back on a random port. Of course, your system will keep track of these random ports automatically so you don't have to worry about those details. When a protocol is configured to use a specific port, it is referred to as binding to that port.

Common ports you should always remember include:

DNS: TCP/UDP port 53

FTP: TCP port 20 and 21

HTTP: TCP port 80

HTTPS: TCP port 443

IMAP: TCP/UDP port 143

LDAP: TCP port 389

POP3: TCP port 110

SMTP: TCP/UDP port 25

Telnet: TCP/UDP port 23

> **+ MORE INFORMATION**
>
> For a list of ports, visit the following websites:
> http://www.iana.org/assignments/portnumbers
> http://en.wikipedia.org/wiki/List_of_TCP_and_UDP_port_numbers
> http://support.microsoft.com/kb/832017

■ Troubleshooting IP Network Problems

THE BOTTOM LINE

While networks can be simple or complex, there are several tools that are invaluable when troubleshooting network connectivity problems. No matter how complex the network is, you should always follow a troubleshooting methodology, which will help you quickly isolate and pinpoint the problem.

CERTIFICATION READY
What tools would you use to troubleshoot network problems?
2.2

If you experience network connectivity problems while using Windows 7, you can use Windows Network Diagnostics to start the troubleshooting process. If there is a problem, Windows Network Diagnostics analyzes the problem and, if possible, presents a solution or a list of possible causes. To run the Windows Network Diagnostics program, right-click the Network and Sharing Center icon in the notification area and select Troubleshoot problems. You can also right-click the adapter under Network Connections and click Diagnose.

If the problem still exists, you can also use the following command-line tools:

- ipconfig
- ping
- tracert
- pathping
- netstat
- telnet
- nslookup

In addition, you should also look at the logs shown in the Event Viewer. Some error messages may be found in the System and Application logs.

Viewing IP Configuration

When you cannot connect to a website or a server, the first thing you should check is the client IP configuration. This can be done by using Network Connections or the *ipconfig command*.

To view your network connections, you can open the Network Connections under the Network and Sharing Center and click Status. The General tab will show if the adapter has IPv4 and IPv6 connectivity, if the adapter is enabled, how long the adapter has been running, and the speed of the adapter. It will also show you the bytes being sent and received from the adapter. If you click the Details button, you can view the network connection details including IP addresses, subnet mask, gateway, WINS and DNS servers, and physical/MAC address.

The **ipconfig** command is one of the most useful commands when troubleshooting network problems. It displays all current TCP/IP network configuration values and refreshes Dynamic Host Configuration Protocol (DHCP) settings. Used without parameters, ipconfig displays the IP address, subnet mask, and default gateway for all adapters. When you execute **ipconfig /all**, it displays the full TCP/IP configuration for all adapters including host name, DNS servers, and the physical/MAC address. See Figure 2-7.

Figure 2-7

Ipconfig command

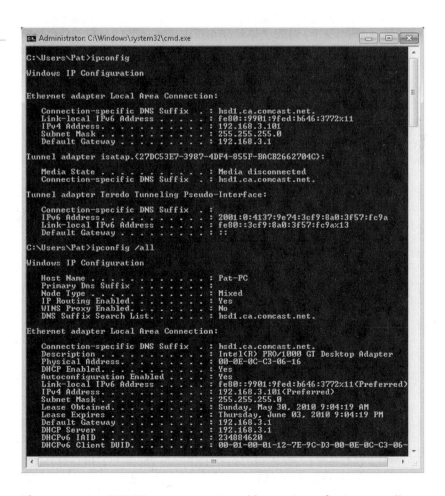

If you are using DHCP servers to assign addresses, **ipconfig /renew** will renew the DHCP configuration from the DHCP server. This parameter is available only on computers with adapters that are configured to obtain an IP address automatically. You can also use **ipconfig /release** to release the DHCP address from a network adapter.

If the IP address is invalid, communication may fail. If the subnet mask is incorrect, you may have problems communicating with local or remote hosts. If the default gateway is invalid, you will have problems communicating with remote hosts, but you can still communicate with local hosts. If the DNS server is incorrect or missing, the computer may not be able to resolve names and communication may fail.

If a computer is configured to receive an IP address from a DHCP server and one does not respond, the computer will use the Automatic Private IP addressing, which generates an IP address in the form of 169.254.xxx.xxx and the subnet mask of 255.255.0.0. When you have an Automatic Private IP address, you can only communicate with computers on the same network/ subnet that have an Automatic private IP address. Therefore, you will most likely not able to communicate with any host on the network without the proper IP address and subnet mask.

Testing Network Connectivity

Assuming that you have the correct IP configuration, you need to determine if you can communicate with the destination host. Windows 7 provides several tools to determine if you have network connectivity and if you don't, to help you pinpoint where the failure is occurring.

An extremely valuable tool in troubleshooting is the ***ping command***. The ping command verifies IP-level connectivity to another TCP/IP computer by sending Internet Control Message Protocol (ICMP) Echo Request messages. The receipt of corresponding Echo Reply messages are displayed, along with round-trip times. Ping is the primary TCP/IP command used to troubleshoot connectivity, reachability, and name resolution. Since it gives you the round-trip times, the ping command can also tell you if the link is slow between your host and the destination host.

To ping a host, you would execute ping followed by a host name or IP address. The ping command also supports the following parameters:

- **–t**: Specifies that ping continue sending Echo Request messages to the destination until interrupted. To interrupt and display statistics, press CTRL-BREAK. To interrupt and quit ping, press CTRL-C.
- **–a**: Specifies that reverse name resolution is performed on the destination IP address. If this is successful, ping displays the corresponding host name.
- **–n** *Count*: Specifies the number of Echo Request messages sent. The default is 4.
- **–l** *Size*: Specifies the length, in bytes, of the data field in the Echo Request messages sent. The default is 32. The maximum size is 65,527.

A "Request Timed Out" response indicates that there is a known route to the destination computer but one or more computers or routers along the path, including the source and destination, are not configured correctly. "Destination Host Unreachable" indicates that the system cannot find a route to the destination system and therefore does not know where to send the packet on the next hop.

Two other useful commands are the **tracert** command and **pathping** command. The tracert command traces the route that a packet takes to a destination and displays the series of IP routers that are used in delivering packets to the destination. If the packets are unable to be delivered to the destination, the tracert command displays the last router that successfully forwarded the packet. The tracert command also uses the ICMP protocol. See Figure 2-8.

Pathping traces a route through the network in a manner similar to tracert. However, pathping also provides more detailed statistics on the individual hops.

Figure 2-8

Ping and tracert commands

```
Administrator: C:\Windows\system32\cmd.exe

C:\Users\Pat>ping 192.168.3.1

Pinging 192.168.3.1 with 32 bytes of data:
Reply from 192.168.3.1: bytes=32 time<1ms TTL=64
Reply from 192.168.3.1: bytes=32 time<1ms TTL=64
Reply from 192.168.3.1: bytes=32 time<1ms TTL=64
Reply from 192.168.3.1: bytes=32 time<1ms TTL=64

Ping statistics for 192.168.3.1:
    Packets: Sent = 4, Received = 4, Lost = 0 (0% loss),
Approximate round trip times in milli-seconds:
    Minimum = 0ms, Maximum = 0ms, Average = 0ms

C:\Users\Pat>tracert 4.2.2.2

Tracing route to vnsc-bak.sys.gtei.net [4.2.2.2]
over a maximum of 30 hops:

  1    <1 ms    <1 ms    <1 ms  LINKSYSWRT350N [192.168.3.1]
  2    18 ms    22 ms    14 ms  c-24-10-40-1.hsd1.ca.comcast.net [24.10.40.1]
  3     7 ms     9 ms     6 ms  ge-5-13-ur01.sacramento.ca.sacra.comcast.net [
.87.212.221]
  4     7 ms     8 ms     7 ms  68.87.221.21
  5    12 ms    16 ms    16 ms  be-60-ar01.oakland.ca.sfba.comcast.net [68.86.
3.25]
  6    31 ms    12 ms    12 ms  pos-0-5-0-0-cr01.sacramento.ca.ibone.comcast.n
[68.86.90.137]
  7    16 ms    14 ms    15 ms  pos-0-6-0-0-cr01.sanjose.ca.ibone.comcast.net
8.86.86.202]
  8    15 ms    17 ms    17 ms  xe-10-1-0.edge1.SanJose1.Level3.net [4.71.118.
  9    38 ms    18 ms    17 ms  vlan69.csw1.SanJose1.Level3.net [4.68.18.62]
 10    14 ms    14 ms    17 ms  ge-10-0.core1.SanJose1.Level3.net [4.68.123.6]
 11    16 ms    33 ms    23 ms  vnsc-bak.sys.gtei.net [4.2.2.2]

Trace complete.

C:\Users\Pat>
```

TAKE NOTE *

Since ICMP packets can be used in Denial of Service (DoS) attacks, some routers and firewalls block ICMP packets. Therefore, when you try to ping a host with the ping, tracert, or pathping command, it may not respond even though the host is connected.

To isolate network connectivity problems, you use the following troubleshooting process:

1. Verify host IP configuration.
2. Use the ping command to gather more information on the extent of the problem:
   - Ping the destination address.
   - Ping the loopback address (127.0.0.1).
   - Ping a local IP address.
   - Ping a remote gateway.
   - Ping a remote computer.
3. Identify each hop (router) between two systems using the tracert or pathping command.

To determine whether you have a network connectivity problem, you should ping the destination by name or by IP address. If the ping command shows you have network connectivity, your problem is most likely with the host requesting the services, or the services on the destination could be down. It should be noted that if you ping by name, you should verify that the correct address was used.

If you appear not to have network connectivity to a server or service, you will need to isolate where the connectivity problem occurs starting with the host computer. Therefore, you should ping the loopback address and local IP address to determine whether your TCP/IP components are functioning. Next, if you ping a local IP address, your results will demonstrate whether you can communicate on the local subnet that you are connected to. If you still have not found the problem, you can then ping the remote gateway (most likely your default gateway) to determine if you can communicate with the router. Next, pinging a remote computer determines if you can communicate through your default gateway to a remote subnet. Finally, you would use the tracert and pathping commands to determine exactly where the problem is.

Testing Name Resolution

Since we often use names instead of addresses, you may need to verify that you have the correct name resolution when specifying a name. Two tools included with Windows 7 are nslookup and nbtstat.

CERTIFICATION READY
What is the primary tool used to test DNS naming resolution?
2.3

Nslookup.exe is a command-line administrative tool for testing and troubleshooting DNS name resolution. Entering *hostname* in nslookup will provide a forward lookup of the host name to IP address. Entering *IP_Address* in nslookup will perform a reverse lookup of IP address to host name. See Figure 2-9.

Figure 2-9

Nslookup command

However, entering nslookup, puts you into an nslookup command environment that allows you to query specific servers using the server command and to query for specific resource records using the set type command.

If you found problems with the DNS, the ipconfig command can be used in certain situations:

- **ipconfig /flushdns:** Flushes and resets the contents of the DNS client resolver cache. During DNS troubleshooting, you can use this procedure to discard negative cache entries from the cache, as well as any other entries that have been added dynamically.

- **ipconfig /displaydns:** Displays the contents of the DNS client resolver cache, which includes both entries preloaded from the local hosts file and any recently obtained resource records for name queries resolved by the computer. The DNS Client service uses this information to resolve frequently queried names quickly, before querying its configured DNS servers.

- **ipconfig /registerdns:** Initiates manual dynamic registration for the DNS names and IP addresses that are configured at a computer. You can use this parameter to troubleshoot a failed DNS name registration or resolve a dynamic update problem between a client and the DNS server without rebooting the client computer. The DNS settings in the advanced properties of the TCP/IP protocol determine which names are registered in DNS.

If you used the nslookup command to test DNS resolution and found a problem with name resolution, you would fix the problem at the DNS server. Unfortunately, previous DNS results that your system processes, such as when you access a web page using a browser, are cached in your memory. Therefore, if you correct the problem, you may need to flush your DNS cache using the ipconfig /flushdns command so that it can query and obtain the corrected values.

TAKE NOTE *

If you decide to use hosts files or lmhosts files, you should check to see if any entries may be incorrect. NSLookup only tests DNS name resolution and will not check to see if a hosts file or lmhosts file is correct.

While WINS is considered a legacy method for name resolution, you still may have a need to troubleshoot WINS problems. Nbtstat.exe is a useful tool for troubleshooting NetBIOS name resolution problems. You can use the **nbtstat.exe** command to remove or correct preloaded entries by typing the command with the following parameters at the command prompt and pressing ENTER:

- **nbtstat –n**: To list the NetBIOS table of the local computer, type nbtstat –n at the command prompt, and then press ENTER. This command displays the names that were registered locally on the computer by programs such as the server and redirector.

- **nbtstat –c**: To list the contents of the NetBIOS name cache, type nbtstat –c at the command prompt, and then press ENTER. This command shows the NetBIOS name cache, which contains name-to-address mappings for other computers. See Figure 2-10.

- **nbtstat –R**: To purge the name cache and reload it from the LMHOSTS file, type nbtstat –R at the command prompt, and then press ENTER.

- **nbtstat –a**: To perform a NetBIOS adapter status command against the computer that you specify by name, type nbtstat –a NetBIOS computer name at the command prompt, and then press ENTER. The adapter status command returns the local NetBIOS name table for that computer and the MAC address of the network adapter.

- **nbtstat –s**: To display a list of client and server connections, type nbtstat –s at the command prompt, and then press ENTER. This command lists the current NetBIOS sessions and their statuses, including statistics.

Figure 2-10

Nbtstat command

Viewing Port Usage

In some situations, you may not be able to test network connectivity with ping or similar utilities because ICMP packets are blocked by a firewall. In addition, even if a computer responds to ICMP packets, it doesn't tell you whether the computer is running the network service that you need to access. Therefore, there are several tools that can be used to look at the client and server network connections and services.

The **netstat** command displays active TCP connections, ports on which the computer is listening, Ethernet statistics, the IP routing table, IPv4 statistics (for the IP, ICMP, TCP, and UDP protocols), and IPv6 statistics (for the IPv6, ICMPv6, TCP over IPv6, and UDP over IPv6 protocols). Used without parameters, netstat displays active TCP connections. See Figure 2-11.

Figure 2-11

Netstat command

Netstat supports the following parameters:

- **−a**: Displays all active TCP connections and the TCP and UDP ports on which the computer is listening.
- **−e**: Displays Ethernet statistics, such as the number of bytes and packets sent and received. This parameter can be combined with −s.
- **−n**: Displays active TCP connections; however, addresses and port numbers are expressed numerically and no attempt is made to determine names.
- **−o**: Displays active TCP connections and includes the process ID (PID) for each connection. You can find the application based on the PID on the Processes tab in Windows Task Manager. This parameter can be combined with −a, −n, and −p.
- **−p** *Protocol*: Shows connections for the protocol specified by Protocol. In this case, the Protocol can be tcp, udp, tcpv6, or udpv6. If this parameter is used with −s to display statistics by protocol, Protocol can be tcp, udp, icmp, ip, tcpv6, udpv6, icmpv6, or ipv6.

- **–s**: Displays statistics by protocol. By default, statistics are shown for the TCP, UDP, ICMP, and IP protocols. If the IPv6 protocol for Windows XP is installed, statistics are shown for the TCP over IPv6, UDP over IPv6, ICMPv6, and IPv6 protocols. The –p parameter can be used to specify a set of protocols.
- **–r**: Displays the contents of the IP routing table. This is equivalent to the route print command.
- *Interval*: Redisplays the selected information every *x* seconds. Press CTRL+C to stop the redisplay. If this parameter is omitted, netstat prints the selected information only once.

Another tool worth mentioning that will help troubleshoot TCP/IP connectivity issues is the **portqry.exe** command-line utility. Portqry.exe reports the port status of TCP and UDP ports on a computer that you select by using the following command:

> portqry –n *destination* –e *portnumber*

For example, the Hypertext Transfer Protocol (HTTP) uses TCP port 80. To test HTTP connectivity to www.microsoft.com, type the following command at the command line:

> portqry –n www.microsoft.com –e 80

Unfortunately, portqry is not included with Windows 7, but it can be downloaded from Microsoft.com.

> **➕ MORE INFORMATION**
>
> For more information and links to download portqry.exe, visit the following website:
> http://support.microsoft.com/default.aspx?scid=kb;en-us;310099

Telnet is a text-based communication program that allows you to connect to a remote server over a network to execute commands at a remote command prompt. Unfortunately, using the telnet command is frowned on in IT because telnet packets are not encrypted. Therefore, it is recommended that you use Secure Shell (SSH). However, you can also use the telnet command to test connectivity to a network service such as checking a web server (port 80), checking a POP3 mail server (port 110), and checking a SMTP mail server (port 25).

> telnet *hostname port*

> **➕ MORE INFORMATION**
>
> If you wish to learn more about using the telnet command for diagnostics, view the following Microsoft websites:
>
> - To request a web page through a telnet client:
>   http://support.microsoft.com/kb/279466
> - To test SMTP communications:
>   http://support.microsoft.com/kb/153119
> - To test POP3:
>   http://support.microsoft.com/kb/196748

Finally, you can find many other tools for troubleshooting from Microsoft and third-party vendors, and you can also find websites that will provide some of the same functionality as the command prompt tools that have been mentioned, such as nslookup.

In 2006, Microsoft purchased SysInternals, which created a wide range of troubleshooting/diagnostic tools. SysInternals tools can be found at:

> http://technet.microsoft.com/en-us/sysinternals/bb545027.aspx

Two networking tools worth mentioning are SysInternals' TCPView and Whois:

- **TCPView:** Active socket command-line viewer.
- **Whois:** See who owns an Internet address.

SKILL SUMMARY

IN THIS LESSON YOU LEARNED:

- When diagnosing network problems, you must first determine the extent of the problem including whether it affects one host or multiple hosts. This will help you determine where to focus your attention.

- If the problem only affects one computer on a subnet, the problem is most likely with the computer itself, the network interface, or the cable that connects them to the switch or hub.

- If the problem is affecting more than one computer, you need to look for a centralized component to those computers.

- A host is any device that connects directly to a network.

- An Internet Protocol (IP) address is a logical address and numerical label that is assigned to a device connected to a computer network.

- Today, most IP addresses are based on the traditional IPv4 addresses that are based on 32-bit numbers.

- The earliest IPv4 addresses used a classful network design where the first three bits of the first octet defined the class—class A, B, and C.

- The subnet masks specify which bits are network bits and which are host bits.

- Classless inter-domain routing (CIDR) was developed to utilize the networks more efficiently. Instead of using the pre-defined subnet masks, CIDR is based on variable-length subnet masking (VLSM) where you can take a network and subdivide the network into smaller subnets.

- Network address translation (NAT) is used with masquerading to hide an entire address space behind a single IP address. In other words, it allows multiple computers on a network to connect to the Internet through a single IP address.

- Private addresses are reserved addresses not allocated to any specific organization. Since these private addresses cannot be assigned to global addresses used on the Internet, you must use a NAT gateway or proxy server to convert between private and public addresses.

- IPv6 provides a number of benefits for TCP/IP-based networking connectivity, including 128-bit address space to provide addressing for every device on the Internet with a globally unique address.

- A default gateway is a device, usually a router, that connects the local network to other networks. In today's networks, you assign logical addresses such as IP addressing. Unfortunately, these addresses tend to be hard to remember.

- DNS, short for Domain Name System, is a hierarchical client/server based distributed database management system that translates domain/host names to an IP address.

- Another name resolution technology is Windows Internet Name Service or WINS, which translates from NetBIOS (computer name) to specify a network resource. Since the growth of the Internet and the scalability of DNS, WINS is considered a legacy system.

- The Network and Sharing Center provides real-time status information about your network. It can be used to configure and manage your network connections including managing your wireless networks, connection types, and the level of access you have to other computers and devices on the network.

- Network discovery allows your computer to see other network computers and devices and makes it visible to other network computers.

- To identify which packets belong to a network service or program, a host uses ports.

- If a computer is configured to receive an IP address from a DHCP server and one does not respond, the computer will use the Automatic Private IP addressing, which generates an IP address in the form of 169.254.xxx.xxx and the subnet mask of 255.255.0.0.

- The ipconfig command, one of the most useful commands when troubleshooting network problems, displays all current TCP/IP network configuration values and refreshes Dynamic Host Configuration Protocol (DHCP) and Domain Name System (DNS) settings.

- The ping command verifies IP-level connectivity to another TCP/IP computer by sending Internet Control Message Protocol (ICMP) Echo Request messages.

- Nslookup.exe is a command-line administrative tool for testing and troubleshooting DNS name resolution.

■ Knowledge Assessment

Fill in the Blank

Complete the following sentences by writing the correct word or words in the blanks provided.

1. Most wired networks are _____ networks.

2. A _____ is any device that connects directly to a network.

3. A _____ is a logical address and numeric label that is assigned to a device connected to a computer network.

4. A _____ specifies which bits are network bits and which are host bits.

5. A _____ address is a single address that refers to multiple network devices.

6. _____ is used to translate domain/host names to an IP address.

7. To identify which packets belong to a network service or program packets, a host uses _____.

8. By default, HTTP uses port _____.

9. The _____ is a device, usually a router, which connects the local network to other networks, allowing a host to communicate with other hosts on remote networks.

10. To view the MAC address, you would use the _____ command.

Multiple Choice

Circle the letter that corresponds to the best answer.

1. IPv4 networks are based on a _____ -bit address.
   a. 8
   b. 24
   c. 32
   d. 48

2. IPv6 networks are based on a _____ -bit address.
   a. 32
   b. 48
   c. 64
   d. 128

3. The default subnet mask in a classful network for a host with the IP address 132.75.3.5
   is _____.
   a. 255.0.0.0
   b. 255.255.0.0
   c. 255.255.255.0
   d. 255.255.255.255

4. You see the following address—183.23.54.2/24. What type of IP addresses does this host use?
   a. Classful
   b. CIDR
   c. NAT
   d. Multicasting

5. You need to connect to a host that is using address 10.75.23.3. What type of address is
   this address?
   a. Public address
   b. Private address
   c. Global address
   d. Firewall address

6. What type of IPv6 address is globally routable and reachable on the IPv6 of the
   Internet?
   a. Global unicast address
   b. Link-local addresses
   c. Unique local addresses
   d. Anycast addresses

7. Which command is used to test name resolution problems with DNS?
   a. ipconfig
   b. ping
   c. nslookup
   d. netstat

8. Which command is used to test network connectivity between two hosts?
   a. ipconfig
   b. ping
   c. nslookup
   d. netstat

9. What port does DNS use?
   a. 25
   b. 53
   c. 80
   d. 443

10. For your Windows 7 computer to be visible on the network by other clients, you will
    need to first enable _____.
    a. Media streaming
    b. Password protected sharing
    c. Network discovery
    d. Public folder sharing

True / False

Circle T if the statement is true or F if the statement is false.

T | F 1. You can only have one http connection at a time.

T | F 2. To clear the DNS cache, you need to execute the ipconfig/clearcache.

T | F 3. IPv4 and IPv6 addresses are interchangeable if you use the newest browser from Microsoft.

T | F 4. The Network and Sharing Center does not show the number of packets being sent and received.

T | F 5. Anycast allows you to communicate with the nearest server.

■ Case Scenarios

Scenario 2-1: Troubleshooting Website Connectivity

You have a computer that is having problems connecting to a website at corporate partner www.acme.com. Explain the steps you would use to troubleshoot this problem.

Scenario 2-2: Researching Ports

Using the Internet, determine which ports use the following protocols:

RPC

NetBIOS Session Service

DHCP Server

SMB

SQL over TCP

Remote Desktop/Terminal Services

3 LESSON

Understanding Workgroups and Active Directory

OBJECTIVE DOMAIN MATRIX

TECHNOLOGY SKILL	OBJECTIVE DOMAIN	OBJECTIVE NUMBER
Troubleshooting Authentication Issues	Identify and resolve logon issues.	2.1

KEY TERMS

Account Lockout Policy	computer account	member server	user account
Active Directory	Credential Manager	object	user profile
auditing	domain	organizational unit	user rights
authentication	domain controller	permission	workgroup
authorization	group policy	Security Accounts Manager (SAM)	
	groups		

After completing this lesson, you will understand the role of Active Directory for an organization and how it relates to Windows 7. You will also be able to understand how a user and Windows 7 authenticate on a local computer and within an Active Directory domain. Last, you will look at how to troubleshoot problems with users logging in to Windows 7.

You work for the Contoso Corporation's Help Desk. You get a call from a user who is very frustrated. When he tries to log in to a computer running Windows 7, Windows will not let him in. He needs to quickly access some reports for a presentation and time is running out. Therefore, he is starting to panic. As part of the Help Desk, you will need to calm the user down so that you can quickly get to the root of the problem and make it possible for the user to access his files.

■ Introducing Workgroups and Non-Domain Computers

↓
THE BOTTOM LINE

As mentioned in Lesson 1, a ***workgroup*** is usually associated with a peer-to-peer network where user accounts are decentralized and stored on each individual computer. Since each computer has its own security database, when you have several users that need access to the computer (while requiring unique username and passwords), you will need to create a user account for each user on the computer.

Understanding Authentication and Logins

Before any user can access a computer or a network resource, that user has to log in to prove they are who they say they are and to determine whether they have the necessary rights and permissions to access the network resources.

Authentication is the process of identifying an individual, usually based on a username and password. After a user is authenticated, users can access network resources based on the user's authorization. ***Authorization*** is the process of giving individuals access to system objects based on their identity. ***Auditing*** is the process of keeping track of a user's activity while accessing the network resources, including the amount of time spent in the network, the services accessed while there, and the amount of data transferred during the session.

A login allows an individual to access a computer system and includes authentication, which proves who they are. A user can authenticate using one or more of the following methods:

- **What they know:** Such as using a password or Personal Identity Number (PIN).
- **What they own or possess:** Such as a passport, smart card, or ID card.
- **What a user is:** Usually using biometric factors based on fingerprints, retinal scans, voice input, or other forms.

The most common method of authentication with computers and networks is the password. A password is a secret series of characters that enables a user to access a file, computer, or program. To make a password more secure, you need to choose a password that nobody can guess. Therefore, it should be long enough and considered a complex or strong password. According to Microsoft, complex passwords:

- Cannot contain the user's account name or parts of the user's full name that exceed two consecutive characters.
- Must be at least six characters in length or the number of characters specified in the Minimum password length policy setting.
- Must contain characters from at least three of the following four categories: English uppercase alphabet characters (A–Z), English lowercase alphabet characters (a–z), base-10 digits (0–9), and non-alphanumeric characters (for example,!$#,%).

You should also change your password regularly.

A ***user account*** enables a user to log on to a computer and domain. As a result, it can used to prove the identity of a user, which can then be used to determine what a user can access and what kind of access a user will have (authorization). It can be used for auditing so that if there is a security problem where something was accessed or deleted, it can be determined who accessed or deleted the object.

On today's Windows networks, there are two types of user accounts:

- The local user account
- The domain user account

A local user account allows a user to log on and gain access to the computer where the account was created. The security table located on the local computer that stores the local user account is known as the *Security Accounts Manager (SAM)* database.

There are three types of local user accounts and each provides the user with different levels of control over the computer:

- **Administrator:** An account that allows complete control over the computer and its settings. It is a member of the Administrators group.
- **Standard:** An account that allows general access to the computer; however, users cannot install software, delete system files, or change settings. If you're working in a Standard account and need to make system changes, the administrator password will be needed.
- **Guest:** A temporary user account that cannot install software, make any changes, or create a password. The guest account is disabled by default. It is a member of the Guests group.

Windows 7 provides two separate interfaces for creating and managing local user accounts:

- User Accounts in the Control Panel
- Local Users and Groups MMC snap-in

Both of these interfaces provide access to the same user and group accounts stored in the SAM, so any changes you make using one interface will appear in the other.

Using the User Accounts Control Panel

When you install Windows 7, an administrator account is created during the Windows 7 installation process. During this time, you are asked for a username and password for the administrator account. In addition, the installation program creates the Administrator and Guest accounts, both of which are disabled by default.

CREATE A NEW USER ACCOUNT

GET READY. To create a new user account with the User Accounts control panel, use the following procedure:

1. Click Start, and then click Control Panel. The Control Panel window appears.
2. Click User Accounts and Family Safety. The User Accounts and Family Safety window appears.
3. Click Add or remove user accounts. The *Choose the account you would like to change* page appears.
4. Click Create a new account. The *Name the account and choose the account type* page appears.
5. Type a name for the new account in the text box, and then choose the appropriate radio button to specify whether the account should be a Standard user or an Administrator.
6. Click Create Account. The *Choose the account you would like to change* page reappears, with the new account added.

TAKE NOTE *

This procedure is valid only on Windows 7 computers that are part of a workgroup. When you join a computer to an AD DS domain, you can only create new local user accounts with the Local Users and Groups snap-in.

The User Accounts control panel refers to an account type that is actually a group membership. Selecting the Standard user option adds the user account to the local Users group, while selecting the Administrator option adds the account to the Administrators group.

Most critically, when you create a new user account with this procedure, the account is not protected by a password. You must modify the account after creating it to specify a password or change any of its other attributes.

➔ MANAGE USER ACCOUNTS

GET READY. To see the modifications you can make to an existing local user account with the User Accounts control panel, use the following procedure:

1. Click Start, and then click Control Panel. The Control Panel window appears.
2. Click User Accounts and Family Safety. The User Accounts and Family Safety window appears.
3. Click Add or remove user accounts. The *Choose the account you would like to change* page appears.
4. Click one of the existing accounts. The *Make changes to [user's] account* page appears. See Figure 3-1.

Figure 3-1

Change an account using the Control Panel

5. Click Change the account name. The *Type a new account name for [user] account* page appears.
6. Type a new name for the account in the text box, and then click Change Name. The *Make changes to [user's] account* page reappears.
7. Click Create a password. The *Create a password for [user's] account* page appears.
8. Type a password in the *New password* and *Confirm new password* text boxes and, if desired, supply a password hint.
9. Click Create password. The *Make changes to [user's] account* page reappears, now with a *Remove the password* option added.
10. Click Remove the password. The *Remove a password* page appears.
11. Click Remove Password. The *Make changes to [user's] account* page reappears.
12. Click Change the picture. The *Choose a new picture for [user's] account* page appears.
13. Select a new picture for the account, or click Browse for more pictures, and then click Change Picture. The *Make changes to [user's] account* page reappears.
14. Click Change the account type. The *Choose a new account type for [user]* page appears.
15. Select the Standard user or Administrator radio button, and then click Change Account Type. The *Make changes to [user's] account* page reappears.
16. Click Delete the account. The *Do you want to keep [user's] files?* page appears.
17. Click Delete Files to delete the user profile, or click Keep Files to save it to the desktop. The *Are you sure you want to delete [user's] account?* page appears.
18. Click Delete Account. The *Choose the account you would like to change* page reappears.
19. Close the User Accounts control panel window.

Using the Local Users and Groups Snap-In

For more control when managing user accounts, you should use the Local Users and Groups snap-in, which is included as part of the Computer Management console.

 CREATE A NEW USER

GET READY. To create a local user account with the Local Users and Groups snap-in, use the following procedure:

1. Click Start, and then click Control Panel. The Control Panel window appears.
2. Click System and Security > Administrative Tools. The Administrative Tools window appears.
3. Double-click Computer Management. The Computer Management window appears.
4. In the scope (left) pane of the console, expand the Local Users and Groups node and click Users. A list of the current local users appears in the details (middle) pane.
5. Right-click the Users folder and, from the context menu, select New User. The New User dialog box appears.
6. In the User name text box, type the name you want to assign to the user account. This is the only required field in the dialog box.
7. Specify a Full name and a Description for the account, if desired.
8. In the Password and Confirm password text boxes, type a password for the account, if desired.
9. Select or clear the four check boxes to control the following functions:
   - **User must change password at next logon:** Forces the new user to change the password after logging on for the first time. Select this option if you want to assign an initial password and have users control their own passwords after the first logon. You cannot select this option if you have selected the *Password never expires* check box. Selecting this option automatically clears the *User cannot change password* check box.
   - **User cannot change password:** Prevents the user from changing the account password. Select this option if you want to retain control over the account password, such as when multiple users are logging on with the same user account. This option is also commonly used to manage service account passwords. You cannot select this option if you have selected the *User must change password at next logon* check box.
   - **Password never expires:** Prevents the existing password from ever expiring. This option automatically clears the *User must change password at next logon* check box. This option is also commonly used to manage service account passwords.
   - **Account is disabled:** Disables the user account, preventing anyone from using it to log on.
10. Click Create. The new account is added to the detail pane and the console clears the dialog box, leaving it ready for the creation of another user account.
11. Click Close.
12. Close the Computer Management console.

 MANAGE A USER

GET READY. To manage a user:

1. Open the Computer Management console.
2. In the console's scope pane, expand the Local Users and Groups subheading, and then click Users. A list of the current local users appears in the details pane.

3. Double-click one of the existing user accounts. The Properties sheet for the user account appears, as shown in Figure 3-2.

Figure 3-2

Local user account properties

4. If desired, modify the contents of the Full name and Description text boxes.
5. Select or clear any of the following check boxes:
   - **User must change password at next logon.**
   - **User cannot change password.**
   - **Password never expires.**
   - **Account is disabled.**
   - **Account is locked out.** When selected, this indicates that the account has been disabled because the number of unsuccessful log on attempts specified in the local system policies has been exceeded. Clear the check box to unlock the account.
6. Click the Member Of tab.
7. To add the user to a group, click the Add button. The Select Groups dialog box appears.
8. Type the name of the local group to which you want to add the user in the text box, and then click OK. The group is added to the Member of list. You can also type part of the group name and click Check Names to complete the name or click Advanced to search for groups.
9. Click the Profile tab. See Figure 3-3.
10. Type a path or filename into any of the following four text boxes as needed:
    - **Profile path:** To assign a roaming or mandatory user profile to the account, type the path to the profile stored on a network share using Universal Naming Convention (UNC) notation, as in the example \\server\share\folder.

Figure 3-3

Local user account Profile tab

- **Logon script:** Type the name of a script that you want to execute whenever the user logs on.
- **Local path:** To create a home folder for the user on a local drive, specify the path in this text box.
- **Connect:** To create a home folder for the user on a network drive, select an unused drive letter and type the path to a folder on a network share using Universal Naming Convention (UNC) notation.

11. Click OK to save your changes and close the Properties sheet.
12. Close the Computer Management console.

Utilizing User Profiles

A **user profile**, which is a collection of folders and data that store the user's current desktop environment and application settings, is associated with each user account. A user profile also records all network connections that are established so when a user logs on to a computer, it will remember the mapped drives to shared folders. When a user logs on to a computer, they will get the same desktop environment that they previously had on the computer.

For Windows 7, the profiles are stored in the C:\Users folder. For example, if jsmith logs in, his or her user profile folders would be c:\Users\jsmith. In each user's folder, some of the folders include Desktop, Documents, Start Menu, and Favorites. So when jsmith is directly accessing the Desktop or My Documents, they are really accessing c:\Users\jsmith\desktop and c:\Users\jsmith\my documents.

By default, users use local profiles. Unfortunately, when you go to a different computer within the domain, you will be using a different profile, which will contain a different Desktop and Documents folder. If users tend to use different computers and need to have access to the files on their Desktop and in their Documents folder, you can use roaming profiles that are stored on a centralized server's shared folder. To configure domain user accounts with roaming user profiles, you simply need to modify the properties of those accounts so that the profiles are stored on a network share instead of on the local machine.

Utilizing Credential Manager

Credential Manager allows you to store credentials, such as usernames and passwords that you use to log on to websites or other computers, on a network. By storing your credentials, Windows can automatically log you on to websites or other computers. Credentials are saved in special folders on your computer called vaults. Windows and programs (such as web browsers) can securely give the credentials in the vaults to other computers and websites.

Windows automatically adds credentials used to connect to shared folders to the Credential Manager. However, you can manually add username and password.

 ADD A PASSWORD TO WINDOWS VAULT

GET READY. To add a password to your Windows vault, use the following procedure:

1. Click to open User Accounts.
2. In the left pane, click Manage your credentials.
3. Click Add a Windows credential.
4. In the Internet or network address box, type the name of the computer on the network that you want to access. This can be the NetBIOS name (example: server1) or DNS name (example: server1.fabrikam.com).
5. In the User name and Password boxes, type the username and password that you use for that computer or website, and then click OK.

 DELETE OR CHANGE CREDENTIALS IN VAULT

GET READY. To delete or change the credentials that you store on your computer for logging on to websites or other computers on a network, use the following procedure:

1. Click User Accounts in the Control Panel.
2. In the left pane, click Manage your credentials.
3. Click the vault that contains the credential that you want to manage.
4. Select the credential you want to manage.
5. Click Edit, make the change you want, and then click Save.

■ Introducing Directory Services with Active Directory

A directory service stores, organizes, and provides access to information in a directory. It is used for locating, managing, administering, and organizing common items and network resources, such as volumes, folders, files, printers, users, groups, devices, telephone numbers, and other objects. A popular directory service used by many organizations is Microsoft's Active Directory.

Active Directory is a technology created by Microsoft that provides a variety of network services, including:

- Lightweight Directory Access Protocol (LDAP)
- Kerberos-based and single sign-on (SSO) authentication
- DNS-based naming and other network information
- Central location for network administration and delegation of authority

Active Directory is often a key component in authentication, authorization, and auditing.

LDAP is an application protocol for querying and modifying data using directory services running over TCP/IP. Within the directory, the sets of objects are organized in a logical hierarchical manner so that you can easily find and manage those objects. The structure can reflect geographical or organizational boundaries, although it tends to use DNS names for structuring the topmost levels of the hierarchy. Deeper inside the directory might appear entries representing people, organizational units, printers, documents, groups of people, or anything else that represents a given tree entry (or multiple entries). LDAP uses TCP port 389.

Kerberos is a computer network authentication protocol, which allows hosts to prove their identity over a non-secure network in a secure manner. It can also provide mutual authentication so that both the user and server verify each other's identity. To make it secure, Kerberos protocol messages are protected against eavesdropping and replay attacks.

Single sign-on (SSO) allows you to log on once and access multiple, related, but independent software systems without having to log in again. As you log on with Windows using Active Directory, you are assigned a token, which can then be used to sign on to other systems automatically.

+ MORE INFORMATION

Another commonly used authentication protocol was NTLM. NTLM is used in various Microsoft network protocol implementations and is also used throughout Microsoft's systems as an integrated single sign-on mechanism. However, Kerberos, is slowing replacing NTLM.

Last, Active Directory allows you to organize all of your network resources including users, groups, printers, computers, and other objects so that you can assign passwords, permissions, rights, and so on to the identity that needs it. You can also assign who can manage a group of objects.

Understanding Active Directory Domains

Active Directory domains, trees, and forests are logical representations of your network organization, which allows you to organize them in the best way to manage them. To connect the domains, trees, forests, and objects within Active Directory, they are tied very closely to DNS and a DNS namespace is assigned to each domain, tree, and forest.

As mentioned in Lesson 1, a Windows *domain* is a logical unit of computers and network resources that defines a security boundary. Different from the local security database that was previous discussed, a domain uses a single Active Directory database to share its common security and user account information for all computers within the domain.

Since some organizations can contain thousands of users and thousands of computers, it might make sense to break an organization into more than one domain. The Active Directory forest contains one or more transitive, trust-linked trees, while a tree is linked in a transitive trust hierarchy so that users and computers from one domain can access resources in another domain. Active Directory is tied very closely to DNS and requires it.

Introducing Domain Controllers

While domains, trees, and forests are logical representation of your organization, sites and domain controllers represent the physical structure of your network.

A *domain controller* is a Windows server that stores a replica of the account and security information of the domain and defines the domain boundaries. After a computer has been promoted to a domain controller, there were will be several MMC snap-in consoles to manage Active Directory. They are:

- **Active Directory Users and Computers:** Used to manage users, groups, computers, and organizational units.
- **Active Directory Domains and Trusts:** Used to administer domain trusts, domain and forest functional levels, and user principal name (UPN) suffixes.
- **Active Directory Sites and Services:** Used to administer the replication of directory data among all sites in an Active Directory Domain Services (AD DS) forest.
- **Active Directory Administrative Center:** Used to administer and publish information in the directory including managing users, groups, computers, domains, domain controllers, and organizational units. Active Directory Administrative Center is new in Windows Server 2008 R2.
- **Group Policy Management Console (GPMC):** Provides a single administrative tool for managing Group Policy across the enterprise. GPMC is automatically installed in Windows Server 2008 and above domain controllers, and it needs to be downloaded and installed on Windows Server 2003 domain controllers.

A server that is not running as a domain controller is known as a ***member server***.

When a user logs on, Active Directory clients locate an Active Directory server (using the DNS SRV resource records) known as a domain controller in the same site as the computer. Each domain will have its own set of domain controllers to provide access to the domain resources such as users and computers. If you receive an error message saying that it cannot locate a domain controller or you get a "RPC Server Unavailable" message, you should make sure you are pointing to the correct DNS server and that the DNS server has the correct SRV resource records for the domain controllers.

To provide fault tolerance, it is recommended for a site to have two or more domain controllers. If a domain controller fails, the other domain controller can still service the clients. When an object such as a username or password is modified, it will be automatically replicated to the other domain controllers within a domain.

While these tools are installed on domain controllers, they can also be installed on client PCs so that you can manage Active Directory without logging on to a domain controller.

Looking at Organizational Units

As mentioned earlier, an organization could have thousands of users and thousands of computers. With Windows NT, the domain could only handle so many objects before you saw some performance issues. With later versions of Windows, the size of the domain was dramatically increased. While you may have several domains with Windows NT to define your organization, you could have one domain to represent a large organization. However, if you have thousands of such objects, you need a way to organize and manage them.

To help organize objects within a domain and minimize the number of domains, you can use ***organizational units***, commonly seen as OU. OUs can be used to hold users, groups, computers, and other organizational units. An organizational unit can only contain objects that are located in a domain. While there is no restriction on how many nested OUs (an OU inside of another OU) you can have, you should design a shallow hierarchy for better performance.

When you first install Active Directory, there are several organizational units already created. They include computers, users, domain controllers, and built-in OUs. Different from OUs that you create, these OUs do not allow you to delegate permissions or assign group policies to them. Group policies will be explained in a little bit. Another OU worth mentioning is the domain controller, which holds the default domain controllers policy.

Containers are objects that can store or hold other objects. They include the forest, tree, domain, and organizational unit. To help you manage your objects, you can delegate authority to a container, particularly the domain or organizational unit.

For example, let's say that you have your domain divided by physical location. You can then assign a site administrator authoritative control to the OU that represents the physical location, and the user will only have administrative control over the objects within the OU. You can also structure your OUs by function or areas of management. For example, you can create a Sales OU to hold all of your sales users. You can also create a Printers OU to hold all of the printer objects and assign a printer administrator.

By delegating administration, you can assign a range of administrative tasks to the appropriate users and groups. You can assign basic administrative tasks to regular users or groups, and leave domain-wide and forest-wide administration to members of the Domain Admins and Enterprise Admins groups. By delegating administration, you can allow groups within your organization to take more control of their local network resources. You also help secure your network from accidental or malicious damage by limiting the membership of administrator groups.

You can delegate administrative control to any level of a domain tree by creating OUs within a domain and delegating administrative control for specific OUs to particular users or groups.

Examining Objects

An **object** is a distinct, named set of attributes or characteristics that represents a network resource. Common objects used within Active Directory are computers, users, groups, and printers. Attributes have values that define the specific object. For example, a user could have the first name John, the last name Smith, and the login name jsmith, all of which identify the user.

When working with objects, administrators will use names of the object such as usernames. However, Active Directory objects are assigned a 128-bit unique number called a globally unique identifier (GUID), sometimes referred to as security identifier (SID) to uniquely identify an object. If a user changes his or her name, you can change the name and he or she will still be able to access all objects and have all of the rights as before since those rights are assigned to the GUID. GUIDs also provide some security; if a user is deleted, you cannot create a new user account with the same username and expect to have access to all of the objects and all of the rights that the previous user had.

The schema of Active Directory defines the format of each object and the attributes or fields within each object. The default schema contains definitions of commonly used objects such as user accounts, computers, printers, and groups. For example, the schema defines that the user account has the first name, last name, and telephone number.

To allow the Active Directory to be flexible so that it can support other applications you can extend the schema to included additional attributes. For example, you could add badge numbers or employee identification numbers to the user object. When you install some applications such as Microsoft Exchange, it will extend the schema, usually by adding additional attributes or fields so that it can support the application.

UTILIZING DOMAIN USERS

A domain user account is stored on the domain controller and allows you to gain access to resources within the domain, assuming you have been granted the permissions needed to access those objects. The administrator domain user account is the only account that is created and enabled by default in Windows when you first create a domain. While the administrator domain user account cannot be deleted, it can be renamed.

When you create a domain user account, you must supply a first name, last name, and a user's login name. The user's login name must be unique with the domain. See Figure 3-4. After the user account is created, you can then open the user account properties and configure a person's username, logon hours, which computers a user can log on to, telephone numbers, addresses, what groups the person is a member of, and so on. You can also specify if a password expires, if the password can be changed, and if the account is disabled. Finally, in the Profile tab, you can define the user's home directory, logon script, and profile path. See Figure 3-5.

Figure 3-4

User account in Active Directory

Figure 3-5

Profile tab

The enhanced user account security settings are located in the Account tab. You can access and make changes to the Logon Hours that a domain user can logon by clicking the Logon Hours button. By default, domain logon is allowed 24 hours a day, 7 days a week. See Figure 3-6. Since this settings is for Active Directory user accounts, it does not affect local computer accounts.

Figure 3-6

Account tab and Logon Hours

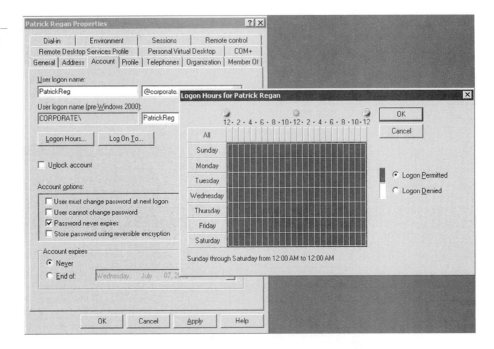

If you want to specify what computers a user can log on to, you would click the Log On To button. By default, a user is able to log on at any workstation computer that is joined to the domain.

In the Account tab, if an account is locked because of too many login attempts, you can deselect the Unlock account box. You can also specify if a user must change password at next logon, user cannot change password, or password never expires. You can also specify a date that an account will automatically be disabled by specifying the date in the Account expires section.

Administrators can also use the Account tab of an AD DS user's properties to restrict logon hours. This is useful when administrators do not want a user to log on outside his normal working hours.

If a user attempts to log on outside his allowed hours, Windows 7 displays the error message "Your account has time restrictions that prevent you from logging on at this time. Please try again later." The only way to resolve this problem is to adjust the user's logon hours by clicking the Logon Hours button on the Account tab of the user's Properties dialog box.

Administrators can disable user accounts to prevent a user from logging on. You should disable accounts when someone leaves the company, is gone for an extended period of time, or when the account has been compromised. To enable a user's disabled account, clear the Account Is Disabled check box in the user's Properties dialog box or right-click the account and select Enable Account.

USING COMPUTER ACCOUNTS

Like user accounts, Windows *computer accounts* provide a means for authenticating and auditing the computer's access to a Windows network and its access to domain resources. Each Windows computer to which you want to grant access to resources must have a unique computer account. It can also be used for auditing purposes specifying what system was used when something was accessed.

Like user accounts, computer accounts are assigned passwords when the computer is added to the domain, and those passwords are automatically maintained between the computer and the domain controllers. Unfortunately, from time to time, a computer account can become untrusted where the security identifier (SID) or password is different from those stored in Active Directory. This happens when:

- You deploy a computer from an image of another computer and you do not use the sysprep tool to reset the SID.
- The computer account is corrupted.
- The computer is not connected to the domain network for long periods of time.

Unfortunately, you cannot reset the password. Instead, the best thing to do is to rejoin the computer to the domain. You can also use the **netdom** command-line tool, which is included with Windows Server 2008 R2.

> **➕ MORE INFORMATION**
>
> For more information about the netdom command, visit the following website:
> http://technet.microsoft.com/en-us/library/cc772217(WS.10).aspx

Using Groups

> A *group* is a collection or list of user accounts or computer accounts. Different from a container, the group does not store the user or computer, it just lists them. The advantage of using groups is to simplify administration, especially when assigning rights and permissions.

A group is used to group users and computers together so that when you assign rights and permissions, you assign the rights and permissions to the group rather than to each user individually. Users and computer can be members of multiple groups, and in some instances, a group can be assigned to another group.

EXAMINING GROUP TYPES

In Windows Active Directory, there are two types of groups: security and distribution. The security group is used to assign rights and permissions and gain access to a network resource. It can also be used as a distribution group. A distribution group is only for non-security functions such as to distribute email to, and you cannot assign rights and permissions to it.

> **TAKE NOTE*** If you are assigning rights or permissions to a group and the group does not appear, you should check to see if it is a distribution group. Distribution groups cannot be assigned rights and permissions.

LOOKING AT GROUP SCOPES

Any group, whether it is a security group or a distribution group, is characterized by a scope that identifies the extent to which the group is applied in the domain tree or forest. The three group scopes are:

- **Domain Local group:** Contains Global and Universal groups, even though it can also contain user accounts and other Domain Local groups. It is usually in the domain where the resource you want to assign permissions or rights to is located.
- **Global group:** Designed to contain user accounts. Global groups can contain user accounts and other Global groups. Global groups are designed to be "global" for the domain. After you place user accounts into Global groups, the Global groups are typically placed into Domain Local or Local groups.

- **Universal group:** This group scope is designed to contain Global groups from multiple domains. Universal groups can contain Global groups, other Universal groups, and user accounts. Since global catalogs replicate Universal group membership, you should limit the membership to Global groups. This way if you change a member within a Global group, the global catalog will not have to replicate the change.

UTILIZING BUILT-IN GROUPS

Similar to the administrators and guest account, Windows has default groups called built-in groups. These default groups have been granted the essential rights and permissions to get you started. Some of the built-in groups include:

- **Domain admins:** Can perform administrative tasks on any computer within the domain. By default, the Administrator account is a member.
- **Domain users:** Windows automatically adds each new domain user account to the Domain Users group.
- **Account operators:** Can create, delete, and modify user accounts and groups.
- **Backup operators:** Can back up and restore all files using Windows Backup.
- **Authenticated users:** Includes all users with a valid user account on the computer or in Active Directory. Use the Authenticated Users group instead of the Everyone group to prevent anonymous access to a resource.
- **Everyone:** All users who access the computer even if the user does not have a valid account.

> ➕ **MORE INFORMATION**
>
> For more information on the available groups, visit the following website:
> http://technet.microsoft.com/en-us/library/cc756898(WS.10).aspx

■ Introducing Group Policies

THE BOTTOM LINE

Group Policy is one of the most powerful features of Active Directory that controls the working environment for user accounts and computer accounts. Group Policy provides the centralized management and configuration of operating systems, applications, and users' settings in an Active Directory environment. For example, you can use group policies to specify how often a user has to change his or her password, what the background image on a person's computer is, or you can specify if spell checking is required before sending an email.

There are literally thousands of settings that can be made to restrict certain actions, make a system more secure, or standardize a working environment. Group Policy can control a computer registry, NTFS security, audit and security policy, software installation, folder redirection, offline folders, and logon and logoff scripts. As each server version is released, Microsoft usually adds additional parameters.

Group policy objects (GPOs) are collections of user and computer settings (see Figure 3-7) including:

- **System settings:** Application settings, desktop appearance, and behavior of system services.
- **Security settings:** Local computer, domain, and network security settings.
- **Software installation settings:** Management of software installation, updates, and removal.
- **Scripts settings:** Scripts for when a computer starts or shuts down and when a user logs on and off.
- **Folder redirection settings:** Storage for users' folders on the network.

Figure 3-7

Group Policy Editor

Group policies can be set locally on the workstation or can be set at different levels (site, domain, or organizational unit) within Active Directory. Generally speaking, you will not find as many settings locally as you do at the site, domain, or OU level. Group policies are applied in the following order:

1. Local
2. Site
3. Domain
4. OU

If you configure a group policy setting at the site, domain, or organization unit level, and that setting contradicts a setting configured at the local policy, the group policy will override the settings at the local policy. Generally speaking, if you have a policy setting that conflicts with a previous executed setting, the more recently executed setting wins.

Since group policies are defined at site, domain, and OU, you may need to determine where the user's domain is and where within the Active Directory domain tree structure those group policies would affect them. A quick way for users to see their context is to run the set command at a command prompt to display all environment variables. The USERDOMAIN will show the users domain. If the user logged on with a local user account, this will be the computer name (shown on the COMPUTERNAME line). If the user logged on with an AD DS user account, this will be the name of the domain. You can also check the LOGONSERVER line to determine whether a domain controller or the local computer authenticated the user. To determine where they are within the Active Directory tree:

1. Open the Active Directory Users and Computers.
2. Open the View menu and select Advanced Features.
3. Right-click the top of the tree and perform a search for the user.
4. Right-click the user account and select Properties.

Since you selected the Advanced Features, the object tab shows the location of the user account.

You can also use the Group Policy Results in the Group Policy Manager console where you can specify the username and computer name to see all group policies and settings that apply to the user logged on to the computer. In addition, you can also execute the gpresults /r command to show all of the group policies for a person who is logged on.

 ACCESS THE LOCAL GROUP POLICY EDITOR

GET READY. You can open the Local Group Policy Editor by using the command line or by using the Microsoft Management Console (MMC). To open the Local Group Policy Editor from the command line:

1. Click Start, type gpedit.msc in the Start Search box, and then press ENTER.
2. To open the Local Group Policy Editor as an MMC snap-in, open MMC. (Click Start, click in the Start Search box, type mmc, and then press ENTER.)
3. On the File menu, click Add/Remove Snap-in.
4. In the Add or Remove Snap-ins dialog box, click Group Policy Object Editor, and then click Add.
5. In the Select Group Policy Object dialog box, click Browse.
6. Click This computer to edit the Local Group Policy object, or click Users to edit Administrator, Non-Administrator, or per-user Local Group Policy objects.
7. Click Finish.

Most times, you just need to access the security settings that you found in the local policy. This can be done by opening the Local Security Policy from Administrative Tools.

Understanding Rights versus Permissions

Specifying what a user can do on a system or to a resource is determined by two things: rights and permissions.

A *user right* authorizes a user to perform certain actions on a computer such as logging on to a system interactively or backing up files and directories on a system. User rights are assigned through local policies or Active Directory group policies. See Figure 3-8.

Some of the user rights policy settings include:

- **Access this computer from the network:** Determines which users can connect to the computer from the network.
- **Add workstations to domain:** Determines which users can add a computer to a specific domain.
- **Allow log on locally:** Determines which users can start an interactive session on the computer. The error message the users will see without this permission is "The local policy of this system does not permit you to log on interactively." Users who do not have this right are still able to start a remote interactive session on the computer if they have the Allow logon through Terminal Services right.

Figure 3-8

Group Policy User Rights
Assignment

- **Allow log on through Terminal Services policy settings:** Determines which users can log on to the computer through a Remote Desktop connection. You should not assign this user right to additional users or groups. Instead, it is a best practice to add users to or remove users from the Remote Desktop Users group to control who can open a Remote Desktop connection to the computer.
- **Back up files and directories:** This policy setting determines which users can circumvent file and directory permissions to back up the computer.
- **Change the system time:** This policy setting determines which users can adjust the time on the computer's internal clock.
- **Load and unload device drivers:** This policy setting determines which users can dynamically load and unload device drivers. This user right is not required if a signed driver for the new hardware already exists in the Driver.cab file on the computer.
- **Log on as a service:** This policy setting determines which service accounts can register a process as a service. In Windows Server 2008 and Windows Vista, only the Network Service account has this right by default. Any service that runs under a separate user account must be assigned this user right.
- **Restore files and directories:** This security setting determines which users can bypass file, directory, registry, and other persistent objects permissions when restoring backed up files and directories, and determines which users can set any valid security principal as the owner of an object.
- **Shut down the system:** This policy setting determines which users can shut down the local computer.
- **Take ownership of files or other objects:** This policy setting determines which users can take ownership of any securable object in the computer, including Active Directory objects, NTFS files and folders, printers, registry keys, services, processes, and threads.

A *permission* defines the type of access that is granted to an object (an object can be identified with a security identifier) or object attribute. The most common objects assigned permissions are NTFS files and folders, printers and Active Directory objects. To keep track of which user can access an object and what the user can do is recorded in the access control list (ACL), which lists all users and groups that have access to the object.

Utilizing Account Lockout Policies

Permissions are covered in more detail in Lessons 7 and 8.

An *Account Lockout Policy* specifies the number of unsuccessful logon attempts that, if made within a pre-defined amount of time, may hint of an unauthorized person trying to access a computer or the network. An Account Lockout Policy can be set to lock the account in question after a specified number of invalid attempts. Additionally, the policy specifies the duration that the account remains locked.

The three policy settings used for account lockout are:

- **Account lockout duration:** How long (in minutes) a locked-out account remains locked out (range is 1 to 99,999 minutes).
- **Account lockout threshold:** How many failed logons it will take until the account becomes locked out (range is 1 to 999 logon attempts).
- **Reset account lockout counter after:** How long (in minutes) it takes after a failed logon attempt before the counter tracking failed logons is reset to zero (range is 1 to 99,999 minutes).

See Figure 3-9.

Figure 3-9

Account lockout policies

If you set the Account lockout duration to 0, the account stays locked until an administrator unlocks it. If the account lockout threshold is set to 0, the account will never be locked out no matter how many failed logons occur.

 CONFIGURE AN ACCOUNT LOCKOUT POLICY

GET READY. To configure a domain-wide account lockout policy:

1. OPEN the GPMC. Click Forest: <Forest Name>, click Domains, click <Domain Name>, and then click Group Policy Objects.
2. Right-click the Default Domain Policy and click Edit. A Group Policy Management Editor window for this policy is displayed.
3. In the left window pane, expand the Computer Configuration node, expand the Policies node, and expand the Windows Settings folder. Then, expand the Security Settings node. In the Security Settings node, expand Account Policies and select Account Lockout Policy. The available settings for this category of the GPO are displayed.
4. In the right windowpane, double-click the Account lockout duration policy setting to view the Properties dialog box.
5. Select the Define This Policy Setting check box. Note the default setting of 30 minutes for Account Lockout Duration. If you want to change the account lockout duration, you may do so here.
6. Click OK to accept the specified lockout duration. The Suggested Value Changes dialog box, which indicates other related settings and their defaults, is displayed.
7. Click OK to automatically enable these other settings or click Cancel to go back to the Account Lockout Duration Properties dialog box.
8. Click OK to accept the additional setting defaults.
9. Make any additional changes, as necessary, to the other individual Account Lockout Policy settings.
10. Close the Group Policy Management Editor window for this policy.

Utilizing Password Control

Group policies can be used to control passwords including how often a user changes a password, how long the password is, and if the password is a complex password.

To help manage passwords, you can configure settings in the Computer Configuration\Windows Settings\Security Settings\Account Policies\Password Policy node of a group policy. The Group Policy Password Policy settings (see Figure 3-10) are:

- **Minimum password length:** Determines the minimum number of characters that a user's password must contain. You can set a value between 1 and 14 characters. To specify that no password is required, set the value to 0.
- **Passwords must meet complexity requirements:** If enabled, password must be at least six characters long, cannot use parts of the user's name, and must be a mix (3 of the 4) of uppercase, lowercase, digits, and non-alphanumeric characters.
- **Maximum password age:** The time before a password expires.
- **Enforce password history:** The number of different passwords that users must have before they can reuse a password.
- **Minimum password age:** The time before users can change their password, which will prevent users from changing the password numerous times to go beyond the enforce password history so that they can reset their password to their original password.

Figure 3-10

Group Policy Password Policy settings

Understanding Auditing

As mentioned before, security can be divided into three areas. Authentication is used to prove the identity of a user, while authorization gives access to the user that was authenticated. To complete the security picture, you need to enable auditing so that you can have a record of the users who have logged in and what the user accessed or tried to access.

It is important that you protect your information and service resources from people who should not have access to them, and at the same time make those resources available to authorized users. Along with authentication and authorization, you should also enable auditing so that you can have a record of:

- Who has successfully logged in
- Who has attempted to login but failed
- Who has changed accounts in Active Directory
- Who has accessed or changed certain files
- Who has used a certain printer
- Who restarted a system
- Who has made some system changes

Auditing is not enabled by default. To enable auditing, you specify what types of system events to audit using group policies or the local security policy (Security Settings\Local Policies\Audit Policy). See Figure 3-11. Table 3-1 shows the basic events to audit that are available in Windows Server 2003 and 2008. Windows Server 2008 has additional options for more granular control. After you enable logging, you then open the Event Viewer security logs to view the security events.

Figure 3-11

Enabling Auditing using Group Policies

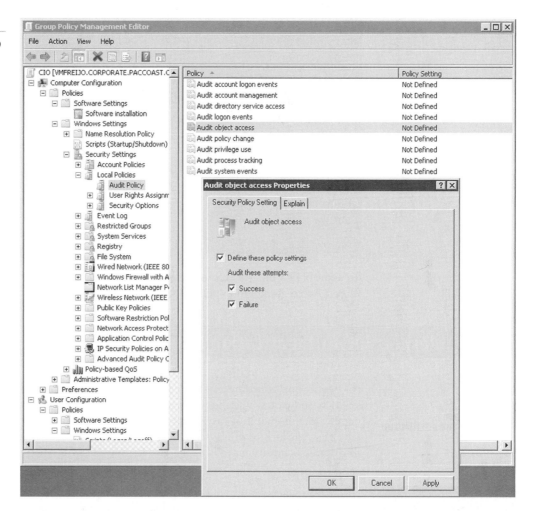

Table 3-1

Audit events

EVENT	EXPLANATION
Account Logon	Determines whether the OS audits each time the computer validates an account's credentials such as account login.
Account Management	Determines whether to audit each event of account management on a computer including changing passwords and creating or deleting user accounts.
Directory Service Access	Determine whether the OS audits user attempts to access Active Directory objects.
Logon	Determines where the OS audits each instance of a user attempting to log on to or log off his or her computer.
Object Access	Determines whether the OS audits user attempts to access non-Active Directory objects including NTFS files and folders and printers.

(continued)

Table 3-1

(continued)

EVENT	EXPLANATION
Policy Change	Determines whether the OS audits each instance of attempts to change user rights assignments, auditing policy, account policy, or trust policy.
Privilege Use	Determines whether to audit each instance of a user exercising a user right.
Process Tracking	Determines whether the OS audits process-related events such as process creation, process termination, handle duplication, and indirect object access. This is usually used for troubleshooting.
System	Determines whether the OS audits if the system time is changed, system startup or shutdown, attempt to load extensible authentication components, loss of auditing events due to auditing system failure, and security log exceeding a configurable warning threshold level.

To audit NTFS files, NTFS folders, and printers is a two-step process. You must first enable Object Access using group policies. Then you must specify which objects you want to audit.

■ Troubleshooting Authentication Issues

THE BOTTOM LINE

Authentication issues are a common problem that everyone has to deal with. The simplest and easiest mistake for users is forgetting their password, which then needs to be reset. A common but easy mistake to make when typing a username or password is to have the caps lock or num lock key on. If the solution isn't that simple, then you need to dig a little bit deeper.

CERTIFICATION READY
What reasons can you think that would prevent a user from logging in to a computer running Windows 7?
2.1

Fortunately when people are logging in and having difficulty, the message generated when a login fails clearly identifies the problem. For example, if the account is disabled or the password expired, you will see a message to that effect. If you log in after hours when you have logon hour restrictions, or from the wrong computer when you have computer restrictions, you will get a message to that effect.

Other items that you should check include:

- When typing in your username and password, always check the caps lock and num lock keys first.
- Make sure you have the correct language defined and that the keyboard is operating fine where all of the buttons click properly.
- If the time is off, authentication can fail. Therefore, you should also check the time and time zone of the computer.
- If your computer is no longer part of the domain or is no longer trusted, you will not be able to log in to the domain.

If you have checked the obvious and you still cannot log on, you should check the Event Viewer next. You should check the security logs if you have enabled login auditing. You should also check the System logs to make sure that there are no errors that would contribute to this problem. Also if you try to access a remote object such as a shared folder or shared printer, you will need to check the computer or host that manages the shared objects and look though the Event Viewer logs.

SKILL SUMMARY

IN THIS LESSON YOU LEARNED:

- A workgroup is usually associated with a peer-to-peer network in which user accounts are decentralized and stored on each individual computer.

- When you create a local user account on a computer running Windows 7, it is stored in the Security Accounts Manager (SAM). SAM is a database stored as a registry file.

- A user account enables a user to log on to a computer and domain. As a result, it can be used to prove the identity of a user, which can then be used to determine what a user can access and what kind of access a user will have (authorization).

- Associated with a user account is the user profile, which is a collection of folders and data that store the user's current desktop environment and application settings.

- Credential Manager allows you to store credentials, such as usernames and passwords that you use to log on to websites or other computers on a network.

- Authentication is the process of identifying an individual, usually based on a username and password. After a user is authenticated, users can access network resources based on the user's authorization.

- Authorization is the process of giving individuals access to system objects based on their identity.

- Auditing is the process of keeping track of a user's activity while accessing the network resources, including the amount of time spent in the network, the services accessed while there, and the amount of data transferred during the session.

- Active Directory is a directory service and technology created by Microsoft that provides a variety of network services, including LDAP, Kerberos-based and single sign-on authentication, DNS-based naming, and other network information, as well as a central location for network administration and delegation of authority.

- A Windows domain is a logical unit of computers and network resources that defines a security boundary. A domain uses a single Active Directory database to share its common security and user account information for all computers within the domain, allowing centralized administration of all users, groups, and resources on the network.

- A server that is not running as a domain controller is known as a member server.

- A domain controller is a Windows server that stores a replica of the account and security information of the domain and defines the domain boundaries.

- To help organize objects within a domain and minimize the number of domains, you can use organizational units (OUs).

- An object is a distinct, named set of attributes or characteristics that represent a network resource. Common objects used within Active Directory are computers, users, groups, and printers.

- A domain user account is stored on the domain controller and allows you to gain access to resources within the domain, assuming you have been granted permissions to access those objects.

- Like user accounts, Windows computer accounts provide a means for authenticating and auditing the computer's access to a Windows network and its access to domain resources.

- A group is a collection or list of user accounts or computer accounts.

- Group Policy provides the centralized management and configuration of operating systems, applications and users' settings in an Active Directory environment.

- A user right authorizes a user to perform certain actions on a computer such as logging on to a system interactively or backing up files and directories on a system.

- A permission defines the type of access that is granted to an object (an object can be identified with a security identifier) or object attribute.

- An Account Lockout Policy specifies the number of unsuccessful logon attempts that, if made within a pre-defined amount of time, may hint of an unauthorized person trying to access a computer or the network.

- To help protect against someone guessing a user's login password, users should change their passwords regularly.

Knowledge Assessment

Fill in the Blank

Complete the following sentences by writing the correct word or words in the blanks provided.

1. _____ is used for authentication, authorization, and auditing.

2. _____ allows you to store credentials, such as usernames and passwords that you can use to log on to websites and other computers on a network.

3. A _____ defines the type of access that is granted to an object such as a user or printer.

4. _____ is a popular directory service with objects in a logical hierarchical manner.

5. To view the security logs for Windows 7, you will use the _____ .

6. The _____ is used to organize the objects within a domain.

7. Printers, users, and computers are examples of _____ in Active Directory.

8. The local security database found on a member server is _____ .

9. A collection or list of users is known as _____ .

10. By default, the user profiles are stored in the _____ folder.

Multiple Choice

Circle the letter that corresponds to the best answer.

1. For Active Directory to function, you need to have _____ .
   a. AD
   b. WINS
   c. DNS
   d. DHCP

2. Which of the following terms describes the process of giving individuals access to system objects based on their identity?
   a. Authentication
   b. Authorization
   c. Auditing
   d. Masquerading

3. What is a logical unit of computers and network resources that define a security boundary?
   a. Server
   b. Group
   c. DNS
   d. Domain

4. To uniquely identify a user or computer, these objects are assigned a _____ .
   a. Domain controller
   b. Group
   c. Security identifier
   d. Owner

5. To enforce users in changing their password, you would use the _____ setting in group policies.
   a. Task scheduler
   b. Maximum password age
   c. Enforce password history
   d. Minimum password age

6. Which of the following would NOT cause a problem with authentication?
   a. Caps lock key
   b. Incorrect time
   c. UAC
   d. Account is disabled

7. The Documents, Desktop, and Favorite folders are part of the _____ .
   a. User profile
   b. Group policy
   c. Software policy
   d. User account collection

8. What can be used to specify how many times a user can give the login with an incorrect password before the account is disabled?
   a. User profile
   b. Group policy
   c. Software policy
   d. User account collection

9. Which of the following can a group policy NOT be applied to directly?
   a. Group
   b. Site
   c. Domain
   d. OU

10. What authorizes a user to perform certain actions on a computer?
    a. Permission
    b. UNC
    c. Right
    d. Task

True / False

Circle T if the statement is true or F if the statement is false.

T | F 1. Roaming profiles are usually kept on the C drive of the local computer running Windows 7.

T | F 2. UAC is used for authentication.

T | F 3. User rights define what actions a person can do on a system.

T | F 4. For a user to log on directly to a computer running Windows 7, the user needs to have the Allow interactive login right.

T | F 5. The SAM is located on domain controllers.

■ Case Scenarios

Scenario 3-1: Looking at User Rights

Open the local security policy on a Windows 7 computer. Open the User Rights Assignment located in the local policies under Computer Configuration. Determine which user rights are assigned to the Administrator or Administrator's group.

Scenario 3-2: Looking at Passwords

Explain the weakness of a password and why it should be changed regularly.

Troubleshooting Mobile Connectivity Problems

OBJECTIVE DOMAIN MATRIX

TECHNOLOGY SKILL	OBJECTIVE DOMAIN	OBJECTIVE NUMBER
Troubleshooting Wireless Connection Problems	Identify and resolve wireless connectivity issues.	4.1
Troubleshooting VPN Client Connectivity	Identify and resolve remote access issues.	4.2

KEY TERMS

802.11

802.11a

802.11b

802.11g

802.11n

bootstrap wireless profile

DirectAccess

Internet Key Exchange version 2 (IKEv2)

IP Security (IPSec)

Layer 2 Tunneling Protocol (L2TP)

Point-to-Point Tunneling Protocol (PPTP)

remote access server (RAS)

Remote Authentication Dial In User Service (RADIUS)

Secure Socket Tunneling Protocol (SSTP)

service set identifier (SSID)

virtual private network (VPN)

Wi-Fi Protected Access (WPA)

Wi-Fi Protected Access 2 (WPA2)

Wired Equivalent Privacy (WEP)

Lesson 4 continues the discussion of how to connect a computer running Windows 7 to the network, specifically how to connect through a wireless connection and how to connect remotely through a VPN connection. In both instances, each sublesson will discuss how to troubleshoot problems relating to wireless and VPN connections.

You just got home from a long day at work and you get a call from your CIO. He took his computer home, and he is having problems getting connected to the Internet with his wireless network card. As a result, the CIO cannot use his VPN connection to connect to the corporate servers so that he can access a report that he needs for an important meeting in the morning. You need to help him connect to his wireless network and connect to the corporation's network using a VPN connection.

■ Introducing Windows 7 and Wireless Technology

THE BOTTOM LINE

Over the last several years, wireless technology has become very common within businesses and home networks allowing computers to roam within the office. Before learning how to configure wireless technology, you must first learn the basics of wireless technology and how they work.

When you purchase a laptop computer today, it will most likely come with a wireless card or wireless interface to connect to an 802.11 wireless network. The IEEE 802 standard is part of the Institute of Electrical and Electronics Engineers (IEEE) standards dealing with local area networks. While the IEEE 802.2 defined logical link control and 802.3 defined Ethernet, the IEEE *802.11* is a set of standards carrying out wireless local area network (WLAN) computer communication in the 2.4, 3.6, and 5 GHz frequency bands.

Understanding Wireless Standards

Most wireless networks used by companies are 802.11b, 802.11g, or 802.11n networks. Wireless devices that are based on these specifications can be Wi-Fi certified to show they have been thoroughly tested for performance and compatibility.

802.11b was the first widely accepted wireless technology, followed by *802.11g* and *802.11n*. See Table 4-1. As a general rule, devices supporting the newer, faster standards are capable of

Table 4-1

Wireless protocols

802.11 PROTOCOL	FREQ. (GHz)	BANDWIDTH (MHz)	DATA RATE PER STREAM (MBIT/S)	ALLOWABLE STREAMS	APPROXIMATE INDOOR RANGE (M)	(FT)	APPROXIMATE OUTDOOR RANGE (M)	(FT)
	2.4	20	1, 2	1	20	66	100	330
a	5	20	6, 9, 12, 18, 24, 36, 48, 54	1	35	115	120	390
	3.7				—	—	5,000	16,000
b	2.4	20	1, 2, 5.5, 11	1	38	125	140	460
g	2.4	20	1, 2, 6, 9, 12, 18, 24, 36, 48, 54	1	38	125	140	460
n	2.4/5	20	7.2, 14.4, 21.7, 28.9, 43.3, 57.8, 65, 72.2	4	70	230	250	820
		40	15, 30, 45, 60, 90, 120, 135, 150		70	230	250	820

falling back to slower speeds when necessary. Therefore, 802.11n is backward compatible with 802.11g, which is backward compatible for 802.11b. It should be noted that *802.11a* is not compatible with 802.11b because each use different frequencies and modulation techniques; although, some network adapters may support both 802.1a and 802.11b.

The 802.11 workgroup currently documents use in three distinct frequency ranges, 2.4 GHz, 3.6 GHz, and 4.9/5.0 GHz bands. Each range is divided into a multitude of channels. Countries apply their own regulations to both the allowable channels, allowed users, and maximum power levels within these frequency ranges.

There are 14 channels designated in the 2.4 GHz range spaced 5 MHz apart (with the exception of a 12 MHz spacing before Channel 14). Because the protocol requires 25 MHz of channel separation, adjacent channels overlap and can interfere with each other. Consequently, using only channels 1, 6, 11, and 14 is recommended to avoid interference.

Wireless adapters can run in one of two operating modes:

- **Independent basic service set (IBSS):** Also known as ad hoc, where hosts connect directly to other computers with wireless adapters.
- **Extended service set (ESS):** Also known as infrastructure, where hosts connects to a wireless access point using a wireless adapter.

When running in ESS mode, the access point will often connect to the organization's network using an Ethernet or connect directly to the Internet using a coaxial cable.

Utilizing Wireless Security

> Since wire technology sends radio waves out into the open, anyone can capture data within the range of the antennas. Therefore, you will need to implement encryption and other security measures to prevent data that are sent over wireless technology from being read.

The first widely used encryption algorithm used on wireless networks is *Wired Equivalent Privacy (WEP)*. WEP is often inaccurately referred to as Wireless Encryption Protocol. With WEP, you encrypt data using 40-bit, 128-bit, 152-bit, or higher bit-length private key encryption. With WEP, all data is encrypted using a symmetric key derived from the WEP key or password before it is transmitted, and any computer that wants to read the data must be able to decrypt it using the key. While WEP was intended to provide confidentiality comparable to that of a traditional wired network, WEP was easily cracked with readily available software within minutes. Therefore, it is recommended that you use WPA or WPA2.

Within a few months after the security weaknesses were identified with WEP, IEEE created *Wi-Fi Protected Access (WPA)* as an interim standard prior to the ratification of 802.11i followed by WPA2. WPA provides strong data encryption via Temporal Key Integrity Protocol (TKIP), while *Wi-Fi Protected Access 2* (*WPA2)* provides enhanced data encryption via Advanced Encryption Standard (AES), which meets the Federal Information Standard (FIPS) 140-2 requirement of some government agencies. To help prevent someone from hacking the key, WPA and WPA2 rotate the keys and change the way keys are derived.

Both WPA and WPA2 can run in both personal and enterprise mode. Personal mode, designed for home and small office networks, provides authentication via a pre-shared key or password. Each wireless network device encrypts the network traffic using a 256-bit key. This key may be entered either as a string of 64 hexadecimal digits, or as a passphrase of 8 to 63 printable ASCII characters. The preshared encryption key is programmed into the access point and all wireless devices, which is used as a starting point to mathematically generate session keys. The session keys are then changed often and handled in the background.

Enterprise mode provides authentication using IEEE 802.1X and Extensible Authentication Protocol (EAP). 802.1X provides an authentication framework for wireless LANs, allowing a user to be authenticated by a central authority such as a RADIUS server (RADIUS is described in more depth later in this lesson). Since it uses EAP, the actual algorithm that is used to determine whether a user is authentic is left open so that multiple algorithms can be used and even added as new ones are developed. Enterprise mode uses two sets of keys: the session keys and group keys. The session keys are unique to each client associated between an access point and a wireless client. Group keys are shared among all clients connected to the same access point. Both sets of keys are generated dynamically and are rotated to help safeguard the integrity of keys over time. The encryption keys could be supplied through a certificate or smart card.

Configuring Wireless Adapters

Now that you understand the basics of wireless adapters, you are going to have to configure Windows 7 to connect to a wireless network.

 WARNING For stronger security, it is recommended that you do not broadcast the SSID.

802.11 wireless networks are identified by the ***service set identifier***, or SSID, which is often broadcasted for all to see. When running Windows 7, the network can be seen in the networking notification icon in the system tray. If the SSID is not broadcasted, you will have to enter the SSID manually. The SSID can be up to 32 characters long.

 CONFIGURE A WIRELESS ADAPTER

GET READY. If the wireless adapter or interface is not built into the computer, you will have to physically install the wireless network adapter by inserting it into a PCI or PC Card slot, or connecting it to a USB port. Then start the computer and log on to Windows 7.

1. Click Start, and then click Control Panel > Network and Internet > Network and Sharing Center. The Network and Sharing Center control panel appears.
2. Click Manage wireless networks. The Manage Wireless Networks window appears.
3. Click Add. The *How do you want to add a network?* page appears.
4. Click Manually create a network profile. The *Enter information for the wireless network you want to add* page appears.
5. In the Network Name text box, type the SSID value for the network. See Figure 4-1.

Figure 4-1

Manually connect to a wireless network

Manually connect to a wireless network

Enter information for the wireless network you want to add

Network name:	TestSSID
Security type:	WPA2-Enterprise
Encryption type:	AES
Security Key:	☐ Hide characters

☑ Start this connection automatically

☐ Connect even if the network is not broadcasting
    Warning: If you select this option, your computer's privacy might be at risk.

Next   Cancel

6. Configure the appropriate security values in the *Security type*, *Encryption type*, and *Security key* fields for your network.

7. Select the *Start this connection automatically* check box and click Next. The *Successfully added* page appears.

8. Click Close. The network you created appears in the list of networks.

 CONNECT TO A WIRELESS NETWORK IN RANGE

GET READY. To connect to a wireless network that is currently in range, follow these steps:

1. Click the networking notification icon in the system tray, and then click the name of the network you want to connect to. If you have never connected to profile the network previously and you want to connect to it automatically, select the *Connect Automatically* check box, and then click Connect.

2. If the Network Security Key dialog box appears, enter the network security key, and then click OK.

To disconnect from all wireless networks, click the networking notification icon in the system tray, click the name of the current network, and then click Disconnect.

When you first connect to a wireless network, Windows 7 creates a wireless profile. If the configuration for the wireless network changes such as a different key or password, you will need to modify the wireless profile.

 CHANGE A WIRELESS NETWORK CONNECTION

GET READY. To change the configuration of a wireless network after the original configuration, perform these steps:

1. Click the networking notification icon in the system tray, and then click Open Network And Sharing Center.

2. In the Network And Sharing Center, click Manage Wireless Networks. See Figure 4-2.

Figure 4-2

Manage wireless networks

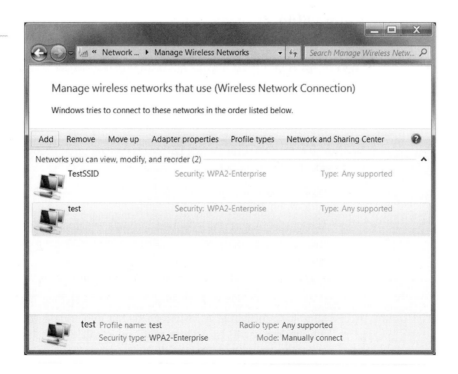

3. Right-click the network you want to reconfigure, and then click Properties. The Wireless Network Properties dialog box appears.

4. Use the Connection tab to specify whether Windows 7 will connect automatically to the network when it is in range and the Security tab to specify the security and encryption types.

5. Click OK.

Of course, any time you create or change a profile, you should immediately test the connection by connecting to the wireless network.

 PRIORITIZE WIRELESS NETWORKS

GET READY. If you have multiple networks available, you can prioritize the wireless networks to make sure that you connect to the correct network when in range. To set the priority of wireless networks, perform these steps:

1. Click the networking notification icon in the system tray, and then click Open Network And Sharing Center.

2. In the Network And Sharing Center, click Manage Wireless Networks.

3. In the Manage Wireless Networks window, click a wireless network profile, and then click Move Up or Move Down.

When multiple networks are available, Windows 7 always connects to the network listed first.

Using Group Policies and Scripts to Configure Wireless Settings

You can also configure wireless networks using Group Policies or scripts. If you use group policies, you can configure a client to automatically connect to your organization's wireless network and keep the computer from connecting to other wireless networks. You can also use the `netsh` command and carry the configuration information using USB flash drives.

USING GROUP POLICIES

To support wireless configuration using group policies when you have a Windows Server 2003 domain controller with SP1, you will need to extend the AD DS schema using the 802.11Schema.ldf file from http://www.microsoft.com/technet/network/wifi/vista_ad_ext .mspx. This features is already included with Windows Server 2008.

 EXTEND THE ACTIVE DIRECTORY SCHEMA

GET READY. To extend the Active Directory schema on Windows Server 2003 domain controllers, follow these steps:

1. From the Windows desktop, click Start, click Programs, click Accessories, and then click Notepad.

2. Select the text of the "Contents of 802.11Schema.ldf" section (not including the section title) from http://technet.microsoft.com/en-us/library/bb727029. aspx#EDAA.

3. Right-click the selected section, and then click Copy.

4. Click the open Notepad window, click Edit, and then click Paste.

5. Click File, click Save As, navigate to the appropriate folder, type 802.11Schema.ldf for the File name. In *Save as type*, select All files, select ANSI for the Encoding, and then click Save.

6. Copy the 802.11Schema.ldf file to a folder on a domain controller.

7. Log on to the domain controller with Domain Admin privileges and open a command prompt.

8. Select the folder containing the 802.11Schema.ldf file, and run the following command (where Dist_Name_of_AD_Domain is the distinguished name of the AD DS domain, such as "DC=contoso,DC=com" for the contoso.com AD DS domain):

```
ldifde -i -v -k -f 802.11Schema.ldf -c DC=X
Dist_Name_of_AD_Domain
```

9. Restart the domain controller.

 CONFIGURE GROUP POLICIES FOR WIRELESS CONNECTIONS

GET READY. To configure the group policy:

1. Open the AD DS Group Policy Object (GPO) in the Group Policy Object Editor.

2. Expand Computer Configuration, Policies, Windows Settings, Security Settings, and then click Wireless Network (IEEE 802.11) Policies.

3. Right-click Wireless Network (IEEE 802.11) Policies, and then click Create A New Wireless Network Policy For Windows Vista And Later Releases (if the server is running Windows Server 2008 R2) or Create A New Windows Vista Policy (if the server is running an earlier version of Windows).

4. The New Wireless Network Policy Properties dialog box appears.

5. To add an infrastructure network, click Add, and then click Infrastructure to open the Connection tab of the New Profile Properties dialog box. In the Network Names list, type a valid internal SSID in the Network Names box, and then click Add. Repeat this to configure multiple SSIDs for a single profile. If the network is hidden, select the *Connect Even If The Network Is Not Broadcasting* check box.

6. In the New Profile Properties dialog box, click the Security tab. Use this tab to configure the wireless network authentication and encryption settings. Click OK.

USING SCRIPTS

While not as common, you can also use the netsh wlan command in scripts to connect to different wireless networks. To list available wireless networks, run the following command:

```
netsh wlan show networks
```

To connect to a wireless network using the netsh command, you must have a saved network profile that contains the SSID and security information. Examples would include:

```
connect name=Profile1 ssid=SSID1

connect name=Profile2 ssid=SSID2

interface="Wireless Network Connection"
```

For more information about the netsh wlan command, execute the following:

```
netsh wlan help
```

USING A USB FLASH DRIVE

If you have multiple computers that must be configured to connect to a wireless network, you can use a USB flash drive to carry the configuration from computer to computer.

SAVE WIRELESS CONFIGURATION TO USB FLASH DRIVE

GET READY. To save your wireless network settings to a USB flash drive, insert a USB flash drive into the computer, and then follow these steps:

1. Open Network and Sharing Center.
2. In the left pane, click Manage wireless networks.
3. Right-click the network, click Properties.
4. Click Copy this network profile to a USB flash drive.
5. Select the USB device, and then click Next. If you only have the one, click the Next button. If you don't have a USB device connected, insert the USB device and click the Next button.
6. When the wizard is complete, click the Close button.

 ADD WIRELESS CONFIGURATION TO WINDOWS 7 USING A USB FLASH DRIVE

GET READY. To add a wireless configuration to a computer running Windows 7 by using a USB flash drive:

1. Plug the USB flash drive into a USB port on the computer.
2. For a computer running Windows 7, in the AutoPlay dialog box, click Connect to a Wireless Network.
3. When it asks if you want to add the network, click the Yes button.
4. When it says it was successful, click the OK button.

Creating a Bootstrap Wireless Profile

When a computer running Windows 7 joins a domain over a wireless network, it uses a single sign on to use the same credentials to join a wireless network as the domain. A ***bootstrap wireless profile*** can be created on the wireless client, which first authenticates the computer to the wireless network and then connects to the network and attempts to authenticate to the domain. Authentication can be done either by using a username and password combination or security certificates from a public key infrastructure (PKI).

 CREATE A BOOTSTRAP WIRELESS PROFILE

GET READY. To configure a bootstrap wireless profile in Windows 7, follow this procedure:

1. In Control Panel, open the Network and Sharing Center.
2. Under Change your networking settings section, click Set up a new connection or network.
3. Under the Choose a connection option, select *Manually connect to a wireless network*. Click Next.
4. Configure the wireless network with network name, security type, and encryption type (WEP, TKIP, or AES). Click Next.
5. Click Change connection settings.
6. On the Security tab, under *Choose a network authentication method*, make sure that Protected EAP (PEAP) is selected.
7. Click Settings and uncheck the box *Validate server certificate*. Leave the authentication method set to the default option Secured password (EAP-MSCHAP v2).
8. Click OK and then click Close to close all the dialog boxes. A sample bootstrap wireless profile can be found at http://msdn.microsoft.com/en-us/library/aa369539%28VS.85%29.aspx.

Troubleshooting Wireless Connection Problems

When problems occur with wireless connections, some of what you learned with wired connections can be applied such as dealing with IP addresses, subnet masks, and the default gateway. However since wireless technology uses radio waves instead of cables, you have other factors to consider.

If your network adapter cannot see any wireless networks, you should make sure:

- The wireless device is on.
- The wireless device is enabled in the Network and Sharing Center.
- The correct wireless device driver is installed and enabled.

You can check to make sure the wireless device is on because most of today's laptops have on/off switches or buttons so that you can quickly turn the wireless device on or off. To enable or disable a wireless device using Windows 7, open the Network and Sharing Center, click Change adapter settings and right-click the device to enable or disable the device. You can use the Device Manager to verify the proper drivers are loaded and enabled.

LOOKING AT SIGNAL STRENGTH

As wireless networks have become common, so have problems with signal strength. The farther you are from a wireless access point, the weaker the signal will be. Since the signal is weaker, you will usually have slower network performance. To view your network signal strength, you can open Network and Sharing Center, click Change adapter settings, right-click the wireless device, and select Status.

If your wireless network connection drops frequently or you suffer from poor performance, you should:

- Check to make sure the wireless access point and wireless device are transmitting at maximum power.
- Try to move closer to the access point or move the access point closer to the client computer.
- Try adjusting the antennas or replace the antenna of the wireless access point to a high-gain antenna.

For larger organizations, you can install additional access points and rearrange your current access points to get the best coverage for your organization.

Besides distance, you also need to look at physical obstacles. While radio waves can transmit through walls and other obstacles, the signals are reduced when this occurs. You also need to move any metal items that might block the wireless signal.

If performance is an issue, you should also check the connection's speeds and if possible, make sure you are using the newest technology such as 802.11n instead of the slower 802.11g or 802.11b. Don't forget that the wireless access point and the wireless device must match each other.

DEALING WITH CONNECTIVITY PROBLEMS

If you cannot connect to a wireless network but you could before, you should verify the wireless profile to make sure the correct settings are being used including the encryption algorithm and the key. You should also verify that the access point is powered on and working properly and that you have sufficient signal strength.

If you maintain steady signal strength and have intermittent connections, you should check for interference from another device that transmits on the same frequency as your wireless network. For example, while 802.11b, 802.11g, and 802.11n use 2.4 GHz, and 802.11a uses 5.8 GHz, you can purchase cordless phones that use one or more of the same frequencies. In addition to consumer wireless devices, you also need to check whether there are other wireless access points nearby that are using the same channel (from 1 to 14). If two wireless access points broadcast on the same channel or on a channel within five channels of another wireless access point, the performance of both can be reduced. For best results, use channels 1, 6, 11, and 14 when wireless access points overlap.

DEALING WITH COMPATIBILITY ISSUES

If you are using a wireless device based on a technology that was not officially standardized when it was purchased, these devices or wireless access points may have some compatibility issues with devices and wireless access points released later. In addition, much like a computer, you may need to upgrade the drivers for the wireless adapters or upgrade the firmware if software glitches exist.

■ Introducing Remote Access

THE BOTTOM LINE

Today, it is very common for an organization to use *remote access server (RAS)*, which enables users to connect remotely using various protocols and connection types. By connecting to RAS over the Internet, users can connect to their organization's network so that they can access data files, read email, and access other applications just as if they were sitting at work even though they are at home.

Virtual private network (VPN) links two computers through a wide-area network such as the Internet. To keep the connection secure, the data sent between the two computers is encapsulated and encrypted. In one scenario, a client connects to the RAS server to access internal resources from offsite. See Figure 4-3. Another scenario is to connect one RAS server on one site or organization to another RAS server on another site or organization so that they can communicate with each other.

Figure 4-3

Connecting remotely through a VPN

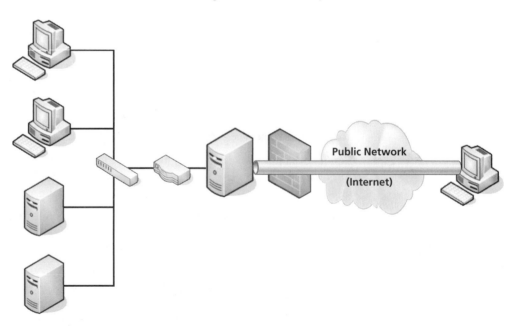

The VPN server in a Windows VPN infrastructure runs Routing and Remote Access Server (RRAS), which in Windows Server 2008 is the Network Policy and Access Service server role. Servers configured with RRAS can receive requests from remote access users located on the Internet, authenticate these users, authorize the connection requests, and finally either block the requests or route the connections to private internal network segments.

Tunneling Protocols

> Tunneling protocols is an encryption mechanism that places one set of packets into the encryption packet and is sent over a public network.

The four types of tunneling protocols used with a VPN server/RAS server running on Windows Server 2008 and Windows 7 include:

- Point-to-Point Tunneling Protocol (PPTP)
- Internet Protocol Security (IPSec)
- Layer 2 Tunneling Protocol (L2TP)
- Internet Key Exchange version 2 (IKEv2)
- Secure Socket Tunneling Protocol (SSTP)

Point-to-Point Tunneling Protocol (PPTP) is based on the legacy Point-to-Point protocol used with modems. Unfortunately, PPTP is easy to set up but is considered to use weak encryption technology.

Internet Protocol Security (IPSec) is a protocol suite for securing Internet Protocol (IP) communications by authenticating and encrypting each IP packet of a data stream. IPSec also includes protocols for establishing mutual authentication between agents at the beginning of the session and negotiation of cryptographic keys to be used during the session. IPSec can be used to protect data flows between a pair of hosts or between a security gateway and a host.

Layer 2 Tunneling Protocol (L2TP) is used with IPSec to provide security and is the industry standard when setting up secure tunnels. Since all clients must be authenticated, a user must connect with either a computer certificate or a preshared key. To define the digital certificate or preshared key, open the Properties dialog box of the VPN connection, click the Security tab, and then click Advanced Settings. Another drawback with L2TP/IPSec is that it does not natively support the traversal of NAT devices. However, you can enable L2TP/IPSec to cross a NAT device by changing a registry value.

✚ MORE INFORMATION

For more information about the registry values for Windows 7 to support NAT, visit the following website: http://support.microsoft.com/kb/926179

IKEv2, short for ***Internet Key Exchange version 2***, is new in Windows 7 and Windows Server 2008 R2. It uses IPSec for encryption while supporting VPN Reconnect (also called Mobility), which enables VPN connections to be maintained when a VPN client moves between wireless cells or switches and to automatically reestablish broken VPN connectivity. Different from L2TP with IPSec, IKEv2 client computers do not need to provide authentication through a machine certificate or a preshared key. In addition, IKEv2 offers improved performance in that the connectivity is established more quickly than L2TP with IPSec.

When you view web pages, you are connecting to the web server using TCP port 80. However, the content is not encrypted and could be read by someone who can access the data stream. Since personal information can be sent over the Internet including credit card numbers, a supplemental protocol was developed called SSL. SSL, short for Secure Sockets Layer, uses TCP port 443, which uses a digital certificate to encrypt the packet so that it cannot be read by anyone else except the source and target. When you are using SSL, the browser URL will start with https.

Secure Socket Tunneling Protocol (SSTP), also introduced with Windows Server 2008, uses HTTPS protocol over TCP port 443 to pass traffic through firewalls and web proxies that might block PPTP and L2TP/IPSec without requiring a client computer certificate or preshared key.

Working with Authentication and Authorization

When connecting to a network through a VPN, the user will have to authenticate, proving who he or she is. If a VPN user is attempting to log on to a domain remotely, the VPN connection must be authenticated, authorized, and established before normal domain logon occurs.

For authentication, RRAS can be configured to forward the authentication request to a RADIUS/Network Policy Server (NPS) server or to use Windows authentication (domain or SAM). RADIUS, short for *Remote Authentication Dial In User Service*, is a networking protocol that provides centralized authentication, authorization, and accounting (AAA) management for computers to connect and use a network service.

When using VPNs, Windows 7 and Windows Server 2008 support the following forms of authentication:

- **Password Authentication Protocol (PAP):** Uses plain text (unencrypted passwords). PAP is the least secure authentication and is not recommended.
- **Challenge Handshake Authentication Protocol (CHAP):** A challenge-response authentication that uses the industry standard md5 hashing scheme to encrypt the response. CHAP was an industry standard for years and is still quite popular.
- **Microsoft CHAP version 2 (MS-CHAP v2):** Provides two-way authentication (mutual authentication). MS-CHAP v2 provides stronger security than CHAP.
- **Extensible Authentication Protocol (EAP-MS-CHAPv2):** A universal authentication framework that allows third-party vendors to develop custom authentication schemes including retinal scans, voice recognition, fingerprint identifications, smart card, Kerberos, and digital certificates. It also provides mutual authentication methods that support password-based user or computer authentication.

After a user is authenticated, the user must then be authorized to connect to the network. Authorization is done by first looking at a user's dial-in properties in the user account followed by looking at the network policy that specifies who can access the network.

 CREATE A VPN TUNNEL

GET READY. To create a VPN tunnel on a computer running Windows 7 so that you can connect to a Remote Access Server:

1. From Control Panel, select Network and Internet to access the Network and Sharing Center.
2. From the Network and Sharing Center choose Set up a new connection or wizard.
3. In the Set Up a Connection or Network choose Connect to a workplace.
4. In the *Connect to a Workplace* page answer the question: Do you want to use a connection that you already have? Choose Create a new connection or choose an existing connection.
5. On the next page choose to Use my Internet connection (VPN).
6. At the next screen, choose your VPN connection or you can specify the Internet Address for the VPN Server and a Destination Name. You can also specify options: use a Smart card for authentication, Allow other people to use this connection and Don't connect now, or just set up so I can connect later.

Sometimes, you may need to do additional configuration of your VPN connection such as specifying the type of protocol, which authentication protocol to use, and the type of encryption.

When the VPN connection is created and configured, to connect using the VPN, you just open the Network and Sharing Center and click on Manage Network Connections. Then right-click your VPN connection and click the Connect button. See Figure 4-4.

Figure 4-4

VPN connection

Using Split Tunneling

When connecting through a VPN, by default the "Use Default Gateway on the Remote Network" option is enabled. As a result, a new default route is created on the VPN client, which forwards data that cannot be sent to the local network to the VPN connection. In other words, if you connect from home to your corporate network, all network traffic including surfing the Internet will be routed through the VPN connection when you are connected through the VPN unless you need to talk to another computer on your home network.

Enabling this option helps protect the corporate network because all traffic will also go through firewalls and proxy servers to help prevent a network from being infected or compromised. When you disable the "Use Default Gateway on Remote Network" option, you are using a split tunnel. With the split tunnel, only traffic that is meant for your corporate network is sent through the default gateway on the remote network. When you want to surf the Internet, you will use your local connection instead of the corporate network.

ENABLE SPLIT TUNNELING

GET READY. To enable split tunneling:

1. Right-click a VPN connection and click Properties.
2. Click the Networking tab.
3. Double-click Internet Protocol Version 4 (TCP/IPv4).
4. Click the Advanced button.
5. Deselect the *Use default gateway on remote network*. See Figure 4-5.

Figure 4-5

Configuring split tunneling

Troubleshooting VPN Client Connectivity

Usually when someone wants to connect to a remote network using a VPN connection, they need to do some work today, either administrating or troubleshooting a server or accessing email, documents, or an internal application. Therefore, you will need to know how to troubleshoot such problems.

CERTIFICATION READY
What should you check if a user cannot connect through a VPN?
4.2

When troubleshooting VPN client connectivity issues you should:

- Make sure that the client computer can connect to the Internet.
- Verify the VPN client connection has the correct server name or IP address. If the connection specification uses the server name, you will need to verify that the server name resolves to the correct IP address.
- Verify that the user has the correct digital certificate and that the digital certificate is valid.
- Make sure that the user is using the proper user credentials including the domain name if necessary.
- Verify the user is authorized for remote access by checking the user properties or by checking the network policies.
- Verify that the correct authentication and encryption methods are selected, especially if you receive a 741/742 encryption mismatch error.

- If you are using LT2P with IPSec going through a NAT device, you need to make sure that you have the proper registry settings. For more information, visit http://support. microsoft.com/kb/926179.

- If you are using any type of firewall and any type of security control software, make sure that the firewall is configured to allow the VPN connection.

- Verify that you have enough PPTP or L2TP ports available to handle the new connection.

Once you are connected, you may have some other problems relating to your VPN connection (mostly configured on the VPN server):

- Verify that routing is configured properly by pinging a remote host through the VPN.

- Verify that you have the proper name resolution for internal resources.

- Verify that the VPN connection has the proper IP configuration including that there are enough DHCP addresses available.

■ Understanding DirectAccess

THE BOTTOM LINE

DirectAccess is a new feature introduced with Windows 7 and Windows Server 2008 R2 that provides seamless intranet connectivity to DirectAccess client computers when they are connected to the Internet. Different from the traditional VPN connections, DirectAccess connections are automatically established.

DirectAccess overcomes the limitations of VPNs by automatically establishing a bi-directional connection from client computers to the corporate network using IPSec and Internet Protocol version 6 (IPv6). As a result, remote client computers are automatically connected to the corporation's network so that they can be easily managed including kept up-to-date with critical updates and configuration changes.

> **➕ MORE INFORMATION**
>
> For more information about DirectAccess, download the Windows 7 and Windows Server R2 DirectAccess Executive Overview:
> http://www.microsoft.com/downloads/details.aspx?FamilyID=D8EB248B-8BF7-4798-A1D1-04D37F2E013C& displaylang=en

To use DirectAccess, you need to have the following:

- One or more DirectAccess servers running Windows Server 2008 R2 with two network adapters: one that is connected directly to the Internet and one that is connected to the intranet. In addition, DirectAccess servers must be a member of an AD DS domain.

- On the DirectAccess server, at least two consecutive, public IPv4 addresses assigned to the network adapter that is connected to the Internet.

- DirectAccess client computers that are running Windows 7 Enterprise or Windows 7 Ultimate. DirectAccess clients must be members of an AD DS domain.

- At least one domain controller and DNS server that is running Windows Server 2003 SP2 or Windows Server 2008 R2. When Forefront Unified Access Gateway (UAG) is used, DirectAccess can be deployed with DNS servers and domain controllers that are running Windows Server 2003 when NAT64 functionality is enabled.

- A public key infrastructure (PKI) to issue computer certificates, and optionally, smart card certificates for smart card authentication and health certificates for NAP.

- Without UAG, an optional NAT64 device to provide access to IPv4-only resources for DirectAccess clients. DirectAccess with UAG provides a built-in NAT64.

Looking at the DirectAccess Connection Process

A DirectAccess connection to a target intranet resource is initiated when the DirectAccess client connects to the DirectAccess server through IPv6. IPSec is then negotiated between the client and server. Finally, the connection is established between the DirectAccess client and the target resource.

This general process can be broken down into the following specific steps:

1. The DirectAccess client computer running Windows 7 Enterprise or Windows 7 Ultimate detects that it is connected to a network.
2. The DirectAccess client computer determines whether it is connected to the intranet. If it is, DirectAccess is not used. If it is not, DirectAccess is used.
3. The DirectAccess client computer connects to the DirectAccess server by using IPv6 and IPSec. If a native IPv6 network is not available (and it probably will not be when the computer is connected to the Internet), the client uses 6to4 or Teredo tunneling to send IPv4-encapsulated IPv6 traffic.
4. If a firewall or proxy server prevents the client computer that is using 6to4 or Teredo tunneling from reaching the DirectAccess server, the client automatically attempts to connect by using the Internet Protocol over Secure Hypertext Transfer Protocol (IP-HTTPS) protocol. IP-HTTPS uses a Secure Sockets Layer (SSL) connection to encapsulate IPv6 traffic.
5. As part of establishing the IPSec session for the tunnel to reach the intranet DNS server and domain controller, the DirectAccess client and server authenticate each other using computer certificates for authentication.
6. If Network Access Protection (NAP) is enabled and configured for health validation, the DirectAccess client obtains a health certificate from a Health Registration Authority (HRA) located on the Internet prior to connecting to the DirectAccess server. The HRA forwards the DirectAccess client's health status information to a NAP health policy server. The NAP health policy server processes the policies defined within the Network Policy Server (NPS) and determines whether the client is compliant with system health requirements. If so, the HRA obtains a health certificate for the DirectAccess client. When the DirectAccess client connects to the DirectAccess server, it submits its health certificate for authentication.
7. When the user logs on, the DirectAccess client establishes the second IPSec tunnel to access the resources of the intranet. The DirectAccess client and server authenticate each other using a combination of computer and user credentials.
8. The DirectAccess server forwards traffic between the DirectAccess client and the intranet resources to which the user has been granted access.

Troubleshooting DirectAccess

Since DirectAccess is a new technology and it depends on several components, it is easy to have problems with it. Of course, you should first verify that you meet system requirements.

When troubleshooting DirectAccess, you should check the following:

1. The DirectAccess client computer must be running Windows 7 Ultimate or Windows 7 Enterprise edition.
2. The DirectAccess client computer must be a member of an Active Directory Domain Services (AD DS) domain and its computer account must be a member of one of the security groups configured with the DirectAccess Setup Wizard.

3. The DirectAccess client computer must have received computer configuration Group Policy settings for DirectAccess.

4. The DirectAccess client must have a global IPv6 address, which should begin with a 2 or 3.

5. The DirectAccess client must be able to reach the IPv6 addresses of the DirectAccess server.

6. The intranet servers have a global IPv6 address.

7. The DirectAccess client on the Internet must correctly determine that it is not on the intranet. You can type the `netsh dnsclient show state` command to view network location displayed in the Machine Location field (Outside corporate network or Inside corporate network).

8. The DirectAccess client must not be assigned the domain firewall profile.

9. The DirectAccess client must be able to reach the organization's intranet DNS servers using IPv6. You can use Ping to attempt to reach the IPv6 addresses of intranet servers.

10. The DirectAccess client must be able to communicate with intranet servers using application layer protocols. If File And Printer Sharing is enabled on the intranet server, test application layer protocol access by typing net view \\IntranetFQDN.

Microsoft also provides the DirectAccess Connectivity Assistant (DCA) to help you streamline end-user support for DirectAccess. The DCA installs on DirectAccess clients and adds an icon to the notification area of the desktop. With DCA, you can determine the intranet connectivity status and get diagnostic information. In addition, it can help users reconnect on their own if problems arise.

 ➕ MORE INFORMATION

For more information, visit the following website:
http://technet.microsoft.com/en-us/library/ff453413(WS.10).aspx

---

SKILL SUMMARY

IN THIS LESSON YOU LEARNED:

- When you purchase laptop computers today, they will most likely come with wireless card to connect to an 802.11 network.

- 802.11 is a set of standards carrying out wireless local area network (WLAN) computer communication in the 2.4, 3.6, and 5 GHz frequency bands.

- 802.11b was the first widely accepted wireless technology, followed by 802.11g and 802.11n.

- It should be noted that 802.11a is not compatible with 802.11b because each use different frequencies and modulation techniques; although, some network adapters may support both 802.1a and 802.11b.

- Wireless adapters can run in one of two operating modes: Independent basic service set (IBSS) and Extended service set (ESS).

- Independent basic service set (IBSS), also known as ad hoc, has hosts connect directly to other computers with wireless adapters.

- Extended service set (ESS), also known as infrastructure, has a host connect to a wireless access point using a wireless adapter.

- Since wire technology sends radio waves out into the open, wireless network signals can be captured by anyone within the range of the antennas. Therefore, you will need to implement encryption and other security measures to prevent the reading of the data sent over the wireless technology.

- The first encryption algorithm widely used on wireless networks is Wired Equivalent Privacy (WEP), which was intended to provide confidentiality comparable to that of a traditional wired network.

- Unfortunately, WEP was easily cracked with readily available software within minutes. Therefore, it is recommended to use WPA or WPA2.

- IEEE created Wi-Fi Protected Access (WPA) as an interim standard prior to the ratification of 802.11i, which provides strong data encryption via Temporal Key Integrity Protocol (TKIP).

- WPA2 provides enhanced data encryption via Advanced Encryption Standard (AES), which meets the Federal Information Standard (FIPS) 140-2 requirement of some government agencies.

- To help prevent someone from hacking the key, WPA and WPA2 rotate the keys and change the way keys are derived.

- 802.1X provides an authentication framework for wireless LANs, allowing a user to be authenticated by a central authority such as a RADIUS server.

- Both WPA and WPA2 can run in both personal and enterprise mode.

- Personal mode, designed for home and small office networks, provides authentication via a pre-shared key or password.

- Enterprise mode provides authentication using IEEE 802.1X and Extensible Authentication Protocol (EAP). The encryption key could be supplied through a certificate or smart card.

- 802.11 wireless networks are identified by the service set identifier, or SSID, which are often broadcast for all to see.

- For better security, it is recommended that you do not broadcast the SSID.

- You can also configure wireless networks using Group Policies, scripts, or a USB flash drive.

- A bootstrap wireless profile can be created on the wireless client, which first authenticates the computer to the wireless network and then connects to the network and attempts to authenticate to the domain.

- If your network adapter cannot see any wireless networks, you need to check whether the wireless device is on, is enabled, and that the correct wireless device is installed.

- The farther away you get from a wireless access point, the weaker the signal will be, which also results in slower network performance.

- If you cannot connect to a wireless network that you could before, it would make sense to check the security settings to make sure the correct settings are being used within wireless profile including any keys.

- If you have an intermittent connection to your wireless network, it is most likely caused by interference with another device that transmits on the same frequency as your wireless network.

- Today, it is very common for an organization to use remote access server (RAS), which allows users to connect remotely using various protocols and connection types.

- Virtual private network (VPN) links two computers through a wide-area network such as the Internet. To keep the connection secure, the data sent between the two computers is encapsulated and encrypted.

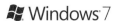

- The four types of tunneling protocols used with a VPN server/RAS server running on Windows Server 2008 and Windows 7 include: Point-to-Point Tunneling Protocol (PPTP), Layer 2 Tunneling Protocol (L2TP), Internet Key Exchange version 2 (IKEv2), and secure socket Tunneling Protocol (SSTP).

- Point-to-Point Tunneling Protocol (PPTP) is based on the legacy Point-to-Point protocol used with modems. Unfortunately, PPTP is easy to set up but uses a weak encryption technology.

- Internet Protocol Security (IPSec) is a protocol suite for securing Internet Protocol (IP) communications by authenticating and encrypting each IP packet of a data stream.

- Layer 2 Tunneling Protocol is used with IPSec to provide security and is the industry standard when setting up secure tunnels. Since all clients must be authenticated, a user must connect with either a computer certificate or a preshared key.

- IKEv2, short for Internet Key Exchange version 2, uses IPSec for encryption while supporting VPN Reconnect (also called Mobility), which enables VPN connections to be maintained when a VPN client moves between wireless cells or switches.

- Unlike L2TP with IPSec, IKEv2 client computers do not need to provide authentication through a machine certificate or a preshared key.

- Secure Socket Tunneling Protocol (SSTP) uses HTTPS protocol over TCP port 443 to pass traffic through firewalls and web proxies that might block PPTP and L2TP/IPSec without requiring client computer certificates or a preshared key.

- RADIUS, short for Remote Authentication Dial In User Service, is a networking protocol that provides centralized authentication, authorization, and accounting (AAA) management for computers to connect and use a network service.

- When using VPNs, Windows 7 and Windows Server 2008 support the following forms of authentication: Password Authentication Protocol (PAP), Challenge Handshake Authentication Protocol (CHAP), Microsoft CHAP version 2 (MS-CHAP v2), and Extensible Authentication Protocol (EAP-MS-CHAPv2).

- When connecting through a VPN, by default the "Use Default Gateway on the Remote Network" option is enabled. As a result, a new default route is created on the VPN client, which forwards data that cannot be sent to the local network to the VPN connection.

- When troubleshooting VPN client connectivity issues make sure that the client computer can connect to the Internet; you have the correct digital certificates; you are using the correct authentication, encryption, and the proper user credentials.

- If you are using LT2P with IPSec going through a NAT device, you need to make sure that you have the proper registry settings.

- DirectAccess is a new feature introduced with Windows 7 and Windows Server 2008 R2 that provides seamless intranet connectivity to DirectAccess client computers when they are connected to the Internet.

- DirectAccess overcomes the limitations of VPNs by automatically establishing a bi-directional connection from client computers to the corporate network using IPSec and Internet Protocol version 6 (IPv6).

- If a native IPv6 network is not available (and it probably will not be when the computer is connected to the Internet), the client uses 6to4 or Teredo to send IPv4-encapsulated IPv6 traffic.

- The Direct Access client must have a global IPv6 address, which should begin with a 2 or 3.

Knowledge Assessment

Fill in the Blank

Complete the following sentences by writing the correct word or words in the blanks provided.

1. 802.11g and 802.11n are backward compatible with _____ .

2. When a wireless adapter connects to a wireless access point, the wireless adapter runs in _____ mode.

3. WPA uses _____ to provide encryption and a rotating key.

4. To identify and connect to a wireless network, you need to specify the _____ .

5. A _____ can be created on a wireless client, which first authenticates the computer to the wireless network and then connects to the network and attempts to authenticate to the domain.

6. _____ links two computers through a wide-area network such as the Internet, while keeping the connection secure.

7. _____ is a networking protocol that provides centralized authentication, authorization, and accounting (AAA) management for computers to connect and use a network service.

8. _____ is a form of authentication that uses plain text.

9. By disabling the "Use the Default Gateway on Remote Network" option, you are using a _____.

10. WPA2 uses _____ for encryption and rotating key.

Multiple Choice

Circle the letter that corresponds to the best answer.

1. 802.11b uses a frequency of _____ .
   a. 2.4 GHz
   b. 3.7 GHz
   c. 5 GHz
   d. 8 GHz

2. Which form of wireless security is easily cracked?
   a. WEP
   b. WPA
   c. WPA2
   d. IPSec

3. _____ provides an authentication framework for wireless LANs.
   a. WEP
   b. WPA
   c. 802.1n
   d. 802.1X

4. A _____ enables users to connect remotely using various protocols and connection types.
   a. DHCP
   b. RAS
   c. BCD
   d. WDS

5. What tunneling protocol used with VPN server is easy to set up but is considered to use a weak encryption?
   a. PPTP
   b. L2TP with IPSec
   c. IKEv2
   d. SSTP

6. Which tunneling protocol used with VPN server supports VPN Reconnect?
   a. PPTP
   b. L2TP with IPSec
   c. IKEv2
   d. SSTP

7. Which tunneling protocol used with VPN server uses HTTP over TCP port 443?
   a. PPTP
   b. L2TP with IPSec
   c. IKEv2
   d. SSTP

8. Direct Access requires IPSec and _____ .
   a. WDS
   b. IPv6
   c. BCD
   d. EMS

9. When you are using DirectAccess, your DirectAccess client must have a global IPv6 address. A global IPv6 address starts with _____ ?
   a. 1
   b. 2 or 3
   c. 5 or 6
   d. 7, 8, or 9

10. If you have an intermittent wireless connection, you should check for _____ .
    a. Wireless adapter is overheating
    b. Interference with another device that is transmitting on the same frequency
    c. A disconnected cable
    d. A low battery

True / False

Circle T if the statement is true or F if the statement is false.

T | F **1.** When you have multiple wireless access points, you should use odd numbered channels to help avoid interference.

T | F **2.** WEP is recommended for most network security situations.

T | F **3.** For better security, you should not broadcast the SSID.

T | F **4.** If you are using L2TP with IPSec through a NAT transversal device, you will need to modify the registry settings within Windows 7.

T | F **5.** 802.11a and 802.11b are interchangeable.

Case Scenarios

Scenario 4-1: Isolating Wireless Interference

You work for the Contoso Corporation as a network administrator. You want to purchase a wireless access point and adapter for your office. However, you want to avoid any interference. How can you determine if you will have any type of interference problems?

Scenario 4-2: Troubleshooting VPN Problems

You are part of a help desk team for the Contoso Corporation. Over the last several months, you decided to count how many help desk phone calls your team received from people who have trouble connecting to your organization's network using a VPN. What do you think the most common problem would be when connected through the VPN?

Troubleshooting Hardware Issues

OBJECTIVE DOMAIN MATRIX

TECHNOLOGY SKILL	OBJECTIVE DOMAIN	OBJECTIVE NUMBER
Troubleshooting Hardware Devices	Identify and resolve hardware failure issues.	3.2
Managing Devices and Device Drivers	Identify and resolve hardware failure issues.	3.2

KEY TERMS

device drivers	Error-checking tool	signed driver
Device Manager	fragmentation	Windows Memory
Devices and Printers folder	Plug and Play (PnP)	Diagnostic
Disk Defragmenter	power-on self-test (POST)	

After completing this lesson, you will understand how device drivers interact with hardware and Windows 7. In addition, you will be able to install, configure, and troubleshoot devices running under Windows 7 and you will be able to troubleshoot common hardware problems.

You arrive in the office and find a message waiting from one of your users. She tried to turn on her computer when she arrived at work this morning and found it wouldn't start. After calling her and asking a series of questions, you discover that the PC is not starting up at all—you're getting neither activity lights nor sounds of any kind from the machine. You decide to visit her cubicle to retrieve her PC, so you can put it on your bench for further troubleshooting.

■ Troubleshooting Hardware Devices

THE BOTTOM LINE

Computers are divided into hardware and software. Software cannot run on hardware that is not working properly. Therefore besides knowing how to troubleshoot Windows and software applications, you also need to troubleshoot hardware problems.

CERTIFICATION READY
What tools are available with Windows 7 that will assist you in troubleshooting hardware problems?
3.2

As mentioned in Lesson 1, the computer is built around the processor. The processor is inserted into a motherboard—a piece of hardware that allows you to connect other components including RAM, storage, video systems, and other devices. If the processor, motherboard, or RAM is faulty, it can cause the entire system to fail, including a computer that won't boot, a system that locks up, or a system that reboots randomly.

Every time you turn on a computer, the computer goes through the ***power-on self-test (POST)***, which initializes hardware and finds an operating system to load. The POST includes the following steps:

1. Computer does a quick power check to make sure it has enough power to start the system.

2. When the processor receives a power good signal, the processor initializes and tests essential PC components as specified in the System ROM BIOS.

3. If a problem is found, it identifies the problem with a series of beeps based on the system ROM BIOS.

4. The processor then initializes the video card and starts sending information to the monitor. The system initializes additional components. If a problem is discovered, it displays a message to indicate the problem.

5. The system next searches for a boot device (such as a hard drive, optical disk, or USB flash drive) to boot from.

6. The system reads the master boot record on a boot device to determine operating system boot files.

WARNING Anytime you open a system, you should unplug the power from the system. You should also be sure to follow steps to avoid discharging electrostatic electricity including using a wrist strap that is attached to ground and using electrostatic bags when transporting electronic devices.

Remember that the ROM BIOS is firmware that occupies a spot halfway between software and hardware. The only difference between the software within the ROM BIOS and a software program is that it is stored within a chip instead of being executed from a disk or drive. Unfortunately, like any software, the BIOS may need to have a bug fixed or may need to be expanded to support a new type of hardware that did not exist when the BIOS was written. Sometimes a newer BIOS version can lead to better system performance. To overcome some problems, you would have to check with your system or motherboard manufacturer to see if they have a new version of your BIOS that you can download and apply to your system. The process of updating your system ROM BIOS is called flashing the BIOS.

Unfortunately, it may be difficult to determine which of the components: processor, RAM, or motherboard is the actual faulty item. Therefore, you may be left with only one option, replacing each component, one by one with a known good device to determine which is the faulty device.

Using Memory Diagnostic Tool

Memory problems can be caused by faulty RAM or a faulty motherboard. Unfortunately, these problems can sometimes be difficult to confirm without special tools. Like Windows Vista, Windows 7 includes the Memory Diagnostic Tool.

If Windows detects possible problems with your computer's memory, it will prompt you to run the ***Windows Memory Diagnostic***. When you run it, the Memory Diagnostics Tool gives you two options. If you choose to restart your computer and run the tool immediately, make sure that you save your work and close all of your running programs. The other option is to turn on or reboot the test the next time you run your computer.

Be aware that it might take several minutes for the tool to finish checking your computer's memory. Once the test is completed, Windows will restart automatically. If the tool detects errors, you should contact your computer manufacturer for information about fixing them, since memory errors usually indicate a problem with the memory chips in your computer or the motherboard that the memory chips are plugged in.

Microsoft recommends that you let the Memory Diagnostics Tool run automatically. However, you can adjust some settings by pressing F1 when the Memory Diagnostic Tool starts. You can then configure the following:

- **Test mix:** Choose what type of test you want to run: Basic, Standard, or Extended. The choices are described in the tool.
- **Cache:** Choose the cache setting you want for each test: Default, On, or Off.
- **Pass count:** Type the number of times you want to repeat the test.

You will then press F10 to start the test.

 CHECK MEMORY WITH THE MEMORY DIAGNOSTICS TOOL

GET READY. To run the Windows Memory Diagnostic:

1. Turn on the computer and press F8 before Windows loads.
2. When the *Advanced Startup* menu appears, select the Repair Your Computer and press Enter.
3. When the *System Recovery Options* dialog box appears, click Next.
4. Specify the administrator username and password and click OK.
5. Click Windows Memory Diagnostic.
6. Select the Restart Now and Check for Problems (Recommended) option. The computer will automatically reboot and start the memory diagnostic. When the diagnostic tool is completed, it will reboot again.

Resolving Faulty Power Problems

The power supply is as important as the processor, memory, and motherboard because the power is connected to it. Without power, the entire system would fail, including not being able to boot, the system locking up, or the system rebooting randomly.

One of the scenarios that you may deal with is that there are no running fans, lights, sounds, or signs of movement when you attempt to start the computer. This problem can be caused by a faulty component, like the processor, RAM, motherboard, or power supply, or possibly another device that is causing a short, overload, or power problem.

If your computer appears to be dead, you should follow these steps to isolate the cause of the problem:

1. Verify that you have power from the wall outlet. This may include making sure that any on/off wall switches are turned on for the wall outlet.
2. Check to make sure that all power cords are connected properly.
3. If the power supply has a voltage selector, make sure you have the correct voltage selected.
4. Confirm that the cables from the power supply are connected properly to the motherboard.
5. Make sure that any other devices are connected properly.
6. If the problem still exists, disconnect any unnecessary devices that are not required for boot up to see if any of those devices are causing a short or overload.
7. You can use a voltmeter/multimeter to see if the power supply is giving the correct output device.
8. If the previous steps do not uncover the source of the problem, replace the power supply.
9. Last, if the problem still exists, try replacing the processor, RAM, and/or motherboard.

If your computer reboots before completing boot up or shuts down before boot, you should verify that your power supply can deliver enough power to all of your devices. You can also use a voltmeter/multimeter to see if the power supply is giving the correct output power. Before you replace the power supply, you should also check that the system is not overheating. If you still cannot figure out the problem, you can replace the power supply.

If the computer shuts off or reboots randomly, you should try the following:

1. Verify that the power supply unit fan, processor fan, and other fans are operating properly. If possible, replace any faulty fans. Also make sure that the dust has been cleared out of your system because excessive dust can cause a heat build up.
2. Verify that the motherboard fan is working. Replace this fan if necessary.
3. Run Windows Memory Diagnostic to check your RAM for hardware faults.
4. Run motherboard diagnostic software (acquired from your motherboard or system manufacturer) to check the functionality of the motherboard.
5. Replace the entire power supply unit.
6. Last, if the problem still exists, try replacing the processor, RAM, and/or motherboard.

If the power supply fan is not spinning or the power supply is making a loud, continuous noise, you should replace the unit.

Testing Drives

When a drive cannot be found during boot up, you will receive disk errors during POST or receive disk read or write errors. You could have a faulty drive, drive cable, or controller (found on its own expansion card or built into the motherboard). Windows includes two useful tools to check disks including error-checking and defragmentation tools.

You can solve some computer problems and improve the performance of your computer just by making sure that your hard disk has no errors. To test your hard disk, use the graphical ***Error-checking tool*** or the chkdsk command at the command prompt.

 RUN THE DISK ERROR-CHECKING TOOL

GET READY. To run the Error-checking tool:

1. Click Start and click Computer.
2. Right-click the hard disk that you want to check, and then click Properties.
3. Click the Tools tab, and then under Error-checking, click Check now. If you are prompted for an administrator password or confirmation, type the password or provide confirmation.
    - To automatically repair problems with files and folders that the scan detects, select Automatically fix file system errors. Otherwise, the disk check will report problems but not fix them.
    - To perform a thorough disk check, select *Scan for and attempt recovery of bad sectors*. This scan attempts to find and repair physical errors on the hard disk itself, and it can take much longer to complete.
    - To check for both file errors and physical errors, select both Automatically fix file system errors and Scan for and attempt recovery of bad sectors. See Figure 5-1.
4. Click Start.

Figure 5-1

Using the Disk Error-checking tool

Depending on the size of your hard disk, this might take several minutes. If you selected Automatically fix file system errors for a disk that is in use (for example, the partition that contains Windows), you'll be prompted to reschedule the disk check for the next time you restart your computer.

Fragmentation makes your hard disk do extra work that can slow down your computer. Removable storage devices such as USB flash drives can also become fragmented. ***Disk Defragmenter*** rearranges fragmented data so your disks and drives can work more efficiently. Disk Defragmenter runs on a schedule, but you can also analyze and defragment your disks and drives manually. You can also use the defrag.exe command at the command prompt.

 DEFRAGMENT A DISK

GET READY. To defragment a disk:

1. Click Start and click Computer.
2. Right-click the hard disk that you want to check, and then click Properties.
3. Click the Defragment now button.
4. Under Current status, select the disk you want to defragment.
5. To determine if the disk needs to be defragmented or not, click Analyze disk. If you are prompted for an administrator password or confirmation, type the password or provide confirmation. Once Windows is finished analyzing the disk, you can check the percentage of fragmentation on the disk in the Last Run column. If the number is above 10%, you should defragment the disk. See Figure 5-2.
6. Click Defragment disk. If you are prompted for an administrator password or confirmation, type the password or provide confirmation.

Figure 5-2

Using the Disk Defragmenter

Disk Defragmenter might take several minutes to a few hours to finish, depending on the size and degree of fragmentation of your hard disk. You can still use your computer during the defragmentation process.

If the disk is already in exclusive use by another program, or if the disk is formatted using a file system other than NTFS file system, FAT, or FAT32, it can't be defragmented.

If a disk that you expect to see under Current status does not show up, it might be because it contains an error. You should try to repair the disk first, and then return to Disk Defragmenter to try again.

Troubleshooting Ports, Video, and Sound

The other common devices that may fail are ports, video systems, and sound systems. Unlike the motherboard, RAM, and processors, these devices don't usually cause the system not to boot unless the device is causing a short or overload.

When troubleshooting devices connected through ports, the video system, or the sound system, you need to verify that the related devices are connected properly, turned on, and that the correct driver is loaded. You can then try replacing the hardware device and related cables to determine if the device is truly faulty or not. You can also try the suspected device in a known good system.

You should also keep in mind that the motherboard is a very complicated device that contains multiple built-in components. For many of these components to function, you have to load the correct driver including the proper chipset driver and USB drivers, all of which are essential for other devices to operate. Note that some of these components can be disabled using the BIOS Setup program, allowing for additional ways to troubleshoot built-in components.

When you have problems with the video system, you should verify that the monitor is plugged in, turned on, and properly connected to the computer. If you have a laptop, you should also make sure that you switch to the correct output device by pressing a specific toggle button or switch. You also need to make sure you have the correct driver for the monitor and video adapter and that you have selected the correct frequency, resolution, and number of colors that is supported by both the monitor and video system.

For the audio system, make sure that you have the correct cables connected to correct audio ports. You also need to make sure that your speakers are turned on and all volume controls are turned on. For laptop computers, that usually includes on/off switches on the computer, on the speakers and within Windows (Volume Control). You also need to make sure you have the correct drivers loaded.

Managing Devices and Device Drivers

↓
THE BOTTOM LINE
Since a computer running Windows 7 can have a wide array of devices, it can sometimes be a challenge to make all devices operate correctly especially since some specialized computers can have non-standard hardware that may require you to manually install or update drivers.

CERTIFICATION READY
What icons show problems within the Device Manager?
3.2

Device drivers are programs that control a device. You can think of them as translators between the device and the operating system and programs that use the device.

Programmers write code that accesses generic commands such as sending sound. The device driver translates those generic commands to specific commands understood by the device, such as a specific sound card. While Windows 7 includes many built-in drivers and others that are included on the installation DVD, device drivers usually come with the device or you may have to go to the manufacturer's website to download them. Since these drivers are software, there may be times where you may need to go to the manufacturer's website to retrieve newer drivers (although sometimes older drivers work better than newer drivers) or download them through Microsoft's updates.

To prevent you from constantly inserting the Windows 7 installation DVD, Windows 7 includes a driver store with an extensive library of device drivers. Drivers will be located in the C:\Windows\System32\DriverStore. In the DriverStore folder, you will find subfolders with driver information such as en-US for US English that will have hundreds of different drivers. When you add a hardware device, Windows can check the driver store for the correct driver.

Using Plug and Play Devices

For years, Windows has benefited from *Plug and Play (PnP)*, a technology that allows you to install or connect a device, have the device automatically recognized and configured with the appropriate driver installed. Today, this technology has been expanded beyond expansion cards to include other technologies.

Years ago, Intel and Microsoft released Plug and Play, a technology that allowed you to insert an expansion card into an expansion slot so that the card was automatically recognized by the system and configured. As a computer technician, this made life a lot easier because you did not have to worry about setting DIP switches or jumpers on the card. Today, if you use Plug and Play hardware combined with a Plug and Play operating system such as Windows, you can plug in the hardware, and Windows searches for an appropriate device driver and automatically configures it to work without interfering with other devices. If Windows 7 does not have a driver available on the device after detection, Windows 7 will prompt you to provide a media or path to the driver. Eventually, the driver will be added to the driver store. Today, Plug and Play has been expanded beyond expansion cards to include USB, IEEE 1394, and SCSI devices.

Today, most devices are Plug and Play. Therefore, when you add or connect a new device, Windows will automatically recognize the device and load the appropriate drivers. When a driver cannot be found, it may ask if you want to connect to the Internet in an attempt to find one or to specify the location of one such as on a disk. You can also open the Control Panel, click Hardware, and select Add a device under the Devices and Printers section. It will then search for any devices that are not currently recognized by Windows.

As part of the configuration process, Windows assigns the following system resources to the device you are installing so that the device can operate at the same time as other expansion cards:

- **Interrupt request (IRQ) line numbers:** A signal sent by a device to get the attention of the processor when the device is ready to accept or send information. Each device must be assigned a unique IRQ number.
- **Direct memory access (DMA) channels:** Memory access that does not involve the processor.
- **Input/output (I/O) port addresses:** A channel through which data is transferred between a device and the processor. The port appears to the processor as one or more memory addresses that it can use to send or receive data.
- **Memory address ranges:** A portion of computer memory that can be allocated to a device and used by a program or the operating system. Devices are usually allocated a range of memory addresses.

Using Signed Drivers

Windows was designed to work with a large array of devices. Unfortunately, in the past, there were times when a device was added and a driver was loaded, and the driver caused problems with Windows. As a result, Microsoft started using signed drivers to help fight faulty drivers. While signed drivers do not fix a faulty driver, they do make sure that the publisher of the driver is identified, the driver has not been altered, and the driver has been thoroughly tested to be reliable so that it will not cause a security problem.

A *signed driver* is a device driver that includes a digital signature, which is an electronic security mark that can indicate the publisher of the software and provide information that can show if a driver has been altered. When signed by Microsoft, a driver has been thoroughly tested to make sure that it will not cause problems with the system's reliability or security.

Drivers that are included on the Windows installation DVD or downloaded from Microsoft's update website are digitally signed. A driver that lacks a valid digital signature, or was altered after it was signed, cannot be installed on 64-bit versions of Windows. If you have problems with a device driver, you should only download drivers from Microsoft's update website or the manufacturer's website.

Windows 7 comes in 32-bit and 64-bit versions. All drivers must be signed for 64-bit versions of Windows 7. If you are using an older version of Windows that is not a 64-bit version, you can use the File Signature Verification program (Sigverif.exe) to check for unsigned device drivers in the system area of a computer.

TAKE NOTE*

On a 64-bit version of Windows 7, you cannot install a driver that lacks a valid digital signature or that has been altered after it was signed.

Using Devices and Printers

Starting with Windows Server 2008 and Windows Vista, Windows includes the Devices and Printers folder to quickly allow users to see all the devices connected to the computer and to configure and troubleshoot these devices. This folder will also allow you to view information about the make, model, and manufacturer and give you detailed information about the sync capabilities of a mobile phone or other mobile devices.

The **Devices and Printers folder** gives you a quick view of all the devices currently connected to your computer that you can connect or disconnect through a port or network connection. This includes mobile devices such as music players, digital cameras, USB devices, and network devices. See Figure 5-3. It does not include items installed inside your computer such as internal disk drives, expansion cards, and RAM, and it will not display legacy devices such as keyboards and mice connected through a PS/2 or serial port.

Figure 5-3

Devices and Printers folder

To open the Devices and Printers folder, open the Control Panel and click View devices and printers under Hardware while in Category view or double-click Devices and Printers in Icon view. You can also open Devices and Printers by clicking the Start button and clicking Devices and Printers.

When you right-click a device icon in the Devices and Printers folder, you can select from a list of tasks that vary depending on the capabilities of the device. For example, you might be able to see what's printing on a network printer, view files stored on a USB flash drive, or open a program from the device manufacturer. For mobile devices that support the new Device Stage feature in Windows, you can also open advanced, device-specific features in Windows from the right-click menu, such as the ability to sync with a mobile phone or change ringtones.

Using Device Manager

Device Manager provides you with a graphical view of the hardware (internal and external) that is installed on your computer and gives you a way to manage and configure your devices. With Device Manager, you can determine whether a device is recognized by Windows and if the device is working properly. You can also enable, disable, or uninstall the device, roll back the previous version of the driver, identify the device driver including its version, and change hardware configuration settings.

To open the Device Manager, you can do one of the following:

- Open the Control Panel in Category view, click Hardware, and click Device Manager.
- Open the Control Panel in Icon view and double-click Device Manager.
- Open the System Properties and click Device Manager.
- Open the Computer Management console and click Device Manager.
- Open the Server Manager and click Device Manager under Diagnostics.
- Execute the following command from a command prompt, Start Search box or Run box: mmc devmgmt.msc.
- Search for Device in the Start menu search box and select Device Manager.

If you are logged on using the built-in Administrator account, Device Manager opens. If you are logged on as the user that is a member of the Administrator group and you have User Account Control enabled, you will have to click Continue to open Device Manager. See Figure 5-4.

Figure 5-4

Device Manager

If you locate and double-click a device or right-click a device and select properties, you can view the details of the driver in the General tab including the status of the device. The Details tab will give you detailed settings of various properties assigned to the hardware device. As a server administrator, most of the items you will need are located at the Driver tab:

1. **Driver file details:** Shows the driver file(s) and their location, the provider of the driver, the version of the file, and the digital signer of the file.
2. **Update device drivers:** Allows you to update the driver software for a device.
3. **Roll back drivers:** Allows you to roll back a driver if problems exist when you update a device driver. If there's no previous version of the driver installed for the selected device, the Roll Back Driver button will be unavailable.
4. **Disable/enable devices:** Instead of uninstalling the driver, you can use the device manger to disable the device.
5. **Uninstall a device:** Used to remove the driver software from the computer.

Additional tabs such as Advanced, Resources (Memory Range, I/O Range, IRQ, and DMA), and Power Management may be shown depending on the type of device. If there is a conflict for your resources, you can try to use Device Manager to change the memory range, I/O range, IRQ, or DMA of the device. In addition, if you right-click a device in Device Manager, you can update driver software, disable the device, uninstall the device, or scan for hardware changes. See Figure 5-5.

Figure 5-5

Device Properties

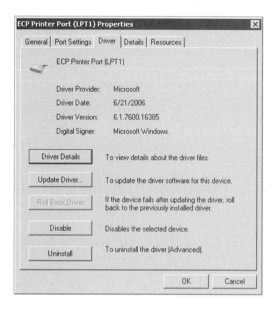

When you use the Device Manager that comes with Windows Vista, Windows 7, and Windows Server 2008, you should note the following:

- A downward pointing black arrow indicates a disabled device. A disabled device is a device that is physically present in the computer and is consuming resources, but does not have a driver loaded.
- A black exclamation point (!) on a yellow field indicates the device is in a problem state.
- You also need to check whether any devices are listed as an unknown device, listed under Other devices, or has a generic name such as Ethernet Controller or PCI Simple Communications Controller, which indicates that the proper driver is not loaded.

If you install a driver and you have problems with the driver, there are several ways which you can roll back or replace the driver. If you can start Windows and get to the Device Manager, you can use the roll back driver button previously mentioned.

If you cannot access the Device Manager, you can start Windows in Safe mode. When you start Windows in Safe mode, you load a minimum set of drivers and services. To access the Advanced Boot Options screen, turn your computer on and press the F8 key before the Windows logo appears. The Advanced Boot Options are discussed in more detail in Lesson 6.

If you load or update a driver and the system does not start, you can access the Advanced Boot Menu and select the Last Known Good Configuration option. The Last Known Good Configuration will start Windows with the last registry and driver configuration that worked successfully when you last logged on successfully.

SKILL SUMMARY

- Every time you turn on a computer, the computer goes through the power-on self-test (POST), which initializes hardware, tests basic hardware devices, and finds an operating system to load.

- If the processor, motherboard, or RAM is faulty, it can cause the entire system to fail. Specific symptoms may include an inability to boot, system lock-ups, or random reboots.

- If there are no running fans, flashing lights, audible sounds, or signs of movement when you attempt to start the computer. It is probably caused by a faulty component, such as a processor, RAM, motherboard, or power supply.

- If Windows detects possible problems with your computer's memory, it will prompt you to run the Memory Diagnostics Tool.

- Windows includes two useful tools to check disks including Error-checking and Defragmentation tools.

- You can solve some computer problems and improve the performance of your computer just by making sure that your hard disk has no errors using the Error-checking tool.

- Fragmentation makes your hard disk do extra work that can slow down your computer. Removable storage devices such as USB flash drives can also become fragmented.

- Disk Defragmenter rearranges fragmented data so your disks and drives can work more efficiently.

- When troubleshooting devices connected through ports, the video system, or the sound system, you need to verify that the related devices are connected properly, turned on, and the correct driver is loaded.

- Device drivers are programs that control a device. You can think of them as a translator between the device and the operating system and programs that use that device.

- To prevent you from constantly inserting the Windows 7 installation DVD, Windows 7 includes a driver store with an extensive library of device drivers.

- For years, Windows has benefited from Plug and Play (PnP), which means the device is automatically recognized, automatically configured, and the appropriate driver installed when you install or connect a device.

- A signed driver is a device driver that includes a digital signature, which is an electronic security mark that can indicate the publisher of the software and provides information that can show if a driver has been altered.

- All installed drivers in the 64-bit version of Windows 7 are required to be signed and unaltered.

- The Devices and Printers folder gives you a quick view of devices connected to your computer that you can connect or disconnect through a port or network connection.

- Device Manager provides you with a graphical view of the hardware (internal and external) that is installed your computer and gives you a way to manage and configure your devices.

■ Knowledge Assessment

Fill in the Blank

Complete the following sentences by writing the correct word or words in the blanks provided.

1. To test your system's RAM, you should use the _____.

2. _____ is technology used in Windows, so that when you install or connect a device, the device is automatically recognized, automatically configured, and the appropriate driver is installed.

3. Drivers used on 64-bit versions of Windows must be _____.

4. To easily manage your external devices and printers, you would use the _____.

5. To keep from always inserting the Windows 7 installation DVD, Windows 7 includes the _____ folder.

6. The component that initializes hardware and finds an operating system to load is the _____.

7. You can use the _____ to check if unsigned device drivers are in the system area of a computer.

8. When you suspect problems with a disk, you should run the _____.

9. A generic name such as Ethernet Control or PCI Simple Communications Controller in the Device Manager usually means that the proper _____ is not loaded.

10. If you suspect a problem with the system ROM BIOS, you should _____ the BIOS.

Multiple Choice

Circle the letter that corresponds to the best answer.

1. Your system does not boot and you have no lights, sounds, or running fans. Which of the following will most likely NOT cause this problem?
   a. Faulty motherboard
   b. Faulty sound card
   c. Faulty memory
   d. Faulty processor

2. Your system performance has slowed over time. What can you use to bring some performance back to your system?
   a. Error-checking tool
   b. Disk Defragmenter
   c. Memory Diagnostics Tool
   d. Windows PE

3. A _____ is a device driver that includes a digital signature, which is an electronic security mark that can indicate the publisher of the software and provide information that can show if a driver has been altered.
   a. PnP driver
   b. Riskless driver
   c. Diagnostic driver
   d. Signed driver

4. To see if a driver is NOT loaded, you should use the _____ .
   a. Devices and Printers folder
   b. Signature Validation tool
   c. Memory Diagnostics Tool
   d. Device Manager

5. To roll back a driver, you would use the _____ .
   a. Registry Viewer
   b. Signature Validation tool
   c. Memory Diagnostics Tool
   d. Device Manager

6. When viewing the Device Manager, a downward pointing black arrow means _____ ?
   a. A disabled device
   b. The device is in a problem state
   c. The proper driver is not loaded
   d. The device is not plugged in or turned on

7. When viewing the Device Manager, a black exclamation point (!) on a yellow field indicates _____ ?
   a. A disabled device
   b. The device is in a problem state
   c. The proper driver is not loaded
   d. The device is not plugged in or turned on

8. You see a device that is listed under Other Devices. What does this mean?
   a. A disabled device
   b. The device is in a problem state
   c. The proper driver is not loaded
   d. The device is not plugged in or turned on

9. When you suspect a faulty device, the best method to test the device is to _____ ?
   a. Replace with a known good device
   b. Replace the driver
   c. Run the Hardware Diagnostics Tool
   d. Run the Windows PE Diagnostics Tool

10. You install a driver and the system no longer boots, you should _____ ?
    a. Use the Last Known Good Configuration option during startup
    b. Restore the C drive from backup
    c. Run the Memory Diagnostic Tool
    d. Run the Windows PE Diagnostic Tool

True / False

Circle T if the statement is true or F if the statement is false.

T | F 1. When you experience problems with the system ROM BIOS, you should not flash the BIOS unless the system will not boot.

T | F 2. If a system intermediately shuts down, your system has not warmed up enough.

T | F 3. Every time you connect a portable drive, your system reboots. Therefore, the system most likely cannot supply enough power.

T | F 4. To make a hard drive faster, you should run the Memory Diagnostic tool.

T | F 5. To automatically configure IRQ and I/O port addresses for a device, the device would be a Plug and Play device.

■ Case Scenarios

Scenario 5-1: Troubleshooting a Device

You work as a desktop technician for the Contoso Corporation. You have a desktop computer running Windows 7. You purchased a new network expansion card that will allow you to tap into a corporation information website. Unfortunately, when you insert the device your system will not start. There are no lights, no sounds, and no running fans. You remove the device and the system still does not boot. What should you do to isolate the problem?

Scenario 5-2: Loading a Driver

You work as a desktop technician for the Contoso Corporation. You have a desktop computer running Windows 7, which you installed last week. While the computer was running fine, you tried to get better performance by downloading and installing the newest driver for your video card from the vendor. Unfortunately, now the device does not work properly. What can you do to overcome this problem?

6 LESSON

Troubleshooting Startup Problems

TECHNOLOGY SKILL	OBJECTIVE DOMAIN	OBJECTIVE NUMBER
Understanding the Boot Process	Identify and resolve hardware failure issues.	3.2

KEY TERMS

Advanced Boot Menu

Boot Configuration Data (BCD)

boot partition

BOOTMGR

Last Known Good Configuration

master boot record (MBR)

safe mode

System Configuration

system partition/volume

volume boot record (VBR)

Windows Preinstallation
Environment (Windows PE)

Windows Recovery
Environment (Windows RE)

Lesson 6 discusses the Windows 7 startup process with a focus on troubleshooting startup problems—including using the Advanced Boot Menu, Safe Mode, Last Known Good Configuration, Windows PE, and Windows RE.

You just got a call from one of your junior administrators. He said he was called to a computer that seemed to be infected by a virus. While he was able to remove the virus, the computer will no longer boot. Therefore, you need to show him what tools are available to make Windows boot again.

■ Understanding the Boot Process

THE BOTTOM LINE

Sometimes due to hardware failure or software corruption because of malware or some other unforeseen circumstance, you may have trouble starting Windows. Therefore, you will need to know how to overcome these problems.

CERTIFICATION READY
What tools can you use
to troubleshoot boot
problems?
3.2

As mentioned in the last lesson, every time you turn on a computer, the computer goes through the power-on self-test (POST), which initializes hardware and finds an operating system to load. The system will search for a boot device (such as a hard drive, optical disk, or USB flash drive [UFD]) to boot from. Eventually, assuming everything goes well, the system will read the master boot record on a boot device to locate and access operating system boot files.

If the system is running Windows 7, the system will go through the following steps:

1. BOOTMGR is loaded and accesses the Boot Configuration Data Store to display the boot menu or to boot from a partition or volume.
2. WINLoad is the operating system boot loader that loads the rest of the operating system.
3. NTOSKERNL.EXE is the main part of Windows, which is responsible for various system services, processes, and memory management.
4. Boot-class device drivers implement a number of functions that are utilized in different ways by different hardware platforms based on processor and chipset.

A *master boot record (MBR)* is the first 512-byte boot sector of a partitioned data storage device such as a hard disk. It contains the disk's primary partition table, and the code to bootstrap an operating system, which usually passes control to the volume boot record and uniquely identifies the disk media. By default, the master boot record contains the primary partition entries in its partition table.

A *volume boot record (VBR),* also known as a volume boot sector or a partition boot sector, is a type of boot sector, stored in a disk volume on a hard disk, floppy disk, or similar data storage device that contains code for booting an operating system such as BOOTMGR.

The active partition is the partition or volume that is marked as the partition to boot from. The active partition or volume that contains the boot file *(BOOTMGR)* is known as the *system partition/volume*. The partition or volume that contains the Windows operating system files (usually the Windows folder) is called the *boot partition*. It is common for computer systems to have one drive and one partition/volume, which makes the partition both the system partition and the boot partition.

The *%SystemRoot%* variable is a special system-wide environment variable found on Microsoft Windows systems. Its value is the location of the system folder, including the drive and path. By default, on a clean installation of Windows 7, the Windows files are placed in the C:\Windows folder.

Using BCDEdit

Boot Configuration Data (BCD) is a firmware-independent database for boot-time configuration data used by Microsoft's Windows Boot Manager found with Windows Vista, Windows 7, and Windows Server 2008. To edit the Boot Configuration, you would typically use Bcdedit.exe.

Unlike previous versions of Windows that used the Boot.ini file to designate the boot configuration, new versions of Windows store the configuration in a \Boot\bcd folder on the system volume on machines that use IBM PC compatible firmware. To edit the Windows Boot Menu Options, use the Boot Configuration Data Editor (Bcdedit).

The Bcdedit.exe command-line tool can be used to add, delete, and edit entries in the BCD store, which contains objects. Each object is identified by a GUID (Globally Unique Identifier).

Some of the options available for the BCDEdit command are:

- **/createstore:** Creates a new empty BCD store.
- **/export:** Exports the contents of the system BCD store to a specified file.

- **/import:** Restores the state of the system BCD store from a specified file.
- **/copy:** Makes copies of boot entries.
- **/create:** Creates new boot entries.
- **/delete:** Deletes boot entries.
- **/deletevalue:** Deletes elements from a boot entry.
- **/set:** Creates or modifies a boot entry's elements.
- **/enum:** Lists the boot entries in a store.
- **/bootsequence:** Specifies a one-time boot sequence.
- **/default:** Specifies the default boot entry.
- **/displayorder:** Specifies the order in which Boot Manager displays its menu.
- **/timeout:** Specifies the Boot Manager Timeout value.
- **/toolsdisplayorder:** Specifies the order in which Boot Manager displays the tools menu.
- **/bootems:** Enables or disables Emergency Management Services (EMS) for a specified boot application.
- **/ems:** Enables or disables EMS for an operating system boot entry.
- **/emssettings:** Specifies global EMS parameters.
- **/store:** Specifies the BCD store upon which a command acts.

To run bcdedit (see Figure 6-1), you must first open a command prompt as an administrator. To view the BCD settings, you would use the following command:

```
bcdedit /enum
```

Figure 6-1

Running the bcdedit /enum command

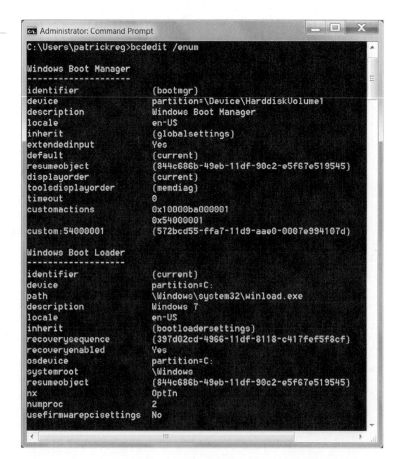

Every drive or partition on the system will have its own GUID that is identified as one of the following:

- **{legacy}:** A drive or partition containing a pre-Windows Vista operating system.
- **{default}:** The drive or partition containing the current default operating system.
- **{current}:** The current drive or partition you are booted to, or for example {c34b751a-ff09-11d9-9e6e-0030482375e7} which describes another drive or partition on which an operating system has been installed.

In addition, you can add the following parameter to the bcdedit /enum command to change the information that is displayed:

- **Active:** Displays all entries in the boot manager display order (default).
- **Firmware:** Displays all firmware applications.
- **Bootapp:** Displays all boot environment applications.
- **Bootmgr:** Displays the boot manager.
- **Osloader:** Displays all operating system entries.
- **Resume:** Displays all resume from hibernation entries.
- **Inherit:** Displays all inherit entries.
- **All:** Displays all entries.

Before you make any changes, you should perform a backup of the BCD settings. To make a backup of your current BCD registry settings, execute the following command:

```
bcdedit /export name_of_file.bcd
```

To restore your BCD registry settings, execute the following command:

```
bcdedit /import name_of_file.bcd
```

To change the default operating system entry, you must first run the bcdedit /enum command to view the existing entries and to record the identifier. To set a new default, run the following command:

```
bcdedit /default <id>
```

where the <id> is the identifier for the new entry.

For example, to configure the Windows Boot Manager to start the previous installation of Windows XP by default (which is identified as {ntldr}), run the following command:

```
bcdedit /default {ntldr}
```

To configure the currently running instance of Windows 7 as the default, run the following command:

```
bcdedit /default {current}
```

To change the timeout on showing the boot menu:

```
bcdedit /timeout 5
```

To change the title of the boot menu entry, you would use the /set option. For example, to change to Windows XP from "Earlier Windows Version," you would type in the following:

```
bcdedit /set {ntldr} description "Windows XP"
```

To change the default OS to boot first:

```
bcdedit /default {ntldr}
```

If {ntldr} was not part of the boot menu when you copied it, you also need to run the following command to add the copied entry to the boot menu:

```
bcdedit /displayorder {NEW-GUID} /addlast
```

Additionally, you might need to configure the operating system's own boot loader.
To remove a boot entry, you would run the following command:

```
bcdedit /displayorder {GUID} /remove
```

+ MORE INFORMATION

For more information about Bcdedit, visit the following websites:
http://technet.microsoft.com/en-us/library/cc709667(WS.10).aspx
http://www.windows7home.net/how-to-use-bcdedit-in-windows-7

When using Windows Vista, Windows 7, and Windows Server 2008, you can modify the
default operating system and the amount of time the list of operating systems appears by
right-clicking Computer, selecting Properties, clicking Advanced system settings, selecting the
Advanced tab, and clicking the Settings button in the Startup and Recovery section. You can
also specify what type of dump occurs during a system failure.

Using the Advanced Boot Menu

When you have some problems that occur during boot up, you may need to take some extra
steps to get the computer in a usable state so that you can fix the problem. Since Windows XP,
you can use the ***Advanced Boot Menu*** to access advanced troubleshooting modes.

To access the Advanced Boot Options screen (see Figure 6-2), turn your computer on and
press F8 before the Windows logo appears. If you have Windows 7, you can then select one
of the following options:

- **Repair Your Computer:** Shows a list of system recovery tools you can use to repair
  startup problems, run diagnostics, or restore your system. This option is available only
  if the tools are installed on your computer's hard disk.
- **Safe Mode:** Starts Windows with a minimal set of drivers and services. If you make a
  change to the system and Windows no longer boots, you can try safe mode.
- **Safe Mode with Networking:** Starts Windows in safe mode and includes the network
  drivers and services needed to access the Internet or other computers on your network.
- **Safe Mode with Command Prompt:** Starts Windows in safe mode with a command
  prompt window instead of the usual Windows interface.
- **Enable Boot Logging:** Creates a file, ntbtlog.txt, that lists all the drivers that are
  installed during startup and that might be useful for advanced troubleshooting.
- **Enable low-resolution video (640×480):** Starts Windows using your current video
  driver and using low resolution and refresh rate settings. You can use this mode to reset
  your display settings.
- **Last Known Good Configuration (advanced):** Starts Windows with the last registry and
  driver configuration that worked successfully, usually marked at the last successful login.
- **Directory Services Restore Mode:** Starts Windows domain controller running Active
  Directory so that the directory service can be restored.
- **Debugging Mode:** Starts Windows in an advanced troubleshooting mode intended for
  IT professionals and system administrators.
- **Disable automatic restart on system failure:** Prevents Windows from automatically
  restarting if an error causes Windows to fail. Choose this option only if Windows is
  stuck in a loop where Windows fails, attempts to restart, and fails again repeatedly.
- **Disable Driver Signature Enforcement:** Allows drivers containing improper signatures
  to be loaded.
- **Start Windows Normally:** Starts Windows in its normal mode.

Figure 6-2

Advanced boot options

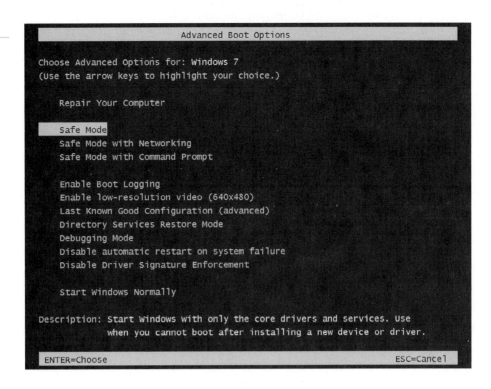

Safe mode and its derivatives, Enable Boot Logging, Enable Low-resolution, Last Known Good Configuration, and Directory Services Restore Mode have been around for years.

Safe mode is useful for troubleshooting problems with programs and drivers that might not start correctly or that might prevent Windows from starting correctly. If a problem doesn't reappear when you start in safe mode, you can eliminate the default settings and basic device drivers as possible causes. If a recently installed program, device, or driver prevents Windows from running correctly, you can start your computer in safe mode and then remove the program that's causing the problem. See Figure 6-3.

Figure 6-3

Windows 7 safe mode

While in safe mode, you use the Control Panel to access the Device Manager, Event Viewer, System Information, command prompt, or Registry Editor.

Devices and drivers that start in safe mode:

- Floppy disk drives (internal and USB)
- Internal CD-ROM drives (ATA, SCSI)
- External CD-ROM drives (USB)
- Internal DVD-ROM drives (ATA, SCSI)
- External DVD-ROM drives (USB)
- Internal hard disk drives (ATA, SATA, SCSI)
- External hard disk drives (USB)
- Keyboards (USB, PS/2, serial)
- Mice (USB, PS/2, serial)
- VGA video cards (PCI, AGP)

Windows services that start in safe mode:

- Windows event log
- Plug and Play
- Remote procedure call (RPC)
- Cryptographic Services
- Windows Management Instrumentation (WMI)

Devices and services that start in safe mode with networking:

- Network adapters (wired Ethernet and wireless 802.11x)
- Dynamic Host Configuration Protocol (DHCP)
- DNS
- Network connections
- TCP/IP-NetBIOS Helper
- Windows Firewall

The *Last Known Good Configuration* feature restores registry information and driver settings that were in effect the last time the computer started successfully and a user logged on successfully. If you install a driver such as for your video adapter or install an application that causes Windows not to boot properly, you can select the Last Known Good Configuration and Windows will restore information in the following registry key:

HKEY_LOCAL_MACHINE\System\CurrentControlSet

Using System Configuration

While safe mode allows you to boot Windows when it would not boot before due to a bad driver, service, or application that loads at boot time, the System Configuration tool allows you to select or deselect the services or applications that automatically start when you start Windows.

System Configuration (msconfig.exe) is a tool that can help isolate problem startup programs or services that prevent Windows from starting correctly. See Figure 6-4. When a problem occurs and assuming you can successfully start and log in to Windows, you can open System Configuration and disable certain startup programs or services. If the problem goes away when you restart Windows, you know that the problem is caused by the program or service that you disabled.

Figure 6-4

System Configuration tool

The following tabs and options are available in System Configuration:

- **General tab:** Shows the startup selection:
  - **Normal startup:** Starts Windows in the usual manner.
  - **Diagnostic startup:** Starts Windows with basic services and drivers only.
  - **Selective startup:** Starts Windows with basic services and drivers and the other services and startup programs that you select.
- **Boot tab:** Shows configuration options for the operating system and advanced debugging settings, including:
  - **Safe boot:Minimal:** On startup, opens the Windows graphical user interface (Windows Explorer) in safe mode running only critical system services. Networking is disabled.
  - **Safe boot:Alternate shell:** On startup, opens the Windows command prompt in safe mode running only critical system services. Networking and the graphical user interface are disabled.
  - **Safe boot:Active Directory repair:** On startup, opens the Windows graphical user interface in safe mode running critical system services and Active Directory.
  - **Safe boot:Network:** On startup, opens the Windows graphical user interface in safe mode running only critical system services. Networking is enabled.
  - **No GUI boot:** Does not display the Windows Welcome screen when starting.
  - **Boot log:** Stores all information from the startup process in the file %SystemRoot%Ntbtlog.txt.
  - **Base video:** On startup, opens the Windows graphical user interface in minimal VGA mode. This loads standard VGA drivers instead of display drivers specific to the video hardware on the computer.
  - **OS boot information:** Shows driver names as drivers are being loaded during the startup process.
  - **Make all boot settings permanent:** Doesn't track changes made in System Configuration. Options can be changed later using System Configuration, but they must be changed manually. When this option is selected, you can't roll back your changes by selecting Normal startup on the General tab.
  - **Advanced boot options:** Allows you to configure Windows to load quicker or slower based on your needs.
  - **Number of processors:** Limits the number of processors used on a multiprocessor system. If the check box is selected, the system boots using only the number of processors in the drop-down list. One processor is selected by default.

- **Maximum memory:** Specifies the maximum amount of physical memory used by the operating system to simulate a low memory configuration. The value in the text box is megabytes (MB).

- **PCI Lock:** Prevents Windows from reallocating I/O and IRQ resources on the PCI bus. The I/O and memory resources set by the BIOS are preserved.

- **Debug:** Enables kernel-mode debugging for device driver development.

- **Services tab:** Lists all of the services that start when the computer starts, along with their current status (Running or Stopped). Use the Services tab to enable or disable individual services at startup so that you can troubleshoot which services might be contributing to startup problems. You can also select the Hide all Microsoft services option to show only third-party applications in the services list.

- **Startup:** Lists applications that run when the computer starts up, along with the name of their publisher, the path to the executable file, and the location of the registry key or shortcut that causes the application to run.

■ Using Windows 7 Repair Tools

THE BOTTOM LINE

When a server does not start, there are several tools that are available to help you fix these problems. Some of them have already been discussed such as booting the computer into safe mode or using the System Configuration tool. Other tools include WinPE and WinRE.

Windows Preinstallation Environment (Windows PE) 3.0 is a minimal Win32 operating system with limited services, built on the Windows 7 kernel. It is used to prepare a computer for Windows installation, to copy disk images from a network file server, and to initiate Windows Setup. Besides being used to deploy operating systems, it is an integral component in recovery technology with Windows Recovery Environment (Windows RE). This is a list of some of the tools included in the Windows PE disk:

- **BCDBoot:** A tool used to quickly set up a system partition, or to repair the boot environment located on the system partition.

- **BCDEdit:** A command-line tool for managing the BCD Store, which describes the boot application and boot application settings such as the boot menu.

- **BootSect:** Used to restore the boot sector on your computer.

- **Deployment Image Servicing and Management (DISM):** Used to service Windows images offline before deployment.

- **DiskPart:** Text-mode command interpreter to manage disks, partitions, and volumes.

- **DrvLoad:** Adds out-of-box drivers.

- **OscdImg:** A command-line tool for creating an image file (.iso) of a customized 32-bit or 64-bit version of Windows PE.

- **Winpeshl:** Controls whether a customized shell is loaded in Windows PE or default Command prompt window. To load a customized shell, create a file named Winpeshl.ini and place it in %SYSTEMROOT%\System32 of your customized Windows PE image.

- **WpeInit:** A command-line tool that initializes Windows PE each time that Windows PE boots. It installs Plug and Play devices, processes Unattend.xml settings, and loads network resources.

- **WpeUtil:** A command-line tool that enables you to run various commands in a Windows PE session.

➕ MORE INFORMATION

For more information about Windows PE and its tools, visit the following websites:
http://technet.microsoft.com/en-us/library/cc749538(WS.10).aspx
http://technet.microsoft.com/en-us/library/cc749055(WS.10).aspx
http://download.microsoft.com/download/5/b/5/5b5bec17-ea71-4653-9539-204a672f11cf/WindowsPE_tech.doc

Windows Recovery Environment (WinRE) is a set of tools included in the Windows Vista, Windows 7, and Windows Server 2008 operating systems to help diagnose and recover from serious errors, which may be preventing Windows from booting successfully. WinRE may be installed and/or booted from many media including hard disks, optical media (such as an operating system installation disc), and PXE (e.g., Windows Deployment Services).

The following options are available when booting from the operating system DVD (see Figure 6-5):

- **Startup Repair:** Automatically finds and fixes boot errors in the Windows 7 Startup Process (including corrupted Boot Configuration Data files).
- **System Restore:** Utilizes the Volume Shadow Copy service to restore the computer to a previous state or restore point. It uses the System Restore feature that was first introduced in Windows ME.
- **System Image Recovery:** Restores the Complete PC Backup disk image.
- **Windows Memory Diagnostic Tool:** Analyzes the computer memory (RAM) for hardware memory problems.
- **Command Prompt:** Gives full command-line access to the file system, volumes and files, unlike the Recovery Console, which was limited in operation.

Figure 6-5

System Recovery options

When installed on the same partition as another Windows operating system, such as Windows 7, Windows Recovery Environment can be accessed by pressing F8 while the computer is booting.

Running Startup Repair

The Startup Repair tool, which is part of the System Recovery tools, is capable of fixing almost any startup problem related to boot sectors, MBRs, or the BCD registry file.

RUN THE SYSTEM RECOVERY TOOLS FROM THE HARD DRIVE

GET READY. To start the System Recovery tools from the hard drive, follow these steps:

1. Restart the computer.
2. If the System Recovery tools do not automatically start, restart the computer again, press F8 before the Starting Windows logo appears, and then choose *Repair Your Computer from the Advanced Boot Options* screen.
3. Select your language and keyboard input method and then click Next.
4. Select your username and type your password. Then, click OK.

RUN THE SYSTEM RECOVERY TOOLS FROM THE WINDOWS DVD

GET READY. If you cannot start the System Recovery tools from the hard drive, insert the Windows DVD and configure the computer to start from the DVD. Then, follow these steps:

1. Insert the Windows DVD in your computer.
2. Restart your computer.
3. When prompted to boot from the DVD, press any key. If you are not prompted to boot from the DVD, you may have to configure your computer's startup sequence.
4. After Windows 7 setup loads, select your regional preferences and keyboard layout when prompted and then click Next.
5. Click Repair Your Computer to start RecEnv.exe.
6. When the System Recovery tools start, System Recovery scans your hard disks for Windows installations.
7. If the standard Windows drivers do not detect a hard disk because it requires drivers that were not included with Windows 7, click Load.

Depending on what problems are detected, you will get different prompts to restore your computer using System Restore or to restart your computer to continue troubleshooting. Either way, when the diagnostic and repair completes, you can click Click Here For Diagnostic And Repair Details. At the bottom of the report, the startup tool will list the problem and the steps it took to repair the problem. In addition, the Log files are stored in the %WinDir%\System32\LogFiles\SRT\SRTTrail.txt file.

Using the BootRec Command

If you prefer to perform a manual repair, you can use the BootRec command, which can repair the MBR or the volume boot sector.

BootRec.exe can be executed from the Command Prompt in the System Recovery tools. BootRec.exe supports the following command-line parameters:

＋ MORE INFORMATION

For more information about the bootrec.exe command, visit the following website:

http://support.microsoft.com/kb/927392

- **/FIXMBR:** This switch writes an MBR to the system partition.
- **/FIXBOOT:** This switch writes a new boot sector onto the system partition.
- **/SCANOS:** This switch scans all disks for Windows installations and displays entries currently not in the BCD store.
- **/REBUILDBCD:** This switch scans all disks for Windows installations and gives you a choice of which entries to add to the BCD store.

If your boot sector gets overwritten by another operating system installation, then you can restore the Windows boot sector by executing the following command from a command prompt in the System Recovery tools:

```
bootsect/NT60 ALL
```

After running this command, if you still need to load earlier versions of Windows that are installed on the same computer, then you will most likely need to add entries to the BCD registry file.

 REINSTALL WINDOWS FOR DATA RECOVERY

GET READY. If the Windows startup files and critical areas become corrupted and cannot be repaired, you can try to reinstall Windows for the purpose of data recovery by following these steps:

1. Insert the Windows DVD in your computer.
2. Restart your computer. When prompted to boot from the CD/DVD, press any key.
3. Windows Setup loads. When prompted, select your regional preferences and then click Next.
4. Click Install Now.
5. When prompted, enter your product key.
6. Select the *I Accept The License Terms* check box and then click Next.
7. Click Custom.
8. On the *Where Do You Want to Install Windows?* page, select the partition containing your Windows installation and then click Next.
9. When prompted, click OK.

Setup will install a new instance of Windows and will move all files from your previous installation into the \Windows.Old folder (including the \Program Files, \Windows, and \Users folders). You can then move the files from your system to a fresh installation of Windows.

Of course, you should always keep in mind that while these repairs can come in handy and save you a lot of time and effort, they do not replace a good backup. You should always be in the habit of performing regular backups. Backups can be used to restore data files that may not be replicable or that you do not have the ability to re-create, and they can be used to quickly restore a system if Windows or the programs become damaged and beyond repair. Backups will be discussed in more detail in Lesson 7.

SKILL SUMMARY

IN THIS LESSON YOU LEARNED:

- The computer goes through the power-on self-test (POST), which initializes hardware and finds an operating system to load. The system will search for a boot device (such as a hard drive, optical disk, or USB flash drive) to boot from.

- If the system is running Windows 7, the system will load the BOOTMGR, WINLoad, and NTOSKERNL.EXE.

- BOOTMGR is loaded and accesses the Boot Configuration Data Store to display the boot menu or to boot from a partition or volume.

- WINLoad is the operating system boot loader that loads the rest of the operating system.

- NTOSKERNL.EXE is the main part of Windows that is responsible for various system services, processes, and memory management.

- A master boot record (MBR) is the first 512-byte boot sector of a partitioned data storage device such as a hard disk. It is used to hold the disk's primary partition table and contains the code to bootstrap an operating system, which usually passes control to the volume boot record and uniquely identifies the disk media.

- A volume boot record (VBR), also known as a volume boot sector or a partition boot sector, is a type of boot sector, stored in a disk volume on a hard disk, floppy disk, or similar data storage device that contains code for booting an operating system such as BOOTMGR.

- The active partition is the partition or volume that is marked as the partition to boot from. The active partition or volume that contains the boot file (BOOTMGR) is known as the system partition/volume.

- The partition or volume that contains the Windows operating system files (usually the Windows folder) is called the boot partition.

- Boot Configuration Data (BCD) is a firmware-independent database for boot-time configuration data used by Microsoft's Windows Boot Manager found with Windows Vista, Windows 7, and Windows Server 2008.

- To edit the Boot Configuration, you typically use Bcdedit.exe.

- To access the Advanced Boot Options screen, turn your computer on and press F8 before the Windows logo appears.

- Last Known Good Configuration starts Windows with the last registry and driver configuration that worked successfully, usually marked at the last successful login.

- Safe mode is useful for troubleshooting problems with programs and drivers that might not start correctly or that might prevent Windows from starting correctly.

- System Configuration (msconfig.exe) is a tool that can help identify problems that might prevent Windows from starting correctly.

- Windows Preinstallation Environment (Windows PE) 3.0 is a minimal Win32 operating system with limited services, built on the Windows 7 kernel.

- Windows Recovery Environment (WinRE) is a set of tools included in the Windows Vista, Windows 7, and Windows Server 2008 operating systems to help diagnose and recover from serious errors that may be preventing Windows from booting successfully.

- The Startup Repair tool, which is part of the System Recovery tools is capable of fixing almost any startup problem related to boot sectors, MBRs, or the BCD registry file.

- To perform a manual repair, use the BootRec command to fix the MBR or the volume boot sector.

- You should always keep in mind that while these repairs can come in handy and save you a lot of time and effort, they do not replace a good backup.

Knowledge Assessment

Fill in the Blank

Complete the following sentences by writing the correct word or words in the blanks provided.

1. _____ is loaded and accesses the Boot Configuration Data Store to display the boot menu or to boot from a partition or volume.

2. The partition or volume that contains the Windows operating system files (usually the Windows folder) is called the _____.

3. _____ is a firmware-independent database for boot-time configuration data used by Microsoft's Windows Boot Manager for Windows 7.

4. To configure the Boot Configuration Data, you would use _____.

5. To access the Safe Mode and Last Known Good Configuration, you would use the
   _____.

6. _____ is a minimal Win32 operating system with limited services built on the
   Windows 7 kernel, which can be used to troubleshoot a wide range of problems.

7. _____ is a set of tools included in Windows 7 to help diagnose and recover from
   serious errors, which may prevent Windows from booting successfully.

8. The _____ tool is part of the System Recovery tool that is capable of fixing almost
   any startup problems related to boot sectors, MBRs, or the BCD registry file.

9. The option to use with the BootRec.exe command to write a new boot sector onto the
   system partition is _____.

10. If you load a driver and the system does not boot, you should restart Windows, load the
    Advanced Boot Options, and select _____.

Multiple Choice

Circle the letter that corresponds to the best answer.

1. What is the main part of Windows that is responsible for various system services and
   process and memory management?
   a. BOOTMGR
   b. WINLoad
   c. NTOSKERNL.EXE
   d. Primary Boot-class Device Driver

2. The _____ is the first 512-byte boot sector of a partitioned data storage device
   such as a hard disk that holds the disk's primary partition table and contains the code
   to bootstrap an operating system?
   a. MBR
   b. VBR
   c. Root folder
   d. BIOS Root file

3. _____ is a tool to help identify problems that might prevent Windows from
   starting correctly.
   a. System Information
   b. System Configuration
   c. MSDebug.exe
   d. WDS

4. Which mode starts Windows with a minimal set of drivers and services?
   a. Safe mode
   b. Last Known Good Configuration
   c. Full mode
   d. Standard mode

5. To access the Advanced Boot Menu, press the _____ key.
   a. F1
   b. F2
   c. F4
   d. F8

6. The command used to fix a MBR or the volume boot sector is _____.
   a. FixMBR
   b. FixBoot

    c. BootSect

    d. BootRec

7. If you install Windows on top of another instance of Windows, the files from the previous installation are _____ .

    a. Deleted

    b. Overwritten

    c. Moved to the \Windows.OLD folder

    d. Moved to the \Windows.BAK folder

8. By default, the %SystemRoot% is _____ ?

    a. C:\

    b. C:\Windows

    c. C:\WINNT

    d. C:\Windows\System32

9. If you load the wrong video driver, you should restart Windows in the _____ mode.

    a. Enable low-resolution video (640x480)

    b. Enable boot logging

    c. Debugging

    d. Safe Mode with command prompt

10. If systems cannot be repaired, you should _____ .

    a. Restore from backup

    b. Repartition the drive

    c. Run the Recovery Console from Windows XP installation disk

    d. Reformat the drive

True / False

Circle T if the statement is true or F if the statement is false.

T | F 1. While repair commands can come in handy and save you a lot of time and effort, they do not replace a good backup.

T | F 2. Safe mode will often load Windows when something prevents Windows from loading.

T | F 3. You can run the BootSect command and the BCDBoot command after booting to WinPE.

T | F 4. Windows Recovery Console is the best way to repair an MBR in Windows 7.

T | F 5. If you've upgraded a driver and the device does not work after you log on, you should use the Last Known Good Configuration.

■ Case Scenarios

Scenario 6-1: Designing Active Directory

You work for the Contoso Corporation. You install a system program that will synchronize some reports when you first start your computer. Unfortunately, when you reboot the computer, the system no longer boots. What can you do to fix this type of problem: you installed the driver and the system no longer reboots?

Scenario 6-2: WinPE and WinRE

You work for the Contoso Corporation. You have a junior help desk person who is having problems repairing a computer that will not load Windows properly. He wants to fix this problem, so you suggest trying WinPE or WinRE. He has not used these tools. Therefore he wants to know when he should use each tool. What do you tell him?

Understanding and Troubleshooting File Access

OBJECTIVE DOMAIN MATRIX

TECHNOLOGY SKILL	OBJECTIVE DOMAIN	OBJECTIVE NUMBER
Understanding NTFS	Identify and resolve new software installation issues.	1.1
Sharing Drives and Folders	Identify and resolve new software installation issues.	1.1
Understanding Backups	Identify causes of and resolve software failure issues.	1.3
Understanding File Access Auditing	Identify causes of and resolve software failure issues.	1.3

KEY TERMS

auditing

administrative share

advanced sharing

backup

effective permissions

explicit permission

homegroup

inherited permission

NTFS file system

NTFS permissions

owner

previous version

public sharing

restore point

shared folder

standard sharing

System Protection

System Restore

Windows Backup

After completing this lesson, you will know how to manage files on a computer running Windows 7 so that they can be accessed by users who log on directly to the computer and who access the files remotely from another computer. This includes configuring permissions to limit who can access the files and creating a record showing who accessed those files.

You are an administrator at the Acme Corporation. You have several reports on your server that your management team needs to access. Therefore, you decide to create a reports folder, move the reports into the reports folder, and share the reports folder. To keep the reports confidential, you configure it so that only the Management team can access the reports folder.

■ Understanding NTFS

THE BOTTOM LINE

NTFS is the preferred file system that supports much larger hard disk and a higher level of reliability than FAT-based file systems. In addition, NTFS offers better security through permissions and encryption.

CERTIFICATION READY
Can you list all of the standard NTFS permissions?
1.1

A permission is a type of access granted to an object such as NTFS files and folders. When files and folders are created on an NTFS volume, a security descriptor known as an Access Control List (ACL) is created, which includes information that controls which users and groups can access the file or folder and the type of access allowed to the users and groups. Each assignment of permissions to a user or group is represented as an access control entry (ACE).

TAKE NOTE *

NTFS permissions are managed by using Windows Explorer (explorer.exe).

Looking at NTFS Permissions

NTFS permissions allow you to control which users and groups can gain access to files and folders on an NTFS volume. The advantage with NTFS permissions is that they affect local users as well as network users.

Usually when assigning NTFS permissions, you would assign the following NTFS Standard permissions:

- **Full Control:** Read, write, modify, and execute files in the folder; change attributes, permissions, and take ownership of the folder or files within.
- **Modify:** Read, write, modify, and execute files in the folder; change attributes of the folder or files within.
- **Read & Execute:** Display the folder's contents; display the data, attributes, owner, and permissions for files within the folder; and run files within the folder.
- **List Folder Contents:** Display the folder's contents; display the data, attributes, owner, and permissions for files within the folder; and run files within the folder.
- **Read:** Display the file's data, attributes, owner, and permissions.
- **Write:** Write to the file, append to the file, and read or change its attributes.

To manage NTFS permissions, you can right-click a drive, folder, or file and select Properties and then select the Security tab. As shown in Figure 7-1, you should see the group and users who have been given NTFS permissions and their respective standard NTFS permissions. To change the permissions, you would click the Edit button.

Each of the standard permissions consists of a logical group of special permissions. The available special permissions are:

- **Traverse Folder/Execute File:** The Traverse Folder allows or denies moving through folders to reach other files or folders, even if the user has no permissions for the traversed folders. By default, the Everyone group is granted the Bypass traverse checking user right. (Applies to folders only.) Execute File allows or denies running program files.

Figure 7-1

NTFS permissions

(Applies to files only.) Setting the Traverse Folder permission on a folder does not automatically set the Execute File permission on all files within that folder.

- **List Folder/Read Data:** List Folder allows or denies viewing filenames and subfolder names within the folder. List Folder affects the contents of that folder only and does not affect whether the folder you are setting the permission on will be listed. (Applies to folders only.) Read Data allows or denies viewing data in files. (Applies to files only.)

- **Read Attributes:** Allows or denies viewing the attributes of a file or folder, such as read-only and hidden.

- **Read Extended Attributes:** Allows or denies viewing the extended attributes of a file or folder. Extended attributes are defined by programs and may vary by program.

- **Create Files/Write Data:** Create Files allows or denies creating files within the folder. (Applies to folders only.) Write Data allows or denies making changes to the file and overwriting existing content. (Applies to files only.)

- **Create Folders/Append Data:** Create Folders allows or denies creating folders within the folder. (Applies to folders only.) Append Data allows or denies making changes to the end of the file but not changing, deleting, or overwriting existing data. (Applies to files only.)

- **Write Attributes:** Allows or denies changing the attributes of a file or folder, such as read-only or hidden. The Write Attributes permission does not imply creating or deleting files or folders; it only includes the permission to make changes to the attributes of a file or folder. To allow (or deny) create or delete operations, see Create Files/Write Data, Create Folders/Append Data, Delete Subfolders and Files, and Delete.

- **Write Extended Attributes:** Allows or denies changing the extended attributes of a file or folder. Extended attributes are defined by programs and may vary by program. The Write Extended Attributes permission does not imply creating or deleting files or folders; it only includes the permission to make changes to the attributes of a file or folder. To allow (or deny) create or delete operations, Create Folders/Append Data, Delete Subfolders and Files, and Delete.

- **Delete Subfolders and Files:** Allows or denies deleting subfolders and files, even if the Delete permission has not been granted on the subfolder or file.

- **Delete:** Allows or denies deleting the file or folder. If you do not have Delete permission on a file or folder, you can still delete it if you have been granted Delete Subfolders and Files on the parent folder.

- **Read Permissions:** Allows or denies reading permissions of the file or folder, such as Full Control, Read, and Write.
- **Change Permissions:** Allows or denies changing permissions of the file or folder, such as Full Control, Read, and Write.
- **Take Ownership:** Allows or denies taking ownership of the file or folder. The owner of a file or folder can always change permissions on it, regardless of any existing permissions on the file or folder.
- **Synchronize:** Allows or denies different threads to wait on the handle for the file or folder and synchronize with another thread that may signal it. This permission applies only to multithreaded, multiprocess programs.

Table 7-1 shows the special permissions assigned to each standard NTFS permission. If for some reason, you need more granular control, you can assign special permissions. To assign special permissions, you right-click a drive, folder, or file, choose Properties, and then select the Security tab. Then click the Advanced button to open the Advanced Security Settings, click the Change Permissions button, and click the Add, Edit, or Remove button. See Figure 7-2.

Table 7-1

NTFS permissions

SPECIAL PERMISSIONS	FULL CONTROL	MODIFY	READ & EXECUTE	LIST FOLDER CONTENTS (FOLDERS ONLY)	READ	WRITE
Traverse Folder/Execute File	X	X	X	X		
List Folder/ Read Data	X	X	X	X	X	
Read Attributes	X	X	X	X	X	
Read Extended Attributes	X	X	X	X	X	
Create Files/ Write Data	X	X				X
Create Folders/ Append Data	X	X				X
Write Attributes	X	X				X
Write Extended Attributes	X	X				X
Delete Subfolders and Files	X					
Delete	X	X				
Read Permissions	X	X	X	X	X	X
Change Permissions	X					
Take Ownership	X					
Synchronize	X	X	X	X	X	X

Figure 7-2

Advanced security settings

Groups or users granted Full Control permission on a folder can delete any files in that folder regardless of the permissions protecting the file. In addition, List Folder Contents is inherited by folders but not files, and it should only appear when you view folder permissions. In Windows 7, the Everyone group does not include the Anonymous Logon group by default, so permissions applied to the Everyone group do not affect the Anonymous Logon group.

To simplify administration, it is recommended that you grant permissions using groups. By assigning NTFS permissions to a group, you are granted permissions to one or more people, reducing the number of entries in each access list, and reducing the amount of effort to configure when multiple people need access to the files or folders.

Understanding Effective NTFS Permissions

The folder/file structure on an NTFS drive can be very complicated with many folders and many nested folders. In addition, since assigning permissions to groups is recommended and you can assign permissions at different levels on an NTFS volume, figuring out the effective permissions of a particular folder or file for a particular user can be tricky.

There are two types of permissions used in NTFS:

- *Explicit permission:* Permissions granted directly to the file or folder.
- *Inherited permission:* Permissions that are granted to a folder (parent object or container) that flow into child objects (subfolders or files inside the parent folder).

When assigning permissions to a folder, by default, the permissions apply to the folder being assigned and the subfolders and files of the folder. To keep permissions from being inherited, you can select the "Replace all existing inheritable permissions on all descendants with inheritable permissions from this object" in the Advanced Security Settings dialog box. It will then ask you if you are sure. You can also clear the "Allow inheritable permissions from parent to propagate to this object" check box. When the check box is clear, Windows will respond with a Security dialog box. When you click on the Copy button, the explicit permission will be copied from the parent folder to the subfolder or file. You can then change the explicit permissions on the subfolder or file. If you click on the Remove button, it removes the inherited permission altogether.

By default, objects within a folder inherit the permissions from that folder when the objects are created. However, explicit permissions take precedence over inherited permissions. So if you grant different permissions at a lower level, the lower level permissions take precedence.

For example, you have a folder called Data. Under the Data folder, you have Folder1, and under Folder1, you have Folder2. If you grant Allow Full Control to a user account, the Allow Full Control permission will flow down to the subfolders and files under the Data folder.

OBJECT	NTFS PERMISSIONS
Data	Allow Full Control (Explicit)
Folder1	Allow Full Control (Inherited)
Folder2	Allow Full Control (Inherited)
File1	Allow Full Control (Inherited)

If you grant Allow Full Control on the Data folder to a user account and Allow Read permission to Folder1, the Allow Read permission will overwrite the inherited permissions and will then be inherited by Folder2 and File1.

OBJECT	NTFS PERMISSIONS
Data	Allow Full Control (Explicit)
Folder1	Allow Read (Explicit)
Folder2	Allow Read (Inherited)
File1	Allow Read (Inherited)

If a user has access to a file, the user will still be able to gain access to a file even if he or she does not have access to the folder containing the file. Of course, since the user doesn't have access to the folder, the user cannot navigate or browse through the folder to get to the file. Therefore, a user would have to use the universal naming convention (UNC) or local path to open the file.

When you view the permissions, they will be one of the following:

- **Checked:** Permissions are explicitly assigned.
- **Cleared (unchecked):** No permissions are assigned.
- **Shaded:** Permissions are granted through inheritance from a parent folder.

Besides granting the Allow permissions, you can also grant the Deny permission. The Deny permission always overrides the permissions that have been granted, including when a user or group has been given Full Control. For example, if the group has been granted read and write, yet a person has been denied the Write permission, the user's effective rights would be the Read permission.

When you combine applying Deny versus Allowed with Explicit versus Inherited permissions, the hierarchy of permission precedence works like this:

1. Explicit Deny
2. Explicit Allow
3. Inherited Deny
4. Inherited Allow

Because users can be members of several groups, it is possible for them to have several sets of explicit permissions to a folder or file. When this occurs, the permissions are combined to form the ***effective permissions***, which are the actual permissions you have when logging in and accessing a file or folder. They consist of explicit permissions plus any inherited permissions.

When you calculate the effective permissions, you must first calculate the explicit and inherited permissions for an individual group and then combine them. When combining user and group permissions for NTFS security, the effective permission is the cumulative permission. The only exception is that Deny permissions always apply.

For example, you have a folder called Data. Under the Data folder, you have Folder 1, and under Folder 1, you have Folder 2. User 1 is a member of Group 1 and Group 2. If you assign the Allow Write permission on the Data folder to User 1, the Allow Read permission on Folder 1 to Group 1, and the Allow Modify Permission on Folder2 to Group 2, then the user's effective permission would be shown as:

Object	User 1 NTFS Permissions	Group 1 Permissions	Group 2 Permissions	Effective Permissions
Data	Allow Write Permission (Explicit)			Allow Write Permission
Folder 1	Allow Write Permission (Inherited)	Allow Read Permission (Explicit)		Allow Read and Write Permission
Folder 2	Allow Write Permission (Inherited)	Allow Read Permission (Inherited)	Allow Modify Permission* (Explicit)	Allow Modify Permission*
File 1	Allow Write Permission (Inherited)	Allow Read Permission (Inherited)	Allow Modify Permission* (Inherited)	Allow Modify Permission*

*The Modify permission includes the Read and Write permissions.

For example, you have a folder called Data. Under the Data folder, you have Folder 1, and under Folder 1, you have Folder 2. User 1 is a member of Group 1 and Group 2. If you assign Allow Write permission on the Data folder to User 1, the Allow Read permission on Folder 1 to Group 1, and the Deny Modified permission on Folder 2 to Group 2, the user's effective permission would be shown as:

Object	User 1 NTFS Permissions	Group 1 Permissions	Group 2 Permissions	Effective Permissions
Data	Allow Write Permission (Explicit)			Allow Write Permission
Folder 1	Allow Write Permission (Inherited)	Allow Read Permission (Explicit)		Allow Read and Write Permission
Folder 2	Allow Write Permission (Inherited)	Allow Read Permission (Inherited)	Deny Modify Permission (Explicit)	Deny Modify Permission
File 1	Allow Write Permission (Inherited)	Allow Read Permission (Inherited)	Deny Modify Permission (Inherited)	Deny Modify Permission

VIEW NTFS EFFECTIVE PERMISSIONS

GET READY. To view the NTFS effective permissions for a file or folder, you would:

1. Right-click the file or folder and select properties.
2. Select the Security tab.
3. Click the Advanced button.
4. Click the Effective Permissions tab. See Figure 7-3.

Figure 7-3

NTFS effective permissions

5. Click Select, type in the name of the user or group you want to view. Click OK.

Copying and Moving Files

When you move or copy files from one location to another, you need to understand what happens to the NTFS permissions.

When copying and moving files, you have the following three scenarios:

- When you **copy a folder or file**, the new folder or file will automatically acquire the permissions of the drive or folder that the folder or file is being copied to.
- When you **move a folder or file within the same volume**, the folder or file will retain the same permissions that were originally assigned to it.
- When you **move a folder or file from one volume to another volume**, the folder or file will automatically acquire the permissions of the drive or folder that the folder or file is being copied to.

Looking at Folder and File Owners

The *owner* of the object controls how permissions are set on the object and to whom permissions are granted. If for some reason, you have been denied access to a file or folder and you need to reset the permissions by taking ownership of a file or folder and modifying the permissions. All administrators automatically have the Take Ownership permission of all NTFS objects.

TAKE OWNERSHIP OF A FILE OR FOLDER

GET READY. To take ownership of a file or folder:

1. Open Windows Explorer, and then locate the file or folder you want to take ownership of.
2. Right-click the file or folder, click Properties, and then click the Security tab.
3. Click Advanced, and then click the Owner tab.
4. Click Edit, and then do one of the following:
    - To change the owner to a user or group that is not listed, click Other users and groups and, in *Enter the object name to select (examples)*, type the name of the user or group, and then click OK.
    - To change the owner to a user or group that is listed, in the *Change owner to* box, click the new owner.
5. To change the owner of all subcontainers and objects within the tree, select the *Replace owner on subcontainers and objects* check box.

■ Sharing Drives and Folders

THE BOTTOM LINE

Most users are not going to log on to a server directly to access their data files. Instead, a drive or folder will be shared (known as a ***shared folder***) and users will access those data files over the network. To help protect against unauthorized access, you will use share permissions along with NTFS permissions (assuming the shared folder is on an NTFS volume). When users need to access a network share, they would use the UNC, which is \\servername\sharename.

CERTIFICATION READY
What are the four methods of file sharing in Windows 7?
1.1

In Windows 7, there are four types of file sharing:

- Homegroups
- Public sharing
- Standard sharing
- Advanced sharing

Of these four models, standard and advanced sharing are preferred because they are more secure than public sharing. However, public sharing is designed to enable users to share files and folders from a single location quickly and easily.

Using Homegroups

X REF

To access computers remotely on a network through shared folders and printers, you need to enable network services under the Advanced Sharing setting in Network and Sharing Center, which includes network discovery and File and Printer Sharing. For more information, see Lesson 2.

Homegroups are new to Windows 7 and are used to make it easier to share files and printers on a home network. A homegroup allows you to share pictures, music, videos, documents, and printers with other people in your homegroup.

Homegroups are only available with Windows 7. You can join a HomeGroup in any edition of Windows 7, but you can only create one in Home Premium, Professional, or Ultimate editions.

When you install Windows 7, a homegroup is created automatically if one doesn't already exist on your home network. If a homegroup already exists, you can join it. After you create or join a homegroup, you can select the libraries that you want to share. Computers that belong to a domain can join a homegroup, but they can't share files with the homegroup. They can only access files shared by others.

You can prevent specific files or folders from being shared, and you can share additional libraries later. You can help protect your homegroup with a password, which you can change at any time.

CHANGE NETWORK LOCATION

GET READY. To join a homegroup, your computer's network location must be set to Home. To change a network location:

1. Open Network and Sharing Center.
2. Click Work network, Home network, or Public network, and then click the network location you want.

JOIN A HOMEGROUP

GET READY. To join a homegroup, you will need the homegroup password. When you join a homegroup, all user accounts on your computer become members of the homegroup. To join a homegroup:

1. Open the Control Panel and click Choose homegroup and sharing options.
2. Click Join now, and then complete the wizard.

CREATE A HOMEGROUP

GET READY. To create a homegroup:

1. Open the Control Panel and click Choose homegroup and sharing options.
2. On the Share with other home computers running Windows 7 page, click a homegroup to start the wizard.

REMOVE A COMPUTER FROM A HOMEGROUP

GET READY. To remove a computer from a homegroup, follow these steps on the computer you want to remove:

1. Open the Control Panel and click Choose homegroup and sharing options.
2. Click Leave the homegroup.
3. Click Finish.

CHANGE HOMEGROUP SETTINGS

GET READY. If your computer is part of a homegroup, you can change settings by following these steps:

1. Open the Control Panel and click Choose homegroup and sharing options.
2. Select the settings you want and then click Save changes.

Options for homegroups include:

- **Share libraries and printers:** Select the libraries and printers you want to share in their entirety with your homegroup.
- **Share media with devices:** Use this setting to share media with all devices on your network. For example, you can share pictures with an electronic picture frame, or share music with a network media player. Unfortunately, shared media is not secure. Anyone connected to your network can receive your shared media.
- **View or print the homegroup password:** View or print the password for your homegroup.

- **Change the password:** Change the password for your homegroup.
- **Leave the homegroup:** Leave your homegroup.
- **Change advanced sharing settings:** Change settings for network discovery, file sharing, Public folder sharing, password-protected sharing, homegroup connections, and file sharing connections.
- **Start the HomeGroup troubleshooter:** Troubleshoot homegroup problems.

 PREVENT A LIBRARY FROM BEING SHARED WHILE CREATING OR JOINING A HOMEGROUP

GET READY. To prevent a library from being shared (while creating or joining a homegroup):

1. Open the Control Panel and click Choose homegroup and sharing options.
2. Do one of the following:
   - To create a new homegroup, click Create a homegroup.
   - To join an existing homegroup, click Join now.
3. On the next screen of the wizard, clear the check box for each library you don't want shared.
4. Click Next, and then click Finish.

 PREVENT A LIBRARY FROM BEING SHARED AFTER CREATING OR JOINING A HOMEGROUP

GET READY. To prevent a library from being shared (after creating or joining a homegroup):

1. Open the Control Panel and click Choose homegroup and sharing options.
2. Clear the check box for each library you don't want shared, and then click Save changes.

 PREVENT A SPECIFIC FILE OR FOLDER FROM BEING SHARED

GET READY. To prevent specific files or folders from being shared (after creating or joining a homegroup):

1. Click the Start button, and then click your username.
2. Navigate to the file or folder you want to exclude from sharing, and then select it.
3. Do one of the following:
   - **To prevent the file or folder from being shared with anyone:** In the toolbar, click Share with, and then click Nobody.
   - **To share the file or folder with some people but not others:** In the toolbar, click Share with, click Specific people by selecting each person you want to share with, and then click Add. Click Share when you are finished.
   - **To change the level of access to a file or folder:** In the toolbar, click Share with, and then select either Homegroup (Read) or Homegroup (Read/Write).

Using Public Sharing

The Public folder is a Windows folder that you can use to share files with other people that either use the same computer, or connect to it over a network. The Public folder is located in the Users folder of your root directory (for example, C:\Users\Public), and it can be accessed through a person's libraries.

The default folders located in the Public folder are:

- Public Documents
- Public Downloads
- Public Music
- Public Pictures
- Public Videos

 CHANGE NETWORK LOCATION

GET READY. When *public sharing* is turned on, anybody on your network can view or open files in your Public folders. To turn on Public folder sharing:

1. Open the Network and Sharing Center.
2. Click the Change advanced sharing settings option.
3. Click the chevron to expand your current network profile.
4. Under Public folder sharing, select one of the following options:
   - Turn on Public folder sharing so anyone with network access can read and write files in the Public folders.
   - Turn off Public folder sharing (people logged on to this computer can still access these folders).
5. Click Save changes. If you're prompted for an administrator password or confirmation, type the password or provide confirmation.

If you wish to limit access to the Public folder to only those people with a user account and password, on Windows 7, you would enable password-protected sharing.

Using Basic Sharing

To make sharing easier, Windows 7 allows you to quickly enable sharing with a standard set of permissions to allow or deny initial access to files and folders over the network.

Similar to public folder sharing, *standard sharing* settings can be enabled or disabled on a per computer basis. To enable file sharing:

1. Open the Network and Sharing Center.
2. Click the Change advanced sharing settings option.
3. To enable file sharing, select Turn on file and printer sharing. To disable file sharing, select Turn off file and printer sharing.
4. Click Save changes.

The easiest way to create a shared folder is to right-click the folder you want to share and click Share with. You can also select Share with from the menu at the top of the window. Then select who you want to share the folder with. Your choices are Nobody, Homegroup (Read), Homegroup (Read/Write), and Specific people. If you select specific people, you can give Read access or Read/Write access.

Using Advanced Sharing

For more control of the shared folders, you would use *advanced sharing*. The options available with advanced sharing are similar to what you would find when sharing a folder on a computer running Windows XP.

You can access advanced sharing by right-clicking a folder, selecting Properties and clicking Advanced Sharing. Shared folders can be shared several times with different names and permissions. Therefore, you can specify the name of the shared folder.

 SHARE A FOLDER

GET READY. To Share a folder follow these steps:

1. In Windows 7, right-click the drive or folder, select properties and select the Sharing tab; then click the Advanced Sharing button. Then follow these steps:
2. Select *Share this folder*.
3. Type the name of the shared folder.
4. If necessary, you can specify the maximum number of people that can access the shared folder at the same time.
5. Click the Permissions button.
6. By default, Everyone is given the Allow Read share permission. You can then remove Everyone, expand the Read Share permission, or add additional people.
7. After the users and groups have been added with the proper permissions, click the OK button to close the Permissions dialog box. See Figure 7-4.
8. Click OK to close the Properties dialog box.

Figure 7-4

Sharing a folder

The share permissions that are available include:

- **Full Control:** Users have Read and Change permissions, as well as the additional capabilities to change file and folder permissions and take ownership of files and folders.
- **Change:** Users have Read permissions and the additional capability to create files and subfolders, modify files, change attributes on files and subfolders, and delete files and subfolders.
- **Read:** Users can view file and subfolder names, access the subfolders of the share, read file data and attributes, and run program files.

Like with NTFS permissions, with share permissions you can allow or deny each share permission. To simplify managing share and NTFS permissions, Microsoft recommends giving Everyone Full Control, and then controlling access using NTFS permissions. In addition, since a user can be member of several groups, it is possible for the user to have several sets of permissions to a shared drive or folder. The effective share permissions are the combination of the user and all group permissions that the user is a member of.

When a person logs on to the server and accesses the files and folders without using the UNC, only the NTFS permissions (not the share permissions) apply. When a person accesses a shared folder using the UNC, you must combine the NTFS and share permissions to see what a user can do. To determine the overall access, first calculate the effective NTFS permissions. Then determine the effective shared permissions. Last, apply the more restrictive permissions between the NTFS and shared permissions.

Looking at Special and Administrative Shares

In Windows, there are several special shared folders that are automatically created by Windows for administrative and system use. Different from regular shares, these shares do not show up when a user browses computer resources using Network Neighborhood, My Network Place, or similar software. In most cases, special shared folders should not be deleted or modified. For Windows Servers, only members of the Administrators, Backup Operators, and Server Operators group can connect to these shares.

An *administrative share* is a shared folder typically used for administrative purposes. To make a shared folder or drive into an administrative share, the share name must have a $ at the end of it. Since the shared folder or drive cannot be seen during browsing, you would have to use a UNC name, which includes the shared name (including the $). By default, all volumes with drive letters automatically have administrative shares (C$, D$, E$, and so on). Other administrative shares can be created as needed for individual folders.

Besides the administrative shares for each drive, you also have the following special shares:

- **ADMIN$:** A resource used by the system during remote administration of a computer. The path of this resource is always the path to the Windows 7 system root (the directory in which Windows 7 is installed, for example, C:\Windows).
- **IPC$:** IPC stands for Interprocess Communications. A resource that shares the named pipes that are essential for communication between programs. It is used during remote administration of a computer and when viewing a computer's shared resources.
- **PRINT$:** A resource used during remote administration of printers.

Troubleshooting File Access Problems

While sharing files gives you the ability to allow multiple people to access files, it can still be frustrating when a user cannot access those files. Therefore, you will need to be able to troubleshoot these problems.

Anytime a user is having problems accessing a shared folder, you should make sure that the computer is available (including proper name resolution), the shared folder is available, and there are no firewall issues (SMB file sharing uses port 139 and 445) on the client and remote computer that would cause the folder to become inaccessible. If the user gets an access denied or similar message, you should verify the NTFS and share permissions.

■ Understanding Backups

THE BOTTOM LINE

Data stored on a computer or stored on the network is vital to the users and probably the organization. It represents hours of work and its data is sometimes irreplaceable. Backups are one of the most essential components of any server design. No matter how much effort, hardware, and software you put into a system, you will eventually have system failures. Sometimes when the downtime occurs, you may have data loss.

CERTIFICATION READY
What is the best method for data recovery?
1.3

A *backup* or the process of backing up refers to making copies of data so that these additional copies may be used to restore the original after a data loss event. They can be used to restore entire systems following a disaster or to restore a small set of files that were accidentally deleted or corrupted.

TAKE NOTE*

The best method for data recovery is Backup, Backup, Backup!

When planning your backups, you also need to plan where backup files are going to be stored. If you have files stored throughout your corporation, including users keeping files on their local computers, it is very difficult to back up all of these files. Therefore, you will most likely need to use some form of technology that keeps your files in a limited number of locations. For example, you can use file redirection for Desktop and My Documents to be stored on a file server by configuring the user profiles.

Defining Backup Items

When a novice thinks of backups, he or she will most likely think of backing up data files such as Microsoft Word or Excel documents. However, there are more than just data files. You have the program files that make computer do what it needs to do. When determining what and how often to backup, you should also look at the time it would take to reinstall, reconfigure, or recover the item.

When planning backups, you should isolate your program files and your data files. Program files usually do not change and so they do not have to be backed up often. Data files change often, so they should be backed up more often. If you isolate them in different areas, you can create different backup policies for each area.

Another item that must be covered is the system state. The Windows system state is a collection of system components that are not contained in a simple file that can be backed up easily. It includes:

- Boot files
- Registry (including COM settings)
- SYSVOL
- User profiles
- COM+ and WMI information
- IIS metabase

Windows backup and most commercial backup software packages will back up the Windows system state. If you want to perform a complete restore of a system running Windows, you will need to back up all files on the drive and the system state.

Understanding Backup Methods

When planning and implementing backups, you will need to determine when and how often you are going to backup, what hardware and software you are going to use, where you are going to store the backups, and how long you are going to store them.

The first question you should ask yourself is "How often should I do a backup?" Your answer should be based on your needs. You must first look at how important your data is and how much effort would be required to recreate the data if that data were lost, assuming it could be re-created at all. You should also consider what the impact to your company would be if the data were lost. Important or critical data should be backed up nightly. Data that does not change much can be backed weekly, and data that does not change at all can be backed up monthly.

The next question you should ask is "How long should I keep my backups?" That question is not easy to answer because it is really based on the needs of your organization, including legal requirements that your organization must follow.

Another consideration you should keep in mind is that backups do fail from time to time. Therefore, you should periodically test your backups by doing a restore to make sure that a backup is working and that you are backing up the necessary files. Second, you should have some type of rotation.

Using Microsoft Windows Backup

Windows Backup allows you to make copies of data files for everyone who uses the computer. You can let Windows choose what to back up or you can select the individual folders, libraries, and drives that you want to back up. By default, your backups are created on a regular schedule. You can change the schedule and manually create a backup at any time. Once you set up Windows Backup, Windows keeps track of the files and folders that are new or modified and adds them to your backup.

To back up your files:

1. Open the Control Panel and click Back up your computer if you are in Category View or Backup and Restore if you are in Icon View. See Figure 7-5. You can also search for Backup in the Start menu search box to quickly find Backup and restore.

Figure 7-5

Windows Backup

2. Do one of the following:
   - If you've never used Windows Backup before, click Set up backup, and then follow the steps in the wizard. If you are prompted for an administrator password or confirmation, type the password or provide confirmation.
   - If you've created a backup before, you can wait for your regularly scheduled backup to occur, or you can manually create a new backup by clicking Back up now. If you are prompted for an administrator password or confirmation, type the password or provide confirmation.

You should not back up your files to the same hard disk that Windows is installed on. Always store media used for backups (external hard disks, DVDs, or CDs) in a secure place to prevent unauthorized people from having access to your files.

After you create your first backup, Windows Backup will add new or changed information to your subsequent backups. If you're saving your backups on a hard drive or network location, Windows Backup will create a new, full backup for you automatically when needed. If you're saving your backups on CDs or DVDs and can't find an existing backup disc, or if you want to create a new backup of all of the files on your computer, you can create a full backup.

To create a new full backup to CDs or DVDs:

1. Open the Control Panel and click Back up your computer if you are in Category View or Backup and Restore while in Icon View.
2. In the left pane, click Create new, full backup.

You can use a system image to restore the contents of your computer if your hard disk or entire computer ever stops working. A system image is an exact copy of a drive. By default, a system image includes the drives required for Windows to run. It also includes Windows and your system settings, programs, and files.

When you restore your computer from a system image, it's a complete restoration; you can't choose individual items to restore. All of your current programs, system settings, and files are replaced with the contents of the system image. Therefore, it is still recommended to backup personal files on a regular basis using Windows Backup.

Using System Protection and Restore Points

> **System Protection** is a feature that regularly creates and saves information about your computer's system files and settings. System Protection uses restore points, which are created just before significant system events, such as the installation of a program or device driver. They're also created automatically once every seven days if no other restore points were created in the previous seven days, but you can create restore points manually at any time.

System Protection is automatically enabled for the drive that Windows is installed on. System Protection can only be turned on for drives that are formatted using the NTFS file system.

System Protection includes **System Restore**, which helps you restore your computer's system files to an earlier point in time by regularly creating and saving **restore points** on your computer. It's a way to undo system changes to your computer without affecting your personal files, such as email, documents, or photos. System Restore comes in handy when the installation of a program or driver causes an unexpected change to your computer or causes Windows to behave unpredictably. If uninstalling doesn't fix the problem, you can try restoring your computer's system to an earlier date when everything worked correctly.

TURN ON SYSTEM PROTECTION

GET READY. To turn on System Protection:

1. Open the System properties using the Control Panel.
2. In the left pane, click System protection. If you are prompted for an administrator password or confirmation, type the password or provide confirmation. See Figure 7-6.

Figure 7-6

System protection

3. Click the drive, and then click Configure.
4. Do one of the following:
   - To turn on the ability to restore system settings and previous version of files, click Restore system settings and previous versions of files.
   - To turn on the ability to restore previous version of files, click Only restore previous versions of files.
5. Click OK.

 CREATE A RESTORE POINT MANUALLY

GET READY. You can create a restore point manually anytime by following these steps:

1. Open System properties using the Control Panel.
2. In the left pane, click System protection. If you are prompted for an administrator password or confirmation, type the password or provide confirmation.
3. Click the System Protection tab, and then click Create.
4. In the System Protection dialog box, type a description, and then click Create.

You cannot delete an individual restore point, but you can either delete all restore points or all but the most recent restore point. Deleting restore points temporarily frees up disk space. As new restore points are created, disk space will be used again. Note: When you delete restore points, previous versions of files are also deleted.

 DELETE ALL RESTORE POINTS

GET READY. You can delete all restore points by following these steps:

1. Click to open System.
2. In the left pane, click System protection. If you are prompted for an administrator password or confirmation, type the password or provide confirmation.

3. Under Protection Settings, click Configure.

4. Under Disk Space Usage, click Delete.

5. Click Continue, and then click OK.

 DELETE ALL BUT THE MOST RECENT RESTORE POINT

GET READY. You can delete all but the most recent restore point by following these steps:

1. Open Disk Cleanup. If prompted, select the drive that you want to clean up, and then click OK.

2. In the Disk Cleanup for (drive letter) dialog box, click Clean up system files. If you are prompted for an administrator password or confirmation, type the password or provide confirmation.

3. If prompted, select the drive that you want to clean up, and then click OK.

4. Click the More Options tab, under System Restore and Shadow Copies, and click Clean up.

5. In the Disk Cleanup dialog box, click Delete.

6. Click Delete Files, and then click OK.

 RESTORE BACK TO AN EARLIER RESTORE POINT

GET READY. To restore back to an earlier restore point, perform the following steps:

1. Click the Start button and select All Programs, select Accessories, select System Tools and select System Restore.

2. When the System Restore wizard starts, click the Next button.

3. Select the appropriate restore point and click the Next button.

4. When the wizard is complete, click the Finish button. The system will restart your computer to apply those changes.

If you don't want Windows to keep *previous versions* of your files, you can turn off System Protection. When you turn off System Protection, you are also turning off the ability to restore your computer's system files using System Restore.

 TURN OFF SYSTEM PROTECTION

GET READY. To restore back to an earlier restore point, perform the following steps:

1. Open the System properties using the Control Panel.

2. In the left pane, click System Protection. If you are prompted for an administrator password or confirmation, type the password or provide confirmation.

3. Click the drive, and then click Configure.

4. Click Turn off system protection, and then click OK.

 RESTORE A PREVIOUS VERSION OF A FILE OR FOLDER

GET READY. To restore a previous version of a file or folder:

1. Locate the file or folder that you want to restore, right-click the file or folder, and click Properties. The Properties dialog box will appear.

2. Click the Previous Versions tab, click the version of the file that you want to restore, and then click Restore. See Figure 7-7. A warning message about restoring a previous version will appear. Click Restore to complete the procedure.

Figure 7-7

Restoring a previous version

Restoring a previous version will delete the current version. If you choose to restore a previous version of a folder, the folder will be restored to its state at the date and time of the version you selected. You will lose any changes that you have made to files in the folder since that time. Instead, if you do not want to delete the current version of a file or folder, click Copy to copy the previous version to a different location.

Understanding File Access Auditing

THE BOTTOM LINE

As mentioned earlier, security can be divided into three areas. Authentication is used to prove the identify of a user. Authorization gives access to the user that was authenticated. To complete the security picture, you need to enable *auditing* so that you can have a record of the users who have logged in and what the user accessed or tried to access.

CERTIFICATION READY
What would you do if you want to determine who is deleting an important report from your server?
1.3

Auditing is not enabled by default. To enable auditing, you specify what types of system events to audit using group policies or the local security policy (Security Settings\Local Policies\Audit Policy). To audit NTFS files, NTFS folders, and printers is a two-step process. You must first enable Object Access using group policies. Then you must specify which files or folders you want to audit. After you enable logging, you then open the Event Viewer security logs to view the security events.

 AUDIT FILES AND FOLDERS

GET READY. To audit files and folders:

1. Open Windows Explorer.
2. Right-click the file or folder that you want to audit, click Properties, and then click the Security tab.
3. Click Edit, and then click Advanced.
4. In the Advanced Security Settings for <object> dialog box, click the Auditing tab.
5. Do one of the following:
   - To set up auditing for a new user or group, click Add. In Enter the object name to select, type the name of the user or group that you want, and then click OK.

- To remove auditing for an existing group or user, click the group or username, click Remove, click OK, and then skip the rest of this procedure.

- To view or change auditing for an existing group or user, click its name, and then click Edit.

6. In the *Apply onto* box, click the location where you want auditing to take place.

7. In the Access box, indicate what actions you want to audit by selecting the appropriate check boxes:

   - To audit successful events, select the Successful check box.

   - To stop auditing successful events, clear the Successful check box.

   - To audit unsuccessful events, select the Failed check box.

   - To stop auditing unsuccessful events, clear the Failed check box.

   - To stop auditing all events, click Clear All.

8. If you want to prevent subsequent files and subfolders of the original object from inheriting these audit entries, select the Apply these auditing entries to objects and/or containers within this container only check box.

9. Click OK to close the Advanced Security Settings dialog box.

10. Click OK to close the Properties dialog box.

SKILL SUMMARY

IN THIS LESSON YOU LEARNED:

- A permission is defined as the type of access that is granted to an object such NTFS files and folders.

- When files and folders are created on an NTFS volume, a security descriptor known as an Access Control List (ACL) is created that includes information that controls which users and groups can access the file or folder and the type of access allowed to the users and groups.

- NTFS permissions allow you to control which users and groups can gain access to files and folders on an NTFS volume.

- By assigning NTFS permissions to a group, you are granting permissions to one or more people, reducing the number of entries in each access list, and reducing the amount of effort to configure when multiple people need access to the files or folders.

- Explicit permissions are permissions granted directly to the file or folder.

- Inherited permissions are permissions that are granted to a folder (parent object or container) that flow into that folder's child objects (subfolders or files inside the parent folder).

- Because users can be members of several groups, it is possible for them to have several sets of explicit permissions to a folder or file. When this occurs, the permissions are combined to form effective permissions, which are the actual permissions when logging in and accessing a file or folder.

- If you copy a file or folder, the new file or folder will automatically acquire the permissions of the drive or folder that the file or folder is being copied to.

- If a folder or file is moved within the same volume, the folder or file will retain the same permissions that were already assigned.

- When a folder or file is moved from one volume to another volume, the folder or file will automatically acquire the permissions of the drive or folder that the folder or file is being copied to.

- In Windows 7, there are four types of sharing: Homegroups, Public sharing, Basic sharing, and Advanced sharing.

- Homegroups are new to Windows 7 and are used to make it easier to share files and printers on a home network. A homegroup allows you to share pictures, music, videos, documents, and printers with other people in your homegroup.

- The Public folder is a Windows folder that you can use to share files with other people that either use the same computer, or connect to it over a network.

- To make sharing easier, Windows 7 allows you to quickly enable sharing with a standard set of permissions to allow or deny initial access to files and folders over the network.

- You can access advanced sharing by right-clicking a folder, selecting Properties, and clicking Advanced Sharing. Shared folders can be shared several times with different names and permissions.

- An administrative share is a shared folder typically used for administrative purposes.

- Anytime a user is having problems accessing a shared folder, you should make sure that the computer is available (including proper name resolution), the shared folder is available, and there are no firewall issues (SMB file sharing uses port 139 and 445) on the client and remote computer that would cause the folder to become inaccessible.

- If the user gets an access denied or similar message, you should verify the NTFS and Share permissions.

- A backup or the process of backing up refers to making copies of data so that these additional copies may be used to restore the original after a data loss event.

- The best method for data recovery is Backup, Backup, Backup.

- The Windows system state is a collection of system components that are not contained in a simple file that can be backed up easily.

- Windows Backup allows you to make copies of data files for everyone who uses the computer. You can let Windows choose what to back up or you can select the individual folders, libraries, and drives that you want to back up.

- System Protection is a feature that regularly creates and saves information about your computer's system files and settings. System Protection also saves previous versions of files that you've modified.

- Along with System Protection is System Restore, which helps you restore your computer's system files to an earlier point in time by regularly creating and saving restore points on your computer.

- Auditing NTFS files, NTFS folders, and printers is a two-step process. You must first enable Object Access using group policies. Then you must specify which files or folders you want to audit.

■ Knowledge Assessment

Fill in the Blank

Complete the following sentences by writing the correct word or words in the blanks provided.

1. The _____ of the object controls how permissions are set on the object and to whom permission are granted.

2. The NTFS special permission that allows you to move through a folder to reach lower files or folders is _____ .

3. The Windows component that allows you to manage shares and NTFS permissions is _____.

4. Permissions that flow from a parent object to a child object are called _____.

5. The _____ are the actual permissions used when a user logs in and accesses a file or folder.

6. _____ make it easier to share files and printers on a home network.

7. For Windows 7 to be seen on the network, you must enable _____.

8. A(n) _____ share is not seen when browsed.

9. The _____ is a Windows folder that can you use to share files with other people who either use the same computer, or connect to it over the network.

10. You would use _____ to restore your computer's system files to an earlier point in time.

Multiple Choice

Circle the letter that corresponds to the best answer.

1. What is the standard NTFS permission needed to change attributes?
   a. Write
   b. Read
   c. Modify
   d. Full Control

2. Which permission takes precedence?
   a. Explicit Deny
   b. Explicit Allow
   c. Inherited Deny
   d. Inherited Allow

3. Which of the following is NOT a share permission?
   a. Full Control
   b. Write
   c. Change
   d. Read

4. In which of the following editions is Homegroups NOT available?
   a. Home Basic
   b. Home Premium
   c. Professional
   d. Ultimate

5. To enable System Protection, you would access _____.
   a. Display properties
   b. File properties
   c. Shared Folders properties
   d. System properties

6. What symbol makes an administrative share NOT seen when browsed?
   a. #
   b. *
   c. !
   d. $

7. Which of the following ports does SMB use?
   a. 169
   b. 445
   c. 142
   d. 80

8. What is the minimum share permissions allowed for you to change file and folder permissions?
   a. Full Control
   b. Change
   c. Read
   d. Manage

9. When you copy files from one folder to another folder within the same volume, you get the _____.
   a. Same permissions as the source
   b. Same permissions as the target
   c. No permissions are set
   d. Everyone has full permission

10. You are an administrator on a computer. Unfortunately, there is a folder that you cannot access because no one has permissions to the folder. What can you do?
   a. Take ownership of the folder
   b. Delete the folder and re-create it
   c. Turn off the Deny attribute
   d. Grant the Everyone Allow Full permission

True / False

Circle T if the statement is true or F if the statement is false.

T | F 1. If Full Control is assigned to a parent object for a user, the Full Control permission will overwrite explicit permissions at a child object.

T | F 2. To see who accesses a file over time, you only have to turn on object access audit events.

T | F 3. When you are looking at NTFS permissions that are grayed out, it means that you don't have permissions to modify the NTFS permissions.

T | F 4. You can encrypt and compress a file within NTFS at the same time.

T | F 5. When calculating the NTFS and share permissions, you would apply the more restrictive permissions between the NTFS and shared permission.

■ Case Scenarios

Scenario 7-1: Creating a Shared Folder

You work for the Contoso Corporation's Help Desk. You are configuring a computer for your manager who is running Windows 7. You have a Data folder that you need to share so that all managers can access and make changes to the documents in the folder and no one else can access it. What should you do to set this folder up?

Scenario 7-2: Auditing the Managers Folder

You work for the Contoso Corporation's Help Desk. You just created a Data folder for your Managers computer that is running Windows 7. You need to verify that it is not getting accessed from anyone who is not supposed to access the files. You also want to know if someone is deleting or making changes to these files. What should you do?

Troubleshooting Printer Problems

OBJECTIVE DOMAIN MATRIX

TECHNOLOGY SKILL	OBJECTIVE DOMAIN	OBJECTIVE NUMBER
Using Printers	Identify and resolve network printer issues.	2.4

KEY TERMS

Devices and Printers

Internet Printing Protocol (IPP)

print device

print driver

print job

print queue

printer

printer permissions

printer pool

spool folder

shared printer

After completing this lesson, you will be able to install, configure, and manage a printer that is connected directly to a computer running Windows 7 or connected through the network. You can also configure printer permissions to control who can print and manage your printers and print queues, and you can enable auditing.

You have a small office with seven users. You just purchased a new printer and connect it to your computer. You would like other people to use your printer so you decide to share the printer.

■ Using Printers

↓
THE BOTTOM LINE

One of the basic network services is network printing where multiple users can share the same printer (***shared printer***). This becomes a cost effective solution while providing printing to everyone who requires it.

As an administrator, you can install two types of printers: a local or a network printer. Today, most local printers are connected using USB ports, while some legacy printers found on servers may use parallel or serial ports. Network printers can be shared local printers or printers that are connected directly to the network with built-in network cards or expandable jet-direct cards.

When you install the physical print device, which Microsoft refers to as *print device*, you must first connect the printer and turn it on. Next, you need to create a logical printer (Microsoft refers to this as *printer*), which will provide a software interface to the print device and/or applications. When you create the printer, you also load a *print driver*, which acts as a translator for Windows and the programs running on Windows so that they do not have to worry about the specifics of the printer's hardware and printer language.

When you print a document in Windows, Windows will convert the document into a language that is understood by the printer. Today, common languages understood by printers include Hewlett Packard's Printer Control Language (PCL) and Adobe's PostScript. The *print job* is then sent to the local spooler, which provides background printing, allowing you to print and queue additional documents whenever the printer is busy.

If the print job is sent to the local print device, the print job is temporarily saved to the local hard drive's spool file. When the physical printer is available, the printer will send the print job to the local print device. If Windows determines the job is for a network print device, Windows sends the job to the print server's spooler. The print server's spooler will save it to the print server's hard drive spool file. When the network print device becomes available, it will print from the spool file to the network print device.

Enhanced Metafile (EMF) is the spool file format used by the Windows operating system. The EMF format is device-independent, which means the EMF file will be the same no matter what printer it is being sent to.

Installing Printers

If you have the correct permissions to add a local printer or remote shared printer, you would use the Add Printer Wizard or the Add a printer button in the Printers and Devices folder to install the printer. After the printer is installed, it will then appear in the **Devices and Printers** folder.

 ADD A LOCAL PRINTER

GET READY. To add a local printer to a Windows 7 computer:

1. Click the Start button and open the Control Panel.
2. Under *Hardware and Sound*, click View Devices and Printers.
3. To start the Add Printer Wizard, click Add a printer.
4. Select *Add a Local Printer*. See Figure 8-1.
5. When the Add Printer dialog box appears, you will then specify which port the printer is connected to. See Figure 8-2. If the port already exists, such as an LPT1, USB, or a network port specified by an IP address, select the port from the *Use an existing port* drop-down list. If the port does not exist, click Create a New Port, select Standard TCP/IP Port, and click Next. For the device type, you can select either auto detect, TCP/IP device, or web services device. Then specify the IP address or DNS name of the printer and the Port Name. If you type the address in hostname or IP address box, it will populate the IP address in the port name. It will then try to communicate with the printer using the address you specified.

Figure 8-1

Selecting local or network printers

Figure 8-2

Adding a local printer

6. If Plug and Play does not detect and install the correct printer automatically, you will be asked to specify the printer driver (printer manufacturer and printer model). If the printer is not listed, you will have to use the *Have Disk* option. See Figure 8-3.

7. When the *Type a Printer Name* dialog box appears, specify the name of the printer. If you want this to be the default printer for the system you are installing the printer on, select the *Set as the default printer* option. Click the Next button.

Figure 8-3

Installing the printer driver

8. On the Printer Sharing dialog box, specify the share name. You can also specify the Location or Comments. Although Windows Server 2008 supports long printer names and share names including spaces and special characters, it is best to keep names short, simple, and descriptive. The entire qualified name, including the server name (for example, \\Server1\HP4100N-1), should be 32 characters or fewer. See Figure 8-4.

Figure 8-4

Sharing the printer

TAKE NOTE *

The TCP/IP printer port uses host port 9100 to communicate.

9. When the printer was successfully added, you can print the standard Windows test page by selecting *Print a test page*. Click the Finish button.

ADD A NETWORK PRINTER

GET READY. To add a network printer to Windows 7:

1. Click the Start button and open the Control Panel.
2. Under Hardware and Sound, click View Devices and Printers.
3. To start the Add Printer Wizard, click Add a printer.

4. Select Add a Network, wireless or Bluetooth printer.

5. If the printer is not automatically found, click The Printer that I want isn't listed option.

6. If you have a printer published in Active Directory (assuming you are part of a domain), you would choose *Find a printer in the directory, based on location or feature*. If you know the UNC, you would select *Select a shared printer by name*. if you know the TCP/IP address choose the last option. See Figure 8-5. Click Next.

Figure 8-5

Finding a network printer

7. In the Type a printer name dialog box, specify the printer name. If you want this to be the default printer for the system you are installing, select *Set as the default printer* option. Click the Next button.

8. When the printer was successfully added, you can print the standard Windows test page by selecting *Print a test page*. Click Finish.

Windows can provide drivers to clients that are printing to a printer if the driver is loaded on the server. For example, if you have a 32-bit version of Windows 7, you can load a 64-bit print driver so that Windows can then provide the driver to other 64-bit Window clients.

 ADD ADDITIONAL PRINT DRIVERS

GET READY. To add additional print drivers in Windows 7:

1. Open Devices and Printers.

2. Click the Print Server button.

3. Select the Drivers tab.

4. Click Change Driver Settings.

5. Click the Add button.

6. When the Welcome to the Add Printer Driver Wizard appears, click Next. See Figure 8-6.

Figure 8-6

Adding a print driver

7. Select the appropriate processor and operating system drivers and click the Next button.

8. If necessary, provide a path for the printer driver and click OK.

9. When the wizard is complete, click the Finish button.

> **TAKE NOTE***
>
> You can also use group policies to install and configure printers.

Network printers are usually used by more than one user. If you have a high volume of print jobs, the printer can become congested, and users will have to wait for their documents to print. Either you can purchase a faster printer or you can create a group of printers called a **printer pool** to act as a single virtual printer with a single **print queue**. Users print to a single printer and the print jobs are distributed among the printers within the pool.

To create a printer pool, you must have two or more print devices that are the same model and use the same printer driver. They can use the same type of ports or different ports. Since you don't know which print job will go to which printer, it is recommended that you place all pooled print devices in the same physical location.

CREATE A PRINTER POOL

GET READY. To create a printer pool:

1. In Control Panel, open the Printers and Faxes folder, right-click the appropriate printer, and click Properties.

2. On the Ports tab, select the *Enable printer pooling* check box.

3. In the list of ports, select the check boxes for the ports connected to the printers that you want to pool.

4. Repeat steps 2 and 3 for each additional printer to be included in the printer pool.

Looking at Printer Properties

With most printers, you have a wide range of options. While these options will vary from printer to printer, they are easily accessible by right-clicking the printer in the Devices and Printers folder and selecting Printer Properties and Printer Preferences.

Every printer manufacturer and software publisher has its own way of doing things. Double-sided or color printing might require you to click a button labeled Properties, Preferences, or even Advanced. The Printer properties dialog box is typically where you'll find specific options related to the printer itself—updating drivers, configuring ports, and other hardware-related customizations.

Printing preferences are the options available on your printer. Some of the choices may include:

- **Page orientation or layout:** Choose between tall (portrait) or wide (landscape).
- **Paper or sheet size:** Letter, legal, A4, or envelope size are common options.
- **Paper or output source:** Selects a paper tray. Printers store different sheets in different trays.
- **Double-sided (duplex) printing:** Print on one, or both, sides of a sheet.
- **Print color:** Color or black-and-white (grayscale) prints.
- **Staple:** A common option on workplace printers.

When you open the Printer Properties, you will find the following options:

- **General tab:** Allows you to configure the printer name, location, and comments, and to print a test page.
- **Sharing tab:** Allows you to share a printer. You can also publish the printer in Active Directory if you chose the List in the directory option. Since the printer on a server can be used by other clients connected to the network, you can add additional drivers by clicking the Additional Drivers button.
- **Ports tab:** Allows you to specify which port (physical or TCP/IP port) the printer will use as well as creating new TCP/IP ports.
- **Advanced tab:** Allows you to configure the driver to use with the printer, the priority of the printer, when the printer is available, and how print jobs are spooled.
- **Security tab:** Allows you to specify the permissions for the printer.
- **Device Settings tab:** Allows you to configure the trays, font substitution, and other hardware settings.

If you click the Printing Preferences button on the General tab, the options for default paper size, paper tray, print quality/resolution, pages per sheet, print order (such as front to back or back to front), and number of copies may be available, depending on your printer. See Figure 8-7.

Figure 8-7

Printer properties and preferences

Understanding Printer Permissions

Printers are considered objects. Because they are similar to NTFS files and folders, you can assign permissions to a printer so you can specify who can use the printer, who can manage the printer, and who can manage the print jobs.

Windows 7 provides three levels of *printer permissions*:

- **Print:** Allows users to send documents to the printer.
- **Manage Printers:** Allows users to modify printer settings and configuration, including the ACL itself.
- **Manage Documents:** Provides the ability to cancel, pause, resume, or restart a print job.

See Figure 8-8.

Figure 8-8

Printer permissions

TAKE NOTE*

Users can delete their own print jobs without having the Manage Documents permission.

By default, the print permission is assigned to the Everyone group. If you need to restrict who can print to the printer, you will need to remove the Everyone group and add another group or user and assign the Allow Print permission to the user or group. Of course, it is still recommended that you use groups instead of users. Just like with file permissions, you can Deny Print permission.

Managing the Print Jobs

The print spooler is an executable file that manages the printing process, which includes retrieving the location of the correct print driver, loading the driver, creating the individual print jobs, and scheduling the print jobs for printing.

On occasion, a print job may have been sent that was not intended or you decide it is not necessary to print. Therefore, you need to delete the print job from the print queue.

VIEW THE PRINT QUEUE

GET READY. To view the print queue, you would:

1. Open the Devices and Printers folder.
2. Double-click the printers on which you want to view the print jobs waiting to print.
3. Click Printer: Ready or <number> document(s) in queue. See Figure 8-9.

Figure 8-9

Viewing the print queue

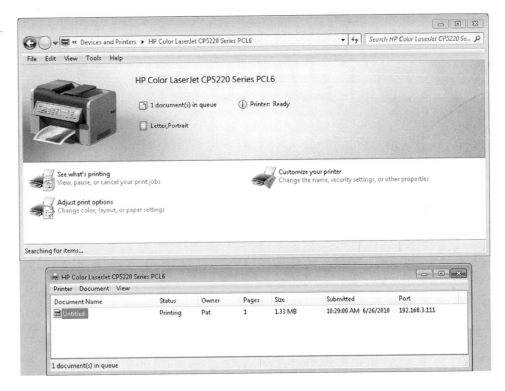

The print queue shows information about a document such as print status, owner, and number of pages to be printed. To pause a document, open the print queue, right-click on the document you want to pause, and select the Pause option. If you want to stop printing the document, right-click on the document that you want to stop printing and select the Cancel option. You can cancel printing of more than one document by holding down the Ctrl key and clicking on each document that you want to cancel.

By default, all users can pause, resume, restart, and cancel their own documents. To manage documents that are printed by other users, however, you must have the Allow Manage Documents permissions.

When the print device is available, the spooler retrieves the next print job from the **spool folder** and sends it to the print device. By default, the spool folder is located at C:\Windows\\System32\Spool\Printers. If you have a server that handles a large number of print jobs or several large print jobs, make sure the drive housing the spool folder has sufficient free disk space.

 CHANGE THE LOCATION OF THE SPOOL FOLDER

GET READY. To change the location of the spool folder in Windows 7:

1. Open the Devices and Printers folder.
2. Click a printer and select the Print server properties.
3. Click the Advanced tab.
4. Click the Change Advanced Settings button.

5. Specify the new location and click the OK button. See Figure 8-10.

Figure 8-10

Changing the location of the spool folder

On occasion, the print spooler may freeze or become unresponsive. You can restart the print spooler by doing the following:

1. Open the Services console located in Administrative Tools.
2. Right-click Print Spooler, and select Restart.

You can also stop and start the service.

Using Printer Priorities and Scheduling

One advantage of using logical printers that point to a physical printer/printer device is that you can use multiple logical printers that point to a single physical printer. You can then schedule some of these logical printers to only print at night. In addition, you can assign priorities to your printers.

By configuring with different priorities, when two print jobs are sent to a printer device through two different printers in Windows, the printer with the higher priority prints before the printer with a lower priority. Printer priority is only evaluated when determining which job to complete next. A printer does not stop processing a job it is already working on, even when the spooler receives a higher priority job, directed to a higher priority printer on the same port.

 CONFIGURE PRINTER PRIORITIES AND SCHEDULING

GET READY. To modify the printer priorities or schedule times that a printer is available:

1. Open Devices and Printers.
2. Right-click the printer and select Printer Properties.
3. Click the Advanced tab.

4. By default, the printer is always available. To change the time that the printer is available, click the *Available from* option and specify the times. See Figure 8-11.

Figure 8-11

Configuring printer priorities and scheduling

5. To change the priority, type in a new number for the priority or use the up arrow or down arrow buttons.

Using Internet Printing

The ***Internet Printing Protocol (IPP)*** provides a standard network protocol for remote printing as well as for managing print jobs, media size, resolution, and so forth over a TCP/IP network. Since it is web printing, it uses the standard TCP ports 80 and 443.

Internet Printing is a server role found on Windows Server 2008 that creates a website hosted by Internet Information Services (IIS). This website enables users to:

• Manage print jobs on the server.
• Use a web browser to connect and print to shared printers on this server by using the Internet Printing Protocol (IPP).

To manage a server by using the website created by Internet Printing, open a web browser and navigate to http://*servername*/printers, where *servername* is the UNC path of the print server.

 ENABLE INTERNET PRINTING CLIENT

GET READY. Internet Printing is not hosted on a computer running Windows 7. But, Windows 7 includes the Internet Printing Client. To enable the Internet Printing Client:

1. Open the Control Panel and click Programs and Features.
2. Click Turn Windows features on or off.

3. Expand Print and Document Services and select the Internet Printing Client check box.
4. Click OK.

Troubleshooting Network Printing

When users have trouble with printing, they can often get frustrated because it does not work as expected. Troubleshooting network printing problems has some similarities to network file access because they both use SMB.

 RUN THE TROUBLESHOOTER FOR PRINTER PROBLEMS

GET READY. If a user cannot print to a network printer, use the Windows 7 troubleshooter for printer problems:

1. Click Start and then click Control Panel.
2. Click System and Security.
3. Under Action Center, click Troubleshoot Common Computer Problems.
4. Under Hardware and Sound, click Use A Printer.
5. The Printer Troubleshooter appears and attempts to diagnose the problem. Follow the steps that appear.
6. On the *Troubleshoot and Help Prevent Computer Problems* page, click Next.
7. On the *Which Printer Would You Like To Troubleshoot?* page, click My Printer Is Not Listed. Click Next.
8. Respond to the prompts that appear to troubleshoot your problem.

As the troubleshooter, you first need to determine the scope of the problem. For example, are multiple users being affected by the problem or is it only affecting one person? Does it affect a certain application or does it affect all applications on a computer? You can also check the event viewer of the client computer and, if applicable, the event viewer of the print server. Last, look at the print queue to make sure that it is running and not stalled on the client computer and the print server.

If the print server appears to be functioning, verify that the printer is running, is online and is connected properly. You should also test connectivity from the print server to the printer. You can also make sure that the IP address on the logical printer port matches the address of the print device. You could test network connectivity by pinging the address of the print device.

To help determine the scope of the problem, you can open the Printer and Faxes folder and double-click the printer to open the printer window. If the printer window opens and shows documents in the print queue, the client is communicating with the print server. If not, you need to check for issues with user authentication, security permissions, or network connectivity. To test shared printers on a server, you can click the Start button, select run, and type in \\printservername to view all of the shared folders and printers. You should also check to make sure there are no firewalls (SMB uses ports 139 and 445 and IPP uses port 80 and port 443) on the client and print server that would cause the network printer to become inaccessible.

If you suspect a problem with the print server itself, you need to make sure that the Print service and the remote procedure call (RPC) service is running. If you cannot access the remote printers, then make sure you don't have the Server service running on the remote computer or the workstation client on the computer trying to print. You might also try to restart the print service and make sure that you have sufficient disk space on the drive where the spool folder is located.

If pages are only partially printed, check that there is sufficient memory on the print device to print the document. If text is missing, verify whether the missing text uses a font that is valid and installed. Of course, another reason might be that you need to replace the print device's toner cartridge.

If your printed documents have garbled data or strange characters, you should verify that you have the correct print driver loaded for the printer. You might also consider reinstalling the drivers since they could be corrupt. Check for bad cables or electromagnetic interference. Finally, most printers have a built-in diagnostic program or test routing that can be used to test their own components.

■ Understanding Printer Auditing

THE BOTTOM LINE

Since printers are considered objects, auditing of printers is similar to auditing file and folder access. You must first enable object auditing and then you need to specify which printer events you want to audit.

To look at spooler and printer activity, look at the logs shown in the Event Viewer that pertain to the printer and spooler activity. By default, the System logs will show printer creation, deletion, and modification. You can also find entries for printer traffic, hard disk space, spooler errors, and other relevant maintenance issues.

→ AUDIT PRINTING

GET READY. To audit printing in Windows 7:

1. Right-click the printer in Devices and Printers and select Printer Properties.
2. Select the Security tab and click the Advanced button.
3. Select the Auditing tab.
4. Click the Add button and
   - To set up auditing for a new user or group, click Add. In *Enter the object name to select*, type the name of the user or group that you want, and then click OK.
   - To remove auditing for an existing group or user, click the group or username, click Remove, click OK, and then skip the rest of this procedure.
   - To view or change auditing for an existing group or user, click its name, and then click Edit.
5. Click OK to close the Advanced Security Settings dialog box.
6. Click OK to close the Properties dialog box.

Because the security log is limited in size, select only those objects that you need to audit and consider the amount of disk space that the security log will need. The maximum size of the security log is defined in Event Viewer by right-clicking Security Log and selecting the Properties option.

SKILL SUMMARY

IN THIS LESSON YOU LEARNED:

- When you install the physical print device, which Microsoft refers to as print device, you must first connect the printer and turn on the printer.
- You need to create a logical printer (Microsoft refers to this as the printer), which will provide a software interface to the print device and or applications.
- When you create the printer, you also load a print driver, which acts as a translator for Windows and the programs running so that they do not have to worry about the specifics of the printer's hardware and printer language.

- When you print a document in Windows, the logical printer and printer driver format the document into a language that is understood by the printer including rendering it into a printer language such as HP's Printer Control Language or Adobe's Postscript to create an enhanced metafile (EMF).

- The print job is then sent to the local spooler, which provides background printing, allowing you to print and queue additional documents while the first one is being printed.

- If the print job is being sent to the local print device, it will temporarily save it to the local hard drive's spool.

- A printer pool is a group of print devices that acts as a single virtual printer with a single print queue file.

- Similar to NTFS files and folders, you can assign permissions to a printer so you can specify who can use the printer, who can manage the printer, and who can manage the print jobs.

- By default, the Print permission is assigned to the Everyone group.

- The print queue shows information about a document such as print status, owner, and number of pages to be printed.

- When the print device is available, the spooler retrieves the next print job and sends it to the print device.

- By default, the spool folder is located at C:\Windows\\System32\Spool\Printers.

- The Internet Printing Protocol (IPP) provides a standard network protocol for remote printing as well as for managing print jobs, media size, resolution, and so forth over a TCP/IP network.

- To enable Internet Printing on a computer running Windows 7, you just need to install the Internet Printing Client feature.

- Troubleshooting network printing problems has some similarities to network file access because they both use SMB.

- By default, the system logs will show printer creation, deletion, and modification. You can also find entries for printer traffic, hard disk space, spooler errors, and other relevant maintenance issues.

■ Knowledge Assessment

Fill in the Blank

Complete the following sentences by writing the correct word or words in the blanks provided.

1. To print to a printer, you need the _____ permission.

2. HP's Printer Control Language and Adobe's Postscript are examples of _____.

3. When you print a document, the document is sent as a _____ so that it can print in the background.

4. Besides manually installing the print drivers, drivers can also be provided by a print _____.

5. If you constantly have a large volume of printing that must be done each day that cannot be handled by a single printer, you should set up a _____.

6. To configure which driver a printer is using or to configure the trays of a printer, you would access the printer's _____.

7. By default, the print permission is assigned to the _____ group.

8. The print _____ shows information about a document such as print status, owner, and number of pages to be printed.

9. If a printer becomes unresponsive, you should restart the _____.

10. The default location of the spool folder is _____.

Multiple Choice

Circle the letter that corresponds to the best answer.

1. Which type of printer is connected directly to the network?
   a. Local printer
   b. Network printer
   c. Providing printer
   d. Job printer

2. With Windows, the physical printer is known as:
   a. Print device
   b. Printer
   c. Printer job
   d. Printer spooler

3. The logical printer that users can access in Windows is known as:
   a. Print device
   b. Printer
   c. Printer job
   d. Printer spooler

4. TCP/IP printers use port _____.
   a. 443
   b. 23
   c. 9100
   d. 3000

5. What is a single virtual printer with a single print queue that consists of two or more printers?
   a. Print collection
   b. Direct printers
   c. Printer group
   d. Printer pool

6. To manage other people's print jobs, you need to assign the _____.
   a. Print permission
   b. Manage printers
   c. Manage documents
   d. Full Control

7. To manage printers used in Internet printing, you would access the _____ website.
   a. http://printername
   b. http://servername
   c. http://servername/printers
   d. http://servername/printqueue

8. Which port do shared printers use?
   a. 80
   b. 139
   c. 143
   d. 443

9. Which port does Internet Printing use?
   a. 80
   b. 139
   c. 143
   d. 25

10. To view who has printed on a printer, you would look in the:
    a. Printer logs in the C:\Windows\System32\Logs folder
    b. System logs in the Event Viewer
    c. Application logs in the Event Viewer
    d. Audit logs in the Event Viewer

True / False

Circle T if the statement is true or F if the statement is false.

T | F **1.** A 64-bit version of Windows cannot provide print drivers to 32-bit versions of Windows.

T | F **2.** To create a printer pool, you must have two or more printers that are the same model and use the same printer driver.

T | F **3.** The Advanced tab in Printer Properties allows you to configure the driver to use with the printer and the priority of the printer.

T | F **4.** You need to assign the Manage Documents permission for a user to delete his or her print jobs.

T | F **5.** To modify printer permissions, you need to have the Full Control permission.

■ Case Scenarios

Scenario 8-1: Giving Print Priority to Users

You work for the Contoso Corporation. You have a small office with 8 users. Sometimes, some of the users print large documents that may make other users wait for their print job. The office manager does not want to wait behind those large print jobs so she asks you to configure it so that she prints before the large print jobs. What can you do to solve this problem?

Scenario 8-2: Having UNIX Users Print to Your Printer

You work for the Contoso Corporation. You have two users running UNIX workstations. They would like to print to your printer. What would you need to set up on the Windows computer so that you can print? Hint: If you don't know, look at Windows Features under Program and Features (Control Panel). Then to fill in the blanks, use the Internet and Windows 7 help files.

Dealing with Software Issues

OBJECTIVE DOMAIN MATRIX

TECHNOLOGY SKILL	OBJECTIVE DOMAIN	OBJECTIVE NUMBER
Configuring Application Compatibility	Identify and resolve new software installation issues.	1.1
Configuring Application Compatibility	Identify and resolve software configuration issues.	1.2
Troubleshooting Applications	Identify cause of and resolve software failure issues.	1.3

KEY TERMS

Application Compatibility
Manager (ACM)

Application Compatibility
Toolkit (ACT)

AppLocker

compatibility settings

Internet Explorer
Compatibility Test Tool

Program Compatibility
Troubleshooter

Setup Analysis Tool (SAT)

software shim

software program

software restrictions

Standard User
Analyzer (SUA)

Windows XP Mode

After completing this lesson, you will be able configure and troubleshoot applications to run on Windows 7, including older applications that were made for older versions of Windows. In addition, you will be able to restrict the applications that can be executed on a Windows 7 computer.

You just purchased several new machines with Windows 7 and need to put the standard accounting program on them. So you double-click on setup.exe, but you get an error message saying that this software is incompatible with your version of Windows. You need to get this software installed quickly so the accountants can do their job.

■ Installing Programs, Roles, and Features

THE BOTTOM LINE

A *software program* is a sequence of instructions written to perform a specified task for a computer. When you install a program on a computer running Windows 7, you are executing an executable (usually a file with a .exe or .msi filename extension). Of course, when you start a program, you double-click an icon which is usually a shortcut to the executable file.

Managing Programs

Since Windows only has a limited number of built-in applications such as Word Pad, you will most likely need to install programs such as Microsoft Office. Therefore, you need to know how to install and uninstall these applications.

If you need to install a program in Windows such as an anti-virus software package or Microsoft office that does not come with Windows 7, you often insert the disk, usually a CD or DVD into the drive and the installation program will automatically start. Others will be downloaded and installed over the Internet or over your organization's network. For other programs, you may need to run a command, download and install using your browser, or double-click on an executable file such as a file with an .exe or a .msi extension.

Most Windows programs allow you to uninstall a program from your computer if you no longer use it or if you want to free up space on your hard disk. For Windows 7, you can use the Control Panel's Programs and Features to uninstall programs or to change a program's configuration by adding or removing certain options.

UNINSTALL OR CHANGE A PROGRAM

GET READY. To uninstall a program or change a program in Windows 7:

1. Open the Control Panel.
2. If you are in Category view, click Programs, and click Programs and Features. If you are in Icon view, double-click Programs and Features.
3. Select a program such as Adobe Acrobat Reader, and then click Uninstall. See Figure 9-1.

Figure 9-1

Programs and Features

If the program you want to uninstall isn't listed, it might not have been certified for or registered with Windows. You should check the documentation for the software.

Some programs include the option to repair the program in addition to uninstalling it, but many simply offer the option to uninstall. To change the program, click Change or Repair. If you are prompted for an administrator password or confirmation, type the password or provide confirmation.

■ Configuring Application Compatibility

THE BOTTOM LINE

Anytime a new version of Windows is released, there is always a chance that some of your applications will have problems running on the new version of Windows. While Windows 7 is considered an improved version of Windows Vista, there are some Windows XP applications that will not run on Windows 7 or require some extra configuration to make the application work. In addition, you may encounter problems with applications that were written for Windows Vista.

CERTIFICATION READY
What tools can you use to resolve problems when installing a program?
1.1

Most programs written for Windows Vista also work in this version of Windows, but some older programs might run poorly or not at all. If a program written for an earlier version of Windows doesn't run correctly, you can try changing the ***compatibility settings*** for the program, either manually or by using the Program Compatibility troubleshooter.

Using Program Compatibility Troubleshooter

CERTIFICATION READY
What options are available that will allow older programs to run on Windows 7?
1.2

The ***Program Compatibility Troubleshooter*** is essentially a wizard that simplifies the process of selecting compatibility mode settings for an executable file.

The Program Compatibility Troubleshooter gives the user an easy method to use to get an older application to work on a computer running Windows 7 by configuring various compatibility mechanisms that are part of Windows 7.

To run the Program Compatibility Troubleshooter, right-click an executable file or a shortcut to an executable file, and select Troubleshoot Compatibility from the context menu. After it tries to determine what is preventing the program from running properly, it will then give two options:

- Try Recommended Settings
- Troubleshoot Program

When you select Troubleshoot Program, it will start a series of questions asking if the program worked in a previous version of Windows, if the program has display problems, and if the program requires additional permissions.

If you have trouble installing a program, you can also use the troubleshooter on the program's setup file such as setup.exe or install.exe. Unfortunately, the troubleshooter is not designed to work on programs that have a .msi filename extension.

Setting Compatibility Modes

Instead of using the Program Compatibility Troubleshooter, you can configure the same compatibility mode settings for the executable.

To change compatibility settings manually for a program, right-click the program icon, click Properties, and then click the Compatibility tab. The compatibility settings include:

- **Compatibility mode:** Runs the program using settings from a previous version of Windows. Try this setting if you know the program is designed for (or worked in) a specific previous version of Windows. The Windows emulation modes are as follows:

- Windows 95
- Windows 98/Windows Me
- Windows NT 4.0 (Service Pack 5)
- Windows 2000
- Windows XP (Service Pack 2)
- Windows XP (Service Pack 3)
- Windows Server 2003 (Service Pack 1)
- Windows Server 2008 (Service Pack 1)
- Windows Vista
- Windows Vista (Service Pack 1)
- Windows Vista (Service Pack 2)

- **Run in 256 colors:** Uses a limited set of colors in the program. Some older programs are designed to use fewer colors.
- **Run in 640 × 480 screen resolution:** Runs the program in a smaller-sized window. Try this setting if the graphical user interface appears jagged or is rendered improperly.
- **Disable visual themes:** Disables themes on the program. Try this setting if you notice problems with the menus or buttons on the title bar of the program.
- **Disable desktop composition:** Turns off transparency and other advanced display features. Choose this setting if window movement appears erratic or you notice other display problems.
- **Disable display scaling on high DPI settings:** Turns off automatic resizing of programs if large-scale font size is in use. Try this setting if large-scale fonts are interfering with the appearance of the program.
- **Run this program as an administrator:** Runs the program as an administrator. Some programs require administrator privileges to run properly. If you are not currently logged on as an administrator, this option is not available.
- **Change settings for all users:** By default, the executable or shortcut you select retains the compatibility mode settings for the user currently logged on. This lets you choose settings that will apply to all users on this computer.

See Figure 9-2.

Figure 9-2

Compatibility tab

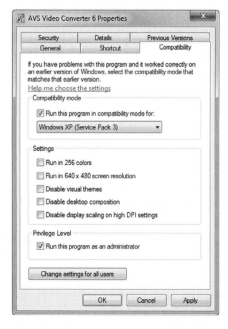

Configuring Application Compatibility Policies

As with many Wind[...] can use group policies to configure compatibility mode settings i[...]pplication compatibility warnings.

[...]n compatibility warnings, administrators can use the Group Policy [...] a GPO at Computer Configuration\Administrative Templates\System\ [...]ng and Diagnostics\Application Compatibility Diagnostics.

[...]pplication Compatibility Diagnostics settings are as follows:

- **Notify blocked drivers:** Specifies whether the Program Compatibility Assistant (PCA) should notify users when drivers are blocked for compatibility reasons.
- **Detect application failures caused by deprecated com objects:** Specifies whether the PCA should attempt to detect the creation of COM objects that no longer exist in Windows 7.
- **Detect application failures caused by deprecated windows DLLs:** Specifies whether the PCA should detect attempts to load DLLs that no longer exist in Windows 7.
- **Detect application install failures:** Specifies whether the PCA should attempt to detect application installation failures and prompt to restart the installation in compatibility mode.
- **Detect application installers that need to be run as administrator:** Specifies whether the PCA should detect application installations that failed due to a lack of administrative privileges and prompt to restart the installation as an administrator.
- **Detect applications unable to launch installers under UAC:** Specifies whether the PCA should detect the failure of child installer processes to launch due to the lack of elevated privileges.

Administrators can also limit users' access to compatibility mode controls using Group Policy. These settings are located in Computer Configuration\Administrative Templates\Windows Components\Application Compatibility.

- **Prevent access to 16-bit applications:** Disables the MS-DOS subsystem on the computer, preventing 16-bit applications from running.
- **Remove Program Compatibility Property Page:** Removes the Compatibility tab from the Properties sheets of executables and shortcuts.
- **Turn off Application Telemetry:** Disables the application telemetry engine, which tracks anonymous usage of Windows system components by applications.
- **Turn off Application Compatibility Engine:** Prevents the computer from looking up applications in the compatibility database, boosting system performance but possibly affecting the execution of legacy applications.
- **Turn off Program Compatibility Assistant:** Disables the PCA, preventing the system from displaying compatibility warnings during application installations and startups.
- **Turn off Program Inventory:** Prevents the system from inventorying programs and files and sending the resulting information to Microsoft.
- **Turn off Switchback Compatibility Engine:** Prevents the computer from providing generic compatibility mitigations to older applications, thus boosting performance.
- **Turn off Problem Steps Recorder:** Prevents the computer from capturing the steps taken by the user before experiencing a problem.

Using the Application Compatibility Toolkit

To assist in resolving compatibility issues, Microsoft has introduced the Microsoft *Application Compatibility Toolkit (ACT)*. Although it is aimed at the corporate environment and is to be used to determine before software deployment whether the software is compatible with Windows 7, it can also be used by individuals.

ACT has the following features:

- Verify your application's, device's, and computer's compatibility with a new version of the Windows operating system, including determining your risk assessment.
- Verify the compatibility of Windows Update, including determining your risk assessment.
- Become involved in the ACT Community, including sharing your application assessment with other ACT users.
- Test your applications for issues related to User Account Control (UAC) by using the Standard User Analyzer (SUA) tool.
- Test your web applications and web sites for compatibility with new releases and security updates to Internet Explorer, by using the Internet Explorer Compatibility Test Tool.

The tools included in the kit are as follows:

- Application Compatibility Manager
- Compatibility Administrator
- Internet Explorer Compatibility Test Tool
- Setup Analysis Tool
- Standard User Analyzer

The *Application Compatibility Manager (ACM)* is a tool that enables you to configure, to collect, and to analyze your data, so that you can fix any issues prior to deploying a new operating system in your organization.

The Compatibility Manager tool enables you to resolve many application-compatibility issues before deploying a new version of the Windows operating system to your organization by:

- Providing individual compatibility fixes, compatibility modes, and AppHelp messages that you can use to resolve specific compatibility issues.
- Enabling you to create custom-compatibility fixes, compatibility modes, AppHelp messages, and compatibility databases.
- Providing a query tool that enables you to search for installed fixes on your local computers.

A *software shim* is a compatibility fix that consists of a small library that transparently intercepts certain application calls and changes the parameters passed, handles the operation itself, or redirects the operation elsewhere so that the application will operate properly. It is usually used for older applications that rely on older functionality that may have been altered for Windows 7.

The Internet Explorer Compatibility Test Tool (IECTT) provides a user interface that collects compatibility information for web pages and web-based applications in real time with Windows Internet Explorer 7 and 8.

To use the *Internet Explorer Compatibility Test Tool*, you simply run the program, click enable, and use Internet Explorer to access the sites you want to test. An icon appears in the IE status bar, indicating that Internet Explorer compatibility evaluation logging is turned on, and log entries begin to appear in the tool's Live Data window.

The *Setup Analysis Tool (SAT)* automates the running of application installations while monitoring the actions taken by each application's installer. The stand-alone version of SAT can monitor any Windows and third-party installers. However, the Virtual SAT tool can only monitor Windows and third-party installers that run unattended.

The **Standard User Analyzer (SUA)** tool enables you to test your applications and monitor API calls to detect potential compatibility issues due to the User Account Control (UAC) feature in both Windows Vista and Windows 7. Since UAC requires that all users run as Standard Users until the application needs administrative permissions, unfortunately, not all applications can run properly with the Standard User role due to the application requiring access and privileges for locations that are unavailable to a Standard User.

✚ MORE INFORMATION

For more information about Application Compatibility Manager, visit the following website:
http://technet.microsoft.com/en-us/library/cc766464(WS.10).aspx

---

Download ✱

To download ACT 5.6, visit the following website:
http://www.microsoft.com/downloads/details.aspx? FamilyId=24DA89E9-B581-47B0-B45E-492DD6DA2971&displaylang=en.

TAKE NOTE ✱

If you are running the 64-bit version of Windows 7, you will not be able to run 16-bit applications.

■ Using Windows XP Mode

↓ THE BOTTOM LINE

If you have an application that you cannot get to run on Windows 7 using the Compatibility settings or ACT, you can use Windows XP Mode to create a virtual machine running Windows XP on a computer running Windows 7.

Virtualization has become quite popular during the last few years. By using virtual machine technology, you can run multiple operating systems concurrently on a single machine, which allows you to separate services and keep costs to a minimum. It can also be used to create a Windows test environment in a safe, self-contained manner.

To run several virtual machines on a single computer, you will need to have sufficient processing power and memory to handle the load. However, since most computers often sit idle, virtualization can help utilize the server's hardware more efficiently.

TAKE NOTE ✱

No matter what processor platform Windows 7 is using, the virtual Windows XP machine is the x86 version of Windows XP Professional SP3. You can therefore only use Windows XP Mode to run x86 applications.

Using **Windows XP Mode**, you can run programs that were designed for Windows XP on computers running Windows 7 Professional, Enterprise, or Ultimate editions. Windows XP Mode runs in a separate window on the Windows 7 desktop like a program, except it's a fully functional version of Windows XP. In Windows XP Mode, you can access your physical computer's CD/DVD drive, install programs, save files, and perform other tasks as if you were using a computer running Windows XP. When you install a program in Windows XP Mode, the program appears in both the Windows XP Mode list of programs and in the Windows 7 list of programs, so you can open the program directly from Windows 7.

To use Windows XP Mode, you need to download and install Windows XP Mode, which is a fully licensed version of Windows XP with Service Pack 3. You also need to download and install Windows Virtual PC, which is the program that runs virtual operating systems on your computer.

⚠ WARNING The hardware requirements may change with future service packs.

To run Windows XP Mode, you need a computer that is capable of hardware virtualization (Intel-VT or AMD-V virtualization) and BIOS that supports hardware virtualization. Virtualization must also be enabled in the BIOS Setup program. It is also recommended that you have 2 GB of memory and an additional 15 GB of hard disk space per virtual Windows environment.

INSTALL WINDOWS XP MODE

GET READY. To install Windows XP Mode:

1. Go to http://www.microsoft.com/windows/virtual-pc/ and click Get Windows XP Mode and Windows Virtual PC now.
2. Under Select your edition of Windows 7 and desired language for installation in step 2, click the Select system drop-down list, and then click the edition of Windows 7 you're currently running.
3. Click the Select language drop-down list, and then click the language you want to use.
4. Under Download and install Windows XP Mode, click Windows XP Mode.
5. Click Open to install the program immediately; or click Save to save the installation file to your computer, double-click the file, and then click Run.
6. In the Welcome to Setup for Windows XP Mode dialog box, click Next.
7. Choose the location for the virtual hard disk file that Windows XP Mode uses, or accept the default location, and then click Next.
8. On the Setup Completed screen, click Finish.

 DOWNLOAD AND INSTALL WINDOWS VIRTUAL PC

GET READY. To download and install Windows Virtual PC:

1. Go to http://www.microsoft.com/windows/virtual-pc/ and then click Get Windows XP Mode and Windows Virtual PC now.
2. Under Select your edition of Windows 7 and desired language for installation in step 2, click the Select system drop-down list, and then click the edition of Windows 7 you're currently running.
3. Click the Select language drop-down list, and then click the language you want to use.
4. Under Download and install Windows XP Mode, click Windows Virtual PC.
5. Click Open to install the program immediately; or click Save to save the installation file to your computer, and then double-click the file.
6. Click Yes to install Update for Windows (KB958559).
7. If you accept the license terms, click I Accept.
8. After installation is complete, click Restart Now to restart your computer.

 SET UP WINDOWS XP MODE

GET READY. To set up Windows XP Mode for first use:

1. Click the Start button, click All Programs, click Windows Virtual PC, and then click Windows XP Mode.
2. If you accept the license terms, click I accept the license terms, and then click Next.
3. On the Installation folder and credentials page, accept the default location where Windows XP Mode files will be stored, or choose a new location.
4. Type a password, type it again to confirm it, and then click Next.
5. On the *Help protect your computer* page, decide whether you want to help protect your computer by turning on automatic updates, and then click Next.
6. Click Start Setup. After setup is complete, Windows XP Mode opens in a separate window.

INSTALL AND USE A PROGRAM IN WINDOWS XP MODE

GET READY. To install and use a program in Windows XP Mode:

1. In Windows 7, click the Start button, click All Programs, click Windows Virtual PC, and then click Windows XP Mode.
2. In Windows XP Mode, insert the program's installation disk into your computer's CD/DVD drive; or browse to the program's installation file, open the file, and follow the instructions to install the program.
3. Click the Close button at the top of the Windows XP Mode window.
4. In Windows 7, click the Start button, click Windows Virtual PC, click Windows XP Mode Applications, and then click the program you want to open.

 If the Windows XP Mode window is open when you try opening a program in Windows XP Mode from Windows 7, you'll be prompted to close the virtual machine. Be sure to save any data you want to keep in Windows XP Mode before closing it. In addition, be aware that anti-virus software isn't included with Windows XP Mode. Even if your computer running Windows 7 already has anti-virus software, you should also install anti-virus software in Windows XP Mode to help defend your computer against viruses.

■ Restricting Applications

 One of the most powerful features of using a Windows environment is group policies, which can be used to configure or manage the user's working environment. To help manage a person's computer, you can use group policies to create a uniform workstation environment while controlling what applications are installed or not installed on a system. By preventing applications from being installed, you can reduce the possibility of malware infiltration as well as any software package that may interfere with the operation of the computer.

Windows 7 supports two mechanisms for restricting applications. They are:

- Software restriction policies
- AppLocker

Understanding Software Restriction Policies

Software restriction policies, which have been included in Windows since Windows XP and Windows Server 2003, are rules that specify which applications users can run. When you use the software restriction policies, you can identify and specify the software that is allowed to run so that you can protect your computer environment from untrusted code or programs.

To create rules, you must open a Group Policy object (GPO) and browse to Computer Configuration\Windows Settings\Security Settings\Software Restriction Policies. Right-click the Software Restriction Polices object and, from the context menu, select Create Software Restriction Policies.

You can create rules based on one of the following:

- **Certificate rules:** Identify applications based on the inclusion of a certificate signed by the software publisher. An application can continue to match this type of rule, even if the executable file is updated, as long as the certificate remains valid.

- **Hash rules:** Identify applications based on a digital fingerprint that remains valid even when the name or location of the executable file changes.
- **Network zone rules:** Identify Windows Installer (.msi) packages downloaded with Internet Explorer based on the security zone of the site from which they are downloaded.
- **Path rules:** Identify applications by specifying a file or folder name or a registry key. The potential vulnerability of this type of rule is that any file can match the rule, as long as it has the correct name or location.

See Figure 9-3.

Figure 9-3

Software Restriction Policies

Software restriction policies can work in three ways, based on the settings you choose for each of the rules. The three possible settings are:

- **Disallowed:** Prevents an application that matches a rule from running.
- **Basic user:** Allows all applications that do not require administrative privileges to run. Allows applications that require administrative privileges to run only if they match a rule.
- **Unrestricted:** Allows an application that matches a rule to run.

If you have defined one or more of the previous rules, and an application does not match any of the rules you defined, it will then apply the default rule. To configure the default rule, you select one of the policies in the Security Levels folder and click Set As Default on its Properties sheet.

The most secure method would be to set the default rule to Disallowed and then create additional Unrestricted rules for the applications you want your users to be able to run. This prevents them from launching any applications other than the ones you specify.

If you have multiple rules that apply to a single application, you may have a conflict. Therefore, the more specific rule takes precedence over the less specific. Thus, the order of precedence is as follows:

1. Hash rules
2. Certificate rules
3. Path rules
4. Zone rules
5. Default rule

Using AppLocker

AppLocker is a new feature in Windows Server 2008 R2 and Windows 7 that enables you to use advanced software restrictions. AppLocker contains new capabilities and extensions that allow you to create rules to allow or deny applications from running based on unique identities of files and to specify which users or groups can run those applications. AppLocker is more flexible than software restriction policies and much easier to administer.

AppLocker helps reduce administrative overhead and the organization's cost of managing computing resources by decreasing the number of help desk calls that result from users running unapproved applications. Using AppLocker, you can:

- Control the following types of applications: executable files (.exe and .com), scripts (.js, .ps1, .vbs, .cmd, and .bat), Windows Installer files (.msi and .msp), and DLL files (.dll and .ocx).
- Define rules based on file attributes derived from the digital signature, including the publisher, product name, filename, and file version.
- Assign a rule to a security group or an individual user.
- Create exceptions to rules.
- Use audit-only mode to deploy the policy and understand its impact before enforcing it.
- Import and export rules.
- Streamline creating and managing AppLocker rules by using Windows PowerShell cmdlets.

The primary disadvantage of AppLocker is that you can only apply the policies to computers running Windows 7 and Windows Server 2008 R2.

The AppLocker settings are located in Group Policy objects in the Computer Configuration\Windows Settings\Security Settings\Application Control Policies\AppLocker container. In the AppLocker container, there are three nodes that contain the basic rule types:

- **Executable Rules:** Contains rules that apply to files with .exe and .com extensions.
- **Windows Installer Rules:** Contains rules that apply to Windows Installer packages with .msi and .msp extensions.
- **Script Rules:** Contains rules that apply to script files with .ps1, .bat, .cmd, .vbs, and .js extensions.

See Figure 9-4.

Figure 9-4

AppLocker settings

Each of the rules you create in each of these containers can allow or block access to specific resources, based on one of the following criteria:

- **Publisher:** Identifies code-signed applications by means of a digital signature extracted from an application file. You can also create publisher rules that apply to all future versions of an application.
- **Path:** Identifies applications by specifying a file or folder name. The potential vulnerability of this type of rule is that any file can match the rule, as long as it has the correct name or location.
- **File Hash:** Identifies applications based on a digital fingerprint that remains valid even when the name or location of the executable file changes. This type of rule functions much like its equivalent in software restriction policies; in AppLocker, however, the process of creating the rules and generating file hashes is much easier.

By default, AppLocker blocks all executables, installer packages, and scripts, except for those specified in Allow rules. Therefore, to use AppLocker, you must create rules that enable users to access the files needed for Windows to run the system's installed applications. The easiest way to do this is to right-click each of the three rules containers and select Create Default Rules from the context menu. To make it more flexible, you can then replicate, modify, and delete the default rules as needed, and you can create your own rules.

While you have to manually create each rule with software restrictions, with AppLocker you can create rules manually or automatically. To create rules automatically, right-click one of the three rules containers and select Create Rules Automatically from the context menu. An Automatically Generate Rules Wizard appears. After specifying the folder to be analyzed and the users or groups to which the rules should apply, a *Rule Preferences* page appears where you select the types of rules you want to create. The wizard then displays a summary of its results in the *Review Rules* page and adds the rules to the container.

To create a rule manually, you can start a wizard-based interface by selecting Create New Rule from the context menu for one of the three rule containers. The wizard prompts you for the following information:

- **Action:** Specifies whether you want to allow or deny the user or group access to the resource. In AppLocker, explicit deny rules always override allow rules.
- **User or group:** Specifies the name of the user or group to which the policy should apply.
- **Conditions:** Specifies whether you want to create a publisher, path, or file hash rule. The wizard generates an additional page for whichever option you select, enabling you to configure its parameters.
- **Exceptions:** Enables you to specify exceptions to the rule you are creating, using any of the three conditions: publisher, path, or file hash.

■ Troubleshooting Applications

THE BOTTOM LINE

When a user is having a problem with an application, you need to stick to a troubleshooting methodology model to determine the real cause and to come up with a fix or workaround to overcome the problem.

CERTIFICATION READY
Where can you look for hints on why an application is failing?
1.3

As with any problem, you should first identify the problem and determine its scope. Does the problem occur on one computer only or does it involve multiple computers. You also need to determine if it is a local application, a network application or a local application that requires network access to fulfill its task. If the problem exists on more than one computer, what do the computers have in common? Check the version and edition of Windows, the Service Pack of Windows, the version of Internet Explorer, and so on.

If the application worked before, you then need to ask if anything has changed. Check for changes to the computer (directly or remotely such as through group policies) or changes to the network or the servers that host network services required by the application. You should also check the Event Viewer, specifically the System and Application logs: check for any logs that the application itself may create and manage on its own. You should also verify the configuration of the software. Before doing more drastic things, try to research the problem on the Internet or with the vendor.

Other things that you should check or try:

- Verify that the application works with the specific operating system and Internet Explorer version.
- Try the Compatibility mode, especially if the application worked in a previous version of Windows. If this does not work, consider trying Windows XP Mode or applying a shim, if one exists.
- If the application requires network connectivity, check firewalls and proxy settings.
- Check whether the application requires any other applications like .NET Framework or Java.
- Try running the application while Windows is in safe mode to determine if another component is causing the application not to run properly.
- If the application depends on a service running on your computer, verify that the service is running.
- Check whether the application requires additional privileges or the NTFS folders require additional permissions.
- Disable UAC if enabled.
- Check whether the application requires licensing and make sure the correct licensing is applied.
- If it is a web application that runs through Internet Explorer, try compatibility mode. You should also determine whether Internet Explorer Protected Mode is affecting the application and related security settings such as Internet zone and security settings. Internet Explorer will be discussed in more detail in later in the book.
- Finally, if the problem is only with the one computer, you can try to reinstall the application. If that does not work, you can try a System Restore or a restore from backup.
- Don't forget to check the vendor's website (as well as the rest of the Internet) for the errors and symptoms to see if they have steps to overcome the problem and to check for patches and hotfixes.

If you are trying to install an application and it fails or will not install, you should try most of the previous list including checking rights and permissions of the user, checking for dependencies, checking for compatibility, and checking for licensing. You should also verify the installation media to make sure it is complete and not corrupt.

SKILL SUMMARY

IN THIS LESSON YOU LEARNED:

- A software program is a sequence of instructions written to perform a specified task for a computer.
- For Windows 7, you can use Programs and Features to uninstall programs or to change a program's configuration by adding or removing certain options.
- The Program Compatibility Troubleshooter gives the user an easy method to configure an older application to work on a computer running Windows 7 by configuring various compatibility mechanisms that are part of Windows 7.

- To run the Program Compatibility Troubleshooter, you right-click an executable file or a shortcut to an executable file and select Troubleshoot Compatibility from the context menu.

- To change compatibility settings manually for a program, right-click the program icon, click Properties, and then click the Compatibility tab.

- As with many Windows Computers, you can use group policies to configure compatibility mode settings including suppressing application compatibility warnings.

- To assist in resolving compatibility issues, Microsoft has introduced the Microsoft Application Compatibility Toolkit (ACT).

- The Application Compatibility Manager (ACM) is a tool that enables you to configure, to collect, and to analyze your data, so that you can fix any issues prior to deploying a new operating system in your organization.

- A shim is a compatibility fix that consists of a small library that transparently intercepts certain application calls and changes the parameters passed, handles the operation itself, or redirects the operation elsewhere so that the application will operate properly.

- If you have an application that you cannot get to run on Windows 7 using the Compatibility settings or ACT, you can use Windows XP Mode to create a virtual machine running Windows XP on your computer running Windows 7.

- To run Windows XP Mode, you need a computer that is capable of hardware virtualization (Intel-VT or AMD-V virtualization) and BIOS that supports hardware virtualization.

- To help manage a person's computer, you can use group policies to create a uniform workstation environment while controlling what applications are installed or not installed on a system.

- By not allowing applications to be installed, you can reduce the possibility of malware infiltration as well as eliminate any software package that may interfere with the operation of the computer.

- When you use the software restriction policies, you can identify and specify the software that is allowed to run so that you can protect your computer environment from untrusted code or programs.

- AppLocker is a new feature in Windows Server 2008 R2 and Windows 7 that enables you to use advanced software restrictions. AppLocker contains new capabilities and extensions that allow you to create rules to allow or deny applications from running based on unique identities of files and to specify which users or groups can run those applications.

- When a user is having a problem with an application, you need to stick to a troubleshooting methodology model to determine the real cause and to come up with a fix or work around to overcome the problem.

■ Knowledge Assessment

Fill in the Blank

Complete the following sentences by writing the correct word or words in the blanks provided.

1. A _____ is a sequence of instructions written to perform a specified task for a computer.

2. If a program written for an earlier version of Windows doesn't run correctly, you can try changing the _____ .

3. To suppress application compatibility warnings, you would use _____ .

4. Application Compatibility Manager (ACM), Compatibility Administrator Tool, and Internet Explorer Compatibility Test Tool are found in _____ .

5. A _____ is a compatibility fix that consists of a small library that transparently intercepts certain application calls and changes the parameters passed, handles the operation itself, or redirects the operation elsewhere so that the application will work properly.

6. If you cannot get an application to run on Windows 7 using the compatibility settings, you can use _____ .

7. Windows XP mode is based on _____ version of Windows XP.

8. Application restrictions are configured using _____ .

9. Windows XP mode requires a computer that is capable of _____ .

10. If you want to limit access to a DLL, you would use _____ .

Multiple Choice

Circle the letter that corresponds to the best answer.

1. Typically to uninstall an application in Windows, you would use _____ from the Control Panel.
   a. Programs and Features
   b. Add/Remove Programs
   c. Remove Programs
   d. Uninstall All

2. What is a wizard that simplifies the process of selecting compatibility mode settings for an executable file?
   a. Mode Settings wizard
   b. Backward Settings
   c. Program Compatibility Troubleshooter
   d. Try Me Now Settings

3. What tool allows you to detect potential compatibility issues due to the User Account Control (UAC) feature?
   a. Application Compatibility Manager
   b. Application Compatibility Toolkit
   c. Internet Explorer Compatibility Test Tool
   d. Standard User Analyzer

4. Which of the following is NOT a compatibility mode you can configure for an application?
   a. Windows 3.1
   b. Windows 95
   c. Windows NT 4.0
   d. Windows Vista

5. Which compatibility settings should you select if you notice problems with menus or buttons on the title bar of the program?
   a. Run in 256 colors
   b. Run in 640 x 480 screen resolution
   c. Disable virtual themes
   d. Disable display scaling on high DPI settings

6. AppLocker is configured using _____ .
   a. Registry Editor
   b. AppLocker Commander

    c. Command prompt

    d. Group policies

7. Which of the following CANNOT be used as a rule when configuring software restriction policies?

    a. Certificate rules

    b. Hash rules

    c. Network zone rules

    d. Location rules

8. When configuring software restriction policies for an application that does not match any of the rules, it should _____.

    a. Use Unrestricted

    b. Use Disallowed

    c. Use the default rule

    d. Remove the application

9. If a program must run as an administrator, you should select _____.

    a. Upgrade

    b. RunAs

    c. Privilege Level

    d. Disable display scaling on high DPI settings

10. AppLocker creates rules based the following except _____.

    a. Publisher

    b. Path

    c. File Hash

    d. Network zone

True / False

Circle T if the statement is true or F if the statement is false.

T | F 1. You decide you don't need a program on your system. Therefore, to remove it, you should delete the folder where the program resides.

T | F 2. When a program will not run under Windows 7 compatibility settings, you should then try Windows XP Mode.

T | F 3. A PIM is a compatibility fix that can correct a wide range of applications.

T | F 4. If an application cannot communicate over the network, you should check the firewalls.

T | F 5. Windows XP Mode is a virtual machine running on your Windows 7 box.

■ Case Scenarios

Scenario 9-1: Working with a 32-bit Application

You work for the Contoso Corporation's Help Desk. You have a 32-bit version graphics drawing program that you cannot install on your 64-bit edition of Windows 7. You last used this application on your computer running Windows XP. What options do you have in trying to get this to work?

Scenario 9-2: IT Department Tools

You work for the Contoso Corporation IT department. The CIO walks up to you and says that he noticed an employee playing a game. He then asks what tools could be used to make sure that games and other unauthorized programs cannot be executed on the corporate computers? What should you tell your CIO?

Dealing with Performance Issues

OBJECTIVE DOMAIN MATRIX

TECHNOLOGY SKILL	OBJECTIVE DOMAIN	OBJECTIVE NUMBER
Troubleshooting Performance Problems	Identify and resolve performance issues.	3.1

KEY TERMS

bottleneck	Performance Monitor (performon.exe)	Resource Monitor
paging file	power management	Task Manager
performance	power plan	virtual memory

After completing this lesson, you will be able understand what components contribute to a computer's performance. You will also be able to use the various tools that come with Windows 7 to determine if any of these components are causing a bottleneck and if a program is hogging the resources on your computer.

You work as a help desk technician for the Acme Corporation. You got a call that a user's computer is running really slow, so slow that he cannot do his work. You go to the user's computer and confirm that the computer is running so slow that when you click on anything, you have to wait at least 3 to 5 seconds for the computer to respond. You need to determine why the machine is running this way.

■ Understanding Performance

THE BOTTOM LINE

Performance is the overall effectiveness of how data moves through the system. Of course, it is important to select the proper hardware (processor, memory, disk system, and network) to satisfy the expected performance goals. Without the proper hardware, bottlenecks limit the effectiveness of software.

When a component limits overall performance, that component is known as a ***bottleneck***. When you relieve one bottleneck, another bottleneck may be triggered. For example, one of the most common bottlenecks is the amount of memory the system has. By increasing the memory, you can often increase the overall performance of a system (up to a point). However, when you add more RAM, then RAM needs to be fed more data from the disk. Therefore, the disk becomes the bottleneck. So, although the system may become faster, if your performance is still lacking, you will have to look for new bottlenecks.

You usually cannot identify performance problems just by taking a quick look at performance. Instead, you need a baseline. You can get one by analyzing the performance when the system is running normally and within design specifications. Then when a problem occurs, you compare the current performance to your baseline to see what is different. Since performance can also change gradually over time, it is highly recommended that you baseline your computer regularly so that you can chart your performance measures and identify trends. This will give you an idea about when the server needs to be upgraded or replaced or the workload of the server reduced.

There are several tools available with Windows for you to analyze performance. They include:

- Windows Experience Index
- Task Manager
- Performance Monitor
- Resource Monitor

Using Windows Experience Index

In today's computer world, it is sometimes hard to figure out which PC is running faster than another PC, which can make it difficult to determine if a computer can run a particular software application. Starting with Windows Vista, Windows client operating systems include the Windows Experience Index. This is a tool that measures the capabilities of your computer's hardware and software configuration and expresses the measurement as a base score.

Since the base score will look at processor, memory, disk, and video performance, it can give you an idea of how well your computer can perform. The scores currently range from 1.0 to 7.9. A higher base score generally means that your computer will perform better and faster than a computer with a lower base score.

 VIEW THE WINDOWS EXPERIENCE INDEX

GET READY. To access the Windows Experience Index:

1. Right-click Computer and select Properties.
2. Click Windows Experience Index. See Figure 10-1.

If you recently upgraded your hardware including changing drivers and want to find out if your score has changed, click Re-run the assessment.

The Windows Experience Index is designed to accommodate advances in computer technology. As hardware speed and performance improve, higher score ranges will be enabled. The standards for each level of the index generally stay the same. However, in some cases, new tests might be developed that can result in lower scores.

Here are general descriptions of the experience you can expect from a computer that receives the following base scores:

- **1.0 or 2.0:** Usually has sufficient performance to do general computing tasks. However a computer with this base score is generally not powerful enough to run Aero.

Figure 10-1

WEI scores

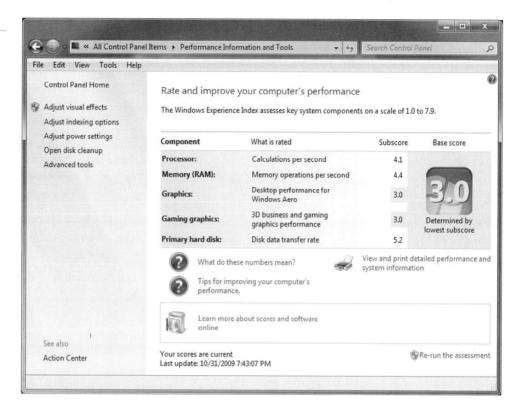

- **3.0:** Can run Aero and many features of Windows 7 at a basic level. Your computer will struggle with a high resolution theme on multiple monitors or struggle to play high-definition television (HDTV) content.
- **4.0 or 5.0:** Can run new features of Windows 7 and can support running multiple programs at the same time.
- **6.0 or 7.0:** Can support high-end, graphics-intensive experiences, such as multiplayer and 3-D gaming and recording and playback of HDTV content.

Understanding Virtual Memory and Paging File

If your computer lacks the RAM needed to run a program or perform an operation, Windows uses *virtual memory* to compensate. Virtual memory combines your computer's RAM with temporary space on your hard disk. When RAM runs low, virtual memory moves data from RAM to space called a *paging file*. Moving data to and from the paging file frees up RAM so your computer can complete its work. Unfortunately, when something needs to be accessed from the virtual memory on hard disk, it is much slower than accessing it directly from RAM. The more RAM you have, the less frequently virtual memory will have to be utilized.

 MANAGE YOUR PAGING FILE

GET READY. To manage your paging file in Windows:

1. Right-click Computer and select Properties.
2. In the left pane, click Advanced system settings. If you are prompted for an administrator password or confirmation, type the password or provide confirmation.
3. On the Advanced tab, under performance, click Settings.
4. Click the Advanced tab, under virtual memory, click Change.

5. Clear the *Automatically manage paging file size for all drives* check box. See Figure 10-2.

Figure 10-2

Configuring the paging file

6. Under Drive [Volume Label], click the drive that contains the paging file you want to change.
7. Click Custom size, type a new size in megabytes in the *Initial size (MB) or Maximum size (MB)* box, click Set, and then click OK.

⚠ **WARNING** When you access the settings for the paging file, Windows 7 will advise you to reboot the computer to accept the new settings. If you don't change anything, you can ignore this warning.

Increases in size usually don't require a restart for the changes to take effect, but if you decrease the size, you will need to restart your computer. It is recommended that you don't disable or delete the paging file.

The default paging file size is equal to 1.5 times the total RAM. However, this default configuration may not be optimal in all cases in particular with 32-bit versions of Windows 7 and some intensive graphic programs. Therefore, unless you have an application that requires a larger paging file, if your system is utilizing more than 1.5 times its RAM, you should considering adding more RAM to your system, assuming that your system can accommodate additional RAM.

In earlier versions of Windows, paging files became essential because RAM was expensive. Today, you can purchase relatively large amounts of RAM for little money. In addition since 64-bit versions of Windows can recognize more than 4 GB of memory, and these systems often have 4 GB or more, it is recommended that you let Windows manage the paging file. The only time you should change the virtual memory settings is when you have multiple physical hard drives. In that case, you can move the paging file to a second drive or have the paging file on both drives.

Using Task Manager

Task Manager gives you a quick glance at performance and provides information about programs and processes running on your computer.

Task Manager is one of the handiest programs you can use to view performance to see which programs are using the most resources on your computer. Using Task Manager, you can see the status of running programs, find programs that have stopped responding, and you can stop a program running in memory.

To start Task Manager, you can right-click the empty space on the taskbar and select Task Manager or you can open the security menu by clicking Ctrl+Alt+Del keys and selecting Start Task Manager. You can also type Ctrl+Shift+Esc to launch the Task Manager directly. When you first start the Task Manager on a computer running Windows 7, there are six tabs:

- **Applications:** Shows the status of currently running programs and programs that have stopped responding. You can end, switch to, or start a program including starting Windows Explorer (explorer.exe) if it stops unexpectedly.

- **Processes:** Shows all processes running in memory and how much processing and memory each process takes up. To see processes owned by other users, you need to select the show processes from all users. To stop a process, right-click the process and select End Process.

- **Services:** Shows all running services.

- **Performance:** Shows the amount of physical memory, CPU usage, and paging file usage.

- **Networking:** Shows how the network interfaces are being used.

- **Users:** Shows the users that are currently logged in and gives you the ability to log off other users.

The Performance tab includes four graphs. The top two graphs show how much CPU is being used both at the moment and for the past few minutes. (If the CPU Usage History graph appears split, your computer either has multiple CPUs, multiple cores, or both.) A high percentage means that programs or processes are requiring a lot of CPU resources, which can slow your computer. If the percentage appears frozen at or near 100%, then a program might not be responding. See Figure 10-3.

Figure 10-3

Performance tab

The bottom two graphs display how much RAM, or physical memory, is being used in megabytes (MB) both at the current moment and for the past few minutes. The percentage of memory being used is listed at the bottom of the Task Manager window. If memory use seems consistently high or slows your computer's performance noticeably, try reducing the number of programs you have open at one time or install more RAM.

To view memory use for individual processes on your computer, click the Processes tab. To view all of the processes currently running on the computer, click Show processes from all users. To end a process, click a process, and then click End Process. See Figure 10-4.

Figure 10-4

Processes tab

If you are an advanced user, you might want to view other advanced memory values on the Processes tab. To do so, click View, click Select Columns, and then select a memory value:

- **Memory—Working Set:** Amount of memory in the private working set plus the amount of memory the process is using that can be shared by other processes.

- **Memory—Peak Working Set:** Maximum amount of working set memory used by the process.

- **Memory—Working Set Delta:** Amount of change in working set memory used by the process.

- **Memory—Commit Size:** Amount of virtual memory that is reserved for use by a process.

- **Memory—Paged Pool:** Amount of committed virtual memory for a process that can be written to another storage medium, such as the hard disk.

- **Memory—Non-paged Pool:** Amount of committed virtual memory for a process that can't be written to another storage medium.

Using Performance Monitor

Windows *Performance Monitor* is a Microsoft Management Console (MMC) snap-in that provides tools for analyzing system performance. It is included in the Computer Management console and it can be executed using perfmon.exe from the Start menu Search box. From a single console, you can monitor application and hardware performance in real time, specify which data you want to collect in logs, define thresholds for alerts and automatic actions, generate reports, and view past performance data in a variety of ways.

Performance Monitor provides a visual display of built-in Windows performance counters, either in real time or as a way to review historical data. You can add performance counters to Performance Monitor by dragging and dropping, or by creating custom data collector sets. It features multiple graph views that enable you to visually review performance log data. You can create custom views in Performance Monitor that can be exported as data collector sets for use with performance and logging features.

Windows Performance Monitor (see Figure 10-5) allows you to combine the following types of information into data collector sets:

- **Performance counters:** Measurements of system state or activity. They can be included in the operating system or can be part of individual applications. Windows Performance Monitor requests the current value of performance counters at specified time intervals.

- **Event trace data:** Collected from trace providers, which are components of the operating system or of individual applications that report actions or events. Output from multiple trace providers can be combined into a trace session.

- **Configuration information:** Collected from key values in the Windows registry. Windows Performance Monitor can record the value of a registry key at a specified time or interval as part of a file.

Figure 10-5

Performance Monitor

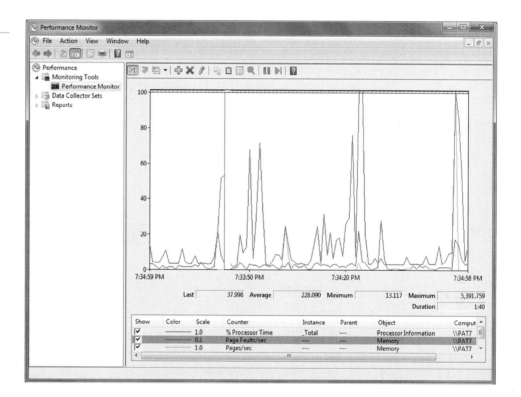

There are hundreds of counters that can be added. Many are included in Task Manager. Others can only be found in the Performance Monitor. They include:

- **%Processor Time:** This counter measures how busy the processor is. Although the processor may jump to 100% usage occasionally, the processor should never stay above 80% all of the time. If the processor usage is consistently high, you should upgrade the processor (use a faster processor or add additional processors) or move some of the services to other systems.

- **Page faults/sec:** A page fault occurs when a process attempts to access a virtual memory page that is not available in its working set in RAM. If the pages/sec is 20 or higher, you should increase the memory.

- **Pages/sec:** If the paging file usage is 1.5 (or higher for specialized applications) you should increase the memory.

- **%Avg. Disk Queue Length:** The average number of read requests or write requests queued for the disk in question. A sustained average higher than 2 indicates that the disk is being over utilized.

- **Interrupts/sec:** The numbers of interrupts generated by hardware the processor was asked to respond to. A sustained value over 1,000 is usually an indication of a problem including poorly configured drivers, errors in drivers, excessive utilization of a device, or hardware failure. Compare this value with the System:Systems Calls/sec or with past threshold values. If the Interrupts/sec is much larger over a sustained period, you probably have a hardware issue.

Using Resource Monitor

Windows Resource Monitor is a system tool that allows you to view information about the use of hardware (CPU, memory, disk, and network) and software (file handles and modules) resources in real time. You can filter the results according to specific processes or services that you want to monitor. In addition, you can use Resource Monitor to start, stop, suspend, and resume processes and services, and to troubleshoot when an application does not respond as expected.

Windows *Resource Monitor* is a powerful tool for understanding how your system resources are used by processes and services. In addition to monitoring resource usage in real time, Resource Monitor can help you analyze unresponsive processes, identify which applications are using files, and control processes and services. To start Resource Monitor, execute the resmon.exe command.

Resource Monitor includes five tabs: Overview, CPU, Memory, Disk, and Network. The Overview tab displays basic system resource usage information; the other tabs display information about each specific resource. Each tab in Resource Monitor includes multiple tables that provide detailed information about the resource featured on that tab. See Figure 10-6.

Figure 10-6

Resource Monitor

IDENTIFY THE PROCESS WITH THE HIGHEST CURRENT CPU USAGE

GET READY. To identify the process with the highest current CPU usage:

1. Click the CPU tab.
2. In Processes, click CPU to sort processes by current CPU resource consumption.

 VIEW SERVICE CPU USAGE

GET READY. To view service CPU usage by process:

1. Click the CPU tab.
2. In Processes, in the Image column, select the check box next to the name of the service for which you want to see usage details. You can select multiple services. Selected services are moved to the top of the column.
3. Click the title bar of Services to expand the table. Review the data in Services to see the list of processes hosted by the selected services, and to view their CPU usage.

 IDENTIFY A PROCESS USING A FILE

GET READY. To identify the process that is using a file:

1. Click the CPU tab, and then click the title bar of Associated Handles to expand the table.
2. Click in the Search Handles box, type the name of the file you want to search for, and then click Search.

 IDENTIFY THE NETWORK ADDRESS THAT A PROCESS CONNECTS TO

GET READY. To identify the network address that a process is connected to:

1. Click the Network tab, and then click the title bar of TCP Connections to expand the table.
2. Locate the process whose network connection you want to identify. If there are a large number of entries in the table, you can click Image to sort by executable filename.
3. Review the Remote Address and Remote Port columns to see which network address and port the process is connected to.

■ Understanding Power Management

THE BOTTOM LINE

Power management is the process of balancing battery life against performance. Windows 7 includes extensive power management capabilities, including support for the Advanced Configuration and Power Interface (ACPI) and the ability to configure these power settings for mobile computers. Windows 7 enables you to fine-tune the power consumption of a mobile computer by configuring individual components to operate at lower power levels. Unfortunately when you conserve power, you usually reduce performance.

As a mobile computer user, when you are not connected to an AC adapter, you are using batteries for power. If you have used a laptop before, you already know that battery life is very limited. In addition, if you were giving a presentation while relying on your computer's battery, and you ran out of power, it could be disastrous. To get the most out of your battery, you need to understand how power settings affect performance so that you can modify the power settings accordingly.

The Power Options control panel is the primary interactive power configuration interface. From this control panel you can select the power plan that the computer should use; modify the settings for the default power plans; and create new, custom power plans of your own.

By default, the Windows 7 desktop contains a power icon in the notification area. The icon will show if the mobile computer is running on AC power or DC power or what percentage of the battery charge currently remains, including an estimated time of power remaining. When you click the icon, it will show the same information mentioned before, and if you right-click the icon, it will show the power plan currently in use. If you click More power options, it will open the Power Options from the Control Panel. You can also right-click the icon to open the Windows Mobility Center or the Power Options control panel.

TAKE NOTE* Some OEMs may include their own power management software and icons. In addition, they often have what they consider an optimal power plan that balances power usage and performance.

Power consumption varies constantly, depending on what you're doing and how long you spend doing it. If you watch a DVD, it will consume more battery power than if you are reading or writing emails. Therefore, the time remaining on the battery meter may sometimes change drastically depending on your activities.

Understanding Power Plans

A *power plan* is a collection of hardware and system settings that manage how your computer uses power. You can use power plans to reduce the amount of power your computer uses, maximize performance, or balance the two.

Windows 7 includes the following power plans to help you manage your computer's power:

- **Balanced:** Offers full performance when you need it and saves power during periods of inactivity. This is the best power plan for most people.
- **Power saver:** Saves power by reducing system performance and screen brightness. This plan can help laptop users get the most from a single battery charge.
- **High performance:** Maximizes screen brightness and might increase the computer's performance in some circumstances. This plan uses a lot more energy and will reduce the amount of time that a laptop battery lasts between charges.

 USE THE HIGH PERFORMANCE POWER OPTION

GET READY. By default, the high performance power option doesn't appear on the battery meter. To turn on High performance:

1. Open Power Options by clicking the Start button, and then clicking Control Panel.
2. In the search box, type power options, and then click Power Options.
3. Under *Select a power plan*, click Show additional plans, and then click High performance.

If you want to use different settings than what is included in these power plans, you can create your own power plan using one of these plans as a starting point. You can change the following settings for individual power plans including how long your computer sleeps after a specified period of inactivity, how long to turn off the display during periods of inactivity, and how to adjust the brightness of your display.

➔ CHANGE A SINGLE POWER PLAN

GET READY. To change settings for a single plan:

1. Open the Power Options in the Control Panel. See Figure 10-7.

Figure 10-7

Power options

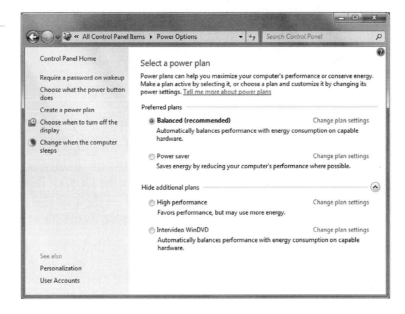

2. Under the plan that you want to change, click Change plan settings.

3. On the *Change settings for the plan* page, choose the display and sleep settings that you want to use when your computer is running on battery (if applicable) and when it's plugged in.

4. For more Advanced options, click the Change advanced power settings option. See Figure 10-8.

Figure 10-8

Power Plan advanced options

In Power Options, some of the links in the left pane open System Settings. When you make changes on this page, changes are automatically made to all of your power plans.

By changing system settings, you can help secure your computer by requiring a password to unlock it when it wakes from sleep. Choose what your computer does when you press the power and sleep buttons on your keyboard or laptop frame or, with some laptops, when you close the lid. For example, when you press the power button, the computer can either do nothing or it can shut down. If the computer supports sleep and hibernate, pressing the power button can also put the computer into one of those power-saving states.

 CHANGE SETTINGS FOR ALL POWER PLANS

GET READY. To change settings that affects all of your power plans (system settings):

1. Open the Power Options in the Control Panel.
2. In the left pane, click Require a password on wakeup, Choose what the power button does, or Choose what closing the lid does (available only on laptops).
3. On the *Define power buttons and turn on password protection* page, choose the settings that you want to use when your computer is running on battery (if applicable), and when it's plugged in.
4. Click Save changes.

You can create your own plan and customize it to suit your needs. For example, if you frequently use a laptop to give presentations, you can create a plan that keeps the display turned on during the presentations and ensures that your computer stays awake.

 CREATE YOUR OWN POWER PLAN

GET READY. To create your own plan:

1. Open the Power Options in the Control Panel.
2. In the left pane, click Create a power plan.
3. On the *Create a power plan* page, select the plan that's closest to the type of plan that you want to create.
4. In the *Plan name* box, type a name for the plan, such as "Giving a presentation," and then click Next.
5. On the *Change settings for the plan* page, choose the display and sleep settings that you want to use when your computer is running on battery and when it's plugged in:
   • **To keep your display turned on during presentations:** Change the Turn off display after setting to Never for both On battery and Plugged in.
   • **To keep your laptop awake during presentations:** Change the Put the computer to sleep setting to Never for both On battery and Plugged in.
6. Click Create. If you're using a laptop, your plan appears under Plans shown on the battery meter. If you're using a desktop computer, your plan appears under Preferred plans. The plan that you based your new plan on is moved, and appears under Additional plans.

The plan that you just created automatically becomes the active plan.

If you created power plans that you no longer use or need, you can delete them. However, you can't delete Balanced, Power saver, High performance, or the plan that you're currently using (the active plan).

→ DELETE A POWER PLAN

GET READY. To delete a plan:

1. Click to open Power Options.
2. If the active plan is the one that you want to delete, make a different plan the active plan.
3. Under the plan that you want to delete, click Change plan settings.
4. On the *Change settings for the plan* page, click Delete this plan.
5. When prompted, click OK.

To select one of the default power plans, you can use any of the following procedures:

- Open the Windows Mobility Center and then, in the Battery Status tile, select one of the plans from the drop-down list.
- Click Start, click Control Panel > Hardware and Sound > Power Options, and then select the radio button for the desired plan.
- Open the Mobile PC Control Panel, click Power Options, and then select the radio button for the desired plan.
- Click the power icon in the notification area, and then select one of the plans from the menu that appears.

Each power plan consists of two sets of settings, one for when the computer is plugged into an AC power source and one for when the computer is running on battery power. Table 10-1 lists the primary settings for each of the power plans.

Table 10-1

Default power plan settings

POWER SETTING	POWER SAVER	BALANCED	HIGH PERFORMANCE
Turn off the display	2 minutes (battery) 5 minutes (AC)	5 minutes (battery) 10 minutes (AC)	10 minutes (battery) 15 minutes (AC)
Put the computer to sleep	10 minutes (battery) 15 minutes (AC)	15 minutes (battery) 30 minutes (AC)	Never (battery) Never (AC)
Turn off hard disk	5 minutes (battery) 20 minutes (AC)	10 minutes (battery) 20 minutes (AC)	20 minutes (battery) 20 minutes (AC)
Minimum processor state	5% (battery) 5% (AC)	5% (battery) 5% (AC)	5% (battery) 100% (AC)
System cooling policy	Passive (battery) Passive (AC)	Passive (battery) Active (AC)	Active (battery) Active (AC)
Maximum processor state	100% (battery) 100% (AC)	100% (battery) 100% (AC)	100% (battery) 100% (AC)
Wireless adapter power saving mode	Maximum Power Saving (battery) Maximum Performance (AC)	Medium Power Saving (battery) Maximum Performance (AC)	Maximum Performance (battery) Maximum Performance (AC)

■ Troubleshooting Performance Problems

THE BOTTOM LINE

Performance problems can be frustrating for anyone and they often happen with no apparent cause. Of course, much like any other problem, to solve performance problems, you would also follow the same troubleshooting methodology used in the previous lessons.

CERTIFICATION READY
What tool should you use to see if a computer is running slowly?
3.1

A good place to start when troubleshooting is to look at what the machine is running including the operating system and active applications. This will give you an idea on the load that it is trying to process. You should then look at how many processors or processor cores the computer currently has, as well as the speed of the processors. You should also look at how much memory you have. As stated in Lesson 1, a 32-bit version of Windows 7 should have a 1 GHz processor and 1 GB of memory. A 64-bit processor should have a 1 GHz processor and 2 GB of memory. Most likely, you should have at least double this for decent performance for basic programs and more if you are using heavy graphics, video editing, or a lot of data processing.

The next thing you should do is open Task Manager to see what programs and processes are running and which processes are taking up the most processor utilization and memory usage. You should also look at how large the paging file currently is, which may give you a clue that you need to add more memory. If you see that there are no applications that seem to be hogging resources, you should check when you last defragged your hard drive. You should also considering rebooting your computer to reset the memory, especially if you have not rebooted your computer in days. If you still cannot figure out the problem, you should then use Performance Monitor to determine where the bottleneck is.

To keep your PC running smoothly, you should also keep your PC up to date with Windows updates and security patches. You need to use up-to-date anti-virus software to keep your PC free from malware that would use up computer resources.

If you find that an application is using too much in computer resources, you should check with the vendor's website for potential problems and updates including memory leaks. A memory leak is when a program grabs some memory for some reason and is not able to release the memory when it is finished with it. As a result, your memory is used up. You can also try a software repair or re-installation of the program.

Finally, if everything is running as expected, there may be times when you will have to upgrade the computer or even replace the computer. Remember, as new software is released, it usually has new features that take up more processing and memory than previous versions.

SKILL SUMMARY

IN THIS LESSON YOU LEARNED:

- Performance is the overall effectiveness of how data moves through the system.
- When a component limits performance, the component is known as a bottleneck.
- When you relieve one bottleneck, you may trigger other bottlenecks.
- If your computer lacks the RAM needed to run a program or perform an operation, Windows uses virtual memory to compensate. Virtual memory combines your computer's RAM with temporary space on your hard disk.
- When RAM runs low, virtual memory moves data from RAM to space called a paging file.
- The default paging file size is equal to 1.5 times the total RAM.

- Unless you have an application that uses a larger paging file, if your system is utilizing more than 1.5 times your RAM, you should considering adding more RAM to your system.

- Task Manager gives you a quick look at performance and provides information about programs and processes running on your computer.

- Windows Performance Monitor is a Microsoft Management Console (MMC) snap-in that provides tools for analyzing system performance. It is included in the Computer Management and Server Manager consoles, and it can be executed using perfmon.

- Windows Resource Monitor is a system tool that allows you to view information about the use of hardware (CPU, memory, disk, and network) and software (file handles and modules) resources in real time.

- Power management is the process of balancing battery life with performance.

- Windows 7 includes extensive power management capabilities, including support for the Advanced Configuration and Power Interface (ACPI) and the ability to configure these power settings.

- A power plan is a collection of hardware and system settings that manage how your computer uses power.

- A good place to start when troubleshooting is to look at what the machine is running, including the operating system and running applications. This will give you an idea on the load that it is trying to process.

- When troubleshooting performance problems, you should look at the number of processors, the number of processor cores, and the speed of those processors, and you should look at how much memory you have.

- To keep your PC running smoothly, you should keep your PC up to date with Windows updates and security patches, and you need to use an up-to-date anti-virus software to keep your PC free from malware that would use up computer resources.

- If you find that an application is using too much of your computer's resources, you should check with the vendor's website for potential problems and updates including memory leaks.

- A memory leak is when a program grabs some memory, for some reason, and is not able to release the memory when it is done with it.

- Finally, if everything is running as expected, there may be times when you will have to upgrade the computer or even replace the computer.

■ Knowledge Assessment

Fill in the Blank

Complete the following sentences by writing the correct word or words in the blanks provided.

1. A _____ is when a component limits overall performance.

2. _____ is the overall effectiveness of how data moves through the system.

3. _____ combines your computer's RAM with temporary space on your hard disk to increase the amount of available memory.

4. Windows _____ is a powerful tool for understanding how your system resources are used by processes and services.

5. _____ is the process of balancing battery life with performance.

6. A _____ is a collection of hardware and system settings that manage how your computer uses power.

7. The default paging file size is _____ times the total RAM.

8. A _____ is when a program grabs some memory for some reason and is not able to release the memory when it is done with it.

9. A _____ is done by analyzing the performance when the system is running normally and within design specifications.

10. _____ is the amount of committed virtual memory for a process that can be written to another storage medium, such as the hard disk.

Multiple Choice

Circle the letter that corresponds to the best answer.

1. Which of the following is NOT typically a bottleneck in a computer running Windows 7?
   a. Processor
   b. Memory
   c. Disk
   d. Audio

2. Virtual memory in Windows 7 is known as a _____.
   a. Page driver
   b. Chipset
   c. Paging file
   d. Memory controller

3. What program gives you a quick glance at a system's performance and provides information about programs and processes running on your computer?
   a. Task Manager
   b. System Information
   c. System Configuration
   d. Event Viewer

4. To terminate a process, you would use _____.
   a. Task Manager
   b. Resource Manager
   c. System Configuration
   d. Event Viewer

5. What MMC snap-in provides tools in analyzing system performance?
   a. Task Manager
   b. Performance Monitor
   c. System Information
   d. System Configuration

6. The processor utilization should NOT be consistently above _____.
   a. 25%
   b. 50%
   c. 60%
   d. 80%

7. The average disk queue length should NOT be more than _____.
   a. 1
   b. 2
   c. 5
   d. 10

8. Which power plan does NOT come with Windows 7?
   a. Balanced
   b. Power Saver
   c. High Performance
   d. Performance Saver

9. What should be the maximum pages/sec?
   a. 5
   b. 10
   c. 20
   d. 50

10. What can make your disk appear slow over time?
    a. Memory leak
    b. Disk defragmentation
    c. Page file growth
    d. Processor virtualization

True / False

Circle T if the statement is true or F if the statement is false.

T | F **1.** Paging files are close to or the same speed as regular memory.

T | F **2.** Sometimes by relieving one bottleneck, you may trigger another bottleneck.

T | F **3.** If the paging file usage is larger than 1.5 times, you should increase the memory.

T | F **4.** To determine where a bottleneck is occurring, you should compare to a baseline.

T | F **5.** A page fault occurs when a process attempts to access a virtual memory page that is not available in its working set of RAM.

Case Scenarios

Scenario 10-1: Working with a 32-bit Application

You work for the Contoso Corporation. You have a user who complains that her computer is running too slow at times. Therefore, you decide you want to graph the processor utilization for a specific process over a couple of days. How would you do this? Hint: you may need to look through the performance monitor counters and research on the Internet.

Scenario 10-2: Configuring Power Settings with GPOs

You work for the Contoso Corporation. You decided to look at using power settings in an attempt to cut the electric bill for your company. Therefore, you want to enforce power settings. What should you do to make sure that every computer is designed to save power? Hint: Open local group policies and hunt around or use the Internet to research.

11 LESSON

Troubleshooting Internet Explorer

OBJECTIVE DOMAIN MATRIX

TECHNOLOGY SKILL	OBJECTIVE DOMAIN	OBJECTIVE NUMBER
Securing Internet Explorer	Identify and resolve Windows Internet Explorer security issues.	5.1

KEY TERMS

accelerators

add-ons

Compatibility View

Content zones

Cookie

dynamic security

InPrivate Browsing

InPrivate Filtering

Internet Explorer

phishing

pop-up windows

Protected Mode

RSS

search providers

Secure Sockets Layer (SSL)

SmartScreen Filter

After completing this lesson, you will have a better idea of the capabilities of Internet Explorer. In addition, you will be able to configure Internet Explorer to protect your computer while surfing the Internet.

You just installed several new computers running Windows 7 for the Acme Corporation. Within the first day, users call saying that when they try to access a couple of intranet websites, the web pages could not be accessed. You need to troubleshoot these problems and figure out why they cannot access those pages.

■ Administering Internet Explorer

THE BOTTOM LINE

One of the most popular applications with users is *Internet Explorer*, Windows standard Internet browser. Besides using Internet Explorer to surf the Internet, many corporate applications are now web based and available on the corporation's intranet.

Windows 7 includes the newest version of Internet Explorer, IE8. When compared to Internet Explorer 6, which was included with Windows XP, IE8 has a streamlined interface that is simpler and less cluttered and introduces tabs that allow you to open multiple web pages in a single browser window. It also adds a zoom feature that allows you to enlarge or reduce the view of a web page. It also fixed some long-standing printer problems by using the default Shrink To Fit setting so that the web page can fit on a single sheet of paper with no text cut off on the right.

Configuring Compatibility Mode

Apart from its performance features, Internet Explorer includes a number of functional enhancements and important security enhancements that protect users from malware incursions and other Internet dangers.

Since Internet Explorer 8 has additional functions and supports newer technology such as cascading style sheets 2.1, Internet Explorer may display web pages designed for older browsers incorrectly. If Internet Explorer recognizes a webpage that isn't compatible, you'll see the *Compatibility View* button on the address bar.

 VIEW COMPATIBILITY VIEW

GET READY. To turn Compatibility View on or off, click the Compatibility View button, or follow these steps:

1. Open Internet Explorer.
2. Click the Tools button, and then click Compatibility View.

The website will be displayed in Compatibility View until you turn it off or the website is updated to display correctly in the current version of Internet Explorer.

When you select Tools/Compatibility View Settings from the Tools menu or the Tools toolbar button, the Compatibility View Settings dialog box appears. In this dialog box, you can maintain a list of web sites for which you want to use Compatibility View all of the time. See Figure 11-1.

Figure 11-1

Compatibility View

Compatibility View Settings	✕

You can add and remove websites to be displayed in Compatibility View.

Add this website:

yahoo.com	Add

Websites you've added to Compatibility View:

google.com	Remove

☑ Include updated website lists from Microsoft
☑ Display intranet sites in Compatibility View
☐ Display all websites in Compatibility View

Close

In addition to the individual list on each computer, Microsoft also maintains its own list of sites that can benefit from Compatibility View. When you select the Include updated website lists from Microsoft check box on the Compatibility View Settings dialog box, IE includes the Microsoft-supplied sites in the computer's list.

Managing Add-Ons

To make Internet Explorer more flexible, Internet Explorer allows you to add *add-ons* such as extra toolbars, animated mouse pointers, stock tickers, and pop-up add blockers to your web browser. Add-ons are downloaded from the Internet and installed as an executable program.

The four basic types of add-ons supported by IE are:

- **Toolbars and Extensions:** Enables the browser to open and manipulate websites or file types that IE does not support natively. Some applications add their own toolbars to IE, enabling you to work with their documents in an IE session.
- **Search Providers:** Enables the user to perform searches directly from the IE interface using search engines on the Internet or the local network.
- **Accelerators:** Enables users to send text or other media they select in an IE browser window to another application, such as an email client, or an Internet resource, such as a blog.
- **InPrivate Filtering:** Enables you to import and export XML files containing InPrivate filters.

 VIEW YOUR CURRENT ADD-ONS

GET READY. To view your current add-ons:

1. Open Internet Explorer.
2. Click the Tools button, and then click Manage Add-ons. See Figure 11-2.

Figure 11-2

Managing add-ons

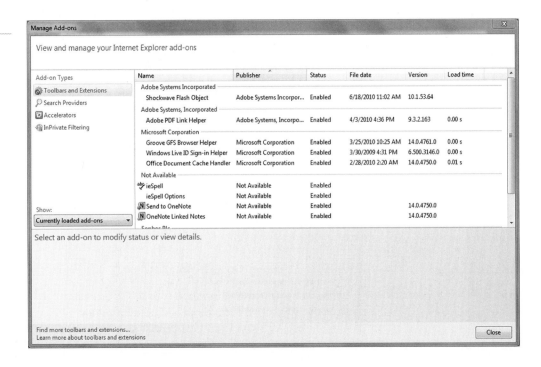

3. Under Add-on Types, click Toolbars and Extensions.
4. Under Show, you can select one of the following views of your add-ons:
   - To display a complete list of the add-ons that reside on your computer, click All add-ons.
   - To display only those add-ons that were needed for the current web page or a recently viewed web page, click Currently loaded add-ons.
   - To display add-ons that were pre-approved by Microsoft, your computer manufacturer, or a service provider, click Run without permission.
   - To display only 32-bit ActiveX controls, click Downloaded controls.
5. When you are finished, click Close.

ActiveX is a technology and framework that enables powerful applications with rich user interfaces to run within a web browser. Some examples of ActiveX components include the Microsoft Update component that scans your computer for missing updates, Shockwave Flash, and the SharePoint component.

In Internet Explorer 8, ActiveX controls are not installed by default. Therefore, when you visit a web page that includes an ActiveX control, you will see an information bar that alerts you that an ActiveX control is required. You then click the information bar and click Install ActiveX Control.

If you are having problems with an add-in, you may choose to disable or delete the ActiveX control. However, you can only delete ActiveX controls that you have downloaded and installed. You cannot delete ActiveX controls that were pre-installed or add-ons of any kind, but you can disable them. To delete an ActiveX control that you have installed, use Manage add-ons. If the add-on cannot be removed in Manage add-ons, you might be able to uninstall it through Control Panel.

 DELETE ACTIVEX CONTROLS

GET READY. To delete ActiveX controls you have installed:

1. Open Internet Explorer.
2. Click the Tools button, and then click Manage Add-ons.
3. Under Show, click Downloaded controls to display all ActiveX controls.
4. Click the ActiveX control you want to delete, and then click More information.
5. In the More Information dialog box, click Remove. If you are prompted for an administrator password or confirmation, type the password or provide confirmation.

 DISABLE ADD-ONS

GET READY. To permanently disable add-ons:

1. Open Internet Explorer.
2. Click the Tools button, and then click Manage Add-ons.
3. Under Show, click All add-ons.
4. Click the add-on you want to disable, and then click Disable.

SEARCH PROVIDERS

To make the Internet usable, search engines were created so that you can find information easily. Instead of always going to a search engine web page, you can search information from the search box via a ***search provider.*** Examples of search providers are Google, Bing, and Wikipedia. You can change the search provider for a specific search (Internet Explorer uses that search provider until you choose another one or until you close Internet Explorer) and you can specify which search provider you prefer to be used by default.

When you first install Internet Explorer, you might have only one provider installed. Bing is the default search provider if you use the express setup for Internet Explorer. If you want to change providers, follow the steps here to add new search providers.

ADD NEW SEARCH PROVIDERS

GET READY. To add new search providers:

1. Open Internet Explorer by clicking the Start button, and then clicking Internet Explorer.
2. Click the arrow to the right of the search box.
3. Click Find More Providers.
4. Click the search providers you would like to add. This opens the Add Search Provider dialog box.
5. If you want the provider that you just added to be used by default when searching from the address bar or search box, select the *Make this my default search provider* check box.
6. If you're using IE8, and the search provider offers search suggestions, select the *Use search suggestions from this provider* check box to receive search suggestions.
7. Click Add.

Some web pages offer search providers. These providers will appear in the search provider list for your current browsing session and are identified with a gold star next to them.

CHANGE THE SEARCH PROVIDER TEMPORARILY

GET READY. To change the search provider temporarily (this session only):

1. Open Internet Explorer by clicking the Start button, and then clicking Internet Explorer.
2. Click the arrow to the right of the search box.
3. Click the search provider you would like to use.
4. In the search box, type the word or phrase you want to search for, and then press ENTER.

That search provider will be used until you close Internet Explorer. When you restart Internet Explorer, your default search provider will be used again.

CHANGE THE DEFAULT SEARCH PROVIDER

GET READY. To change the default search provider:

1. Open Internet Explorer by clicking the Start button, and then clicking Internet Explorer.
2. Click the arrow to the right of the search box.
3. In Internet Explorer 8, click Manage Search Providers.
4. In Internet Explorer 8, click the search provider you would like to set as the default, click Set as default, and then click Close.

REMOVE A SEARCH PROVIDER

GET READY. To remove a search provider:

1. Open Internet Explorer by clicking the Start button, and then clicking Internet Explorer.
2. Click the arrow to the right of the search box.

3. Click Manage Search Providers.

4. Click a search provider in the list, click Remove, and then click Close.

IE supports virtually any type of search provider, not just the well-known web search engines such as Google. You can also add search providers for specific topics or sites, such as Wikipedia and the *New York Times*. Finally, you can add internal search engines of your own design, so that users can search your corporate intranet.

CONFIGURING ACCELERATORS

Another feature of Internet Explorer 8 is accelerators. **Accelerators** are a form of selection-based search that allows you to start an online service from any other page using only the mouse. For example, you might right-click text on a web page to access a third-party service such as a search engine, map service, dictionary service, or news service without the need to copy and paste content between web pages. You can use accelerators with text that you select on a web page to perform such tasks as opening a street address in a mapping website or looking up the dictionary definition for a word.

When you first start Internet Explorer, you can accept a selection of default accelerators, or you can choose your own from an online list. The list of new accelerators is frequently updated, so be sure to check back from time to time.

 USE AN ACCELERATOR

GET READY. To use an Accelerator, follow these steps:

1. Open Internet Explorer.

2. Go to the web page that contains the text that you want to use with an Accelerator, and select the text.

3. Click the Accelerator button to display a list of Accelerators and select the Accelerator you want to use.

While Internet Explorer comes with a selection of accelerators to get you started, you might want to take a look at some of the other accelerators that are available.

 FIND NEW ACCELERATORS

GET READY. To find new accelerators, follow these steps:

1. Open Internet Explorer.

2. Click the Tools button, and then click Manage Add-ons.

3. In Manage Add-ons, under Add-on Types, click Accelerators to display a list of your current Accelerators.

4. At the bottom of the screen, click Find More Accelerators.

5. On the Internet Explorer Gallery web page, click the Accelerator you want to install, and then click Install Accelerator.

6. In the Add Accelerator dialog box, do one of the following:

   • If you're adding a new Accelerator, click Add. When you add an Accelerator, you can also select the *Make this my default provider for this Accelerator Category* check box.

   • If you're replacing an existing Accelerator, click Replace.

   • If you're not sure you trust the website listed in the From field, click Cancel.

Looking at RSS Feeds

RSS, short for Really Simple Syndicating, allows users to subscribe to a website and get timely updates from that website or to aggregate feeds from many sites into one place, assuming the website supports RSS feeds. RSS feeds can be read using software called an "RSS reader," "feed reader," or "aggregator," which can be web based, desktop based, or mobile device based including Internet Explorer and Microsoft Outlook.

Before you can receive RSS feeds with IE, however, you must subscribe to them. Subscription is the term used to refer to the process of configuring the RSS client to receive transmissions from a particular site. When you access a web page, IE automatically searches for RSS feeds. If IE locates feeds as part of the page, the RSS button on the toolbar changes its color to red. To subscribe to a feed, use the following procedure.

 SUBSCRIBE TO AN RSS FEED

GET READY. Log on to Windows 7.

1. Click Start, and then click Internet Explorer. The Internet Explorer window appears.
2. Browse to the web site providing the feed to which you want to subscribe. When IE detects a feed, the Feeds button in the toolbar turns red.
3. Click the Feeds button. If there is more than one feed associated with the page, select one from the Feeds submenu. The feed page appears. You can always read the current contents of the feed on this page, whether you are subscribed or not.
4. Click the Subscribe to this feed link. A *Subscribe to this Feed* dialog box appears.
5. In the Name text box, type a name you want to assign to the feed (if it differs from the default).
6. Select the folder to which you want to add the feed, or click New folder to create one. Then click Subscribe. The feed page changes to indicate that you have successfully subscribed to the feed.

Once you have subscribed to RSS feeds, you can view their contents at any time.

 VIEW RSS FEEDS

GET READY. Log on to Windows 7.

1. Click Start, and then click Internet Explorer. The Internet Explorer window appears.
2. Click the Favorites button. The Favorites Center pane appears.
3. In the *Favorites Center* pane, click the Feeds tab. The pane displays a list of your currently subscribed feeds. To leave the Favorites Center pane open so you can browse through a list of subscriptions, click the Pin the Favorites Center button, on the right side of the menu bar.
4. Click one of your subscribed feeds to display its contents in the main IE window.

When you subscribe to an RSS feed using Internet Explorer, the content is updated once every day, by default. You can modify the default update setting for all feeds or for individual feeds.

CONFIGURE DEFAULT FEED SETTINGS

GET READY. Log on to Windows 7.

1. Click Start, and then click Internet Explorer. The Internet Explorer window appears.
2. Click the Tools button, and then select Internet Options. The Internet Options dialog box appears.
3. Click the Content tab and then, in the Feeds section, click Settings. The *Feed and Web Slice Settings* dialog box appears.
4. In the *Every* drop-down list, specify the interval at which IE should check the subscribed RSS feeds for updates. Then click OK to close the Feed Settings dialog box.
5. Click OK to close the Internet Options dialog box.

To configure the settings for an individual feed, use the following procedure.

CONFIGURE INDIVIDUAL FEED SETTINGS

GET READY. Log on to Windows 7.

1. Click Start, and then click Internet Explorer. The Internet Explorer window appears.
2. Click the Favorites button. The Favorites Center pane appears.
3. In the *Favorites Center* pane, click the Feeds button. The pane displays a list of your currently subscribed feeds.
4. Right-click one of your feed subscriptions and then, from the context menu, select Properties. The *Feed Properties* dialog box appears.
5. To change the update schedule, select the Use custom schedule radio button and then, in the *Frequency* drop-down list, select the desired interval.
6. When subscribing to an RSS feed that includes podcasts, you must also select the Automatically download attached files check box.
7. To change the Archive settings for the feed, change the *Number of items* spin box to specify the number of new content items you want to retain in the feed window, or select the Keep maximum items radio button.
8. Click OK to close the Feed Properties dialog box.

■ Securing Internet Explorer

THE BOTTOM LINE

One of the current complaints about Internet Explorer 6.0 is its security. Internet Explorer offers a number of features to protect your security and privacy while you browse the web including a Phishing Filter, Protected Mode, Pop-Up Blocker, Add-on Manager, download files or software notification, use of digital signatures and 128-bit secure (SSL) connections when using secure websites.

CERTIFICATION READY
What features does Internet Explorer 8 include that will protect your system?
5.1

With the Internet, you can use your web browser to reach around the world. Unfortunately, on the Internet, there are lots of opportunities for your computer or private information to be compromised.

Utilizing Cookies and Privacy Settings

When you use a browser to surf the Internet, a lot can be revealed about a person's personality and personal information. Therefore, you need to take steps to ensure that this information cannot be read or used without your knowledge.

USING COOKIES

A *cookie* is a piece of text stored by a user's web browser. It can be used for a wide range of items including user identification, authentication, and storing site preferences and shopping cart contents. While cookies can give a website a lot of capability, it can be used by spyware programs and websites to track people. Unfortunately, some websites will not operate without cookies.

 DELETE COOKIES

GET READY. To delete cookies, follow these steps:

1. Open Internet Explorer.
2. Click the Tools button, and then click Internet Options.
3. On the General tab, under Browsing history, click Delete. See Figure 11-3.

Figure 11-3

Deleting cookies and temporary files

4. Select the *Cookies* check box, and then check Delete if it isn't already checked. Clear or select check boxes for any other options you also want to delete. If you want to keep cookies for your saved favorites, select the *Preserve Favorites website data* check box.

USING INPRIVATE BROWSING

Being aware of how your private information is used when browsing the web is important to help prevent targeted advertising, fraud, and identity theft.

 CHANGE PRIVACY SETTINGS

GET READY. To change Internet Explorer privacy settings, follow these steps:

1. Open Internet Explorer.
2. Click the Tools button, and then click Internet Options.
3. Click the Privacy tab. See Figure 11-4.

Figure 11-4

Privacy tab

To change your privacy settings, adjust the tab slider to a new position on the privacy scale. The default level is Medium; it is recommended to configure Medium or higher. If you click on the Advanced button, you can override certain settings, and if you click the Edit button, you can allow or block cookies from individual websites.

To prevent Internet Explorer from storing data about your browsing session, Internet Explorer 8 includes *InPrivate Browsing.* This helps prevent anyone else who might be using your computer from seeing where you visited and what you looked at on the web.

When you start InPrivate Browsing, Internet Explorer opens a new window. The protection that InPrivate Browsing provides is only in effect during the time that you use that window. You can open as many tabs as you want in that window, and they will all be protected by InPrivate Browsing. However, if you open another browser window, that window will not be protected by InPrivate Browsing. To end your InPrivate Browsing session, close the browser window.

 TURN ON INPRIVATE BROWSING

GET READY. To turn on InPrivate Browsing, do any of the following:

1. Click the Safety button, and then click InPrivate Browsing. See Figure 11-5.

Figure 11-5

Configuring InPrivate Browsing

2. Open a new tab, and then, on the new tab page, click Open an InPrivate Browsing window.

3. Press Ctrl+Shift+P.

USING INPRIVATE FILTERING

When you enable InPrivate Filtering, which is different from InPrivate Browsing, it will block tracking ads or web content while using Internet Explorer 8.

InPrivate Filtering helps prevent website content providers from collecting information about sites you visit. Many web pages use content, such as advertisements, maps, or web analysis tools, from websites other than the one you are visiting. These websites are called content providers or third-party websites. When you visit a website with third-party content, some information about you is sent to the content provider. If a content provider offers content to a large number of the websites you visit, the content provider could develop a profile of your browsing preferences. Profiles of browsing preferences can be used in a variety of ways, including for analysis and serving targeted advertisements.

InPrivate Filtering works by analyzing web content on the web pages you visit, and if it sees the same content being used on a number of websites, it will give you the option to allow or block that content. You can also choose to have InPrivate Filtering automatically block any content provider or third-party website it detects, or you can choose to turn off InPrivate Filtering.

 TURN ON INPRIVATE FILTERING

GET READY. To turn on InPrivate Filtering for the first time, follow these steps:

1. Open Internet Explorer by clicking the Start button, and then clicking Internet Explorer.
2. Click the Safety button, click InPrivate Filtering, and then do one of the following:
   - Click Block for me to block websites automatically.
   - Click Let me choose which providers receive my information to choose content to block or allow.
3. When you're finished, click OK.

 MANAGE INPRIVATE FILTERING SETTINGS

GET READY. To manually block or allow content provider or third-party websites that could be in the position to know which websites you've visited, follow these steps:

1. Open Internet Explorer by clicking the Start button, and then clicking Internet Explorer.
2. Click the Safety button, and then click InPrivate Filtering Settings.
3. Click Choose content to block or allow, click one or more websites, and then click Allow or Block.
4. To set the number of websites you visit that share content before they are put in the list, type a new number in the *Show content from providers used by this number of websites you've visited* box. You can set the number from 3 to 30. The default setting is 10, which means at least 10 different websites must share the same content provider before it is displayed and you can block or allow it.
5. When you're finished, click OK.

USING POP-UP BLOCKER

Pop-up windows are very common. While some pop-up windows are useful website controls, most are simply annoying advertisements, with a few attempting to load spyware or other malicious programs on your machine. To help protect your computer, Internet Explorer has the capability to suppress some or all pop-ups. To configure the Pop-Up Blocker, use the following procedure.

CONFIGURE THE POP-UP BLOCKER

GET READY. Log on to Windows 7.

1. Click Start, and then click Control Panel. The Control Panel window appears.
2. Select Network and Internet>Internet Options. The Internet Properties sheet appears.
3. Click the Privacy tab.
4. Click Settings. The Pop-Up Blocker Settings dialog box appears.
5. To allow pop-ups from a specific website, type the URL of the site in the *Address of website to allow* text box, and then click Add. Repeat the process to add additional sites to the *Allowed sites* list.
6. Adjust the *Blocking level* drop-down list to one of the following settings:
   - **High:** Block all pop-ups.
   - **Medium:** Block most automatic pop-ups.
   - **Low:** Allow pop-ups from secure sites.
7. Click Close to close the Pop-Up Blocker Settings dialog box.
8. Click OK to close the Internet Properties sheet.

Examining Content Zones

To help manage Internet Explorer security when visiting sites, Internet Explorer divides your network connection into four ***content zones***. For each of these zones, a security level is assigned.

The security for each security zone is assigned based on dangers associated with that zone. For example, it is assumed that when you connect to a server within your own corporation it is safer than connecting to a server on the Internet.

The four default content types are:

- **Internet Zone:** Anything that is not assigned to any other zone and anything that is not on your computer, or your organization's network (intranet). The default security level of the Internet zone is Medium.

- **Local Intranet Zone:** Computers that are part of the organization's network (intranet) that do not require a proxy server, as defined by the system administrator. These include sites specified on the Connection's tab, network, paths such as \\computername\ foldername, and local intranet sites such as http://internal. You can add sites to this zone. The default security level for the Local intranet zone is Medium=Low, which means Internet Explorer will allow all cookies from websites in this zone to be saved on your computer and read by the website that created them. Finally, if the website requires NTLM or integrated authentication, it will automatically use your username and password.

- **Trusted Sites Zone:** Contains trusted sites that you believe you can download or run files from without damaging your computer or data, or sites that you do not consider security risks. You can assign sites to this zone. The default security level for the Trusted sites zone is Low, which means Internet Explorer will allow all cookies from websites in this zone to be saved on your computer and read by the website that created them.

- **Restricted Sites Zone:** Contains sites that you do not trust from which downloading or running files may damage your computer or data, or sites that you consider security risks. You can assign sites to this zone. The default security level for the Restricted sites zone is High, which means Internet Explorer will block all cookies from websites in this zone.

To tell which zones the current web page falls into, look at the right side of the Internet Explorer status bar.

 MODIFY SECURITY LEVEL FOR WEB CONTENT ZONE

GET READY. To modify the security level for a web content zone:

1. Click the Tools button, and then click Internet Options.
2. In the Internet Options dialog box, on the Security tab, click the zone on which you want to set the security level. See Figure 11-6.

Figure 11-6

Configuring security content zones

3. Drag the slider to set the security level to High, Medium, or Low. Internet Explorer describes each option to help you decide which level to choose. You are prompted to confirm any reduction in security level. You can also choose the custom Level button for more detailed control.
4. Click OK to close the Internet Options dialog box.

For each of the web content zones, there is a default security level. The security levels available in Internet Explorer are:

- **High:** Excludes any content that can damage your computer.
- **Medium:** Warns you before running potentially damaging content.
- **Low:** Does not warn you before running potentially damaging content.
- **Custom:** A security setting of your own design.

The easiest way to modify the security settings that Internet Explorer imposes on a specific website is to manually add the site to a different security zone. The typical procedure is to add a site to the Trusted Sites zone to increase its privileges, or add it to the Restricted Sites zone to reduce its privileges. To do this, use the following procedure.

 ADD A SITE TO A SECURITY ZONE

GET READY. Log on to Windows 7.

1. Click Start, and then click Control Panel. The Control Panel window appears.
2. Select Network and Internet > Internet Options. The Internet Properties sheet appears.

3. Click the Security tab.

4. Select the zone, either Trusted sites or Restricted sites, to which you want to add a site.

5. Click Sites. The *Trusted sites* or *Restricted sites* dialog box appears.

6. Type the URL of the website you want to add to the zone into the *Add this website to the zone* text box, and then click Add. The URL appears in the websites list.

7. Click Close to close the *Trusted sites* or *Restricted sites* dialog box.

8. Click OK to close the Internet Properties sheet.

To modify the security properties of a zone, use the following procedure.

 MODIFY SECURITY ZONE SETTINGS

GET READY. Log on to Windows 7.

1. Click Start, and then click Control Panel. The Control Panel window appears.

2. Select Network and Internet > Internet Options. The Internet Properties sheet appears.

3. Click the Security tab.

4. Select the zone for which you want to modify the security settings.

5. In the *Security level for this zone* box, adjust the slider to increase or decrease the security level for the zone. Moving the slider up increases the protection for the zone and moving the slider down decreases it.

6. Select or clear the Enable Protected Mode check box, if desired.

7. To exercise more precise control over the zone's security settings, click Custom level. The Security Settings dialog box for the zone appears.

8. Select radio buttons for the individual settings in each of the security categories. The radio buttons typically make it possible to enable a setting, disable it, or prompt the user before enabling it.

9. Click OK to close the Security Settings dialog box.

10. Click OK to close the Internet Properties sheet.

Using Dynamic Security and Protected Mode

Internet Explorer offers multiple security features to defend against malware and data theft including dynamic security and Protected Mode. ***Dynamic security*** is a set of tools and technology that protects your computer as you browse the Internet with Internet Explorer. It includes ActiveX opt-in, Security Status Bar, Phishing Filter, address bar protection, and Protected Mode.

The Security Status Bar keeps you notified of the website security and privacy settings by using color-coded notifications next to the address bar. Some of these features include:

• Address bar turns green to show a website bearing new High Assurance certificates, indicating the site owner has completed extensive identity verification checks.

• Phishing Filter notifications, certificate names, and the gold padlock icon are now also adjacent to the address bar for better visibility.

• Certificate and privacy detail information can easily be displayed with a single click on the Security Status Bar.

- The address bar is displayed to the user for every window, whether it's a pop-up or standard window, which blocks malicious sites from emulating trusted sites.
- To help protect you against phishing sites, Internet Explorer warns you when you are visiting potential or known fraudulent sites, and it blocks the site if appropriate. The opt-in filter is updated several times per hour with the latest security information from Microsoft and several industry partners.
- International Domain Name Anti-Spoofing notifies you when visually similar characters in the URL are not expressed in the same language.

When Internet Explorer is still using its original settings, you'll see the Information bar in the following circumstances:

- If a website tries to install an ActiveX control on your computer or run an ActiveX control in an unsafe manner.
- If a website tries to open a pop-up window.
- If a website tries to download a file to your computer.
- If a website tries to run active content on your computer.
- If your security settings are below recommended levels.
- If you access an intranet web page, but have not turned on intranet address checking.
- If you started Internet Explorer with add-ons disabled.
- If you need to install an updated ActiveX control or add-on program.
- The web address can be displayed with native language letters or symbols but you don't have the language installed.

To help protect your computer, Internet Explorer ***Protected Mode*** runs as a low integrity procedure, which means that Internet Explorer writes to only low-integrity disk locations such as the Temporary Internet Files folder and the standard IE storage areas, including the History, Cookies, and Favorites folders. As a result, Protected Mode is a feature that makes it more difficult for malicious software to be installed on your computer.

TAKE NOTE* Protected Mode is not a complete defense against malware. Therefore, it is recommended to use an up-to-date anti-virus package with anti-spyware capability and to keep your system up to date with Windows and Internet Explorer security updates and patches.

 ENABLE PROTECTED MODE

GET READY. You need to enable UAC for Protected Mode to be enabled. Then to enable Protected Mode:

1. Open Internet Explorer.
2. Open the Tools menu and select Internet Options.
3. Select the Security tab.
4. Select Enable Protected Mode.

Unfortunately, some web-based applications designed to run on IE6 or earlier versions might not run properly because the application is designed to write to a disk area that is inaccessible while in Protected Mode.

Understanding SmartScreen Filters and Phishing

Phishing is a technique based on social engineering. With phishing, users are sent (usually through email or other websites) to convincing-looking websites that urge users to supply personal information, such as passwords and account numbers.

To help protect against phishing, Internet Explorer 8 includes a *SmartScreen Filter* that examines traffic for evidence of phishing activity and displays a warning to the user if it finds any. It also sends the address back to the Microsoft SmartScreen service to be compared against lists of known phishing and malware sites. If SmartScreen Filter discovers that a website you're visiting is on the list of known malware or phishing sites, Internet Explorer will display a blocking web page and the address bar will appear in red. From the blocking page, you can choose to bypass the blocked website and go to your home page instead, or you can continue to the blocked website, although this is not recommended. If you decide to continue to the blocked website, the address bar will continue to appear in red.

To protect your privacy, information that is submitted to the SmartScreen web service is transmitted in encrypted format over HTTPS. This information is not stored with your IP address or other personally identifiable information, and will not be used to identify, contact, or provide advertising to you.

When you run IE8 for the first time, you can elect to set up the browser by using express settings, or by configuring settings individually. The express settings option enables the SmartScreen Filter, but you can disable it at any time by clicking the Safety button on the toolbar and selecting SmartScreen Filter > Turn off SmartScreen Filter, to display the Microsoft SmartScreen Filter dialog box.

Even without SmartScreen Filter turned on, you can remain safe from phishing attempts as long as you follow one simple rule: Don't trust hyperlinks. Never supply a password or any other confidential information to a website unless you type the URL yourself and you are sure that it is correct.

Working with SSL and Certificates

When you surf the Internet, there are times when you need to transmit private data over the Internet such as credit card numbers, social security numbers, and so on. During these times, you should be using http over SSL (https) to encrypt the data sent over the Internet. By convention, URLs that require an SSL connection start with https instead of http.

Secure Sockets Layer (SSL) is a cryptographic system that uses two keys to encrypt data—a public key known to everyone and a private or secret key known only to the recipient of the message. The public key is published in a digital certificate, which also confirms the identity of the web server.

When you connect to a site that is secured using SSL, a gold lock appears in the address bar, along with the name of the organization to which the CA issued the certificate. Clicking the lock icon displays more information about the site, including the identity of the CA that issued the certificate. For even more information, you can click the View Certificate link to open the Certificate dialog box.

When visiting certain websites, Internet Explorer may find problems with the digital certificate such as that the certificate has expired, it is corrupted, it has been revoked, or it does not match the name of the website. When this happens, IE will block access to the site and display a warning stating that there is a problem with the certificate. You then have a chance to close the browser window or ignore the warning and continue on to the site. Of course, if you chose to ignore the warning, make sure you trust the website and you believe that you are communicating with the correct server.

SKILL SUMMARY

- Windows 7 includes the newest version of Internet Explorer, IE8.

- Internet Explorer may display web pages designed for older browsers incorrectly. If Internet Explorer recognizes a web page that isn't compatible, you'll see the Compatibility View button on the address bar.

- To make Internet Explorer more flexible, Internet Explorer allows you to use add-ons such as extra toolbars, animated mouse pointers, stock tickers, and pop-up ad blockers on your web browser.

- Search Providers enable the user to perform searches directly from the IE interface using search engines on the Internet or the local network.

- Accelerators enable users to send text or other media they select in an IE browser window to another application, such as an email client, or an Internet resource, such as a blog.

- ActiveX is a technology and framework that enables powerful applications with rich user interfaces to run within a web browser.

- Really Simple Syndicating (RSS) allows users to subscribe to a website and get timely updates from the website or to aggregate feeds from many sites into one place, assuming the websites support RSS feeds.

- Before you can receive RSS feeds with IE, however, you must subscribe to them.

- A cookie is a piece of text stored by a user's web browser. It can be used for a wide range of items including user identification, authentication, storing site preferences and shopping cart contents.

- InPrivate Browsing helps prevent anyone else who might be using your computer from seeing where you went and what you looked at on the web.

- InPrivate Filtering, different from InPrivate Browsing, helps prevent website content providers from collecting information about the sites you visit.

- Pop-up windows are very common. While some pop-up windows are useful web site controls, most are simply annoying advertisements, with a few attempting to load spyware or other malicious programs.

- To help protect your computer, Internet Explorer has the capability to suppress some or all pop-ups.

- To help manage Internet Explorer security when visiting sites, Internet Explorer divides your network connection into four content types. For each of these zones, a security level is assigned.

- The Security Status Bar keeps you notified about web site security and privacy settings by using color-coded notifications next to the address bar.

- Phishing is a technique based on social engineering. With phishing, users are sent (usually through email or other websites) to convincing-looking websites that urge users to supply personal information, such as passwords and account numbers.

- To help protect against phishing, Internet Explorer 8 includes a SmartScreen Filter that examines traffic for evidence of phishing activity and displays a warning to the user if it finds any.

- There are times when you need to transmit private data over the Internet such as credit card numbers, social security numbers, and so on. During these times, you should be using http over SSL (https) to encrypt the data sent over the Internet.

- By convention, URLs that require an SSL connection start with https instead of http.

- Secure Sockets Layer (SSL) is a cryptographic system that uses two keys to encrypt data—a public key known to everyone and a private or secret key known only to the recipient of the message.

- The public key used in SSL is published in a digital certificate, which also confirms the identity of the web server.

- When you connect to a site that is secured using SSL, a gold lock appears in the address bar, along with the name of the organization to which the CA issued the certificate.

■ Knowledge Assessment

Fill in the Blank

Complete the following sentences by writing the correct word or words in the blanks provided.

1. When a web page cannot be displayed properly, you should click the _____ button.

2. The _____ technology and framework extends the ability of Internet Explorer but must be approved by you before being executed.

3. _____ allows you to do a quick search using a search engine without opening a search engine web page.

4. _____ allows you to subscribe to a website so that you can receive updates from the website.

5. A _____ is a text file used to keep track of web page settings and history.

6. _____ prevents other people from seeing your browsing history.

7. Protected Mode requires _____ to be on.

8. _____ tries to trick you into supplying personal information on a website that looks like a trusted website.

9. _____ uses public and private keys to encrypt data sent over the Internet.

10. When connected to SSL, a _____ appears in the address bar and allows you to access the digital certificate associated with the SSL connection.

Multiple Choice

Circle the letter that corresponds to the best answer.

1. Which of the following is NOT a basic type of add-on?
   a. Toolbar and Extensions
   b. Search Providers
   c. Privacy Plug-in
   d. Accelerators

2. When an ActiveX component needs to be approved, a _____ bar will appear.
   a. Orange
   b. Red
   c. Yellow
   d. Blue

3. What is the default search provider for Internet Explorer?
   a. Bing
   b. Google
   c. Yahoo
   d. MSN

4. What allows you to select text and open an online server for the selected text?
   a. Toolbar
   b. Search engine
   c. ActiveX
   d. Accelerator

5. By default, RSS feeds update once per _____.
   a. Hour
   b. Day
   c. Week
   d. Month

6. What technology is used to prevent websites from collecting information about the sites you visit?
   a. InPrivate Browsing
   b. InPrivate Filtering
   c. Pop-up blocking windows
   d. Content zones

7. Which content zone automatically uses your username and password to access websites that require authentication?
   a. Internet Zones
   b. Local Intranet Zone
   c. Trusted Sites Zone
   d. Restricted Sites Zone

8. What technology is used to protect against phishing?
   a. InPrivate Browsing
   b. InPrivate Filtering
   c. SmartScreen
   d. SSL

9. When using SSL, the public key is found in a _____.
   a. Digital certificate
   b. Cookie
   c. SmartFilter
   d. Accelerator

10. Which technology used with IE prevents Internet applications from writing to the system files' locations?
    a. SmartScreen
    b. Protected Mode
    c. InPrivate Browsing
    d. InPrivate Filtering

True / False

Circle T if the statement is true or F if the statement is false.

T | F **1.** Compatibility View will fix all web pages that do not display properly with IE8.

T | F **2.** SmartScreen is the only protection against phishing.

T | F **3.** Protected Mode will protect you against all spyware.

T | F **4.** All websites support RSS.

T | F **5.** Accelerators cache web pages so that they are faster when accessing in the future.

■ Case Scenarios

Scenario 11-1: Protected Mode

Explain why UAC is needed for Protected Mode to work.

Scenario 11-2: Proxy Settings

How would you configure a default proxy setting for all users within your organization?

12 LESSON

Resolving Security Issues

OBJECTIVE DOMAIN MATRIX

TECHNOLOGY SKILL	OBJECTIVE DOMAIN	OBJECTIVE NUMBER
Looking at Malicious Software	Identify and resolve issues due to malicious software.	5.2
Understanding Encryption	Identify and resolve encryption issues.	5.3
Understanding Windows Updates	Identify and resolve software update issues.	5.4

KEY TERMS

Action Center

BitLocker

BitLocker To Go

data recovery agent (DRA)

decryption

Encrypting File System (EFS)

encryption

firewall

malicious software (malware)

rootkit

security

social engineering

spyware

Trojan horse

virus

virus hoax

Windows Defender

Windows Firewall

Windows Update

worm

After completing this lesson, you will have a basic understanding of computer security. In addition, you will know how to configure Windows to make it more secure.

You work as a desktop administrator for the Acme Corporation. You get a call from your CIO to visit him in his office. He says that a new virus has been floating around on the Internet that is causing havoc to many corporations. He wants to know what steps you are taking to keep the computers secure and not affected by the virus.

▪ Introducing Security

↓
THE BOTTOM LINE

Computer *security* is the protection of information and property from theft, corruption, or natural disaster, while allowing the information and property to remain accessible and productive to its intended users. If you have worked with Windows for long and you access the Internet on a regular basis, you know that the world is filled with viruses, worms, and hackers and other types of criminals. Therefore, you need to take steps to protect your computer.

To keep a system secure:

- Always require usernames and passwords so that if someone tries to access your computer, he or she will need to provide a username and password.
- Don't give your password to anyone.
- Change your passwords frequently so that if a password becomes compromised, it will be changed.
- If your password is compromised, change your password immediately.
- Don't allow people to watch you type in your password.
- Do not write your password down near the computer. You will be amazed how often this happens.
- When you leave your computer unattended, log off or lock your computer. You can also enable a screen saver to come on after a few minutes of inactivity, which will require a password to resume working within the session.
- Use a password-protected screen saver so that if you unexpectedly walk away from your computer, if someone tries to access your computer, he or she will have to provide your password.
- Use strong passwords (passwords that are at least 8 characters long and are a mix of lowercase, uppercase, digits, and special characters).
- Do not use obvious passwords.
- Don't always assign full permissions to resources. Only assign the permissions that people need to perform their job or task.
- When you are not with your computer, be sure it is physically secure.
- Do not always log on as an administrator. Instead, log in as a standard user and then elevate to an administrator as needed by using the runas command or by right-clicking an icon while pressing the Shift key and selecting Runas Administrator.

If you are a network administrator for a corporation, you should establish written policies and require your corporate users to read and follow the guidelines and you should use group policies whenever possible to enforce the settings. In addition, training that highlights computer security could not hurt.

Before getting into other technology that comes with Windows, you should be aware of one of the biggest threats to any computer or network. *Social engineering* is the act of manipulating people into performing actions or divulging confidential information. Rather than using technology to break through security technology, social engineering is used to bypass the security. With social engineering, you trick someone into giving their username, password, or other private information such as credit card numbers and social security numbers,

Social engineering is not new—people use social engineering (when they act as a friend or co-worker or act as if they are having a problem that only you can help them with) to unlock a locked building or room. Of course, many of these skills can be used in tricking a person into giving rights or permissions to someone or resetting passwords. Often, the social engineering skills of these criminals are well-rehearsed, very realistic looking, and extremely effective. Most companies do not prepare their staff for this type of deception.

Social engineering can be described with the following scenarios:

- **Pretexting:** The act of creating and using an invented scenario (the pretext) to engage a targeted victim in a manner that increases the chance the victim will divulge information or perform actions that would be unlikely in ordinary circumstances. To make pretexting work, the person may do research on the Internet or dumpster dive (going through trash in the hope of gathering personal or private information about a company or person) so that they can impersonate someone or to establish legitimacy in the mind of the target.

- **Phishing:** A technique of fraudulently obtaining private information. Typically, the phisher sends an email that appears to come from a legitimate business and requests verification such as your bank account information or social security number. They may go as far as establishing a realistic website where you would input the information, which is then gathered by the criminals. Phishing was also discussed in Lesson 11.

- **Baiting:** Using curiosity or greed of the victim to access a disk or website that acts as a real-world Trojan Horse to give someone access to your system. They may leave a legitimate-looking disk where it can be easily found with an alluring label such as "Executive Salary Summary." As people find the disk, they may be curious and access the disk on their computer, running some form of malware that will infect or compromise their system, and possibly the entire company's system.

- **Quid pro quo:** Means something for something. An attacker calls random numbers at an organization, saying they are from technical support. Eventually, they will reach someone with a legitimate problem and are glad that someone contacted him or her. The attacker will then trick the person into loading something on their machine or simply ask for the person's username and password.

So how do you avoid attacks involving social engineering? Typically, you use common sense, a little due diligence, and awareness. Remember, that if something is too good to be true, it most likely is not true. You should use extreme caution if you cannot verify someone's identity. Finally, one of the steps to combat social engineering is to include training for your IT staff and end users with examples of social engineering and the various scams that exists.

■ Looking at Malicious Software

THE BOTTOM LINE

Malicious software, sometimes called malware, is software designed to infiltrate or affect a computer system without the owner's informed consent. It is usually associated with viruses, worms, Trojan horses, spyware, rootkits, and dishonest adware. As a network administrator and computer technician, you will need to know how to identify malware, how to remove malware, and how to protect a computer from malware.

Identifying Types of Malware

CERTIFICATION READY
How do you defend your system from malware?
5.2

Since it is quite common for a computer to be connected to the Internet, there are more opportunities than ever for your computer to be infected by malware. In addition, over the last couple of years, the amount of malware produced has reached staggering proportions.

Many early forms of malware were written as experiments or practical jokes (known as pranks). Most of the time, these were intended to be harmless or merely annoying. However, as time passed, malware turned more into vandalism or as a tool to compromise private information. In addition, malware can be used as a denial of service (DoS) tool to attack other systems, networks, or websites causing those to have performance problems or become inaccessible.

As mentioned before, malware can be divided into:

- Viruses
- Worms
- Trojan horses
- Spyware and dishonest adware
- Rootkits
- Backdoors
- Scamware/scareware

A computer *virus* is a program that can copy itself and infect a computer without the user's consent or knowledge. Early viruses had some form of executable code that was hidden in the boot sector of a disk or as an executable file (with a .exe or .com filename extension).

Later, as macro languages were used in software applications such as word processors and spreadsheets to enhance the programs' power and flexibility, macro programs were embedded within the documents. Unfortunately, these documents can infect other documents and can cause a wide range of problems on a computer system when the macro code is executed by someone opening the document.

When accessing websites over the Internet, today's website can be written in various programming and scripting languages and can include executable programs. Therefore, as you access the Internet, your system is under constant threat.

A *worm* is a self-replicating program that replicates itself to other computers over the network without any user intervention. Different from a virus, a worm does not corrupt or modify files on a target computer. Instead, it consumes bandwidth and processor and memory resources, slowing your system down or causing your system to be unusable. Worms usually spread by using security holes found in the operating system or TC/IP software implementations.

A *Trojan horse* is a program named after the Trojan horse story in Greek mythology. A Trojan horse program is an executable that appears as a desirable or useful program. Since it appears to be a desirable or useful program, users are tricked into loading and executing the program on their system. After the program is loaded, it can cause your computer to become unusable or it can bypass your system's security allowing your private information to be read including passwords, credit card numbers, and social security numbers, and it may execute adware.

Spyware is a type of malware that is installed on computers and collects personal information or browsing habits often without the user's knowledge. It can also install additional software, and redirect your web browser to other sites or change your home page.

One type of spyware is the keylogger, which records every key pressed. Therefore when you type in credit card numbers, social security numbers, and passwords, that information gets recorded and is eventually sent to or read by someone without the user's knowledge. It should be noted that not all keyloggers are bad since some corporations used them to monitor their corporate users.

Adware is any software package that automatically plays, displays, or downloads advertisements to a computer after the software is installed on it or while the application is being used. While adware may not necessarily be bad, it is often used with ill intent.

A *rootkit* is a software or hardware device designed to gain administrator-level control over a computer system without being detected. Similar to adware, while a rootkit is not necessarily bad, it is often used with ill intent to gain access to systems and private information or used as part of a DoS attack on another system. Rootkits can target the BIOS, hypervisor, boot loader, kernel, or less commonly, libraries or applications.

A backdoor is a program that gives some remote user, unauthorized control of a system or initiates an unauthorized task. Some backdoors have been installed by viruses or other forms of malware. Other backdoors may be created by programs on commercial applications or with a customized application made for an organization.

Scamware or scareware are software applications or pop-ups that show up when you are visiting some web pages. You may get a message that says that the system has detected a bogus infection and it can fix the bogus infection. This is a method of preying on buyers' fears to sell them software that they don't need, and sometimes the software may contain other forms of malware as well.

Identifying Symptoms of Malware

The first step in removing malware is detecting that you have malware. Sometimes it is easy to see that you are infected with malware. Other times, you may never know your machine has it.

Some of the symptoms of malware include:

- Poor system performance
- Your system has less available memory than it should
- Poor performance while connected to the Internet
- Computer stops responding frequently
- Computer takes longer to start up
- Browser closes unexpectedly or stops responding
- Default home or default search pages change in your browser
- Unexpected pop-up advertising windows
- Unexpected additional toolbars added to the browser
- Unexpected programs automatically start
- Cannot start a program
- Components of Windows or other programs no longer work
- Programs or files are suddenly missing
- Unusual messages or displays on your monitor
- Unusual sounds or music played at random times
- Unknown programs or files have been created or installed
- Your browser has unexpected add-ons
- Files have become corrupted
- File size unexpectedly changes

Of course, to see these symptoms, you may need to actively look for them. For example, when your machine slows down, it is logical that you start Task Manager to view processor and memory utilization. You would then look at the processes to see which process is using the most processor and memory resources. You should also review the processes and services in memory (again, you can use Task Manager). You can also use the System Configuration tool (msconfig.exe). Of course, to make the most of determining which processes and services are rogue, you need to have a baseline of what processes and services usually run on the system so that you have something to compare to. Finally, the best way to detect malware is to use an up-to-date anti-virus program and an up-to-date anti-spyware package, which can scan an entire system and look for malware in real time as you open files and access websites.

Protecting Yourself from Malware

> With most of today's computers connecting to the Internet, it is easy to understand why you have to protect your system from all types of malware threats. Of course, a little common sense can go a long way in protecting you.

USING SECURITY UPDATES AND ANTI-VIRUS SOFTWARE

Some viruses, worms, rootkits, spyware, and adware are made possible because they exploit some security hole in Windows, Internet Explorer, or Microsoft Office. Therefore, to protect yourself against malware, you first need to keep your Windows (as well as other Microsoft products such as Microsoft Office) system up to date with the latest service packs, security patches, and other critical fixes.

Second, you should use an up-to-date anti-virus software package. In addition, if your anti-virus software does not include an anti-spyware component, you should install an anti-spyware software package. You should also run your anti-virus software at least once a week and do a full scan.

Windows Defender is a software product from Microsoft that prevents, removes, and quarantines spyware in Microsoft Windows. It protects your computer against pop-ups, slow performance, and security threats caused by spyware and other unwanted software by detecting and removing known spyware from your computer. Windows Defender features Real-Time Protection, a monitoring system that recommends actions against spyware when it is detected, minimizes interruptions, and helps you stay productive. Like any anti-virus package, you must keep Windows Defender up to date.

Download * Windows Defender can be downloaded from the following website: http://www.microsoft.com/windows/products/winfamily/defender/default.mspx

USING UAC

While keeping your system up to date with security patches and using an up-to-date anti-virus package are necessary, there are a couple of other tools that will help protect your system. User Account Control (UAC), discussed in Lesson 1, is a feature that helps prevent unauthorized changes to your computer. So if you download software from the Internet, and the software starts making changes to your system, UAC will notify you of those changes. Also remember that to use Protected Mode in IE, you need to have UAC.

USING WINDOWS FIREWALL

A firewall is an important security tool. A ***firewall*** is software or hardware that checks information coming from the Internet or a network, and then either blocks it or allows it to pass through to your computer, depending on your firewall settings. A firewall can help prevent hackers or malicious software (such as worms) from gaining access to your computer through a network or the Internet. A firewall can also stop your computer from sending malicious software to other computers.

+ MORE INFORMATION

For more information on available computer firewalls and their product rankings, visit
http://www.matousec.com/projects/proactive-security-challenge/results.php

Early firewalls were only packet filters, which block packets based on IP addresses and ports. Windows Firewall is a stateful, host-based firewall that filters incoming and outgoing connections based on its configuration. A stateful firewall is a firewall that keeps track of the state of network connections. The firewall then determines which packets are legitimate based on the current network connections. Only packets matching a known connection state will be allowed by the firewall; others will be rejected.

Microsoft recommends that you always use the ***Windows Firewall.*** However, since some security packages and anti-virus packages include their own firewall, you should only use one firewall.

 ENABLE AND DISABLE WINDOWS FIREWALL

GET READY. To enable or disable Windows Firewall:

1. Open the Control Panel.
2. If you are in Category view, click System and Security and click Windows Firewall. If you are in Icon view, double-click Windows Firewall.
3. In the left pane, click Turn Windows Firewall on or off. If you are prompted for an administrator password or confirmation, type the password or provide confirmation.
4. Click Turn on Windows Firewall under the appropriate network location to enable Windows Firewall or click Turn off Windows Firewall (not recommended) under the appropriate network location to disable Windows Firewall. See Figure 12-1. You would typically want to block all incoming traffic when you connect to a public network in a hotel or airport or when a computer worm is spreading over the Internet. When you block all incoming connections, you can still view most web pages, send and receive email, and send and receive instant messages.

Figure 12-1

Windows Firewall

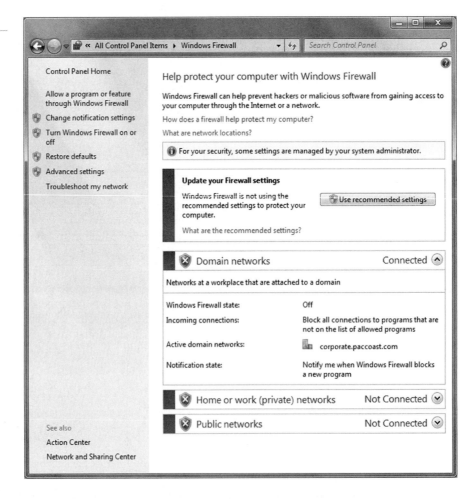

5. If desired, Block all incoming connections, including those in the list of allowed programs and choose Notify me when Windows Firewall blocks a new program.
6. Click the OK button.

By default, most programs are blocked by Windows Firewall to help make your computer more secure. To work properly, some programs might require you to allow them to communicate through the firewall.

 ALLOW A PROGRAM TO COMMUNICATE THROUGH WINDOWS FIREWALL

GET READY. To allow a program to communicate through Windows Firewall:

1. Open Windows Firewall.
2. In the left pane, click Allow a program or feature through Windows Firewall.
3. Click Change settings. If you are prompted for an administrator password or confirmation, type the password or provide confirmation.
4. Select the check box next to the program you want to allow, select the network locations you want to allow communication on, and then click OK.

 OPEN A PORT IN WINDOWS FIREWALL

GET READY. If the program isn't listed, you might need to open a port:

1. Open Windows Firewall.
2. In the left pane, click Advanced settings. If you are prompted for an administrator password or confirmation, type the password or provide confirmation.
3. In the Windows Firewall with Advanced Security dialog box, in the left pane, click Inbound Rules, and then, in the right pane, click New Rule.
4. Select Port and click the Next button. See Figure 12-2.

TAKE NOTE* For a list of ports, visit http://support.microsoft.com/default.aspx?scid=kb;en-us; 832017 and http://en.wikipedia.org/wiki/List_of_TCP_and_UDP_port_numbers.

Figure 12-2

Inbound Rules options

5. Specify TCP or UDP and specify the port numbers. Click the Next button. See Figure 12-3.

Figure 12-3

Open a port in the Firewall

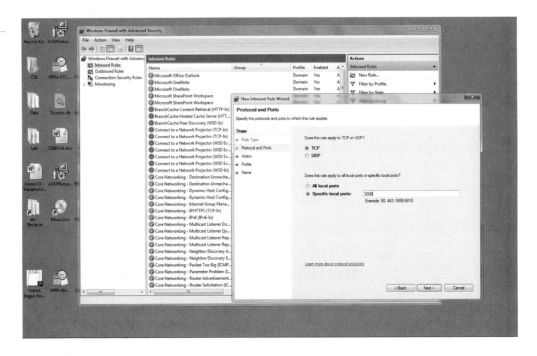

6. Select the Allow the connection, Allow the connection if it is secure or Block the connection. Click the Next button.

7. By default, the rule will apply to all domains. If you don't want the rule to apply to a domain, deselect the domain. Click the Next button.

8. Specify a name for the rule and a description if desired. Click the Finish button.

USING INTERNET EXPLORER SECURITY FEATURES

As explained in Lesson 11, Internet Explorer has multiple security features. These features included InPrivate Browsing, InPrivate Filtering, pop-up blocker, content zones, and Protected Mode.

USING COMMON SENSE WITH MALWARE

To avoid malware, don't forget common sense. Follow these steps:

1. Don't install unknown software or software from a disreputable source.

2. Don't open unexpected or unsolicited email attachments.

3. Don't click on hyperlinks in messages from unknown people without knowing what the link is supposed to do. That applies to messengers too.

4. If your email client supports auto launch, turn it off. Otherwise you might automatically activate a computer virus just by opening the email.

5. Don't visit questionable websites, especially from sites that include downloading software, music and video piracy sites, and porn sites.

6. If your web browser alerts you that a site is known for hosting malware, pay attention to these warnings.

7. If you surf the Internet and you get browser pop-ups that you need to download the newest driver or you need to check your system for viruses, use caution.

8. Don't forget to perform regular backups. So if you get a virus and lose data, you can restore from backup.

USING WINDOWS 7 ACTION CENTER

In Lesson 1 we discussed the Windows 7 *Action Center,* which is a central place to view alerts and take actions to keep Windows running. Like the Network and Sharing Center, the Action Center is a centralized console that enables users and administrators to access, monitor, and configure the various Windows 7 security mechanisms. The primary function of the Action Center is to provide an automatic notification system that alerts users when the system is vulnerable. See Figure 12-4.

Figure 12-4

Windows 7 Action Center

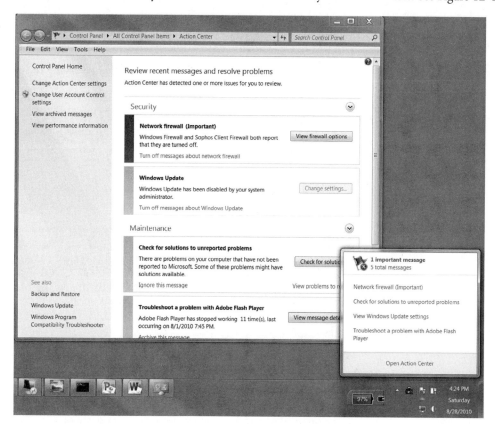

Removing Malware

If you start seeing some of the symptoms listed earlier in this lesson, you need to try to detect and remove the malware.

TAKE NOTE*

Be sure that your anti-virus software is up to date. If it is not kept current, it will not know about newer viruses.

The first step in removing malware would be to run an anti-virus software package and perform a full scan. If you don't have one, it will be a good time to purchase one. If you cannot download it with the computer, you will have to download it from another machine and copy it to an optical disk such as a CD or DVD or use a thumb drive to transfer it to your system. If it finds malware and removes the malware, you should reboot your computer and run it again to be sure your system is clean. If it keeps finding different malware, you should keep running it until you are all clear. You may also consider using online malware scanners from reputable anti-virus companies.

If your anti-virus software package keeps finding the same malware, you need to make sure you are not accessing a disk or other device that would keep infecting the system. You also need to reboot Windows into safe mode and try another scan. If you have the option, you can also try to boot from a CD or DVD and run the scan.

If the malware cannot be removed, you should then do a little bit of research on the Internet. Often, you can find step-by-step instructions in removing malware including deleting files and deleting keys in the registry. Of course, be sure that the instructions are from a reliable source and that you follow the instructions precisely.

TAKE NOTE*

If you have purchased an anti-virus software package and you have trouble removing malware, don't be afraid to contact the company to get assistance.

TAKE NOTE*

Since some malware has key logging capabilities, you may want to update your login information for your online accounts.

Remember, that if your anti-virus package does not have an anti-spyware component, you should install an anti-spyware package to check for spyware. Don't forget about Windows Defender.

Microsoft also includes a Malicious Software Removal Tool, which checks computers running Windows for infections by specific, prevalent malicious software. So when you run updates, you should always run this tool. Microsoft releases an updated version of this tool on the second Tuesday of each month, and as needed to respond to security incidents. The tool is available from Microsoft Update, Windows Update, and the Microsoft Download Center.

Finally, don't forget to use the following tools when trying to remove unknown malware:

- Use Task Manager to view and stop unknown processes and to stop unknown or questionable services.
- Use the Services MMC to stop unknown or questionable services.
- Use System Configuration to disable unknown or questionable services and startup programs.
- Disable unknown or questionable Internet Explorer add-ons.

Looking at a Virus Hoax

A **virus hoax** is a message warning the recipient of a nonexistent computer virus threat, usually sent as a chain email that tells the recipient to forward it to everyone he or she knows.

Virus hoaxes are a form of social engineering that plays on people's ignorance and fear and includes emotive language and encouragement to forward the message to other people. Some hoaxes are harmless that create only fear or use network resources as people forward the emails to other people. However, some hoaxes may tell people to delete key system files that make the system work properly or tell you to download software from the Internet to clean the virus. But instead, they install some form of malware. Anti-virus specialists agree that recipients should delete virus hoaxes when they receive them, instead of forwarding them.

■ Understanding Windows Updates

THE BOTTOM LINE

After installing Windows, check **Windows Update** to see if Microsoft has any updates including fixes, patches, service packs, and device drivers and apply them to the Windows system. By adding fixes and patches, you will keep Windows stable and secure. If there are many fixes or patches, Microsoft releases them together as a service pack or a cumulative package.

CERTIFICATION READY
Why is it important to keep your system updated with patches from Microsoft?
5.4

To update Windows 7, Internet Explorer, and other programs that ship with Windows, go to Windows Update in the Control Panel, or click the Start button, select All Programs and select Windows Update. Then in the left pane, click Check for updates. See Figure 12-5. Windows will then scan your system to determine what updates and fixes your system still needs. You then have the opportunity to select, download, and install each update.

Figure 12-5

Windows Update

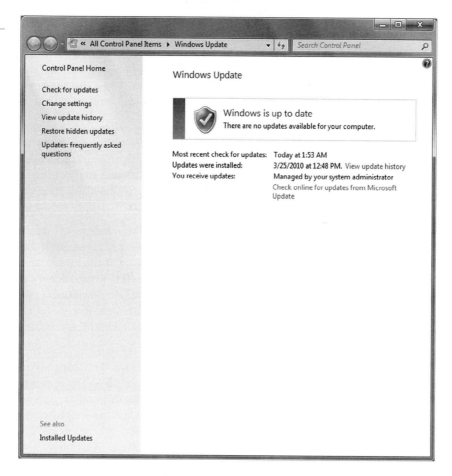

Microsoft routinely releases security updates on the second Tuesday of each month on what is known as "Patch Tuesday." Most other updates are released as needed, which are known as "out of band" updates. Since computers are often used as production systems, you should test updates to make sure they do not cause problems for you. While Microsoft does intensive testing, occasionally problems do occur either through a bug or a compatibility issue with a third-party software. Therefore, you should also make sure you have a good backup of your system and data files before you install patches so that you have a back out plan if necessary.

Updates are classified as Important, Recommended, or Optional:

- **Important updates:** Offer significant benefits, such as improved security, privacy, and reliability. They should be installed as they become available and can be installed automatically with Windows Update.

- **Recommended updates:** Address noncritical problems or help enhance your computing experience. While these updates do not address fundamental issues with your computer or Windows software, they can offer meaningful improvements. These can be installed automatically.

- **Optional updates:** Can include updates, drivers, or new software from Microsoft to enhance your computing experience. You need to install these manually.

Depending on the type of update, Windows Update can deliver:

- **Security updates:** A broadly released fix for a product-specific security-related vulnerability. Security vulnerabilities are rated based on their severity, which is indicated in the Microsoft security bulletin as critical, important, moderate, or low.

- **Critical updates:** A broadly released fix for a specific problem addressing a critical, nonsecurity-related bug.

- **Service Packs:** A tested, cumulative set of hotfixes, security updates, critical updates, and updates, as well as additional fixes for problems found internally since the release of the product. Service Packs might also contain a limited number of customer-requested design changes or features. When an operating system is released, many corporations consider the first service pack as a time when the operating system matures enough to be used throughout the organization.

Not all updates can be retrieved through Windows Update. Sometimes, if you are researching a specific problem, Microsoft may have a fix for the problem by installing a hotfix or cumulative patch. A hotfix is a single, cumulative package that includes one or more files that are used to address a problem in a software product such as a software bug. Typically, hotfixes are made to address a specific customer situation and often have not gone through extensive testing as other patches retrieved through Windows Updates.

For small organizations, you can configure your system to perform Auto Updates to ensure that critical, security, and compatibility updates are made available for installation automatically without significantly affecting your regular use of the Internet. Auto Update works in the background when you are connected to the Internet to identify when new updates are available and to download them to your computer. When download is completed, you will be notified and prompted to install the update. You can install it then, get more details about what is included in the update, or let Windows remind you about it later. Some installations may require you to reboot, but some do not.

To change the Windows Update settings, click the Change settings option in the left pane of the Windows Update window. See Figure 12-6. The options allow you to specify whether to download and let you specify which ones to install, specify which updates to install and then download, or just disable Windows Update all together. You can also specify if Windows Update will check for other Microsoft products other than the operating system and also install software that Microsoft recommends.

Figure 12-6

Windows Update settings

If Windows Update fails to get updates, you should check your proxy settings in Internet Explorer to see if it can get through your proxy server (if any) or firewall. You should also check to see if you can access the Internet such as accessing the http://www.microsoft.com website.

To see all updates that have been installed, click the View Update History link on the left pane. If you suspect a problem with a specific update, you can then click Installed Updates at the top of the screen that will open the Control Panel's Programs. From there, you will then see the all installed programs and installed updates. If the option is available, you can then remove the update.

■ Understanding Encryption

THE BOTTOM LINE

> **Encryption** is the process of converting data into a format that cannot be read by another user. Once a user has encrypted a file, it automatically remains encrypted when the file is stored on disk. **Decryption** is the process of converting data from encrypted format back to its original format.

CERTIFICATION READY
What can cause decryption of a document to fail?
5.3

Encryption algorithms can be divided into three classes:

- Symmetric
- Asymmetric
- Hash function

Symmetric encryption uses a single key to encrypt and decrypt data. Therefore, it is also referred to as secret-key, single-key, shared-key, and private-key encryption. To use symmetric key algorithms, you need to initially send or provide the secret key to both sender and receiver.

Asymmetric key, also known as public-key cryptography, uses two mathematically related keys. One key is used to encrypt the data while the second key is used to decrypt the data. Unlike symmetric key algorithms, it does not require a secure initial exchange of one or more secret keys to both sender and receiver. Instead, you can make the public key known to anyone and use the other key to encrypt or decrypt the data. The public key could be sent to someone or could be published within a digital certificate via a Certificate Authority (CA). Secure Sockets Layer (SSL)/Transport Layer Security (TLS) and Pretty Good Privacy (PGP) use asymmetric keys.

For example, say you want a partner to send you data. Therefore, you send the partner the public key. The partner will then encrypt the data with the key and send you the encrypted message. You then use the private key to decrypt the message. If the public key falls into someone else's hands, that person still could not decrypt the message.

The last type of encryption is the hash function. Different from the symmetric and asymmetric algorithms, a hash function is meant as a one-way encryption. That means that after it has been encrypted, it cannot be decrypted. It can be used to encrypt a password that is stored on disk. Anytime a password is entered, the same hash calculation is performed on the entered password and compared to the hash value of the password stored on disk. If the two match, the user must have typed in the password. This avoids storing the passwords in a readable format that a hacker might try to access.

No matter what encryption algorithm you choose, they all use keys to encrypt data. The key must be long enough so that an attacker cannot try all possible combinations to figure out what the key is. Therefore, a key length of 80 bits is generally considered the minimum for strong security with symmetric encryption algorithms. 128-bit keys are commonly used and considered very strong.

Using File Encryption with NTFS

If someone steals a hard drive that is protected by NTFS permissions, they could take the hard drive, put it in a system in which they are an administrator of and access all files and folders on the hard drive. Therefore, to truly protect a drive that could be stolen or accessed illegally, you can encrypt the files and folders on the drive.

Windows 7 offers two file encrypting technologies, Encrypting File System (EFS) and BitLocker Drive Encryption. EFS protects individual files or folders, while BitLocker protects entire drives.

Encrypting File System (EFS) can encrypt files on an NTFS volume that cannot be used unless the user has access to the keys required to decrypt the information. After a file has been encrypted, you do not have to manually decrypt an encrypted file before you can use it. Once you encrypt a file or folder, you work with the encrypted file or folder just as you do with any other file or folder.

EFS is keyed to a specific user account, using the public and private keys that are the basis of the Windows public key infrastructure (PKI). The user who creates a file is the only person who can read it. As the user works, EFS encrypts the files he or she creates using a key generated from the user's public key. Data encrypted with this key can be decrypted only by the user's personal encryption certificate, which is generated using his or her private key.

 ENCRYPT A FOLDER OR FILE USING EFS

GET READY. To encrypt a folder or file:

1. Right-click the folder or file you want to encrypt, and then click Properties.
2. Click the General tab, and then click Advanced.
3. Select the Encrypt contents to secure data check box, click OK, and then click OK again. See Figure 12-7.

TAKE NOTE*

You can only encrypt or compress NTFS files when using EFS; you can't do both.

Figure 12-7

Encrypting data with EFS

DECRYPT A FOLDER OR FILE

GET READY. To decrypt a folder or file:

1. Right-click the folder or file you want to decrypt, and then click Properties.
2. Click the General tab, and then click Advanced.
3. Clear the Encrypt contents to secure data check box, click OK, and then click OK again.

The first time you encrypt a folder or file, an encryption certificate is automatically created. If your certificate and key are lost or damaged and you don't have a backup, you won't be able to use the files that you have encrypted. Therefore, you should back up your encryption certificate.

BACK UP AN EFS CERTIFICATE

GET READY. To back up your EFS certificate:

1. Execute the certmgr.msc. If you are prompted for an administrator password or confirmation, type the password or provide confirmation.
2. In the left pane, click Personal.
3. Click Certificates.
4. In the main pane, click the certificate that lists Encrypting File System under Intended Purposes. If there is more than one EFS certificate, you should back up all of them.
5. Click the Action menu, point to All Tasks, and then click Export.
6. In the Certificate Export wizard, click Next, click Yes, export the private key, and then click Next.
7. Click Personal Information Exchange, and then click Next.
8. Type the password you want to use, confirm it, and then click Next. The export process will create a file to store the certificate.
9. Type a name for the file and the location (include the whole path) or click Browse, navigate to a location, type a filename, and then click Save.
10. Click Next, and then click Finish.

You should then place the certificate in a safe place.

If for some reason, a person leaves the company and you cannot read encrypted files, you can set up a recovery agent who can recover encrypted files for a domain.

ADD RECOVERY AGENTS

GET READY. To add new users as recovery agents, they must first have recovery certificates issued by the enterprise CA structure:

1. Open the Active Directory Users and Computers console.
2. Right-click the domain, and select Properties.
3. Select the Group Policy tab.
4. Select the Default Domain Policy and click Edit.
5. Expand Computer Configuration\Windows Settings\Security Settings\Public Key Policies\Encrypted Data Recovery Agents.
6. Right-click Encrypted Data Recovery Agents, and select Add.
7. Click Next to the Add Recovery Agent Wizard.

8. Click Browse Directory. Locate the user and click OK.

9. Click Next.

10. Click Finish.

11. Close the Group Policy Editor.

Using Disk Encryption with Windows 7

Unlike EFS, BitLocker allows you to encrypt entire disks. Therefore, if a drive or laptop is stolen, the data is still encrypted even if the thief installs it in another system for which they are an administrator.

BitLocker Drive Encryption is the feature in Windows 7 that makes use of a computer's TPM. A Trusted Platform Module (TPM) is a microchip that is built into a computer. It is used to store cryptographic information, such as encryption keys. Information stored on the TPM can be more secure from external software attacks and physical theft. BitLocker Drive Encryption can use a TPM to validate the integrity of a computer's boot manager and boot files at startup, and to guarantee that a computer's hard disk has not been tampered with while the operating system was offline. BitLocker Drive Encryption also stores measurements of core operating system files in the TPM.

The system requirements of BitLocker are:

- Because BitLocker stores its own encryption and decryption key in a hardware device that is separate from your hard disk, you must have one of the following:
  - A computer with Trusted Platform Module (TPM). If your computer was manufactured with TPM version 1.2 or higher, BitLocker will store its key in the TPM.
  - A removable USB memory device, such as a USB flash drive. If your computer doesn't have TPM version 1.2 or higher, BitLocker will store its key on the flash drive.
- Have at least two partitions: a system partition (which contains the files needed to start your computer and must be at least 200 MB) and an operating system partition (which contains Windows). The operating system partition will be encrypted, and the system partition will remain unencrypted so that your computer can start. If your computer doesn't have two partitions, BitLocker will create them for you. Both partitions must be formatted with the NTFS file system.
- Your computer must have a BIOS that is compatible with TPM and supports USB devices during computer startup. If this is not the case, you will need to update the BIOS before using BitLocker.

BitLocker has five operational modes, which define the steps involved in the system boot process. These modes, in descending order from most to least secure, are as follows:

- **TPM + startup PIN + startup key:** The system stores the BitLocker volume encryption key on the TPM chip, but an administrator must supply a personal identification number (PIN) and insert a USB flash drive containing a startup key before the system can unlock the BitLocker volume and complete the system boot sequence.
- **TPM + startup key:** The system stores the BitLocker volume encryption key on the TPM chip, but an administrator must insert a USB flash drive containing a startup key before the system can unlock the BitLocker volume and complete the system boot sequence.
- **TPM + startup PIN:** The system stores the BitLocker volume encryption key on the TPM chip, but an administrator must supply a PIN before the system can unlock the BitLocker volume and complete the system boot sequence.

TAKE NOTE*

BitLocker is a feature of Windows 7 Enterprise and Windows 7 Ultimate. It is not supported on other editions of Windows 7.

- **Startup key only:** The BitLocker configuration process stores a startup key on a USB flash drive, which the administrator must insert each time the system boots. This mode does not require the server to have a TPM chip, but it must have a system BIOS that supports access to the USB flash drive before the operating system loads.
- **TPM only:** The system stores the BitLocker volume encryption key on the TPM chip, and accesses it automatically when the chip has determined that the boot environment is unmodified. This unlocks the protected volume and the computer continues to boot. No administrative interaction is required during the system boot sequence.

When you enable BitLocker using the BitLocker Drive Encryption control panel, you can select the TPM + startup key, TPM + startup PIN, or TPM only option. To use the TPM + startup PIN + startup key option, you must first configure the *Require additional authentication at startup* Group Policy setting, found in the Computer Configuration\Policies\Administrative Templates\Windows Components\BitLocker Drive Encryption\Operating System Drives container.

ENABLING BITLOCKER

 DETERMINE WHETHER YOU HAVE TPM

GET READY. To find out if your computer has Trusted Platform Module (TPM) security hardware:

1. Open the Control Panel, click System and Security and click BitLocker Drive Encryption.
2. In the left pane, click TPM Administration. If you are prompted for an administrator password or confirmation, type the password or provide confirmation.

The TPM Management on Local Computer snap-in tells you whether your computer has the TPM security hardware. See Figure 12-8. If your computer doesn't have it, you'll need a removable USB memory device to turn on BitLocker and store the BitLocker startup key that you'll need whenever you start your computer.

Figure 12-8

TMP Management console

 TURN ON BITLOCKER

GET READY. Log on to Windows 7 using an account with administrative privileges.

1. Click Start, then click Control Panel > System and Security > BitLocker Drive Encryption. The BitLocker Drive Encryption control panel appears.
2. Click Turn on BitLocker for your hard disk drives. The *Set BitLocker startup preferences* page appears. See Figure 12-9.

Figure 12-9

Turning On BitLocker

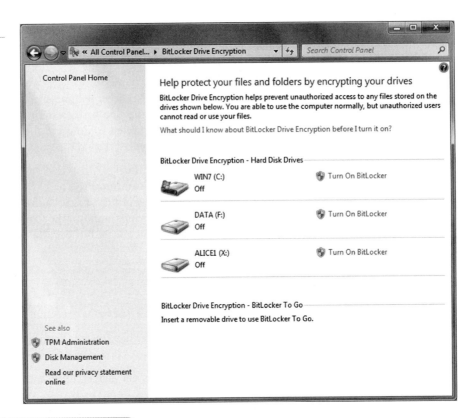

+ MORE INFORMATION

If your computer has a TPM chip, Windows 7 provides a Trusted Platform Module (TPM) Management console that you can use to change the chip's password and modify its properties.

3. Click Require a Startup key at every startup. A *Save your Startup key* page appears.
4. Insert a USB flash drive into a USB port and click Save. The *How do you want to store your recovery key?* page appears.
5. Select one of the options to save your recovery key and click Next. The *Are you ready to encrypt this drive?* page appears.
6. Click Continue. The wizard performs a system check and then restarts the computer.
7. Log on to the computer. Windows 7 proceeds to encrypt the disk.

Once the encryption process is completed, you can open the BitLocker Drive Encryption control panel to ensure that the volume is encrypted, or turn off BitLocker, such as when performing a BIOS upgrade or other system maintenance.

The BitLocker control panel applet enables you to recover the encryption key and recovery password at will. You should consider carefully how to store this information, because it will allow access to the encrypted data. It is also possible to escrow this information into Active Directory.

USING DATA RECOVERY AGENTS AND BITLOCKER

If for some reason, the user loses the startup key and/or startup PIN needed to boot a system with BitLocker, the user can supply the recovery key created during the BitLocker configuration process and regain access to the system. If the user loses the recovery key you can use a data recovery agent designated with active Directory to recover the data on the drive.

A *data recovery agent (DRA)* is a user account that an administrator has authorized to recover BitLocker drives for an entire organization with a digital certificate on a smart card. In most cases, administrators of Active Directory Domain Services (AD DS) networks use

DRAs to ensure access to their BitLocker-protected systems, to avoid having to maintain large numbers of individual keys and PINs.

To create a DRA, you must first add the user account you want to designate to the Computer Configuration\Policies\Windows Settings\Security Settings\Public Key Policies\BitLocker Drive Encryption container in a GPO or to the system's Local Security Policy. Then, you must configure the Provide The Unique Identifiers For Your Organization policy setting in the Computer Configuration\Policies\Administrative Templates\Windows Components\BitLocker Drive Encryption container with unique identification fields for your BitLocker drives.

Finally, you must enable DRA recovery for each type of BitLocker resource you want to recover, by configuring the following policies:

- Choose How BitLocker-Protected Operating System Drives Can Be Recovered
- Choose How BitLocker-Protected Fixed Drives Can Be Recovered
- Choose How BitLocker-Protected Removable Drives Can Be Recovered

These policies enable you to specify how BitLocker systems should store their recovery information, and also enable you to store it in the AD DS database.

USING BITLOCKER TO GO

BitLocker To Go is a new feature in Windows 7 that enables users to encrypt removable USB devices, such as flash drives and external hard disks. While BitLocker has always supported the encryption of removable drives, BitLocker To Go enables you to use the encrypted device on other computers without having to perform an involved recovery process. Because the system is not using the removable drive as a boot device, a TPM chip is not required.

To use BitLocker To Go, you insert the removable drive and open the BitLocker Drive Encryption control panel. The device appears in the interface, with a *Turn on BitLocker* link just like that of the computer's hard disk drive.

SKILL SUMMARY

IN THIS LESSON YOU LEARNED:

- Computer security is the protection of information and property from theft, corruption, or natural disaster, while allowing the information and property to remain accessible and productive to its intended users.

- Social engineering is the act of manipulating people into performing actions or divulging confidential information.

- Social engineering can be avoiding by using common sense, and a little due diligence and awareness.

- Malicious software, sometimes called malware, is software designed to infiltrate or affect a computer system without the owner's informed consent. It is usually associated with viruses, worms, Trojan horses, spyware, rootkits, and dishonest adware.

- A computer virus is a program that can copy itself and infect a computer without the user's consent or knowledge.

- A worm is a self-replicating program that replicates itself to other computers over the network without any user intervention.

- A Trojan horse program is a program named after the Trojan horse story in *The Iliad* (Greek mythology).

- Spyware is a type of malware that is installed on computers and collects personal information or browsing habits often without the user's knowledge.

- Adware is any software package that automatically plays, displays, or downloads advertisements to a computer after the software is installed on it or while the application is being used.

- A rootkit is a software or hardware device designed to gain administrator-level control over a computer system without being detected.

- Most viruses, worms, rootkits, spyware, and adware are made possible because they exploit some security hole with Windows, Internet Explorer, or Microsoft Office.

- The first step in protecting yourself against malware is to keep your system up to date with Windows (as well as other Microsoft products such as Microsoft Office) by downloading the latest service packs, security patches, and other critical fixes.

- The second step to protect your computer from malware is to use an up-to-date anti-virus software package. Make sure you keep your anti-virus software current. If you don't, it will not know about newer viruses.

- If your anti-virus software does not include an anti-spyware component, you should install an anti-spyware software package.

- Windows Defender is a software product from Microsoft that prevents, removes, and quarantines spyware in Microsoft Windows.

- A firewall is software or hardware that checks information coming from the Internet or a network, and then either blocks it or allows it to pass through to your computer, depending on your firewall settings.

- A firewall can help prevent hackers or malicious software (such as worms) from gaining access to your computer through a network or the Internet.

- By default, most programs are blocked by Windows Firewall to help make your computer more secure. To work properly, some programs might require you to allow them to communicate through the firewall.

- The Windows 7 Action Center is a central place to view alerts and take actions that keep Windows running.

- The first step in removing malware would be to run an anti-virus software package and perform a full scan.

- A virus hoax is a message warning the recipient of a nonexistent computer virus threat, usually sent as a chain email that tells the recipient to forward it to everyone he or she knows.

- After installing Windows, check to see if Microsoft has any Windows updates including fixes, patches, service packs, and device drivers, and apply them to the Windows system.

- Microsoft routinely releases security updates on the second Tuesday of each month on what is known as "Patch Tuesday." Most other updates are released as needed, which are known as "out of band" updates.

- Encryption is the process of converting data into a format that cannot be read by another user. Once a user has encrypted a file, it automatically remains encrypted when the file is stored on disk.

- Decryption is the process of converting data from encrypted format back to its original format.

- Encrypting File System (EFS) can encrypt files on an NTFS volume that cannot be used unless the user has access to the keys required to decrypt the information.

- Unlike EFS, BitLocker allows you to encrypt entire disks. Therefore, if a drive or laptop is stolen, the data is still encrypted even if the thief installs it in another system in which they are an administrator.

- A Trusted Platform Module (TPM) is a microchip that is built into a computer. It is used to store cryptographic information, such as encryption keys. Information stored on the TPM is more secure from external software attacks and physical theft.

- A data recovery agent (DRA) is a user account that an administrator has authorized to recover BitLocker drives for an entire organization with a digital certificate on a smart card.

- BitLocker To Go is a new feature in Windows 7 that enables users to encrypt removable USB devices, such as flash drives and external hard disks.

■ Knowledge Assessment

Fill in the Blank

Complete the following sentences by writing the correct word or words in the blanks provided.

1. A nontechnical method to gain access to network resources is known as _____.

2. _____ is software designed to compromise a person's computer without the user's consent.

3. _____ is a self-replicating program that replicates to other computers while consuming network resources.

4. Microsoft's anti-spyware program is _____.

5. For anti-virus software to be effective, it must be _____.

6. The _____ gives you a single place to look at all security components in Windows.

7. An example of a _____ is a message saying to delete the win.com file because it is a virus.

8. The process of converting data into a format that cannot be read by others is _____.

9. To encrypt content on a USB drive, you should use _____.

10. The chip used by BitLocker is known as _____.

Multiple Choice

Circle the letter that corresponds to the best answer.

1. What is a form of malware that copies itself onto other computers without the owner's consent and will often delete or corrupt files?
   a. Virus
   b. Worm
   c. Trojan horse
   d. Spyware

2. What type of malware collects personal information or browsing history often without the user's knowledge?
   a. Virus
   b. Worm

    c. Trojan horse

    d. Spyware

3. Your computer seems to be slow and you notice that you have a different default web page. What is most likely the problem?

    a. Your ISP has slowed your network connection.

    b. Your computer has been infected with malware.

    c. You did not update your computer.

    d. You accidentally clicked the turbo button.

4. Besides installing an anti-virus software package, the best thing to do is to _____ to protect your computer against malware.

    a. Keep your machine up to date with the latest security patches.

    b. Reboot your computer on a regular basis.

    c. Change your password on a regular basis.

    d. Spoof your IP address.

5. _____ is required to run protected mode in IE.

    a. Runas Administrator

    b. UAC

    c. Fully patched system

    d. A running Protected Mode service

6. Where can you quickly see if you are using a firewall, a current anti-virus package, and if your computer has the newest security patches from Microsoft?

    a. System Configuration

    b. Event Viewer

    c. Services console

    d. Action Center

7. What technology is used to encrypt individual files on an NTFS volume?

    a. BitLocker

    b. BitLocker To Go

    c. EFS

    d. DFS

8. What technology is used to encrypt an entire volume?

    a. BitLocker

    b. BitLocker To Go

    c. EFS

    d. DFS

9. You encrypted a file using EFS. The next day, you decide to compress the file because of its large size. Later you notice that it was not encrypted anymore. What is the problem?

    a. You cannot compress and use EFS on a file at the same time.

    b. The file is not on an NTFS volume.

    c. You have malware.

    d. The file was backed up and the archive attribute was turned off.

10. If your machine does not have a TPM chip, you can still use BitLocker if you use _____ .

    a. The C drive to store the keys

    b. A USB Flash drive

    c. A floppy disk

    d. A read-write CD

True / False

Circle T if the statement is true or F if the statement is false.

T | F   1. No matter what technology you use to secure your laptop, social engineering can still bypass that security.

T | F   2. The best way to protect your system is to use an up-to-date anti-virus and to keep your system up to date with the newest security patches.

T | F   3. If the patches are released on Microsoft Patch Tuesday, you don't have to test the patches before deploying on your production systems.

T | F   4. BitLocker requires a TPM chip.

T | F   5. If a user loses his or her password and key, they will never be able to access their encrypted files if they are encrypted with BitLocker.

■ Case Scenarios

Scenario 12-1: Keys and Password

You work for the Contoso Corporation. Your CIO walks up to you and says that he just got a message on his computer saying that he has to change his password. He wants to know why he has to change the password to a relatively long password on a regular basis. What do you tell him?

Scenario 12-2: Social Engineering

You work for the Contoso Corporation. Your manager wants to put a training class together for end user security. He wants you to research on the Internet for three cases or instances where someone used social engineering to break into a system and list how they attempted to get access.

Appendices Brief Contents

Introduction to Networking Concepts

■ Understanding TCP/IP Addressing

THE BOTTOM LINE

From as early as the 1950s, one of the main challenges in the field of computer science has been finding ways to allow different computers to communicate with one another. Before networking technologies became prevalent, files would be transferred manually from one computer to another using portable media such as a floppy disk. Over time, this process was replaced by various networking technologies that allowed computers to communicate using different types of network cables, which are the physical means of communicating, as well as *network protocols*, which provide the logical "language" for communication. Just like two human beings must speak the same language in order to communicate, two computers must be configured with the same network protocols in order to communicate and transfer information. Numerous networking protocols have gained varying levels of prevalence over the years, but the most common networking protocol in use today is *Transmission Control Protocol/Internet Protocol (TCP/IP)*. Rather than a single network protocol, TCP/IP consists of a suite of different protocols that work in concert to allow computers to communicate on a TCP/IP network. TCP/IP networks are arranged in a hierarchical fashion that allows for a great deal of flexibility and scalability; by subdividing TCP/IP networks into smaller groupings called *subnets*, the administration of a TCP/IP network can be as centralized or as decentralized as the needs of a particular organization might dictate. (You can see this in action in the largest TCP/IP network in the world, which is "owned" and administered by hundreds and thousands of separate entities. The name of this TCP/IP network? The Internet.) This lesson introduces fundamental concepts related to TCP/IP networking, including the fundamentals of IP network addressing, and the distinction between IPv4 and IPv6. The lesson also introduces the basic concepts of various TCP/IP network services such as DHCP, DNS, and *routing*, the process of transferring data across a network from one LAN to another.

In order for any computer or *host*, a computer, printer, or other device configured with a network interface, to communicate on a TCP/IP network, it must be configured with a valid *IP address*. This IP address, analogous to the postal address of a house or an office building, provides a way to identify a device that is connected to a TCP/IP network and provides a means for one computer to contact another in order to transmit information. Each IP address consists of two components:

- *network address*—This portion of the IP address is shared by all TCP/IP hosts on a particular network or subnet.
- *host address*—This comprises the portion of the IP address that is unique to a particular computer or host. The combination of the network address plus the host address creates the IP address as a whole, each of which must be unique across an entire TCP/IP network.

In addition to the IP address, each TCP/IP host must be configured with the following:

- *subnet mask*—Used to identify which network the TCP/IP host resides on by defining where the network address stops and the host address begins.

- *default gateway*—Allows a host to communicate with devices that reside on a remote network or location. (On the extremely rare occasion when you are configuring hosts that never need to communicate outside of their own subnet, a default gateway is not required; however, with the prevalence of Internet connectivity, you will almost always find a default gateway configured on TCP/IP-enabled devices.)

Introducing TCP/IP Addressing

The TCP/IP protocol suite has undergone several revisions since it was first developed in the 1960s. The version of TCP/IP that is most commonly used on modern networks is *IP version 4(IPv4)*. *IP version 6 (IPv6)* is a new TCP/IP implementation that is increasing in prevalence, as it addresses a number of shortcomings that have appeared in IPv4 over time. IPv4 was the first implementation of the Internet Protocol (IP) to be widely deployed, predating the public Internet. It uses 32 bits (four bytes, or *octets*) for addressing, thus providing a mathematical limit of 2^{32} possible addresses. Some of the possible addresses are reserved (for example, for private networks or multicast addresses), so that the maximum number of possible network addresses is somewhat less than the theoretical maximum. IPv4 addresses are commonly represented using what is called *dotted-decimal notation*, in which the decimal value of each byte is shown, using periods to separate the bytes; for example, 192.1.120.84 or 192.5.18.102 would be IPv4 addresses in dotted-decimal notation.

When IPv4 was first introduced, only the first octet was used for the network number and the remaining three octets were used for the host number. This limited the number of possible networks to a maximum of 254, which was quickly seen to be inadequate. The next revision defined what is termed *classful addressing*, in which the field for the network number was a different length for different classes of network, and the remaining bits were used for the host number, so each network class had a different maximum number of nodes. As shown in Table A-1, the first one to four bits identified the network class, and the remaining bits comprised the network and host address fields. Class A networks had the most significant bit as "0" and used the remainder of the first octet for the network number. Thus there were 126 Class A networks, with a maximum of 16,777,214 hosts in each. Note that the number of valid networks and hosts available is always $2^N - 2$ (where N is the number of bits used, and the 2 adjusts for the special function of the first and last address in each network). Class B networks had the two most significant bits as "10," with the remainder of the first two octets, or fourteen bits, representing the network number. Thus there were 16,384 Class B networks, with a maximum of 65,534 hosts in each. Class C networks had the three most significant bits as "110," with the remainder of the first three octets as the network number and the last octet as the host number. Thus there were 2,097,152 Class C networks, each with a maximum of 254 host addresses. Network addresses with the four most significant bits "1110" (Class D, multicast) and "1111" (Class E, reserved) were also defined.

Table A-1

IP Network Classes

Network Class	Leading Bits	Bits for Network Number	Number of Networks	Bits for Host Number	Maximum Hosts
Class A	0	7	126	24	16,777,214
Class B	10	14	16,384	16	65,534
Class C	110	21	2,097,152	8	254
Class D (multicast)	1110				
Class E (reserved)	1111				

Using this classful addressing scheme created a few large networks with many possible host addresses, and a much larger number of small networks with fewer possible host addresses, so it was considerably more flexible. However, there were still problems and limitations in this design. Some networks required more host addresses than their network class allowed, and other networks had many more host addresses than they used.

To overcome these issues and to improve flexibility for public ***Internet Service Providers (ISPs)*** to allocate many small networks to their customers, ***Classless Inter-Domain Routing (CIDR)*** evolved. CIDR creates a hierarchical addressing structure by breaking the network address space into CIDR blocks, which are identified by the leading bit string, similar to the classful addressing just described. However, the length of the bit string identifying a CIDR block is specified as part of the block name, using ***CIDR notation***. CIDR notation describes a network by specifying the base address and the number of bits used for the network portion; i.e., 10.0.0.0/8 would describe a network using 24 bits for host numbering and thus having a maximum of $2^{24} - 2$ possible host addresses. The CIDR notation can be viewed as representing a bitmask dividing the routing (network) information and a block of local addresses. The classful networking address structure can also be described using CIDR notation, as shown in Table A-2.

Table A-2

CIDR Representation of Classful Addresses

Network Class	Starting Address	Ending Address	CIDR Block	Bitmask
Class A	0.0.0.0	127.255.255.255	/8	255.0.0.0
Class B	128.0.0.0	191.255.255.255	/16	255.255.0.0
Class C	192.0.0.0	223.255.255.255	/24	255.255.255.0
Class D (multicast)	224.0.0.0	239.255.255.255	/4	
Class E (reserved)	240.0.0.0	255.255.255.255	/4	

This hierarchical structure can be even further divided by ***subnetting***. Subnetting refers to the logical partitioning of an organization's network address range into smaller blocks, by using a subnet mask to further distinguish the contents of the network address as a subnet number and a subnet address block. CIDR can be viewed as a method of subnetting the entire public IP address space, essentially carving it up into blocks that can be managed by service providers. A subnet mask is analogous to defining CIDR blocks within internal networks, allowing ISPs to delegate address management within the blocks assigned to their customers. Thus the CIDR block number contains information required for external routing, and the subnet mask distinguishes information required for routing internally from the host numbers (or hierarchical subnet addresses) contained within the subnet.

A big advantage of subnetting is that systems within a subnet need not be burdened with information about external network addressing. Systems within the same subnet share the same network address, so they can communicate directly without additional information about the external network. A default gateway is then used to route traffic for addresses outside the local subnet. Only the gateway requires any information about external network addressing.

For convenience, several network address blocks were reserved for private networks, and they were defined to be non-routable outside of the private network. Hosts using private network addresses can communicate with public networks only by using ***network address translation (NAT)***, which enables routing by mapping their private network address to a different, routable network address. The private IPv4 network address ranges are shown in Table A-3.

Table A-3

Private Network Address Ranges

ADDRESS RANGE	DESCRIPTION	MAXIMUM ADDRESSES	CLASSFUL DESCRIPTION	CIDR DESCRIPTION
10.0.0.0 – 10.255.255.255	24-bit block	16,777,216	Single Class A network	10.0.0.0/8
172.16.0.0 – 172.31.255.255	20-bit block	1,048,576	16 contiguous Class B networks	172.16.0.0/12
169.254.0.0 – 169.254.255.255	16-bit block	65,536	256 contiguous Class C networks	169.254.0.0/16
192.168.0.0 – 192.168.255.255	16-bit block	65,536	256 contiguous Class C networks	192.168.0.0/16

Introducing IP version 6 (IPv6)

With the popularization of the public Internet, the limitations of the address space, that is, the list of usable TCP/IP addresses, provided by IPv4 became a concern. When IPv4 reached prevalence in the 1960s, no one foresaw the Internet explosion of the 1990s that would threaten to exhaust even the 4-billion-plus IP addresses available through IPv4. While the use of private IP networks and NAT have alleviated the problem somewhat, a long-term solution is still required. To this end, *IPv6*, the next generation of the TCP/IP protocol, was developed to provide a significantly larger address space for current and future implementations of TCP/IP networks.

IPv6 uses 128 bits, or 16 bytes, for addressing, thus providing 2^{128} (about 340 billion) unique addresses. To put this in perspective, the IPv6 address space would allow each human being on the planet Earth to possess multiple IPv6 IP addresses that were assigned only to them, without ever being re-used.

IPv6 address notation is noticeably different from the dotted-decimal of IPv4, using eight groups of four hexadecimal digits, separated by colons. IPv6 includes a few other enhancements for performance and security. Notably, IP security through the use of IPSec is an integral part of IPv6, whereas it was an optional feature under IPv4.

Unlike IPv4 addresses, which are 32 bits in length and expressed in dotted-decimal notation, IPv6 addresses are 128 bits in length and expressed in hexadecimal notation. For example, `192.168.1.101` is an example of an IPv4 IP address, while `2001:0db8:85a3:08d3:13 19:8a2e:0370:7334` is an example of an IPv6 IP address. If an IPv6 address contains a series of sequential zeroes, the address can be shortened to use a single zero in each group, or else the entire grouping can be represented using a double colon (`::`). So the following three strings all represent the same IPv6 address:

- `2001:0000:0000:0000:0000:0000:0000:7334`
- `2001:0:0:0:0:0:0:7334`
- `2001::7334`

IPv6 addresses have retained from IPv4 the delineation between host address and network address, and IPv6 networks can be expressed using CIDR notation such as `2001:0db8:1234::/48` to represent the `2001:0db8:1234` network configured with a 48-bit subnet mask.

IPv6 has been supported in the Windows operating systems since Windows Server 2003; however, Windows Vista and Windows Server 2008 are the first Microsoft operating systems to have IPv6 support turned on right out of the box. IPv6 can be managed using the Network and Sharing Center graphical user interface, or using the netsh command-line utility.

TAKE NOTE*

The loopback address in IPv4 is written as `127.0.0.1`; in IPv6 it is written as `::1`.

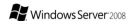

■ Introducing the Domain Name System (DNS)

THE BOTTOM LINE

For network devices, such as computers and printers, to communicate on the Internet or within your organization's TCP/IP network, they must be able to locate one another. This ability is provided by the IP address, as we discussed in the previous section. But it is cumbersome to use IP addresses as the only means of identifying systems. A more common practice is to use human-readable names as a more convenient way for humans to refer to systems. Thus, in order for Computer A to communicate with Computer B using TCP/IP, Computer A must obtain the IP address of Computer B. It is also convenient to be able to refer to a network, or part of a network, by its name instead of its address range.

The Domain Name System (DNS) provides the mechanism for associating meaningful host names with network addresses. Because DNS plays such a key role in Microsoft Windows Server 2008 and the public Internet, it is critical that you have a strong grasp of its concepts, processes, and methods of configuration. Without DNS, your network will most likely not function—clients won't be able to resolve names to Internet Protocol (IP) addresses. In addition, Active Directory clients use DNS to locate domain controllers; therefore, it is important that you understand key DNS concepts and how to properly configure DNS for your network.

The process of obtaining an IP address for a computer name (for example, "ComputerA") is called *name resolution*. Originally, before the evolution of what we now know as the Internet, name resolution was handled by text files called *HOSTS files*. The text file listed each name of the host and its corresponding IP address within the HOSTS file. Whenever a new host was added to the network, the HOSTS file was updated with the host name and IP address. Periodically, all systems would download and then use the updated HOSTS file. Because the HOSTS file was flat, rather than hierarchical, every host name using this system had to be unique. There was no method for creating namespaces such as DNS domains like *www.adatum.com*.

Another problem with HOSTS files was an inability to distribute the workload that resulted from parsing this file across multiple computers. Every HOSTS file listed every available host, which meant that every computer that parsed the HOSTS file did all of the work to resolve client names into IP addresses. Clearly, this was inefficient, and a better name resolution system had to be devised.

Using DNS for Name Resolution

DNS was developed to provide a method of associating such names with network addresses. DNS provides mechanisms for communicating names and network addresses publicly, so that system names can be resolved to network addresses from anywhere that the address would be reachable. Because DNS is designed as a distributed database with a hierarchical structure, it can serve as the foundation for host name resolution in a TCP/IP network of any size, including the Internet. The distributed nature of DNS enables the name resolution workload to be shared among many computers. Today, most internetworking software, such as e-mail programs and Web browsers, use DNS for name resolution. Also, because of the hierarchical design of DNS, it provides a means of naming networks as well as end devices.

In a Windows Server 2008 network, the primary means of identifying network devices and network services is through the use of DNS. Although DNS is most commonly associated with the Internet, private networks also use DNS because of the following benefits:

* Scalability—Because DNS is capable of distributing workload across several databases or computers, it can scale to handle any level of name resolution required.

- Transparency—Host names remain constant even when associated IP addresses change, which makes locating network resources much easier.
- Ease of use—Users access computers using easy-to-remember names such as www. microsoft.com rather than a numerical IP address, such as 192.168.1.100.
- Simplicity—Users need to learn only one naming convention to find resources on either the Internet or an intranet.

To understand the importance of DNS and how it functions within a Windows Server 2008 networking environment, you must understand the following components of DNS:

- DNS namespace
- DNS zones
- Types of DNS name servers
- DNS resource records

The DNS namespace is a hierarchical, tree-structured namespace, starting at an unnamed root used for all DNS operations. In the DNS namespace, each node and leaf object in the domain namespace tree represents a named domain. Each domain can have additional child domains. Figure A-1 illustrates the structure of an Internet domain namespace.

Figure A-1

Internet DNS namespace

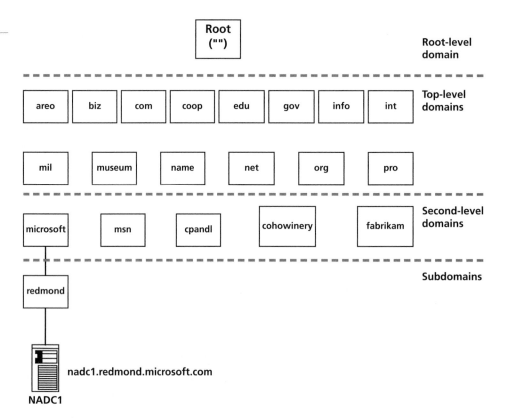

The DNS namespace has a hierarchical structure, and each DNS domain name is unique. In Figure A-1, at the top of the Internet DNS namespace is the root domain. The root domain is represented by "." (a period). Under the DNS root domain, the top-level domains, or first-level domains, are organizational types such as .org, .com, and .edu, or country codes such as .uk (United Kingdom), .de (Germany), and .it (Italy). The Internet Assigned Numbers Authority (IANA) assigns top-level domains. Table A-4 lists several top-level domain names and their uses.

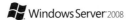

Table A-4

Generic Top-Level Domain Names

Domain Name	Use
.aero	Exclusively reserved for the aviation community
.biz	A top-level domain that is aimed at large and small companies around the world
.com	Commercial organizations, such as microsoft.com for the Microsoft Corporation
.coop	A top-level domain for cooperatives
.edu	Educational institutions, now mainly four-year colleges and universities, such as wustl.edu for Washington University in St. Louis
.gov	Agencies of the U.S. federal government, such as fbi.gov for the U.S. Federal Bureau of Investigation
.info	An unrestricted domain aimed at providing information for worldwide consumption
.int	Organizations established by international treaties, such as nato.int for NATO
.mil	U.S. military, such as af.mil for the U.S. Air Force
.museum	A domain restricted to museums and related organizations and individuals
.name	A global domain for use by individuals that possibly develops into a global digital identity for users
.net	Computers of network providers, organizations dedicated to the Internet, Internet service providers (ISPs), and so forth, such as internic.net for the Internet Network Information Center (InterNIC)
.org	A top-level domain for groups that do not fit anywhere else, such as nongovernmental or nonprofit organizations (for example, w3.org, which is the World Wide Web Consortium)
.pro	A top-level domain for professionals, such as doctors, lawyers, and accountants

DNS uses a ***fully qualified domain name (FQDN)*** to map a host name to an IP address. The FQDN describes the exact relationship between a host and its DNS domain. For example, *computer1.sales.adatum.com* represents a host name, *computer1*, in the *sales* domain, in the *adatum* second-level domain, and in the *.com* top-level domain, which is under the "." root domain.

Second-level DNS domains are registered to individuals or organizations, such as *microsoft.com*, the Microsoft Corporation in the corporate (.com) domain; or *wustl.edu*, which is Washington University of St. Louis in the education (.edu) domain; or *gov.au*, the domain for the Australian government. Second-level DNS domains can have many subdomains, and any domain can have hosts. A host is a specific computer or other network device within a domain, such as *computer1* in the *sales* subdomain of the *microsoft.com* domain.

One benefit of the hierarchical structure of DNS is that it is possible to have two hosts with the same host names that are in different locations in the hierarchy. For example, two hosts named computer1—*computer1.sales.adatum.com* and *computer1.cpandl.microsoft.com*—can both exist without conflict because they are in different locations in the namespace hierarchy.

As previously noted, another benefit of the DNS hierarchical structure is that workload for name resolution is distributed across many different resources, through the use of DNS caching, DNS zones, and delegation of authority through the use of appropriate resource records. DNS zones, name servers, and resource records are discussed in more detail later in this book. For now, it is sufficient to understand that DNS is the way that IP addresses can be given a unique name.

■ Introducing the Dynamic Host Configuration Protocol (DHCP)

THE BOTTOM LINE

It is very important to understand that address assignments are not arbitrary. The address specifies both the system identification and also its location within the network. Thus, each IP address must be both valid and unique within the host's entire internetwork. This requirement presents a challenge for network administrators. The process of assigning, changing, retiring, and reassigning addresses must be carefully monitored to ensure that each host has a unique IP address. Private network address ranges help, but addresses within private networks must still be unique within that network. The ***Dynamic Host Configuration Protocol (DHCP)*** provides a mechanism for conveniently assigning network addresses and other network configuration parameters to a system upon request, usually when it is first bootstrapped or attached to the network. This greatly simplifies network management.

When administering TCP/IP hosts, you can assign ***static IP addresses***, which must be configured and maintained manually. This can become a daunting, tedious task as the number of systems grows to larger numbers. Organizations with significant numbers of workstations requiring IP address configurations would have great difficulty managing IP addressing manually. Dynamic Host Configuration Protocol (DHCP) simplifies the problem by automating the assigning, tracking, and reassigning of IP addresses.

DHCP allows administrators to configure TCP/IP by automatically assigning unique IP addresses while preventing duplicate address assignment and also to provide other important settings such as the default gateway, subnet mask, DNS, etc. Ideally, this would be accomplished without having to manually list every device on the network. DHCP is based heavily on the Bootstrap Protocol (BOOTP), a protocol still in use today that provides IP configuration information to diskless workstations that cannot store information locally and need to store their IP information in volatile memory upon each system boot. DHCP may be based on BOOTP, but it extends its predecessor in several ways. Rather than push preconfigured parameters to expected clients, DHCP can dynamically allocate an IP address from a pool of addresses and then reclaim it when it is no longer needed. Because this process is dynamic, no duplicate addresses are assigned by a properly configured DHCP server and administrators can move computers between subnets without manually configuring them. In addition, a large number of standard configuration and platform-specific parameters can be specified and dynamically delivered to the client. Thus, DHCP provides important functions beyond simply bootstrapping diskless workstations, and it is often used to automatically configure networking after systems are booted.

Understanding DHCP

DHCP is an open, industry-standard protocol that reduces the complexity of administering networks based on TCP/IP. It provides a mechanism for automatically assigning IP addresses and reusing them when they are no longer needed by the system to which they were assigned. It also provides mechanisms for providing associated configuration information when systems are first assigned IP addresses. DHCP is defined by the Internet Engineering Task Force (IETF) Requests for Comments (RFCs) 2131 and 2132.

➕ MORE INFORMATION

DHCP is an IETF standard and is defined in RFCs 2131 and 2132, which can be looked up at www.rfc-editor.org/rfcsearch.html. Requests For Comments (usually referred to in abbreviated form as RFC) is the process by which the IETF arrives at a consensus standard for fundamental internet technologies. New RFC numbers are assigned sequentially, and are conventionally used to identify the resulting standard.

IP addressing is complex, in part because each host connected to a TCP/IP network must be assigned at least one unique IP address and subnet mask in order to communicate on the network. Additionally, most hosts will require additional information, such as the IP addresses of the default gateway and the DNS servers. DHCP frees system administrators from manually configuring each host on the network. The larger the network, the greater the benefit of using DHCP. Without dynamic address assignment, each host has to be configured manually and IP addresses must be carefully managed to avoid duplication or misconfiguration.

Managing IP addresses and host options is much easier when configuration information can be managed from a single location rather than coordinating information across many locations. DHCP can automatically configure a host while it is booting on a TCP/IP network, as well as change settings while the host is connected to the network. All of this is accomplished using settings and information from a central DHCP database. Because settings and information are stored centrally, you can quickly and easily add or change a client setting (for example, the IP address of an alternate DNS server) for all clients on your network from a single location. Without a centralized database of configuration information, it is difficult to maintain a current view of the host settings or to change them.

All Microsoft Windows clients automatically install the DHCP Client service as part of TCP/IP, including Microsoft Windows Vista, Microsoft Windows XP, Microsoft Windows 2000, Microsoft Windows NT 4, Microsoft Windows Millennium Edition (Windows Me), and Microsoft Windows 98.

In brief, DHCP provides five key benefits to those managing and maintaining a TCP/IP network:

- Centralized administration of IP configuration—DHCP IP configuration information can be stored in one location, enabling the administrator to centrally manage it. A DHCP server tracks all leased and reserved IP addresses and lists them in the DHCP console. You can use the DHCP console to determine the IP addresses of all DHCP-enabled devices on your network. Without DHCP, not only would you need to manually assign addresses, but you would also be required to devise a method of tracking and updating them.

- Dynamic host configuration—DHCP automates the host configuration process for key configuration parameters. This eliminates the need to manually configure individual hosts when TCP/IP is first deployed or when IP infrastructure changes are required.

- Seamless IP host configuration—The use of DHCP ensures that DHCP clients get accurate and timely IP configuration parameters, such as the IP address, subnet mask, default gateway, IP address of the DNS server, and so on, without user intervention. Because the configuration is automatic, troubleshooting of misconfigurations, such as mistyped numbers, is largely eliminated.

- Scalability—DHCP scales from small to large networks. DHCP can service networks with ten clients as well as networks with thousands of clients. For very small, isolated networks, Automatic Private IP Addressing (APIPA) can be used, which is a component of Windows networking that automatically determines the client IP configuration without access to an external DHCP server.

- Flexibility—Using DHCP gives the administrator increased flexibility, allowing the administrator to more easily change IP configurations when the infrastructure changes.

X REF

APIPA is defined and discussed in more detail later in this appendix.

USING THE DHCP RELAY AGENT

DHCP relies heavily on broadcast messages. Broadcast messages are generally limited to the subnet in which they originate and are not forwarded to other subnets. This poses a problem if a client is located on a different subnet from the DHCP server. A DHCP relay agent can solve this problem.

A ***DHCP relay agent*** is either a host or an IP router that listens for DHCP (and BOOTP) client messages being broadcast on a subnet and then forwards those DHCP messages to a DHCP server on a remote subnet. The DHCP server sends DHCP response messages back to the relay agent, which then broadcasts them onto the local subnet for the DHCP client. Using DHCP relay agents eliminates the need to have a DHCP server on every subnet.

To support and use the DHCP service across multiple subnets, routers connecting each subnet should comply with the DHCP/BOOTP relay agent capabilities described in RFC 1542. To comply with RFC 1542 and provide relay agent support, each router must be able to recognize BOOTP and DHCP protocol messages and relay them appropriately. Because routers typically interpret DHCP messages as BOOTP messages, a router with only BOOTP relay agent capability relays DHCP packets and any BOOTP packets sent on the network.

The DHCP relay agent is configured with the address of a DHCP server. The DHCP relay agent listens for DHCPDISCOVER, DHCPREQUEST, and DHCPINFORM messages that are broadcast from the client. The DHCP relay agent then waits a previously configured amount of time and, if no response is detected, sends a unicast message to the configured DHCP server. The server then acts on the message and sends the reply back to the DHCP relay agent. The relay agent then broadcasts the message on the local subnet, allowing the DHCP client to receive it. This is depicted in Figure A-2.

Figure A-2

DHCP messages are forwarded by a DHCP relay agent

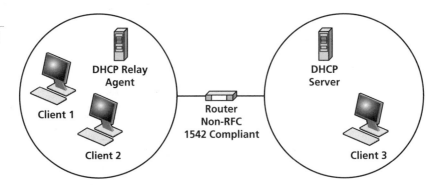

1. Client 1 Broadcasts a DHCPDISCOVER packet
2. Relay agent forwards DHCPDISCOVER packet to DHCP server
3. Server sends a DHCPOFFER packet to the DHCP relay agent
4. Relay agent broadcasts the DHCPOFFER packet
5. Client 1 broadcasts a DHCPREQUEST packet
6. Relay agent forwards the DHCPREQUEST packet to the DHCP server
7. Server broadcasts a DHCPACK packet which is picked up by the DHCP relay agent
8. Relay agent broadcasts the DHCPACK packet

CONFIGURING CLIENTS WITHOUT DHCP

Client systems need to obtain an IP address in order to join the network. DHCP is the usual solution, but it is possible that no DHCP server would be accessible (for example, a remote server could become inaccessible if the relay agent went down). As mentioned previously, clients can be configured automatically determine their IP configuration in cases where they cannot access an external DHCP server. This automatic configuration facility is called *Automatic Private IP Addressing (APIPA)*.

In most cases, DHCP clients find a server either on a local subnet or through a relay agent. To allow for the possibility that a DHCP server is unavailable, Windows Vista, Windows Server 2008, Windows Server 2003, Windows XP, Windows 2000, and Windows 98 provide Automatic Private IP Addressing (APIPA). APIPA is a facility of the Windows TCP/IP implementation that allows a computer to determine IP configuration information without a DHCP server or manual configuration.

APIPA avoids the problem of IP hosts being unable to communicate if for some reason the DHCP server is unavailable. Figure A-3 illustrates different IP address assignment outcomes

Figure A-3

How IP addresses are assigned using APIPA or an alternate configuration

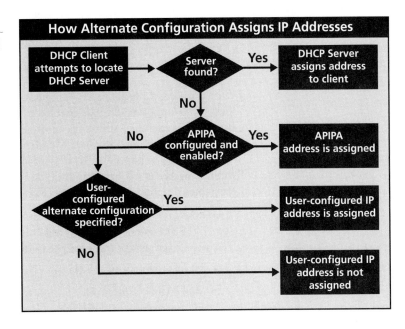

when a DHCP client attempts to find a DHCP server. In the case where a DHCP server is not found and APIPA is configured and enabled, an APIPA address is assigned. APIPA is useful for small workgroup networks where no DHCP server is implemented. Because autoconfiguration does not support a default gateway, it works only with a single subnet and is not appropriate for larger networks.

If the DHCP client is unable to locate a DHCP server and is not configured with an alternate configuration (as shown in Figure A-4), the computer configures itself with an IP address randomly chosen from the Internet Assigned Numbers Authority (IANA)–reserved class B network 169.254.0.0 and with the subnet mask 255.255.0.0. The autoconfigured computer then tests to verify that the IP address it has chosen is not already in use by using a gratuitous ARP broadcast. If the chosen IP address is in use, the computer randomly selects another address. The computer makes up to ten attempts to find an available IP address.

Figure A-4

Alternate configuration properties page

Once the selected address has been verified as available, the client is configured to use that address. The DHCP client continues to check for a DHCP server in the background every five minutes, and if a DHCP server is found, the configuration offered by the DHCP server is used.

Windows Vista, Windows XP, Windows Server 2008, and Windows Server 2003 clients can be configured to use an alternate configuration, which the DHCP client uses if a DHCP server cannot be contacted. The alternate configuration includes an IP address, a subnet mask, a default gateway, DNS, and additional configuration information.

One purpose of the alternate configuration is as a solution for portable computers that move between a corporate, DHCP-enabled network and a home network where static IP addressing is used. For example, Janice has a portable computer she uses at work and at home. At work, her portable computer obtains IP address information using DHCP, but she does not use a DHCP server at home. Janice can use alternate configuration to hold her home IP address, subnet mask, default gateway, and DNS server information so that when she connects her portable computer to her home network, it is configured automatically.

If you use DHCP with an alternate configuration, and the DHCP client cannot locate a DHCP server, the alternate configuration is used to configure the network adapter. No additional discovery attempts are made except under the following conditions:

- The network adapter is disabled and then enabled again.
- Media (such as network cabling) is disconnected and then reconnected.
- The TCP/IP settings for the adapter are changed, and DHCP remains enabled after these changes.

If a DHCP server is found, the network adapter is assigned a valid DHCP IP address lease.

To display the Alternate Configuration tab shown in Figure A-4, the network adapter must be configured to obtain an IP address automatically. To view the Alternate Configuration tab, follow these steps:

1. Open the Control Panel, and double-click Network and Internet.
2. Double-click Network and Sharing Center.
3. In the Network Connections window, right-click Local Area Connection, and then click Properties.
4. In the Local Area Connection Properties page, click Internet Protocol (TCP/IP), and then click Properties.
5. In the Alternate Configuration tab, specify your IP address settings.

Using the Routing and Remote Access Service (RRAS)

THE BOTTOM LINE

Routing, or the process of transferring data across a network from one LAN to another, provides the basis for TCP/IP communications on the Internet and nearly all other corporate networks. Routing plays a key role in every organization that is connected to the Internet or that has more than one network segment. Routing can be a complex process, but if you understand some key concepts such as authentication, authorization, static routing, and policies, you can effectively configure, monitor, and troubleshoot routing and remote access for your organization.

As the name implies, the RRAS server role provides two key services for your network clients:

- Routing—By configuring two network interface cards (NICs) within a Windows Server 2008 server, the server can provide a means of transmitting data from one network to another.

TAKE NOTE*

For larger networks, the processing demands of network routing are typically handled by dedicated hardware-based routers. The routing service included with Windows Server 2008 is better suited for a smaller network or one with a small amount of network traffic that needs to pass between subnets.

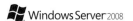

- Remote Access—A Windows Server 2008 computer can act as a remote access server, which can allow remote network clients to access resources on a network as though they were physically connected to the LAN. The Windows Server 2008 remote access server can provide remote access using either dial-up connections via a modem, or else through a Virtual Private Network (VPN) connection over the Internet or another public network.

■ Introducing Network Access Protection (NAP)

↓
THE BOTTOM LINE

One of the principal challenges in corporate networks is the ability to secure networks against unwarranted access. In addition to configuring perimeter firewalls, network administrators also need to protect the network against "inside threats," laptop computers that are physically brought inside the corporate network or that gain access to the company network through remote access technologies such as Virtual Private Networks (VPNs.) For network administrators, this creates a challenge of enforcing corporate security standards such as up-to-date anti-virus protection definitions and a consistent firewall configuration. To assist with this endeavor, Windows Server 2008 provides the Network Access Protection platform, which provides a policy enforcement mechanism to control access to a 2008 network.

Network Access Protection is a new feature in Windows Server 2008 that allows network administrators to specify one or more policies that define the conditions under which network access will or will not be permitted. For example, consider a user who brings his home laptop into the office, and this laptop does not have anti-virus software installed. By connecting this laptop to the corporate network, this user runs the risk of propagating a network virus or worm throughout the corporate network, because the perimeter firewall does not offer any protection against a computer that is located inside of the perimeter. If Network Access Protection is in place, this laptop can be placed into a "quarantine" area where it cannot cause harm to the remainder of the computers on the network.

Appendix B
Overview of Active Directory Domain Services

■ Introducing Active Directory Domain Services

 THE BOTTOM LINE

The Active Directory Domain Services (AD DS) service in Windows Server 2008 provides a centralized authentication service for Microsoft networks. Some of the benefits of Active Directory DS include a hierarchical organizational structure, multimaster authentication (the ability to access and modify AD DS from multiple points of administration) to create fault tolerance and redundancy, a single point of access to network resources, and the ability to create trust relationships with external networks running previous versions of Active Directory and even UNIX. Windows Server 2008 includes a number of new features to improve Active Directory, including the introduction of the Read-Only Domain Controller (RODC), fine-grained password policies, an improved graphical user interface (GUI), improved auditing of Active Directory modification and deletions, the ability to start and stop Active Directory as a service without needing to completely restart the domain controller for maintenance, and the introduction of Server Core, a minimal installation of Windows Server 2008 that has a greatly reduced attack footprint relative to a full install of the server operating system.

Identifying Active Directory's Functions and Benefits

Microsoft introduced the Active Directory service in Windows Server 2000 to provide the main repository for information about network users, computers, services, and other resources on a Microsoft network. Although subsequent versions of Active Directory in Windows Server 2003 and Windows Server 2008 have introduced new functionality and security features, the basic premise of the service remains the same: to provide a centralized authentication and authorization repository for large and small organizations alike.

A *directory service* allows businesses to define, manage, access, and secure network resources, including files, printers, people, and applications. Without the efficiency of a directory service, businesses would have difficulty keeping up with demands for fast-paced data exchange. As corporate networks continue to grow in complexity and importance, businesses require more and more from the networks that facilitate this automation. In Windows Server 2008, Microsoft provides two separate roles that can provide directory services:

- *Active Directory Domain Services (AD DS)* provides the full-fledged directory service that was referred to as *Active Directory* in Windows Server 2003 and Windows 2000.
- **Active Directory Lightweight Directory Services (AD LDS)** provides a lightweight, flexible directory platform that can be used by Active Directory developers without incurring the overhead of the full-fledged Active Directory DS directory service. For example, an application developer might use AD LDS to provide a directory of employee photographs that integrate with AD DS, without actually needing to store hundreds or thousands of graphics files throughout the company.

A Windows Server 2008 computer that has been configured with the Active Directory DS role is referred to as a *domain controller (DC)*. A domain controller is a server that stores the

Active Directory database and authenticates users with the network during logon. Each domain controller actively participates in storing, modifying, and maintaining the Active Directory database information that is stored on each domain controller in a file called ntds.dit. Active Directory is a *multimaster database*, which means that administrators can update the ntds.dit from any domain controller. The process of keeping each domain controller in synch with changes that have been made elsewhere on the network is called *replication*. When a domain controller transmits replication information to other domain controllers on the network, this is called *outbound replication*. Conversely, when a domain controller receives updates to the Active Directory database from other domain controllers on the network, this is called *inbound replication*.

Consider a small network with three domain controllers: DC1, DC2, and DC3. A user changes her password, updating the ntds.dit database on DC1. DC1 must then replicate this change to DC2 and DC3. Domain controllers automatically replicate with other domain controllers in the same domain to ensure that the Active Directory database is consistent. Windows Server 2008 relies on one or more domain controllers to manage access to network services.

Active Directory is designed to enable scalability by handling organizations of any size, from small businesses to global enterprises. In fact, Active Directory is theoretically scalable to holding 4,294,967,041 (2^{32} - 255) separate objects. From a practical standpoint, this means that the maximum size of an Active Directory database is really only limited by the processing power of the hardware that has been deployed onto the domain controllers.

The major benefits of the high-powered Active Directory Domain Services include:

- Centralized resource and security administration
- Single logon for access to global resources
- Fault tolerance and redundancy
- Simplified resource location

Centralizing Resource and Security Administration

Active Directory provides a single point from which administrators can manage network resources and their associated security objects. An organization can administer Active Directory based on an organizational model, a business model, or the types of functions being administered. For example, an organization could choose to administer Active Directory by logically dividing the users according to the departments in which they work, their geographical location, or a combination of these characteristics.

Active Directory can simplify the security management of all network resources and extend interoperability with a wide range of applications and devices. Management is simplified through centralized access to the administrative tools and to the Active Directory database of network resources. Interoperability with prior versions of Microsoft Windows is available in Windows Server 2008 through the use of *functional levels*.

When Active Directory is installed and configured, it includes a number of GUI and command-line tools that can be used to administer network services, resources, and security at a detailed level. These administrative tools can be accessed from any domain controller in the network or an administrative workstation that has these tools installed. When you configure a Windows 2008 Server as an Active Directory domain controller, you will see the following tools added to the Administrative Tools folder:

- Active Directory Users and Computers
- Active Directory Domains and Trusts
- Active Directory Sites and Services
- ADSI Edit

You will see these administrative tools described throughout this book. As you are introduced to new concepts, the tools that should be used with each associated task will be noted. This will allow you to build your administrative knowledge at a manageable pace.

X REF

See "Using Forest and Domain Functional Levels" later in this appendix for information on functional levels.

TAKE NOTE*

Unlike Active Directory in Windows 2000 and Windows Server 2003, Windows Server 2008 no longer supports the use of Windows NT domain controllers.

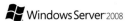

Providing a Single Point of Access to Resources

Prior to the introduction of directory services into corporate networks, all users were required to log on to many different servers in order to access a variety of different resources. This required users to enter their authentication information multiple times, and an administrator had to maintain duplicate user accounts on every server in the organization. Imagine how enormous the task of managing a separate username and password on each server would be if your organization contained 10 servers and 10 users per server. Now imagine how much *more* difficult that would become with 10 servers and 500 users per server. You would have to create and maintain 5,000 user accounts, with all of the associated security assignments, if you were maintaining separate authentication for each individual server.

Active Directory provides a single point of management for network resources. Active Directory uses a single sign-on to allow access to network resources located on any server within the domain. The user is identified and authenticated by Active Directory once. After this process is complete, the user signs on once to access the network resources that are authorized for the user according to his or her assigned roles and privileges within Active Directory.

Benefiting from Fault Tolerance and Redundancy

A system is said to be *fault tolerant* if it is capable of responding gracefully to a software or hardware failure. For example, a server is fault tolerant if it can continue to function when a power supply or a hard drive suffers a mechanical failure. An authentication system such as Active Directory is considered fault tolerant when it has the ability to continue providing authentication services even if one or more servers that provide authentication services (in the case of AD DS domain controllers) experience hardware failure or a loss of network connectivity. In this way, Active Directory can offer a redundant solution which can continue to provide authentication services without any adverse effects noticed by users, workstations, or other services.

TAKE NOTE

It can take anywhere from a few seconds to several hours for changes to replicate throughout a given environment, which means that each individual domain controller may contain slightly different information until the replication process has been completed. Because of this, the Active Directory database is said to maintain *loose consistency*.

Active Directory builds in fault tolerance through its multimaster domain controller design. This fault tolerance is created due to the fact that all domain controllers in an Active Directory domain share a common database file called ntds.dit; any change that is made on one domain controller is replicated to all other domain controllers in the environment. This ensures that all domain controllers have consistent information about the domain.

Windows Server 2008 introduces the *Read-Only Domain Controller* (**RODC**), a domain controller that contains a copy of the ntds.dit file that cannot be modified and that does not replicate its changes to other domain controllers within Active Directory. Microsoft introduced this type of domain controller as a way to increase security in branch-office deployments because many companies find it necessary to deploy domain controllers in far-removed locations that are not secured as well as a centralized data center. The Read-Only Domain Controller protects Active Directory against unauthorized changes made from these remote locations.

Because the entire Active Directory database is duplicated on all domain controllers, it is still possible for authentication and resource access to take place via another domain controller if one domain controller fails. Because a single-domain-controller environment does not offer the fault tolerance described here, Microsoft recommends configuring at least two domain controllers in every environment.

Simplifying Resource Location

Imagine you are a user in a 10-server environment, where every server has a different set of resources that you need to do your job. If you were in this situation, identifying which server provided each resource would not be an easy task. This is even more complicated when you have mobile users, such as an employee visiting from another site who needs to locate printers and other devices to become productive at the new site.

Active Directory simplifies this process by allowing file and print resources to be published on the network. *Publishing* an object allows users to access network resources by searching the Active Directory database for the desired resource. This search can be based on the resource's name, description, or location. For example, a shared folder can be found by clicking the appropriate search button using My Network Places in Windows XP or Microsoft Windows Server 2003 or the Network and Sharing Center in Windows Vista. Generally, a user can configure the search scope. The shared folder name and keyword do not need to be search criteria. Providing more search information creates more specific results. For example, if you've configured the word "accounting" as a keyword for 100 folders, a search for that keyword will return 100 results that a user would need to sort through to find the desired folder.

Categorizing Active Directory Components

Active Directory consists of a number of components that allow flexibility in the design, scalability, administration, and security of an Active Directory network. Some of these components can be changed and scaled to fit a future design. Others are more difficult to change after the initial configuration, so organizations need to have a clear plan in place for the design of an Active Directory environment before beginning the installation and configuration process.

Each component in Active Directory can be categorized as either a *container object* or a *leaf object*. A container object is one that can have other objects housed within it; these can be additional container objects as well as leaf objects. A leaf object, by contrast, cannot contain other objects and usually refers to a resource such as a printer, folder, user, or group. To begin, let's discuss the following container objects:

- Forests
- Domain trees
- Domains
- OUs

Seeing the Forest

The largest container object within Active Directory is the *forest*. The forest container defines the fundamental security boundary within Active Directory, which means that a user can access resources across an entire Active Directory forest using a single logon/password combination. An additional logon would be required to access resources across more than one forest.

To improve the efficiency of Active Directory, Active Directory divides information into multiple *partitions*, also called *naming contexts (NCs)*. Each domain controller's copy of the ntds.dit database file will contain a minimum of three NCs (sometimes more depending on the configuration of a particular domain controller). The following two NCs are replicated forest-wide and are thus stored in the ntds.dit file on every domain controller in a forest:

- The schema partition, or *Schema NC*, contains the rules and definitions that are used for creating and modifying object classes and attributes within Active Directory.
- The configuration partition, or *Configuration NC*, contains information regarding the physical topology of the network, as well as other configuration data that must be replicated throughout the forest.

Because the Schema NC is replicated forest-wide, each Active Directory forest has a single schema that is shared by every domain and domain tree within the forest. The information in the Configuration NC is similarly shared by all domains in a single forest.

Each domain controller also stores a copy of the *Domain NC*, which is replicated to each DC within a single domain. The Domain NC consists of user, computer, and other resource information for a particular Active Directory domain.

Deploying Domain Trees and Domains

> Within a forest, Active Directory relies on domain trees and domains to create smaller administrative boundaries. These partitions divide the database into manageable pieces that separate forest-wide information from domain-specific information.

An Active Directory **domain tree** is a logical grouping of network resources and devices that can contain one or more **domains** configured in a parent–child relationship. Each Active Directory forest can contain one or more domain trees, each of which can in turn contain one or more domains. Active Directory domains create an administrative boundary of resources that can be managed together as a logical unit. Figure B-1 depicts a simple Active Directory structure that includes a parent domain, lucernepublishers.com, and a child domain, tokyo. lucernepublishers.com.

Figure B-1

Simple Active Directory structure

lucernepublishers.com

tokyo.lucernepublishers.com

Every Active Directory domain has an associated domain partition, or Domain NC, that is replicated to each domain controller within a particular domain. Each domain's Domain NC contains information about the objects that are stored within that domain: users, groups, computers, printers, OUs, and more. This Domain NC is replicated to all domain controllers in a single domain with the forest-wide Schema and Configuration NCs. Active Directory information within a domain is replicated to all domain controllers within the domain to provide redundancy, fault tolerance, and load balancing for resources within the domain.

Although not considered to be a formal partition, the Active Directory global catalog also needs to be replicated throughout the forest. In contrast to the Domain NC, the global catalog does not replicate to all domain controllers. Rather, it replicates only to domain controllers that have been specifically configured to hold the global catalog. These domain controllers are known as global catalog servers.

The example shown in Figure B-1 would include the following replication information:

- Each domain controller in the lucernepublishers.com domain replicates a copy of the Schema NC, the Configuration NC, and the lucernepublishers.com Domain NC.
- Each domain controller in the tokyo.lucernepublishers.com domain replicates a copy of the Schema NC, the Configuration NC, and the tokyo.lucernepublishers.com Domain NC.
- Each domain controller in the entire forest that has been configured as a global catalog replicates a copy of the global catalog.

Working with Organizational Units

> An Active Directory domain can contain one or more *organizational units (OUs)* that can further subdivide users and resources. An OU is a container that represents a logical grouping of resources that have similar security or administrative guidelines.

Like the parent–child relationships possible with domains, OUs can be nested in a hierarchical fashion in which a parent OU can contain one or more child OUs. Each child OU can be a parent to child OUs of its own. However, although it is possible to create a nested OU structure containing a number of parent–child relationships, you must consider that these subsequent relationships can make the administration of OUs difficult if they are nested too deeply.

An Active Directory OU structure can reflect the logical structure of the organization by modeling the company's organizational chart, depicting employees and their respective departments, or by organizing users according to their resource needs. For example, all users who have similar resource needs can be placed in an OU for ease of management if this best supports the business needs of the organization. By default, security settings that are applied to an OU will be inherited by all child objects of the container. This simplifies management by allowing you to apply a security setting once at the OU level rather than applying a setting individually to dozens or hundreds of user or computer objects contained within that OU.

Administration of an OU also can be delegated to a departmental supervisor or manager and thus can allow that person to manage day-to-day resource access or more mundane tasks, such as resetting passwords. This is referred to as *delegation* of control. Each container or OU can be created with custom security guidelines in mind, allowing detailed administrative control.

OUs can contain the following objects:

- Users
- Groups
- Contacts
- Printers
- Shared folders
- Computers
- OUs
- InetOrgPerson

Beginning in Windows Server 2003, Active Directory also includes a fourth partition type called an *application partition*. Application partitions provide fine control. Administrators can direct where information is replicated to a domain or forest. This results in greater flexibility and better control over replication performance. For example, the DomainDNSZones application partition will replicate information to every DNS server within a single domain; the ForestDNSZones application partition will replicate data to every DNS server in a forest.

Understanding the Schema

> The Active Directory schema defines what different types of objects look like within Active Directory. What is a user? What properties does a group have? Active Directory comes with a prepopulated base schema, and it can be modified or extended to meet the needs of custom applications.

Every resource in Active Directory is represented as an *object*, and each object has a set of *attributes* that are associated with it. In Active Directory, each object is defined within the Active Directory *schema*. The schema is a master database that contains definitions of all objects in the Active Directory—in a way, it defines what Active Directory *is*. The schema has two components: object classes and attributes. Each object that is represented in Active Directory—for example, the user John and the printer Laserprinter—is an instance of the user and printer object classes, respectively.

Each object class in the schema is further defined according to a list of attributes that make the object class unique within the database. The list of attributes is defined only once in the schema, but the same attribute can be associated with more than one object class. Some attributes are *required* attributes that are necessary for the object to be created, such as a user account logon name. Other *optional* attributes, such as street address and phone number, provide additional details that can be published for user and administrative purposes.

When Active Directory is installed, a number of object classes are created automatically. Some of these object classes include:

- Users
- Groups
- Computers
- Domain controllers
- Printers

All object classes have a common set of attributes that help to uniquely identify each object within the database. Some of these common attributes are as follows:

- **Unique name.** This name identifies the object in the database. A unique name is given to the object upon its creation and includes references to its location within the directory database. This will be explained later in this lesson.
- *Globally unique identifier (GUID).* The GUID is a 128-bit hexadecimal number that is assigned to every object in the Active Directory forest upon its creation. This number does not change, even when the object itself is renamed. The number is not used again, even if an object is deleted and recreated with the same display name.
- **Required object attributes.** These attributes are required for the object to function. In particular, the user account must have a unique name and a password entered upon creation.
- **Optional object attributes.** These attributes add information that is not critical to the object in terms of functionality. This type of information is "nice to know" as opposed to "need to know." An example of an optional object attribute would be a phone number or street address for a user account.

As you will see, the schema can be modified to include additional objects and attributes when necessary. Each object in the schema is protected by access control lists (ACLs) so that only authorized administrators can access and modify the schema. ACLs are implemented by the administrator and used by the directory to keep track of which users and groups have permission to access specific objects and to what degree they can use or modify them.

Creating Active Directory Sites and Subnets

A *site* is defined as one or more IP subnets that are connected by fast links. In most circumstances, all computers that are connected via a single LAN will constitute a single site. Within Active Directory, sites are used to optimize the replication of Active Directory information across small or large geographic areas.

All domain controllers within the same site will use intrasite replication to replicate information as changes are made to Active Directory, whereas intersite replication takes place at regularly scheduled intervals that are defined by an administrator. An internal Active Directory process known as the *Knowledge Consistency Checker (KCC)* automatically creates and maintains the replication topology. The KCC operates based on the information provided by an administrator in the Active Directory Sites and Services snap-in, which is located in the Administrative Tools folder on a domain controller or an administrative workstation that has had the Administrative Tools installed.

Figure B-2

lucernepublishing.com domain, OUs, and leaf objects

lucernepublishers.com

ou = Sales

cn = jsmith

TAKE NOTE *

For further information on the objects defined by LDAP, search for LDAP on the RFC Editor search page at www.rfc-editor.org/rfc-search.html.

Using Active Directory Naming Standards

Active Directory's scalability and integration capabilities result from its use of industry standards for naming formats and directory functions, specifically the *Lightweight Directory Access Protocol (LDAP)*. LDAP was developed in the early 1990s by the Internet Engineering Task Force (IETF) to facilitate the implementation of X.500 in email. (X.500 is the standard that defines how global directories should be structured and organized.)

Since the introduction of LDAP, this protocol has become an industry standard that enables data exchange between directory services and applications. The LDAP standard defines the naming of all objects in the Active Directory database and therefore provides a directory that can be integrated with other directory services, such as Novell *eDirectory*, and Active Directory–aware applications, such as Microsoft Exchange.

Queries and modifications of Active Directory objects take place almost exclusively via LDAP. For this reason, it is necessary to understand how objects are referenced in Active Directory. Consider the following example in Figure B-2.

LDAP refers to an object using its *distinguished name (DN)*, which references an object in the Active Directory directory structure using its entire hierarchical path, starting with the object itself and including all parent objects up to the root of the domain. LDAP defines the naming attributes that identify each part of the object's name. These attributes are listed in Table B-1.

Table B-1

Active Directory Object Classes and Naming Attributes

Object Class	LDAP Naming Attribute	Definition of Naming Attribute
User or any leaf object	Cn	Common name
Organizational unit object	Ou	Organizational unit name
Domain	Dc	Domain components, one for each part of the DNS name

When Figure B-2 is used as a reference, JSmith has the following distinguished name:

cn=JSmith, ou=sales, dc=lucernepublishing, dc=com

Not all Active Directory management tools require you to specify the full distinguished name of an object to manage it. In many cases, you can specify a shortened account name like "jsmith." However, it is important to understand how a distinguished name is structured for those times when one is required. For example, you might need to restore an object that has been accidentally deleted from the Active Directory database. In this situation, understanding how a distinguished name is structured is critical to accomplishing the desired restore.

In addition to understanding the significance of DNS and LDAP in Active Directory name formats, it is important to understand the use of User Principal Names (UPNs) in Windows Server 2008. UPNs follow the format of *username@lucernepublishing.com*. This convention provides a simple solution to a complex domain structure, in which it can be difficult for users to remember the distinguished name. It also provides an opportunity to create consistency between the user's email name and his or her logon name.

Understanding DNS

You will often hear Active Directory administrators say that "Active Directory lives and dies by DNS." After the introduction of Active Directory in Windows 2000, the *Domain Name System (DNS)* has been Active Directory's default name resolution method. Configuring DNS correctly is a critical task for any Active Directory administrator because the health of an Active Directory environment will largely depend on how well DNS is functioning to support Active Directory.

> **TAKE NOTE***
>
> This four-octet IP address is an *IP version 4 (IPv4)* address. This refers to version 4 of IP, which is the most widely deployed version of IP at present. Windows Server 2008 and Windows Vista also natively support *IPv6*, which is the next generation of IP. For more details about IPv6, see the MOAC 642 guide.

In most modern networks, TCP/IP is the primary networking protocol used to communicate between systems. All devices on an IP network use a unique number to identify themselves and their location on the network. This is called an IP address. *IP addresses* are four octets long and are commonly expressed in dotted-decimal notation, such as 192.168.10.1.

One way to access a resource is through its IP address. However, when a computer system identifies resources using 32-bit numbers, expecting a user to access a resource by using its IP address would be cumbersome at best. This is where DNS comes into play. DNS is a distributed name resolution service that provides name resolution for an Active Directory domain. In addition to an IP address, all computers are given a DNS host name upon installation. Although the host name helps you define a device's location or purpose, it needs to be translated into a value that computers can understand. This is why you need DNS. DNS maps a computer's host name to its IP address. When a user or application references a computer's host name, DNS provides the translation of the host name to an IP address, thereby allowing the traffic to be routed appropriately to the correct destination.

Integrating DNS and Active Directory

> DNS is a foundational requirement for Active Directory; the domain controller role cannot be installed onto a server unless that server can locate an appropriate DNS server on the same machine or somewhere on the network.

In addition to providing computer host name–to–IP address mappings on the network, DNS plays a much larger role in the functionality of Active Directory. Active Directory relies on DNS to provide a *locator service* for clients on the network. This locator service provides direction for clients that need to know which server performs what function. For example, if a user were attempting to log on to the network, the locator service would attempt to provide the client with the host name and IP address of the domain controller located in the same site as the client workstation if possible.

This locator service is necessary within Active Directory because Active Directory is a multimaster directory service. Therefore, network services might not always be provided by the same server. Fault tolerance, load balancing, and redundancy are among the reasons for setting up every network, even a small network, with multiple servers, which makes this locator service essential for clients to be able to access domain controllers and other Active Directory resources.

> **TAKE NOTE***
>
> SRV records are supported by BIND DNS versions 4.9.7 and later. Dynamic updates are supported by BIND DNS version 8.2.2 and later.

In many cases, organizations will rely on the built-in DNS server role within Windows Server 2008 to provide DNS name resolution for Active Directory. In some cases, though, a company may already have a third-party DNS service in place, such as the BIND DNS service offered by UNIX. When deploying Active Directory with third-party DNS, you need to ensure that the DNS server can support *SRV records*. SRV records are the locator records within DNS that allow clients to locate an Active Directory domain controller or global catalog. Without the ability to resolve SRV records, clients will be unable to authenticate against Active Directory.

In addition to the required support of SRV records, modern DNS implementations also have the ability to support dynamic updates. Dynamic updates permit DNS clients to automatically register and update their information in the DNS database. When a domain controller is added to the forest, for example, its SRV and A records can be added dynamically to the DNS database via dynamic updates to keep the DNS locator service up to date. Dynamic DNS provides a convenient method to assist in keeping the database current. Dynamic updates are not required for Active Directory to function, but taking advantage of this feature can make it much simpler to administer.

Using Forest and Domain Functional Levels

Forest and domain functional levels are designed to offer support for Active Directory domain controllers running various supported operating systems. As you decommission legacy domain controllers, you can modify these functional levels to expose new functionality within Active Directory. Some features in Active Directory cannot be activated, for example, until all domain controllers in a forest are upgraded to the Windows Server 2003 family, and some domain-wide Active Directory functionality can only exist in a domain that is at the Windows Server 2008 functional level.

As corporate enterprises expand and update their networks, they typically do not upgrade their entire network at the same time. The upgrade strategy chosen will depend on the size of the network and the impact an upgrade will have on users' productivity and access to the network. Because of this, Microsoft has created functional levels that will allow enterprises to migrate their Active Directory domain controllers gradually, based on the need and desire for the new functionality. You can change the functional level for a single domain within a multi-domain environment without requiring other domains to make the same change. This allows *rolling upgrades* as time, budget, and application compatibility factors permit.

Note that forest and domain functional levels will not change automatically. Even if all domain controllers in a particular domain are running the Windows Server 2008 operating system, for example, the domain functional level will not switch to Windows Server 2008 until an administrator makes the change manually. This is due to the fact that functional level changes are *irreversible*; once you have upgraded a functional level, you cannot return to a previous one without performing a domain- or forest-wide restore of the Active Directory database. Because of the permanent nature of this change, Active Directory requires manual intervention on an administrator's part in order to change the forest or domain functional level of an Active Directory environment.

Raising Domain Functional Levels

Windows Server 2008 supports three domain functional levels, depending on the operating systems of domain controllers that are deployed in the domain. As you raise the domain functional level, additional functionality becomes available within Active Directory.

Within Active Directory, domain functional levels are configured on a per-domain basis. This allows different domains within the forest to be at different phases in the process of transitioning to Windows Server 2008—a parent domain can exist at the Windows Server 2003 domain functional level while a child domain has been raised to the Windows Server 2008 functional level. Windows Server 2008 supports Windows 2000, Windows Server 2003, and Windows Server 2008 domain controllers. Windows NT 4.0 domain controllers are *no longer supported*.

The following domain functional levels are available in Windows Server 2008:

- **Windows 2000 native.** This level allows backward compatibility with Microsoft Windows 2000. It also allows Windows 2000, Windows Server 2003, and Windows Server 2008 domain controllers.
- **Windows Server 2003.** This functional level allows Windows Server 2003 and Windows Server 2008 domain controllers only. It does not allow the presence of Windows 2000 domain controllers.

- **Windows Server 2008.** This functional level allows no backward compatibility. Only Windows Server 2008 domain controllers are supported.

At the Windows 2000 native domain functional level, the following basic Active Directory functionality is available:

- **Install from Media.** This feature, introduced in Windows Server 2003, allows you to promote a server to domain controller status using a backup from an existing domain controller.

- **Application partitions.** As you already learned, application partitions allow you to exert greater control over how application information is replicated throughout Active Directory.

- **Drag-and-drop user interface.** This feature allows you to drag and drop objects from one container to another within tools, such as Active Directory Users and Computers as well as Active Directory Sites and Services. (This feature was not available in Windows 2000.)

- **Global Group nesting and Universal Security groups.** This feature allows greater flexibility in creating Active Directory group objects.

- **SIDHistory.** Each Active Directory user, group, and computer possesses a Security Identifier (SID) that is used to grant or deny access to resources within Active Directory, file servers, and Active Directory–aware applications. SIDHistory allows a user to retain access to these SIDs when an object is migrated from one domain to another.

At the Windows Server 2003 domain functional level, a domain can contain Windows Server 2003 and Windows Server 2008 domain controllers. All of the features available in the Windows 2000 native mode are available, as well as the following features:

- **lastLogonTimestamp attribute.** lastLogonTimestamp is an attribute of the user class that allows administrators to keep track of logon times for computers and users within the domain.

- **Passwords for inetOrgPerson objects.** Windows Server 2003 introduced support for the inetOrgPerson object class, which can be used for interoperability with other directory services, such as *openLDAP*. At the Windows Server 2003 domain functional level, inetOrgPerson objects can be configured with passwords and permissions just like Active Directory user objects.

- **Domain rename.** As the name suggests, this feature allows you to rename an Active Directory domain, such as renaming a domain from example.com to cohowinery.com. This operation still has several restrictions placed on it. For example, you cannot use domain rename to restructure a child domain into the parent domain of a separate domain tree. Even in a single-domain environment, renaming a domain is a nontrivial operation that needs to be extensively planned and tested before attempted in a production environment.

At the highest domain functional level of Windows Server 2008, all possible Active Directory features are available to you. To support this advanced functionality, this functional level requires you to have only Windows Server 2008 domain controllers throughout your entire domain. All of the features available in the previous two domain functional levels are available, as well as the following features:

- **SYSVOL replication using DFSR instead of NTFRS.** SYSVOL is a file share that is created on every Active Directory domain controller, the contents of which are replicated to every domain controller in the domain. Windows Server 2008 allows the use of the new Distributed File System Replication (DFSR) replication protocol to replicate SYSVOL instead of the legacy NT File Replication Service (NTFRS) protocol, which has proven cumbersome and difficult to troubleshoot and maintain in previous versions of Active Directory.

- **Additional encryption mechanisms for Active Directory authentication.** This includes support for 256-bit Advanced Encryption Services (AES) encryption for the Kerberos authentication protocol.

- **Improved auditing of user logon information.** This includes recording a user's last successful logon and which computer they logged into, as well as recording the number of failed logon attempts for a user and the time of the last failed logon attempt.

Additionally, the Windows Event Viewer can now capture "before and after" information when a change is made to Active Directory. If you change a user's first name from "William" to "Larry," the Event Viewer can show you the old value ("William") and the value that it was changed to ("Larry").

• **Multiple password policies per domain.** This is an exciting new feature of Windows Server 2008 Active Directory. In previous versions of Active Directory, you could only configure a single password policy per domain. For example, if you configured domain passwords with an eight-character minimum length that would expire every 42 days, you could not configure a more stringent policy setting for administrative accounts in your domain. At the Windows Server 2008 domain functional level, you can now configure multiple password policies within a single domain.

• **Read-Only Domain Controller.** Windows Server 2008 introduces the concept of the Read-Only Domain Controller (RODC), a special type of domain controller that maintains a read-only copy of the Active Directory database and does not perform any outbound replication of its own. To deploy an RODC in a Windows Server 2008 network, your domain must be at the Windows Server 2003 functional level or higher and you need to have at least one writeable 2008 domain controller deployed in the domain.

> **TAKE NOTE** *
>
> To raise the domain functional level, you need to be a member of the Domain Admins group for the domain in question.

Before you can raise the domain functional level, you need to ensure that all domain controllers within that domain are running the required version of the Windows operating system. For example, to raise the domain functional level to Windows Server 2003, you must upgrade or retire any remaining Windows 2000 domain controllers in your environment.

Table B-2 provides a summary of the different functional levels available in Windows Server 2008.

Table B-2

Summary of Domain Functional Levels

DOMAIN FUNCTIONAL LEVEL	SUPPORTED OPERATING SYSTEMS	WINDOWS SERVER 2003 FEATURES
Windows 2000 native	Windows 2000	Install from Media
	Windows Server 2003	Application Directory partitions
	Windows Server 2008	Drag-and-drop user interface
		Universal groups
Windows Server 2003	Windows Server 2003	All Windows 2000 native features and the following:
	Windows Server 2008	Replicated lastLogonTimestamp attribute
		User password on inetOrgPerson
		Domain rename
Windows Server 2008	Windows Server 2008	All Windows Server 2003 native features and the following:
		Improved SYSVOL replication
		Improved encryption for authentication methods
		Improved auditing of user logons
		Multiple password policies per domain

Using Forest Functional Levels

In most respects, forest functional levels are treated like domain functional levels. Advancing from a lower to a higher forest functional level is a one-way process that cannot be reversed.

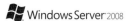

Note that although domain functional levels can be independent of other domains in the forest, the forest functional level applies to all domains within that forest. Three forest functional levels are available within Windows Server 2008: Windows 2000, Windows Server 2003, and Windows Server 2008. As when dealing with domain functional levels, Windows Server 2008 Active Directory supports only domain controllers that are running Windows 2000, Windows Server 2003, and Windows Server 2008. Windows NT 4.0 domain controllers are *no longer supported*.

Windows 2000 is the default forest functionality enabled when the first Windows Server 2008 domain controller is introduced into the network. Just as in Windows 2000 native domain functionality, Windows 2000 forest functionality supports domain controllers running Windows 2000, Windows Server 2003, and Windows Server 2008. Windows 2000 is the default forest functional level for installations of new Windows Server 2008 Active Directory forests. The Windows 2000 forest functional features include:

- **Install from Media.** This is the same feature that was described in the Windows 2000 native domain functional level. It allows servers to be promoted to domain controllers using a backup replica from another domain controller.
- **Universal group caching.** This feature allows users to log on to a domain at a remote site without having a global catalog server present in that site.
- **Application Directory partitions.** Like the Windows 2000 native domain functionality, this allows a separate replication partition for application data that does not need to be globally available. It allows greater control over the scope of replication within a network.

The next forest functional level is Windows Server 2003, which requires that all domain controllers have Windows Server 2003 or Windows Server 2008 installed. Before raising the forest functional level, it is important to ensure that support for Windows 2000 domain controllers is no longer required. Raising the forest functional level is an irreversible procedure like raising the domain functional level. The Windows Server 2003 forest functional level includes all Windows Server 2000 features, as well as the following features:

- **Improved replication of group objects.** In Windows 2000, whenever you make a change to the member list of a group object, the entire member list is replicated throughout the domain. By raising the forest functional level to Windows Server 2003, Active Directory can take advantage of *link-value replication*, which will replicate only the portions of the member list that have actually been added, modified, or deleted.
- **Dynamic auxiliary class objects.** This is a new schema modification option that provides support for dynamically linking auxiliary classes to individual objects. Prior to this functionality, an auxiliary class object could be linked only to an entire class of objects.
- **User objects can be converted to inetOrgPerson objects.** The inetOrgPerson object is used by non–Microsoft LDAP directory services, such as Novell. This new base object in Windows Server 2003 allows easier migration of objects from these other platforms.
- **Schema deactivations.** Windows Server 2003 allows you to deactivate (though not delete) classes or attributes that have been added to the schema.
- **Domain rename.** Domains can be renamed within this functional level to accommodate major design changes on your network.
- **Cross-forest trusts permitted.** This trust type was introduced in Windows Server 2003 and allows resources to be shared between Active Directory forests. Trust relationships are described in the next section.
- **Improved Intersite Topology Generator (ISTG).** ISTG is the process used to initiate the creation and management of the replication topology between sites. In Windows 2000, this feature was limited by the number of sites in the forest. In Windows Server 2003, this feature scales to allow a greater number of sites.

The Windows Server 2003 forest functional level assumes that all domains have been raised to Windows Server 2003 before the forest is raised. All new features and enhancements become available. However, note that all new domain controllers introduced into the domain must be installed as a Windows Server 2003 product.

TAKE NOTE *

In a forest that is configured at the Windows Server 2003 forest functional level, any new child domains will automatically be created at the Windows Server 2003 domain functional level.

The highest available forest functional level is Windows Server 2008. In the present release of Active Directory, the Windows Server 2008 functional level does not unlock any new functionality within Active Directory. Its primary purpose is to ensure that once the forest functional level has been raised to Windows Server 2008, any new child domains that are added to the forest will automatically be created at the Windows Server 2008 domain functional level. This ensures that all new child domains have immediate access to the advanced functionality of the Windows Server 2008 domain functional level, as well as preventing any down-level domain controllers from being added to the forest.

Use the following guidelines to raise the forest functional level:

- To raise the functional level of a forest, you must be logged on as a member of the Enterprise Admins group.
- The functional level of a forest can be raised only by connecting to the DC that holds the Schema Master role. This server is the authority for all schema changes.
- All domain controllers in the entire forest must be running an operating system supported by the targeted forest functional level.
- Raising the forest functional level to the highest level, Windows Server 2008, requires that all domains within the forest be at the Windows Server 2008 functional level.
- During a forest functional level advancement, all domains will automatically be raised to support the new forest functional level.
- Raising the forest functional level is an irreversible procedure.

Table B-3 provides a summary of the forest functional levels and the included features.

Table B-3

Summary of Forest Functional Levels

Forest Functional Level	Supported Operating Systems	Windows Server 2003 Features
Windows 2000	Windows 2000 Windows Server 2003	Install from Media Universal group caching
	Windows Server 2008	Application Directory partitions Enhanced user interface
Windows Server 2003	Windows Server 2003 Windows Server 2008	All Windows 2000 functionality and the following: Linked-value replication Improved ISTG functionality User objects can be converted to inetOrgPerson objects Schema modifications to attributes and classes Can create instances of Dynamic Auxiliary class objects called dynamicObjects Domain renaming Cross-forest trusts All new domains will be created at the Windows Server 2003 domain functional level
Windows Server 2008	Windows Server 2008	All new domains will be created at the Windows Server 2008 domain functional level

Understanding Active Directory Trust Models

Active Directory uses ***trust relationships*** to allow access between multiple domains and/or forests, either within a single forest or across multiple enterprise networks. As the name implies, a trust relationship allows administrators from a particular domain to grant access to their domain's resources to users in other domains.

To see trust relationships in action, consider this example. A book publisher called Lucerne Publishing has entered into a business agreement with Wingtip Toys, a child's toy manufacturer, in preparation for an anticipated merger. To allow the Wingtip Toys R&D department to access design files on the Lucerne Publishing file servers, the administrators of the Lucerne Publishing domain need to establish a trust relationship with the Wingtip Toys Active Directory.

To ease the Active Directory administrative process, certain trust relationships are created automatically during the Active Directory installation process. Beginning with the first domain installed in an Active Directory forest, each new domain has a two-way transitive trust with every other domain in the forest. A two-way trust means that users from Domain A can access resources in Domain B, and users in Domain B can simultaneously access resources in Domain A. A transitive trust relationship harkens back to days of middle-school mathematics—it means that if Domain A trusts Domain B and Domain B trusts Domain C, then Domain A automatically trusts Domain C. The trust relationships in an Active Directory forest are structured as follows:

- When a child domain is created, it automatically receives a two-way transitive trust with its parent domain. So the sales.tokyo.lucernepublishers.com child domain has a two-way transitive trust with its tokyo.lucernepublishers.com parent domain. And, because of trust transitivity (tokyo.lucernepublishers.com has a two-way transitive trust with its lucernepublishers.com parent domain), the users in the sales "grandchild" domain can access resources in the lucernepublishers.com "grandparent" domain and vice versa.

- When a new domain tree is created, the root domain in the new tree automatically receives a two-way transitive trust with the root domain of all other domain tree root domains in the forest. So, if the graphicdesigninstitute.com forest includes a separate domain tree called fineartschool.net, a two-way transitive trust is configured between the root domains. Due to the transitive nature of the trust, any child domains in the graphicdesigninstitute.com tree will be able to access resources in child domains in the fineartschool.net tree and vice versa.

Figure B-3 illustrates the transitive nature of trust relationships between domains in an Active Directory forest. Note that each child domain is linked to its parent domain, continuing up

Figure B-3

Domain trust model

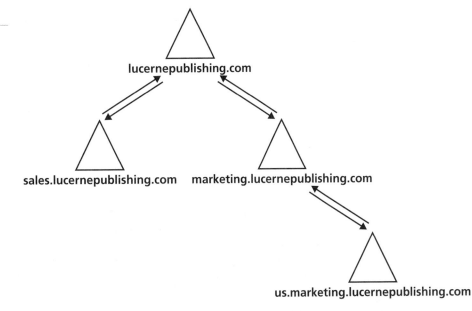

to the forest root domain. If a user in sales.lucernepublishing.com needs access to a resource in us.marketing.lucernepublishing.com, the request is sent up from the sales child domain to the lucernepublishing root domain. From there, it is sent to the marketing child domain and finally to its destination in the us.marketing.lucernepublishing.com domain. This process is called tree-walking.

If the domains within a forest are separated by slow WAN links and this tree-walking process takes an exceedingly long time to allow user authentication across domains, you can configure a ***shortcut trust*** along a commonly used "trust path." Therefore, if users in tokyo. lucernepublishing.com require frequent access to resources in marketing.us.tailspintoys.com, you can create a shortcut trust to "short-circuit" the tree-walking process and form a direct trust path between the two domains, as shown in Figure B-4.

Figure B-4

Shortcut trust

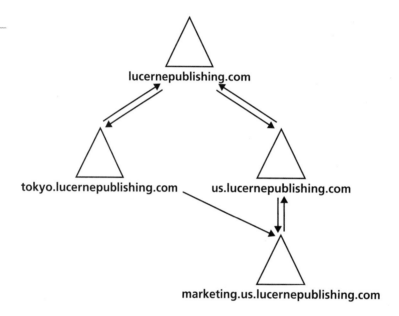

These shortcut trusts are nontransitive, which means that they only apply to the two domains that have been specifically configured within the shortcut trust. For example, if a user from us.sales.wingtiptoys.com needs to access resources in us.marketing.wingtiptoys.com, that user cannot utilize the shortcut trust between the sales and us.marketing child domains. They will follow the default tree-walking trust path shown in Figure B-3. Shortcut trust are also *one-way*, which means that creating a shortcut trust from sales to us.marketing will allow users from sales to authenticate against us.marketing. However, users from us.marketing will *not* be able to use the shortcut trust to authenticate against sales unless a second shortcut trust is created in the opposite direction.

Another type of trust that you can create is an ***external trust*** with a Windows NT domain or a Windows 2000 domain in a separate forest. Similar to shortcut trusts, external trusts are one-way, nontransitive trusts. If users in your domain are able to access resources in a remote domain, users in the remote domain will *not* be able to access resources in your domain unless you create a second trust relationship in the opposite direction. Similarly, if your organization creates a trust with Vendor A and Vendor A subsequently creates a trust relationship with Vendor B, your users will *not* be able to access resources on Vendor B's network. You would need to create a separate trust directly linking your Active Directory with Vendor B's Active Directory. Also, in the case of a remote Windows 2000 Active Directory domain, because an external trust is nontransitive, you will only have access to the specific domain for which the trust has been configured. If you configure a trust with the tokyo.lucernepublishing.com domain, you will not be able to access resources in the lucernepublishing.com domain without configuring a separate trust with lucernepublishing.com directly.

Beginning at the Windows Server 2003 functional level, you also have the ability to create a new type of trust called a ***cross-forest trust***. With Windows NT or Windows 2000 domain controllers in place, it is not possible to create a transitive trust path between forests. Resource access from one forest to another was unsupported. When you are establishing a trust between two forests that are both running at the Windows Server 2003 forest functional level or better, cross-forest trust relationships are transitive in nature and they can be configured as either a one-way or two-way relationship. This means that every domain in Forest A trusts every resource in Forest B and (in the case of a two-way cross-forest trust) every domain in Forest B trusts every resource in Forest A, as shown in Figure B-5.

Figure B-5

Cross-forest trust

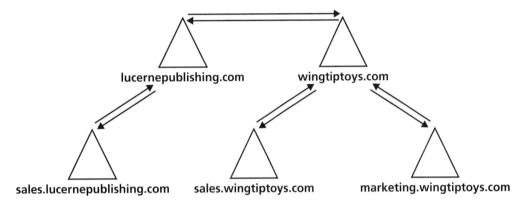

WARNING The transitivity of a cross-forest trust does not extend beyond two forests. This means that if you've configured a cross-forest trust between Forest A and Forest B and a second cross-forest trust between Forest B and Forest C, Forest A would *not* be able to access resources in Forest C unless you configure a third trust relationship directly between Forest A and Forest C.

Once the trust is established, administrators can select users and groups from a trusted forest and include them on the ACL of an object. When a resource is accessed via the cross-forest trust, the user is not required to reenter any logon credentials; you have achieved "single sign-on" across forest boundaries. This advanced feature allows corporations to share resources with partners or new acquisitions without a complete design change or migration.

Installing a New Active Directory Forest

The first Active Directory domain on the network is the forest root domain. The forest root domain is critical to the functioning of Active Directory because it needs to remain online and in place for the lifetime of an Active Directory installation. You can add and remove child domains and additional domain trees as the needs of your organization grow and change, but the forest root domain must remain in place.

You can launch the Active Directory Installation Wizard using the dcpromo.exe command-line tool or from the ***Server Manager*** utility that's installed in the Administrative Tools folder of each Windows Server 2008 server. The Server Manager utility launches automatically at startup after you close the Initial Configuration Tasks utility, or you can access it manually through the shortcut provided in the Administrative Tools folder or directly from the Start menu. The advantage of the Server Manager interface is that it will allow you to view any other roles the server might be performing. However, using dcpromo will allow you to script or automate the installation process.

The first domain controller installed in a new Active Directory forest will hold all of the ***Flexible Single Master Operations (FSMO)*** roles, which are specific server roles that work together to enable the multimaster functionality of Active Directory. The dcpromo process assigns per-forest and per-domain FSMO roles in each new domain that you add to Active Directory. By default, all forest-wide FSMOs will be configured on the first domain controller installed in the entire forest, and all domain-wide FSMOs will be configured on the first domain controller installed in a new domain. For example, modifying the schema is a per-forest role because the Active Directory schema is shared among all domains in a forest. The server holding the Schema Master operations role must be accessible to all domains in the forest. After the initial domain controller creation, additional domain controllers can be installed and the roles can be transferred to the new domain controllers.

 INSTALL A NEW ACTIVE DIRECTORY FOREST

GET READY. You must be logged on as a member of the local Administrators group to begin this process; the server computer should be configured with a static IP address.

1. Click the **Start** menu and select **Server Manager**.
2. Click **Roles** and then click **Add Roles** under the Roles Summary section.
3. Read the Before You Begin window and click **Next**.
4. On the Select Server Roles window, select **Active Directory Domain Services**, as shown in Figure B-6.

Figure B-6

Select server role

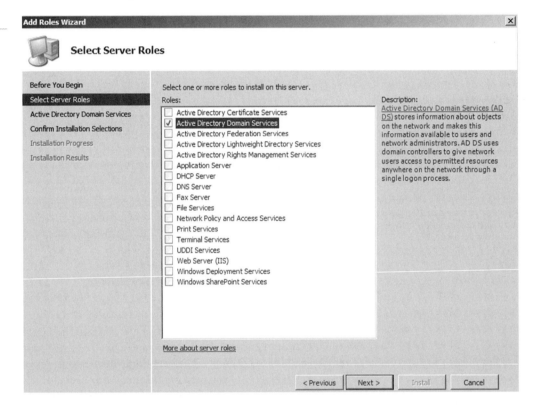

5. Click **Next** to continue. You are presented with an introduction to Active Directory Domain Services that provides a number of helpful hints for installing and administering Active Directory. The tips include the following points:
   • Be sure to install more than one domain controller in each Active Directory domain so that clients can log on even if a single domain controller fails.
   • Active Directory requires an available DNS server on the network.
   • Installing Active Directory will also add the following prerequisite services to the server: *DFS Namespace, DFS Replication*, and the *File Replication Service*.
6. Click **Next** after you read the Introduction to AD Domain Services window.
7. Click **Install** to begin the installation process. The Server Manager will appear to pause for a few minutes because the actual executable files or **binaries** that are needed to install Active Directory are being copied to the system drive. A significant security improvement in Windows Server 2008 is that these binaries (installation files) are not actually installed until you choose to install Active Directory; this prevents any viruses or worms from targeting these files if the server is not configured as a domain controller because the files in question are not present on the hard disk.

8. After the AD DS binaries have installed, click **Close**. You are returned to Server Manager, which will now resemble the window shown in Figure B-7. Notice that the Active Directory Domain Services role is listed, but it has a red 'X' next to it. This indicates that the AD DS binaries have been installed on the server, but Active Directory has not been completely configured.

Figure B-7

Active Directory Domain Services role installed but not configured

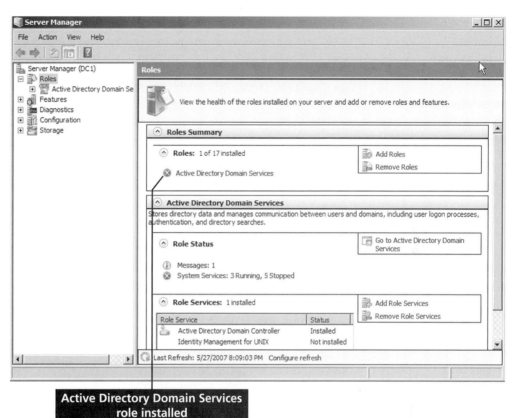

9. Drill down to the Active Directory Domain Service role, which will take you to a window similar to the one shown in Figure B-8.

Figure B-8

Active Directory Domain Services summary

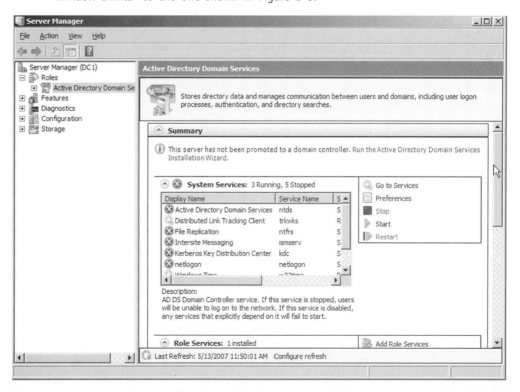

10. Follow the instructions you see on the window and click **Run the Active Directory Domain Services Wizard.** The Active Directory Domain Services Installation Wizard will launch as shown in Figure B-9. Place a checkmark next to **Use Advanced Mode Installation.**

Figure B-9

Active Directory Domain
Services Wizard

11. Read the information and click **Next** in two windows to display the window shown in Figure B-10.

Figure B-10

Choose a deployment
configuration

12. To create the first domain controller in a new Active Directory forest, select **Create a new domain in a new forest** and click **Next.**

13. You are prompted to enter the domain name of the Active Directory forest root domain. In this case, key **lucernepublishing.com** and click **Next.**

14. You are prompted to fill in the ***domain netBIOS name*** for this domain. The domain netBIOS name is limited to 15 characters and is maintained for legacy compatibility with older applications that cannot use DNS for their name resolution. In most cases, this name will simply be the first portion of the ***fully qualified domain name (FQDN)***—LUCERNEPUBLISHING in the case of the lucernepublishing.com FQDN or SALES in the case of sales.lucernepublishing.com. However, because LUCERNEPUBLISHING is longer than 15 characters, you must select a shorter name. Enter **LP** as the domain netBIOS name as shown Figure B-11 and click **Next.**

Figure B-11

Enter the Domain NetBIOS name

15. You are prompted to select the forest functional level (FFL) and domain functional level (DFL) of the new domain and the new forest. As discussed in Lesson 1, the FFL and DFL are used to control what operating systems can be installed as domain controllers within a domain or forest. Raising the DFL or FFL will enable more functionality within Active Directory because it reduces the need to coexist with legacy operating systems. Select **Windows Server 2003** as the forest functional level and then click **Next**.

16. Select **Windows Server** 2003 as the domain functional level and then click **Next**.

17. Next, you could select one or more of the following domain controller options for this domain controller:

   • **DNS Server.** This option is checked by default and will allow the domain controller to perform DNS name resolution. Leave this box selected.

   • *Global Catalog.* This option is selected and grayed out for the first domain controller in a new domain because Active Directory requires that at least one global catalog be installed in each domain.

   • **Read-Only Domain Controller (RODC).** This option is unavailable for the first domain controller in a new domain because the first domain controller cannot be an RODC.

   As shown in Figure B-12, the DNS Server option is selected by default. Click **Next** without making any changes.

Figure B-12

Choose additional domain controller options

TAKE NOTE*

You may receive a dialog box in step 17 that says "A delegation for this DNS Server will not be created because the authoritative parent zone cannot be found or it does not support dynamic updates. To ensure this DNS Server can be resolved as authoritative for the domain test.com, you can create a delegation to this DNS Server manually in the parent zone. Do you want to continue?" Click Yes to continue. This is a new step in the dcpromo process to ensure that your parent DNS zone (if you have one) contains a delegation for the DNS zone that you are creating. See the article, *Configuring DNS for the Forest Root Domain* on the Microsoft TechNet site for more information.

18. In the window shown in Figure B-13, you can select the disk locations for the Active Directory database, log files, and the SYSVOL shared folder. Click **Next** to accept the default locations.

Figure B-13

Choose disk locations

19. You are prompted to enter the Directory Services Restore Mode (DSRM) password that is used to access Directory Services Restore Mode to perform maintenance and disaster-recovery operations on your domain controller. Enter a strong password and click **Next** to continue.

TAKE NOTE*

The DSRM password is not stored in Active Directory. Be sure to keep a record of this password in a secure location for later access.

20. In Figure B-14, you see the Summary window, which will allow you to review your configuration choices before configuring this server as a domain controller. Pay special attention to the Export Settings button on this window. You can use this button to create a text file that can be used to automate the installation of additional domain controllers from the command line. For now, click **Next** to begin the installation process.

Figure B-14

Review selections

PAUSE. After the installation process has completed, click **Finish** and **Restart Now to** reboot the newly configured domain controller when prompted.

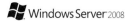

Establishing and Maintaining Trust Relationships

> Trust relationships exist to make resource accessibility easier between domains and forests. Many trust relationships are established by default during the creation of the Active Directory forest structure, as well as other trusts that you can create manually.

In addition to the default trust relationships that exist between parent and child domains and between root domains of domain trees within a forest, four trust types can be manually established in Windows Server 2008:

- **Shortcut trusts.** As discussed in Lesson 1, shortcut trusts can be used to shorten the "tree-walking" process for users who require frequent access to resources elsewhere in the forest.
- **Cross-forest trusts.** This trust relationship was introduced in Windows Server 2003; it allows you to create two-way transitive trusts between separate forests.
- **External trusts.** External trusts are used to configure a one-way nontransitive trust with a Windows 2000 domain or a single domain in an external organization.
- **Realm trusts.** These trusts allow you to configure trust relationships between Windows Server 2008 Active Directory and a UNIX MIT Kerberos realm, which is the UNIX equivalent to an Active Directory domain allowing centralized user and password administration on a UNIX network.

Use the Active Directory Domains and Trusts MMC snap-in to establish manual trust relationships. When using the New Trust Wizard in this utility, you can decide if the trust will be one-way incoming, one-way outgoing, or two-way. A one-way incoming trust establishes that users from another domain, external trust source, or realm can gain access to resources in your domain. However, users in your source domain would not be able to gain access to resources in the trusted external domain. For example, suppose a company wishes to allow a vendor or other subsidiary to gain access to certain resources, such as product lists or order information. Generally, the access would be limited, but allow the vendor or supplier to gain access to necessary business-related data. It may not be necessary or desirable for the vendor to allow the same permissions for your company to access their data. A one-way trust allows this type of situation to take place securely.

A one-way outgoing trust is the exact opposite of a one-way incoming trust. The vendor or supplier wishes to allow your organization accessibility, but you do not want them to gain access to your resources. If both organizations choose to allow access, a two-way trust is available and would achieve the same goal as establishing a one-way incoming *and* a one-way outgoing trust.

CREATING A TRUST RELATIONSHIP

If you have the appropriate administrative privileges in the source and target forest or domain, you can create both sides of the trust relationship. To create a cross-forest trust, each forest must be able to resolve the DNS names and SRV records contained in the other forest through the use of secondary zones, stub zones, or conditional forwarding.

 CREATE A TRUST RELATIONSHIP

GET READY. Before you begin these steps, you must be logged on as a member of the Domain Admins group of the local domain. You also need to have a second Active Directory domain configured and have administrative credentials available for the remote domain.

1. Open Active Directory Domains and Trusts from the Administrative Tools folder.
2. In the console tree on the left, right-click the domain for which you wish to establish a trust and select **Properties**.
3. Click the **Trusts** tab and click **New Trust** to begin the New Trust Wizard. Click **Next** to continue.
4. On the Trust Name page, key the DNS name of the domain and click **Next**.

5. On the Trust page, select the desired trust type.

6. On the Direction of Trust page, select the type and direction of the desired trust. On the Sides of Trust page, select whether you wish to create both sides of the trust simultaneously. (You must have administrative credentials on both the source and remote domains.) On the Trust Password page, enter a strong password to confirm the trust relationship; the same password must be entered when creating the other side of the trust on the remote domain. As a final step, you will be prompted to confirm the outgoing and incoming trusts; only perform these steps if the trust relationship has also been created on the remote domain.

PAUSE. You created a trust relationship.

In the previous exercise, you created a trust relationship between an Active Directory domain and an external network.

VERIFYING A TRUST RELATIONSHIP

After you establish a manual trust, you can verify the trust using either Active Directory Domains and Trusts or the *netdom* command-line tool that is used to create, delete, verify, and reset trust relationships from the Windows Server 2008 command line. Because automatic trusts are part of the default functionality provided by Active Directory, you can only use this process to verify shortcut, external, and cross-forest trusts.

 VERIFY A TRUST RELATIONSHIP USING ACTIVE DIRECTORY

GET READY. Before you begin these steps, you must be logged on as a member of the Domain Admins group.

1. In Active Directory Domains and Trusts, right-click the domain for which you want to verify trusts, and select **Properties**.

2. On the Trusts tab, select **Domains Trusted By This Domain (Outgoing)** or **Domains that Trust This Domain (Incoming)**. Select the appropriate trust and click **Properties**.

3. Click **Validate**. You will be prompted to choose to validate only one side of the trust or validate both sides of the trust simultaneously. Select **Yes** to validate both sides of the trust. You will be prompted to supply an administrative user account and password on the target domain. Select **No** to manually log on to the target domain to validate the other side of the trust relationship.

PAUSE. You used Active Directory Domains and Trusts to verify a trust relationship.

In the previous exercise, you verified the validity of a trust relationship within the Active Directory Domains and Trusts MMC snap-in.

 VERIFY A TRUST RELATIONSHIP USING NETDOM

GET READY. Before you begin these steps, you must be logged on as a member of the Domain Admins group.

1. Open a command prompt and key the following text:

   netdom trust *TrustingDomainName/d:TrustedDomainName*/verify

   Replace *TrustingDomainName* with the domain that is allowing access to resources. *TrustedDomainName* is the domain that needs to gain access.

2. Press ⏎ Enter .

PAUSE. You used netdom to verify a trust relationship.

In the previous exercise, you verified the validity of an Active Directory trust relationship from the command line using the netdom tool.

REVOKING A TRUST RELATIONSHIP

In some cases, it may be necessary to remove an established trust. If a corporation relinquishes its business relationship with a supplier that was trusted, you will need to revoke the trust to prevent unwanted access to network resources. Just like creating trust relationships, you can use Active Directory Domains and Trusts or netdom to revoke a trust.

 REVOKE A TRUST USING ACTIVE DIRECTORY DOMAINS AND TRUSTS

GET READY. Before you begin these steps, you must be logged on as a member of the Domain Admins group.

1. In Active Directory Domains and Trusts, right-click the domain for which you want to verify trusts and select **Properties**.
2. On the Trusts tab, select **Domains Trusted By This Domain (Outgoing)** or **Domains That Trust This Domain (Incoming)**. Select the appropriate trust and click **Properties**.
3. Click **Remove** and follow the prompts to revoke the trust relationship.
4. Repeat steps 1 through 3 for the other end of the trust relationship.

PAUSE. You used Active Directory Domains and Trusts to revoke a trust relationship.

In the previous exercise, you removed an Active Directory trust relationship using the Active Directory Domains and Trusts MMC snap-in.

 REVOKE A TRUST USING NETDOM

GET READY. Before you begin these steps, you must be logged on as a member of the Domain Admins group.

1. Open a command prompt and enter the following text:

    netdom trust *TrustingDomainName*/d:*TrustedDomainName*/**remove**
2. Press **Enter**.
3. Repeat steps 1 and 2 for the other end of the trust relationship.

PAUSE. You used netdom to revoke a trust relationship.

In the previous exercise, you removed an Active Directory trust relationship using the netdom command-line tool.

Changing the Default Suffix for User Principal Names

As your organization grows due to normal expansion, acquisitions, mergers, and new geographic locations, the Active Directory structure can become difficult to navigate. Users needing access to more than one tree structure within the forest can find it cumbersome to recall what is contained in each domain. The distributed system can be cumbersome to navigate. To alleviate this confusion and provide a simple means for users to gain global access to the forest structure, Active Directory supports User Principal Names.

A *User Principal Name (UPN)* is stored in the global catalog, which allows the UPNs to be available forest-wide. In addition, if a cross-forest trust exists, a UPN can be used to gain access to resources in a trusting forest. A UPN follows a naming convention that can reflect the forest root domain or another alias that you configure that follows the format of *username@domainname*. One common practice is to configure the UPN to match the email ID of the user. In the case of a company with different internal and external domain names, using the external name for the UPN is preferred so that entering the correct UPN is simpler to the user. In larger organizations, this may mean that you will need to modify the default UPN suffix when creating users. To modify the default suffix for a UPN, you must have Enterprise Administrator credentials because this is a forest-wide operation.

CHANGE THE DEFAULT SUFFIX FOR USER PRINCIPAL NAMES

GET READY. Before you begin these steps, you must be logged on as a member of the Enterprise Admins group

1. Open Active Directory Domains and Trusts from the Administrative Tools folder.

2. Right-click **Active Directory Domains and Trusts** and choose **Properties**.

3. Click the **UPN Suffix** tab, key the new suffix, and click **Add**. The window shown in Figure B-15 is displayed.

Figure B-15

UPN Suffixes window

4. Key more than one suffix if your forest has more than one tree. Click **OK**.

END. You changed the default UPN suffix.

When creating a new user account, the new suffixes will be available for you to assign to users, as shown in Figure B-16.

Figure B-16

New Object—User window

⚠ WARNING Removing a UPN suffix that is in use will cause users to be unable to log on to the domain. You will receive a warning message if you attempt to remove a UPN.

Appendix C
Server Roles

■ Configuring the DHCP Server Role

THE BOTTOM LINE

In order to communicate with other hosts on a network, all Transmission Control Protocol/Internet Protocol (TCP/IP) hosts must be correctly configured. Each host must have an Internet Protocol (IP) address and a subnet mask, and if communicating outside the local subnet, each must also have a default gateway. Each IP address must be valid and unique within the host's internetwork. This requirement can present a challenge for network administrators. If it is done manually, accurate and timely records must be kept of each host, noting where the host is located and what IP address and subnet mask have been assigned to it. This can quickly become a daunting, tedious task. Organizations with large numbers of workstations requiring IP addresses would have great difficulty managing IP addressing manually. The Dynamic Host Configuration Protocol (DHCP) simplifies this process by automating the assigning, tracking, and reassigning of IP addresses.

IP addressing is complex, in part because each host (a computer, printer, or other device with a network interface) connected to a TCP/IP network must be assigned at least one unique IP address and subnet mask in order to communicate on the network. Additionally, most hosts will require additional information, such as the IP addresses of the default gateway and the DNS servers. DHCP frees system administrators from manually configuring each host on the network. The larger the network, the greater the benefit of using a dynamic address assignment. Without this, each host must be configured manually and IP addresses must be carefully managed to avoid duplication or misconfiguration.

Since the advent of TCP/IP, several solutions have been developed to address the challenge of configuring TCP/IP settings for organizations with a large number of workstations. The *Reverse Address Resolution Protocol (RARP)* was designed for diskless workstations that had no means of permanently storing their TCP/IP settings. RARP, as its name suggests, was essentially the opposite of ***Address Resolution Protocol (ARP)***. ARP was used to discover the Media Access Control (MAC) address (an address unique to a Network Interface Card) that corresponds to a particular IP address. RARP clients broadcast the MAC address. A RARP server then responds by transmitting the IP address assigned to the client computer.

Because RARP failed to provide other much-needed settings to the client, such as a subnet mask and a default gateway, it gave way to another solution, the Bootstrap Protocol (BOOTP). BOOTP, which is still in use today, enables a TCP/IP workstation to retrieve settings for all the configuration parameters it needs to run, including an IP address, a subnet mask, a default gateway, and Domain Name System (DNS) server addresses. Using ***Trivial File Transfer Protocol (TFTP)***, a lightweight version of FTP that uses the UDP protocol, a workstation also can download an executable boot file from a BOOTP server. The major drawback of BOOTP is that an administrator still must specify settings for each workstation on the BOOTP server. A better way to administer TCP/IP would be to automatically assign unique IP addresses while preventing duplicate address assignment and while providing other important settings such as the default gateway, subnet mask, DNS, Windows Internet Naming Service (WINS) server, and so on. Ideally, this would be accomplished without having to manually list every device on the network. To address this issue, server administrators can deploy DHCP.

DHCP is based heavily on BOOTP, but rather than pushing preconfigured parameters to expected clients, DHCP can dynamically allocate an IP address from a pool of addresses and then reclaim it when it is no longer needed. Because this process is dynamic, no duplicate addresses are assigned by a properly configured DHCP server, and administrators can move computers between subnets without manually configuring them. In addition, a large number of standard configuration and platform-specific parameters can be specified and dynamically delivered to the client. DHCP is an open, industry-standard protocol that reduces the complexity of administering networks based on TCP/IP. It is defined by the *Internet Engineering Task Force (IETF)* in **Requests for Comments (RFCs)** 2131 and 2132.

Managing IP addresses and host options is much easier when configuration information can be managed from a single location rather than coordinating information across many locations. DHCP can automatically configure a host while it is booting on a TCP/IP network, as well as change settings while the host is connected to the network. All of this is accomplished using settings and information from a central DHCP database. Because settings and information are stored centrally, you can quickly and easily add or change a client setting (for example, the IP address of an alternate DNS server) for all clients on your network from a single location. Without a centralized database of configuration information, it is difficult to maintain a current view of the host settings or to change them.

Each Microsoft Windows Server 2008 edition (the Standard Edition, Enterprise Edition, and Datacenter Edition) include the DHCP Server service, which is an optional installation. All Microsoft Windows clients automatically install the DHCP Client service as part of TCP/IP, including Windows Server 2008, Windows Server 2008, Microsoft Windows Vista, and Microsoft Windows XP.

In brief, DHCP provides four key benefits to those managing and maintaining a TCP/IP network:

- Centralized administration of IP configuration—DHCP IP configuration information can be stored in a single location and enables the administrator to centrally manage all IP configuration information. A *DHCP server* tracks all leased and reserved IP addresses and lists them in the DHCP console. You can use the DHCP console to determine the IP addresses of all DHCP-enabled devices on your network. Without DHCP, not only would you need to manually assign addresses, you would also need to devise a method of tracking and updating them.

- Dynamic host configuration—DHCP automates the host configuration process for key configuration parameters. This eliminates the need to manually configure individual hosts when TCP/IP is first deployed or when IP infrastructure changes are required.

- Seamless IP host configuration—The use of DHCP ensures that DHCP clients get accurate and timely IP configuration parameters, such as the IP address, subnet mask, default gateway, IP address of the DNS server, and so on, without user intervention. Because the configuration is automatic, troubleshooting of misconfigurations, such as mistyped numbers, is largely eliminated.

- Flexibility and scalability—Using DHCP gives the administrator increased flexibility, allowing the administrator to more easily change IP configurations when the infrastructure changes. DHCP also scales from small to large networks. DHCP can service networks with ten clients as well as networks with thousands of clients. For very small, isolated networks, Automatic Private IP Addressing (APIPA) can be used. (APIPA is discussed later in this lesson.)

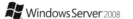

Understanding How DHCP Works

> The core function of DHCP is to assign addresses. DHCP functions at the ***Application Layer*** of the ***Open System Interconnection (OSI)*** reference model, as defined by the International Organization for Standardization (ISO) and the Telecommunication Standards Section of the International Telecommunications Union (ITU-T). The OSI model is used for reference and teaching purposes; it divides computer networking functions into seven layers. From top to bottom, the seven layers are application, presentation, session, transport, network, data-link, and physical. For more information about the OSI reference model, see the *Network + Certification Training Kit,* Second Edition (Microsoft Press, 2001).

As discussed previously, the key aspect of the DHCP process is that it is dynamic. What this means to the network administrator is that the network can be configured to allocate an IP address to any device that is connected anywhere on the network. This allocation of addresses is achieved by sending messages to, and receiving application layer messages (messages from the Application Layer of the OSI model) from, a DHCP server. All DHCP messages are carried in ***User Datagram Protocol (UDP)*** datagrams using the well-known port numbers 67 (from the server) and 68 (to the client). UDP operates at the Transport Layer of the OSI model and is a low-overhead protocol because it does not use any type of packet acknowledgement.

Before learning how address allocation works, you should understand some terminology related to the DHCP server role: DHCP clients, servers, and leases. These terms are defined as follows.

- *DHCP client*—A computer that obtains its configuration information from DHCP.
- *DHCP server*—A computer that provides DHCP configuration information to multiple clients; the IP addresses and configuration information that the DHCP server makes available to the client are defined by the DHCP administrator.
- *DHCP lease*—This defines the duration for which a DHCP server assigns an IP address to a DHCP client. The lease duration can be any amount of time between 1 minute and 999 days, or it can be unlimited. The default lease duration is eight days.

In addition to this terminology, you should also be familiar with the various *DHCP message types* that are used by DHCP clients and servers on a TCP/IP network.

- ***DHCPDISCOVER***—Sent by clients via broadcast to locate a DHCP server. Per RFC 2131, the DHCPDISCOVER message may include options that suggest values for the network address and lease duration.
- ***DHCPOFFER***—Sent by one or more DHCP servers to a DHCP client in response to DHCPDISCOVER, along with offered configuration parameters.
- ***DHCPREQUEST***—Sent by the DHCP client to signal its acceptance of the offered address and parameters. The client generates a DHCPREQUEST message containing the address of the server from which it is accepting the offer, along with the offered IP address. Because the client has not yet configured itself with the offered parameters, it transmits the DHCPREQUEST message as a broadcast. This broadcast notifies the server that the client is accepting the offered address and also notifies the other servers on the network that the client is rejecting their offers.
- ***DHCPDECLINE***—Sent by a DHCP client to a DHCP server, informing the server that the offered IP address has been declined. The DHCP client will send a DHCPDECLINE message if it determines that the offered address is already in use. After sending a DHCPDECLINE, the client must begin the lease or renewal process again.
- ***DHCPACK***—Sent by a DHCP server to a DHCP client to confirm an IP address and to provide the client with those configuration parameters that the client has requested and the server is configured to provide.

- *DHCPNACK*—Sent by a DHCP server to a DHCP client to deny the client's DHCPREQUEST. This might occur if the requested address is incorrect because the client was moved to a new subnet or because the DHCP client's lease expired and cannot be renewed. After receiving a DHCPNACK message, the client must begin the lease or renewal process again.

- *DHCPRELEASE*—Sent by a DHCP client to a DHCP server to relinquish an IP address and cancel the remaining lease. This message type is sent to the server that provided the lease.

- *DHCPINFORM*—Sent from a DHCP client to a DHCP server to ask only for additional local configuration parameters; the client already has a configured IP address. This message type is also used to detect unauthorized DHCP servers.

The initial DHCP lease process is accomplished using a series of exchanges between a DHCP client and DHCP server that utilize four messages, DHCPDISCOVER, DHCPOFFER, DHCPREQUEST, and DHCPACK, as shown in Figure C-1. You can remember this four-step sequence of the DHCP lease process with the acronym DORA, for "Discover, Offer, Request, Acknowledgement," as described here:

Figure C-1

The DHCP lease process

DHCP client   DHCP server

1. DHCPDISCOVER. The client broadcasts a DHCPDISCOVER message to find a DHCP server. Because the client does not already have an IP address or know the IP address of the DHCP server, the DHCPDISCOVER message is sent as a local area broadcast, with 0.0.0.0 as the source address and 255.255.255.255 as the destination address. The DHCPDISCOVER message is a request for the location of a DHCP server and IP addressing information. The request contains the client's MAC address and computer name so that the DHCP servers know which client sent the request. After broadcasting its DHCPDISCOVER message, the DHCP client waits 1 second for an offer. If an offer is not received, the client will not be able to initialize, and the client will rebroadcast the request three times (at 9-, 13-, and 16-second intervals, plus a random offset between 0 milliseconds and 1 second). If an offer is not received after four tries, the client continuously retries in five-minute intervals. If DHCP fails, Windows Server 2008, Windows Vista, Windows XP, and Windows Server 2003 can use APIPA to obtain a dynamically assigned IP address and subnet mask. Clients can also use an alternate configuration, which assigns predefined settings if a DHCP server cannot be located. APIPA and alternate configurations are described in the "Using APIPA and Alternate Configurations" section later in this appendix.

2. All DHCP servers that receive the DHCPDISCOVER message and that have a valid configuration for the client will broadcast a DHCPOFFER message with the following information:

- Source (DHCP server) IP address

- Physical (MAC) address of the requesting client (this is sent to the broadcast IP address of 255.255.255.255 because the client has not yet been configured with IP information)

- An offered IP address

- Client hardware address

- Subnet mask

- Length of lease
- A server identifier (the IP address of the offering DHCP server)

3. After the client receives an offer from at least one DHCP server, it broadcasts a DHCPREQUEST message to all DHCP servers with 0.0.0.0 as the source address and 255.255.255.255 as the destination address. The broadcast DHCPREQUEST message contains the following information:
   - The IP address of the DHCP server chosen by the client
   - The requested IP address for the client
   - A list of requested parameters (subnet mask, router, DNS server list, domain name, vendor-specific information, WINS server list, NetBIOS node type, NetBIOS scope)

4. The DHCP server with the accepted offer sends a successful acknowledgement to the client in the form of a DHCPACK message. This message contains a valid lease for an IP address, including the renewal times (T1 and T2, which are discussed next) and the duration of the lease (in seconds).

A DHCP client will perform the initial lease process in the following situations:

- The very first time the client boots
- After releasing its IP address
- After receiving a DHCPNACK message, in response to the DHCP client attempting to renew a previously leased address

Because each DHCP lease has a finite lifetime, the client must periodically renew the lease after obtaining it. Windows DHCP clients attempt to renew the lease either at each reboot or at regular intervals after the DHCP client has initialized. The lease renewal involves just two DHCP messages, as shown in Figure C-2—DHCPREQUEST (either broadcast or unicast) and DHCPACK. If a Windows DHCP client renews a lease while booting, these messages are sent through broadcast IP packets. If the lease renewal is made while a Windows DHCP client is running, the DHCP client and the DHCP server communicate using unicast messages. (In contrast with broadcast messages, unicast messages are point-to-point messages between two hosts.)

Figure C-2

The DHCP lease renewal process

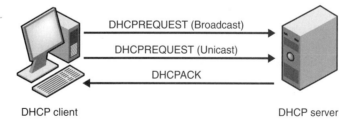

DHCP client   DHCP server

A DHCP client first attempts to reacquire its lease at half the lease time, which is known as *T1*. The DHCP client obtains the value of T1 from the DHCPACK message that confirmed the IP lease. If the lease reacquisition fails at T1, the DHCP client attempts a further lease renewal at 87.5 percent of the lease time, which is known as *T2*. Like T1, T2 is specified in the DHCPACK message. If the lease is not reacquired before it expires (if, for example, the DHCP server is unreachable for an extended period of time), the client immediately releases the IP address as soon as the lease expires and attempts to acquire a new lease.

If the DHCP client requests a lease through a DHCPREQUEST message that the DHCP server cannot fulfill (for example, when a portable computer is moved to a different subnet, as shown in Figure C-3), the DHCP server sends a DHCPNACK message to the client. This informs the client that the requested IP lease will not be renewed. The client then begins the acquisition process again by broadcasting a DHCPDISCOVER message. When a Windows

Figure C-3

A DHCP client booting in a new subnet

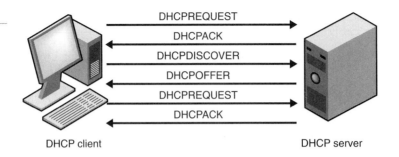

DHCP client boots in a new subnet, it broadcasts a DHCPREQUEST message to renew its lease. The DHCP renewal request is broadcast on the subnet so all DHCP servers that provide DHCP addresses will receive the request. This DHCP server responding on the new subnet is different from the server that provided the initial lease. When the DHCP server receives the broadcast, it compares the address the DHCP client is requesting with the scopes configured on the server and the subnet.

If it is not possible to satisfy the client request, the DHCP server issues a DHCPNACK message, and the DHCP client then begins the lease acquisition process again. If the DHCP client is unable to locate any DHCP server when rebooting, it issues an ARP broadcast for the default gateway that was previously obtained, if one was provided. If the IP address of the gateway is successfully resolved, the DHCP client assumes that it remains located on the same network from which it obtained its current lease and continues to use its lease. Otherwise, if the IP address of the gateway is not resolved, the client assumes that it has been moved to a network that has no DHCP services currently available (such as a home network), and it configures itself using either APIPA or an alternate configuration. Once it configures itself, the DHCP client tries to locate a DHCP server every five minutes in an attempt to renew its lease.

Using the DHCP Relay Agent

DHCP relies heavily on broadcast messages. Broadcast messages are generally limited to the subnet in which they originate and are not forwarded to other subnets. This poses a problem if a client is located on a different subnet from the DHCP server. A *DHCP relay agent* is either a host or an IP router that listens for DHCP (and BOOTP) client messages being broadcast on a subnet and then forwards those DHCP messages to a DHCP server. The DHCP server sends DHCP response messages back to the relay agent, which then broadcasts them onto the subnet for the DHCP client. Using DHCP relay agents eliminates the need to have a DHCP server on every subnet.

To support and use the DHCP service across multiple subnets, routers connecting each subnet should comply with the DHCP/BOOTP relay agent capabilities described in RFC 1542. To comply with RFC 1542 and provide relay agent support, each router must be able to recognize BOOTP and DHCP protocol messages and relay them appropriately. Because routers typically interpret DHCP messages as BOOTP messages, a router with only BOOTP relay agent capability relays DHCP packets and any BOOTP packets sent on the network.

The DHCP relay agent is configured with the address of a DHCP server. The DHCP relay agent listens for DHCPDISCOVER, DHCPREQUEST, and DHCPINFORM messages that are broadcast from the client. The DHCP relay agent then waits a previously configured amount of time and, if no response is detected, sends a unicast message to the configured DHCP server. The server then acts on the message and sends the reply back to the DHCP relay agent. The relay agent then broadcasts the message on the local subnet, allowing the DHCP client to receive it.

Using APIPA and Alternate Configurations

In most cases, DHCP clients find a server either on a local subnet or through a relay agent. To allow for the possibility that a DHCP server is unavailable, Windows clients can obtain their IP configuration using Automatic Private IP Addressing (APIPA). APIPA is a feature of the Windows TCP/IP implementation that allows a computer to determine IP configuration information without a DHCP server without relying on manual configuration of the TCP/IP stack.

WARNING Because APIPA does not configure clients with a default gateway, it works only with a single subnet and is not appropriate for larger networks.

APIPA avoids the problem of IP hosts being unable to communicate if for some reason the DHCP server is unavailable. In the case where a DHCP server is not found and APIPA is configured and enabled, an APIPA address is assigned. APIPA is useful for small workgroup networks where no DHCP server is implemented.

If the DHCP client is unable to locate a DHCP server and is not configured with an alternate configuration (discussed next), the computer configures itself with an IP address randomly chosen from the Internet Assigned Numbers Authority (IANA)–reserved class B network 169.254.0.0 and with the subnet mask 255.255.0.0. The auto-configured computer then tests to verify that the IP address it has chosen is not already in use by using a gratuitous ARP broadcast. If the chosen IP address is in use, the computer randomly selects another address. The computer makes up to ten attempts to find an available IP address.

Once the selected address has been verified as available, the client is configured to use that address. The DHCP client continues to check for a DHCP server in the background every five minutes, and if a DHCP server is found, the configuration offered by the DHCP server is used.

Windows clients can also be configured to use an alternate configuration, which the DHCP client uses instead of APIPA if a DHCP server cannot be contacted. The alternate configuration includes an IP address, a subnet mask, a default gateway, DNS, and WINS server addresses.

One purpose of the alternate configuration is as a solution for portable computers that move between a corporate, DHCP-enabled network and a home network where static IP addressing is used. For example, Janice has a portable computer she uses at work and at home. At work, her portable computer obtains IP address information using DHCP, but she does not use a DHCP server at home. Janice can use alternate configuration to hold her home IP address, subnet mask, default gateway, and DNS server information so that when she connects her portable computer to her home network, it is configured automatically.

If you use DHCP with an alternate configuration and the DHCP client cannot locate a DHCP server, the alternate configuration is used to configure the network adapter. No additional discovery attempts are made except under the following conditions:

- The network adapter is disabled and then enabled again
- Media (such as network cabling) is disconnected and then reconnected
- The TCP/IP settings for the adapter are changed, and DHCP remains enabled after these changes

If a DHCP server is found, the network adapter is assigned a valid DHCP IP address lease.

To display the Alternate Configuration tab in Windows Server 2008, as shown in Figure C-4, the network adapter must be configured to obtain an IP address automatically. To view the Alternate Configuration tab, follow these steps:

1. Open the Control Panel, and double-click Network and Sharing Center. In the Network and Sharing section, click Manage Network Connections.
2. In the Network Connections window, right-click Local Area Connection, and then click Properties.
3. In the Local Area Connection Properties page, click Internet Protocol version 4 (TCP/IPv4), and then click Properties.

Figure C-4

Viewing the Alternate
Configuration screen

4. Ensure that the Obtain an IP Address Automatically radio button is selected. In the Alternate Configuration tab, specify your IP address settings.

Installing the DHCP Server Role

Windows Server 2008 has introduced the Server Manager utility as a single point of reference for managing all components of the Windows operating system, as well as installing, managing, and uninstalling various server roles such as Active Directory Domain Services, DHCP, DNS, and others. Adding the DHCP server role is largely wizard-driven, and allows you to configure basic DHCP settings at the same time that you install the role.

INSTALL THE DHCP SERVER ROLE

GET READY. This exercise assumes that you have installed Windows Server 2008, Enterprise Edition, and that you have local administrator access to the computer. In Part A we will add the DHCP server role on a full installation of Windows Server 2008. In Part B we will add the DHCP server role on a Server Core installation of Windows Server 2008.

PART A—Adding the DHCP Server Role on a Full Installation of Windows Server 2008

1. Press **Ctrl** + **Alt** + **Del** on the Windows Server 2008 computer and log on as the default administrator of the local computer.
2. The Server Manager screen will appear automatically. Expand the Server Manager window to full-screen if necessary.
3. In the left-hand pane of Server Manager, double-click **Roles**.
4. Click **Add Role**. Click **Next** to bypass the initial Welcome screen.
5. The Select Server Roles screen appears. Place a checkmark next to **DHCP Server**. Click **Next**.
6. The Introduction to DHCP Server screen appears. Read the information about the DHCP Server role and click **Next**.
7. The Specify IPv4 DNS Server Settings screen appears. Enter the appropriate information for your network configuration and click **Next**.
8. The Specify IPv4 WINS Server Settings screen appears. Select the appropriate configuration for your network and click **Next**.
9. The Add or Edit DHCP Scopes screen appears. Click **Add** to create a DHCP scope for your network.

10. The Add Scope screen appears. Enter the appropriate information for your network configuration, for example:
    - *Name:* 70-642 Lab Network
    - *Starting IP Address:* 192.168.1.100
    - *Ending IP Address:* 192.168.1.254
    - *Subnet Mask:* 255.255.255.0
    - *Default Gateway:* 192.168.1.1
    - *Subnet type:* Wired

11. Ensure that there is a checkmark next to **Activate this scope**, and then click **OK**.

12. Click **Next**. The Configure DHCPv6 Stateless Mode screen appears. Select **Enable DHCPv6 stateless mode** and click **Next**.

13. The Specify IPv6 DNS Server Settings screen appears. Enter the appropriate information for your network configuration and click **Next**.

14. The Authorize DHCP Server screen appears. Select **Skip authorization of this DHCP server in AD DS** and click **Next**.

15. The Confirm Installation Selections screen appears. Click **Install**.

PART B—Adding the DHCP Server Role on a Server Core Installation of Windows Server 2008

1. Press (Ctrl) + (Alt) + (Del) on the Server Core computer and log on as the default administrator of the local computer.

2. From the command prompt, enter the following command and press **Enter**:

    Start /w ocsetup DHCPServerCore

STOP. When the installation is completed, log off of the Windows Server 2008 computer.

In the previous exercise, you installed the DHCP Server role on a Windows Server 2008 computer. In the next section, we will discuss the process of authorizing DHCP servers within Active Directory.

Authorizing a DHCP Server

In implementations of DHCP prior to Windows 2000, any user could create a DHCP server on the network, an action that could lead to conflicts in IP address assignments. For example, if a client obtains a lease from an incorrectly configured DHCP server, the client might receive an invalid IP address, which prevents it from communicating on the network. This can prevent users from logging on. In Windows Server 2000 and later, an unauthorized DHCP server (also referred to as a *rogue DHCP server*) is simply a DHCP server that has not been explicitly listed in the Active Directory Domain Service as an authorized server. You must *authorize* a DHCP server in Active Directory before the server can issue leases to DHCP clients.

At the time of initialization, the DHCP server contacts Active Directory to determine whether it is on the list of servers that are currently authorized to operate on the network. One of the following actions then occurs:

- If the DHCP server is authorized, the DHCP Server service starts.
- If the DHCP server is not authorized, the DHCP Server service logs an error in the system event log, does not start, and, of course, will not respond to client requests.

Let's examine two scenarios. In the first scenario, the DHCP server is part of a domain and is authorized. In the second scenario, the DHCP server is not in a domain and, consequently, not authorized.

In the first scenario, the DHCP server initializes and determines if it is part of the directory domain. Since it is, it contacts the directory service to verify that it is authorized. The directory service confirms the server is authorized. After receiving this confirmation, the server broadcasts a DHCPINFORM message to determine if other directory services are available and repeats the authorization process with each directory service that responds. After this is completed, the server begins servicing DHCP clients accordingly.

In the second scenario, the server is not a part of a domain. When the server initializes, it checks for DHCP member servers. If no DHCP member servers are located, the server begins servicing DHCP clients and continues to check for member servers by sending a DHCPINFORM message every five minutes. If a DHCP member server is located, the server shuts down its DHCP service and, of course, stops servicing DHCP clients.

Active Directory must be present to authorize DHCP servers and block unauthorized servers. If you install a DHCP server on a network without Active Directory, no authorization will take place. If you subsequently add Active Directory, the DHCP server will sense the presence of Active Directory; however, if it has not been authorized, the server will shut itself down. DHCP servers are not authorized by default; they must be explicitly authorized.

When a DHCP server that is not a member server of the domain (such as a member of a workgroup) initializes, the following happens:

1. The server broadcasts a DHCPINFORM message on the network.
2. Any other server that receives this message responds with a DHCPACK message and provides the name of the directory domain it is part of.
3. If a workgroup DHCP server detects a member DHCP server of a domain on the network, the workgroup DHCP server assumes itself to be unauthorized on that network and shuts itself down.
4. If the workgroup DHCP server detects the presence of another workgroup server, it ignores it; this means multiple workgroup servers can be active at the same time as long as there is no directory service.

> **TAKE NOTE***
>
> To authorize a DHCP server, a user must be a member of the Enterprise Admins group, which exists in the root domain of the forest.

Even when a workgroup server initializes and becomes authorized (because no other domain member server or workgroup server is on the network), it continues to broadcast DHCPINFORM every five minutes. If an authorized domain member DHCP server initializes later, the workgroup server becomes unauthorized and stops servicing client requests.

⊙ AUTHORIZE A DHCP SERVER

GET READY. This exercise assumes that you have installed the DHCP Server role on a Windows Server 2008 computer in an Active Directory domain, and that you have local administrator rights to the DHCP server.

1. Press **Ctrl** + **Alt** + **Del** on the Windows Server 2008 computer and log on as the default administrator of the local computer.
2. Click **Start→Administrative Tools→DHCP**.
3. In the console tree, right-click **DHCP**, and then click **Manage Authorized Servers**.
4. In the Manage Authorized Servers dialog box, select **Authorize**.
5. In the Authorize DHCP Server dialog box, key the name or IP address of the DHCP server to be authorized, and then click **OK**.
6. The computer will list the IP and full computer name and then ask for confirmation. Click **OK** to continue.

STOP. You can close the DHCP administrative console or leave it open for a subsequent exercise. To authorize a DHCP server from a Server Core computer, use the netsh command using the following syntax: **netshdhcp add server <Server IP Address>**

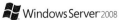

In this exercise, you authorized a DHCP server within an Active Directory domain. In the next section we will discuss creating and configuring DHCP scopes to issue specific DHCP configurations to your network clients.

Configuring DHCP Scopes

A DHCP scope determines which IP addresses are allocated to clients. A scope defines a set of IP addresses and associated configuration information that can be supplied to a DHCP client. A scope must be defined and activated before DHCP clients can use the DHCP server for dynamic TCP/IP configuration. You can configure as many scopes on a DHCP server as needed for your network environment.

A DHCP administrator can create one or more scopes on one or more Windows Server 2008 servers running the DHCP Server service. However, because DHCP servers do not communicate scope information with each other, you must be careful to define scopes so that multiple DHCP servers are not assigning the same IP address to multiple clients or assigning addresses that are statically assigned to existing IP hosts.

The IP addresses defined in a DHCP scope must be contiguous and are associated with a subnet mask. If the addresses you want to assign are not contiguous, you must create a scope encompassing all the addresses you want to assign and then exclude specific addresses or address ranges from the scope. You can create only one scope per subnet on a single DHCP server. To allow for the possibility that some IP addresses in the scope might have been already assigned and are in use, the DHCP administrator can specify an *exclusion range*—one or more IP addresses in the scope that are not handed out to DHCP clients. An exclusion range is a limited sequence of IP addresses within a scope range that are to be excluded from DHCP service offerings. Where exclusion ranges are used, they ensure that any addresses within the defined exclusion range are not offered to clients of the DHCP server. You should exclude all statically configured IP addresses within a particular IP address range.

Once a DHCP scope is defined and exclusion ranges are applied, the remaining addresses form what is called an *available address pool* within the scope. Pooled addresses can then be dynamically assigned to DHCP clients on the network.

 CONFIGURE A DHCP SCOPE

GET READY. This exercise assumes that you have installed the DHCP Server role on a Windows Server 2008 computer, and that you have administrative rights to that server.

1. Press (Ctrl) + (Alt) + (Del) on the Windows Server 2008 computer and log on as the default administrator of the local computer.

2. Click **Start→Administrative Tools→DHCP**.

3. To configure an IPv4 DHCP scope, drill down to the server name, followed by IPv4.

4. Right-click **IPv4** and select **New scope**. Click **Next** to bypass the initial Welcome screen.

5. The Scope Name screen appears. Enter a name and description for the DHCP scope and then click **Next**.

6. The IP Address Range screen appears. Enter the starting and ending IP address and the subnet mask for the scope and then click **Next**.

7. The Add Exclusions screen appears. Enter any necessary exclusions and then click **Next**.

8. The Lease Duration screen appears. Enter the length of the DHCP lease and click **Next**.

9. The Configure DHCP Options screen appears. Click **Yes, I want to configure these options now** and click **Next**.

10. The Router (Default Gateway) screen appears. Enter the default gateway for the scope, click **Add,** and then click **Next**.

11. The Domain Name and DNS Servers screen appears. Enter the DNS domain and DNS servers as appropriate for the scope. Click **Next**.

12. The WINS Servers screen appears. Enter the WINS servers as appropriate for the scope and then click **Next**.

13. The Activate Scope screen appears. Click **Yes, I want to activate this scope now** and then click **Next**.

14. Click **Finish** to complete creating the DHCP scope.

PAUSE. You can close the DHCP management console or else leave it open for a subsequent exercise. To configure a DHCP scope from a Server Core computer, use the netsh command.

In the previous exercise you created and configured a DHCP server on a Windows Server 2008 computer. In the next section we will discuss creating DHCP reservations within a DHCP scope.

TAKE NOTE *

A DHCP *superscope* is an administrative grouping of scopes that is used to support *multinets*, or multiple logical subnets (subdivisions of an IP network) on a single network segment (a portion of the IP internetwork bounded by IP routers). Multinetting commonly occurs when the number of hosts on a network segment grows beyond the capacity of the original address space. By creating a logically distinct second scope and then grouping these two scopes into a single superscope, you can double your physical segment's capacity for addresses. (In multinet scenarios, routing is also required to connect the logical subnets.) In this way, the DHCP server can provide clients on a single physical network with leases from more than one scope. Superscopes contain only a list of member scopes or child scopes that can be activated together; they are not used to configure other details about scope use.

Configuring a DHCP Reservation

Network administrators can use DHCP *reservations* for DHCP-enabled hosts that need to have static IP addresses on your network. Examples of hosts that require static IP addresses are e-mail servers and application servers. File and print servers may also require static or reserved IP addresses if they are accessed by their IP addresses.

DHCP reservations enable permanent address lease assignment by the DHCP server. Where reservations are used, they ensure that a specified hardware device on the network can always use the same IP address. Reservations must be created within a scope and must not be excluded from the scope. Excluded addresses are not available for assignment to clients even if reserved for a client. An IP address is set aside, or reserved, for a specific network device that has the *Media Access Control (MAC)* address (the hard-coded hexadecimal hardware address associated with a Network Interface Card) associated with that IP address. Therefore, when creating a reservation, you must know the MAC address for each device for which you are reserving an address. The MAC address can be obtained by keying **ipconfig /all** at the command line, which will result in output similar to the following:

```
Ethernet adapter Wireless Network Connection:

Connection-specific DNS Suffix.:

Description......................:   Dell Wireless 1390 WLAN Mini-Card

Physical Address.................:   00-1A-92-9F-D7-DC
```

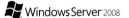

Dhcp Enabled.....................:	Yes
Autoconfiguration Enabled...:	Yes
IP Address.........................:	192.168.1.100
Subnet Mask......................:	255.255.255.0
Default Gateway.................:	192.168.1.1
DHCP Server.....................:	192.168.1.1
DNS Servers.....................:	192.168.1.210
	192.168.1.215
Lease Obtained.................:	Sunday, December 02, 2007 4:54:47 PM
Lease Expires...................:	Monday, December 03, 2007 4:54:47 PM

The MAC address in this example is 00-1A-92-9F-D7-DC.

CONFIGURE A DHCP RESERVATION

GET READY. This exercise assumes that you have configured a DHCP Server on a Windows Server 2008 computer and have configured at least one DHCP scope.

1. Press **Ctrl** + **Alt** + **Del** on the Windows Server 2008 computer and log on as the default administrator of the local computer.
2. Click **Start→Administrative Tools→DHCP**.
3. To configure an IPv4 DHCP scope, drill down to the server name, followed by IPv4, followed by the scope name, and then expand the **Reservations** node.
4. Right-click the **Reservations** node and click **New Reservation....**
5. The New Reservation screen appears. Enter a descriptive name for the reservation, followed by the desired IP address.
6. Enter the MAC address of the computer that should receive this reservation, and an optional description.
7. Click **Add** and then click **Close**.

PAUSE. You can close the DHCP administration console, or else leave it open for a subsequent exercise. To configure a DHCP scope from a Server Core computer, use the netsh command.

In the previous exercise, you configured a DHCP reservation within a DHCP scope. In the next exercise, we will discuss configuring DHCP options to fine-tune the configuration of computers receiving their IP address configuration from a Windows Server 2008 DHCP server.

Configuring DHCP Options

DHCP options are additional client-configuration parameters that a DHCP server can assign when serving leases to DHCP clients. DHCP options are configured using the DHCP console and can apply to scopes and reservations. For example, IP addresses for a router or default gateway, WINS servers, or DNS servers are commonly provided for a single scope or globally for all scopes managed by the DHCP server.

Many DHCP options are predefined through RFC 2132, but the Microsoft DHCP server also allows you to define and add custom options. Table C-1 describes some of the options that can be configured.

Table C-1

DHCP Options

OPTION	DESCRIPTION
Router (default gateway)	The addresses of any default gateway or router. This router is commonly referred to as the default gateway.
Domain name	A DNS domain name defines the domain to which a client computer belongs. The client computer can use this information to update a DNS server so that other computers can locate the client.
DNS and WINS servers	The addresses of any DNS and WINS servers for clients to use for network communication.

DHCP options can be assigned to all scopes, one specific scope, or to a specific machine reservation. There are four types of DHCP options in Windows Server 2008:

- *Server options*—apply to all clients of the DHCP server. Use these options for parameters common across all scopes on the DHCP server.
- *Scope options*—apply to all clients within a scope and are the most often used set of options. Scope options override server options.
- *Class options*—provide DHCP parameters to DHCP clients based on type—either vendor classes or user classes.
- *Client options*—apply to individual clients. Client options override all other options (server, scope, and class).

User classes are created at the discretion of the DHCP administrator. Vendor classes are defined by the machine's vendor and cannot be changed. Using vendor and user classes, an administrator can then configure the DHCP server to assign different options, depending on the type of client receiving them. For example, an administrator can configure the DHCP server to assign different options based on type of client, such as desktop or portable computer. This feature gives administrators greater flexibility in configuring clients. If client class options are not used, default settings are assigned. Vendor class and vendor options are described in RFC 2132 and can be looked up at *http://www.rfc-editor.org/rfcsearch.html*.

Configuring the DHCP Relay Agent

When the DHCP client and the DHCP server are on the same subnet, the DHCPDISCOVER, DHCPOFFER, DHCPREQUEST, and DHCPACK messages are sent by means of broadcast traffic. When the DHCP server and DHCP client are not on the same subnet, the connecting router or routers must support the forwarding of DHCP messages between the DHCP client and the DHCP server, or a BOOTP/DHCP relay agent must be installed on the subnet where the client is located. This is because BOOTP and DHCP protocols rely on network broadcasts to perform their work, and routers in normal routed environments do not automatically forward broadcasts from one interface to another.

In this section, we will discuss the two options available to you to allow a DHCP server on one subnet to service client requests from remote subnets. First, if the routers separating the DHCP server and clients are RFC 1542 compliant, the routers can be configured for BOOTP forwarding. Through BOOTP forwarding, routers forward DHCP broadcasts between clients and servers and inform servers on the originating subnet of the DHCP requests. This process allows DHCP servers to assign addresses to the remote clients from the appropriate scope.

The second way to allow remote communication between DHCP servers and clients is to configure a DHCP relay agent on the subnet containing the remote clients. DHCP relay agents intercept DHCPDISCOVER packets and forward them to a remote DHCP server whose address has been pre-configured. A DHCP relay agent is either a router or a host computer configured to listen for DHCP/BOOTP broadcast messages and direct them to a specific DHCP server or servers. Using relay agents eliminates the necessity of having a DHCP server on each physical network segment or having RFC 2131–compliant routers. Relay agents not only direct local DHCP client requests to remote DHCP servers, but also return remote DHCP server responses to the DHCP clients. Although the DHCP relay agent is configured through the Routing and Remote Access server role, the computer that is hosting the agent does not need to be functioning as an actual router between subnets. RFC 2131–compliant routers (supersedes RFC 1542) contain relay agents that allow them to forward DHCP packets.

Let's examine a scenario in which a DHCP client on Subnet 2 attempts to obtain its IP address from a DHCP server on Subnet 1:

1. The DHCP client broadcasts a DHCPDISCOVER message on Subnet 2 as a UDP datagram over UDP port 67, which is the port reserved and shared for BOOTP and DHCP server communication.

2. The relay agent, in this case a DHCP/BOOTP relay–enabled router, examines the gateway IP address field in the DHCP/BOOTP message header. If the field has an IP address of 0.0.0.0, the relay agent fills it with its own IP address and forwards the message to Subnet 1, where the DHCP server is located.

3. When the DHCP server on Subnet 1 receives the DHCPDISCOVER message, it examines the gateway IP address field for a DHCP scope to determine whether it can supply an IP address lease. If the DHCP server has multiple DHCP scopes, the address in the gateway IP address field identifies the DHCP scope from which to offer an IP address lease.

For example, if the gateway IP address field has an IP address of 192.168.45.2, the DHCP server checks its DHCP scopes for a scope range that matches the Class C IP network that includes the gateway IP address of the computer. In this case, the DHCP server checks to see which scope includes addresses between 192.168.45.1 and 192.168.45.254. If a scope exists that matches this criterion, the DHCP server selects an available address from the matched scope to use in an IP address lease offer (DHCPOFFER) response to the client. The DHCP Relay Agent process continues as follows:

4. The DHCP server sends a DHCPOFFER message directly to the relay agent identified in the gateway IP address field.

5. The router relays the address lease offer (DHCPOFFER) to the DHCP client as a broadcast since the client's IP address is still unknown.

After the client receives the DHCPOFFER, a DHCPREQUEST message is relayed from client to server, and a DHCPACK message is relayed from server to client in accordance with RFC 1542.

Managing the DHCP Database

DHCP plays a key role in an organization's network infrastructure. Without an accessible DHCP server, most clients completely lose network connectivity. Therefore, like any key resource in your organization, you must carefully manage the DHCP server. Proper management of a DHCP server helps prevent server downtime and aids in quick recovery after a server failure.

Your network is constantly changing. New servers are added and existing servers are changing roles or are removed from the network altogether. Because of this, you must both monitor and manage the DHCP service to ensure it is meeting the needs of the organization. Specifically, you must manage the DHCP database by performing the following database functions:

- Backup and restore
- Reconciliation
- Compacting the database
- Removing the database

The DHCP server database is a dynamic database, which is a data store that is updated as DHCP clients are assigned or as they release their TCP/IP configuration parameters. Because the DHCP database is not a distributed database like the DNS server database, maintaining the DHCP server database is less complex. DNS is stored hierarchically across many different servers, with each server containing a part of the overall database. DHCP, by contrast, is contained in a few files on one server.

The DHCP server database in the Windows Server 2008 family uses the *Joint Engine Technology (JET)* storage engine. When you install the DHCP service, the files shown in Table C-2 are automatically created in the %systemroot%\System32\Dhcp directory.

Table C-2

DHCP Service Database Files

FILE	DESCRIPTION
Dhcp.mdb	The DHCP server database file.
Temp.edb	A file used by the DHCP database as a temporary storage file during database index maintenance operations. This file sometimes resides in the %systemroot%\System32\Dhcp directory after a system failure.
J50.log and J50#####.log	A log of all database transactions. The DHCP database uses this file to recover data when necessary.
J50.chk	A *checkpoint file* indicates the location of the last information that was successfully written from the transaction logs to the database. In a data recovery scenario, the checkpoint file indicates where the recovery or replaying of data should begin. The checkpoint file is updated when data is written to the database file (Dhcp.mdb).

There is virtually no limit to the number of records a DHCP server stores; the size of the database is primarily dependent upon the number of DHCP clients on the network. The size of the DHCP database is not directly proportional to the number of active client lease entries, though, because over time some DHCP client entries become obsolete or deleted. This space is not immediately reclaimed and therefore some space remains unused. To recover the unused space, the DHCP database must be *compacted*; that is, the database must be optimized to reclaim unused space that has been left by adding and removing records. Dynamic database compaction occurs on DHCP servers as an automatic background process during idle time or after a database update.

Backing Up and Restoring the DHCP Database

Windows Server 2008 DHCP servers support automatic and manual backups. To provide fault tolerance in the case of a failure, it is important to back up the DHCP database. This enables you to restore the database from the backup copy if the hardware fails.

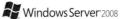

When you perform a backup, the entire DHCP database is saved, including the following:

- Scopes, including superscopes and multicast scopes
- Reservations
- Leases
- Options, including server options, scope options, reservation options, and class options

By default, the DHCP service automatically backs up the DHCP database and related registry entries to a backup directory on the local drive. This occurs every 60 minutes. By default, automatic backups are stored in the %systemroot%\System32\Dhcp\Backup directory. The administrator can also change the backup location. Automatic backups can use only ***automatic restores***, which are performed by the DHCP service when corruption is detected.

You can also back up the DHCP database manually. By default, manual backups are stored in the %systemroot%\System32\Dhcp\Backup\ directory, or you can specify an alternate location. You can manually back up the DHCP database while the DHCP service is running. The backup destination must be on the local disk; remote paths are not allowed, and the backup directory is created automatically if it does not already exist. The administrator can then copy the backed up DHCP files to an offline storage location such as a tape or a disk.

 BACK UP AND RESTORE THE DHCP DATABASE

GET READY. This exercise assumes that you have installed the DHCP Server role on a Windows Server 2008 computer, and that you have administrative rights to that server.

1. In the DHCP console, in the console tree, select the appropriate DHCP server.
2. Right-click the server and click **Backup**.
3. In the Browse For Folder dialog box, select the appropriate folder to back up to, and then click **OK**.
4. To restore the DHCP database, right-click the server and click **Restore**.
5. In the Browse For Folder dialog box, select the folder where the backup resides and then click **OK**.
6. In the DHCP dialog box, click **Yes** to stop and then restart the service.
7. If the status of the service does not update, press **F5** to refresh the DHCP console.

PAUSE. You can close the DHCP administrator console, or else leave it open for subsequent exercises.

In the previous exercise you performed a manual backup and restore of the DHCP database. Next we will discuss reconciling the DHCP database.

Reconciling the DHCP Database

> When you reconcile a server or a scope, the DHCP service uses both the summary information in the registry and the detailed information in the DHCP database to reconstruct the most current view of the DHCP service. You can choose to reconcile all scopes on the server by selecting the DHCP server, or you can reconcile one scope by selecting the appropriate scope.

Reconciliation is the process of verifying DHCP database values against DHCP registry values. You should reconcile your DHCP database in the following scenarios:

- The DHCP database values are configured correctly, but they are not displayed correctly in the DHCP console.
- After you have restored a DHCP database, but the restored DHCP database does not have the most recent values.

For example, assume your existing database was deleted and you have to restore an older version of the database. If you start DHCP and open the console, you will notice that the scope and options display, but the active leases do not. Reconciliation populates the client lease information from the registry to the DHCP database.

Before using the Reconcile feature to verify client information for a DHCP scope from the registry, the server computer needs to meet the following criteria:

- You must restore the DHCP server registry keys, or they must remain intact from previous service operations on the server computer.
- You must generate a fresh copy of the DHCP server database file in the %systemroot%\System32\Dhcp folder on the server computer.

⚠️ **WARNING** Be sure to have a valid backup of the DHCP database before deleting any files.

You can generate a fresh copy of the DHCP server database file by stopping the DHCP server service, deleting all of the database files in the current database path folder, and then restarting the DHCP server service.

Once the registry and database meet the previous criteria, you can restart the DHCP service. Upon opening the DHCP console, you might notice that scope information is present, but that there are no active leases displayed. To regain your active leases for each scope, use the Reconcile feature. You can reconcile a single scope or the entire server by right-clicking on the appropriate node and then clicking Reconcile.

When viewing properties for individual clients displayed in the list of active leases, you might notice client information displayed incorrectly. When the scope clients renew their leases, the DHCP Manager corrects and updates this information.

■ Configuring the Domain Name System (DNS) Service

↓ **THE BOTTOM LINE**

This appendix introduces fundamental concepts related to Domain Name System (DNS) name resolution in Microsoft Windows Server 2008. The appendix also explains key DNS concepts such as the DNS namespace, DNS zones, types of DNS servers, DNS resource records, and DNS resolvers. Also discussed is the process of configuring DNS servers, the types and process of DNS queries, and forwarding. Because DNS plays such a key role in Windows Server 2008, it is critical that you have a strong grasp of its concepts, processes, and methods of configuration. Without DNS, your network will most likely not function—clients won't be able to resolve names to Internet Protocol (IP) addresses. In addition, Active Directory clients use DNS to locate domain controllers; therefore, it is important that you understand key DNS concepts and how to properly configure DNS for your network.

For network devices such as computers and printers to communicate on the Internet or within your organization's network, they must be able to locate one another. In a Windows Server 2008 network, the primary means of locating network devices and network services is through the use of the Domain Name System, or DNS. For example, in order for COMPUTERA to communicate with COMPUTERB over a Transmission Control Protocol/Internet Protocol (TCP/IP) network, COMPUTERA must obtain the IP address of COMPUTERB. The process of mapping an IP address to a computer name (for example, COMPUTERA) is called *name resolution*. Windows Server 2008 includes both the DNS and Windows Internet Naming System (WINS) name resolution services to allow 2008 computers to translate between human-readable names, which are easy for users to understand, and numerical IP addresses, which are difficult for users to comprehend but are necessary for TCP/IP communications.

Before you can design and configure DNS for your Windows Server 2008 network, it is important to have an understanding of how DNS name resolution was developed for use on TCP/IP networks. Before the growth of the ARPANET into what we now know as the Internet, name resolution was handled through the use of text files called *HOSTS files* that were stored locally on each computer. The HOSTS file listed each name of the host and its corresponding IP address. Whenever a new host was added to the network, an administrator would manually update the HOSTS file with the new host name or IP address information. Periodically, all ARPANET users would then download and use the updated HOSTS file. Because the HOSTS file was flat, rather than hierarchical, it was impossible to organize hosts into separate domain structures. There was no method for creating hierarchical namespaces such as domains.

Another problem with HOSTS files was the size of the file and the inability to distribute the workload that resulted from parsing this file across multiple computers. Every HOSTS file listed every available ARPANET host, which meant that every computer that parsed the HOSTS file did 100 percent of the work to resolve client names into IP addresses. Clearly, this was inefficient and a better name resolution system had to be devised. In 1984, when the number of hosts on ARPANET reached 1,000, DNS was introduced. Because DNS is designed as a distributed database with a hierarchical structure, it can serve as the foundation for host name resolution in a TCP/IP network of any size, including the Internet. The distributed nature of DNS enables the name resolution workload to be shared among many computers. Today, most internetworking software, such as electronic mail programs and Web browsers, uses DNS for name resolution.

Although DNS is most commonly associated with the Internet, private networks also use DNS because of the following benefits:

- Scalability—Because DNS is capable of distributing workload across several databases or computers, it can scale to handle any level of name resolution required.

- Constancy—Host names remain constant even when associated IP addresses change, which makes locating network resources much easier.

- Ease of Use—Users access computers using easy-to-remember names such as *www. microsoft.com* rather than a numerical IP address, such as 192.168.1.100.

- Simplicity—Users need to learn only one naming convention to find resources on either the Internet or an intranet.

To understand the importance of DNS and how it functions within a Windows Server 2008 environment, you must understand a number of different components within DNS.

Introducing DNS Namespaces

A *DNS namespace* is a hierarchical, tree-structured list of DNS host names, starting at an unnamed root that is used for all DNS operations. Each domain can have additional child domains: a typical DNS namespace might be the *contoso.com* domain, which contains the *us.contoso.com* and *ee.contoso.com* child domains within the same namespace, and host names (also called *leaf objects*) representing individual TCP/IP-enabled devices such as *server1.austin.us.contoso.com*, *hplaserjet.sales.ee.contoso.com*, or *www.us.contoso.com*. Figure C-5 illustrates the structure of a typical DNS namespace that you might find on the Internet.

Figure C-5

Viewing a typical DNS namespace

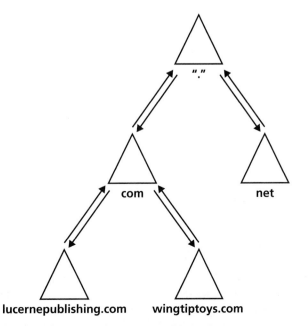

The DNS namespace has a hierarchical structure, and each DNS domain name is unique within a namespace. In Figure C-5, at the top of the Internet DNS namespace is the root domain. The root domain is represented by "." (a period). Under the DNS root domain, the **top-level domains**, or first-level domains, are organizational types such as .org, .com, and .edu. There are three types of top-level domains:

- Generic—See Table C-3 for examples of generic, top-level domain names.
- *Country code*—Examples of country code domain names are .uk., .jp, and .us.
- Infrastructure domain—.arpa is the Internet's infrastructure domain name.

Table C-3

Generic Top-Level Domain Names

DOMAIN NAME	USE
.aero	Exclusively reserved for the aviation community
.biz	A top-level domain that is aimed at large and small companies around the world
.com	Commercial organizations, such as *microsoft.com* for the Microsoft Corporation
.coop	A top-level domain for cooperatives
.edu	Educational institutions, now mainly four-year colleges and universities, such as *wustl.edu* for Washington University in St. Louis.
.gov	Agencies of the U.S. federal government, such as *fbi.gov* for the U.S. Federal Bureau of Investigation
.info	An unrestricted domain aimed at providing information for worldwide consumption
.int	Organizations established by international treaties, such as *nato.int* for NATO
.mil	U.S. military, such as *af.mil* for the U.S. Air Force
.museum	A domain restricted to museums and related organizations and individuals
.name	A global domain for use by individuals that possibly develops into a global digital identity for users
.net	Computers of network providers, organizations dedicated to the Internet, Internet service providers (ISPs), and so forth, such as *internic.net* for the Internet Network Information Center (InterNIC)
.org	A top-level domain for groups that do not fit anywhere else, such as non-governmental or nonprofit organizations (for example, *w3.org*, which is the World Wide Web Consortium)
.pro	A top-level domain for professionals, such as doctors, lawyers, and accountants

DNS uses the fully qualified domain name (FQDN) to map a host name to an IP address. An FQDN describes the exact relationship between a host and its DNS domain. For example, *computer1.sales.microsoft.com* represents a fully qualified domain name: the computer1 host, located in the sales domain, located in the Microsoft second-level domain, located in the .com top-level domain.

Second-level domains are registered to individuals or organizations, such as *microsoft.com*, the Microsoft Corporation domain; or *wustl.edu*, which is Washington University in the St. Louis domain; or *gov.au*, the domain for the Australian government. Second-level DNS domains can have many *subdomains*, and any domain can have hosts. A host is a specific computer or other network device within a domain, such as *computer1* in the *sales* subdomain of the *microsoft.com* domain.

One benefit of the hierarchical structure of DNS is that it is possible to have two hosts with the same host name that are in different locations in the hierarchy. For example, two hosts named *computer1*—*computer1.sales.microsoft.com* and *computer1.cpandl.microsoft.com*—can both exist without conflict because they are in different locations in the namespace hierarchy.

Deploying DNS Servers

As you might expect from the name, *DNS servers* are Windows Servers that host the DNS server role and are classified by the type of zones that they host. A DNS server can host primary zones, secondary zones, stub zones, or no zones. (A DNS *zone* is a collection of host name–to–IP address mappings for hosts in a contiguous portion of the DNS namespace, such as *contoso.com* or *austin.contoso.com*.) A DNS server is called the *primary name server* for any primary zones it hosts and a *secondary name server* for the secondary zones it hosts. A *caching-only server* hosts no zones.

DNS zones will be discussed more fully in the next section: "Introducing DNS zones."

DNS server types are determined by the type of zone or zones they host, and by the functions they perform. A DNS server may host either primary or secondary zones or both. If the server doesn't host any zones, it is referred to a *caching-only server*. A server is said to be **authoritative** for a particular zone if it hosts a primary or secondary zone for a particular DNS domain. These three types of servers are supported in Windows Server 2003 and Windows Server 2008, and are discussed as follows:

- Primary name server—Primary name servers have been configured with one or more primary DNS zones. In the case of standard or file-backed zones, when a change is made to the zone data, such as adding resource records to the zone, the changes must be made on the primary server for that zone; these changes will then propagate to secondary name servers. In the case of AD-integrated zones, there is no distinction between primary and secondary servers.

- Secondary name server—A secondary name server hosts one or more secondary zone databases. Because a zone transfer is used to create a secondary zone, the primary name server and zone already must exist to create a secondary name server.

- Caching-only server—Caching-only servers do not host any zones and are not authoritative for any domain. Caching-only DNS servers start with an empty cache, and then add resource record entries as the server fulfills client requests. This information is then available from its cache when answering subsequent client queries. A caching-only DNS server is valuable at a site when DNS functionality is needed locally but when creating a separate domain or zone is not desirable.

Installing the DNS Server Role

To enjoy the benefits of DNS, you must, of course, install DNS. Before you install DNS, it is recommended that you configure your computer to use a static IP address. If the DNS server is assigned its IP address from Dynamic Host Configuration Protocol (DHCP), its IP address may change. If the DNS server's IP address changes, queries sent by DNS clients configured with the old IP address will fail. Windows Server 2008 provides several wizards and other tools to install DNS quickly and easily. One method of installing DNS is by using the Server Manager page. The Server Manager page enables you to add or remove server roles, such as file server, print server, DHCP server, and DNS server. The following procedure explains how to use the Server Manager console to add the DNS server role. It will also cover the steps needed to create a zone and one or more resource records within a zone, now that we have covered the theory behind each of these concepts.

→ INSTALL THE DNS SERVER ROLE

GET READY. This exercise assumes that you are logged onto a Windows Server 2008 computer that has been configured with a static IP address, and that the Initial Configuration Tasks for this server have already been completed.

Install the DNS server role

1. Log onto the server using administrative credentials.
2. Click the **Start** button, and then click **Server Manager**. Expand the Server Manager console to full-screen, if necessary.
3. In the left-hand pane, click **Roles**. In the right-hand pane, click **Add Roles**.
4. The Before You Begin screen appears. Read the preliminary information and click **Next**.
5. The Select Server Roles screen appears. Place a checkmark next to **DNS Server** and click **Next**.
6. The DNS Server screen appears. Read the information presented about the DNS server role and click **Next**.
7. The Confirm Installation Selections screen appears. Click **Install** to install the DNS server role.
8. After a few minutes, the Installation Results screen will appear. Click **Close**.

PAUSE. Close the DNS console and log off of the Windows Server 2008 server.

In the previous exercise, you installed the DNS server role. In upcoming exercises you will configure DNS zones, create DNS resource records, and perform a number of other common configuration tasks on a Windows Server 2008 DNS server.

Introducing DNS Zones

As previously noted, another benefit of the DNS hierarchical structure is that workload for name resolution is distributed across many different resources. For administrative purposes, DNS domains can be organized into zones. A zone is a collection of host name–to–IP address mappings for hosts in a contiguous portion of the DNS namespace. Just like DNS resource records, DNS zones can be created and configured using the Windows Server 2008 DNS MMC snap-in, or else the *dnscmd* DNS management command-line utility.

A DNS zone can hold the resource records for one domain, or it can hold the resource records for multiple domains. A zone can host more than one domain only if the domains are contiguous—that is, connected by a direct parent-child relationship. One reason to divide a namespace into zones is to delegate authority for different portions of it, as one very large domain could be difficult to administer if contained in a single zone.

For each DNS domain name included in a zone, the zone becomes the authoritative source for information about that domain. When a zone is authoritative over a portion of the namespace, it means that it hosts the resource records for that portion of the namespace. It does not necessarily mean, however, that the server can update or modify the zone.

DNS zones are classified by where they are stored, whether they are writable, and by what information they receive and return. Zones can be stored either in text files or in Active Directory. When you configure a DNS server, you can configure it either with several zone types or with none at all, depending on the type of role that the DNS server has in the network. By using different zones, you can configure your DNS solution to best meet your needs. For example, it is recommended that you configure a primary zone and a secondary zone on separate DNS servers to provide fault tolerance should one server fail. You can also configure a stub zone if the zone is maintained on a separate DNS server to allow local DNS servers to stay up-to-date whenever remote DNS server information for a particular zone is updated.

In brief, zone data is maintained on a DNS name server and is stored in one of two ways:

- As a text-based zone file containing lists of mappings, called a ***standard zone*** or a ***file-backed zone***
- Within an Active Directory database, called an *Active Directory–integrated zone*

In terms of the types of queries that a DNS zone (either standard or AD-integrated) can respond to, each zone can be either a ***forward lookup zone*** or a ***reverse lookup zone***. In turn, each forward or reverse lookup zone can be one of three types:

- Primary zone
- Secondary zone
- Stub zone

As you can see, there are numerous possible combinations of each zone type that you can configure on a DNS server. For example, a single DNS server can host:

- A standard primary forward lookup zone
- A standard secondary forward lookup zone
- An Active Directory–integrated stub zone
- A standard secondary reverse lookup zone

…and so on.

When configuring a DNS server, you can configure a single server to host multiple zones if desired, and you can mix and match between different zone types. For example, a single DNS server might host a primary zone for *contoso.com*, as well as a secondary zone for *lucernepublishing.com* to allow improved name resolution for a remote network's resources, as might be necessary in the case of cross-departmental or cross-organizational projects that require access to resources across multiple organizations.

Configuring Standard Zones

> You can configure DNS zones in a number of different ways to meet the requirements of your network topology, administrative model, and the size of your DNS namespace. Typical DNS server operation involves three standard zones (primary, secondary, and in-addr.arpa). Windows Server 2003 and Windows Server 2008 provide a fourth option, stub zones.

Let's look at each of the standard zone types that can be configured on a Windows Server 2008 server.

- Standard primary zone—A standard primary zone hosts a read/write copy of the DNS zone in which resource records are created and managed. Only one server can host and load the master copy of the zone; no additional primary servers for the zone are permitted, and only the server hosting the primary zone is allowed to accept dynamic updates and process zone changes. When setting up DNS servers to host the zones for a domain, the primary server normally is located where it will be accessible for administering the zone file.

- Standard secondary zone—A copy of the zone file may be stored on one or more servers to balance network load, provide fault tolerance, or avoid forcing queries across a slow, wide area network (WAN) link. This standard secondary zone is a read-only copy of the standard primary DNS zone. In standard zones, information from a primary zone is transmitted to a secondary zone by performing a **zone transfer**, which is done by copying the zone file from the primary server to a secondary server. A zone transfer can be a **full zone transfer** (called an **AXFR**), in which the entire contents of the zone is copied from the primary server to the secondary server during each zone transfer, or an **incremental zone transfer** (called an **IXFR**), in which only changed information is transmitted after an initial AXFR, in order to cut down on bandwidth usage between primary and secondary servers. When a secondary zone is created, you must specify the IP address of one or more master DNS servers from which you want to copy the zone; these can be the Primary DNS server for the zone or another Secondary DNS server. These copies are referred to as *secondary zone database files*. The secondary zone database files are updated regularly from the primary zone database.

- Reverse lookup zone—Most queries sent to a DNS server are forward queries; that is, they request an IP address based on a DNS name. DNS also provides a reverse lookup process, which enables a host to determine another host's name based on its IP address. For example, a query contains the equivalent of "What is the DNS domain name of the host at IP address 192.168.100.1?" To answer this query, the **in-addr.arpa domain** is consulted in combination with the IP address in question. As you read the IP address from left to right, the network portion is some number of bits on the left, and the host portion is some number of bits on the right, based on the subnet mask. For example, 192.168.100.2, with a default subnet mask of 255.255.255.0, means the network portion is 192.168.100, and the host address is 2. Because the higher-level portion of the address is on the right, it must be reversed when building the domain tree. In short, because FQDNs go from specific to general, and IP addresses go from general to specific, that is, reading left to right, to facilitate reverse lookup, the IP address is reversed when concatenated with the in-addr.arpa domain. For example, the reverse lookup zone for the subnet 192.168.100.0 is 100.168.192.in-addr.arpa. The in-addr.arpa domain tree makes use of the *pointer (PTR) resource record*, which is used to associate the IP address with the host name. This lookup should correspond to an *address (A) resource record* for the host in a forward lookup zone. Reverse lookup queries often are used by network applications for verification rather than identification or as a tool for monitoring and troubleshooting the DNS service. The in-addr.arpa domain is used only for Internet Protocol version 4 (IPv4)-based networks. In the DNS console for Windows Server 2003, the DNS server's New Zone Wizard uses this domain when it creates a new reverse lookup zone. Internet Protocol version 6 (IPv6)-based reverse lookup zones are based on the **ip6.arpa domain**, which provides the same functionality as the in-addr.arpa domain for IPv6 networks.

- Stub zone—A DNS server running Windows Server 2003 or Windows Server 2008 also supports a new type of zone called a **stub zone**. A stub zone is a copy of a zone that contains only those resource records necessary to identify the authoritative DNS servers for that zone. A stub zone is a pointer to the DNS server that is authoritative for that zone, and it is used to maintain or improve DNS resolution efficiency. The stub zone contains a subset of zone data consisting of an SOA, an NS, and an A record. Like a standard secondary zone, resource records in the stub zone cannot be modified; they must be modified at the primary zone. Stub zones enable a DNS server to resolve DNS queries by using the stub zone's list of name servers without needing to query the Internet or internal root server for the DNS namespace. Using stub zones throughout your DNS infrastructure enables you to distribute a list of the authoritative DNS servers for a zone without using secondary zones. However, stub zones do not serve the same purpose as secondary zones and should not be considered as a solution to address redundancy and load sharing.

In the following exercises, we will configure a standard primary zone, secondary zone, and stub zone.

CONFIGURE A STANDARD PRIMARY ZONE

GET READY. This exercise assumes that you have installed the DNS server role as described in a previous exercise, and that you are logged onto the Windows Server 2008 computer with administrative privileges. In this exercise, we will create a forward lookup zone for the *contoso. com* domain on a server named DNSPRI.

1. Click the **Start** button, then click **Administrative Tools** and then **DNS**.
2. Expand the DNS console to full-screen, if necessary.
3. Drill down to **DNSPRI→Forward Lookup Zones**.

4. Right-click **Forward Lookup Zones** and click **New Zone**....

5. The Welcome to the New Zone Wizard screen appears. Click **Next**.

6. The Zone Type screen appears. Select the **Primary zone** radio button and click **Next**.

7. The Zone Name screen appears. In the *Zone name:* text box, enter **contoso.com** and then click **Next**.

8. The Zone File screen appears. Ensure that the *Create a new file with this file name:* radio button is selected and then click **Next**.

9. The Dynamic Update screen appears. Ensure that the *Do not allow dynamic updates* radio button is selected and then click **Next**.

10. The Completing the New Zone Wizard appears. Click **Finish**.

PAUSE. Close the DNS MMC snap-in and log off of the DNSPRI Windows Server 2008 server.

In the previous exercise, you configured a standard primary zone for the *contoso.com* DNS domain. In the next exercise, you will configure a secondary zone for load balancing on a second Windows Server 2008 computer called DNSSEC.

 CONFIGURE A STANDARD SECONDARY ZONE

GET READY. This exercise assumes that you have installed the DNS server role on a Windows Server 2008 computer called DNSSEC that has been configured with a static IP address, and that the Initial Configuration Tasks for this server have already been completed, This exercise assumes that you are logged onto DNSSEC with administrative privileges. You must also have the IP address of the DNSPRI server available.

1. Click the **Start** button, then click **Administrative Tools** and then **DNS**.

2. Expand the DNS console to full-screen, if necessary.

3. Drill down to **DNSSEC→Forward Lookup Zones**.

4. Right-click **Forward Lookup Zones** and click **New Zone**....

5. The Welcome to the New Zone Wizard screen appears. Click **Next**.

6. The Zone Type screen appears. Select the **Secondary zone** radio button and click **Next**.

7. The Zone Name screen appears. In the *Zone name:* text box, enter **contoso.com** and then click **Next**.

8. The Zone File screen appears. Ensure that the *Create a new file with this file name:* radio button is selected and then click **Next**.

9. The Master DNS Servers screen appears. Key the IP address of **DNSPRI** and then press (**Enter**). Ensure that the Validated column shows a status of "OK," and then click **Next**.

10. The Completing the New Zone Wizard appears. Click **Finish**.

PAUSE. Close the DNS MMC snap-in and log off of the DNSSEC Windows Server 2008 server.

In the previous exercise, you configured a standard secondary zone for the *contoso.com* DNS domain. In the next exercise, you will configure a stub zone on a Windows Server 2008 computer called DNSSEC.

 CONFIGURE A STUB ZONE

GET READY. This exercise assumes that you have installed the DNS server role on a Windows Server 2008 computer called DNSSEC that has been configured with a static IP address, and that the Initial Configuration Tasks for this server have already been completed, This exercise assumes that you are logged onto DNSSEC with administrative privileges. You must also have the IP address of the DNSPRI server available.

1. Click the **Start** button, then click **Administrative Tools** and then **DNS**.
2. Expand the DNS console to full-screen, if necessary.
3. Drill down to **DNSSEC➔Forward Lookup Zones**.
4. Right-click **Forward Lookup Zones** and click **New Zone....**
5. The Welcome to the New Zone Wizard screen appears. Click **Next**.
6. The Zone Type screen appears. Select the **Stub zone** radio button and click **Next**.
7. The Zone Name screen appears. In the *Zone name:* text box, enter **contoso.com** and then click **Next**.
8. The Master DNS Servers screen appears. Key the IP address of **DNSPRI** and then press **Enter**. Ensure that the Validated column shows a status of "OK," and then click **Next**.
9. The Completing the New Zone Wizard appears. Click **Finish**.

PAUSE. Close the DNS MMC snap-in and log off of the DNSSEC Windows Server 2008 server.

In the previous exercise, you configured a standard stub zone for the *contoso.com* DNS domain. In the next section, we will discuss configuring Active Directory–integrated DNS zones to improve the replication efficiency and security of your DNS data.

Configuring Active Directory–Integrated Zones

Storing zones in Active Directory is a Microsoft proprietary method of managing, securing, and replicating DNS zone information. An Active Directory–integrated zone is a DNS zone contained within Active Directory. Zones stored in text files are typically referred to as *standard* or *file-backed zones*, while zones that are stored in Active Directory are referred to as *Active Directory–integrated zones*.

Storing a zone in Active Directory has the following benefits:

- Fault tolerance—Redundant copy of DNS zone information can be stored on multiple servers.
- Security—DNS zones stored in Active Directory can take advantage of increased security by modifying its **discretionary access control list (DACL)**. The DACL enables you to specify which users and groups may modify the DNS zones. You can also configure **secure dynamic updates** for Active Directory–integrated zones, which will only allow records to be updated by the client that first registered the record.
- Zones are multimaster—This means that zones can be updated in more than one location, i.e., from more than one server. All domain controllers where the zone is stored can modify the zone, and changes to the zone are then replicated to the other domain controllers that contain the zone file.
- Efficient replication—Zone transfers are replaced by more efficient Active Directory replication. This can be especially important over networks with slow links because Active Directory compresses replication data that passes between sites.
- Maintain use of secondary zones—Zones that are stored in Active Directory can also be transferred to standard secondary servers to create secondary zones in the same way that file-backed secondary zones are transferred.

Windows Server 2003 and Windows Server 2008 provide a more efficient method of replicating DNS zone information than does Microsoft Windows 2000 Server. In Microsoft

Windows 2000, updates to Active Directory zones were replicated to all domain controllers in that domain, whether or not they were also configured as DNS servers.

With Windows Server 2003 and Windows Server 2008, Active Directory–integrated zones can be configured with one of three different *replication scopes*, which is to say that their information can be replicated in three different ways:

- To all domain controllers in the domain (this is the only replication scope available that was available in Windows 2000)
- To all domain controllers that are DNS servers in the local domain, also known as the ***DomainDNSZones*** application partition
- To all domain controllers that are also DNS servers in the entire forest, also known as the ***ForestDNSZones*** application

You can create two types of Active Directory–integrated zones: forward lookup zones and reverse lookup zones.

An *Active Directory–integrated forward lookup zone* is similar to a standard primary zone. Outside of Active Directory, primary and secondary servers are necessary because they follow a single-master update model, where only one server contains a writable copy of the zone database. However, Active Directory–integrated zones follow a multimaster update model, meaning all Active Directory–integrated zones contain a read/write copy of the zone and can make changes to the zone information. Therefore, primary and secondary distinctions are not necessary.

An *Active Directory–integrated reverse lookup zone* is used for resolving an IP address to a name and is similar to the standard in-addr.arpa zone. The reverse lookup zone is stored and updated in the same manner as the Active Directory–integrated forward lookup zone.

Configuring DNS Delegation

Initially, a zone stores information about a single DNS domain name. As other domains are added, you must make a decision about whether or not the domain will be part of the same zone. If you choose to add the subdomain, you may manage the subdomain as part of the original zone, or else delegate management of the subdomain to a different zone.

For example, Figure C-6 shows the *contoso.com* domain, which contains domain names for Contoso, Ltd. When the *contoso.com* domain is first created at a single server, it is configured as a single zone for all of the Contoso DNS namespace. If, however, the *contoso.com* domain needs to use subdomains, those subdomains must be included in the zone or delegated away to another zone.

Figure C-6

Viewing a DNS zone configuration

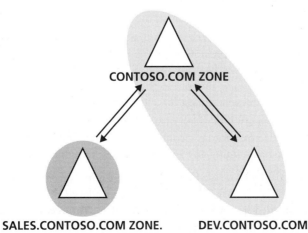

CONTOSO.COM ZONE

SALES.CONTOSO.COM ZONE.   DEV.CONTOSO.COM

In this example, the *contoso.com* domain shows a new subdomain—the *sales.contoso.com* domain—delegated away from the *contoso.com* zone and managed in its own zone. However, the *contoso.com* zone needs to contain a few resource records to provide the delegation information that references the DNS servers that are authoritative for the delegated *sales.contoso.com* subdomain. If the *contoso.com* zone does not use delegation for a subdomain, the data for the subdomain remains part of the *contoso.com* zone. For example, the subdomain *dev.contoso.com* is not delegated away, but is managed by the *contoso.com* zone.

Configuring DNS Zone Transfers

Zone transfers are the complete or partial transfer of all data in a zone from the primary DNS server hosting the zone to a secondary DNS server hosting a copy of the zone. The copy of the zone hosted on a secondary DNS server is initially created using a zone transfer. When changes are made to the zone on a primary DNS server, the primary DNS server notifies the secondary DNS servers that changes have occurred and the changes are replicated to all the secondary DNS servers for that zone using zone transfers.

In the original DNS specifications, only one form of zone transfer was available, the full zone transfer (AXFR). Windows 2000, Windows Server 2003, and Windows Server 2008 DNS also support incremental zone transfers in addition to full zone transfers. This section describes both types of zone transfers, as well as the notification process known as *DNS Notify*.

The following events trigger zone transfers:

- A transfer is manually initiated using the console at the secondary server.
- The zone refresh interval expires.
- The DNS Server service is started at the secondary server.
- The master server notifies the secondary server of a zone change or changes.

Zone transfers are always initiated at the secondary server for a zone and sent to the server's configured master server, which acts as its source for the zone. A master server can be any other DNS server that loads the zone, such as either the primary server for the zone or another secondary server. When the master server receives the request for the zone, it can reply with either an incremental (IXFR) or full (AXFR) transfer of the zone to the secondary server.

In a full zone transfer, the primary DNS server hosting the primary zone transfers a copy of the entire zone database to the secondary DNS server hosting a copy of the zone. Whether a full or incremental transfer, the following process takes place:

See the "Configuring DNS Resource Records" section of this appendix for information about the Start of Authority (SOA) record.

1. When the value of the Refresh field in the Start of Authority (SOA) resource record for the zone hosted on the secondary DNS server expires, the secondary DNS server queries the primary DNS server for the SOA record of the primary zone.

2. The primary DNS server for the zone replies to the query with the SOA resource record.

3. The secondary DNS server for the zone compares the serial number in the returned SOA record to the serial number in the SOA record for the local copy of the zone. If the serial number sent by the primary DNS server for the zone is higher than the serial number for its local zone, the zone needs to be updated, and the secondary DNS server sends an AXFR request (a request for a full zone transfer) to the primary DNS server.

4. The primary DNS server receives the request for the zone transfer and sends the full zone database to the secondary DNS server, essentially re-creating the copy of the zone while maintaining any zone settings.

If the primary DNS server for the zone does not respond to the request for a zone transfer sent from the secondary DNS server, the secondary DNS server continues to retry for the interval specified in the Retry field in the SOA resource record for the zone. If there is still no answer after the interval specified in the Expire field in the SOA resource record for the zone expires, the secondary DNS server discards its zone.

Incremental zone transfers were designed to reduce the amount of network traffic generated by full zone transfers. Rather than sending a copy of the entire zone file, an incremental zone transfer sends only records that have changed since the last zone update. Windows 2000, Windows Server 2003, and Windows Server 2008 all support incremental zone transfers.

Although an incremental zone transfer saves network bandwidth, it uses additional disk space on the server to record the version history. The primary DNS server for the zone maintains a recent version history of the zone, which observes any record changes that occurred in the most recent version updates of the zone. To conserve disk space, DNS servers store only the most recent updates. The Windows Server 2008 DNS Server service stores these updates in a log file that resides in *the %systemroot%\System32\Dns* folder. The log file is named by using the name of the zone file with .log appended. For example, if the zone file for the *contoso.com* domain is stored in the file *Contoso.com.dns,* the log file is named *Contoso.com.dns.log.*

An incremental zone transfer uses the following process:

1. Initially, when a secondary server is first configured, it sends a full zone transfer request (AXFR) to its master DNS server. The master (source) server responds by sending a full copy of the zone to the secondary (destination) server.

2. Each zone delivery has a version indicated by a serial number in the properties of the SOA resource record and a refresh interval (by default, 900 seconds). The refresh interval indicates at what interval the secondary server should request another copy of the zone from the source server.

3. After the interval expires, the destination server submits an SOA query to request an incremental zone transfer.

4. The source server answers the query by sending its SOA record, which contains the aforementioned serial number.

5. The destination server compares the serial number from the SOA record to its current local serial number. If the numbers are equal, no transfer is requested, and the refresh interval is reset.

6. If the value of the serial number in the SOA response is higher than its current local serial number, records on the source are newer than the local records and an IXFR query is sent to the source server. This query contains the local serial number so the source server can determine which records the destination server needs.

7. Depending on several factors, the source server responds with either an incremental or full transfer of the zone. The primary DNS server for a zone is not required to perform an incremental zone transfer. It can choose to perform a full zone transfer under the following conditions:

   • The primary DNS server does not support incremental zone transfers.

   • The primary DNS server does not have all the necessary data for performing an incremental zone transfer.

   • An incremental zone transfer uses more network bandwidth than a full zone transfer.

When the secondary DNS server receives an incremental zone transfer, it creates a new version of the zone and begins replacing outdated resource records with the updated resource records from the source server, applying oldest to newest. When all the updates are completed, the secondary DNS server replaces its old version of the zone with the new version of the zone.

By default, Windows Server 2008 will only permit zone transfers on standard zones to those servers that have been configured as name servers for the zone in question. Before you can configure an additional name server, it must be configured with a valid FQDN that is resolvable by the server in question.

In the following exercise, we will configure DNSPRI to permit zone transfers to take place to the secondary zone configured on DNSSEC, and we will then force a zone transfer to take place between DNSPRI and DNSSEC.

CONFIGURE A STANDARD SECONDARY ZONE

GET READY. This exercise assumes that you have configured DNSPRI with a primary zone for the *contoso.com* domain, and DNSSEC with a secondary zone for the *contoso.com* domain. This exercise assumes that you are logged onto DNSPRI and DNSSEC with administrative privileges. Parts A and C of this exercise will be performed on DNSSEC; Part B will be performed on DNSPRI. You must have the IP address of both servers available.

PART A—Confirm that zone transfers are not currently functional on DNSSEC

1. Log onto DNSSEC as a local administrator on the computer.
2. Click the **Start** button, then browse to **Administrative Tools→DNS**.
3. The DNS MMC snap-in opens. Browse to **DNSSEC→Forward Lookup Zones**.
4. Click the plus sign next to contoso.com. Notice that a red 'X' appears next to the zone name in the left-hand column, and the right-hand pane indicates that the DNS zone was not loaded by the server.

PART B—Configure zone transfers to DNSSEC from DNSPRI.

1. Log onto DNSPRI as a local administrator on the computer.
2. Click the **Start** button, then browse to **Administrative Tools→DNS**.
3. The DNS MMC snap-in opens. Browse to **DNSSEC→Forward Lookup Zones**.
4. Click the plus sign next to contoso.com. Right-click **contoso.com** and click **New Host (A or AAAA)....** The New Host screen appears.
5. In the Name (uses parent domain name if left blank): field, enter **DNSSEC**. In the IP address: field, enter the IP address of the DNSSEC server.
6. Click **Add Host** and then click **OK** followed by **Done**. Notice that an A record for DNSSEC now appears in the contoso.com zone.
7. Right-click **contoso.com** and click **Properties**. The **contoso.com** Properties screen appears.
8. Click the **Name Servers** tab. You will see the screen shown in Figure C-7. Notice that only DNSPRI is listed as a Name Server for the contoso.com zone.

Figure C-7

Configuring DNS name servers

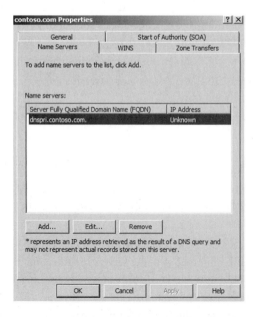

9. Click **Add.** The New Name Server Record screen appears.

WARNING The new name server will appear with a red 'X' next to it at this point, because it is not authoritative for the contoso.com zone. This error can be safely ignored for now because DNSSEC does not yet host the contoso.com zone.

10. In the Server fully qualified domain name (FQDN): text box, enter **DNSSEC.contoso.com**. Click **Resolve**.

11. Click **OK** twice to save your changes.

PART C—Confirm that zone transfers are now taking place on DNSSEC

1. Log onto DNSSEC as a local administrator on the computer.

2. Click the **Start** button, then browse to **Administrative Tools→DNS**.

3. The DNS MMC snap-in opens. Browse to **DNSSEC→Forward Lookup Zones**.

4. Click the plus sign next to contoso.com. Notice that the contents of the contoso.com zone have been transferred to DNSSEC.

PAUSE. Close the DNS MMC snap-in on each server, and then log off of both servers.

Using DNS Notify

Windows-based DNS servers support DNS Notify, an update to the original DNS protocol specification that permits a means of initiating notification to secondary servers when zone changes occur (RFC 1996). Servers that are notified can then initiate a zone transfer as described previously to request zone changes from their master servers and update their local replicas of the zone. This process improves consistency of zone data.

The list of secondary DNS servers that a primary DNS server will notify is maintained in the notify list, which is a list of the IP addresses for those secondary servers. When the zone is updated, the primary DNS server for the zone notifies only DNS servers on the notify list. For secondary DNS servers to be notified by the DNS server acting as their configured source for a zone, each secondary server must first have its IP address in the notify list of the source server. In Windows Server 2008 DNS, you can use the DNS Notify dialog box to set the notify list.

In addition to notifying the listed servers, the DNS console permits you to use the contents of the notify list as a means to restrict or limit zone transfer access to only those secondary servers specified in the list. This can help prevent an undesired attempt by an unknown or unapproved DNS server to pull, or request, zone updates.

When the zone on a primary DNS server is updated, the following events occur:

TAKE NOTE *

For replication of Active Directory–integrated zones, DNS notification is not needed. This is because DNS servers that load a zone from Active Directory automatically poll the directory (as specified by the SOA resource record's refresh interval) to update and refresh the zone. In these cases, configuring a notify list can actually degrade system performance by causing unnecessary, additional transfer requests for the updated zone.

- The Serial Number field in the SOA record is incremented to indicate that a new version of the zone is written to a disk.
- The primary DNS server sends a notify message to the DNS servers that are specified in its notify list.
- A secondary DNS server for the zone that receives the notify message responds by sending an SOA-type query back to the notifying primary DNS server to determine if the zone on the primary DNS server is a later version than the copy of the zone currently stored on the secondary DNS server.
- If a notified secondary DNS server determines that the serial number specified in the SOA record of the zone on the primary DNS server is higher than the serial number specified in the SOA record for its current zone copy (the zone contains more recent updates), the notified secondary DNS server requests a zone transfer (AXFR or IXFR).

Configuring DNS Resource Records

A DNS *resource record* is information that is related to a DNS domain; for example, the host record defining a host IP address. Resource records are represented in binary form in packets when queries and responses are made using DNS. In DNS zone files, however, resource records are represented as text entries. In Windows Server 2008, resource records can be created using the DNS console or the dnscmd command-line utility.

Most resource records are represented as single-line text entries. If an entry is going to span more than one line, you can use parentheses to encapsulate the information. For readability, blank lines and comments often are inserted in the zone files and are ignored by the DNS server. Comments always start with a semicolon (;) and end with a carriage return.

Resource records have the following syntax:

Owner [TTL] Class Type RDATA

Table C-4 describes the common set of information in resource records.

Table C-4

Typical Resource Record Fields

NAME	DESCRIPTION
Owner	Identifies the host or the DNS domain to which this resource record belongs.
TTL (Time to Live)	A 32-bit integer representing the maximum time, in seconds, that a DNS server or client caches this resource record before it is discarded. This field is optional, and if it is not specified, the client uses the minimum TTL in the SOA record.
Class	Defines the protocol family in use, which is IN for the Internet system.
Type	Identifies the type of resource record. For example, A indicates that the resource record stores host address information.
Resource Record Data (RDATA)	Contains RDATA. The RDATA field is a variable-length field that represents the information being described by the resource record. For example, in an A resource record, the data contained in this field is the 32-bit IP address that represents the host identified by the owner.

The DNS database consists of resource records that relate different information about the names in the database. A resource record for a DNS name can identify a single resource within the network, such as the network host that uses that name, or that there is a service running on that network host, such as electronic mail.

Different types of resource records provide DNS data about computers on a TCP/IP network. The most common resource records are described in Table C-5 and in detail in the following sections. This discussion includes resource records specific to Windows 2000, Windows Server 2003, and Windows Server 2008 DNS implementations.

Table C-5

Resource Record Types

DESCRIPTION	CLASS	TTL	TYPE	DATA
Start of Authority (SOA record)	Internet (IN)	60 minutes	SOA	Owner name, primary name server FQDN, serial number, refresh interval, retry interval, expire time, and minimum TTL
Host (A) Record	Internet (IN)	TTL of the SOA in the same zone	A	Owner name (host DNS name) and host IPv4 address
Host (AAAA) Record	Internet (IN)	TTL of the SOA in the zone	AAAA	Owner name (host DNS name) and host IPv6 address
Name Server (NS Record)	Internet (IN)	TTL of the SOA in the same zone	NS	Owner name and DNS server name

(continued)

Table C-5 (continued)

DESCRIPTION	CLASS	TTL	TYPE	DATA
Mail Exchanger (MX Record)	Internet (IN)	TTL of the SOA in the same zone	MX	Owner name, Mail Exchanger (MX) server DNS name, and preference number
Canonical Name (CNAME Record, alias record)	Internet (IN)	TTL of the SOA in the same zone	CNAME	Owner name (alias name) and host DNS name
Service Locator Record (SRV)	Internet (IN)	TTL of the SOA in the same zone	SRV	Domain name associated with the service, Service Name (LDAP, KDC, etc.), Protocol, Weight, Priority, Port number

Start of Authority (SOA) Resource Record

Every zone contains an SOA resource record at the top of the zone file. An SOA resource record indicates the starting point or original point of authority for information stored in a zone. It contains all the zone-specific information for the DNS server to use when maintaining the zone. The SOA resource record is the first resource record that is created when creating a new zone.

The RDATA field for the SOA resource record contains the fields shown in Table C-6.

Table C-6

RDATA Fields for the SOA Resource Record

RDATA FIELDS	DESCRIPTION
Authoritative server	Contains the name of the primary DNS server authoritative for the zone.
Responsible person	Shows the e-mail address of the administrator who is responsible for the zone. This field takes a period (.) instead of an at (@) sign.
Serial number	Shows how many times the zone is updated. When a zone's secondary server contacts its master server to determine whether it needs to initiate a zone transfer, the zone's secondary server compares its own serial number with that of the master. If the serial number of the master server is higher, the secondary server initiates a zone transfer.
Refresh	Shows how often the secondary server for the zone checks to see whether the zone data is changed.
Retry	After sending a zone transfer request, shows how long (in seconds) the zone's secondary server waits before sending another request.
Expire	After a zone transfer, shows how long (in seconds) the zone's secondary server continues to respond to zone queries before discarding its own zone as invalid.
Minimum TTL	Applies to all the resource records in the zone whenever a TTL value is not specified in a resource record or is shorter than the minimum TTL specified in the zone's SOA record. Whenever a DNS client queries the server, the server sends back resource records containing a record-specific TTL or the minimum TTL. Negative responses are cached for the minimum TTL of the SOA resource record of the authoritative zone.

The following output is an example of an SOA resource record:

```
na.contoso.com. IN SOA (
nadc1.na.contoso.com.; authoritative server for the zone
administrator.na.contoso.com.; zone admin e-mail;
(responsible person)
5099;    serial number
3600;    refresh (1 hour)
600;     retry (10 mins)
86400;   expire (1 day)
60 );    minimum TTL (1 min)
```

Name Server (NS) Resource Record

The name server (NS) resource record identifies a DNS server that is authoritative for a zone; that is, a DNS server that hosts a primary or secondary copy of the DNS zone in question. The name of the DNS server that is authoritative for a zone is stored in the RDATA field. NS records are used to indicate both primary and secondary DNS servers for the zone specified in the SOA resource record and to indicate the DNS servers for any delegated zones. If a zone has multiple authoritative servers (for example, a primary server and one or more secondary servers), you need to have an NS record for each server.

TAKE NOTE*

Every zone must contain at least one NS record.

The Windows Server 2008 DNS Server service automatically creates the first NS record for a zone when the zone is created. You can add additional NS records by using DNS or the dnscmd command-line tool.

For example, if the administrator for *contoso.com* delegates authority for the *us.contoso.com* subdomain to the *usdc1.us.contoso.com* server, the following line is added to the *contoso.com* and *na.contoso.com* zones:

```
us.contoso.com. IN NS usdc1.us.contoso.com.
```

Using Delegation and Glue Records

Delegation and glue records are resource records that you add to a zone to delegate a subdomain to a separate zone hosted on a different DNS server. A delegation record is represented by the NS record in the parent zone that lists the authoritative DNS server hosting the child zone for the delegated subdomain. A glue record is the A record in the parent zone for the authoritative DNS server hosting the child zone for the delegated subdomain.

For example, the DNS server that hosts the zone for the domain *contoso.com* will delegate authority for the subdomain *us.contoso.com* to the DNS server *ns2.us.contoso.com*, which is where a zone for the domain *us.contoso.com* is hosted. To create this delegation, the following records are added to the parent zone *contoso.com*:

```
us.contoso.com.          IN NS ns2.us.contoso.com
ns2.us.contoso.com.      IN A 172.16.54.1
```

When a DNS client submits a query for a name in the child zone to the DNS server that is authoritative for the parent zone, the authoritative DNS server for the parent zone checks its zone. The delegation resource records tell it which DNS server is authoritative for the child zone. The authoritative DNS server for the parent zone can then return a referral containing the delegation records to the DNS client.

A glue record is necessary in this example because *ns2.us.contoso.com* is a member of the delegated domain *us.contoso.com*. However, if it was a member of a different domain, such as *lucernepublishing.com*, the DNS client can perform standard name resolution to resolve the name of the authoritative DNS server to an IP address, in which case a glue record is not required. Separate domain configurations are less common.

Incorrect delegations are a major source of name resolution failure for DNS because an incorrect delegation removes a branch of the DNS namespace tree, and the other nodes in the tree cannot locate the DNS names in and under the branch. For this reason, it is recommended that you verify delegations periodically, and that administrators responsible for parent and child zones communicate any modifications that can affect delegation.

IPv4 Host Records (A) and IPv6 Host Records (AAAA)

> The IPv4 *host (A)* resource record maps a FQDN to an IPv4 address. The IPv6 *host (AAAA) resource record* performs the same function, except that it maps an FQDN to an IPv6 address.

For example, the following A resource record is located in the zone *us.contoso.com* and maps the FQDN of a server to its IP address:

```
usdc1.us.contoso.com.    IN A 172.16.48.1
```

The A resource record contains the following fields:

- The Owner, TTL, Class, and Type fields, which are described in Table C-4, "Typical Resource Record Fields," earlier in this appendix.
- The RDATA field is the IP address of the owner.

PTR Resource Record

> The *PTR resource record* performs the reverse function of the A resource record by mapping an IP address to an FQDN. For example, the following PTR resource record maps the IP address 172.16.48.1 of *usdc1.us.contoso.com* to its FQDN:

```
1.48.16.172.in-addr.arpa. IN PTR usdc1.us.contoso.com.
```

PTR resource records contain the following fields:

- The Owner, TTL, Class, and Type fields, which are described in Table C-4, "Typical Resource Record Fields," earlier in this appendix.
- The RDATA field is the host name of the host with the IP address contained in the Owner field.

Canonical Name (CNAME) Resource Record

> The *canonical name (CNAME) resource record* creates an alias for a specified FQDN. You can use CNAME records to hide the implementation details of your network from the clients that connect to it. For example, if you want to put a File Transfer Protocol (FTP) server named *ftp1.us.contoso.com* on your *us.contoso.com* subdomain, but you know that in six months you might move it to a computer named *ftp2.us.contoso.com* and you do not want your users to have to know about the change, do the following: create an alias called *ftp.us.contoso.com* that points to *ftp1.us.contoso.com*. When you move your computer, you need to change only the CNAME record to point to *ftp2.us.contoso.com*.

For example, the following CNAME resource record creates an alias for *ftp1.na.contoso.com*:

```
ftp.us.contoso.com. IN CNAME ftp1.us.contoso.com.
```

After a DNS client queries for the name for *ftp.na.contoso.com*, the DNS server finds the CNAME resource record, resolves the query for *ftp1.us.contoso.com*, and returns both the A and CNAME resource records to the client.

CNAME resource records contain the following fields:

- The Owner, TTL, Class, and Type fields. The Owner field for CNAME records is the alias.
- The RDATA field is the name of the host to which the alias points. (A CNAME record cannot be created unless the A record that it is pointing to already exists.)

Mail Exchanger (MX) Resource Record

> The ***mail exchanger (MX) resource record*** specifies a server that is configured to act as a mail server for a DNS name. The mail server identified by an MX record is a host that either processes or forwards mail for a DNS domain name. Processing the mail means either delivering it to the addressee or passing it to a different type of mail transport. Forwarding the mail means sending it to its final destination server, sending it by using Simple Mail Transfer Protocol (SMTP) to another mail exchange server that is closer to the final destination, or queuing it for a specified amount of time.

To improve the reliability of the mail service for a domain, you can designate secondary mail servers that can store mail for a domain. If the primary mail server stops responding, the secondary servers can hold the mail and then forward it when the mail server comes back into service. An SMTP smart host (a host capable of using MX records) uses multiple mail servers, provided you configure multiple MX resource records.

The following example shows MX resource records for the mail servers for the domain *na.contoso.com*:

```
@ IN MX 5 mailserver1.us.contoso.com.
@ IN MX 10 mailserver2.us.contoso.com.
@ IN MX 20 mailserver3.us.contoso.com.
```

MX resource records contain the following fields:

- The Owner, TTL, Class, and Type fields, which are described in Table C-4, "Typical Resource Record Fields," earlier in this lesson.

The following data is stored in the RDATA field of the MX resource record:

- The fourth field in the MX record is the mail server preference value. The preference value specifies the preference given to the MX record among other MX records. Records with lower priority numbers (which are higher priority) are preferred. Thus, when a mail client needs to send mail to a certain DNS domain, it first contacts a DNS server for that domain and retrieves all the MX records. It then contacts the mailer with the lowest preference value.
- The final field is the name of the mail server to contact.

For more information about how mail is routed in the domain system, see RFC 974, which can be accessed at *http://www.rfc-editor.org/rfcsearch.html*.

For example, suppose Holly Holt sends an e-mail message to *loviatt@us.contoso.com* on a day that mailserver1 is down, but mailserver2 is working. Her e-mail client tries to deliver the message to mailserver1 because it has the lowest preference value, but it fails because mailserver1 is down. In this case, Holly's e-mail client chooses mailserver2 because its preference value is the second lowest. If mailserver2 is operating, the mail is successfully delivered to mailserver2.

To prevent mail loops, if the e-mail client is on a host that is listed as an MX for the destination host, the e-mail client can deliver only to an MX with a lower preference value than its own host. If a mail server receives multiple MX records with equal priority, the choice of which MX record to use depends on implementation.

Service Locator (SRV) Resource Record

Service locator (SRV) resource records enable you to specify the location of servers that provide a specific network service over a specific protocol and in a specific domain. SRV records allow you to have several servers offering a network service and to move services between servers without changing the client configuration. For example, if you have two application servers in your domain, you can create SRV resource records in DNS that specify which hosts serve as application servers. Client applications that support SRV records will use DNS to retrieve the SRV resource records for the application servers.

Active Directory is an example of an application that relies on SRV resource records. An example of an application that supports SRV resource records is the Windows 2000, Windows Server 2003, and Windows Server 2008 Netlogon service. On Windows 2000, Microsoft Windows XP, Windows Server 2003, Windows Server 2008, and Windows Vista, client computers use SRV resource records to locate domain controllers for an Active Directory domain.

The format for an SRV record is as follows:

```
_Service_Protocol.Name [TTL] Class SRV Priority Weight Port Target
```

Table C-7 outlines the SRV resource record fields.

Table C-7

SRV Resource Record Fields

FIELD NAME	DESCRIPTION
Service	Specifies the name of the service, such as http or telnet.
Protocol	Specifies the protocol, such as Transmission Control Protocol (TCP) or User Datagram Protocol (UDP).
Name	Specifies the domain name to which the resource record refers.
TTL	Uses a 32-bit integer to represent the maximum time, in seconds, that a DNS server or client caches this entry before it is discarded. This field is optional, and if it is not specified, the client uses the minimum TTL in the SOA record.
Class	Defines the protocol family in use, which is usually IN for the Internet system. The other value defined in RFC 1034 is CH for the Chaos system, which was used experimentally at the Massachusetts Institute of Technology.

Table C-8 describes the data stored in the RDATA field of the SRV resource record.

Table C-8

SRV Record RDATA Fields

FIELD NAME	DESCRIPTION
Priority	Specifies the priority of the host. Clients attempt to contact the host with the lowest priority number.
Weight	Performs load balancing. When the Priority field is the same for two or more records in the same domain, clients must try records with higher weights more often, unless the clients support some other load-balancing mechanism.
Port	Shows the port for the service on this host.
Target	Shows the FQDN for the host providing the service.

The following example shows SRV records for two domain controller servers:

```
_ldap._tcp.contoso.com. IN SRV 0 0 389 dc1.contoso.com.
_ldap._tcp.contoso.com. IN SRV 10 0 389 dc2.contoso.com.
```

This example does not specify a TTL. Therefore, the DNS client uses the minimum TTL specified in the SOA resource record.

If a computer needs to locate a Lightweight Directory Access Protocol (LDAP) server in the *contoso.com* domain, the DNS client sends an SRV query for the following name:

```
_ldap._tcp.contoso.com.
```

The DNS server replies with the SRV records listed in the previous example. The DNS client then chooses between DC1 and DC2 by looking at their priority values. Because DC1 has the lower priority value, the LDAP client chooses DC1. In this example, if the priority values were the same but the weight values were different, the client would choose a domain controller randomly with a probability proportional to the Weight field value.

Next, the DNS client requests the A record for *DC1.contoso.com*, and the DNS server sends the A record. Finally, the client attempts to contact the domain controller using the IP address in the A record.

Using Wildcard Resource Records

In some DNS designs, you might need to use a large number of resource records in a zone. However, you might find it difficult to manually add the records. In such cases, you can define a wildcard DNS resource record.

The following is an example of a wildcard address from the *contoso.com* domain:

```
* IN A 172.16.54.1
```

If the preceding A record is in DNS, all queries for a host in the *contoso.com* domain not explicitly defined in the zone file receive a reply for 172.16.54.1. Windows 2000, Windows Server 2003, and Windows Server 2008 DNS support wildcard resource records.

 CONFIGURE DNS RESOURCE RECORDS

GET READY. This exercise assumes that you have configured DNSPRI with a primary zone for the *contoso.com* domain. This exercise assumes that you are logged onto DNSPRI with administrative privileges.

1. In the DNS console, drill down to **DNSPRI→Forward Lookup Zones→contoso.com**.
2. Right-click **contoso.com** and click **New Host Record (A or AAAA)....**
3. The New Host window appears. In the Name (uses parent domain name if blank): field, enter **SERVER1**. In the IP Address field, enter an IP address appropriate for your environment, such as *192.168.52.150*.
4. Click **Add Host**. Read the DNS window that appears. Click **OK** and then click **Done**.
5. Right-click **contoso.com** and click **New Mail Exchanger (MX)....**
6. The New Resource Record window appears. In the host or child domain: text box, enter **mail.** In the Fully Qualified Domain Name (FQDN) of mail server: text box, enter *SERVER1.contoso.com*.
7. Click **OK**.

PAUSE. Close the DNS MMC snap-in and log off of the Windows Server 2008 computer before continuing.

In the previous exercise, you configured DNS resource records on a Windows Server 2008 computer. In the following section, you will learn about the process of allowing clients to dynamically update their own resource records on a Windows Server 2008 DNS server.

Configuring DNS Dynamic Updates

Windows Server 2008 DNS supports the DNS dynamic update protocol (RFC [Request for Comments] 2136), which enables DNS clients to dynamically update their resource records in DNS zones. You can specify that the DHCP server in your network dynamically update DNS when it configures a DHCP client computer. This reduces the administration time that is necessary when manually administering zone records. You use the dynamic update feature in conjunction with DHCP to update resource records when a computer releases or updates its IP address.

Client computers running Windows 2000 or later attempt to update address (A) resource records directly, but they utilize the DHCP server to dynamically update their pointer (PTR) resource records. DHCP-enabled client computers running earlier versions of Microsoft operating systems are unable to update or register their DNS resource records directly. These DHCP clients must use the DHCP service provided with Windows 2000, Windows Server 2003, and Windows Server 2008 to register and update both their A and PTR resource records on behalf of these down-level clients.

Although dynamic updates allow clients to update DNS resource records, this is not a secure method. A more secure way of updating DNS resource records is using secure dynamic updates. The server attempts the update only if the client can prove its identity and has the proper credentials to make the update. Secure dynamic updates are available only through Active Directory domain service and when Active Directory–integrated DNS is enabled. By default, Active Directory–integrated zones only allow secure dynamic updates, though this setting can be modified when you create the zone. If you created the zone as a standard primary zone, and then you converted it into an Active Directory–integrated zone, it preserves the primary zone dynamic update configuration, which can be changed using the DNS MMC console.

You can configure dynamic updates for a DNS zone to use one of the following options:

- None—No dynamic updates permitted, all DNS entries must be created manually. This is the default dynamic updates setting for a standard DNS zone.
- Nonsecure and secure—Allows clients to first attempt a nonsecure dynamic update, and only if that fails to attempt a secure dynamic update. Because clients will attempt a nonsecure update first, configuring this setting is effectively the same as permitting all dynamic updates to occur in a nonsecure fashion.
- Secure only—This option is only available on DNS zones that have been configured on Active Directory domain controllers.

Configuring Aging and Scavenging of DNS Records

Traditionally, the DNS administrator manually added or deleted resource records from DNS zone files as required. With dynamic update, individual computers and services are able to automatically add, update, and delete DNS resource records. For example, the Windows XP, Windows Vista, Windows 2000, Windows Server 2003, and Windows Server 2008 DNS Client services register their clients' A and pointer (PTR) resource records in DNS at start time and every 24 hours thereafter. Dynamic update ensures that the records are up-to-date and guards against accidental deletion of resource records by the DNS administrator.

Over time, stale resource records accumulate in the DNS database. Records become stale, for example, when computers, especially those of mobile users, abnormally disconnect from the network. Stale records provide outdated and inaccurate information to clients, take up unnecessary space, and can possibly degrade server performance. Windows Server 2008 provides a mechanism called *scavenging* to remove these records as they become out-of-date.

Windows Server 2008 adds a time stamp to dynamically added resource records in primary zones where aging and scavenging are enabled. Records added manually are time stamped with a value of zero, which indicates those records should be excluded from the aging and scavenging process. Since secondary name servers receive a read-only copy of the zone data from primary name servers, only primary zones are eligible to participate in this process (or Active Directory–integrated zones, in the case of AD-integrated DNS). Servers can be configured to perform recurring scavenging operations automatically, or you can initiate a manual and immediate scavenging operation at the server.

DNS Scavenging depends on the following two settings:

- No-Refresh Interval—The time between the most recent refresh of a record time stamp and the moment when the time stamp may be refreshed again. When scavenging is enabled, this is set to 7 days by default.
- Refresh Interval—The time between the earliest moment when a record time stamp can be refreshed and the earliest moment when the record can be scavenged. The refresh interval must be longer than the maximum record refresh period. When scavenging is enabled, this is set to 7 days by default.

A DNS record becomes eligible for scavenging after both the no-refresh and refresh intervals have elapsed, for a total of 14 days by default. Scavenging is enabled on a per-zone basis, and is disabled by default. You should not enable DNS resource record scavenging unless you are absolutely certain that you understand all the parameters and have configured them correctly. Otherwise, you might accidentally configure the server to delete records that it should retain. If a name is accidentally deleted, not only do users fail to resolve queries for that name, but also a different user can create and own that name, even on zones configured for secure dynamic update.

Introducing the DNS Name Resolution Process

The DNS *resolver* refers to the DNS client software that exists on a Windows computer regardless of whether it is running a client or a server operating system. In this way it is important not to confuse the notion of a DNS client resolver with a client operating system such as Windows XP or Windows Vista; a Windows Server 2008 computer contains DNS client software and will often function as a DNS client when attempting to resolve DNS queries. When any DNS client needs to look up a fully qualified domain name to obtain its corresponding IP address, it forms a *DNS query* that contains the DNS domain name (stated as an FQDN), the query type specifying the resource records to be returned (A, SRV, and so on), and the DNS domain name class, which is IN for the Internet system. The query is first passed to the local DNS resolver client service for resolution. If the query cannot be resolved locally, it is sent to the preferred DNS server as configured in the client's TCP/IP properties. If the query does not match an entry in the cache, the resolution process continues with the client querying a DNS server to resolve the name.

When a query is sent to a DNS server, the server can respond in a number of ways. Following are the most common responses to DNS queries:

- An ***authoritative answer***—An authoritative answer is a positive answer returned to the client and delivered with the authority bit set in the DNS message to indicate the answer was obtained from a server with direct authority for the queried name.
- A positive answer—A positive answer can consist of the queried resource record or a list of resource records (also known as a *resource record set*) that fits the queried DNS domain name and record type specified in the query message. Positive answers may or may not be authoritative.

- A referral answer—A referral answer contains additional resource records not specified by the name or type in the query. This type of answer is returned to the client if the recursion process is not supported. The records are meant to act as helpful reference answers that the client can use to continue the query using iteration. A referral answer contains additional data, such as resource records, that are other than the type queried. For example, if the queried host name was "www" and no A resource records for this name were found in this zone, but a CNAME resource record for "www" was found instead, the DNS server can include that information when responding to the client. If the client is able to use iteration, it can make additional queries using the referral information in an attempt to fully resolve the name.

- A negative answer—A negative answer from the server can indicate that one of two possible results was encountered while the server attempted to process and recursively resolve the query fully and authoritatively: An authoritative server reported that the queried name does not exist in the DNS namespace, or an authoritative server reported that the queried name exists but no records of the specified type exist for that name. The resolver passes the query response back to the requesting program and caches the response.

In addition to the zones configured on a DNS server, a server can also use two additional methods to respond to a client query. These additional name resolution methods involve the use of root hints, and the *DNS server cache*, described in the following sections.

Using Root Hints

DNS servers resolve DNS queries using local authoritative or cached data. But if the server does not contain the requested data and is not authoritative for the name in a query, it may perform recursive resolution or return a referral to another DNS server depending on whether the client requested recursion. The DNS Server service must be configured with ***root hints*** to resolve queries for names that it is not authoritative for or for which it contains no delegations. Root hints contain the names and IP addresses of the DNS servers authoritative for the root zone. You can use the DNS console to manage the list of root servers, as well as the dnscmd command-line utility.

By default, DNS servers use a root hints file, called *cache.dns,* on Microsoft DNS servers. The cache.dns file is stored in the *%systemroot%\System32\Dns* folder on the server computer. When the server starts, cache.dns is preloaded into server memory. By using root hints to find root servers, a DNS server is able to complete recursive queries. This process is designed to enable any DNS server to locate the servers that are authoritative for any other DNS domain name used at any level in the namespace tree.

When you use the Windows Server 2008 GUI to configure a DNS server, it sends an NS query for the root domain (.) to the preferred and alternate DNS servers for the server. The query response is placed into the root hints of the DNS server. If no root servers are detected, the wizard sends the same query to the DNS servers specified in the cache.dns file that correspond to the root servers on the Internet. If no root servers are detected, the wizard prompts the user to either make the server a root server or to manually specify root hints. Updating root hints enables the server to function more efficiently. You should update root hints whenever a new server is added or changed.

Configuring Name Server Caching

As DNS servers make recursive queries on behalf of clients, they temporarily cache resource records. Cached resource records contain information obtained from DNS servers that are authoritative for DNS domain names learned while making iterative queries (discussed in the next section) to search and fully answer a recursive query performed on behalf of a client. Later, when other clients place new queries that request resource record information matching cached resource records, the DNS server can use the cached resource record information to answer them.

Caching provides a way to speed the performance of DNS resolution for subsequent queries of popular names, while substantially reducing DNS-related query traffic on the network. When information is cached, a ***Time to Live (TTL)*** value applies to all cached resource records. As long as the TTL for a cached resource record does not expire, a DNS server can continue to cache and use the resource record again when answering queries by its clients that match these resource records. Caching TTL values used by resource records in most zone configurations are assigned the minimum (default) TTL, which is set in the zone's SOA resource record. By default, the minimum TTL is 3,600 seconds (one hour) but can be adjusted, or, if needed, individual caching TTLs can be set at each resource record.

To reduce the amount of traffic to the DNS server or servers, the DNS resolver on each client will cache resource records that are obtained from query responses. These resource records are used to resolve repeated client queries and reduce redundant queries to the DNS server. Each entry in the cache has a specified TTL, typically set by the query response. When the TTL expires, the entry is purged from the cache. When the resolver is unable to answer a query using its own cache, the resolver sends the query to one or more DNS servers configured in the TCP/IP properties of the server. If a HOSTS file is configured on the client, it is preloaded into the resolver cache.

To view the DNS resolver cache on any Windows computer, key the following at a command prompt:

```
ipconfig /displaydns
```

To purge the cache, key the following at a command prompt:

```
ipconfig /flushdns
```

Using Iterative and Recursive DNS Queries

Queries from DNS resolvers (whether originating from a client or a server-based operating system) can take one of two forms: an *iterative query* or a *recursive query*. An iterative query is a DNS query sent to a DNS server in which the querying host requests it to return the best answer it can provide using its own information, and without seeking further assistance from other DNS servers.

WARNING Do not confuse *recursion*, which is used by *iterative queries*, with *recursive queries*, which are discussed next!

For example, in Figure C-8, a host queries the primary DNS server, which checks its records and refers the client to Server A. Server A checks its names cache, does not find an answer, and sends a referral to Server B instead. The host receives the response and submits a query to Server B, which responds with a referral to Server C. The original host queries Server C and receives a response. The process of a DNS server performing this "tree-walking" of DNS servers to locate the answer to a query is referred to as *recursion*.

As shown in Figure C-8, the querying host is responsible for issuing additional queries until it obtains a definitive answer. In the example that follows, the host issues three queries before receiving the requested information. The process is as follows:

1. The first step of the query process is to convert a name request into a query and then pass it to the DNS Client service for resolution that uses locally cached information.

   If the query can be answered from the local cache, the process is complete. Otherwise, the client submits an iterative query to its preferred DNS server.

Figure C-8

Viewing a typical iterative query

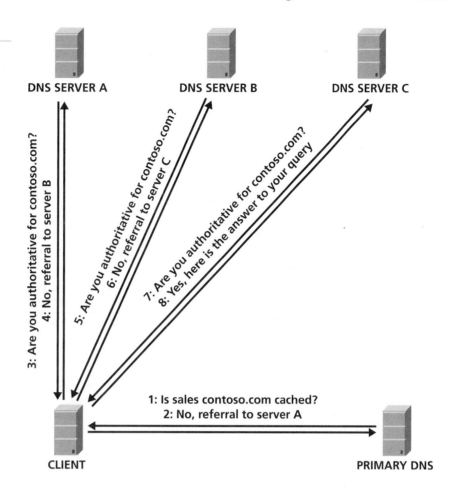

DNS SERVER A   **DNS SERVER B**   **DNS SERVER C**

3: Are you authoritative for contoso.com?
4: No, referral to server B

5: Are you authoritative for contoso.com?
6: No, referral to server C

7: Are you authoritative for contoso.com?
8: Yes, here is the answer to your query

1: Is sales contoso.com cached?
2: No, referral to server A

CLIENT   **PRIMARY DNS**

2. The primary DNS server checks to see if it has authority for that domain. In this example, it does not have authority, but it does contain information that points to the .com top-level domain DNS servers. The primary server responds with a referral to the .com top-level domain servers.

3. The DNS client submits an iterative query to DNS Server A.

4. DNS Server A responds with a referral to DNS Server B.

5. The client submits an iterative query to DNS Server B for *sales.contoso.com*.

6. DNS Server B responds with a referral to DNS Server C.

7. The client submits an iterative query to DNS Server C.

8. DNS Server C is authoritative for the *sales.contoso.com* domain and responds with a definitive answer to the client query (in this case, the A record for *sales.contoso.com*).

A recursive query is a DNS query sent to a DNS server in which the querying host asks the DNS server to provide a definitive answer to the query, even if that means contacting other servers to provide the answer. When sent a recursive query, the DNS server iteratively queries other DNS servers to obtain an answer. In Figure C-9, the querying host issues only one query before receiving the requested information.

To centralize the workload and reduce network traffic, host computers typically issue recursive queries to DNS servers. A network of 1,000 clients iteratively querying DNS servers is clearly less efficient than centralizing queries to a handful of DNS servers. Centralizing queries means each client sends a single recursive query rather than each client sending multiple iterative queries. DNS servers generally issue iterative queries against other DNS servers if they are

Figure C-9

Viewing the recursive query
process

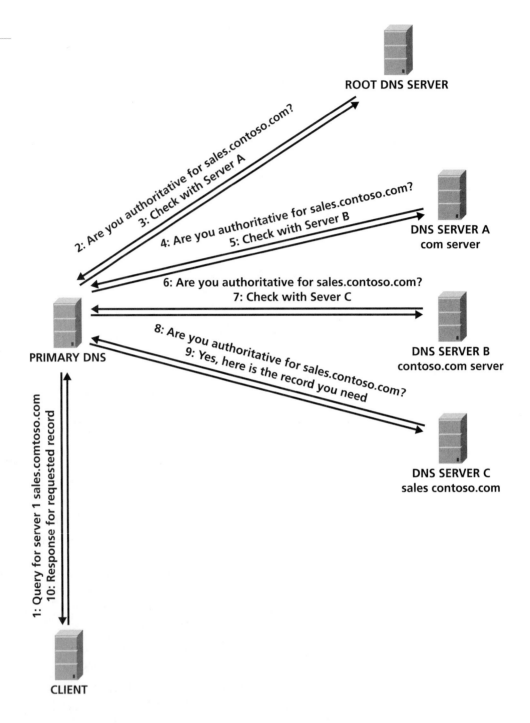

ROOT DNS SERVER

2: Are you authoritative for sales.contoso.com?
3: Check with Server A

4: Are you authoritative for sales.contoso.com?
5: Check with Server B

DNS SERVER A
com server

6: Are you authoritative for sales.contoso.com?
7: Check with Sever C

8: Are you authoritative for sales.contoso.com?
9: Yes, here is the record you need

DNS SERVER B
contoso.com server

PRIMARY DNS

1: Query for server 1 sales.comtoso.com
10: Response for requested record

DNS SERVER C
sales contoso.com

CLIENT

unable to answer a recursive query from cached information. By using recursive queries, the
workload of resolving DNS names can be concentrated to a few servers and thereby achieve
much greater efficiency. Figure C-9 illustrates the client submitting a recursive query and
receiving a definitive answer. The process is as follows:

1. The first step of the query process is to convert a name request into a query and then
   pass it to the DNS Client service for resolution using locally cached information. If
   the query can be answered from the local cache, the process is complete. Otherwise,
   the query is passed to the local DNS server.

2. The local name server checks to see if it has authority for that domain. In this example, it does not have authority, but it does contain root hints. The local name server
   uses the root hints to begin a search for the name server that has authority for the
   domain *sales.contoso.com*. It then queries the root name server.

3. The root name server sends IP addresses of name servers for the .com top-level domain back to the local DNS server.

4. The local DNS server submits an iterative query to DNS Server A (.com) for *sales .contoso.com*.

5. DNS Server A responds with a referral to the *contoso.com* name server, DNS Server B.

6. The local DNS server submits another iterative query to DNS Server B, *contoso.com*.

7. DNS Server B responds with the IP address for the authoritative server, DNS Server C.

8. The local DNS server submits an iterative query to DNS Server C.

9. DNS Server C responds with a definitive answer (in this case the A record).

10. The local DNS server responds to the DNS client with a definitive answer. The client can now establish a TCP/IP connection with *sales.contoso.com*. From the client's perspective, one request was submitted to and fulfilled by the local DNS server. The information obtained by the local DNS server is cached to answer subsequent queries.

By default, DNS servers use timings for retry intervals and time-out intervals. These are as follows:

• A recursion retry interval of three seconds. This is the length of time the DNS service waits before retrying a query made during a recursive lookup.

• A recursion time-out interval of 15 seconds. This is the length of time the DNS service waits before failing a recursive lookup that has been retried.

Configuring Forwarders

A ***forwarder*** is a DNS server on a network used to forward DNS queries for external DNS names to DNS servers outside of that network. A ***conditional forwarder*** forwards queries on the basis of domain name; for example, by forwarding queries for hosts within the *contoso.com* DNS domain to one set of DNS servers, but forwarding queries for the *lucernepublishing.com* domain to a different set of servers.

A DNS server on a network is designated as a forwarder by having the other DNS servers in the network forward the queries they cannot resolve locally to that DNS server. By using a forwarder, you can manage name resolution for names outside of your network, such as names on the Internet, and you improve the efficiency of name resolution for the computers in your network. For example, to use forwarders to manage the DNS traffic between your network and the Internet, configure the firewall used by your network to allow only one DNS server to communicate with the Internet. When you have configured the other DNS servers in your network to forward queries they cannot resolve locally to that DNS server, it will act as your forwarder. Because external network traffic is going through a single DNS server, that server builds up a large cache of DNS data, which, over time, decreases Internet traffic and provides faster response times to clients.

Without having a specific DNS server designated as a forwarder, all DNS servers can send queries outside of a network using their root hints. As a result, a lot of internal, and possibly critical, DNS information can be exposed on the Internet. In addition to this security and privacy issue, this method of resolution can result in a large volume of external traffic that is costly and inefficient for a network with a slow Internet connection or a company with high Internet service costs.

A DNS server configured to use a forwarder will behave differently than a DNS server that is not configured to use a forwarder. A DNS server configured to use a forwarder behaves as follows:

1. When the DNS server receives a query, it attempts to resolve this query by using the primary and secondary zones that it hosts and by using its cache.

2. If the query cannot be resolved using this local data, it will forward the query to the DNS server designated as a forwarder.

3. The DNS server will wait briefly for an answer from the forwarder before attempting to contact the DNS servers specified in its root hints.

4. Rather than send the standard iterative query, when a DNS server forwards a query to a forwarder, by default, it sends a recursive query to the forwarder.

Each domain name used for forwarding on a DNS server is associated with the IP addresses of one or more DNS servers. A DNS server configured for forwarding will use its forwarders list after it has determined that it cannot resolve a query using its authoritative data (primary or secondary zone data) or cached data. If the server cannot resolve a query using forwarders, it may attempt recursion to the root hint servers.

The order of the IP addresses listed determines the sequence in which the IP addresses are used. After the DNS server forwards the query to the forwarder with the first IP address associated with the domain name, it waits a short period for an answer from that forwarder (according to the DNS server's time-out setting) before resuming the forwarding operation with the next IP address associated with the domain name. It continues this process until it receives a positive answer from a forwarder or until it has tried all addresses in the list.

When a DNS server configured to use conditional forwarding receives a query for a domain name, it compares that domain name with its list of domain name conditions and uses the longest domain name condition that corresponds to the domain name in the query. For example, a DNS server receives a query for *www.qualitycontrol.research.wingtiptoys.com*.

It compares that domain name with both *wingtiptoys.com* and *research.wingtiptoys.com*. The DNS server determines that *research.wingtiptoys.com* is the domain name that more closely matches the original query.

Conditional forwarding enables a DNS server to forward queries to other DNS servers based on the DNS domain names in the queries. With conditional forwarding, a DNS server could be configured to forward all the queries it receives for names ending with *research.wingtiptoys .com* to a specific DNS server's IP address or to the IP addresses of multiple DNS servers.

For example, when two companies, *fabrikam.com* and *wingtiptoys.com*, merge or collaborate, they may want to allow clients from the internal namespace of one company to resolve the names of the clients from the internal namespace of another company.

The administrators from one organization (*fabrikam.com*) may inform the administrators of the other organization (*wingtiptoys.com*) about the set of DNS servers that they can use to send DNS queries for name resolution within the internal namespace of the first organiza-tion. In this case, the DNS servers in the *wingtiptoys.com* organization will be configured to forward all queries for names ending with *fabrikam.com* to the designated DNS servers.

One important configuration item to note is that a DNS server cannot perform conditional forwarding for any domain names for which that server is authoritative. For example, the authoritative DNS server for the zone *widgets.microsoft.com* cannot forward queries according to the domain name *widgets.microsoft.com*. If the DNS server were allowed to do this, it would nul-lify the server's capability to respond to queries for the domain name *widgets.microsoft.com*. The DNS server authoritative for *widgets.microsoft.com* can forward queries for DNS names that end with *hr.widgets.microsoft.com*, if *hr.widgets.microsoft.com* is delegated to another DNS server.

The conditional forwarder setting consists of the following:

- The domain names for which the DNS server will forward queries
- One or more DNS server IP addresses for each domain name specified

A DNS server can also be configured as a ***forwarding-only server***, which will not perform recursion after the forwarders fail; if it does not get a successful query response from any of the servers configured as forwarders, it sends a negative response to the DNS client. This option to prevent recursion can be set for each conditional forwarder in Windows Server 2008. For example, a DNS server can be configured to perform recursion for the domain name *research .wingtiptoys.com*, but not to perform recursion for the domain name *wingtiptoys.com*.

A new feature of Windows Server 2008 is that conditional forwarder information can be integrated into Active Directory when DNS is installed on a domain controller. This allows you to replicate conditional forwarder information among multiple DNS servers on your network. A conditional forwarder in an Active Directory environment can be replicated to any of the following:

- All DNS servers in the forest
- All DNS servers in the domain
- All domain controllers in the domain

In the following exercise, we will configure both forwarders and conditional forwarders on a Windows Server 2008 DNS server.

 CONFIGURE FORWARDERS

GET READY. This exercise assumes that you have configured DNSPRI with a primary zone for the *contoso.com* domain. This exercise assumes that you are logged onto DNSPRI with administrative privileges. In Part A you will configure a DNS forwarder; in Part B you will configure conditional forwarders based on domain name.

PART A—Configure a forwarder for a DNS Server

1. Click the **Start** button, then browse to **Administrative Tools→DNS**.
2. Click the plus sign (+) next to DNSPRI. Right-click **DNSPRI** and select **Properties**.
3. Click the **Forwarders** tab. You will see the screen shown in Figure C-10.

Figure C-10

Configuring DNS forwarders

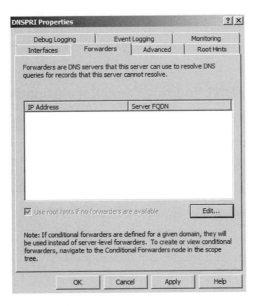

4. Click **Edit**. Enter the IP address of a remote DNS server and click **OK**.
5. To prevent this DNS server from using recursion, remove the checkmark next to Use root hints if no forwarders are available, and then click **OK**.

PART B—Configure a conditional forwarder

1. In the left-hand pane of the DNS MMC snap-in, select the **Conditional Forwarders** node.

2. Right-click the **Conditional Forwarders** node and click **New Conditional Forwarder....**
You will see the screen shown in Figure C-11.

Figure C-11

Configuring conditional
forwarders

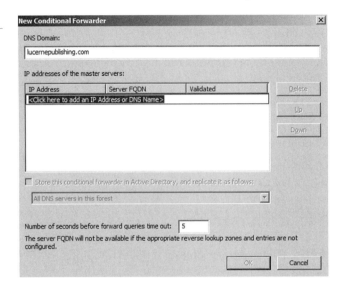

3. In the DNS Domain: text box, enter the name of the remote domain for which you wish to set up conditional forwarding; for example, enter *lucernepublishing.com*.

4. In the IP addresses of the master servers: field, enter the IP address of a server that is authoritative for the lucernepublishing.com zone and press (**Enter**).

5. Click **OK** to save your changes.

PAUSE. Close the DNS MMC snap-in and log off of the Windows Server 2008 computer before continuing.

In the previous exercise, you configured forwarders and conditional forwarders on a Windows Server 2008 DNS server. In the next section, we will discuss the ongoing administration and troubleshooting of the DNS server role using both graphical user interface (GUI) and command-line tools.

Troubleshooting DNS and the Name Resolution Process

DNS is a key service in Microsoft Windows Server 2008 networks. If DNS fails, clients often lose connectivity to the Internet or to other clients and Active Directory fails. Effective management and monitoring procedures mitigate the possibility of DNS server failure. This section introduces you to the tools, concepts, and procedures necessary to manage and monitor DNS name resolution. Topics in this section include securing DNS, monitoring and troubleshooting DNS with tools such as the DNS Event Viewer and DNS debug log, and using tools such as Nslookup and Dnscmd.

Several tools are useful for managing and monitoring DNS services. These tools include the following:

- The DNS MMC snap-in, which is part of Administrative Tools. The DNS console is the primary tool for configuring DNS.

- Nslookup, which can be used to query DNS zone information to verify existing and proper configuration of resource records.

- Logging features, such as DNS events that are logged to the Windows Event Viewer, which you can view with the DNS MMC snap-in, Server Manager, or the Windows Event Viewer. File-based logs also can be used temporarily as an advanced debugging option to log and trace selected service events.

- Dnscmd, which enables you to use the command line to perform most of the tasks you can perform using the DNS console.

You can use the DNS console to manually or automatically test DNS servers by submitting two different types of queries:

- A simple query, or iterative query. The DNS resolver (client) on the server computer queries the local DNS servers, which are located on the same computer.
- A recursive query to other DNS servers. The DNS resolver (client) on the server computer queries the local DNS server, but instead of submitting an iterative query, it submits a recursive query. Specifically, the client asks the server to use recursion to resolve a name server (NS)–type query for the root of the DNS domain namespace. This type of query typically requires additional recursive processing and can be helpful in verifying that server root hints or zone delegations are properly set.

These settings are accessed by clicking the Monitoring tab in the DNS server properties window. You can perform the test by clicking the Test Now button or specify an interval for performing the test.

Using NsLookup

Nslookup is a command-line tool built into TCP/IP that is available in Windows Server 2008 to perform DNS queries and enable examination of the content of zone files on local and remote servers. Nslookup is often used to verify the configuration of DNS zones and to diagnose and solve name resolution problems. In order for Nslookup to be used to troubleshoot DNS name resolution, a reverse lookup zone must be configured for the DNS domain that is being queried.

Nslookup can be run at the command prompt (in command prompt mode) or as a program that accepts serial commands and queries (in interactive mode). To look up a single host name, you would typically enter a single command at the command prompt. For example, executing the following command at the command prompt returns the Internet Protocol (IP) addresses associated with the fully qualified domain name (FQDN) *www.microsoft.com* (output results will vary):

```
C:\.nslookup www.microsoft.com
Server: usdc1.us.contoso.com
Address: 192.168.0.100
Non-authoritative answer:
Name: www.microsoft.akadns.net
Addresses: 207.46.134.155,   207.46.134.190, 207.46.249.222,
207.46.249.27
207.46.249.190
Aliases: www.microsoft.com
```

To resolve the query, the Nslookup utility submits the name to the DNS server specified for the primary connection on the local client computer. This DNS server can then answer the query from its cache or through recursion.

If you submit a query for a host name that does not exist, you receive the following response:

```
C:\.nslookup thisdoesnotexist.contoso.com
Server: usdc1.us.contoso.com
Address: 192.168.0.100
*** usdc1.us.contoso.com can't find thisdoesnotexist.contoso.com:
Non-existent domain
```

If you troubleshoot a specific DNS server instead of the one specified for the primary connection on the local client computer, you can specify that DNS server using the Nslookup command. For example, the following command executed at the command prompt queries the DNS server at 192.168.52.141 for the name *www.microsoft.com*:

```
C:\.nslookup www.microsoft.com 192.168.52.141
```

You can also use Nslookup to resolve IP addresses to host names. For example, the following command executed at the command prompt returns the FQDN associated with the address 192.168.141.22, as shown in this output:

```
C:\.nslookup 192.168.141.22
Server: localhost
Address: 127.0.0.1
Name: www.contoso.com
Address: 192.168.141.22
```

Use the following syntax for Nslookup in the command prompt mode:

```
nslookup [-opt...] [{Host| [Server]}]
```

The Nslookup command uses the following switches:

- -opt—Specifies one or more Nslookup subcommands as a command-line option.
- Host—Looks up information for Host using the current default DNS name server (NS), if no other server is specified. To look up a computer not in the current DNS domain, append a period to the name.
- Server—Specifies to use this server as the DNS name server. If you omit Server, the default DNS name server is used.

When issuing multiple Nslookup commands, it is generally more efficient to use Nslookup in interactive mode. To enter interactive mode, open a command prompt, key nslookup, and press Enter. In interactive mode, Nslookup accepts commands that allow the program to perform a variety of functions, such as displaying the specific contents of messages included in DNS exchanges, simulating a zone transfer, or searching for records of a specific type on a given server. These commands can be displayed by keying the help or ? command.

When you are in interactive mode, you can also use the Set command to configure Nslookup options that determine how the resolver carries out queries. One option is to use the debug command. By default, Nslookup is set to nodebug. Keying set debug while in interactive mode enters debug mode, which enables Nslookup to display the DNS response messages communicated from the DNS server. You can view the options currently configured for Nslookup by running the *set all* command.

WARNING Nslookup commands entered while in interactive mode are case-sensitive and must be keyed in lowercase.

Table C-9 describes the most common options configured with the Set command.

Table C-9

Command-Line Options Available with the Set Command

Option	Purpose	Example (Interactive Mode)
set all	Shows the configuration status of all options.	>set all
set [no]debug	Puts Nslookup in debug mode. With debug mode turned on, more information is printed about the packet sent to the server and the resulting answer.	>set debug Or >set nodebug
set [no]d2	Puts Nslookup in verbose debug mode so you can examine the query and response packets between the resolver and the server.	>set d2 Or >set nod2

(continued)

Table C-9 *(continued)*

Option	Purpose	Example (Interactive Mode)
set domain=<domain name>	Tells the resolver which domain name to append for unqualified queries (for example, sales is an unqualified query as opposed to *sales.fabrikam.com*), including all queried names not followed by a trailing dot.	>set domain=bottinc.com
set timeout=<time-out value>	Tells the resolver what time-value to use, in seconds. This option is useful for slow links on which queries frequently time out and the wait time must be lengthened.	>set timeout=5
set type=<record type> or set querytype=<record type> or set q=<record type>	Tells the resolver which type of resource records to search for (for example, address [A], pointer [PTR], or service locator [SRV] records). If you want the resolver to query for all types of resource records, key set type=all.	>set type=A >set q=MX

By default, names queried for in Nslookup return only matching host address (A) resource records. To look up different data types within the domain namespace, use the Set Type command or set querytype (set q) command at the command prompt. For example, to query for mail exchanger (MX) resource records only instead of A resource records, key set q=mx. To query for a record of any type, execute the Nslookup command set q=any.

TAKE NOTE*

The first time a query is made for a remote name, the answer is authoritative, but subsequent queries are nonauthoritative. This pattern appears for the following reason: the first time a remote host is queried, the local DNS server contacts the DNS server that is authoritative for that domain. The local DNS server then caches that information so that subsequent queries are answered nonauthoritatively out of the local server's cache.

To query another name server directly, use the *server* or *lserver* commands to switch to that name server. The *lserver* command uses the local server to get the address of the server to switch to, whereas the *server* command uses the current default server to get the address.

After you execute either of these commands, all subsequent lookups in the current Nslookup session are performed at the specified server until you switch servers again. The following syntax illustrates what you would key to initiate a server switch:

```
C:\> nslookup
Default Server: nameserver1.contoso.com
Address: 10.0.0.1
> server nameserver2
Default Server: nameserver2.contoso.com
Address: 10.0.0.2
```

You can use the Nslookup subcommand ls to list information for a DNS domain. However, when you issue an Nslookup command with the ls subcommand, you effectively are requesting a zone transfer, so if the DNS server does not permit zone transfers to the IP address that you are running Nslookup from, this command will fail. The syntax for the ls command is as follows:

```
ls [- a | d | t type] domain [> filename]
```

Table C-10 lists valid options for the ls subcommand.

Table C-10

Nslookup ls Options

OPTION	PURPOSE	EXAMPLE
-t QueryType	Lists all records of a specific type.	>ls –t cname contoso.com
-a	Lists aliases of computers in the DNS domain (equivalent to -t CNAME).	>ls –a contoso.com
-d	Lists all records for the DNS domain (equivalent to -t ANY).	>ls –d contoso.com
-h	Lists central processing unit (CPU) and operating system information for the DNS domain (equivalent to—t HINFO).	>ls –h contoso.com
-s	Lists well-known services of computers in the DNS domain (equivalent to -t WKS).	>ls –s contoso.com

The following output demonstrates the use of the ls command in interactive mode:

```
>ls contoso.com
[nameserver1.contoso.com]
nameserver1.contoso.com.   NS server = ns1.contoso.com
nameserver2.contoso.com    NS server = ns2.contoso.com
nameserver1                A 10.0.0.1
nameserver2                A 10.0.0.2
```

Using Dnscmd

You can use the Dnscmd command-line tool to perform most of the tasks that you can do from the DNS console. This tool can be used to script batch files, to help automate the management and updates of existing DNS server configurations, or to perform setup and configuration of DNS servers.

Dnscmd is provided as a built-in command-line tool for managing DNS servers in Windows Server 2008. The Dnscmd command allows you to perform a large number of DNS-related tasks, including the following:

- Create, delete, and view zones and records.
- Reset server and zone properties.
- Perform zone maintenance operations, such as updating the zone, reloading the zone, refreshing the zone, writing the zone back to a file or to Active Directory, and pausing or resuming the zone.
- Clear the cache.
- Stop and start the DNS service.
- View statistics.

For example, to display a complete list of the zones configured on a DNS server by using Dnscmd, at the command prompt, key dnscmd [ComputerName] /enumzones. A sample output of this command follows:

```
C:\>dnscmd localhost /enumzones
Enumerated zone list:
Zone count = 5
```

```
Zone name                        Type        Storage Properties
.                                Cache       AD-Legacy
_msdcs.contoso01.com             Primary     AD-Forest Secure
1.1.10.in-addr.arpa              Primary     AD-Legacy Secure Rev
computer01.contoso.com           Primary     AD-Legacy
contoso01.com                    Primary     AD-Domain Secure
Command completed successfully.
```

To display information about a specific zone that is configured on a DNS server by using Dnscmd, at the command prompt, key the following:

```
dnscmd [ComputerName] /zoneinfo [zone]
```

Sample output of this command follows below:

```
C:\>dnscmd localhost /zoneinfo contoso01.com
Zone query result:
Zone info:
        ptr                    = 00083050
        zone name              = contoso01.com
        zone type              = 1
        update                 = 2
        DS integrated          = 1
        data file              = (null)
        using WINS             = 0
        using Nbstat           = 0
        aging                  = 0
        refresh interval       = 168
        no refresh             = 168
        scavenge available     = 3529116
        Zone Masters
        NULL IP Array.
        Zone Secondaries
        NULL IP Array.
        secure secs            = 3
        directory partition    = AD-Domain flags 00000015
        zone DN                = DC=contoso01.com,cn=MicrosoftDNS,
                                 DC=DomainDnsZones, DC=contoso01,
                                 DC=com

Command completed successfully.
```

Configuring Advanced DNS Server Properties

Advanced DNS server properties refer to the settings that can be configured in the Advanced tab of the DNS Server Properties dialog box (shown in Figure C-12). These properties relate to server-specific features, such as disabling recursion, handling resolution of multi-homed hosts, and achieving compatibility with non-Microsoft DNS servers.

Figure C-12

Viewing advanced DNS server properties

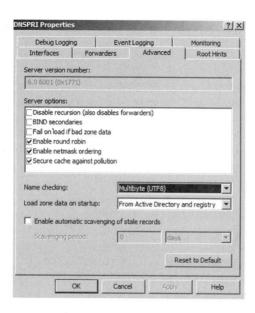

The default installation settings of the DNS server role include six server options, which are either on or off, and three other server features with various selections for configuration. Table C-11 shows the default settings for all nine features.

Table C-11

Default DNS Installation Settings

PROPERTY	SETTING
Disable Recursion (also disables forwarders)	Off
BIND Secondaries	Off
Fail On Load If Bad Zone Data	Off
Enable Round Robin	On
Enable Netmask Ordering	On
Secure Cache Against Pollution	On
Name Checking	Multibyte (UTF-8)
Load Zone Data On Startup	From Active Directory And Registry
Enable Automatic Scavenging Of Stale Records	Off (requires configuration when enabled)

In most situations, these installation defaults are acceptable and do not require modification. However, when needed, you can use the DNS console to modify these advanced parameters and accommodate special deployment needs and situations. You can restore these default settings at any time using the Advanced tab by clicking the Reset To Default button on the Advanced tab.

We'll now describe each available configuration option in more detail.

- Disable Recursion—The Disable Recursion server option is disabled by default (meaning that recursion is enabled). When the Disable Recursion option is enabled, the DNS Server service does not answer queries for which it is not authoritative or which it has not already answered and placed in its cache. Instead, the DNS Server service provides the client with referrals, which are resource records that allow a DNS client to perform iterative queries to resolve an FQDN. Do not disable recursion on a server if any other name servers are using this server as a forwarder. You should only disable recursion when you want to create a server that does not query any other servers to resolve client DNS queries.

- BIND Secondaries—The BIND Secondaries option controls whether a fast transfer format is used during a DNS zone transfer. Berkeley Internet Name Domain (BIND) is a common implementation of DNS written and ported to most available versions of the UNIX operating system. Fast transfer format is an efficient means of transferring zone data that provides data compression and allows multiple records to be transferred per individual Transmission Control Protocol (TCP) message. Fast zone transfer is always used among Windows-based DNS servers, so the BIND Secondaries option does not affect communications among Windows servers. However, only BIND versions 4.9.4 and later can handle these fast zone transfers. For BIND versions earlier than 4.9.4, DNS servers running Windows Server 2003 can be configured to transfer a zone using the slower, uncompressed transfer format. When you select the BIND Secondaries check box in the Advanced tab of the Server Properties dialog box, no fast transfers are made. If you know your DNS server will be performing zone transfers with DNS servers using BIND version 4.9.4 or later, you should disable this option to allow fast zone transfers to occur.

- Fail On Load If Bad Zone Data—DNS servers running on Windows Server 2008 will, by default, load a zone even if that zone contains errors. In that scenario, errors are logged and ignored. Enabling Fail On Load If Bad Zone Data prevents a zone with errors from being loaded.

- Enable Round Robin—*DNS round robin* is a load balancing mechanism used by DNS servers to share and distribute network resource loads. If multiple resource records satisfy a query, you can use round robin to rotate the order of resource record types returned to the client. By default, DNS uses round robin to rotate the order of resource record data returned in query answers in which multiple resource records of the same type exist for a queried DNS domain name. This feature provides a simple method for load balancing client use of Web servers and other frequently queried multi-homed computers.

Consider this example of DNS round robin: The Web server named *server1.contoso.com* has three network adapters and three distinct IP addresses. In the stored zone (either in a database file or in Active Directory), the three A resource records mapping the host name to each of its IP addresses appear in this fixed order:

```
server1 IN A 10.0.0.1
server1 IN A 10.0.0.2
server1 IN A 10.0.0.3
```

The first DNS client—Client1—that queries the server to resolve this host's name receives the list in this default order. However, when a second client—Client2—sends a subsequent query to resolve this name, the list is rotated as follows:

```
server1 IN A 10.0.0.2
server1 IN A 10.0.0.3
server1 IN A 10.0.0.1
```

When you clear the Enable Round Robin check box, round robin is disabled for the DNS server. If round robin is disabled for a DNS server, the order of the response for these queries is based on a static ordering of resource records in the answer list as they are stored in the zone (either its zone file or Active Directory).

- Enable Netmask Ordering—Netmask ordering is a method DNS uses to give ordering and preference to IP addresses on the same network when a requesting client queries for a host name that has multiple A resource records. This is designed so that the client program will attempt to connect to a host using the closest (and, therefore, presumably fastest) IP address available. When returning more than one IP address to a client when Netmask Ordering is enabled, IP addresses most closely matching the client's subnet mask are placed at the top of the response list. The Enable Netmask Ordering option is selected by default.

For an example of netmask ordering in action, consider the following scenario: a multihomed computer, *server1.contoso.com*, has three A resource records for each of its three IP addresses in the *contoso.com* zone. These three records appear in the following order in the zone—either in the zone file or in Active Directory:

```
server1 IN A 192.168.1.27
server1 IN A 10.0.0.14
server1 IN A 172.16.20.4
```

When a DNS client resolver at IP address 10.4.3.2 queries the server for the IP addresses of the host *server1.contoso.com*, the DNS Server service notes that the originating IP network address (10.0.0.0) of the client matches the network (class A) ID of the 10.0.0.14 address in the answer list of resource records. The DNS Server service then reorders the addresses in the response list as follows:

```
server1 IN A 10.0.0.14
server1 IN A 192.168.1.27
server1 IN A 172.16.20.4
```

If the network ID of the IP address of the requesting client does not match any of the network IDs of the resource records in the answer list, the list is not reordered.

- Secure Cache Against Pollution—By default, the Secure Cache Against Pollution option is enabled. This setting allows the DNS server to protect its cache against referrals that are potentially polluting or nonsecure. When the setting is enabled, the server caches only those records with a name that corresponds to the domain for which the original queried name was made. Any referrals received from another DNS server along with a query response are simply discarded. For example, if a query is originally made for the name *example.lucernepublishing.com*, and a referral answer provides a record for a name outside the *lucernepublishing.com* domain name tree (such as *msn.com*), that name is discarded if the Secure Cache Against Pollution option is enabled. This setting helps prevent unauthorized computers from impersonating another network server. When this option is disabled, however, the server caches all the records received in response to DNS queries—even when the records do not correspond to the queried-for domain name.

- Name Checking—By default, the Name Checking dropdown list box in the Advanced tab of the DNS Server Properties dialog box is set to Multibyte (UTF-8). Thus, the DNS service, by default, verifies that all domain names handled by the DNS service conform to the UCS Transformation Format (UTF). Unicode is a 2-byte encoding scheme, compatible with the traditional 1-byte American Standard Code for Information Interchange (ASCII) format, that allows for binary representation of most human languages. Table C-12 lists and describes the four name-checking methods.

Table C-12

Name-Checking Methods

Method	Description
Strict RFC (American National Standards Institute [ANSI])	Uses strict checking of names. These restrictions, set in Request for Comments (RFC) 1123, include limiting names to uppercase and lowercase letters (A–Z, a–z), numbers (0–9), and hyphens (-). The first character of the DNS name can be a number.
Non RFC (ANSI)	Permits names that are nonstandard and that do not follow RFC 1123 Internet host naming specifications.
Multibyte (UTF-8)	Permits recognition of characters other than ASCII, including Unicode, which is normally encoded as more than one octet (8 bits) in length. With this option, multibyte characters can be transformed and represented using UTF-8 support, which is provided with Windows Server 2003.

(continued)

Table C-12 *(continued)*

METHOD	DESCRIPTION
	Names encoded in UTF-8 format must not exceed the size limits stated in RFC 2181, which specifies a maximum of 63 octets per label and 255 octets per name. Character count is insufficient to determine size because some UTF-8 characters exceed one octet in length. This option allows for domain names using non-English alphabets.
All Names	Permits any naming conventions.

TAKE NOTE *

Windows Server 2008 has made improvements in the way that Active Directory–integrated zones are loaded when a domain controller that's running the DNS Server role starts up. This improvement, called *background zone loading*, allows DNS servers in large organizations to begin responding to DNS queries much earlier in the boot process than in previous versions of the Windows server operating systems.

Despite the flexibility of the UTF-8 name-checking method, you should consider changing the Name Checking option to Strict RFC when your DNS servers perform zone transfers to non-Windows servers that are not UTF-8-aware. Although DNS server implementations that are not UTF-8-aware might be able to accept the transfer of a zone containing UTF-8-encoded names, these servers might not be capable of writing back those names to a zone file or reloading those names from a zone file.

You should use the other two name-checking options, Non RFC and All Names, only when a specific application requires them.

- Load Zone Data On Startup—By default, the Load Zone Data On Startup property is set to the From Active Directory And Registry option. Thus, by default, DNS servers in Windows Server 2003 initialize with the settings specified in the Active Directory database and the server registry. You can also load zone data using two other settings: From Registry and From File. The From Registry option forces the DNS server to initialize by reading parameters stored in the Windows registry. The From File option forces the DNS server to initialize by reading parameters stored in a boot file. The boot file must be a text file named Boot located on the local computer in the *%systemroot%\ System32\Dns* folder. When a boot file is used, settings in the file are applied to the server, overriding the settings stored in the registry on the DNS server. However, for parameters that are not configurable using boot file directives, registry defaults (or stored reconfigured server settings) are applied by the DNS Server service.

Appendix D
Configuring the User and Computer Environment Using Group Policy

■ Configuring Security Policies Using Group Policy Objects

THE BOTTOM LINE

In this appendix, you will take a closer look at account security policies, folder redirection, offline file abilities, and disk quotas that can be implemented using Group Policy. It is important for you to know the difference between user and computer settings. In addition to learning about these settings and categorizing them based on where they are applied, you will also look at the default policy refresh process. Specifically, this appendix discusses how the policy refresh process works and how to invoke a manual refresh of Group Policies when necessary.

Centralized management of security settings for users and computers can be accomplished using Group Policy. Most of the settings that pertain to security are found in the Windows Settings folder within the Policies node in the Computer Configuration node of a Group Policy Object (GPO). Security settings can be used to govern how users are authenticated to the network, the resources they are permitted to use, group membership policies, and events related to user and group actions recorded in the event logs. Table D-1 briefly describes some of the security settings that can be configured within the Policies node in the Computer Configuration node.

Table D-1

Policies Node in the Computer Configuration Node Security Settings

SETTING	DESCRIPTION
Account Policies	Includes settings for Password Policy, Account Lockout Policy, and Kerberos Policy. A domain-wide policy, such as the Default Domain Policy GPO, also includes Kerberos Policy settings. In Windows 2000 and Windows Server 2003, the Password Policy and Account Lockout Policy could only be configured at the domain level. In Windows Server 2008, you can configure Fine-Grained Password Policies to allow multiple password policies in a single domain.
Local Policies	Contains three subcategories that pertain to the local computer policies. These subcategories include Audit Policy, User Rights Assignment, and Security Options.
Event Log Policy	These settings pertain to Event Viewer logs, their maximum size, retention settings, and accessibility.
Restricted Groups Policy	This setting gives administrators control over the Members property and Members Of property within a security group.
System Services Policy	These settings can be used to define the startup mode and access permissions for all system services. Each service can be configured as disabled, start automatically, or start manually. Also, the access permissions can be set to Start, Stop, or Pause.

D-1

Table D-1 (continued)

Setting	Description
Registry and File System Policies	These settings can be used to set access permissions and audit settings for specific registry keys or file system objects.
Wireless Network (IEEE 802.11) Policies	Allows definition of a policy for an IEEE 802.11 wireless network. Settings include preferred networks and authentication types, in addition to several other security-related options.
Public Key Policies	This node includes options to create an Encrypted File System (EFS), automatic certificate request, trusted root certificates, and an enterprise trust list.
Software Restriction Policies	This policy can specify software that you wish to run on computers. Also, it can prevent applications from running that might pose a security risk to the computer or organization.
IPSec Policy on Active Directory	Includes policy settings that allow an administrator to define mandatory rules applicable to computers on an IP-based network.

In the previous lesson, you learned that policy settings created within the Policies node in the Computer Configuration node apply to a computer; it does not matter who is logging on to it. More security settings can be applied to a specific computer than can be applied to a specific user. Table D-2 describes the security settings that can be applied within the Policies node in the User Configuration node of Group Policy.

Table D-2

Security Settings Applied in the Policies Node in the User Configuration Node

Setting	Description
Public Key Policies	Includes the Enterprise Trust policy that allows an administrator to list the trusted sources for certificates. Also, auto-enrollment settings can be specified for the user within this node.
Software Restriction Policies	This policy can be used to specify software that you wish to run for the user. Specifically, it can be used to disallow applications that might pose a security risk if run.

The next several sections discuss many of these settings in detail. In addition, examples will be presented to help you understand when and how to implement these policy settings.

Configuring Account Policies

Account policies influence how a user interacts with a computer or a domain. They are specified within the Policies node in the Computer Configuration node of a GPO that is linked to a particular domain, either the Default Domain Policy or one that you create manually. This account policy is applied to all accounts throughout the domain by default, unless you create one or more *Fine-Grained Password Policies (FGPP)* that override the domain-wide policy. These Fine-Grained Password Policies can be applied to one or more users or groups of users, allowing you to specify a more or less stringent password policy for this subset than the password policy defined for the entire domain. Fine-Grained Password Policies are a new feature in Windows Server 2008; in Windows 2000 and Windows Server 2003, you could only configure a single password policy and a single account lockout policy within each Active Directory domain.

The three subcategories within the Account Policies category of the security settings are *Password Policies*, *Account Lockout Policies*, and *Kerberos Policies*. Figure D-1 shows the expanded Password Policy category within the security settings of the Default Domain Policy GPO for lucernepublishing.com. Note that the figure shows default settings for this policy. Settings in this category focus on enforcing password length, password history, and so on. Password Policies can be applied to domain and local user accounts.

Figure D-1

The Default Domain Password Policy in Windows Server 2008

DEFINE A DOMAIN-WIDE ACCOUNT POLICY

1. **OPEN** the GPMC. Click **Forest: <Forest Name>**, click **Domains**, click **<Domain Name>**, and then click **Group Policy Objects**.

2. Right-click the Default Domain Policy and click **Edit**. A Group Policy Management Editor window for this policy is displayed.

3. In the left window pane, expand the Computer Configuration node, expand the Policies node, and expand the Windows Settings folder. Then, expand the Security Settings node. In the Security Settings node, expand Account Policies and select **Password Policy**. This displays the available settings for this category of the GPO, similar to what you saw in Figure D-1. All settings reflect the implemented defaults when the domain was created.

4. To modify a setting, double-click the setting in the right window pane to open the Properties dialog box for the setting. Then, make the desired value changes. For example, double-click the **Enforce password history** setting, change the value to **22** and then click **OK** to change the domain-wide password history from 24 remembered passwords to 22.

5. Click **OK** to close the setting's Properties dialog box.

6. Close the Group Policy Management Editor window for this policy.

PAUSE. You can close the GPMC MMC snap-in or leave it open for the next exercise.

Figure D-2 illustrates the expanded Account Lockout Policy category within the security settings of the Default Domain Policy GPO for lucernepublishing.com. Account Lockout Policies can be used for domain and local user accounts. An Account Lockout Policy specifies the number of unsuccessful logon attempts that, if made within a contiguous time frame, may constitute a potential security threat from an intruder. An Account Lockout Policy can be set to lock the account in question after a specified number of invalid attempts. Additionally, the policy specifies the duration that the account remains locked.

Figure D-2

The Default Domain Account Lockout Policy in Windows Server 2008

CONFIGURE A DOMAIN-WIDE ACCOUNT LOCKOUT POLICY

1. **OPEN** the GPMC. Click **Forest: <Forest Name>**, click **Domains**, click **<Domain Name>**, and then click **Group Policy Objects**.

2. Right-click the Default Domain Policy and click **Edit**. A Group Policy Management Editor window for this policy is displayed.

3. In the left window pane, expand the Computer Configuration node, expand the Policies node, and expand the Windows Settings folder. Then, expand the Security Settings node. In the Security Settings node, expand Account Policies and select **Account Lockout Policy**. The available settings for this category of the GPO are displayed.

4. In the right window pane, double-click the **Account lockout duration** policy setting to view the Properties dialog box.

5. Select the **Define This Policy Setting** checkbox. Note the default setting of 30 minutes for Account Lockout Duration. If you want to change the account lockout duration, you may do so here.

6. Click **OK** to accept the specified lockout duration. The Suggested Value Changes dialog box, which indicates other related settings and their defaults, is displayed.

7. Click **OK** to automatically enable these other settings or click **Cancel** to go back to the Account Lockout Duration Properties dialog box.

8. Click **OK** to accept the additional setting defaults.

9. Make any additional changes, as necessary, to the other individual Account Lockout Policy settings.

10. Close the Group Policy Management Editor window for this policy.

PAUSE. LEAVE the GPMC open for the following exercise.

You have now configured a domain-wide password policy that will configure consistent password settings across an entire domain.

Configuring Fine-Grained Password Policies

Prior to Windows Server 2008, an Active Directory administrator was only able to configure a single Password Policy and Account Lockout Policy for any Active Directory domain. If you were faced with a subset of users whose password policy requirements were different, you were left with the choice of configuring a separate domain or forcing all users within the domain to conform to a single password policy. Beginning in Windows Server 2008, you can configure Fine-Grained Password Policies, which allow you to define multiple password policies within a single domain.

To enable Fine-Grained Password Policies, Windows Server 2008 introduces a new object type called *msds-PasswordSettings*, also called a ***Password Settings Object (PSO)***. Each PSO has the following mandatory attributes:

- **cn.** The common name for the PSO, such as "ServiceAccountNoLockout."

- **msDS-PasswordSettingsPrecedence.** In a case where multiple PSOs apply, this attribute of the PSO is used as a tie-breaker to determine which PSO should apply: a PSO with a precedence of 1 will be applied over a PSO with a precedence of 5, a PSO with a precedence of 10 will be applied over a PSO with a precedence of 100, and so on.

- **msDS-PasswordReversibleEncryptionEnabled.** This attribute indicates whether the PSO allows passwords to be stored in Active Directory using reversible encryption. This setting should only be enabled if a particular application requires it, because it presents a significant security risk.

- **msDS-PasswordHistoryLength.** This attribute indicates the number of passwords that Active Directory should retain in memory before allowing someone to reuse a previously used password. Setting this attribute to a value of "2," for example, would prevent someone from reusing the previous two passwords that they had configured for their user account. This setting corresponds to the ***Enforce Password History*** setting in Group Policy.

- **msDS-PasswordComplexityEnabled.** This attribute indicates whether the PSO requires a complex password; that is, a password that uses a mixture of uppercase and lowercase letters, numbers, and symbols. The default password policy in Windows Server 2008 requires the use of complex passwords.

- **msDS-MinimumPasswordLength.** This attribute indicates the minimum length of a password defined by this PSO.

- **msDS-MinimumPasswordAge.** This attribute is a negative number that indicates the number of milliseconds old a password must be before it can be changed. The default value is −864000000000, which equates to one day.

- **msDS-MaximumPasswordLength.** As the name indicates, this attribute identifies the maximum length of a password defined by this PSO.

- **msDS-MaximumPasswordAge.** This attribute is a negative number that indicates in milliseconds when a password will expire. The default value is −36288000000000, or 42 days.

- **msDS-LockoutThreshold.** This attribute indicates the number of bad login attempts permitted before an account is locked out.

- **msDS-LockoutObservationWindow.** This attribute is a negative number that indicates the number of milliseconds that must pass before the counter for failed logon attempts should be reset.

- **msDS-LockoutDuration.** This attribute is a negative number expressed in milliseconds that indicates how long an account will remain locked out. A value of "0" indicates that the account will stay locked out until it is manually unlocked by an administrator.

You can create one or more PSOs within a domain and then configure each PSO to apply to one or more user or group accounts within the domain; these objects are not created using the Group Policy Management Editor, but by manually creating the object using ADSIEdit or LDIFDE. When a user logs on to the domain, Windows Server 2008 uses the following steps to determine the user's effective password requirements:

1. Are one or more PSOs assigned to the individual user account? If so, use the PSO that has the winning precedence. If not, continue to step 2.

2. Are one or more PSOs assigned to a group that has the user account as a member, either directly or through nested group membership? If so, use the PSO that has the winning precedence. If not, continue to step 3.

3. If PSOs are not assigned to the user or to any group that has the user as a member, apply the domain-wide password policy and account lockout requirements.

Configuring the Kerberos Policy

For domain accounts only, the Kerberos Policy allows you to configure settings that govern how Active Directory authentication functions. Several settings are available within this security setting on a domain-linked GPO.

Kerberos is the default mechanism for authenticating domain users in Windows Server 2008, Windows Server 2003, and Microsoft Windows 2000. Kerberos is a ticket-based system that allows domain access by using a ***Key Distribution Center (KDC)***, which is used to issue Kerberos tickets to users, computers, or network services. These tickets have a finite lifetime and are based in part on system time clocks. Note that Kerberos has a 5-minute clock skew tolerance between the client and the domain controller. If the clocks are off by more than 5 minutes, the client will not be able to log on. Another main setting, Enforce User Logon Restrictions, is enabled by default, as shown in Figure D-3. This setting tells Windows Server 2008 to validate each request for a session ticket against the rights associated with the user account. Although this process can slow the response time for user access to resources, it is an important security feature that should not be overlooked or disabled.

Figure D-3

Configuring the domain-wide Kerberos Policy

CONFIGURE THE KERBEROS POLICY

1. **OPEN** the GPMC. Click **Forest: <Forest Name>**, click **Domains**, click **<Domain Name>**, and then click **Group Policy Objects**.

2. Right-click the Default Domain Policy and click **Edit**. A Group Policy Management Editor window for this policy is displayed.

3. In the left window pane, expand the Computer Configuration node, expand the Policies folder and expand the Windows Settings folder. Then, expand the Security Settings node. In the Security Settings node, expand Account Policies and select **Kerberos Policy**. The available settings for this category of the GPO are displayed. All settings reflect the defaults that were implemented when the domain was created.

4. To modify a setting, double-click the setting in the right window pane to open the Properties dialog box for the setting. Make the desired value changes. For example, double-click **Maximum lifetime for service ticket** and change the existing setting to 480 minutes to change the maximum Kerberos ticket lifetime from 10 hours to 8 hours.

5. Click **OK** to close the setting's Properties dialog box.

6. Close the Group Policy Management Editor window for this policy.

PAUSE. You can close the GPMC or leave it open for the following exercise.

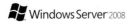
You have now configured the Kerberos Policy for a Windows Server 2008 domain, including configuring the maximum ticket lifetime for a Kerberos ticket and the maximum clock skew that can be tolerated by a 2008 Active Directory network.

Defining Local Policies

Local Policies allow administrators to set user privileges on the local computer that govern what users can do on the computer and determine if these actions are tracked within an event log. Tracking events that take place on the local computer, a process referred to as *auditing*, is another important part of monitoring and managing activities on a Windows Server 2008 computer.

The Local Policies setting area of a GPO has three subcategories: *User Rights Assignment*, *Security Options,* and *Audit Policy*. As discussed in each of the following sections, keep in mind that Local Policies are local to a computer. When they are part of a GPO in Active Directory, they affect the local security settings of computer accounts to which the GPO is applied.

As shown in Figure D-4, the User Rights Assignment settings are extensive and include settings for items that pertain to rights needed by users to perform system-related tasks. For example, logging on locally to a domain controller requires that a user has the Log On Locally right assigned to his or her account or be a member of the Account Operators, Administrators, Backup Operators, Print Operators, or Server Operators group on the domain controller. Other similar settings included in this collection are related to user rights associated with system shutdown, taking ownership privileges of files or objects, restoring files and directories, and synchronizing directory service data.

Figure D-4

User Rights Assignments in Group Policy

The Security Options category includes security settings related to interactive log on, digital signing of data, restrictions for access to floppy and CD-ROM drives, unsigned driver installation behavior, and logon dialog box behavior. The Security Options category also includes options to configure authentication and communication security within Active Directory through the use of the following settings:

- **Domain controller: LDAP server signing requirements** controls whether LDAP traffic between domain controllers and clients must be signed. This setting can be configured with a value of **None** or **Require signing**.
- **Domain member: Digitally sign or encrypt or sign secure channel data (always)** controls whether traffic between domain members and the domain controllers will be signed and encrypted at all times.
- **Domain member: Digitally encrypt secure channel data (when client agrees)** indicates that traffic between domain members and the domain controllers will be encrypted only if the client workstations are able to do so.
- **Domain member: Digitally sign secure channel data (when client agrees)** indicates that traffic between domain members and the domain controllers will be signed only if the client services are able to do so.
- **Microsoft network client: Digitally sign communications (always)** indicates that Server Message Block (SMB) signing will be enabled by the SMB signing component of the SMB client at all times.
- **Microsoft network client: Digitally sign communications (if server agrees)** indicates that SMB signing will be enabled by the SMB signing component of the SMB client only if the corresponding server service is able to do so.
- **Microsoft network server: Digitally sign communications (always)** indicates that SMB signing will be enabled by the SMB signing component of the SMB server at all times.
- **Microsoft network server: Digitally sign communications (if server agrees)** indicates that SMB signing will be enabled by the SMB signing component of the SMB server only if the corresponding client service is able to do so.

From this section, you can also enforce the level of NT LAN Manager (NTLM) authentication that will be allowed on your network. Although Kerberos is the default authentication protocol in an Active Directory network, NTLM authentication will be used in certain situations. The original incarnation of NTLM authentication was called LAN Manager (LM) authentication, which is now considered a weak authentication protocol that can easily be decoded by network traffic analyzers. Microsoft has improved NTLM authentication over the years by introducing first NTLM and subsequently NTLMv2. NTLM authentication levels are controlled by the Network security: NTLM authentication levels security setting, which allows you to select one of the following options:

- **Send LM and NTLM responses**
- **Send LM and NTLM—use NTLMv2 session security if negotiated**
- **Send NTLM response only**
- **Send NTLMv2 response only**
- **Send NTLMv2 response only. Refuse LM**
- **Send NTLMv2 response only. Refuse LM and NTLM**

By allowing only the most stringent levels of NTLM authentication on your network, you can improve the overall communications security of Active Directory. The final key component in defining Local Policies is planning and configuring an *Audit Policy* for a Windows Server 2008 Active Directory network, which we will discuss in-depth in the following section.

Planning and Configuring an Audit Policy

The Audit Policy section of GPO Local Policies allows administrators to log successful and failed security events, such as logon events, account access, and object access. Auditing can be used to track user activities and system activities. Planning to audit requires that you determine the computers to be audited and the types of events you wish to track.

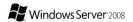

When you specify an event to audit, such as account logon events, you determine whether you wish to audit success events, failure events, or both. Tracking successful events allows you to find out how often resources are accessed. This information can be valuable in planning your resource usage and budgeting for new resources when necessary. Tracking failed events can help you determine when security breaches should be resolved. For example, if you notice frequent failed logon attempts using a specific user account, you may want to investigate further. Figure D-5 illustrates the policy settings available for auditing.

Figure D-5

Audit Policies in the Default Domain Policy

When an audited event occurs, Windows Server 2008 writes an event to the security log on the domain controller or computer where the event took place. If it is an account logon attempt or other Active Directory–related event, the event is written to the domain controller. If it is a computer event, such as floppy drive access, the event is written to the local computer's event log.

Auditing is turned off by default and, as a result, you must decide which computers, resources, and events you want to audit. It is important to balance the need for auditing against the potential information overload that would be created if you audited every possible event type. The following guidelines will help you plan your audit policy:

- **Audit only pertinent items.** Determine the events you want to audit and consider whether it is more important to track successes or failures of these events. You should only plan to audit events that will help you gather network information. When auditing object access, be specific about the type of access you want to track. For example, if you want to audit read access to a file or folder, only audit the read events, not Full Control. Auditing of Full Control would trigger writes to the log for every action on the file or folder. Auditing does use system resources to process and store events. Therefore, auditing unnecessary events will create overhead on your server and make it more difficult to monitor.

- **Archive security logs to provide a documented history.** Keeping a history of event occurrences can provide you with supporting documentation. Such documentation can be used to support the need for additional resources based on the usage of a particular resource. In addition, it provides a history of events that might indicate past security breach attempts. If intruders have administrative privileges, they can clear the log, leaving you without a history of events that document the breach.

- **Configure the size of your security logs carefully**. You need to plan the size of your security logs based on the number of events that you anticipate logging. Event Log Policy settings can be configured under the Computer Configuration\Policies\Windows Settings\Security Settings\Event Log node of a GPO.

Security logs are viewed using the Event Viewer and can be configured to monitor any number of event categories, including the following:

- **System events.** Events that trigger a log entry in this category include system startups and shutdowns; system time changes; system event resources exhaustion, such as when an event log is filled and can no longer append entries; security log cleaning; or any event that affects system security or the security log. In the Default Domain Controllers GPO, this setting is set to log successes by default.

- **Policy change events.** By default, this policy is set to audit successes in the Default Domain Controllers GPO. Policy change audit log entries are triggered by events such as user rights assignment changes, establishment or removal of trust relationships, IPSec policy agent changes, and grants or removals of system access privileges.

- **Account management events.** This policy setting is set to audit successes in the Default Domain Controllers GPO. This setting triggers an event that is written based on changes to account properties and group properties. Log entries written due to this policy setting reflect events related to user or group account creation, deletion, renaming, enabling, or disabling.

- **Logon events.** This setting logs events related to successful user logons on a computer. The event is logged to the Event Viewer Security Log on the computer that processes the request. The default setting is to log successes in the Default Domain Controllers GPO.

- **Account logon events.** This setting logs events related to successful user logons to a domain. The event is logged to the domain controller that processes the request. The default setting is to log successes in the Default Domain Controllers GPO.

Implementation of your plan requires awareness of several factors that can affect the success of your Audit Policy. You must be aware of the administrative requirements to create and administer a policy plan. Two main requirements are necessary to set up and administer an Audit Policy. First, you must have the Manage Auditing and Security Log user right for the computer on which you want to configure a policy or review a log. This right is granted by default to the Administrators group. However, if you wish to delegate this task to a subadministrator, such as a container administrator, the subadministrator must possess the specific right. Second, any files or folders to be audited must be located on NTFS volumes. This requirement is carried over from prior Windows operating system versions, such as Windows 2000 and Windows Server 2003.

Implementation of your plan requires that you specify the categories to be audited and, if necessary, configure objects for auditing. Configuring objects for auditing is necessary when you have configured either of the two following event categories:

- **Audit Directory Service Access.** This event category logs user access to Active Directory objects, such as other user objects or OUs.

- **Audit Object Access.** This event category logs user access to files, folders, registry keys, and printers.

Each of these event categories requires additional setup steps, which are described in the following exercise.

 CONFIGURE AN AUDIT POLICY

GET READY. To perform this exercise, you will need to be logged on to the Active Directory domain using Domain Administrator credentials.

1. **OPEN** the GPMC. Click **Forest: <Forest Name>**, click **Domains**, click **<Domain Name>**, and then click **Group Policy Objects**.

2. Right-click the Default Domain Policy and click **Edit**. A Group Policy Management Editor window for this policy is displayed.

3. In the left window pane, expand the Computer Configuration node, expand the Policies node, and expand the Windows Settings folder. Then, expand the Security Settings node.

In the Security Settings node, expand Local Policies, and select **Audit Policy**. The available settings for this category of the GPO are displayed.

4. In the right window pane, double-click the Audit Policy setting you want to modify; for example, double-click **Audit system events**. The Properties dialog box for the chosen setting is displayed. Select the **Define This Policy Setting** checkbox.

5. Select the appropriate checkboxes to audit Success, Failure, or both under the Audit These Attempts heading.

6. Click **OK** to close the setting's Properties dialog box.

7. Close the Group Policy Management Editor window for this policy.

PAUSE. LEAVE the GPMC open for the following exercise.

You have now configured an Audit Policy within the GPMC.

 CONFIGURE AN ACTIVE DIRECTORY OBJECT FOR AUDITING

GET READY. To perform this exercise, you will need to be logged on to the Active Directory domain using Domain Administrator credentials.

1. In Active Directory Users and Computers (MMC snap-in), click the **View** menu, and then click **Advanced Features**.

2. Navigate to the object that you wish to audit. Right-click the object and select **Properties**.

3. Click the **Security** tab, and then click **Advanced**. The Advanced Security Settings dialog box for the object is displayed.

4. On the Auditing tab, click **Add**.

5. Select the users or groups to be audited for Active Directory object access and click **OK**. The Auditing Entry dialog box for the object is displayed.

6. Select the events you want to audit on this object. Select the tab for object access or property access. Select the **Successful** checkbox, the **Failed** checkbox, or both checkboxes, depending on what you want to track.

7. In the Apply Onto list, specify which objects are audited. By default, *This Object And All Child Objects* is selected.

8. Click **OK** to return to the Advanced Security Settings dialog box for the object.

9. Choose whether you wish auditing entries from parent objects to be inherited to this object by selecting or clearing the **Allow Inheritable Auditing Entries From Parent To Propagate To This Object** checkbox. If the checkboxes in the Access box are shaded in the Auditing Entry dialog box for the object, or if Remove is unavailable in the Advanced Security Settings dialog box for the object, auditing has been inherited from the parent object.

10. Click **OK** to complete this process.

11. Open a command prompt and enter the following command to enable auditing for Active Directory changes, as shown in Figure D-6:

```
auditpol /set /subcategory: "directory service changes" /success:
enable
```

PAUSE. CLOSE the Active Directory Users and Computers MMC snap-in.

Figure D-6

Enable auditing for Active
Directory changes

Beginning in Windows Server 2008, new options are available for Active Directory auditing that will indicate that a change has occurred and provide the old value and the new value. For example, if you change a user's description from "Marketing" to "Training," the Directory Services Event Log will record two events containing the original value and the new value.

 CONFIGURE FILES AND FOLDERS FOR AUDITING

GET READY. To perform this exercise, you must be logged on to the Active Directory domain using Domain Administrator credentials.

1. In Windows Explorer, right-click the file or folder you want to audit and select **Properties**.

2. On the Security tab in the Properties dialog box for the selected file or folder, click **Advanced**.

3. In the Advanced Security Settings dialog box for the file or folder, select the **Auditing** tab, and then click **Add**. Select the users and groups to be audited for file or folder access and then click **OK**. The Auditing Entry dialog box for the file or folder is displayed.

4. Select **Successful**, **Failed**, or both checkboxes for the events you wish to audit.

5. In the Apply Onto list, specify which objects are to be audited. This box is set to *This Folder, Subfolder And Files* by default. This means that changes you make are inherited to lower levels in the file system directory.

6. Click **OK** to return to the Advanced Security Settings dialog box for the object.

7. Choose whether you wish auditing entries from parent objects to be inherited to this object by selecting or deselecting the **Allow Inheritable Auditing Entries From Parent To Propagate To This Object And All Child Objects** checkbox. If the checkboxes in the Access box are shaded in the Auditing Entry dialog box for the object or if Remove is unavailable in the Advanced Security Settings dialog box for the object, auditing has been inherited from the parent object.

8. Click **OK** to complete this process.

9. Close the Group Policy Management Editor window for this policy.

PAUSE. CLOSE the Windows Explorer window.

You have now configured auditing for files and folders within the Windows operating system.

Customizing Event Log Policies

The Event Log Policy settings area allows administrators to configure settings that control the maximum log size, retention, and access rights for each log. Depending on the services you install, the number of logs you have can vary on Windows Server 2008. For example, if your server is configured as a domain controller, you will have a Directory Service log that contains Active Directory–related entries. In addition, if your server is configured as a Domain Name System (DNS) server you will have a DNS log that contains entries specifically related to DNS.

The Event Log Policy settings area includes settings for the three primary log files: the Application, Security, and System logs. In addition to using Event Log Group Policy settings to modify the default log sizes, you can also manually configure the log sizes and actions to be taken when the log reaches its maximum size.

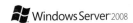 **CUSTOMIZE EVENT LOG POLICIES**

GET READY. To perform this exercise, you must be logged onto the Active Directory domain using Domain Administrator credentials.

1. From the Administrative Tools menu, open Event Viewer.
2. Right-click the log for which you want to view or modify the settings, and select **Properties**.
3. Modify the desired settings and click **OK**.

PAUSE. CLOSE the Event Viewer before continuing to the next exercise.

In the previous exercise, you configured Event Log Policies for a Windows Server 2008 computer.

See "Maintaining and Optimizing Group Policy" later in this appendix for information on the refresh process for restricted groups.

Understanding Restricted Groups

The ***Restricted Groups*** policy setting allows an administrator to specify group membership lists. Using this policy setting, you can control membership in important groups, such as the local Administrators and Backup Operators groups. This policy setting allows you to configure the group members and the groups in which the specified group is nested.

Consider an example: You wish to configure the default administrator account, Scott Seely and John Smith, as members of the built-in Administrators group. As shown in Figure D-7, you would add these users to the Members Of section of this group list for the restricted Administrators group. If another user is added to the Administrators group using Active Directory Users and Computers (MMC snap-in) for malicious or other reasons, the manually added users are removed when the Group Policy is reapplied during the refresh cycle. Only those users who are part of the Restricted Group membership list within the policy setting will be applied.

Figure D-7

Configuring Restricted Groups

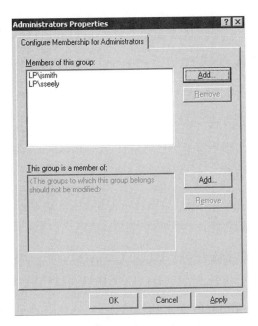

In addition, the Restricted Groups setting can be used to populate a local group's membership list with a domain group, such as Domain Administrators. This allows administrative privileges to be transferred to the local workstations, making management and access to resources easier. This "Member of" functionality is nondestructive, in that it will add users or groups to the membership of a particular group without removing any existing group members that have been configured.

Customizing System Services, Registry, and File System Settings

The *System Services* category is used to configure the startup and security settings for services running on a computer. Figure D-8 shows this policy area within the Default Domain Controllers Policy GPO. The service startup options are Automatic, Manual, and Disabled. Each functions as follows: *Automatic* starts a service automatically during system startup; *Manual* starts a service only by user intervention; and *Disabled* configures the service so that it cannot start.

Figure D-8

Configuring System Services

When using the Automatic setting for service startup, you should test the setting to make sure that the service starts automatically as expected. If certain services do not start as expected, users may not have the desired network functionality, and this may result in unnecessary downtime for users.

In addition to startup settings, the System Services Policy area also allows administrators to determine who has permissions to a particular service. For example, you may need to give certain users the ability to stop and restart a service that is malfunctioning, which includes start, stop, and pause permissions to the service. Permissions are defined by clicking Edit Security after defining the policy. Figure D-9 shows the Security page for a System Services Policy setting.

Figure D-9

Configuring Security for System Services

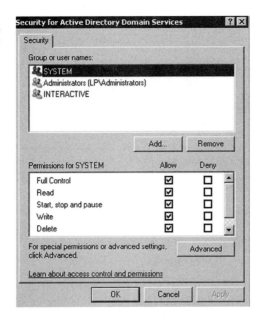

The Registry and File System areas of Group Policy are discussed together because they are similar in function. The Registry security area is used to configure security on registry keys. The File System security area is used to configure security for file system objects. Both of these areas allow administrators to set user permissions that reflect certain registry keys or files and the permissions users have to view and modify them. In addition, you can also set auditing on both of these items so that changes can be tracked for reference later.

Configuring Folder Redirection

Folder Redirection is a Group Policy folder located within the User Configuration node of a Group Policy linked to an Active Directory container object. Folder redirection provides administrators with the ability to redirect the contents of certain folders to a network location or to another location on the user's local computer. Contents of folders on a local computer located in the Documents and Settings folder, including the Documents, Application Data, Desktop, and Start Menu folders, can be redirected.

Depending on the folder being redirected, user data can be redirected to a dynamically created folder, a specified folder created by the administrator, the user's home directory, or the local user profile location. Redirection of the data from a user's local computer to a network location provides the following benefits:

- Files can be backed up during the normal network server backup process. Note that typical users do not back up their own data. Folder redirection eliminates the problems that arise when a local computer fails and a user has stored all documents on the local hard drive. When the data is redirected to a server hard drive, the data is backed up, and therefore is not lost due to hardware failure.

- When users log on to the network from a workstation other than their own, they have access to their files, because files are stored on a network server rather than on the local computer.

Redirecting a folder and files to a separate drive on the local computer can allow administrators to automatically redirect data files to a location separate from the operating system files. In this case, if the operating system must be reinstalled, the data files would not need to be deleted, nor would they be automatically overwritten by anything else. Figure D-10 shows the Folder Redirection Policy setting within the User Configuration node of a GPO.

Figure D-10

Viewing Folder Redirection settings

CONFIGURE FOLDER REDIRECTION

GET READY. Before you begin these steps, you must be logged on using an account with Domain Admin credentials.

1. Create a GPO or modify an existing GPO with the necessary Folder Redirection Policy setting. Using the Group Policy Management Editor for the desired GPO, locate the Folder Redirection policy extension in the User Configuration/Policies/Windows Settings/node.

2. Right-click the **Documents** folder in the left window pane and select **Properties**.

3. As shown in Figure D-11, use the Setting drop-down box of the Target tab to select one of the following options in the My Documents Properties dialog box:

   - **Basic–Redirect Everyone's Folder To The Same Location.** If you select this option, you must create a shared folder to which all subfolders are appended. This will be discussed in further detail later in this section. If this setting is chosen, proceed to step 4 now.

   - **Advanced–Specify Locations For Various User Groups.** Select this option to redirect folders to specified locations based on security group membership. For example, use this option to redirect the Application Data folder for accounting group users to one location and the Application Data folder for engineering group users to a different location. If you select this setting, proceed to step 5 now.

Figure D-11

Configuring folder redirection

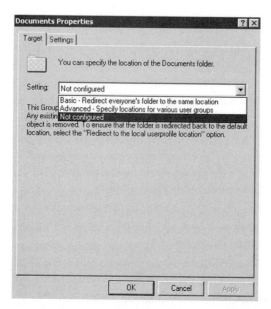

4. If you chose *Basic–Redirect Everyone's Folder To The Same Location*, you must specify the Target folder location in the Settings dialog box. Choose from the following options:

- **Create A Folder For Each User Under The Root Path.** This option is the default. When a user's folders are redirected using this setting, a subfolder is automatically created using the username based on the %username% variable and the folder name of the redirected folder. Allowing the system to create the subfolder structure automatically ensures that the appropriate user permissions are implemented. However, for the subfolder structure creation to work, each user must have appropriate permissions on the shared folder to create a folder. For the root path, use a Universal Naming Convention (UNC) name, rather than a drive letter–referenced path, which may change.

- **Redirect To The Following Location.** This option allows you to specify the path used to redirect the Documents folder. Use this option to redirect the folder to a server share or to another valid local path. When specifying a path, use a UNC name, rather than a drive letter–referenced path, which may change.

- **Redirect To The User's Home Directory.** This option redirects the Documents folder to a preconfigured home directory for the user. This setting is not recommended unless you have already deployed home directories in your organization and wish to maintain them. Security is not checked automatically using this option, and the assumption is made that the administrator has placed appropriate permissions on the folders. Administrators have full control over the users' My Documents folders when they are redirected to the user's home directory, even if the *Grant The User Exclusive Rights To Documents* checkbox is selected.

- **Redirect To The Local User Profile Location.** This option allows administrators to return redirected folders to their original default locations. This setting copies the contents of the redirected folder back to the user profile location. The redirected folder contents are not deleted. The user continues to have access to the content of the redirected folder, but access is provided from the local computer, instead of the redirected location.

5. If you chose *Advanced–Specify Locations For Various User Groups* in step 3, you must specify the target folder location for each group that you add in the Settings dialog box. The choices are the same as those outlined in step 4; however, you need to associate each group selected with a specific target location. Click **Add** to select the groups and choose the target folder location for redirected files.

6. The Settings tab for the Documents Properties dialog box provides several additional selections. Select the **Grant The User Exclusive Rights To Documents** and **Move The Contents Of Documents To The New Location** checkboxes, if necessary. If you will be supporting down-level clients running Windows 2000, Windows XP, or Windows Server 2003, place a checkmark next to **Also apply redirection policy to Windows 2000, Windows 2000 Server, Windows XP, and Windows Server 2003 operating systems**.

7. Select from the following options in the Policy Removal box of the Settings tab:

- **Leave The Folder In The New Location When Policy Is Removed.** This option keeps the redirected folder in its redirected location, without doing anything to the data. If the policy is removed, the user continues to have access to the contents at the redirected folder.

- **Redirect The Folder Back To The Local Userprofile Location When Policy Is Removed.** With this option enabled, the folder and its contents are copied back to their user profile location. The user can continue to access the contents on the local computer. With this option disabled, the folder returns to its user profile location, but the contents are not copied or moved back with the redirection process. The user can no longer see or access the files.

8. Click **OK**.

PAUSE. CLOSE the Group Policy Management Editor window.

⚠️ **WARNING** Although the Start Menu folder is an option in the Folder Redirection policy extension, the contents of each user's Start Menu folder on Windows XP computers is not copied to the redirected location. To configure Start Menu options, use alternate Group Policy settings to control the Start Menu content by using the Administrative Templates\Start Menu and Taskbar extension.

If the policy is changed to Not Configured, it will have no bearing on the redirection of user data. Data continues to be redirected until the policy removal setting is changed to redirect the folder to the user profile location. This is an example of *tattooing* with Group Policy. Tattooing means that the setting continues to apply until it is reversed using a policy that overwrites the setting.

Configuring Offline Files

Offline Files is a separate Group Policy category that can allow files to be available to users, even when the users are disconnected from the network. The Offline Files feature works well with Folder Redirection: When Offline Files is enabled, users can access necessary files as if they were connected to the network. When the network connection is restored, changes made to any documents are updated to the server. Folders can be configured so that either all files or only selected files within the folder are available for offline use. When it is combined with Folder Redirection, users have the benefits of being able to redirect files to a network location and still have access to the files when the network connection is not present.

Offline Files is configured on the Sharing tab of a folder. As shown in Figure D-12, on a Windows XP or Windows 2000 Professional workstation, shared folders can be set for Manual Caching Of Documents, Automatic Caching Of Documents, or Automatic Caching Of Programs And Documents. In contrast, as shown in Figure D-13, on a Windows Server 2003 or Windows Server 2008 family computer, the following options are available:

Figure D-12

Offline Files in Windows 2000 and Windows XP

Figure D-13

Offline Files in Windows Server 2003 and Windows Server 2008

• **Only The Files That Users Specify Will Be Available Offline.** This option is equivalent to the previously mentioned Manual Caching feature. As the default selection, it provides offline caching of only those files that have been selected. Users can choose the files they wish to have available when they are disconnected from the network.

- **All Files And Programs That Users Open From The Share Will Be Automatically Available Offline.** This option replaces the previously mentioned Automatic Caching Of Programs And Documents and the Automatic Caching Of Documents options. All files that have been previously opened in the shared folder are available for offline use.

- **Files Or Programs From The Share Will Not Be Available Offline.** This option stops any files in a shared folder from being available offline. This setting is particularly useful in preventing users from storing files for offline use.

Group Policy allows administrators to define the behavior of offline files for users in an Active Directory domain. For example, in Windows XP, Windows Server 2003, and Windows Server 2008, all redirected folders are automatically cached by default. This default behavior can be changed by enabling the Do Not Automatically Make Redirected Folders Available Offline policy setting in the User Configuration\Policies\Administrative Templates\Network\Offline Files extension. When this policy setting is enabled, users must manually choose which files to cache for offline use. Figure D-14 displays the available User Configuration node Group Policy settings for Offline Files. Note that most of the policy settings are available in both the User Configuration and Computer Configuration nodes of Group Policy.

Figure D-14

Configuring Offline Files in Group Policy

WARNING Allowing users to choose the files they want to cache locally can be a security concern. In high-security networks, offline file caching is disabled to prevent the possibility of sensitive data leaving the corporate environment. Consider exploring policy settings such as At Logoff, Delete Local Copy Of Users Offline Files, and Prohibit User Configuration Of Offline Files.

Using Disk Quotas

Use *disk quotas* to limit the amount of space available on the server for user data. By implementing disk quotas when folder redirection is also configured, administrators can control the amount of information that is stored on the server. This is important for a couple of reasons. For example, when information is stored on a server, your backup strategy and the amount of resources that it takes to implement it must take into account the amount of data that needs to be backed up. Disk quotas can minimize the resources required in this regard.

TAKE NOTE *

If a user compresses a file using the compression utility in Windows 2000, Windows XP, Server 2003, or Server 2008, the original uncompressed size of the file is used to determine the amount of data utilizing quota space because Windows will need at least that amount of space to uncompress the file.

Backup resources include the hardware involved, such as a tape backup device, and tapes or media to store the data. A network backup strategy usually takes into consideration the time required to back up information, the amount of media that is used, and the time it takes to restore the information if necessary. Considering all of this, disk quotas allow administrators to have control over the amount of information that is backed up for each user. When a disk quota limit is reached, the users cannot store additional data until either their limit is increased or they clean up allocated space by deleting unnecessary files or archiving old files to make room for new data.

Disk quotas can be implemented manually through the Properties dialog box of a drive volume, as shown in Figure D-15. This requires individual configuration of quotas for each volume that the administrator wishes to limit. The disk quota feature is only available on volumes formatted with the NTFS file system.

Figure D-15

Configuring disk quotas at the volume level

Using Group Policy to configure disk quotas enables all NTFS volumes on all computers running Windows 2000, Windows XP, Windows Server 2003, Windows Vista, and Windows Server 2008 affected by the GPO to be configured with consistent disk quota settings. This policy setting is located in the Computer Configuration\Policies\Administrative Templates\System\Disk Quotas extension of a GPO. Figure D-16 shows the available settings within this GPO extension.

Figure D-16

Configuring disk quotas using Group Policy

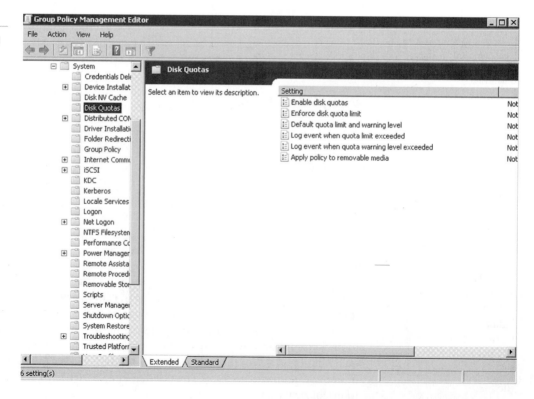

The following list describes each policy setting within this GPO area:

- **Enable Disk Quotas.** This setting enables or disables disk quota management on all NTFS volumes of computers affected by the GPO.
- **Enforce Disk Quota Limit.** Enabling this setting enforces the space limitations designated by the Default Quota Limit and Warning Level setting for all users on the volume from that point forward. Existing files on the volume owned by the user are not counted against the user's quota limit. When a limit is set, the same limit applies to all users on all volumes. If this setting is not configured and disk quotas are enabled, users are able to write data to the volume until it is full. Allowing this to occur defeats the purpose of enabling disk quotas.
- **Default Quota Limit And Warning Level.** This setting requires that the previous setting of Enforce Disk Quota Limit is enabled. This setting allows administrators to determine the space limitation and warning settings when the limit is reached.
- **Log Event When Quota Limit Exceeded.** When enabled, this setting allows quota limit events to be logged to the Application log in Event Viewer. This setting requires that the Default Quota Limit and Warning Level setting is configured.
- **Log Event When Quota Warning Level Exceeded.** When enabled, this setting writes an event to the Application log that indicates when a user is approaching the user's disk quota limits.
- **Apply Policy To Removable Media.** This setting allows the policy settings to be applied to NTFS volumes located on removable media such as external drives.

When applying disk quotas to your network, careful planning of the necessary amount of disk space required by each user is very important. Realistic expectations of drive usage should be calculated. Because the Group Policy settings for disk quotas enforce the same limits to all users, it is better to plan for a larger space limit than to inconvenience users who need more space with error messages stating that the drive is full. When disk quota policy changes are made, you need to restart the server for them to take effect.

Maintaining and Optimizing Group Policy

The final sections of this appendix will discuss the Group Policy refresh process, manual policy refresh procedures, and recommendations for policy settings to increase performance. This includes understanding and configuring the Group Policy refresh rate for member servers and domain controllers, as well as modifying the configuration of GPOs to optimize logon performance for your users and workstations.

Computer Configuration policies are applied by default when a computer starts up. User Configuration policies are applied during user logon. Both of these policies are also refreshed at regular points throughout the day. When a policy is refreshed, all settings are reprocessed, enforcing all of their policy settings. For example, settings that were previously enabled and are set to disabled are overwritten by the new setting and vice versa. In addition, settings that were previously enabled and set to Not Configured are simply ignored, leaving the setting in the registry unchanged. Each policy type has a default refresh cycle that takes place in the background to ensure that the most recent policy changes are applied, even if the system is not restarted or the user does not log off and back on. Although this is generally true, some policy settings will only process on initial startup or during user logon. For example, a policy that is used to install an application may interfere with another application's files for a program that is currently running on the user's computer. This could cause the installation to be incomplete or to fail. For this reason, software installation policies are only processed during computer startup. In addition, Folder Redirection policies are only processed during user logon. In the next sections, you will look at each policy type, the default refresh period, and where administrators can change the default refresh period.

- **Computer Configuration Group Policy Refresh Interval.** The setting for the refresh interval for computers is located in the Computer Configuration\Policies\Administrative Templates\System\Group Policy node in the Group Policy Object Editor window for a GPO. By default, computer policies are updated in the background every 90 minutes, with a random offset of 0 to 30 minutes.

- **Domain Controllers Group Policy Refresh Interval.** The setting for the refresh interval for domain controllers is located in the Computer Configuration\Policies\ Administrative Templates\System\Group Policy node in the Group Policy Object Editor. By default, domain controller group policies are updated in the background every 2 minutes.

- **User Configuration Group Policy Refresh Interval.** The setting for the refresh interval for user policy settings is located in the User Configuration\Policies\Administrative Templates\System\Group Policy node in Group Policy Object Editor for a GPO.

The available period that each background refresh process can be set to ranges from 0 to 64,800 minutes (45 days). If you set the ***refresh interval*** to zero, the system attempts to update the policy every 7 seconds. This can cause a significant amount of traffic and overhead on a production network and should be avoided except in a lab or test environment. However, setting a policy refresh interval to 45 days is also extreme and should not be implemented unless network bandwidth is at a premium. It is also possible to turn off the background refresh of a Group Policy entirely. This setting is available in the Computer Configuration\Policies\Administrative Templates\System\Group Policy node. This setting prevents any policy refreshes, except when a computer is restarted.

Manually Refreshing Group Policy

When you modify settings that you wish to be immediately invoked without requiring a restart, a new logon session, or waiting for the next refresh period, you can force a manual refresh. This process uses the ***gpupdate.exe*** tool. This command-line tool was introduced in Windows Server 2003, and it is used in Windows Server 2003 and Windows Server 2008 to replace the secedit/refreshpolicy command that was used in Windows 2000.

An example of the syntax necessary for *gpupdate.exe* to refresh all the user settings affected by the User Configuration node of the Default Domain GPO is as follows:

```
gpupdate/target:user
```

To refresh the Computer Configuration node policy settings, the syntax would be as follows:

```
gpupdate/target:computer
```

Without the /target switch, both the user and computer configuration policy settings are refreshed.

Optimizing Group Policy Processing

When processing a policy that uses computer or user settings, but not both, the setting area that is not configured should be disabled for faster processing. For example, if you wish to configure a computer policy that applies to all computers within an OU, you should disable the User Configuration node settings so that the policy processing is faster. When one part of the policy is disabled, that section is ignored and the settings are disregarded. This speeds up the completion of the policy processing, because each setting does not need to be read for changes.

OPTIMIZE GROUP POLICY PROCESSING

GET READY. To perform this exercise, you must be logged on to the Active Directory domain using Domain Administrator credentials.

1. Open the Group Policy Management Console (GPMC). Click **Forest: <Forest Name>**, click **Domains**, click **<Domain Name>**, and then click **Group Policy Objects**.

2. Select the Default Domain Policy and click **Edit**.

3. Right-click the Default Domain Policy node at the top of the left window pane. Click **GPO Status**, and place a checkmark next to **User Configuration Settings Disabled**, **Computer Configuration Settings Disabled**, or **All Settings Disabled**.

PAUSE. CLOSE the GPMC.

You have now modified a GPO to optimize its performance at computer startup and shutdown or user logon and logoff.

Appendix E
Configuring Print Services

This appendix covers the concepts required to deploy the Print Services role on a Windows Server 2008 server. We begin with a discussion of the terminology used to describe local and network printers, including print servers, print queues, and printer pools. We then discuss the specific steps required to install, configure, and secure printers on a server that is running the Print Services role.

■ Deploying a Print Server

THE BOTTOM LINE

As with the file sharing functions discussed in the previous lesson, print device sharing is another one of the most basic applications for which local area networks were designed. Installing, sharing, monitoring, and managing a single network print device is relatively simple, but when you are responsible for dozens or even hundreds of print devices on a large enterprise network, these tasks can be overwhelming.

Printing in Microsoft Windows typically involves the following four components:

- *Print device*—A print device is the actual hardware that produces hard copy documents on paper or other print media. Windows Server 2008 supports both *local print devices*, which are directly attached to computer ports, and *network interface print devices*, which are connected to the network, either directly or through another computer.

- *Printer*—In Windows parlance, a printer is the software interface through which a computer communicates with a print device. Windows Server 2008 supports numerous physical interfaces, including Universal Serial bus (USB), IEEE 1394 (FireWire), parallel (LPT), serial (COM), Infrared Data Access (IrDA), and Bluetooth ports; and network printing services such as lpr, standard TCP/IP ports, and the *Internet Printing Protocol (IPP)*, which allows clients to print via HTTP traffic, either over an intranet or via the World Wide Web.

- *Print server*—A print server is a computer (or standalone device) that receives print jobs from clients and sends them to print devices that are either locally attached or connected to the network.

- *Printer driver*—A printer driver is a device driver that converts the print jobs generated by applications into an appropriate string of commands for a specific print device. Printer drivers are designed for a specific print device and provide applications with access to all of the print device's features.

These four components work together to process the print jobs produced by Windows applications and turn them into hard copy documents, as shown in Figure E-1.

The flexibility of the Windows print architecture is manifested in the different ways that you can deploy the four printing components. A single computer can perform all of the roles (except for the print device, of course), or you can distribute them about the network. The following sections describe four fundamental configurations that are the basis of most Windows printer deployments. You can scale these configurations up to accommodate a network of virtually any size.

Figure E-1

The Windows print architecture

The simplest form of print architecture consists of one print device connected to one computer, also known as a ***locally-attached print device***, as shown in Figure E-2. When you connect a print device directly to a Windows Server 2008 computer and print from an application running on that system, the computer supplies the printer, printer driver, and print server functions.

Figure E-2

A locally-attached print device

However, in addition to printing from an application running on that computer, you can also share the printer (and the print device) with other users on the same network. In this arrangement, the computer with the locally-attached print device functions as a print server. The other computers on the network are the print clients, as shown in Figure E-3.

Figure E-3

Sharing a locally-attached printer

In the default Windows Server 2008 printer sharing configuration, each client uses its own printer and printer driver. As before, the application, running on the client computer, sends the print job to the printer and the printer driver renders the job, based on the capabilities of the print device. In this arrangement, the printer driver creates a job file using one of two interim formats, as follows:

- *Enhanced Metafile (EMF)*—A standardized, highly portable print job format that is the default format used by the Windows 2000, Windows XP, and Windows Server 2003 print subsystems. The printer driver converts the application data into an EMF file, and the printer sends it to the print server, which stores it in the spooler. The spooler then uses the printer driver on the print server to render the job into the final PCL format understood by the print device.
- *XML Paper Specification (XPS)*—A new, platform-independent document format included with Windows Server 2008 and Windows Vista, in which print job files use a single XPS format for their entire journey to the print device, rather than being converted first to EMF and then later to PCL.

The main advantage of this printing arrangement is that multiple users, located anywhere on the network, can send jobs to a single print device, connected to a computer functioning as a print server. The downside is that processing the print jobs for many users can impose a significant burden on the print server. Although any Windows computer can function as a print server, it is recommended that you only use a workstation for this purpose when you have no more than a handful of print clients to support, or a very light printing volume.

When you use a server computer as a print server, you must be conscious of the system resources that the print server role will require. Dedicating a computer solely to print server duties is only necessary when you have a lot of print clients or a high volume of printing to support. In most cases, Windows servers that run the Print Services role perform other functions as well. However, you must be judicious in your role assignments.

For example, it is common practice for a single server to run both the Print Services and File Services roles. The usage patterns for these two roles complement each other, in that they both tend to handle relatively brief transactions from clients. Running the Print Services role on a domain controller is seldom a good idea, however, because network clients are constantly accessing the domain controller; their usage patterns are more conflicting than complementary.

Using Networked Printers

The printing solutions discussed thus far all involve print devices that are connected directly to a computer, using a USB or other port. Print devices do not necessarily have to be attached to computers, however. You can connect a print device directly to the network instead. Many print device models are equipped with network interface adapters, enabling you to attach a standard network cable. Some others have expansion slots, into which you can install a network printing adapter purchased separately. Finally, for print devices with no networking capabilities, there are standalone network print servers available, to which you can attach one or more print devices and connect to the network. Print devices so equipped have their own IP addresses, and typically an embedded Web-based configuration interface, also.

With *network-attached print devices,* the primary deployment decision that the administrator must make is to decide which computer will function as the print server. One simple, but often less than practical, option is to let each print client function as its own print server,

---

TAKE NOTE*

The format used depends on whether the client computer is running a newer XPS driver, or an older driver that uses the EMF interim format. In addition to Windows Server 2008 and Vista, XPS is also available for Windows Server 2003 and XP as part of the .NET Framework package.

as shown in Figure E-4. Each client processes and spools its own print jobs, connects to the print device using a TCP (Transmission Control Protocol) port, and sends the jobs directly to the device for printing.

Figure E-4

A network-attached print device with multiple print servers

The advantage of this arrangement is that it is simple to set up, even by individual end users with no administrative assistance. However, the disadvantages are many, including the following:

- Users are oblivious of the other users accessing the print device. They have no way of knowing what other jobs have been sent to the print device, or how long it will be until the print device completes their jobs.
- Users examining the print queue see only their own jobs.
- Administrators have no way of centrally managing the print queue, because there are many print queues, one for each client.
- Administrators cannot implement advanced printing features, such as printer pools or remote administration.
- Error messages appear only on the computer that originated the job the print device is currently processing.
- All print job processing is performed by the client computer, rather than being partially offloaded to an external print server.

For these reasons, this arrangement is suitable only for small workgroup networks that do not have dedicated administrators supporting them.

The other, far more popular, option for network-attached printing is to designate one computer as a print server and use it to service all of the print clients on the network. To do this, you install a printer on one computer, the print server, and configure it to access the print device directly, through a TCP port. Then you share the printer, just as you would a locally-attached print device, and configure the clients to access the print share.

As you can see in Figure E-5, the physical configuration is exactly the same as in the previous arrangement, but the logical path the print jobs take on the way to the print device is different. Instead of going straight to the print device, the jobs go to the print server, which spools them and sends them to the print device in order.

With this arrangement, virtually all of the disadvantages of the multiple print server arrangement become advantages, as follows:

- All of the client jobs are stored in a single print queue, so that users and administrators can see a complete list of the jobs waiting to be printed.

Figure E-5

A network-attached print device with a single, shared print server

Physical Connections

Print Traffic Flow

- Part of the job rendering burden is shifted to the print server, returning control of the client computer to the user more quickly.
- Administrators can manage all of the queued jobs from a remote location.
- Print error messages appear on all client computers.
- Administrators can implement printer pools and other advanced printing features.
- Administrators can manage security, auditing, monitoring, and logging functions from a central location.

The printing configurations that we've just described are the building blocks that administrators can use to create printing solutions for their networks. There are a multitude of possible variations that you can use to create a network printing architecture that supports your organization's needs. Some of the more advanced possibilities are as follows:

- You can connect a single print server to multiple print devices, creating what is called a *printer pool.* On a busy network with many print clients, the print server can distribute large numbers of incoming jobs among several identical print devices to provide more timely service and fault tolerance.
- You can connect multiple print devices that support different forms and paper sizes to a single print server, which will distribute jobs with different requirements to the appropriate print devices.
- You can connect multiple print servers to a single print device. By creating multiple print servers, you can configure different priorities, security settings, auditing, and monitoring parameters for different users. For example, you can create a high-priority print server for company executives, while junior users send their jobs to a lower priority server. This ensures that the executives' jobs get printed first, even if the print servers are both connected to the same print device. Steps needed to modify print server priorities are discussed later in the lesson.

Sharing a Printer

Using Windows Server 2008 as a print server can be a simple or a complex matter, depending on how many clients the server has to support and how much printing they do. For a home or small business network, in which a handful of users need occasional access to the printer, no special preparation is necessary. However, if the computer must support heavy printer use, additional memory, hard drive space, and processing power may be required for the print server.

Before you can share a printer on a Windows Server 2008 computer, you must enable the appropriate settings in the Network and Sharing Center, just as you have to do to share files and folders. To share printers, the following Network Sharing and Discovery settings must be turned on:

- Network Discovery
- Printer Sharing

You can typically share a printer as you are installing it, or at any time afterwards. Older printers require you to initiate the installation process by launching the Add Printer Wizard from the Printers control panel. However, most of the print devices on the market today use either a USB connection to a computer or an Ethernet connection to a network.

In the case of a USB-connected printer, plugging the print device into a USB port on the computer and turning the device on initiates the installation process. Manual intervention is required only when Windows Server 2008 does not have a driver for the print device.

For network-attached print devices, an installation program is typically supplied with the product that locates the print device on the network, installs the correct drivers, creates a printer on the computer, and configures the printer with the proper IP address and other settings.

Once the printer is installed on the Windows Server 2008 computer that will function as your print server, you can share it with your network clients, using the following procedure.

 SHARE A PRINTER

GET READY. Log on to Windows Server 2008 using a domain account with Administrator privileges. When the logon process is completed, close the Initial Configuration Tasks window and any other windows that appear.

1. Click **Start**, and then click **Control Panel→Printers**. The Printers window appears.
2. Right-click the icon for the printer you want to share and, from the context menu, select **Sharing**. The printer's Properties sheet appears, with the Sharing tab selected, as shown in Figure E-6.

Figure E-6

The Sharing tab of a printer's Properties sheet

3. Select the **Share this printer** checkbox. The printer name appears in the Share name text box. You can accept the default name or supply one of your own.

4. Select one or both of the following optional checkboxes:

- **Render print jobs on client computers**—Minimizes the resource utilization on the print server by forcing the print clients to perform the bulk of the print processing.

- **List in the directory**—Creates a new printer object in the Active Directory database, enabling domain users to locate the printer by searching the directory. This option appears only when the computer is a member of an Active Directory domain, so your screen may differ slightly from Figure E-6.

5. Click **Additional Drivers**. The Additional Drivers dialog box appears, as shown in Figure E-7. This dialog box enables you to load printer drivers for the Itanium and × 64 versions of the operating system. When you install the alternate drivers, the print server supplies them to clients running those operating system versions automatically.

Figure E-7

The Additional Drivers dialog box

6. Select any combination of the available checkboxes and click **OK**. For each checkbox you selected, Windows Server 2008 displays a Printer Drivers dialog box.

7. In each Printer Drivers dialog box, key or browse to the location of the printer drivers for the selected operating system, and then click **OK**.

8. Click **OK** to close the Additional Drivers dialog box.

9. Click **OK** to close the Properties sheet for the printer.

STOP. The printer icon in the Printers control panel now includes a symbol indicating that it has been shared.

Configuring Printer Security

Just as with folder shares, clients must have the proper permissions to access a shared printer. Printer permissions are much simpler than NTFS permissions; they basically dictate whether users are allowed to merely use the printer, manage documents submitted to the printer, or manage the properties of the printer itself.

To assign permissions for a printer, use the following procedure.

 ASSIGN PRINTER PERMISSIONS

GET READY. Log on to Windows Server 2008 using a domain account with Administrator privileges. When the logon process is completed, close the Initial Configuration Tasks window and any other windows that appear.

1. Click **Start**, and then click **Control Panel.→Printers**. The Printers window appears.

2. Right-click one of the printer icons in the window and, from the context menu, select **Properties**. When the printer's Properties sheet appears, click the **Security**

tab, as shown in Figure E-8. The top half of the display lists all of the security principals currently possessing permissions to the selected printer. The bottom half lists the permissions held by the selected security principal.

Figure E-8

The Security tab of a printer's Properties sheet

3. Click **Add**. The Select Users, Computers, or Groups dialog box appears, as shown in Figure E-9.

Figure E-9

The Select Users, Computers, or Groups dialog box

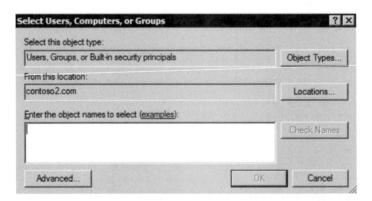

4. In the *Enter the object names to select* text box, key a user or group name, and then click **OK**. (If you have not created any users or groups of your own, select a built-in group such as Administrators.) The user or group appears in the Group or user names list.

5. Select the user or group you added, and select or clear the checkboxes in the bottom half of the display to Allow or Deny the user any of the standard permissions shown in Table E-1.

6. Click **OK** to close the Properties sheet.

STOP. You can log off of the Windows Server 2008 computer or remain logged on for subsequent exercises.

TAKE NOTE* This procedure assumes that the Windows Server 2008 computer is a member of an Active Directory domain. When you assign printer permissions on a standalone server, you select local user and group accounts to be the security principals that receive the permissions.

Table E-1

Standard Printer Permissions

Permission	Capabilities	Special Permissions	Default Assignments
Print	• Connect to a printer • Print documents • Pause, resume, restart, and cancel the user's own documents	• Print • Read Permissions	Assigned to the Everyone special identity
Manage Printers	• Cancel all documents • Share a printer • Change printer properties • Delete a printer • Change printer permissions	• Print • Manage Printers • Read Permissions • Change Permissions • Take Ownership	Assigned to the Administrators group
Manage Documents	• Pause, resume, restart, and cancel all users' documents • Control job settings for all documents	• Manage Documents • Read Permissions • Change Permissions • Take Ownership	Assigned to the Creator Owner special identity

TAKE NOTE *

As with NTFS permissions, there are two types of printer permissions: standard permissions and special permissions. Each of the three standard permissions consists of a combination of special permissions.

WARNING If for any reason the Everyone special identity group is denied the print permission or even completely removed from a printer's permissions list, then users with the Manage Documents permission will not be able to print to that printer. This is because the Manage Documents permission does not include the Print permission, and it is only because of the default configuration of Everyone–Print that users with the Manage Documents permission have the print permission to the printer. The Manage Printers permission, on the other hand, includes the Print permission.

Managing Documents

By default, all printers assign the Allow Print permission to the *Everyone* special identity, which enables all users to access the printer and manage their own documents. Users that possess the Allow Manage Documents permission can manage any users' documents. Managing documents refers to pausing, resuming, restarting, and cancelling documents that are currently waiting in a print queue. Windows Server 2008 provides a print queue window for every printer, which enables you to view the jobs that are currently waiting to be printed.

To manage documents, use the following procedure.

MANAGE DOCUMENTS

GET READY. Log on to Windows Server 2008 using any user account. When the logon process is completed, close the Initial Configuration Tasks window and any other windows that appear.

1. Click **Start**, and then click **Control Panel→Printers**. The Printers window appears.

2. Double-click one of the printer icons. A print queue window named for the printer appears, as shown in Figure E-10.

Figure E-10

A Windows Server 2008 print queue window

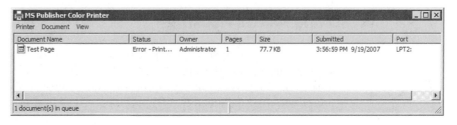

3. Select one of the menu items listed in Table E-2 to perform the associated function.

4. Close the print queue window.

STOP. You can log off of the Windows Server 2008 computer, or else remain logged on for subsequent exercises.

Table E-2

Document Management Menu Commands

MENU ITEM	FUNCTION
Printer > Pause Printing	Causes the print server to stop sending jobs to the print device until you resume it by selecting the same menu item again. All pending jobs remain in the queue.
Printer > Cancel All Documents	Removes all pending jobs from the queue. Jobs that are in progress complete normally.
Printer > Use Printer Offline	Enables users to send jobs to the printer, where they remain in the queue, unprocessed, until you select the same menu item again.
Printer > Properties	Opens the Properties sheet for the printer.
Document > Pause	Pauses the selected document, preventing the print server from sending the job to the print device.
Document > Resume	Causes the print server to resume processing a selected document that has previously been paused.
Document > Restart	Causes the print server to discard the current job and restart printing the selected document from the beginning.
Document > Cancel	Causes the print server to remove the selected document from the queue.
Document > Properties	Opens the Properties sheet for the selected job.

TAKE NOTE*

When managing documents, keep in mind that the commands accessible from the print queue window affect only the jobs waiting in the queue, not those currently being processed by the print device. For example, a job that is partially transmitted to the print device cannot be completely cancelled. The data already in the print device's memory will be printed, even though the remainder of the job was removed from the queue. To stop a job that is currently printing, you must clear the print device's memory (by resetting it or power cycling the unit), as well as clear the job from the queue.

Managing Printers

Users with the Allow Manage Printers permission can go beyond just manipulating queued documents; they can reconfigure the printer itself. Managing a printer refers to altering the operational parameters that affect all users and controlling access to the printer.

Generally speaking, most of the software-based tasks that fall under the category of managing a printer are those you perform once, while setting up the printer for the first time. Day-to-day printer management is more likely to involve physical maintenance, such as clearing print jams, reloading paper, and changing toner or ink cartridges. However, the following sections examine some of the printer configuration tasks that typically are the responsibility of a printer manager.

SETTING PRINTER PRIORITIES

In some cases, you might want to give certain users in your organization priority access to a print device so that when print traffic is heavy, their jobs are processed before those of other users. To do this, you must create multiple printers, associate them with the same print device, and then modify their priorities, as described in the following procedure.

➡ **SETTING A PRINTER'S PRIORITY**

GET READY. Log on to Windows Server 2008 using an account with the Manage Printer permission. When the logon process is completed, close the Initial Configuration Tasks window and any other windows that appear.

1. Click **Start**, and then click **Control Panel→Printers**. The Printers window appears.
2. Right-click one of the printer icons and then, from the context menu, select **Properties**. The Properties sheet for the printer appears.
3. Click the **Advanced** tab, as shown in Figure E-11.

Figure E-11

The Advanced tab of a printer's Properties sheet

4. Set the **Priority** spin box to a number representing the highest priority you want to set for the printer. Higher numbers represent higher priorities. The highest possible priority is 99.
5. Click the **Security** tab.
6. Add the users or groups that you want to provide with high-priority access to the printer and assign them the **Allow Print permission**.
7. Revoke the **Allow Print permission** from the Everyone special identity.
8. Click **OK** to close the Properties sheet.
9. Create an identical printer using the same printer driver and pointing to the same print device. Leave the Priority setting to its default value of 1 and leave the default permissions in place.
10. Rename the printers, specifying the priority assigned to each one.
11. Inform the privileged users that they should send their jobs to the high-priority printer. All jobs sent to that printer will be processed before those sent to the other, low-priority printer.

STOP. You can log off of the Windows Server 2008 computer, or else remain logged on for subsequent exercises.

TAKE NOTE*

The values of the Priority spin box do not have any absolute significance; they are pertinent only in relation to each other. As long as one printer has a higher priority value than another, the server will process its print jobs first. In other words, it doesn't matter if the higher priority value is 9 or 99, as long as the lower priority value is less than 9.

SCHEDULING PRINTER ACCESS

Sometimes, you might want to limit certain users' access to a printer to specific times of the day or night. For example, your organization might have a color laser printer that the company's graphic designers use during business hours, but which you permit other employees to use after 5:00 P.M. To do this, you associate multiple printers with a single print device, much as you did to set different printer priorities.

After creating two printers, both pointing to the same print device, you configure their scheduling using the following procedure.

 CONFIGURING A PRINTER'S SCHEDULE

GET READY. Log on to Windows Server 2008 using an account with the Manage Printer permission. When the logon process is completed, close the Initial Configuration Tasks window and any other windows that appear. In this exercise you will configure different permissions and availability for two separate printers: one called Designers to be made available to members of a "GraphicsDesign" group at all hours, and one called "AllUsers" to be made available to the EVERYONE special identity from 5 P.M. – 7 P.M., Monday through Friday. This exercise assumes that you have created a security group called "GraphicsDesign," either on the local computer or within the Active Directory domain as appropriate.

1. Click **Start**, and then click **Control Panel→Printers**. The Printers window appears.
2. Right-click the printer icon for the GraphicsDesign printer and then, from the context menu, select **Properties**. The Properties sheet for the GraphicsDesign printer appears.
3. Click the **Security** tab.
4. Add the GraphicsDesign security group and grant them the **Allow Print permission**.
5. Revoke the **Allow Print permission** from the Everyone special identity.
6. Click **OK** to close the Properties sheet.
7. Right-click **AllUsers printer** and then, from the context menu, select **Properties**. The Properties sheet for the AllUsers printer appears.
8. Click the **Advanced** tab.
9. Select the **Available from** radio button and then, in the two spin boxes provided, select the range of hours you want the printer to be available to all users. Notice that you do not need to modify the security settings for the AllUsers printer as this printer is available to the Everyone special identity; you are merely restricting the hours during which the printer is available to the Everyone group.
10. Click **OK** to close the Properties sheet.

STOP. You can log off of the Windows Server 2008 computer, or stay logged on for subsequent exercises.

CREATING A PRINTER POOL

As mentioned earlier, a printer pool is an arrangement that increases the production capability of a single printer by connecting it to multiple print devices. When you create a printer pool, the print server sends each incoming job to the first print device it finds that is not busy. This effectively distributes the jobs among the available print devices, providing users with more rapid service.

To create a printer pool, you must have at least two identical print devices, or at least print devices that use the same printer driver. The print devices must be in the same location, because there is no way to tell which print device will process a given document. You must also connect all of the print devices in the pool to the same print server. If the print server is a Windows Server 2008 computer, you can connect the print devices to any viable ports.

To configure a printer pool, use the following procedure.

CREATE A PRINTER POOL

GET READY. Log on to Windows Server 2008 using an account with the Manage Printer permission. When the logon process is completed, close the Initial Configuration Tasks window and any other windows that appear.

1. Click **Start**, and then click **Control Panel→Printers**. The Printers window appears.

2. Right-click one of the printer icons and then, from the context menu, select **Properties**. The Properties sheet for the printer appears.

3. Click the **Ports** tab, and then select all of the ports to which the print devices are connected.

4. Select the **Enable printer pooling** checkbox, and then click **OK**.

STOP. You can log off of the Windows Server 2008 computer, or stay logged on for subsequent exercises.

■ Using the Print Services Role

 THE BOTTOM LINE All of the printer sharing and management capabilities discussed in the previous sections are available on any Windows Server 2008 computer in its default installation configuration. However, installing the Print Services role on the computer provides additional tools that are particularly useful to administrators involved with network printing on an enterprise scale.

When you install the Print Services role using Server Manager's Add Roles Wizard, a Role Services page appears, as shown in Figure E-12, enabling you to select from the options listed in Table E-3.

Figure E-12

The Select Role Services page for the Print Services role

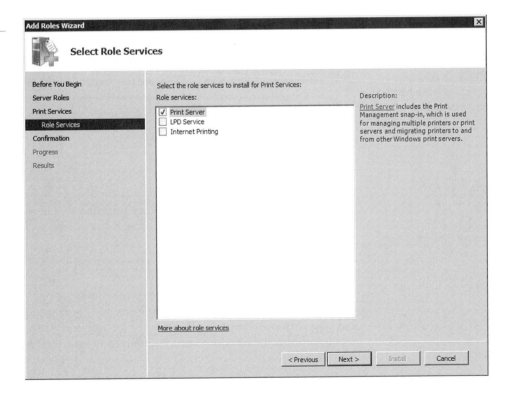

Table E-3

Role Service Selection for the Print Services Role

ROLE SERVICE	WIZARD PAGES ADDED	SYSTEM SERVICES INSTALLED	DESCRIPTION
Print Server	[None]	Print Spooler (Spooler)	• Installs the Print Management console for Microsoft Management Console (MMC), which enables administrators to deploy, monitor, and manage printers throughout the enterprise. • This is the only role service that is required when you add the Print Services role.
LPD Service	[None]	TCP/IP Print Server (LPDSVC)	• Enables UNIX clients running the LPR (line printer remote) program to send their print jobs to Windows printers.
Internet Printing	[None]	• World Wide Web Publishing Service (w3svc) • IIS Admin Service (iisadmin)	• Creates a Web site that enables users on the Internet to send print jobs to shared Windows printers.

To install the Internet Printing role service, you must also install the Web Server (IIS) role, with certain specific role services, as well as the Windows Process Activation Service feature. The Add Roles Wizard enforces these dependencies by displaying an *Add role services and features required for Internet Printing?* message box, as shown in Figure E-13, when you select the Internet Printing role service. Clicking *Add Required Role Services* causes the wizard to select the exact role services within Web Server (IIS) role that the Internet Printing service needs.

Figure E-13

The Add role services and features required for Internet Printing? message box

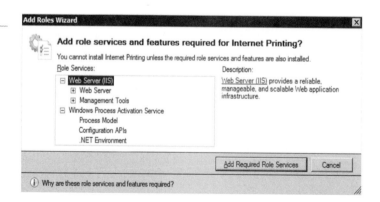

As always, Windows Server 2008 adds a new node to the Server Manager console when you install a role. The Print Services node contains a filtered view of print-related event log entries, a status display for the role-related system services and role services, and suggestions for recommended configuration tasks and best practices, as shown in Figure E-14.

Figure E-14

The Print Services node in
Server Manager

Using the Print Management Console

> The Print Management snap-in for MMC is an administrative tool that consolidates the controls for the printing components throughout the enterprise into a single console. With this tool, you can access the print queues and Properties sheets for all of the network printers in the enterprise, deploy printers to client computers using Group Policy, and create custom views that simplify the process of detecting print devices that need attention due to errors or depleted consumables.

Windows Server 2008 installs the Print Management console when you add the Print Services role to the computer. You can also install the console without the role by adding the Print Services Tools feature, found under Remote Server Administration Tools➜Role Administration Tools in Server Manager.

When you launch the Print Management console, the default display, shown in Figure E-15, includes the following three nodes in the scope (left) pane:

- *Custom Filters*—Contains composite views of all the printers hosted by the print servers listed in the console, regulated by customizable filters.
- Print Servers—Lists all of the print servers you have added to the console, and all of the drivers, forms, ports, and printers for each print server.
- Deployed Printers—Lists all of the printers you have deployed with Group Policy using the console.

The following sections demonstrate some of the administration tasks you can perform with the Print Management console.

E-16 | Appendix E

Figure E-15

The Print Management console

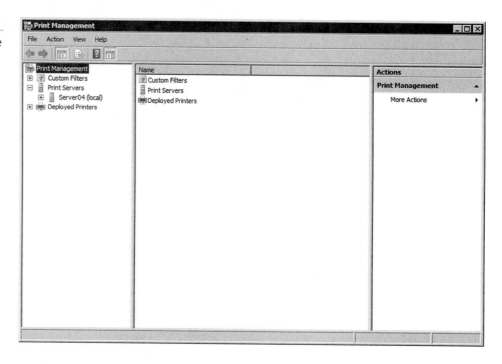

Adding Print Servers

By default, the Print Management console displays only the local machine in its list of print servers. Each print server listed has four nodes beneath it, as shown in Figure E-16, listing the drivers, forms, ports, and printers associated with that server.

Figure E-16

A print server display in the Print Management console

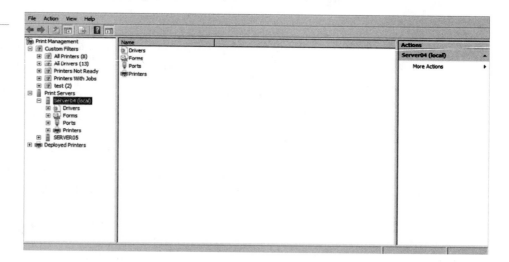

To manage other print servers and their printers, you must add them to the console, using the following procedure.

➔ ADD A PRINT SERVER

GET READY. Log on to Windows Server 2008 using a domain account with Administrator privileges. When the logon process is completed, close the Initial Configuration Tasks window and any other windows that appear. In this exercise you will add the Print Server Role and then add a print server. This exercise assumes that there is another server available on your network that is also running a print server, and that network discovery has been enabled on your network. If you do not have a second server available, you will not be able to complete Steps 5–7.

1. If Server Manager does not open automatically, click **Start**, and then click **Server Manager**. In the left-hand pane, click **Roles**.

2. In the right-hand pane, click **Add roles**. Click **Next** to bypass the initial Welcome screen.

3. The Select Server Roles screen appears. Place a checkmark next to **Print Services**. Click **Next** twice to continue.

4. The Select Role Services screen appears. Accept the default selection and click **Next**.

5. Click **Install** to install the Print Services server role. When the installation completes, click **Close**.

6. Click **Start**, and then click **Administrative Tools→Print Management**. The Print Management console appears.

7. Right-click the **Print Servers** node and, from the context menu, click **Add/Remove Servers**. The Add/Remove Servers dialog box appears, as shown in Figure E-17.

Figure E-17

The Add/Remove Servers dialog box

8. In the Specify Print Server box, click **Browse**. The Select Print Server dialog box appears, as shown in Figure E-18.

Figure E-18

The Select Print Server dialog box

9. Select the print server you want to add to the console and click **Select Server**. The server you selected appears in the Add Server text box on the Add/Remove servers dialog box.

10. Click **Add to List**. The server you selected appears in the Print Servers list.

11. Click **OK**. The server appears under the Print Servers node.

STOP. You can log off of the Windows Server 2008 computer, or else remain logged on for subsequent exercises.

Viewing Printers

One of the major problems for printing administrators on large enterprise networks is keeping track of dozens or hundreds of print devices, all in frequent use, and all needing attention on a regular basis. Whether the maintenance required is a major repair, replenishing ink or toner, or just filling the paper trays, print devices will not get the attention they need until an administrator is aware of the problem.

The Print Management console provides a multitude of ways to view the printing components associated with the print servers on the network. To create views, the console takes the complete list of printers and applies various filters to it, to select which printers to display. Under the Custom Filters node, there are four default filters, as follows:

- All Printers—Contains a list of all the printers hosted by all of the print servers added to the console.

- All Drivers—Contains a list of all the printer drivers installed on all of the print servers added to the console.

- Printers Not Ready—Contains a list of all printers that are not reporting a Ready status.

- Printers With Jobs—Contains a list of all the printers that currently have jobs waiting in the print queue.

Views such as Printer Not Ready are a useful way for administrators to determine what printers need attention, without having to browse individual print servers or search through a long list of every printer on the network. In addition to these defaults, you can create your own custom filters with the following procedure.

 CREATE A CUSTOM FILTER

GET READY. Log on to Windows Server 2008 using a domain account with Administrator privileges. When the logon process is completed, close the Initial Configuration Tasks window and any other windows that appear.

1. Click **Start**, and then click **Administrative Tools→Print Management**. The Print Management console appears.

2. Right-click the **Custom Filters** node and, from the context menu, select **Add New Printer Filter**. The New Printer Filter Wizard appears, as shown in Figure E-19.

3. In the Name text box, key a name for the filter, and optionally, key a description for the filter in the Description text box. If you want the number of printers in the filtered list to appear next to the filter name, select the **Display the total number of filters next to the name of the printer filter** checkbox. Then click **Next**. The Define a printer filter page appears, as shown in Figure E-20.

Figure E-19

The New Printer Filter Wizard

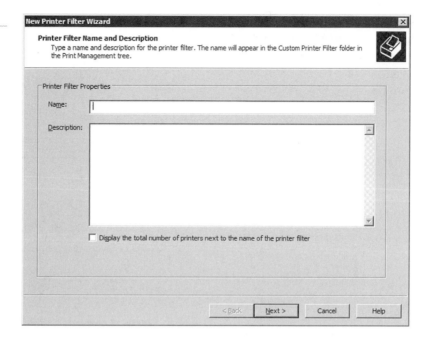

Figure E-20

The Define a printer filter page

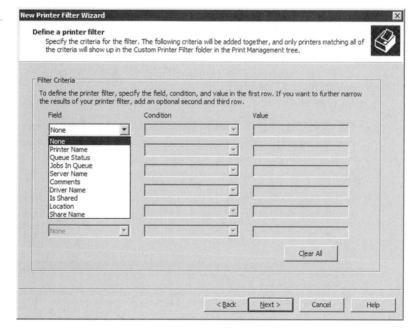

4. In the topmost row of boxes, select values for the **Field,** Condition, and Value fields. Then, select values for additional rows of boxes, if desired. Then click **Next.** The Set Notifications page appears, as shown in Figure E-21.

5. Select the **Send e-mail notification** checkbox to send a message to a specific person when there are printers meeting the criteria you specified on the Define a printer filter page. Use the text boxes provided to specify the sender's and recipient's e-mail addresses, the Simple Mail Transfer Protocol (SMTP) server that will send the message, and the text of the message itself.

6. Select the **Run script** checkbox to execute a particular script file when there are printers meeting the criteria you specified on the Define a printer filter page. Use the text boxes provided to specify the path to the script and any additional arguments you want the system to pass to the script when running it.

7. Click **Finish**. The new filter appears under the Custom Filters node.

Figure E-21

The Set Notifications page

STOP. You can log off of the Windows Server 2008 computer, or else remain logged on for subsequent exercises.

When creating filters, each entry in the Field drop-down list has its own collection of possible entries for the Condition drop-down list, and each Condition entry has its own possible entries for the Value setting. There are, therefore, many thousands of possible filter combinations.

For example, when you select Queue Status in the Field list, the Condition drop-down list presents two options: *is exactly* and *is not exactly*. After you select one of these Condition settings, you choose from the Value list, which displays all of the possible queue status messages that the print server can report, as shown in Figure E-22.

If you create a filter with the settings Queue Status, is exactly, and Error, the filter will display all of the printers that are currently reporting an error condition. A filter like this can be a

Figure E-22

Filter status values

useful tool for detecting printers reporting one specific condition, but there are many different status messages that indicate a print device stoppage. For the busy printer administrator, a better combination might be a filter with the settings Queue Status, is not exactly, and Ready. This way, the filter will display all of the printers suffering from abnormal conditions. These are the printers that need administrative attention.

Managing Printers and Print Servers

Once you have used filtered views to isolate the printers you want to examine, selecting a printer displays its status, the number of jobs currently in its print queue, and the name of the print server hosting it. If you right-click the filter in the scope pane and, from the context menu, select Show Extended View, an additional pane appears containing the contents of the selected printer's queue, as shown in Figure E-23. You can manipulate the queued jobs just as you would from the print queue window on the print server console.

Figure E-23

The Print Management console's extended view

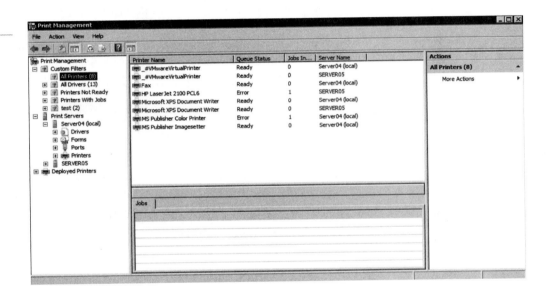

The Print Management console also enables administrators to access the configuration interface for any printer or print server appearing in any of its displays. Right-clicking a printer or print server anywhere in the console interface, and selecting Properties from the context menu, displays the exact same Properties sheet you would see on the print server computer itself. This enables administrators to configure printers and print servers without having to travel to the site of the print server or even establish a Remote Desktop connection to the print server.

Deploying Printers with Group Policy

Configuring a print client to access a shared printer is a simple matter of browsing the network or the Active Directory tree and selecting the printer you want the client to use. However, when you have to configure hundreds or thousands of print clients, the task becomes more complicated. One way to simplify the process of deploying printers to large numbers of clients is to use Active Directory.

Listing printers in the Active Directory database enables users and administrators to search for printers by name, location, or model (as long as you populate the Location and Model fields in the printer object). To create a printer object in the Active Directory database, you can either select the List in the directory checkbox while sharing the printer, or right-click a printer in the Print Management console and, from the context menu, select List in Directory.

To use Active Directory to deploy printers to clients, you must configure the appropriate policies in a Group Policy Object (GPO). You can link a GPO to any domain, site, or organizational unit (OU) in the Active Directory tree. When you configure a GPO to deploy a printer, all of the users or computers in that domain, site, or OU will receive the printer connection when they log on.

To deploy printers with Group Policy, use the following procedure. (The following exercise assumes that you are working in an Active Directory environment.)

 DEPLOY PRINTERS WITH GROUP POLICY

GET READY. Log on to Windows Server 2008 using a domain account with Administrator privileges. When the logon process is completed, close the Initial Configuration Tasks window and any other windows that appear.

1. Click **Start**, and then click **Administrative Tools→Print Management**. The Print Management console appears.

2. Right-click a printer in the console's scope pane and, from the context menu, select **Deploy with Group Policy**. The Deploy with Group Policy dialog box appears, as shown in Figure E-24.

Figure E-24

The Deploy with Group Policy dialog box

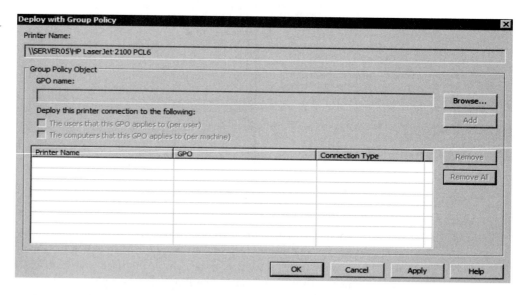

3. Click **Browse**. The Browse for a Group Policy Object dialog box appears, as shown in Figure E-25.

Figure E-25

The Browse for a Group Policy Object dialog box

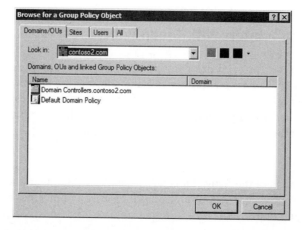

TAKE NOTE *

Clients running earlier versions of Windows, including Windows XP and Windows Server 2003, do not support automatic policy-based printer deployments. To enable the GPO to deploy printers on these computers, you must configure the systems to run a utility called Push-Printer Connections.exe. The most convenient way to do this is to configure the same GPO you used for the printer deployment to run the program from a user logon script or machine script.

4. Select the group policy object you want to use to deploy the printer and click **OK**. The GPO you selected appears in the GPO Name field.

5. Select the appropriate checkbox to select whether to deploy the printer to the users associated with the GPO, the computers, or both. Then click **Add**. The new printer/GPO associations appear in the table.

    Deploying the printer to the users means that all of the users associated with the GPO will receive the printer connection, no matter what computer they use to log on. Deploying the printer to the computers means that all of the computers associated with the GPO will receive the printer connection, no matter which users log on to them.

6. Click **OK**. A Print Management message box appears, informing you that the operation has succeeded.

7. Click **OK**, then click **OK** again to close the Deploy with Group Policy dialog box.

STOP. Close any open windows and log off of the Windows Server 2008 computer.

The next time the Windows Server 2008 or Windows Vista users and/or computers associated with the GPO refresh their policies or restart, they will receive the new settings, and the printer will appear in the Printers control panel.

Understanding the Global Catalog

THE BOTTOM LINE

Although the global catalog is not one of the five FSMO roles, the services it provides are of critical importance to the functionality of the Active Directory network. The global catalog holds a subset of forest-wide Active Directory objects and acts as a central repository by holding a complete copy of all objects from the host server's local domain along with a partial copy of all objects from other domains within the same forest, called the **partial attribute set (PAS)**. This partial copy of forest-wide data includes a subset of each object's attributes. The attributes included in this subset are necessary to provide functionality such as logon, object searches, and universal group memberships.

Understanding the Functions of the Global Catalog

By default, the first domain controller installed in the forest root domain is designated as a global catalog server. However, any or all domain controllers in a domain can be designated as global catalog servers. As an Active Directory administrator, you need to carefully weigh the benefits of designating additional domain controllers in your environment as global catalogs against the resulting performance implications.

The global catalog has four main functions in an Active Directory environment:

- **Facilitating searches for objects in the forest.** When a user initiates a search for an object in Active Directory, the request is automatically sent to TCP port 3268, which is used by Active Directory to direct these requests to a global catalog server. One of the SRV records used by Active Directory refers to the global catalog, or _gc_, service, which listens on port 3268 to respond to these requests.
- **Resolving User Principal Names (UPNs).** UPNs allow users to log on to domains across the forest using a standardized naming format that matches the format used for email addresses, such as jsmith@lucernepublishing.com. When a local domain controller receives a request for logon via a UPN, it contacts a global catalog server to complete the logon process. For example, assume the user account for jsmith resides in the lucernepublishing.com domain, and jsmith is currently working from the tokyo. lucernepublishing.com location. Because jsmith travels frequently between the various corporate locations, he uses the UPN, jsmith@lucernepublishing.com, to log on to his network account and his email account. Upon receiving a logon attempt from jsmith, a local domain controller searches for a global catalog server to resolve jsmith@ lucernepublishing.com to a username. The global catalog server stores enough information about the user to permit or deny the logon request. For example, if a time restriction allows logons only during business hours and jsmith is attempting to log on after hours, the global catalog will have a copy of that information and, therefore, jsmith's logon request will be denied. Because of this need to allow user authentication across domains, Active Directory must be able to contact a global catalog (or have a mechanism

to cache global catalog information as you will see shortly) to process any user logon, even in a single-domain environment.

UPN logons also are possible between forests that have a cross-forest trust established.

WARNING If the user has successfully logged on in the past and you have enabled *cached credentials* in your environment, a user will be able to log on using a cached copy of his or her logon credentials that have been stored on his or her local workstation. Allowing these credentials to be cached on a local computer can pose a security threat for certain companies. For example, if you have a computer that is shared by multiple users with different access permissions, cached credentials could be used for an account to allow an unauthorized user to gain access to a resource.

• **Maintaining universal group membership information.** Active Directory users can be permitted or denied access to a resource based on their group memberships. This information is an important part of a user's security token, which is used to determine which resources a user can and cannot access. Domain local and global group memberships are stored at the domain level; universal group memberships are stored in the global catalog. A *universal group* can contain users, groups, and computers from any domain in the forest. In addition, universal groups, through their membership in domain local groups, can receive permissions for any resource anywhere in the forest. A user who is a member of a universal group can be granted or denied permission to access resources throughout the forest. This presents another reason why a global catalog is required for a successful first-time logon to Active Directory. Without the global catalog available to query universal group memberships, a complete picture of the user's group memberships cannot be created and the logon process would be incomplete.

• **Maintaining a copy of all objects in the domain.** A domain controller that has been configured as a global catalog will contain a copy of its own domain NC, as well as a copy of the partial attribute set (PAS) of every other domain NC in the forest. Each object class has a certain list of attributes that are included in the PAS. This is defined within the Active Directory schema. You can add attributes to the PAS by modifying the attribute so that it is *indexed*, which means that it will be stored in the PAS and replicated to all global catalog servers in the forest.

For sites that do not have a global catalog server available, Windows Server 2003 and 2008 offer a feature called *universal group membership caching*. This stores universal group memberships on a local domain controller that can be used for logon to the domain, eliminating the need for frequent access to a global catalog server. The universal group membership caching feature allows domain controllers to process a logon or resource request without the presence of a global catalog server. For universal group membership caching to function, a user must have successfully logged on when a global catalog server was available and universal group membership caching was enabled. Universal membership caching records each user's information individually. For example, if universal group caching is not available to record the user's information into cache and the global catalog server goes offline, the logon attempt will fail.

Universal group membership caching is enabled on a per-site basis. The information in the cache is refreshed every eight hours, by default, using a confirmation request sent by the local domain controller to a global catalog server. Universal group caching has the following benefits:

• It eliminates the need to place a global catalog in a remote location where the link speed is slow or unreliable.

• It provides better logon performance for users with cached information. If the global catalog is located across a WAN link, cached credentials can replace the need to have logon traffic sent across a slow or unreliable link.

• It minimizes WAN usage for replication traffic because the domain controller does not have to hold information about forest-wide objects. In addition, these remote domain controllers are not listed in DNS as providers of global catalog services for the forest, further reducing bandwidth constraints.

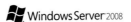

Table F-1 summarizes the logon process with regard to the global catalog and universal group membership caching.

Table F-1

Logon Process Summary

LOGON REQUEST SCENARIO	RESPONSE
The forest mode is set to Windows 2000 or above. A global catalog server is available.	The domain controller receiving the authentication request attempts to locate a global catalog server. A global catalog server is queried for the user's universal group memberships. The user is granted or denied access based on supplied credentials and the associated ACLs.
The forest mode is set to Windows 2000 or above. A global catalog server is not available. It is not functioning or inaccessible due to a connectivity problem or a down WAN link. Universal group membership caching is not enabled.	The domain controller receiving the authentication request attempts to locate a global catalog. The user logon is denied because the global catalog server cannot be contacted.
The forest mode is set to Windows 2000 or above. A global catalog server is not available. Universal group membership caching is enabled.	The domain controller receiving the authentication request attempts to locate a global catalog server. This query fails. If the user has successfully logged on in the past when the global catalog server was online and universal group membership caching was enabled, the logon is processed and the user is granted or denied access based on supplied credentials and ACLs. If the user has not logged on in the past when a global catalog server was available and universal group membership caching was enabled, the logon will be denied.

 ENABLE UNIVERSAL GROUP MEMBERSHIP CACHING

GET READY. Before you begin these steps, you must be logged on as a member of the Domain Admins group in the forest root domain or as an Enterprise Admin.

1. Open Active Directory Sites and Services.
2. Select the site from the console tree for which you want to enable universal group membership caching.
3. In the details window, right-click **NTDS Site Settings** and select **Properties**.
4. Select the **Enable Universal Group Membership Caching** checkbox, as shown in Figure F-1.

Figure F-1

Enabling universal group
membership caching

5. In the Refresh Cache From field, select a site that you wish this site to receive updates from or leave it at <Default> to refresh from the nearest site that contains a global catalog server. Click **OK**.

PAUSE. CLOSE the Active Directory Sites and Services MMC snap-in.

You have just enabled universal group membership caching for a single site within Active Directory. This setting must be enabled for each site that you wish to configure for universal group membership caching.

Configuring Additional Global Catalog Servers

By default, the first domain controller in a forest is a global catalog server. Therefore, your initial site will already contain a global catalog server.

The following guidelines will help you decide when you should add a global catalog server.

- Each site should contain a global catalog server to facilitate user logons. If a remote site is located across an unreliable or slow WAN link, a locally deployed global catalog server will allow logons and Active Directory searches to take place regardless of the state of the WAN link. If this is not possible, consider enabling universal group membership caching.

- When placing a global catalog at a remote site, consider the amount of bandwidth necessary to replicate global catalog information. Responding to logon requests from other sites increases the demands on bandwidth for the remote site.

- The domain controller that hosts the global catalog must have enough space on the hard drive to house the global catalog. As a rule of thumb, you should estimate 50 percent of the size of the ntds.dit file of every other domain in the forest when sizing hardware for a global catalog server.

- A site that contains an application using port 3268 for global catalog queries should contain a global catalog server. Port 3268 is used for Active Directory object searches.

 CONFIGURE AN ADDITIONAL GLOBAL CATALOG SERVER

GET READY. Before you begin these steps, you must be logged on as a member of the Domain Admins group.

1. On the domain controller where you want the new global catalog, open **Active Directory Sites and Services** from the Administrative Tools folder.

2. In the console tree, double-click **Sites**, and then double-click the site name that contains the domain controller for which you wish to add the global catalog.

3. Double-click the **Servers** folder and select your domain controller. Right-click **NTDS Settings** and select **Properties**.

4. On the General tab, select the **Global Catalog** checkbox, as shown in Figure F-2, to assign the role of global catalog to this server. Click **OK**.

Figure F-2

Configuring an additional global catalog server

PAUSE. CLOSE the Active Directory Sites and Services MMC snap-in.

You have just configured a domain controller as an additional global catalog within an Active Directory domain. You can enable some or all domain controllers in a forest as additional global catalog servers in your environment. You will need to allow sufficient time for the account and schema information to replicate to the new global catalog server. The length of time this process takes will vary depending on the number of objects to be replicated and the speed of the link used for the transfer. The Directory Services Event Viewer will display Event ID 1119 when the computer is ready to advertise itself as a global catalog server.

TAKE NOTE*

You also have the option to configure an RODC to host the Global Catalog Server role.

■ Using Certificates

THE BOTTOM LINE

Public key encryption uses two keys, one public and one private, to provide digital signing and data encryption services. Windows Server 2008 relies heavily on this *public key infrastructure (PKI)* for many of its security mechanisms.

There is one important question about the PKI that we have not yet addressed, and that is the distribution of the public keys. For the system to be truly secure, there must be some way to confirm that the public keys being distributed actually belong to the individual they purport to identify.

If you receive an email from Alice that has been encrypted using your public key, the fact that you can decrypt it using your private key confirms that no one has intercepted the message and read its contents. But how do you know that it actually came from Alice, when your public key is freely available to anyone? For that matter, what is there to stop someone from issuing a public key in your name, causing people to send messages intended for you to someone else?

One of the most common answers to these questions is digital certificates. A ***digital certificate*** is a digitally signed document, issued by a third party called a ***certification authority (CA),*** that binds a user, computer, or service holding a private key with its corresponding public key. When both parties involved in a transaction trust the CA to properly authenticate users before handing out certificates, and believe that the CA protects the privacy of its certificates and keys, then they can both trust in the identity of the certificate holder.

Understanding Certificates

The trustworthiness of the CA is a critical element of a certificate's usefulness, and the selection of the CA that will issue certificates is dependent on the application that requires them.

For example, suppose Litware, Inc. wants to run Remote Access servers to enable its employees to telecommute from home, using EAP-TLS authentication. To use EAP-TLS, both the clients and the Remote Access servers must have certificates, and in this case, the organization could create its own CA and issue its own certificates by installing the Active Directory Certificate Services role on a Windows Server 2008 computer. This is an acceptable solution in this case because the internal CA is trusted by both the clients and the servers.

However, consider another scenario in which Litware wants to distribute an ActiveX control to Internet users through its Web site. The users on the Internet would understandably want to confirm that the software is indeed coming Litware, so they expect the software to be digitally signed using a certificate. Litware could conceivably use its own CA to issue the certificate for the software, but the users would be foolish to accept them. What good is an affirmation of identity that comes from the party whose identity you are trying to affirm? Anyone could install their own CA using the name Litware, and digitally sign any piece of software they want.

The key to using certificates is for both parties to trust the CA, so in this case, the certificates must come from a third party that both the client and the server trust. In most cases, this means that Litware must contact one of the commercial certification authorities, such as VeriSign, Inc., to obtain a certificate for its software. They pay a fee to the CA, and use the certificate to digitally sign the software. The clients accessing the Litware Web site are then informed, before they download the software, that it is digitally signed by VeriSign. Recognizing and trusting the VeriSign name, the user then proceed with the download.

UNDERSTANDING CERTIFICATE FUNCTIONS

Digital certificates can perform a variety of functions, including the following:

- Digital signatures—Certificates can confirm that the individual sending a message, file, or other data is actually the person he or she claims to be. Digital signatures do not protect the data itself from compromise, they only verify the identity of the sender.

- Encrypting File System (EFS) user and recovery certificates—EFS enables users to store data on disk in encrypted form, to prevent other users from accessing it. To prevent a loss of data resulting from users leaving the organization or losing their encryption keys, EFS allows designated recovery agents to create public keys that can decode the encrypted information. As with IPsec, EFS does not have to use the PKI for its encryption keys, but the use of a PKI simplifies the implementation of EFS.

- Internet authentication—You can use the PKI to authenticate clients and servers as they establish connections over the Internet. This enables servers to identify the clients connecting to them and enables clients to confirm that they are connecting to the correct servers.

- IP Security (IPsec)—The IP Security extensions enable you to encrypt and digitally sign communications, to prevent intruders from compromising them as they are transmitted

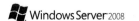

over a network. The Windows Server 2008 IPsec implementation does not have to use a PKI to obtain its encryption keys, but you can use the PKI for this purpose.

- Secure email—Internet email protocols transmit mail messages in plain text, making it relatively easy to intercept them and read their contents. With a PKI, you can secure email communications by encrypting the actual message text using the recipient's public key, and you can digitally sign the messages using your private key.

- Smart card logon—Windows Server 2008 can use a smart card as an authentication device that verifies the identity of a user during logon. The smart card contains the user's certificate and private key, enabling the user to log on to any workstation in the enterprise securely.

- Software code signing—Microsoft's Authenticode is one technology that uses certificates to confirm that the software user's download and install actually come from the publisher and have not been modified.

- Wireless network authentication—The increasing popularity of wireless local area networking (WLAN) technologies, such as those based on the 802.11 standards, raises an important security issue. When you install a WLAN, you must make sure only authorized users can connect to the network and that no one can eavesdrop on the wireless communications. You can use the Windows Server 2008 PKI to protect a wireless network by identifying and authenticating users before they are granted access to the network.

UNDERSTANDING CERTIFICATE COMPONENTS

Digital certificates carry information about their functions and capabilities in a variety of fields, including the following:

- Version—Identifies the version of the X.509 standard used to format the certificate
- Serial number—Specifies a value assigned by the CA that uniquely identifies the certificate
- Signature algorithm—Specifies the algorithm that the CA used to calculate the certificate's digital signature
- Issuer—Specifies the name of the entity that issued the certificate
- Valid from—Specifies the beginning of the period during which the certificate is valid
- Valid to—Specifies the end of the period during which the certificate is valid
- Subject—Specifies the name of the entity for which the certificate is issued
- Public key—Specifies the type and length of the public key associated with the certificate
- Enhanced key usage—Specifies the functions for which the certificate can be used
- Key usage—Specifies additional functions for which the certificate can be used
- Thumbprint algorithm—Specifies the algorithm used to generate a digest of the certificate data
- Thumbprint—Contains a digest of the certificate data, used for digital signing
- Friendly name—Specifies a common name for the entity listed in the Subject field
- Certificate policies—Describes the policy that the CA followed to originally authenticate the subject
- CRL distribution points—Specifies the location of the ***certificate revocation list (CRL),*** a document maintained and published by a CA that lists certificates that have been revoked

> **TAKE NOTE***
>
> Not every certificate has all of the fields listed here. The information within a given certificate is based on its origin and its intended purpose.

To view the information in a certificate's fields in Windows Server 2008, you must open it in the Certificates snap-in for Microsoft Management Console (MMC). There is no shortcut to the Certificates snap-in in the Start menu. You must open a blank MMC console and add the Certificates snap-in to it. When you do this, you have to specify the focus of the snap-in as the current user's account, a computer account, or a service account. When you select the current user account option, the snap-in creates an interface like the one shown in Figure F-3.

Figure F-3

The Certificates snap-in

When you double-click one of the certificates listed in the console, a Certificate dialog box appears, containing the following tabs:

- General—Displays a list of the functions the certificate is capable of performing, plus the issuer, the recipient, and the dates of validity, as shown in Figure F-4
- Details—Displays the values for all of the certificate's fields, as shown in Figure F-5

Figure F-4

The General tab in a Certificates dialog box

Figure F-5

The Details tab in a Certificates dialog box

• Certification Path—Contains a tree display of the certificate's issuing CA, and all of its trusted certification authorities leading back to the root, as shown in Figure F-6

Figure F-6

The Certification Path tab in a Certificates dialog box

Planning a CA Deployment

After you decide that you have reason to install your own certification authorities, there are a number of decisions you must make to ensure that the CAs you install can perform the tasks you require from them.

Windows Server 2008 supports two basic types of CAs, as follows:

• *Enterprise CA*—Enterprise CAs are integrated into the Windows Server 2008 Active Directory environment. They use certificate templates, publish their certificates and CRLs to Active Directory, and use the information in Active Directory to approve or deny certificate enrollment requests automatically. Because the clients of an enterprise CA must have access to Active Directory to receive certificates, enterprise CAs are not suitable for issuing certificates to clients outside the enterprise.

• *Standalone CA*—Standalone CAs do not use certificate templates or Active Directory; they store their information locally. In addition, by default, standalone CAs do not automatically respond to certificate enrollment requests, as is the case with enterprise CAs. Requests wait in a queue for an administrator to manually approve or deny them. Standalone CAs are intended for situations in which users outside the enterprise submit requests for certificates.

In addition, you can configure each enterprise or standalone CA to function as either a root CA or a subordinate CA. The first CA you install in your organization must always be a root CA. A *root CA* is the parent that issues certificates to the *subordinate CAs* beneath it. If a client trusts the root CA, it must also trust all the subordinate CAs that have been issued certificates by the root CA. The certification path included in every certificate traces the hierarchy from the issuing CA up through any additional CAs to the root.

Every CA must have a certificate of its own, which authorizes it to issue certificates. Root CAs are the only CAs that do not have a certificate issued by a higher authority. A root CA issues its own self-signed certificate, which functions as the top of the certificate chain for all the certificates issued by all the CAs subordinate to the root. When you install a subordinate CA, you must specify the name of a parent CA, which will issue a certificate to the subordinate. The parent does not have to be the root CA.

Because the root CA is the ultimate seat of trust in the public key infrastructure, its security is crucial. If the root CA is compromised, then all of the certificates it issues and all of the certificates issued by the subordinate CAs are compromised as well. For this reason, many administrators install a root CA solely for the purpose of issuing certificates to subordinate CAs, and then shut it down and physically secure it for its own protection, leaving the task of issuing end-user certificates to the subordinates.

TAKE NOTE *

> The increasing use of server virtualization in the enterprise has made this root protection strategy less costly, and more appealing. You can create a Windows Server 2008 virtual machine, configure it as your root CA, and shut the root CA virtual machine down. Then you can use the computer to run other virtual machines, and activate the root CA only when you need it.

Depending on the size and layout of the organization, you might decide to create many CAs, in multiple levels and in different locations. If your organization has multiple sites, you might decide to create a CA in each office, to give users local access to new certificates, just as you can do with domain controllers. You might also create separate CAs to perform different functions.

As a result of these options, there are four different types of CAs that you can create on a Windows Server 2008 computer:

- Enterprise root
- Enterprise subordinate
- Standalone root
- Standalone subordinate

DETERMINING THE CERTIFICATE LIFE CYCLE

Certificate holders cannot continue to use the same certificates indefinitely. The longer a certificate remains in use, the more time attackers have to work on penetrating the corresponding private key. Certificates have a predefined life cycle and expire at the end of this life cycle. Administrators exercise control over certificates; they can extend the lifetime of a certificate by renewing it, or end the usefulness of a certificate before the expiration date by revoking it.

Administrators should consider a number of factors when choosing the length of a certificate's lifetime, such as the type of certificate, the security requirements of the organization, the standard practices in the industry, and government regulations. In general, using longer encryption keys makes it possible to have longer certificate lifetimes and key lifetimes. Using longer certificate lifetimes reduces administrative overhead, which in turn reduces costs.

When planning certificate and key lifetimes, administrators must consider how vulnerable the keys are to compromise and what the potential consequences of their compromise are. The following factors can influence the lifetimes that an administrator chooses for certificates and keys:

- The length of private keys for certificates—Because longer keys are more difficult to break, they justify longer safe key lifetimes.
- The security of the CAs and their private keys—In general, the more secure the CA and its private key, the longer the safe certificate lifetime. CAs that are kept offline and stored in locked vaults or data centers are the most secure.

- The strength of the technology used for cryptographic operations—In general, stronger cryptographic technology supports longer key lifetimes. You can extend key lifetimes if you enhance private key storage by using smart cards and other hardware-based cryptographic service providers. Some cryptographic technologies provide stronger security, in addition to support for stronger cryptographic algorithms.

- The vulnerability of the CA certification chain—In general, the more vulnerable your CA hierarchy is to attack, the longer the CA private keys should be and the shorter the key lifetimes.

- The users of your certificates—Organizations typically trust their own employees more than they trust employees of other organizations. If you issue certificates to external users, you might want to shorten the lifetimes of those certificates to reduce the time window during which an individual can abuse a compromised private key.

- The number of certificates that have been signed by a dedicated CA—The wider the distribution of the public key that a CA uses to sign its issued certificates, the more vulnerable it becomes to attempts to break its private key.

A CA defines an expiration date for each certificate it issues. An enterprise CA issues certificates with lifetimes that are based on the certificate template for the requested certificate type.

PLANNING CA VALIDITY PERIODS

Because a CA must have a certificate of its own to operate—either self-issued, in the case of a root CA, or issued by a parent—the expiration of the CA's certificate causes the CA itself to expire. This also means that the expiration date of a CA's certificate is more important to the continued function of the PKI than those of other certificates. In addition, a CA cannot issue certificates with expiration dates that are valid beyond the expiration date of its own certificate. Therefore, when a CA's certificate reaches the end of its validity period, all of the certificates it has ever issued also expire. Because of this, if you deliberately do not renew a CA's certificate, you can be assured that all the certificates the now-expired CA issued are no longer usable. In other words, there can be no orphaned certificates that are still valid, when the CA that issued them is no longer valid.

Because a CA that is approaching the end of its own validity period must issue certificates valid for increasingly shorter periods of time, administrators should have a policy in place to renew the CA well before it expires. For example, in the case of Windows Server 2008, a root CA's self-generated certificate defaults to a validity period of five years. Administrators should renew it every four years, however, to prevent the CA from publishing new certificates with lifetimes shorter than a year.

Administrators can reduce the time required to administer a PKI by increasing the validity period of the root CA. As with any certificate, it is best to choose a validity period shorter than the time required for an attacker to break the root CA key's cryptography. Given the current state of computer technology, one can estimate that a 4096-bit private key would take decades to crack. While a determined attacker can eventually crack any private key, the end result is useless if the certificate expires before the attack is successful.

UNDERSTANDING CERTIFICATE REVOCATION

A certificate has a specified lifetime, but CAs can reduce this lifetime by a process known as *certificate revocation*. Every CA publishes a certificate revocation list (CRL) that lists the serial numbers of certificates that it considers to be no longer valid. The specified lifetime of CRLs is typically much shorter than that of a certificate. The CA might also include in the CRL a code specifying the reason the certificate has been revoked. A revocation might occur because a private key has been compromised, because a certificate has been superseded, or because an employee has left the company. The CRL also includes the date the certificate was revoked.

During signature verification and other activities that require certificate access, applications typically check the revocation list on the certificate's CA to determine whether the certificate and its key pair are still trustworthy. Applications can also determine whether the reason for the revocation or the date it occurred affects the use of the certificate in question. For example, if an application is using the certificate to verify a signature, and the date on the signature precedes the date of the revocation of the certificate by the CA, the application can consider the signature to still be valid.

To reduce the number of requests sent to a CA, clients typically cache CRLs, and use them until they expire. If a CA publishes a new CRL, applications that have a valid CRL do not usually use the new CRL until the one they have expires.

Installing Certification Authorities

When you install the Active Directory Certificate Services Role on a Windows Server 2008 computer, you can create any one of the four types of CA listed earlier.

When you select the CA type, the Add Roles Wizard changes to include various additional configuration pages depending on the type you select. On most enterprise networks that use certificates for their internal applications, the first CA they install will be an enterprise root CA. The following sections describe the process of installing a CA and managing the templates you use to create certificates.

INSTALLING AN ENTERPRISE ROOT CA

To install the first CA on an enterprise network, the enterprise root CA, use the following procedure.

 INSTALL AN ENTERPRISE ROOT CA

GET READY. Log on to Windows Server 2008 using an account with administrative privileges. When the logon process is completed, close the Initial Configuration Tasks window and any other windows that appear.

1. Click **Start,** and then click **Administrative Tools** > **Server Manager.** The Server Manager console appears.
2. Select the **Roles** node and, in the details pane, click **Add Roles.** The Add Roles Wizard appears.
3. Click **Next** to bypass the *Before You Begin* page. The *Select Server Roles* page appears.
4. Select the **Active Directory Certificate Services** checkbox and click **Next.** The *Introduction to Active Directory Certificate Services* page appears.

TAKE NOTE* Although the role is called Active Directory Certificate services, Active Directory is not required to install and run a CA. As noted earlier, standalone CAs need not use Active Directory in any way, and can provide certificates to Internet and other clients outside the enterprise network.

5. Click **Next** to bypass the introduction page. The *Select Role Services* page appears, as shown in Figure F-7.

Figure F-7

The Select Role Services page of the Add Roles Wizard

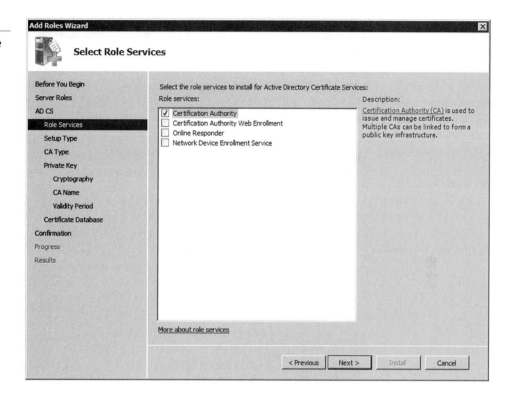

6. Leave the Certification Authority role service selected and click **Next.** The *Specify Setup Type* page appears, as shown in Figure F-8.

Figure F-8

The Specify Setup Type page of the Add Roles Wizard

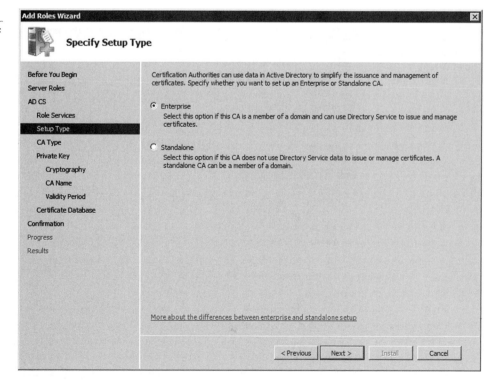

7. Select the **Enterprise** option and click **Next.** The *Specify CA Type* page appears, as shown in Figure F-9.

Figure F-9

The Specify CA Type page of the Add Roles Wizard

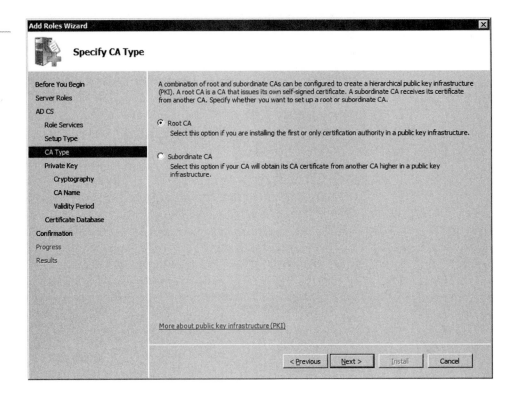

8. Select the **Root CA** option and click **Next.** The *Set Up Private Key* page appears, as shown in Figure F-10.

Figure F-10

The Set Up Private Key page of the Add Roles Wizard

9. Select the **Create a new private key** option and click **Next.** The *Configure Cryptography for CA* page appears, as shown in Figure F-11.

Figure F-11

The Configure Cryptography for CA page of the Add Roles Wizard

TAKE NOTE *

The Create a New Private Key option instructs the wizard to create a new private key for the CA. The Use Existing Private Key option instructs the wizard to use the private key associated with an existing certificate or stored on the server, which you must import in the *Select Existing Certificate* page. This option adds to the wizard. Select this option when you are reinstalling a CA.

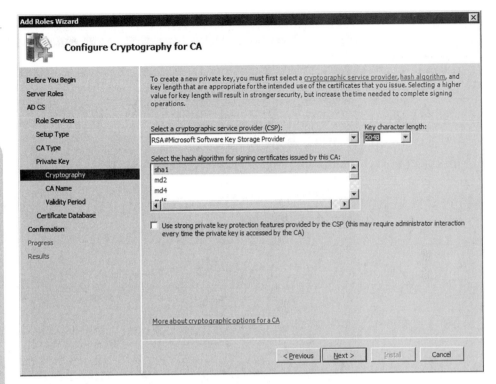

10. Select a cryptographic service provider and a hashing algorithm from the lists provided. Then, specify the **Key character length** you want the CA to use, and click **Next.** The *Configure CA Name* page appears, as shown in Figure F-12.

Figure F-12

The Configure CA Name page of the Add Roles Wizard

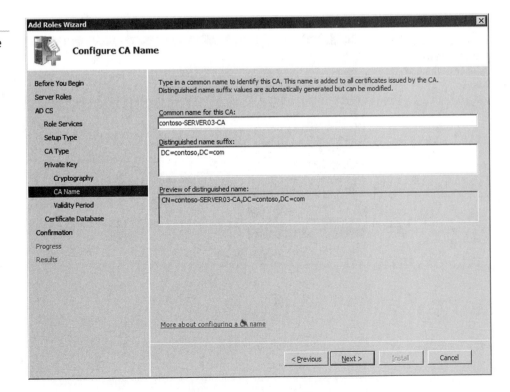

11. The wizard uses the server's name to form the common name of the CA. Specify a different name, if desired, and click **Next**. The *Set Validity Period* page appears, as shown in Figure F-13.

Figure F-13

The Set Validity Period page of the Add Roles Wizard

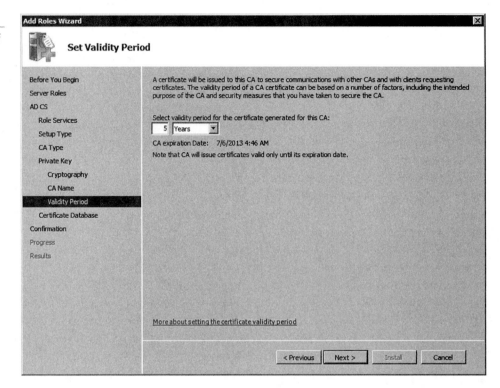

12. Specify a validity period for the certificate that will be self-generated by the CA and click **Next**. The *Configure Certificate Database* page appears, as shown in Figure F-14.

Figure F-14

The Configure Certificate Database page of the Add Roles Wizard

13. Click **Next** to accept the default database location settings. The *Confirm Installation Selections* page appears.

14. Click **Install.** When the installation is complete, click **Close.**

CLOSE the Server Manager console.

Once you have created an enterprise root CA on your network, you can proceed to create as many enterprise subordinate CAs as you need.

INSTALLING AN ENTERPRISE SUBORDINATE CA

The only difference in the installation procedure for an enterprise subordinate CA is the inclusion of a *Request Certificate from a Parent CA* page in the Add Roles Wizard, as shown in Figure F-15, in place of the *Set Validity Period* page.

Figure F-15

The Request Certificate from a Parent CA page of the Add Roles Wizard

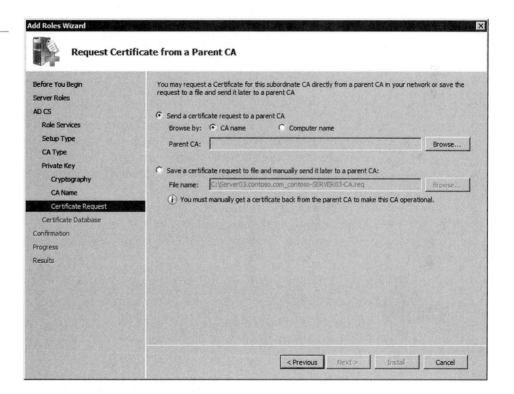

When you create a root CA, the computer generates its own certificate, so the Set Validity Period enables you to specify the life span of that certificate, and consequently the CA's life span. When you create a subordinate CA, you specify the name of a parent CA instead, from which the computer will obtain the certificate it needs to operate as a subordinate. The parent CA can be a root CA or another subordinate CA.

CREATING A CA HIERARCHY

While even a single CA constitutes a PKI, it is common for organizations to use multiple CAs, arranged in a hierarchy, much like Active Directory forests. In a hierarchical CA structure, there is a single root CA at the top, and one or more subordinate CAs beneath it, as shown in Figure F-16. The root CA provides certificates to the subordinate CAs, which in turn can generate certificates for additional subordinate CAs or for end users. In an Active Directory hierarchy, domains in the same tree automatically trust each other. In a CA hierarchy, ***trust chaining*** enables clients that trust the root CA to also trust certificates issued by any other CAs subordinate to the root.

Figure F-16

A simple CA hierarchy

While a CA hierarchy can have just two levels, larger organizations might have three or more levels. When this is the case, there are two distinct types of subordinate CAs, as follows:

- *Intermediate CAs*—Intermediate CAs do not issue certificates to end users or computers; they issue certificates only to other subordinate CAs below them in the certification hierarchy. Intermediate CAs are not required, but using them enables you to take your root CA offline, which greatly increases its security.

- *Issuing CAs*—Issuing CAs provide certificates to end users and computers. Root and intermediate CAs are capable of issuing certificates to end users, but in a three-level arrangement, they typically do not.

TAKE NOTE*

Unlike the strictly defined root, subordinate, enterprise, and standalone CAs discussed earlier, intermediate and issuing servers are not roles that you select when you install Active Directory Certificate Services on a Windows Server 2008 computer. These are instead more informal roles that are dictated only by the use you make of a CA you have already installed.

Figure F-17 displays the relationships between root, intermediate, and issuing CAs in a three-level hierarchy, and the users and computers who use certificates.

TAKE NOTE*

All of the information about installing CAs found in the previous sections is applicable to standalone, as well as enterprise, CAs. However, the following information, on certificate templates, applies only to enterprise CAs.

Managing Certificate Templates

Enterprise CAs might have to issue thousands of certificates to users and computers. If administrators had to provide the configuration settings for each certificate manually, they could easily spend all of their time issuing certificates—and would probably make a large number of mistakes in the process. Fortunately, administrators can use certificate templates to simplify the process of creating certificates and to ensure that they are created consistently across an organization.

Figure F-17

A three-level CA hierarchy

Certificate templates are sets of rules and settings that define the format and content of a certificate based on the certificate's intended use. Certificate templates also provide the client with instructions on how to create and submit a valid certificate request. In addition, certificate templates define which security principals are allowed to read, enroll for, or autoenroll for certificates based on that template.

Windows Server 2008 includes a large collection of predefined certificate templates, supporting a variety of functions and applications. You can also customize each template for a specific use or create your own templates to suit the needs of your organization. Only enterprise CAs can issue certificates based on certificate templates; standalone CAs cannot. When an administrator defines a certificate template, the definition must be available to all CAs in the forest. To make the definition available, administrators publish the template in Active Directory and let the Active Directory replication engine propagate the template throughout the enterprise.

WORKING WITH CERTIFICATE TEMPLATES

To modify and publish certificate templates, you use the Certificate Templates snap-in for Microsoft Management Console (MMC), as shown in Figure F-18, which is only available on a CA server, or a server with the Certification Authority Tools feature installed. Using this snap-in, you can modify templates to suit your needs and deploy them on the network.

As with the Certificates snap-in mentioned earlier, Windows Server 2008 does not have a shortcut to a Certificate Templates console in the Start menu. You must add the Certificate Templates snap-in to an MMC console yourself to manage templates.

Figure F-18

The Certificate Templates snap-in for MMC

MANAGING CERTIFICATE TEMPLATE PERMISSIONS

Every certificate template has an access control list (ACL) that you can use to allow or deny security principals permission to Read, Write, Enroll, and Autoenroll the certificate template. You set permissions on certificate templates by using the Certificate Templates snap-in to open a template's Properties sheet and click the Security tab, as shown in Figure F-19. The process of assigning permissions is the same as on any of Windows Server 2008's other permission systems; only the permissions themselves are different.

Figure F-19

The Security tab of a certificate template's Properties sheet

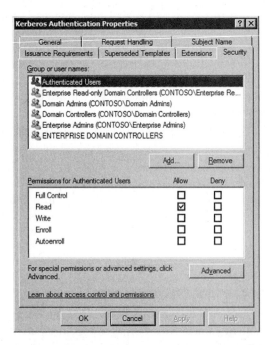

You can allow or deny security principals any combination of the following certificate template permissions:

- Full Control—Enables a security principal to modify all attributes of a certificate template, including its permissions.
- Read—Enables a security principal to find the certificate template in Active Directory when enrolling for a certificate.

- Write—Enables a security principal to modify all the attributes of a certificate template, except for its permissions.
- Enroll—Enables a security principal to enroll for a certificate based on the certificate template. To enroll for a certificate, the security principal must also have the Allow Read permission for the certificate template.
- Autoenroll—Enables a security principal to receive a certificate based on the template through the autoenrollment process. Autoenrollment also requires that the user have both the Allow Read and Allow Enroll permissions.

For autoenrollment to function correctly, you must ensure that all three of the required permissions (Allow Read, Allow Enroll, and Allow Autoenroll) are granted to the same user or group. If you assign Allow Read and Allow Enroll to one group and Allow Autoenroll to another group, users will not be allowed to autoenroll for certificates, even if they have membership in both groups.

This is because permissions for a certificate template are not additive, as they are in the NTFS file system. In this example, because a user is a member of two groups, the CA will treat the group with Allow Read and Allow Enroll permissions separately from the group with Allow Autoenroll permissions. For best results, create a global or universal group for each certificate template. Then, grant the global or universal group all three permissions, and then add the necessary user groups to this group.

UNDERSTANDING CERTIFICATE TEMPLATE VERSIONS

Windows Server 2008's Active Directory Certificate Services role supports three types of certificate templates: version 1, version 2, and version 3. Version 1 templates provide backward compatibility for CAs running Windows Server 2003, Standard Edition and Windows 2000 family operating systems. Version 1 templates have a major limitation, however: the information they contain is hard-coded in the certificate. You cannot modify version 1 certificate template properties, such as certificate lifetime and key size. With version 2 certificate templates, you can modify these properties.

When you install the first enterprise CA in a forest, most of the templates supplied with Certificate Services are version 1 templates. These version 1 templates provide an immediate certificate solution you can use as soon as the CA is installed because they support many general needs for subject certification. For example, using the default version 1 templates, a CA can create certificates that allow EFS encryption recovery, client authentication, smart card logon, and server authentication. Windows 2000 Server and Windows Server 2003, Standard Edition CAs support only version 1 templates.

Some of the default templates supplied with Active Directory Certificate Services are version 2, however, and you can only use them to issue certificates with a CA running Windows Server 2003, Enterprise Edition; Windows Server 2003, Datacenter Edition; or Windows Server 2008. Version 3 can be issued only by CAs running Windows Server 2008, and can be issued only to clients running Windows Vista and Windows Server 2008.

The certificate templates included with Windows Server 2008's Active Directory Certificate Services role are listed in Table F-2.

Table F-2

Windows Server 2008 Certificate Templates

TEMPLATE NAME	TEMPLATE VERSION	SUBJECT TYPE	KEY USAGE	TEMPLATE FUNCTION
Administrator	1	User	Signature and Encryption	Allows user authentication, EFS encryption, secure email, and certificate trust list signing.
Authenticated Session	1	User	Signature	Authenticates a user to a Web server. Uses the private key to sign the authentication request.

(continued)

Table F-2 *(continued)*

Template Name	Template Version	Subject Type	Key Usage	Template Function
Basic EFS	1	User	Encryption	Encrypts and decrypts data by using EFS. Uses the private key to decrypt the file encryption key (FEK) that encrypts and decrypts the EFS-protected data.
CA Exchange	2	Computer	Encryption	Used to store keys that are configured for private key archival.
CEP Encryption	1	Computer	Encryption	Enables the certificate holder to act as a registration authority (RA) for Simple Certificate Enrollment Protocol (SCEP) requests.
Code Signing	1	User	Signature	Used to digitally sign software.
Computer	1	Computer	Signature and Encryption	Provides both client and server authentication abilities to a computer account. The default permissions for this template allow enrollment only by computers running Windows 2000 and Windows Server 2008 family operating systems that are not domain controllers.
Cross-Certification Authority	2	Cross-certified CA	Signature	Used for cross-certification and qualified subordination.
Directory E-mail Replication	2	DirEmailRep	Signature and Encryption	Used to replicate email within Active Directory.
Domain Controller	2	DirEmailRep	Signature and Encryption	Provides both client and server authentication abilities to a computer account. Default permissions allow enrollment by only domain controllers.
Domain Controller Authentication	2	Computer	Signature and Encryption	Used to authenticate Active Directory computers and users.
EFS Recovery Agent	1	User	Encryption	Enables the subject to decrypt files previously encrypted with EFS.
Enrollment Agent	1	User	Signature	Used to request certificates on behalf of another subject.
Exchange Enrollment Agent (Offline request)	1	User	Signature	Used to request certificates on behalf of another subject and supply the subject name in the request.
Exchange Signature Only	1	User	Signature	Used by Exchange Key Management Service to issue certificates to Microsoft Exchange Server users for digitally signing email.
Exchange User	1	User	Encryption	Used by Exchange Key Management Service to issue certificates to Exchange users for encrypting email.
IPsec	1	Computer	Signature and Encryption	Provides certificate-based authentication for computers by using IP Security (IPsec) for network communications.

(continued)

Table F-2 *(continued)*

Template Name	Template Version	Subject Type	Key Usage	Template Function
IPsec (Offline request)	1	Computer	Signature and Encryption	Used by IPsec to digitally sign, encrypt, and decrypt network communication when the subject name is supplied in the request.
Kerberos Authentication	2	Computer	Signature and Encryption	Used to authenticate Active Directory computers and users.
Key Recovery Agent	2	Key Recovery Agent	Encryption	Recovers private keys that are archived on the certification authority.
OCSP Response Signing	3	Computer	Signature	Used by an Online Responder to sign responses to certificate status requests.
RAS and IAS Server	2	Computer	Signature and Encryption	Enables Remote Access Services (RAS) and Internet Authentication Services (IAS) servers to authenticate their identities to other computers.
Root Certification Authority	2	CA	Signature	Used to prove the identity of the certification authorities
Router (Offline request)	1	Computer	Signature and Encryption	Used by a router when requested through SCEP from a certification authority that holds a Certificate Enrollment Protocol (CEP) Encryption certificate.
Smartcard Logon	1	User	Signature and Encryption	Authenticates a user with the network by using a smart card.
Smartcard User	1	User	Signature and Encryption	Identical to the Smartcard Logon template, except that it can also be used to sign and encrypt email.
Subordinate Certification Authority	2	CA	Signature	Used to prove the identity of the certification authorities.
Trust List Signing	1	User	Signature	Enables the holder to digitally sign a trust list.
User	1	User	Signature and Encryption	Used for email, EFS, and client authentication.
User Signature Only	1	User	Signature	Enables users to digitally sign data.
Web Server	1	Computer	Signature and Encryption	Authenticates the Web server to connecting clients. The connecting clients use the public key to encrypt the data that is sent to the Web server when using Secure Sockets Layer (SSL) encryption.
Workstation Authentication	2	Computer	Signature and Encryption	Enables client computers to authenticate their identities to servers.

TAKE NOTE*

In the Certificate Templates snap-in, you can tell the version of a template by looking at the value in the Minimum Supported CAs column. Templates with Windows 2000 in this column are version 1; templates with Windows Server 2003, Enterprise Edition are version 2; and templates with Windows Server 2008 are version 3.

You cannot modify or remove the default version 1 templates installed with Active Directory Certificate Services, but you can duplicate them. When you create a duplicate of a version 1 template, the result is a version 2 template, which you can modify as needed.

The version 1 certificate templates provided by Windows Server 2008 Active Directory Certificate Services are completely compatible with previous versions of Certificate Services. Therefore, a Windows Server 2008 CA installation can work alongside an existing Windows CA infrastructure.

WORKING WITH CERTIFICATE TEMPLATES

Certificates are simply mechanisms for carrying information about users or computers, and as such, they have the potential for use by a wide variety of applications. It is up to the operating system and the applications to use that information to perform functions such as encrypting messages and authenticating connections.

Windows Server 2008's Active Directory Certificate Services includes many different templates designed to create certificates that applications can use for various purposes. To specify how the certificates created with a certificate template can be used, you configure its application policies. Application policies, sometimes known as extended key usage or enhanced key usage, give you the ability to specify which certificates can be used for which purposes. This enables you to issue certificates without being concerned that they will be misused.

For example, when you open the Smartcard User template in the Certificate Templates snap-in, click the Extensions tab, and select Enhanced Key Usage, you can see that a system can use a certificate based on this template to send secure email, to perform client authentication, and to log on by using a smart card, as shown in Figure F-20. By default, the certificate cannot authenticate a server to a client, recover files, encrypt files, or perform many other tasks that rely on a certificate. Further, the CA can issue the certificate only to a user, not to a computer.

Figure F-20

The default capabilities of the Smartcard User template

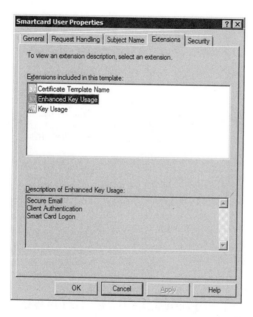

You will notice also that there is no way to modify the policies on the Extensions tab, and if you click on the other tabs, you cannot modify their settings either. This is because Smartcard User is a version 1 certificate template. However, if you create a duplicate of the Smartcard User template, by right-clicking it and selecting Duplicate Template from the context menu, you can choose whether to create a copy that is a version 2 or version 3 template, using the interface shown in Figure F-21.

Figure F-21

The Duplicate Template
dialog box

When you look at the duplicate template you have created, you can see that the same capabilities appear as application policies by default, but in this case you can modify the template by adding any of the additional application policies shown in the Edit Application Policies Extension dialog box, shown in Figure F-22. You can also modify any of the template's other settings, and even create new application policies of your own.

Figure F-22

Adding application policies to
a duplicate template

You have no choice but to create a copy of a version 1 template if you want to modify its properties. However, even if you are working with one of the version 2 templates included with Active Directory Certificate Services, it is a good idea to make a copy before attempting any modifications so that you retain a backup of the original configuration.

Using certificate templates with multiple functions is an excellent way to reduce the number of certificates that administrators have to create and manage to fill an organization's needs. Many certificate templates, however, are single-function only. Single-function certificate templates are typically designed for sensitive operations that have unique requirements. For example, you might want to issue certificates for a sensitive operation, such as key recovery, with a short certificate lifetime of two months. In this case, a single-function template is preferable, because you would not want to combine this function with other functions that are less sensitive, and which can have a much longer lifetime.

You can modify a version 2 or version 3 certificate template at any time. After you make changes, all of the new certificates the CA issues using that template will have the new settings. This is an excellent way to make sweeping changes to certificates deployed to users and computers in your organization. For example, if you discover that a certificate could be compromised in less than one year, you can modify the validity period of the certificate to six months. However, modifying a template does not affect the certificates that the CA has already issued. To ensure that all clients using certificates issued before you modified the template receive the new settings, you must make sure that the CA issues a new certificate to each client. You can do this in two ways:

- Use the Certificates snap-in on each client computer to renew the certificate or request a new certificate.
- Use the Certification Authority snap-in to revoke the old certificates, forcing the client to request a new enrollment.

Enrolling and Revoking Certificates

> Certificate *enrollment* is the process by which a client requests a certificate and a CA generates one.

Although enrollment options might be restricted by network connectivity issues or by the use of a standalone CA, the certificate enrollment process always follows the same high-level procedure, which is as follows:

1. Generating keys—When a client generates a request for a new certificate, the operating system passes the request information to a *Cryptographic Service Provider (CSP)* that is installed on the computer. The CSP generates the private key and the public key—referred to as a key pair—for the certificate request. If the CSP is software-based, it generates the key pair on the client computer. If the CSP is hardware-based, such as a smart card CSP, the CSP instructs the hardware device to generate the key pair. The client might also be assigned a key pair by some authority in the organization.

2. Collecting required information—The client collects the information the CA requires to issue a certificate. For an internal CA, this can be authentication information or data stored in the Active Directory database. For an external CA, such as a commercial provider, the information could include the applicant's email address, birth certificate, fingerprints, or other notarized documents—whatever materials the CA needs to confirm the identity of the applicant. CAs with stringent identification requirements produce certificates with high assurance; that is, their certificates generate a high level of confidence. CAs themselves are said to be of high, medium, or low assurance.

3. Requesting the certificate—The client sends a certificate request, consisting of the public key and the additional required information, to the CA. The certificate request might be encrypted using the CA's own public key. Clients can submit certificate enrollment requests to a CA in several ways: automatically, by an application; explicitly, using email, a Web site, or a client program; or by a postal or courier service, when the certificate request or other documents must be notarized.

4. Verifying the information—The CA uses a policy module to process the applicant's certificate request. A *policy module* is a set of rules the CA uses to determine whether it should approve the request, deny it, or mark it as pending for later review by an administrator. The policy module also adds an attribute to the certificate containing the source of the CA's own certificate. This enables the client to verify the newly issued certificate by checking the credentials of the CA that issued it. As with the identification requirements, the rules in a CA's policy module influence the amount of confidence generated by the certificates it issues.

5. Creating the certificate—The CA creates a document containing the applicant's public key and other appropriate information and digitally signs it using its own private key. The signed document is the certificate. The digital signature of the CA authenticates the binding of the subject's name to the subject's public key. It enables anyone receiving the certificate to verify its source by obtaining the CA's public key.

6. Sending or posting the certificate—The CA uses an *exit module* to determine how it should make the new certificate available to the applicant. Depending on the CA type, the exit module might cause the CA to publish the new certificate in the Active Directory directory service, send it to the applicant in an email message, or store it in a specified folder for later retrieval.

UNDERSTANDING CERTIFICATE ENROLLMENT METHODS

Active Directory Certificate Services supports several certificate enrollment methods. A client's choice of enrollment method for obtaining certificates is typically dictated by the type of CA the client is requesting the certificate from and whether the client and CA can communicate across a network.

When requesting certificates from an enterprise CA, a client can use the following methods:

- *Autoenrollment*—Applications automatically issue a certificate enrollment request and send it to the CA. The CA then evaluates the request and issues or denies a certificate. When everything works properly, the entire process is invisible to the end user.
- *Web enrollment*—When you install Active Directory Certificate Services with the Certification Authority Web Enrollment role service, the setup wizard creates a Web site that clients can use to request certificates from the CA. Although standalone CAs are more likely to use Web enrollment, enterprise CAs support it as well.
- Certificates snap-in—The Certificates snap-in for MMC enables users to manually request certificates, as well as view the certificates they already possess.

Clients requesting certificates from standalone CAs are more limited in their options. Standalone CAs cannot use certificate templates, do not interact with Active Directory, and therefore do not support autoenrollment. Clients also cannot use the Certificates snap-in with a standalone CA, because the snap-in can communicate only with a CA using Active Directory. As a result, clients must use the Web enrollment interface to request a certificate from a standalone CA, and the CA holds the requests in a queue until an administrator evaluates each one individually and either issues or denies the certificate.

Additionally, a client computer that is not connected to the network cannot automatically enroll for a certificate because autoenrollment requires the client to communicate directly to the enterprise CA. In these circumstances, the client must submit all certificates requests to the CA manually.

USING AUTOMATIC ENROLLMENT

Autoenrollment enables organizations to automatically deploy certificates to both users and computers. The autoenrollment feature enables administrators to centrally manage all aspects of the certificate life cycle, including certificate enrollment, certificate renewal, and the modification and superseding of certificates. Autoenrollment also enables faster deployment of PKI applications, such as smart card logon, EFS, SSL, and Signed Multipurpose Internet Mail Extensions (S/MIME), within an Active Directory environment by eliminating the need for interaction with the end user.

Even when clients are manually requesting certificates, using Web enrollment or the Certificates snap-in, autoenrollment enables the CA to automatically issue the certificate without an administrator having to manually grant the request. To control whether a CA should autoenroll clients or queue their requests for manual approval, administrators can allow or deny the Autoenroll permission on the certificate template for the users and groups that will request certificates based on that template.

Some types of certificate enrollment require user interaction to proceed, even when autoenrollment is enabled. For example, smart card certificates require the user to insert the smart card before the CA can generate the certificate. In these cases, you can still use autoenrollment by configuring the version 2 certificate template to prompt the user during enrollment. On the certificate template's Properties sheet, click the Request Handling tab and then select either Prompt The User During Enrollment or Prompt The User During Enrollment And Require User Input When The Private Key Is Used, as shown in Figure F-23. When a client is autoenrolled, a message window appears, informing the user that interaction is required.

USING MANUAL ENROLLMENT

If you have client computers running operating systems earlier than Windows 2000, you must manually enroll these clients for certificates, even with an enterprise CA, because these client operating systems do not support Group Policy, and therefore cannot take advantage of

Figure F-23

The Request Handling tab on a certificate template's Properties sheet

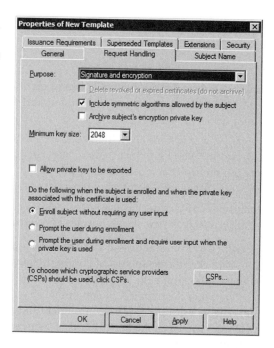

autoenrollment. As discussed in the previous section, you can manually enroll for certificates by using the Web enrollment interface or the Certificates snap-in.

USING WEB-BASED ENROLLMENT

As mentioned earlier, to manually enroll clients using the Web interface, you must install the Certification Authority Web Enrollment role service on a CA, which causes the Add Role Services Wizard to add the Web Services (IIS) role as well. This configures the computer to function as a Web server, with the Active Server Pages support needed to support Web-based enrollment.

Once the installation is complete, clients can connect to the CA from any Web browser using the URL *http://servername/certsrv*. The Web interface, shown in Figure F-24, enables users to create enrollment requests and retrieve certificates that the CA has issued.

Figure F-24

The Certification Authority Web Enrollment interface

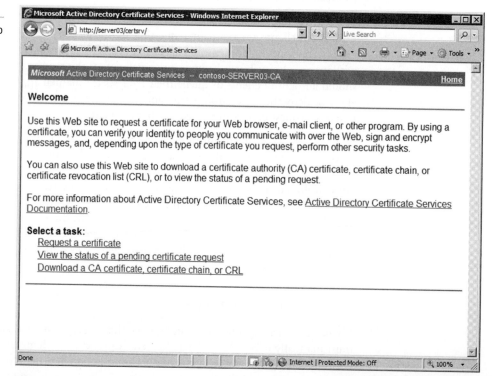

With an enterprise CA, Web-based enrollment can require no interaction from the administrator, as long as the proper policy settings and permissions are in place. For a standalone CA, however, an administrator must manually approve all Web enrollment requests, using the Certification Authority console.

USING THE CERTIFICATES SNAP-IN

Clients can also enroll for certificates by using the Certificate Enrollment Wizard in the Certificates snap-in to request certificates from an enterprise CA, as shown in Figure F-25.

Figure F-25

The Certificate Enrollment Wizard

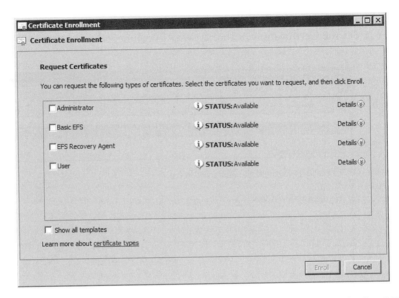

The Certificates snap-in displays the client's active certificates and other PKI client properties, such as trusted root CAs and existing certificate trust lists. Users with administrative privileges on the computer running the snap-in can manage certificates that are issued to users, computers, and services. Users without administrative privileges can manage only their own user certificates.

ISSUING CERTIFICATES MANUALLY

When users send enrollment requests to an enterprise CA using the Certification Authority Web Enrollment interface, the response is usually immediate, because enterprise CAs use autoenrollment. With a standalone CA, however, the CA queues the requests until an administrator evaluates them and manually issues a certificate or denies the request, using the Certification Authority console.

To manually process an enrollment request, use the following procedure.

 ISSUE CERTIFICATES MANUALLY

GET READY. Log on to Windows Server 2008 using an account with administrative privileges. When the logon process is completed, close the Initial Configuration Tasks window and any other windows that appear.

1. Click **Start,** and then click **Administrative Tools** > **Certification Authority.** The Certification Authority console appears.
2. In the scope (left) pane, expand the node representing your server and click the **Pending Requests** folder, as shown in Figure F-26.
3. In the detail (right) pane, right-click a certificate request and, in the context menu, click **All Tasks** > **Issue.** The request moves to the Issued Certificates folder.

CLOSE the Certification Authority console.

Figure F-26

The Pending Requests folder of the Certification Authority console

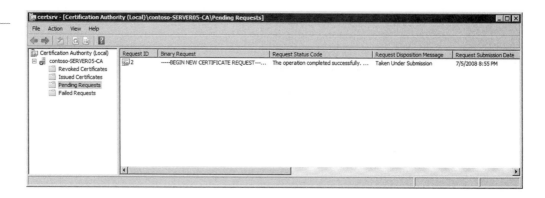

Once the administrator has issued the certificate, the user can check the status of the request in the Certification Authority Web Enrollment site, as shown in Figure F-27.

Figure F-27

The Certificate Issued page in the Certification Authority Web Enrollment site

REVOKING CERTIFICATES

Administrators might occasionally need to revoke a certificate because a user has left the organization, because they have decommissioned a computer, or because a private key has been compromised. There are two ways to revoke certificates:

- By using the Certification Authority snap-in
- By using the Certutil.exe command-line program

To revoke a certificate using the Certification Authority snap-in, you select the Issued Certificates node; right-click the certificate you want to revoke; and, from the context menu, select All Tasks > Revoke Certificate to display the Certificate Revocation dialog box, as shown in Figure F-28.

Figure F-28

The Certificate Revocation
dialog box

You must choose a reason for revoking the certificate, which will be included in the CRL. You can choose from the following reason codes, which are self-explanatory:

- Unspecified
- Key Compromise
- CA Compromise
- Change Of Affiliation
- Superseded
- Cease Of Operation
- Certificate Hold

TAKE NOTE*

The CRLs that a CA publishes contain the reason codes administrators select when they revoke certificates. Before you select a reason code, think about whether you really want everyone who can access the CRL to know why you revoked it. If you did have a key compromise or a CA compromise, do you want that to be public information? If not, just select Unspecified. In most cases, the reason you select for revoking a certificate has no bearing on the applications that use the certificate.

Applications discover that a certificate has been revoked by retrieving the certificate revocation list (CRL) from the CA. There are two kinds of CRLs: full CRLs, which contain a complete list of all of a CA's revoked certificates, and delta CRLs. *Delta CRLs* are shorter lists of certificates that have been revoked since the last full CRL was published. After an application retrieves a full CRL, it can then download the shorter delta CRL to discover newly revoked certificates.

PUBLISHING CRLS

When you have to download a file from a server, you can often access the file in several different ways. If you are logged onto the computer locally, you can use Windows Explorer to navigate to the folder containing the file. If you are on a different computer on the same network, you might map a drive to the server and download the file from a shared folder. If the server is behind a firewall and running IIS, you can open a Web browser to retrieve the file.

Having multiple ways to retrieve a file from a server is important, especially when the server will be accessed by a variety of different clients. Active Directory Certificate Services enables clients to retrieve CRLs using a variety of different protocols, including the following:

- Shared folders
- Hypertext Transfer Protocol (HTTP)
- File Transfer Protocol (FTP)
- Lightweight Directory Access Protocol (LDAP)

By default, CRLs are published in three different locations.

- The *Servername*\CertEnroll share—Created automatically when you install Active Directory Certificate Services, clients on the network can access this share, as long as they have the required permissions.

- CN=CAName,CN=CAComputerName,CN=CDP,CN=Public Key Services, CN=Services,CN=Configuration,DC=ForestRootNameDN—Clients who need to retrieve the CRL by using LDAP can access it from this address.
- http://*servername*/certenroll—Web clients can retrieve the CRLs from this URL.
- file://*servername*/certenroll—Web clients can also retrieve the CRLs using the file prefix.

Though these default locations are sufficient for most organizations, you can add locations if necessary. In particular, you must add a location if you are using an offline root CA, since the CA will not be accessible by clients under normal circumstances. Additionally, if clients use your certificates outside your private network and your CA is behind a firewall, you should publish the CRL to a publicly accessible location.

To simplify administration, you can use variable names when entering CRL locations. After you click the Add button, the Add Location dialog box appears and provides a list of variables that you can use, as shown in Figure F-29. Descriptions for each variable are provided in the Description Of Selected Variable box.

Figure F-29

The Add Location dialog box

After you revoke a certificate, the CA must publish a new CRL before clients can discover that the certificate has been revoked. By default, Windows Server 2008 CAs publish delta CRLs daily, and full CRLs weekly. You can change these settings using the Certification Authority snap-in by right-clicking the Revoked Certificates node, opening its Properties sheet, and then clicking the CRL Publishing Parameters tab, as shown in Figure F-30. This tab also shows you when the next scheduled updates will occur.

Figure F-30

The Properties sheet for a CA's Revoked Certificates node

■ Updating Servers

THE BOTTOM LINE

One of the most important ongoing tasks faced by server administrators is keeping the network's servers updated with the latest operating system hotfixes and service packs. Windows Server 2008 includes an Automatic Updates feature that can download and install updates with no user intervention, but this is not always an ideal solution for enterprise network servers.

When enabled, the default behavior of Automatic Updates is to connect to the Microsoft Update Web site at regular intervals and then download and install any new operating system updates. However, this behavior is often not desirable, especially for servers.

First, having each computer download the same updates independently compounds the amount of Internet bandwidth the systems utilize. In the case of service packs, which can run to hundreds of megabytes, the bandwidth needed to update hundreds of computers can be enormous.

Second, Automatic Updates does not give administrators an opportunity to evaluate the updates before deploying them on production servers and workstations. Many administrators prefer to wait some time before installing new updates, to see if any problems arise, while others test the updates themselves on laboratory computers.

Windows Server Update Services (WSUS) is a solution to both these problems. WSUS is a program that downloads updates from the Microsoft Update Web site and stores them for administrative evaluation. An administrator can then select the updates to deploy and computers on the network download them using a reconfigured Automatic Updates client.

Understanding WSUS Architectures

There are several architectural configurations you can use when deploying WSUS on an enterprise network, depending on its size and the number of remote locations.

There are four basic WSUS architecture configurations, as follows:

- Single WSUS server
- Multiple independent WSUS servers
- Multiple synchronized WSUS servers
- Multiple disconnected WSUS servers

USING A SINGLE WSUS SERVER

In the simplest configuration, a single WSUS server downloads updates from the Microsoft Update Web site and all of the other computers on the network download the updates from that WSUS server, as shown in Figure F-31. A single WSUS server can support as many as 25,000 clients, so this configuration is suitable for most enterprise networks.

USING MULTIPLE INDEPENDENT WSUS SERVERS

For enterprise networks with remote locations, it might be preferable to run a separate WSUS server at each site. In the multiple independent architecture, each of the WSUS servers has its own connection to the Microsoft Update site, as shown in Figure F-32, and maintains its own updates. Administrators at each site manage their own WSUS server configuration and designate the updates they want to release to the production network.

Figure F-31

The WSUS single server
architecture

Figure F-32

The WSUS multiple independent
server architecture

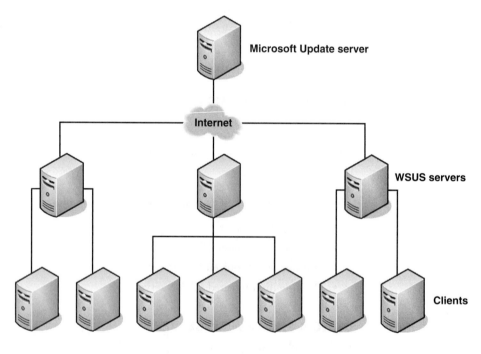

USING MULTIPLE SYNCHRONIZED WSUS SERVERS

It is also possible to use multiple WSUS servers in a synchronized manner. In this configuration, one central WSUS server downloads updates from the Microsoft Update Web site, and the other WSUS servers obtain their updates from that first server, as shown in Figure F-33. This minimizes the amount of Internet bandwidth expended and enables the administrators of the central server to manage the updates for the entire enterprise.

Figure F-33

The WSUS multiple synchronized
server architecture

Both of these multiple server architectures are becoming increasingly unnecessary, as the Windows Server 2008 and Windows Vista operating systems become more prevalent in the enterprise. Both of these operating systems support a feature that you can enable with Group Policy called ***Background Intelligent Transfer Service (BITS) peer-caching,*** which enables computers to share their updates with each other on a peer-to-peer basis, rather than download them all from a WSUS server. As a result, even in the case of remote sites with slow, expensive wide area network (WAN) connections, the update process generates relatively little inter-site communication.

USING MULTIPLE DISCONNECTED WSUS SERVERS

The multiple disconnected WSUS server architecture is the same as the multiple synchronized architecture, except that instead of the central WSUS server transmitting updates directly to the secondary servers, administrators save the updates to an offline medium, such as DVD-ROMs, and ship them to the remote sites.

Deploying WSUS

WSUS 3.0 Service Pack 1 is the first WSUS release that can run on Windows Server 2008.

WSUS 3.0 SP1 is not supplied with the Windows Server 2008 operating system. However, it is a free download from the Microsoft Downloads Web site. You must also download Microsoft Report Viewer 2005 or later and install it before using WSUS.

Automatic Updates clients connect to a WSUS server by accessing a Web site, just as they do when connecting to the Microsoft Update site directly. Therefore, before you install WSUS, you must add the Web Server (IIS) role to the computer. In addition to the default role services, you must also select the following:

- Windows Authentication
- ASP.NET
- IIS 6.0 Management Compatibility
- IIS 6.0 Metabase Compatibility

WSUS requires a database, and if desired, you can use SQL Server 2005 SP1 or later for this purpose. This is optional, however. If there is no database manager installed on the server, WSUS installs the Windows Internal Database feature automatically.

INSTALLING WSUS

Once you have downloaded the WSUS 3.0 SP1 executable and installed all of the prerequisite components, you can proceed with the WSUS installation, using the following procedure.

 INSTALL WSUS

GET READY. Log on to Windows Server 2008. When the logon process is completed, close the Initial Configuration Tasks window and any other windows that appear.

1. Click **Start**, and then click **Run.** The Run dialog box appears.
2. Click **Browse** and, in the **Browse** combo box, locate and select the WSUS executable file you downloaded. Then, click **Open.**
3. In the Run dialog box, click **OK.** The Windows Server Update Services 3.0 SP1 Setup Wizard appears.
4. Click **Next** to bypass the Welcome page. The *Installation Mode Selection* page appears, as shown in Figure F-34.

Figure F-34

The Installation Mode Selection page in the Windows Server Update Services 3.0 SP1 Setup Wizard

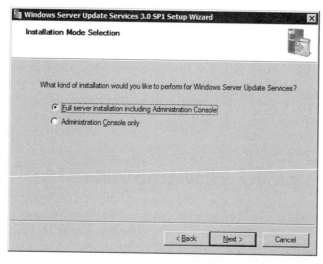

5. Leave the **Full server installation including Administration Console** option selected and click **Next.** The *License Agreement* page appears.
6. Select the **I accept the terms of the License agreement** option and click **Next.** The *Select Update Source* page appears, as shown in Figure F-35.

Figure F-35

The Select Update Source page in the Windows Server Update Services 3.0 SP1 Setup Wizard

7. Leave the **Store Updates Locally** checkbox selected and specify the name of the folder where you want to store the updates the server downloads from the Microsoft Update Web site. Then, click **Next**. The *Database Options* page appears, as shown in Figure F-36.

Figure F-36

The Database Options page in the Windows Server Update Services 3.0 SP1 Setup Wizard

8. Leave the **Install Windows Internal Database On This Computer** option selected and specify the name path to the folder where you want to store the database. Then, click **Next**. The *Web Site Selection* page appears, as shown in Figure F-37.

Figure F-37

The Web Site Selection page in the Windows Server Update Services 3.0 SP1 Setup Wizard

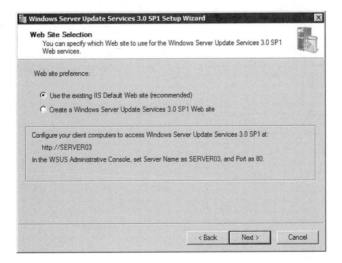

TAKE NOTE*

If you have SQL Server 2005 SP1 or later installed on your network, you can select the Use an existing database server on a remote computer option and specify the database instance you want to use instead of the Windows Internal Database.

9. Specify whether you want to use the default IIS Web site to host WSUS or create a new Web site and click **Next**. The *Ready To Install Windows Server Update Services 3.0 SP1* page appears.

10. Click **Next**. The Wizard installs WSUS and the *Completing the Windows Server Update Services 3.0 SP1 Setup Wizard* page appears.

11. Click **Finish**.

PAUSE as the Windows Server Update Services 3.0 SP1 Setup Wizard closes and the Windows Server Update Services Configuration Wizard appears.

When the wizard completes the WSUS installation, it automatically launches the configuration wizard, as described in the next section.

CONFIGURING WSUS

To configure WSUS, use the following procedure.

 CONFIGURE WSUS

GET READY. Log on to Windows Server 2008. When the logon process is completed, close the Initial Configuration Tasks window and any other windows that appear. Complete the WSUS installation procedure described in the previous section. When the installation is finished, the Windows Server Update Services Configuration Wizard appears, displaying the *Before You Begin* page.

1. Click **Next** twice to bypass the *Before You Begin* page and the *Join the Microsoft Update Improvement Program* page. The *Choose Upstream Server* page appears, as shown in Figure F-38.

Figure F-38

The Choose Upstream Server page in the Windows Server Update Services Configuration Wizard

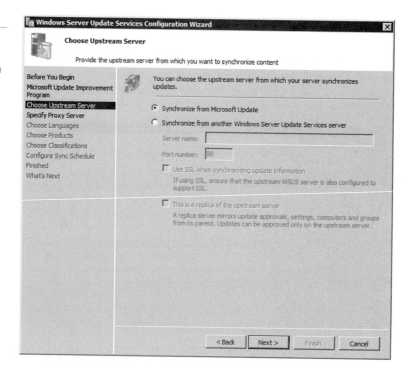

2. Select from the following options:
   - Synchronize from Microsoft Update—Configures the server to obtain updates directly from the Microsoft Update Web site on the Internet.
   - Synchronize from another Windows Server Update Services server—Configures the server to obtain updates from the WSUS server on the internal network whose Server Name and Port Number you specify in the text boxes provided.
   - Use SSL when synchronizing update information—Configures the server to use Secure Sockets Layer (SSL) encryption when communicating with the upstream WSUS server.
   - This is a replica of the upstream server—Configures the server to replicate all configuration settings and update approvals from the upstream WSUS server.
3. Click **Next**. The *Specify Proxy Server* page appears, as shown in Figure F-39.

Figure F-39

The Specify Proxy Server page in the Windows Server Update Services Configuration Wizard

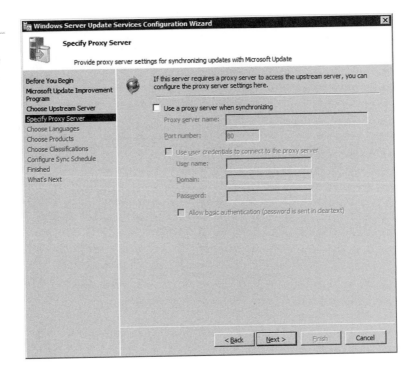

4. If your computer must use a proxy server to connect to the Internet or to the upstream WSUS server, select the **Use a proxy server when synchronizing** option and supply the name, port number, and credentials for the proxy server. Click **Next** to continue. The *Connect To Upstream Server* page appears, as shown in Figure F-40.

Figure F-40

The Connect To Upstream Server page in the Windows Server Update Services Configuration Wizard

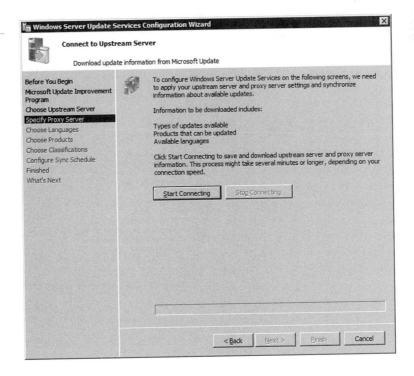

5. Click **Start Connecting**. The wizard connects to the Microsoft Update or upstream WSUS server and downloads information about the updates that are available. When the download is complete, click **Next**. The *Choose Languages* page appears, as shown in Figure F-41.

Figure F-41

The Choose Languages page in the Windows Server Update Services Configuration Wizard

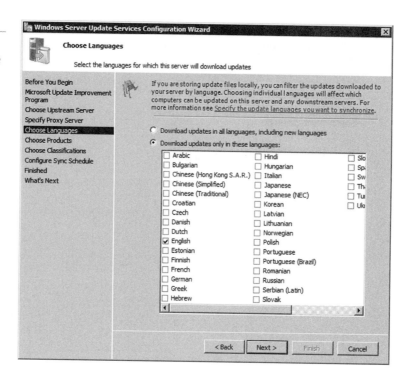

6. Select the checkboxes for any additional languages the computers on your network use and click **Next**. The *Choose Products* page appears, as shown in Figure F-42.

Figure F-42

The Choose Products page in the Windows Server Update Services Configuration Wizard

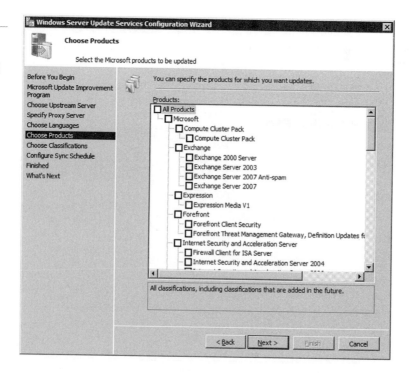

7. Select the checkboxes for the products you want WSUS to update and click **Next**. The *Choose Classifications* page appears, as shown in Figure F-43.

Figure F-43

The Choose Classifications page in the Windows Server Update Services Configuration Wizard

8. Select the types of updates you want WSUS to download and click **Next**. The *Set Sync Schedule* page appears, as shown in Figure F-44.

Figure F-44

The Set Sync Schedule page in the Windows Server Update Services Configuration Wizard

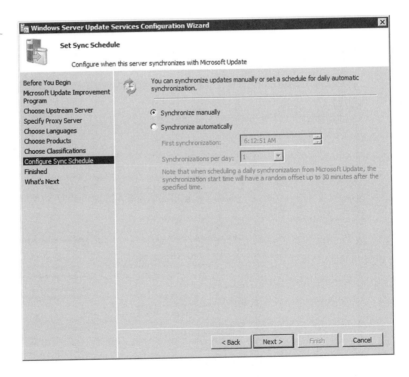

9. To create a synchronization schedule, select the **Synchronize automatically** option and specify a time for the first synchronization and the number of times per day you want WSUS to synchronize. Then, click **Next**. The *Finished* page appears, as shown in Figure F-45.

Figure F-45

The Finished page in the Windows Server Update Services Configuration Wizard

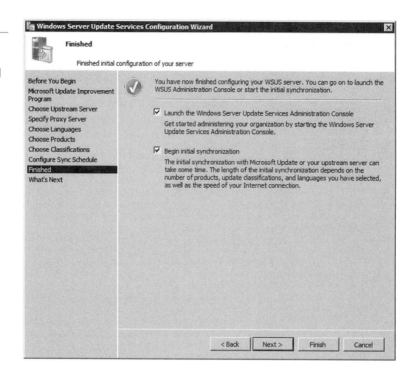

10. Click **Next**. The *What's Next* page appears.
11. Click **Finish**. The Update Services console appears, as shown in Figure F-46, and WSUS begins its first synchronization.

CLOSE the Update Services console.

Figure F-46

The Update Services console

Once the server completes its initial synchronization, an administrator must examine the downloaded updates, as shown in Figure F-47, and approve the ones to be distributed to clients on the network.

Figure F-47

The All Updates display in the Update Services console

CONFIGURING WSUS CLIENTS

Before the client computers on the network can download updates from the WSUS server, you configure their Automatic Updates clients. The Automatic Updates controls in the Windows operating systems do not provide any means of configuring the client to use an internal WSUS server instead of the Microsoft Update Web site, and even if they did, individual client configuration would not be a practical solution for a large enterprise network. To configure the Automatic Updates clients on your network you must use Group Policy.

To configure Automatic Updates using Group Policy, the recommended practice is to create a new group policy object (GPO); configure the required policy settings; and link the GPO to an appropriate domain, site, or organizational unit object. If you are using multiple WSUS servers, you can distribute the client load among them by creating a separate GPO for each server and linking them to different objects.

The Group Policy settings that control the behavior of the Automatic Updates client are found in the Computer Configuration > Policies > Administrative Templates > Windows Components > Windows Update folder in the Group Policy Management Editor console.

To configure clients to download updates from the WSUS server, enable the Specify intranet Microsoft update service location policy, as shown in Figure F-48, and specify the URL of your WSUS server in the two text boxes provided.

To configure the behavior of your Automatic Updates clients, enable the Configure Automatic Updates policy, as shown in Figure F-49, and specify the download options, update frequency, and time of day values for your clients.

Figure F-48

The Specify intranet Microsoft update service location policy

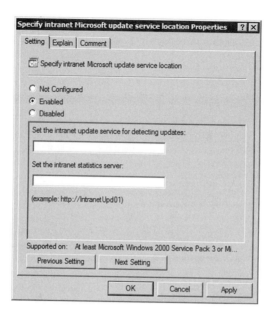

Figure F-49

The Configure Automatic Updates policy

Using the Event Viewer Console

THE BOTTOM LINE

The Event Viewer console has been enhanced in Windows Server 2008 to provide easier access to a more comprehensive array of event logs.

It is common practice for software products to save information about their ongoing activities to chronological lists called logs. By examining the logs, administrators can track the activity of the software, document errors, and extract analytical information. Logs are traditionally text files, which administrators open in an editor application, but the Windows operating systems have long used a graphical application for this purpose.

The operating system component that generates the Windows logs is called Windows Eventing. The primary function of the Windows Eventing engine, as always, is to record information about system activities as they occur and package that information in individual units called *events.* The application you use to view the events is called Event Viewer. In Windows Server 2008, Event Viewer takes the form of a Microsoft Management Console (MMC) snap-in.

The *Event Viewer* snap-in appears in Windows Server 2008 as a separate console, accessible from the Administrative Tools program group, and as part of other consoles, including Server Manager, under the Diagnostics node, and Computer Management, under System Tools. As with all snap-ins, you can also add Event Viewer to a custom MMC console. However you choose to access it, the Event Viewer snap-in looks the same and operates in the same way.

Introducing the Windows Server 2008 Event Viewer

Through many of its previous versions, Windows has maintained the same three basic logs: a System log, a Security log, and an Application log. Servers performing certain roles have additional logs, such as those tracking DNS and File Replication activities. The format of these logs has remained consistent, although the Event Viewer application has undergone some changes. It was in the Windows Server 2003 and Windows XP releases that Event Viewer first took the form of an MMC snap-in, rather than an independent application.

Windows Server 2008 and Windows Vista represent the most comprehensive overhaul of the Windows Eventing engine in many years. Windows Eventing 6.0 includes the following enhancements:

- Events now stored in XML format
- The addition of a Setup log documenting the installation and configuration history of applications
- New logs for key applications and services, including DFS Replication and the Key Management Service
- Individual logs for Windows components
- Enhanced querying capabilities that simplify the process of locating specific events
- The ability to attach scheduled tasks to events
- The ability to create subscriptions that enable administrators to collect and store specific types of events from other computers on the network
- Event log sizes now limited only by available disk space

When you first launch the Event Viewer console, you see the Overview and Summary display shown in Figure F-50.

Figure F-50

The Overview and Summary screen in the Event Viewer console

The Summary of Administrative Events displays the total number of events recorded in the last hour, day, and week, sorted by event type. When you expand an event type, the list is broken down by event ID, as shown in Figure F-51.

Figure F-51

The Event ID breakdown in the Event Viewer console

When you double-click one of the event IDs, the console creates a filtered custom view that displays only the events having that ID, as shown in Figure F-52.

Figure F-52

A custom view in the Event Viewer console

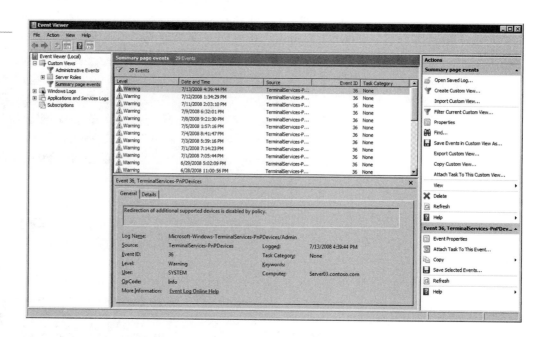

Viewing Windows Logs

In Windows Server 2008, Event Viewer contains more than the three original logs.

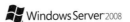

When you expand the Windows Logs folder in the Event Viewer console, you see the following logs:

- Application—Contains events generated by specific programs running on the computer, as determined by the application developer. Many of the applications included with Windows Server 2008 record events to this log, as do many other Microsoft applications. Third-party applications can utilize the log, but they are under no obligation to do so. In Windows Server 2008, the Applications and Services Logs folder usually contains more detailed information about application conditions than the Applications log.

- Security—Contains information about security-related events, such as failed logons, attempts to access protected resources, and success or failure of audited events. The events recorded in this log are determined by audit policies, which administrators can enable using Group Policy.

- Setup—Contains information about the installation and setup of roles, services, and applications.

- System—Contains information about events generated by the operating system components, such as services and device drivers. For example, a failure of a service to start or a driver to load during system startup is recorded in the System log.

- Forwarded Events—Contains events received from other computers on the network via subscriptions.

Selecting one of the logs causes a list of the events it contains to appear in the details pane, in reverse chronological order, as shown in Figure F-53.

TAKE NOTE*

The System log is the primary Windows Server 2008 operational log. You should always view this log first when looking for general information about system problems.

Figure F-53

Contents of a log in the Event Viewer console

The Windows event logs contain different types of events, which are identified by icons. The four event types are as follows:

- Information—An event that describes a change in the state of a component or process as part of a normal operation.

- Error—An event that warns of a problem that is not likely to affect the performance of the component or process where the problem occurred, but that could affect the performance of other components or processes on the system.

- Warning—An event that warns of a service degradation or an occurrence that can potentially cause a service degradation in the near future, unless you take steps to prevent it.

- Critical—An event warning that an incident resulting in a catastrophic loss of functionality or data in a component or process has occurred.

When you select one of the events in the list of events, its properties appear in the preview pane at the bottom of the list. You can also double-click an event to display a separate Event Properties dialog box, such as that shown in Figure F-54.

Figure F-54

An Event Properties dialog box

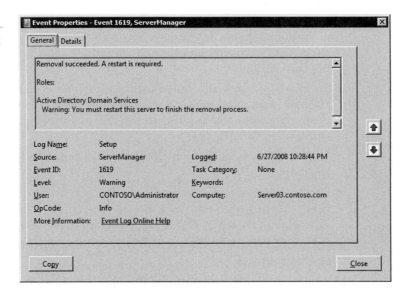

VIEWING APPLICATIONS AND SERVICES LOGS

The Event Viewer console contains a great deal of information, and one of the traditional problems for system administrators and desktop technicians is finding the events they need amidst an embarrassment of riches. Windows Eventing 6.0 includes a number of innovations that can help in this regard, including separate logs for the applications and services running on the computer.

When you expand the Applications and Services Logs folder in the console, you find additional logs for the various applications and services installed on the computer. Many of the roles and features that you can add to a Windows Server 2008 computer include their own logs that appear in this folder. For example, domain controllers include a Directory Service log.

The four types of logs that can appear in this folder are as follows:

- Admin—Contains events targeted at end users or administrators that indicate a problem and offer a possible solution.
- Operational—Contains events that signify a change in the application or service, such as the addition or removal of a printer.
- Analytic—Contains a high volume of events tracking application operation activities.
- Debug—Contains events used by software developers for troubleshooting purposes.

By default, only the Admin and Operational logs are visible in the Event Viewer console, because these are the logs that can be useful to the average administrator. The Analytic and Debug logs are disabled and hidden, because they typically contain large amounts of information that is of interest only to developers and technicians. To display and enable these log types, use the following procedure.

➔ DISPLAY ANALYTIC AND DEBUG LOGS

GET READY. Log on to Windows Server 2008. When the logon process is completed, close the Initial Configuration Tasks window and any other windows that appear.

1. Click **Start.** Then, click **Administrative Tools** > **Event Viewer.** The Event Viewer console appears.
2. Expand the **Applications and Services Logs** folder, as shown in Figure F-55.

Figure F-55

The Applications and Services Logs folder in the Event Viewer Console

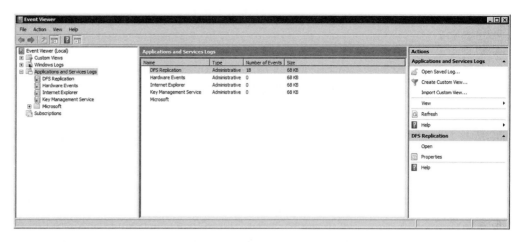

3. Click **View** > **Show Analytic and Debug Logs.** The additional logs appear in new subfolders in the Applications and Services Logs folder, as shown in Figure F-56, as well as in the \Microsoft\Windows subfolders.

Figure F-56

The Analytic and Debug log folders in the Event Viewer Console

4. Select one of the new subfolders. Then, right-click one of the logs and, from the context menu, select **Properties.** The Properties sheet for the log appears, as shown in Figure F-57.

Figure F-57

The Properties sheet for an Analytic log

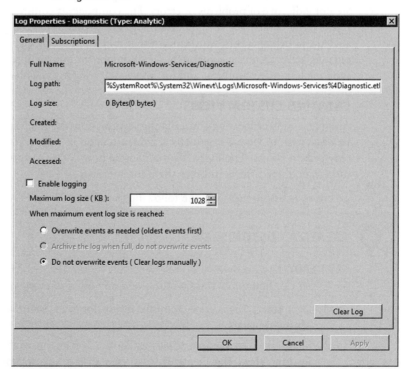

5. Select the **Enable Logging** checkbox and click **OK.**

CLOSE the Event Viewer console.

Analytic logs in particular can generate large amounts of information, so be careful to configure appropriate values for the maximum log size and the overwriting behavior.

VIEWING ADDITIONAL LOGS

Another one of the new logging features in Windows Server 2008 is component-specific logs that enable you to examine the events for a particular operating system component or application. Any component that is capable of recording events in the System log or Application log can also record events in a separate log dedicated solely to that component.

The Event Viewer console comes preconfigured with a large collection of additional logs for Windows Server 2008. When you expand the Microsoft and Windows folders in the Applications and Services Logs folder, you see a long list of Windows components, as shown in Figure F-58. Each of these components has a pathway, called a *channel,* to its own separate log.

Figure F-58

Windows component logs in the Event Viewer console

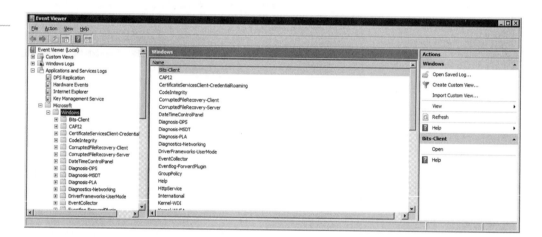

In most cases, the events in the component logs are non-administrative, meaning that they are not indicative of problems or errors. The components continue to save the administrative events to the System log or Application log. The events in the component logs are operational, analytic, or debug events, which means that they are more descriptive entries that document the ongoing activities of the component. The component logs are intended more for use in troubleshooting long-term problems and for software developers seeking debugging information.

CREATING CUSTOM VIEWS

Another means of locating and isolating information about specific events is to create custom views. A custom view is essentially a filtered version of a particular log, configured to display only certain events. The Event Viewer console now has a Custom Views folder, in which you can create filtered views and save them for later use.

To create a custom view, use the following procedure.

 CREATE A CUSTOM VIEW

GET READY. Log on to Windows Server 2008. When the logon process is completed, close the Initial Configuration Tasks window and any other windows that appear.

1. Click **Start.** Then, click **Administrative Tools** > **Event Viewer.** The Event Viewer console appears.

2. Right-click the **Custom Views** folder and, from the context menu, select **Create Custom View.** The Create Custom View dialog box appears, as shown in Figure F-59.

Figure F-59

The Create Custom View
dialog box

 ANOTHER WAY   You can also create custom views of specific logs by right-clicking a log and selecting Create Custom View from the context menu.

3. From the **Logged** dropdown list, select the time interval from which you want to display events.

4. In the Event Level area, select the checkboxes for the types of events you want to display.

5. From the **By Log** dropdown list, select the log(s) from which you want to display events. Alternatively, select the **By Source** option and then select the checkboxes for the components about which you want to display events.

6. Optionally, you can then specify event ID numbers, task categories, keywords, and user credentials to narrow your search.

7. Click **OK.** The Save Filter to Custom View dialog box appears, as shown in Figure F-60.

Figure F-60

The Save Filter to Custom View
dialog box

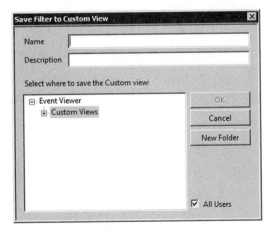

8. Enter a name for the view in the **Name** text box; enter a description, if desired; and select the folder in which you want to create your custom view. You can also create new folders to organize your custom views, if desired. Then, click **OK.** The console adds your view to the folder you selected and displays the view in the detail pane.

CLOSE the Event Viewer console.

Once you have created and saved a custom view, you can access it at any future time from the Custom Views folder.

Appendices Index